D1609073

Commercial Arbitration at Its Best

Commercial Arbitration at Its Best

Successful Strategies for Business Users

A Report of the CPR Commission
on the Future of Arbitration

Thomas J. Stipanowich, editor
Peter H. Kaskell, associate editor

CPR Institute for
Dispute Resolution

American Bar Association
Section of Business Law
Section of Dispute Resolution

The materials contained herein represent the opinions of the authors and editors and should not be construed to be the action of the American Bar Association or the Section of Business Law unless adopted pursuant to the bylaws of the Association.

Nothing contained in this book is to be considered as the rendering of legal advice for specific cases, and readers are responsible for obtaining such advice from their own legal counsel. This book is intended for educational and informational purposes only.

Library of Congress Cataloging-in-Publication Data

CPR Commission on the Future of Arbitration.
    Commercial arbitration at its best : successful strategies for business users : a report of the CPR
 Commission on the Future of Arbitration / Thomas J. Stipanowich, Peter H. Kaskell.
      p. cm.
    Includes bibliographical references and index.
    ISBN 1-57073-814-9 (hbk.)
     1. Arbitration and award--United States. I. Stipanowich, Thomas J., 1952- II. Kaskell, Peter H.
III. Title.

KF9085 .C68 2000
346.7307'0269--dc21

00-049336

Cover design by Catherine Zaccarine

Discounts are available for books ordered in bulk. Special consideration is given to state and local bars, CLE programs, and other bar-related organizations. Inquire at Book Publishing, American Bar Association, 750 North Lake Shore Drive, Chicago, Illinois 60611

04 03 02 01 00   5 4 3 2 1

Summary of Chapters

Contents

Foreword

In 1998, CPR convened the CPR Commission on the Future of Arbitration, consisting of more than 50 of the nation's most respected arbitrators, arbitration practitioners, corporate users of arbitration and legal academics. Their charge was to conduct a very thoughtful, constructive examination of how best to assure that commercial arbitration's promise of a fair, speedy and economical process with a just result is met.

Professor Thomas J. Stipanowich, the William L. Matthews Professor of Law at the University of Kentucky, one of the leading scholars of arbitration, agreed to direct this highly important project, assisted by CPR Vice President Peter Kaskell. In connection with the project, Professor Stipanowich was appointed to be the first CPR-Hewlett Scholar, a position initiated by the William and Flora Hewlett Foundation.

It was agreed that the Commission's core product would be a concise guidebook, discussing significant issues and providing guidance to lawyers, business people and arbitrators on how to make the most of the commercial arbitration process.

The Commission members were divided into five working groups that analyzed the various phases of the arbitration process. Though very busy professionals, they attended numerous meetings of their working groups. As drafts of chapters were circulated, they made invaluable comments.

CPR is deeply indebted to the many members of the Commission who participated in the development of this book. Professor Stipanowich conducted the working group meetings with great skill, making these meetings stimulating as well as productive. He spent innumerable hours as the lead draftsman of this landmark book. All of us learned to appreciate Tom's enthusiasm, his dedication, his ability to forge consensus and his good humor.

Also deserving of special note are the many contributions of Peter Kaskell, who for seventeen years has had primary responsibility for CPR's Committees, Industry Projects and Model Procedures. Peter was instrumental in all aspects:

he organized the CPR Commission on the Future of Arbitration, attended to logistics, co-chaired meetings and made invaluable contributions to the writing and editing of this book.

Commercial arbitration remains full of promise. This book will go a long way toward fulfilling that promise.

James F. Henry
President
CPR Institute for Dispute Resolution

Members of the CPR Commission on the Future of Arbitration

Prof. Thomas J. Stipanowich—
Director
University of Kentucky College of Law
Lexington, KY

Gerald Aksen (C)(E)
Thelen, Reid & Priest LLP
New York, NY

Tom Arnold (B)
Arnold, White & Durkee, P.C.
Houston, TX

Charles A. Beach (C)(E)
Counsel
ExxonMobil Corporation
Irving, TX

Mark T. Bobak (A)
Vice President
Deputy General Counsel
Anheuser-Busch Companies, Inc.
St. Louis, MO

Paul J. Bschorr (C)(E)
Dewey Ballantine
New York, NY

Stephen B. Burbank (D)
University of Pennsylvania
School of Law
Philadelphia, PA

James H. Carter (A)(E)
Sullivan & Cromwell
New York, NY

Zela G. Claiborne (B)
Bronson, Bronson & McKinnon
San Francisco, CA

A. Stephens Clay (D)(E)
Kilpatrick Stockton LLP
Atlanta, GA

Robert S. Clemente (A)(B)
New York Stock Exchange
New York, NY

Steven J. Comen (B)
Goodwin, Procter & Hoar
Boston, MA

Ferderic K. Conover (C)
The Faegre Group
Denver, CO

Louis A. Craco (C)(E)
Willkie Farr & Gallagher
New York, NY

Dr. Bernardo M. Cremades (E)
B. Cremades y Asociados
Madrid, Spain

John D. Curtin, Jr. (C)
Bingham Dana LLP
Boston, MA

Hon. James F. Davis (A)
Howrey & Simon
Washington, DC

Thomas P. Devitt (B)
Thelen, Reid & Priest LLP
San Francisco, CA

Linda D. Fienberg (C)
Executive Vice President
NASD Regulation, Inc.
Washington, DC

Dana H. Freyer (C)
Skadden, Arps, Slate, Meagher & Flom
New York, NY

Hon. Stuart M. Gerson (D)
Epstein, Becker & Green
Washington, DC

Prof. Whitmore Gray (D)(E)
LeBoeuf, Lamb, Greene & MacRae
New York, NY

Dana Haviland (C)
Wilson, Sonsini, Goodrich & Rosati
Palo Alto, CA

Harold Hestnes (D)
Hale and Dorr
Boston, MA

Bud G. Holman (A)(D)
Kelley Drye & Warren
New York, NY

Thomas S. Kilbane (C)
Squire, Sanders & Dempsey
Cleveland, OH

Edward V. Lahey, Jr. (A)
Essex, CT
Chair of the Executive Committee
of the American Arbitration
Association, formerly Vice
President & General Counsel of Pepsico

Joseph M. Manko (B)
Manko Gold & Katcher
Bala Cynwyd, PA

Hon. Thomas A. Masterson (C)(D)
Thomas A. Masterson &
   Associates, P.C.
Norristown, PA

Deborah Masucci (B)
JAMS
New York, NY

Hon. Frank H. McFadden (D)
Capell & Howard, P.C.
Montgomery, AL

Hon. Frank J. McGarr (C)
Foley & Lardner
Chicago, IL

Joseph T. McLaughlin (B)(E)
Managing Director,
   Executive Vice President
Legal & Regulatory Affairs
Credit Suisse First Boston
New York, NY

Paul J. Mode, Jr. (C)
Wilmer, Cutler & Pickering
Washington, DC

Hon. Joseph W. Morris (A)
Gable & Gotwals
Tulsa, OK

Carroll E. Neesemann (A)(C)(D)
Morrison & Foerster LLP
New York, NY

David W. Plant (B)(E)
New London, NH
(formerly of Fish & Neave)

Charles R. Ragan (D)
Pillsbury, Madison & Sutro LLP
Palo Alto, CA

Hon. Charles B. Renfrew (E)
Law Offices of Charles B. Renfrew
San Francisco, CA

Barbara P. Robinson (B)
Debevoise & Plimpton
New York, NY

Donald Lee Rome (B)
Robinson & Cole LLP
Hartford, CT

Robert N. Sayler
Covington & Burling
Washington, DC

Hon. Abraham D. Sofaer
The Hoover Institution
Stanford University
Stanford, CA

John M. Townsend (A)(E)
Hughes Hubbard & Reed LLP
Washington, DC

Dean Paul R. Verkuil (B)(D)
Benjamin N. Cardozo School of Law
New York, NY

P. Elippardo Villarreal (A)(C)
Counsel—Litigation and Legal Policy
General Electric Company
Fairfield, CT

Robert B. von Mehren (A)(C)(D)(E)
New York, NY
formerly of Debevoise & Plimpton

Hon. William H. Webster (C)
Milbank, Tweed, Hadley & McCloy
Washington, DC

Charles Weiss
Bryan Cave LLP
St. Louis, MO

Thomas A. Welch
Brobeck, Phleger & Harrison
San Francisco, CA

Prof. James J. White
Robert A. Sullivan Professor of Law
University of Michigan Law School
Ann Arbor, MI

Clifford L. Whitehill-Yarza (C)
Darden Restaurants, Inc.
Orlando, FL

John H. Wilkinson (A)
Fulton, Rowe, Hart & Coon
New York, NY

Jerome T. Wolf (C)
Sonnenschein Nath & Rosenthal
Kansas City, MO

Stephen P. Younger (B)
Patterson, Belknap, Webb & Tyler
New York, NY

CPR STAFF:
Peter H. Kaskell
Vice President

ADDITIONAL MEMBERS OF
THE WORKING GROUP ON
INTERNATIONAL ARBITRATION

Stephen D. Butler
Managing Counsel
Bechtel Group, Inc.
San Francisco, CA

Matthieu de Boisseson
Darrois Villey Maillot Brochier
Paris, France

L. Yves Fortier CC,QC
Ogilvy Renault
Montreal, Quebec, Canada

Dr. Hanno Goltz
Oppenhoff & Radler
Cologne, Germany

Richard H. Kreindler
Jones, Day, Reavis & Pogue—
    Frankfurt
Frankfurt, Germany

William R. Park
Ropes & Gray
Boston, MA

WORKING GROUPS ON WHICH
MEMBERS SERVED:

(A) Working Group A:
     Qualified Arbitrators
(B) Working Group B:
     Interface Between Arbitration
     and Other ADR
(C) Working Group C:
     The Arbitration Process
(D) Working Group D:
     Finality and Reviewability
     of Awards
(E) Working Group E:
     International Arbitration

Acknowledgments

The CPR Commission on the Future of Arbitration is indebted to several organizations that made this publication possible. These include our sponsor, the CPR Institute for Dispute Resolution; the William and Flora Hewlett Foundation, which provided funding for the Commission's activities through the CPR-Hewlett Scholar Program; the American Bar Association Section of Business Law and the ABA Section of Dispute Resolution, our publishers; and the University of Kentucky College of Law, which provided research stipends and other support.

A number of individuals deserve special mention. These include, first and foremost, CPR President Jim Henry, who conceived and oversaw the project; and Vice President Kathleen Scanlon, who assisted mightily in the editing of this book. Anne Ferguson, administrative assistant to Mr. Kaskell, and Bonnie Detzel, staff assistant to Professor Stipanowich, rendered invaluable support throughout the project, devoting considerable time and effort to preparations for meetings of Commission working groups and typing a veritable mountain of drafts. Significant research assistance was provided by Joanna Decker (UK Law Class of 2001), Darren Embry (Class of 2001), and Alex Lubans-Otto (Class of 2002).

Many others also assisted the Commission in its efforts. Our discussions benefited from the input of President William Slate and the staff of the American Arbitration Association (AAA) and from representatives of Judicial Arbitration and Mediation Services (JAMS).

This book was brought to press under the guidance of Jacqueline McGlamery, Executive Editor, Book Development & Publishing, of the ABA Section of

Business Law. The Section's Director of Marketing, Planning & Promotion, Sandra Eitel, ably spearheaded the marketing efforts with the assistance of Rosemarie Yu of the CPR Institute. Many thanks are also due to Jack Hanna of the ABA Section of Dispute Resolution for his efforts to promote the book.

Thomas J. Stipanowich, Director
Peter Kaskell, Associate Director
CPR Commission on the Future of Arbitration

About This Book

Commercial arbitration has evolved along many lines. It has expanded beyond the conventional settings—construction, maritime, insurance, commodities, apparel industry, and the like—where particular expertise was expected of an arbitrator and relatively well cabined disputes were anticipated. It now covers commercial disputes of all possible configurations, including vast, complex matters with high stakes. It has become virtually indispensable in the international field, where the home court advantage and forum selection are unattractive disincentives to litigation as a method for resolving commercial conflicts. These developments have led to a proliferation of providers, rules and regimes, more involvement by attorneys, and much more complexity. Arbitration has become a legalistic method of adjudication. At the same time some seek to de-legalize the process and restore elements of what was before, others look for ways to control the risks of runaway procedures and unexpected outcomes in bet-the-company cases. Commercial arbitration remains full of promise as a means of resolving disputes. At this moment in its evolution, ongoing creative work is moving us toward full realization of that promise.

—Louis Craco, Esq.
CPR Commission on the Future
of Arbitration

A recent survey of leading U.S. corporations reaffirms that *binding arbitration*—the adjudication of disputes by a private tribunal or panel—remains a widely used method for resolving disputes that arise out of domestic and international commercial transactions.[1] Arbitration usually occurs pursuant to pre-

---

1. *See generally* DAVID B. LIPSKY & RONALD L. SEEBER, THE APPROPRIATE RESOLUTION OF CORPORATE DISPUTES: A REPORT ON THE GROWING USE OF ADR BY U.S. CORPORATIONS, Cornell/PERC Institute on Conflict Resolution (1998).

arranged terms in the business agreement.[2] Courts acting under federal or state law broadly enforce commercial arbitration agreements and the arbitral awards rendered pursuant to those agreements.[3]

Businesses choose arbitration because of its perceived advantages over going to court: speed, economy, flexibility, ability to choose one's own decisionmaker, and privacy.[4] But for many potential users questions about arbitration procedures, arbitrators, and their decisions (awards) overshadow the potential benefits: *Does arbitration provide a more efficient, satisfactory path to justice and fairness? What are the attendant risks, and how should they be addressed?* Lack of information often discourages parties from agreeing to arbitration or prevents them from achieving maximum satisfaction from the process.

The CPR Commission on the Future of Arbitration

In 1998, the CPR Institute for Dispute Resolution brought together over fifty of the nation's leading experts to provide answers to lawyers' and business persons' questions and concerns about binding arbitration. These individuals, all of whom have extensive experience with arbitration as arbitrators, practitioners, clients, or academics, report a relatively high level of satisfaction with the process. Their positive experience is no accident, but the result of a thorough understanding of the possibilities as well as the limitations of arbitration. The CPR Commission on the Future of Arbitration channeled the commissioners' collective experience into a series of guidelines for those using or considering the use of arbitration.

The Commission was organized into working groups addressing four categories of issues in commercial arbitration:

- Arbitration in the ADR Landscape
- Arbitrator Qualifications, Selection, and Ethics
- The Arbitration Process
- Arbitration Remedies, Awards, and Review

A fifth group, comprised of specialists in international arbitration, concentrated on the problems particular to that arena.

---

2. *Id.* at 15, Chart 4.
3. *See generally* IAN R. MACNEIL, RICHARD E. SPEIDEL & THOMAS J. STIPANOWICH, FEDERAL ARBITRATION LAW: AGREEMENTS, AWARDS & REMEDIES UNDER THE FEDERAL ARBITRATION ACT (1994).
4. *See* LIPSKY & SEEBER, *supra* note 1, at 18.

This book is the result of many months of discussion and deliberation by the Commission working groups. Organized in a question-and-answer format, it applies the collective wisdom of Commission experts to the most frequently asked questions of business users about arbitration.

Helpful insights by individual commissioners are interspersed throughout the book. These comments were recorded in the course of the working groups' discussions and are presented without attribution to individual Commissioners as a way of emphasizing that they represent the Commissioners' general experience.

An overview of arbitration benefits and concerns

Perceived benefits of arbitration

Throughout this book are numerous references to various perceived advantages of binding arbitration over traditional litigation. A recent Cornell/PERC survey of Fortune 1,000 corporations identifies many of the reasons businesses agree to arbitrate instead of going to court.

Reasons Businesses Choose Arbitration[5]

Reason	*Percent of respondents*
Saves money	68.6%
Saves time	68.5%
More satisfactory process	60.5%
Limited discovery	59.3%
Neutral expertise	49.9%
Preserves confidentiality	43.2%
Preserves good relations	41.3%
Avoids legal precedents	36.9%
More satisfactory settlements	34.8%
More durable resolution	28.3%

Efficiency, economy, expertise, privacy, finality, more satisfying and durable outcomes are all perceived benefits frequently identified with arbitration. Whether such expectations are fulfilled depends largely on the ability of parties to tailor arbitration procedures to their particular needs and goals. As the Fortune 1,000 survey suggests, these needs and goals vary by company, by transaction, and by dispute. Ultimately, many business users regard *control over the process*—the flexibility to make arbitration what you want it to be—as the single most important advantage of binding arbitration and other forms of ADR.[6]

---

5. *Id.* at 17.
6. *Id.* at 8.

Concerns about arbitration

The Fortune 1,000 survey also identified a number of perceived barriers to the use of arbitration by businesses.

Business Perceptions of Barriers to the Use of Arbitration[7]

	Percent of Respondents by Frequency of Arbitration Use				
	Very frequently	Frequently	Occasionally	Rarely	Never
Difficult to appeal	49%	64%	55%	52%	40%
Compromise outcomes	34%	55%	51%	55%	48%
Lack of confidence in arbitrator	29%	44%	45%	53%	48%
Lack of qualified arbitrators	20%	30%	26%	29%	35%
Too costly	0%	14%	14%	18%	0%
Too complicated	3%	5%	7%	15%	0%

These statistics are a curious counterpoint to those dealing with perceived benefits of arbitration. While many business persons see the use of expert arbitrators as a major advantage, many others are concerned about arbitrator qualifications and arbitrators' ability to produce a rational award. While many use arbitration precisely because it is simpler, quicker, and more final than litigation, others worry about giving up procedural safeguards such as the right to appeal.[8]

The importance of tailoring arbitration to suit specific needs and goals

The Fortune 1,000 survey results reinforce the point that "one size does not fit all" in arbitration. Process characteristics favored by some companies will be viewed with disfavor by others. As one Commission member puts it:

> In the modern environment arbitration deals with a much broader range of conflict than in the "old days," including big cases involving complex legal issues. While parties may see the virtues of a private substitute for court trial in many different kinds of cases, the nature of that private alternative will vary with the circumstances. Arbitration may mean anything from a rudimentary, expedited, non-lawyered process involving a quality determination by a technical expert to a much more formal proceeding with many of the trappings of court trial.

7. *Id.* at 28. *See* Table 24.
8. *Id.* at 25.

To summarize:

(1) business needs and goals for arbitration vary with the circumstances;
(2) business parties enjoy considerable *flexibility* and *autonomy* in fashioning their own arbitration agreements; and
(3) businesses should tailor arbitration and other conflict management approaches to their specific needs and goals.

This book encourages users to take an active role in arbitration and conflict management and it seeks to enable them to make better-informed choices to fashion the process to suit their needs.

Summary of chapters

The eight chapters of this book deal with the most important issues parties using or contemplating arbitration must address. The first seven chapters are organized chronologically, from planning and drafting a dispute resolution provision including arbitration through participation in the arbitration process, final award, and avenues of appeal; the eighth chapter deals with international arbitration.

Chapter 1. Arbitration in the ADR Landscape sets forth general guideposts for businesses on conflict management, explores the use of negotiation and mediation as preliminaries to the use of arbitration, and discusses the role of arbitrators in encouraging settlement of disputes.

Chapter 2. Dispute Resolution Provisions provides a checklist of considerations for those preparing negotiation, mediation, and arbitration provisions, with primary emphasis on the latter.

Chapter 3. Finding the Right Arbitrators discusses mechanisms for qualifying and selecting commercial arbitrators and professional standards for arbitrators. Special attention is paid to the problems associated with "tripartite" panels in which each party chooses an arbitrator and the two party-arbitrators agree upon a third who chairs the tribunal.

Chapter 4. Preparing for the Hearing considers the often critical steps that pave the way for arbitration hearings, with special emphasis on the benefits of pre-hearing conferences.

Chapter 5. The Hearing explores ways to insure that arbitration hearings proceed efficiently and civilly.

Chapter 6. Preserving Confidentiality examines methods of protecting the privacy of arbitration and establishing safeguards for proprietary information.

Chapter 7. The Arbitration Award: Finality versus Reviewability considers the broad authority of arbitrators to tailor awards to the issues before them and commensurate limits on judicial review of awards under state and federal law. Special emphasis is placed on approaches for controlling or limiting arbitrator discretion, on enhanced judicial review of arbitration awards, and the option of appealing awards to a private appellate tribunal.

Chapter 8. International Arbitration considers the foregoing issues in the context of international commercial arbitration.

Rules Appendices. These appendices collect the CPR and AAA rules and procedures that are referenced throughout the book.

Statutory Appendices. The texts of the federal and uniform acts are printed here.

Glossary of Relevant Terms and Arbitration Laws. The book also contains a short glossary of frequently used terms, including forms of conflict resolution, laws governing arbitration and leading institutions sponsoring arbitration.

Bibliography. For those desiring additional information, including more detailed treatment of legal issues touched upon in this volume, a topical bibliography is in the back of the book.

Index. Key terms and phrases are indexed.

Chapter organization

Questions addressed. Each chapter begins with a list of key questions that will be the focus of the chapter. These questions are indexed by page, permitting the reader to find the pertinent discussion readily.

Summary of recommendations. An "executive summary" of recommendations or main points from the chapter's discussion follows the list of key questions.

Appendices. Each chapter is supplemented by appendices containing additional valuable information. These include model provisions for drafters and charts comparing institutional arbitration rules.

Issues not addressed in this book

Labor and employment, consumer arbitration

This book focuses on the use of arbitration in transactions between businesses, the traditional realm of binding arbitration. Although businesses often employ arbitration and other private dispute resolution processes in collective bargaining, individual employment and consumer contracts, all of these topics are beyond the scope of this book.

While sharing some of the characteristics of commercial arbitration, labor arbitration—arbitration pursuant to the terms of a collective bargaining agreement—is a discrete setting animated by unique policies and practices. Arbitration under individual employment contracts and consumer contracts, although significantly closer to the model of arbitration between businesses, often implicates issues of bargaining power and fairness that require special treatment.[9]

Specific commercial settings

One of the lessons of this book is that parties should not rely on "one-size-fits-all" arbitration solutions, but should attempt to craft an arbitration clause that meets their specific needs and goals. Although the Commission's recommendations should be of significant value to planners, drafters, and advocates in all commercial venues, the recommendations do not address specific commercial transaction types. Therefore, decisionmakers are urged to supplement this information by consulting transaction-specific sources. Some of these sources are identified in the Annotated Bibliography at the end of this volume.

Finer points of law

Although this volume is intended for the benefit of business persons and counsel, it is not a treatise on the law of arbitration. Treatises and other helpful writings on legal issues are referenced in the Annotated Bibliography.

A final note

This book reflects the collective efforts of more than fifty individuals representing a wide range of experience and a commensurate range of opinion. In the interest of achieving a general consensus on best practices and providing maximum benefit for users, however, Commission members occasionally deferred to the realities of the marketplace. Although a number of Commission members, for example, would never personally encourage the use of provisions for expanded judicial review of arbitration awards, the increasing incorporation of such provisions in business agreements led the Commission to consider appropriate guidelines.

---

9. *See generally* AAA CONSUMER DISPUTES ADVISORY COMMITTEE, CONSUMER DUE PROCESS PROTOCOL (1998).

Arbitration in the ADR Landscape

Chapter Summary

Arbitration in the ADR Landscape

Arbitration in the ADR Landscape

1.1

Why does a book devoted to arbitration begin with a chapter dealing with topics such as mediation and conflict management?

Today, businesses are more interested than ever in finding appropriate ways to resolve conflicts out of court. They recognize that

(1) most commercial disputes are settled informally; resort to court process is often unnecessary; and
(2) there are cheaper, speedier, more predictable, more private, more flexible, less formal, and generally more appropriate ways to resolve problems.

On the other hand, business persons often lack sound information regarding the growing number of alternative dispute resolution (ADR) options available to them—binding arbitration, mediation, neutral or expert evaluation, mini-trial, and so on.[1] Several of the major ADR options are defined in the Glossary.

This book focuses on *binding arbitration*, which is essentially a substitute for adjudication in court by a judge or jury. Agreeing to have arbitrators decide disputes may save time and money, and allows participants to choose their own decision-makers and procedures. On the other hand, it leaves the ultimate resolution of disputes in the hands of third parties. Most business persons would rather work problems out themselves, even if the assistance of a third party mediator is needed to facilitate negotiations. Binding arbitration, like court trial, is usually a last resort. (Indeed, a recent survey of leading litigators and house counsel reflected a marked preference for mediated negotiation over arbitration.[2]) Therefore, we begin this book with a discussion of the subject of conflict management to give a clear picture of arbitration's place in the "ADR landscape."

The essence of this chapter is captured in the following CPR tenets of conflict resolution:

1. Most disputes are best resolved privately and by agreement.
2. Principals should play a key role in dispute resolution and should approach a dispute as a problem to be solved, not a contest to be won.
3. A skilled and respected neutral third party can play a critical role in bringing about agreement.
4. Efforts should first be made to reach agreement by unaided negotiation.

---

1. For a thorough discussion of the full array of options available to businesses, *see generally*, KATHLEEN M. SCANLON, CPR INSTITUTE FOR DISPUTE RESOLUTION, MEDIATOR'S DESKBOOK (1999).
2. *See* Lisa Brennan, *What Lawyers Like: Mediation*, THE NATIONAL LAW JOURNAL, Nov. 15, 1999, at A1.

5. If such efforts are unsuccessful, resolution by a non-adjudicative procedure, such as mediation or the mini-trial, should next be pursued. These procedures remain available even while litigation or arbitration is pending.
6. If adjudication by a neutral third party is required, a well-conducted arbitration proceeding usually is preferable to litigation.
7. During an arbitration proceeding the door to settlement should remain open; arbitrators should encourage the parties to discuss settlement; if appropriate, employing a mediator.

1.2

When and how should businesses identify appropriate dispute resolution options for commercial relationships?

1. Conflict management should be on the checklist for transactional planning

It is critical to address the management of potential conflict as a part of contract planning and negotiation. Such issues need to be considered prior to the emergence of disputes; otherwise, decisions regarding conflict resolution are likely to be hampered by a lack of cooperation between the parties. In the absence of an agreement regarding conflict resolution options, disputes will probably end up in court.

Given the amount of time and money that businesses spend resolving conflicts, they should carefully consider such issues in contract planning. Unfortunately, parties negotiating business agreements often spend little or no time discussing how disputes will be handled in the course of their relationship. One reason is time pressure; another is an understandable reluctance to introduce a negative note into discussions with a prospective partner. New business partners often have overly optimistic expectations for their relationship.

In light of these realities, *prior* to contract negotiations, companies should develop policies regarding the use of arbitration and other conflict resolution approaches, and prepare ADR drafting templates for use in business agreements. Rather than an awkward "add-on," conflict resolution provisions should be a standard element on the agenda of transactional planners, who should come to the table with specific proposals (or a range of options) for resolution of contract disputes.

2. Conflict management should be a matter of company policy and practice

Explaining why the growing use of ADR is not accidental in large companies,[3] two experienced business attorneys noted that

> ADR is an integral part of corporate policy, selected as one among several measures that they [corporate planners] use to achieve corporate objectives. Indeed, there are a variety of objectives that ADR is well suited to support.[4]

These objectives include:

- saving time and money ("No company is in business to participate in lawsuits"[5]),
- adapting a problem solving approach to fit the problem, thereby assuring control and reducing uncertainty and risk,
- maintaining privacy and confidentiality, and
- preserving business relationships.[6]

Business needs and objectives may vary with the transaction. Such variations dictate the need for several different "model" ADR provisions for use in company contracts. In light of the great flexibility parties enjoy in adapting ADR approaches to their specific goals, there is considerable room for creativity in planning the process. In various commercial settings, parties have devoted considerable time and energy to designing multistep conflict management programs; the usual result has been that conflict is resolved early and informally, with relatively minor diversion of financial and human resources.[7]

Long-term relationships involving significant financial stakes may justify more deliberate conflict management efforts that go beyond traditional ADR. For example, many public and private owners of major construction projects have found it advantageous to "partner" with contractors, design professionals, and other persons involved in the project.[8] Effective partnering permits parties to clarify and prioritize goals and expectations, anticipate critical performance problems, enhance communications among key personnel, and establish a blueprint for resolving conflict at the earliest possible time. Such concepts are readily adaptable to other commercial arenas involving long-term performance and a high potential for disputes, such as joint ventures involving technology-sharing or development.

---

3. Marc J. Sonnenfeld & Paul J. Greco, *ADR as Good Corporate Policy*, 6 Metro. Corp. Couns., Sept. 1998, at 8, col 1.

4. *Id.*

5. *Id. See* also Brennan, *supra* note 2, at A1 (four out of five outside lawyers and house counsel responding to recent survey say they use mediation because it saves time and money).

6. *See* Brennan, *supra* note 2, at A1 (approximately half of outside lawyers and house counsel say that mediation preserves relationships).

7. *See* Thomas J. Stipanowich, *The Multi-Door Contract and Other Possibilities*, 13 Ohio St. J. on Dispute Resolution 303, 378 (1998)(describing partnering approaches and conflict management programs).

8. *See generally Dispute Prevention Through Partnering*, Construction, CPR Institute for Dispute Resolution MAPP Series (1998)(discussing examples of "partnering" programs in the construction industry).

3. Effective conflict management depends upon the commitment of company principals, acting upon advice by informed counsel

Effective conflict management depends upon the commitment of company principals, who must rely in turn on the advice of informed counsel. Corporate attorneys should ordinarily play a primary role in identifying and analyzing appropriate dispute resolution alternatives. Many businesses and their legal representatives are coming to understand that effective legal counsel requires a thorough appreciation of the possibilities and limitations of mediation, arbitration, and other approaches. (Some commentators now equate ignorance or failure to advise of these alternatives with malpractice.[9])

Although some legal advisors may be able to rely on firsthand experience in advising on company ADR policies and contract language, some lawyers who specialize in transactional planning lack personal experience with mediation, arbitration, neutral evaluation, mini-trial, and other approaches. Those we have traditionally called "litigators" are more likely to have some background in ADR, although their experience may be limited.

Those who need outside assistance should consult dispute resolution experts—lawyers or business persons with broad and deep experience in getting problems resolved through ADR. Additional sources of information include educational and training programs and written materials published by the CPR Institute for Dispute Resolution (CPR), the American Arbitration Association (AAA), and other organizations.[10] The Bibliography at the back of this volume provides an extensive list of references on arbitration and other conflict resolution approaches.

Model dispute resolution provisions abound; many of them were developed by industry, trade, or professional associations for specific commercial settings.[11] Chapter 2 contains general guidelines for drafters of commercial dispute resolution agreements. Parties should review existing models in light of their own needs and make appropriate modifications. Some companies have on file several different conflict resolution provisions tailored to different kinds of commercial transactions; these serve as a "menu" from which transactional negotiators/planners can choose. One Commissioner reports:

> As an advocate who is a member of a good-sized law firm, I found one of the problems was that many of these ADR issues were addressed by my transactional corporate partners, who didn't like me tinkering with the ADR provisions at the end of deals so they couldn't close the transaction. Unfortunately, the clauses they used were often taken out of form books and not really discussed between the parties. Now, we have begun to change the culture so that the transactional lawyers call me and consult about ADR language. They

---

9. *See* Donald Lee Rome, *It's a New Day for ADR: From Boilerplate to Professional Responsibility*, 8 Bus. Law Today, Jan. /Feb. 1999, at 11.

10. Many helpful insights and examples are provided in Catherine Cronin-Harris, Building ADR into the Corporate Law Department: ADR Systems Design (CPR 1997).

11. *See generally id.* (discussing source materials for specific commercial transaction types).

don't just stick something in out of a form book, but consult someone who can actually help tailor a clause to the particular circumstances.

A valuable resource for businesses establishing ADR programs is the CPR Institute's *Building ADR into the Corporate Law Department* by Cathy Cronin-Harris.[12] Another useful tool is the CPR ADR Suitability Screen.[13] The following case study describes one among the many current examples of successful corporate ADR programs.

A Case Study:
A Corporate ADR Program[14]

After years of resolving business disputes by "liti-gotiation" (that is, filing pleadings, conducting discovery, and negotiating a settlement), one large company instituted a number of reforms in the way they managed conflict. Among other things, the managers established a company policy to employ tailored dispute resolution agreements in commercial contracts, and to evaluate business disputes at an early stage to determine whether some form of ADR might be employed to settle the case. A member of the legal department was assigned to oversee this effort. Today, although a few cases still go to trial, many more are resolved more quickly and less expensively, with little or no discovery. The program works because, among other things,

—there was a commitment by top management, including the assignment of an in-house person to oversee and implement the policy;

—company counsel developed the necessary expertise to appreciate and use ADR approaches (through training, written materials, and experience);

—dispute resolution provisions were developed for use in commercial agreements; and

—results of different approaches were patiently evaluated over time and "benchmarked" for future reference.

1.3

Are stand-alone arbitration provisions a good idea, or should dispute resolution agreements provide for steps preceding arbitration?

For many decades simple, stand-alone, standardized arbitration clauses have been included by rote in innumerable business agreements. As explained in the

---

12. *See supra* note 10.
13. *See CPR ADR Suitability Screen*, in CPR MODEL ADR PROCEDURES AND PRACTICES, (1998).
14. *See generally* Phillip M. Armstrong, *Case Study: Georgia-Pacific's Aggressive Use of Early Case Evaluation and ADR*, 16 No. 6 ACCA DOCKET, Nov./Dec. 1998, at 42.

introductory "About This Book," this is primarily because businesses perceived *binding arbitration*—the referral, by agreement, of disputes to a private tribunal for hearing and binding decision—as preferable to going to court. But while arbitration may offer certain advantages as a substitute for trial before a judge or jury, it is still a *form of trial.* In other words:

- it is an adversarial proceeding in which parties typically act through their attorneys;
- it may be preceded by lengthy pre-hearing practice, including discovery;
- it is left to the arbitrators to decide the issues in dispute and render an award (and remedy, if any).

While this approach may be necessary to put an end to a dispute that cannot be resolved any other way, other means are available that keep resolution of the dispute in the hands of the parties. Our Commission believes that binding arbitration normally should be the *final* step in dispute resolution. It normally should be preceded by *direct negotiations* between executives, and, if such negotiations do not resolve the matter, by *mediation.* As one Commissioner puts it:

> In conventional litigation, you usually have a number of opportunities to settle prior to court trial—often through mediation. I think many of us are trying to make arbitration work better, and some providers of dispute resolution services are starting to ask people at the beginning of the process, "Do you want to mediate or use another approach to try to help resolve the issues short of arbitration?"

These perceptions are echoed in a recent survey of litigators and Fortune 500 general counsel which shows that mediation is usually preferable to arbitration as a dispute resolution method.[15]

1.4

Should business parties include a clause calling for good faith negotiations between the parties as an initial step in dispute resolution?

1. A provision for good faith negotiation acknowledges the way most disputes are resolved

Most contract disputes lend themselves to resolution by direct negotiations. Contract provisions calling for parties to negotiate in good faith during a "cooling

---

15. *See* Brennan, *supra* note 2.

off" period merely acknowledge the usual starting point for dispute resolution. Such clauses should emphasize the critical importance of having authoritative decisionmakers at the table—in many cases, principal officers of the company.

2. It takes the onus off a party who wishes to "start the ball rolling"

By expressing the parties' mutual commitment to such discussions, clauses calling for good faith negotiations permit parties to call for such discussions without fear that their actions will be interpreted as a sign of weakness or lack of confidence in their position. In the interest of ensuring that settlement discussions bear fruit, such provisions may call for the participation of individuals at a higher level than the persons responsible for administering the agreement. The negotiators should possess settlement authority.

3. It provides an opportunity for crafting an appropriate dispute resolution process

It is often difficult to predict with certainty what kinds of disputes will arise under major commercial contracts. Direct negotiations afford parties a "window of opportunity" to discuss not only substantive issues, but to agree on an appropriate dispute resolution process for issues that cannot be dealt with immediately.

4. Drafting considerations

Drafting considerations for negotiation provisions and a sample clause are set forth in Chapter 2.

1.5

What are the particular advantages of mediation? Should it precede arbitration in the typical dispute resolution agreement?

As a rule, the business agreement should require the parties to *mediate* if direct negotiations do not resolve their dispute within a specified period of time.

Mediation—a flexible, non-binding process in which a neutral third person facilitates negotiations and helps create solutions—offers parties an excellent chance to settle their claims amicably on a business basis and to avoid much of the cost, delay, and adversarial practice associated with arbitration or court trial.[16] Leading providers of mediation services report that the great majority of commercial disputes they submit to mediation are settled through that process. Even if a dispute is not settled during mediation, the process usually lays the groundwork for later resolution of the issues. Even where disputes proceed to arbitration, mediation can set the stage for that process by narrowing and defining issues, facilitating information exchange, and enabling the parties to agree on specific procedures. The differences between these processes are outlined below.

Commonly cited advantages of mediation include:

- retaining control by the parties over the process, including the selection of an appropriate mediator and the ultimate resolution;
- reducing legal fees and other litigation expenses;
- facilitating prompt resolution, saving time and energy of executives;
- circumventing common barriers to negotiation;
- identifying and prioritizing interests (long and short term economic interests, political concerns, social issues, personal interests, etc., as well as legal interests);
- allowing the parties to speak directly to one another and to the issues;
- permitting the parties to fashion their own solutions, including creative, business-driven "win-win" solutions not available in court;
- preserving business and personal relationships;
- maintaining privacy and confidentiality; and
- retaining the option to arbitrate or litigate if the parties do not reach an agreement, and sometimes tailoring of dispute resolution to the particular circumstances with the assistance of the mediator as "process architect."[17]

One attorney who handles complex international business issues says, "I would recommend mediation in nearly every case."[18]

To understand better why mediation should be attempted prior to arbitration, consider the ways in which the processes differ:

In mediation...	**In arbitration...**
The parties to the dispute can play a central role as active participants in the process.	Presentations are made through attorneys; the parties play a secondary role.

---

16. *See generally* CPR Institute for Dispute Resolution, MEDIATION IN ACTION: RESOLVING A COMPLEX BUSINESS DISPUTE, VIDEOTAPE AND VIDEOTAPE STUDY GUIDE (1994)(excellent multi-media package touching on many aspects of commercial mediation). *See also* Brennan, *supra* note 2 (describing results of survey of litigators and general counsel strongly supporting use of mediation).

17. *See generally* Brennan, *supra* note 2. *See also* Stephanie Morse-Shamosh, *Preparing Your Client for Mediation of a Securities Arbitration Claim: An In-House Counsel's Perspective, in* SECURITIES ARBITRATION 1999 at 617 (Practicing Law Institute, 1999).

18. Brennan, *supra* note 2, at A1 (quoting Robert L. King, Esq., Debevoise & Plimpton).

In mediation...	**In arbitration...**
The process is highly informal and extremely flexible.	Though often less formal than the courtroom, the process may retain many of its trappings.
The parties control the ultimate resolution of disputes.	The ultimate resolution of disputes is in the hands of the arbitrator(s), not the parties.
The emphasis is often on the interests of the parties and/or their future relationship—"resolving problems in a principled fashion and moving on from here."	The focus is on past events or circumstances, and determining issues of fact and/or law.
Solutions are limited only by the willingness and the imagination of the participants, and may be anything from monetary settlements to unique forward-looking business arrangements.	Solutions are limited by the original agreement of the parties and the requests for relief, and usually consist of money damages or, more rarely, an injunction or other equitable relief.

Effective mediators function in very different ways from arbitrators:

Mediators...	**Arbitrators...**
Are appointed to facilitate negotiations of issues between the parties.	Are appointed to adjudicate disputes.
Work directly with the parties, often meeting confidentially with individual parties in the interest of encouraging full and frank discussion of the issues and the parties' needs and goals.	Are required to receive information from the parties in open hearings, and to avoid ex parte discussions.
May promote broadly focused discussions which encompass business and personal needs and goals, and may or may not dwell on legal or factual issues.	Are required to focus on the issues presented to them by the parties and no others, usually issues of fact and/or law.

Mediation usually entails few risks since the parties have the option of ending the process and proceeding to arbitration or trial. Although there is the possibility that mediation will fail to resolve the issues between the parties, effective use of the process usually proves valuable to participants. A good mediation may be the ideal foundation for an effective, efficient arbitration.

Case Study
A Successful Corporate Mediation Program[19]

A major manufacturer of lawn and garden equipment claims to have saved at least $50 million in litigation costs through the use of an aggressive ADR program using mediated settlement conferences early in the dispute resolution process. Although the program initially focused on personal injury claims, it has now expanded to encompass warranty, commercial, and breach of contract matters. The settlement rate of claims handled through the program has climbed from 90% to 95%; the total average cost of handling a claim has dropped from $115,000 to $30,600 and the average claim file life span has dropped from two years to three months.

Table 1. A
Pros and Cons of a Pre-Dispute Agreement to Mediate Disputes

Pros	*Cons*
Avoids post-dispute wrangling over whether to mediate and takes the onus off a party proposing the process.	Prevents a case-by-case determination of the appropriateness of mediation.
Only commits parties to sit down at the table together; they are not required to reach a settlement.	May delay ultimate resolution of issues, particularly if there is not a default mechanism for selecting a mediator, and for concluding mediation and moving on to arbitration.
May well result in resolution of some or all of the substantive issues.	If it fails, may actually heighten conflict between the parties.
Even if substantive issues cannot be resolved, may help to set the stage for arbitration (process design, facilitation of information exchange, selection of arbitrators) and, possibly, later settlement.	

Commission members generally believe the advantages of a pre-dispute agreement provision requiring participation in mediation substantially outweigh potential problems. The Commission recommends language requiring the parties to mediate prior to arbitration.

---

19. *See generally* Miguel A. Olivella, Jr., *Toro's Early Intervention Program, After Six Years, Has Saved $50M*, 17 ALTERNATIVES TO THE HIGH COST OF LITIGATION 65 (Apr. 1999).

1.6

What issues should be considered in approaching mediation?

Mediation is a very informal and flexible process, and extensive written rules are inappropriate. As one strong mediation proponent on the Commission explains:

> The *very point* of mediation is to avoid reliance on rules in favor of an informal, flexible approach based on the needs of the problem.

Having said this, CPR, the AAA, JAMS, and other organizations have developed mediation procedures that reflect the advice of leading mediators and that provide very useful ground rules. The CPR Mediation Procedures appear in Rules Appendix R.1; the CPR Rules for Non-Administered Arbitration are in Rules Appendix R.2; the AAA Commercial Dispute Resolution Procedures, including mediation procedures, appear in Rules Appendix R.3.

The rest of this section is a short list of issues to consider in approaching mediation.

1. Mediator selection

Mediator selection is the most important step in the process, because mediators vary considerably in experience, style, and technique.

- *All-purpose mediator or specialty mediator?* There is no substitute for experience with the mediation process. In certain situations (e.g, patent disputes, etc.), the parties are likely to prefer a mediator with subject matter expertise. In other types of disputes specific subject matter expertise is often of secondary importance.

- *Facilitative or evaluative approach?* Some mediators avoid any expression of opinion on issues in dispute in the belief that stating an opinion would undermine their mediative role. Others, emphasizing their role as agent of reality, tend to be more evaluative, and convey clear impressions regarding the strengths and weaknesses of a position or the reasonableness of a monetary claim.[20] Many mediators insist that they adjust their approach to the circumstances at hand: one experienced commercial mediator describes herself as "facilitative in the morning and evaluative in the afternoon." While some Commission members believe that the latter approach is often desired by business parties,[21] expressions of opinion must be offered with great care. A

---

20. *See, e.g.*, David L. Sandborg, *Multistep ADR Gets Creative At Hong Kong's New Airport*, 17 ALTERNATIVES TO THE HIGH COSTS OF LITIGATION 3, 41, 59 (Mar. 1999) (describing evaluative mediation process).

21. *See* Stipanowich, *supra* note 7, at 367–368 (summarizing findings in survey of construction attorneys).

judgment "from the hip" based on fragmentary information may be worse than nothing. Among other things, it may limit the mediator's viability in the event negotiations continue. Some mediators attempt to serve as an agent of reality without revealing their own perspective by effective questioning.[22]

- *Broad or narrow emphasis?* Mediation can be very effective in focusing discussions on broad business issues as opposed to narrow legal questions. Some mediators are more adept than others at expanding the discussion beyond the immediate issues in dispute.

2. Presence of key decisionmakers

As in unassisted settlement negotiations, a key to meaningful mediation is the presence of principals with broad authority to resolve the dispute. They can help identify and overcome obstacles to business solutions, pave the way for improved communications, and fashion an acceptable solution. It is helpful if the spokespersons on each side hold relatively similar positions.

3. Confidentiality

Confidentiality is usually critical to the success of mediation with respect to proprietary information and statements uttered during settlement discussions. To encourage candor in their discussions with the mediator, parties must have faith that their communications will be effectively shielded. Although a growing number of jurisdictions have court rules or statutes offering some protection for mediation-related communications, they vary greatly. The CPR Mediation Procedures and other leading procedures contain confidentiality provisions; parties may wish to supplement such provisions with additional agreements between the parties and the mediator that further protect communications in mediation.[23] Confidentiality issues in arbitration are treated in Chapter 6.

3. Memoranda; information exchange

In the interest of briefing the mediator, clarifying issues, and saving time, parties often prepare memoranda briefing the mediator on issues in dispute prior

---

22. The use of evaluation is discussed in Scanlon, *supra* note 1, at 81–83, 104–05. *See Symposium, Evaluative Versus Facilitative Mediation: A Discussion*, 24 FLA. ST. U. L. REV. 919 (1997), Kimberlee K. Kovach & Lela P. Love, *"Evaluative"Mediation Is an Oxymoron*, 14 ALTERNATIVES TO THE HIGH COST OF LITIGATION 31 (1996); John Bickerman, *An Evaluative Mediator Responds*, 14 ALTERNATIVES TO THE HIGH COST OF LITIGATION 70 (1996).

23. *See generally* Scanlon, *supra* note 1, at 27–36, 97–103.

to meeting with the mediator. (It is rarely appropriate to establish specific criteria for such memoranda in a pre-dispute mediation agreement.[24]) The nature and scope of the memoranda will ultimately depend upon the nature of the issues. Moreover, the mediator may have specific suggestions regarding the scope and form of the memoranda, which may provide an opportunity to explain to the mediator a party's interests and needs as well as legal and other objective standards for resolving the issues.

One or both parties may also believe that settlement negotiations will be facilitated by an information exchange. Again, because the needs of the parties are difficult to anticipate and because little or no information exchange may be necessary, the parties should avoid placing specific criteria in the pre-dispute mediation agreement. The mediator may help in bringing about an agreement between the parties on these issues.[25]

4. Deadlines; concluding the process

The CPR Mediation Procedure permits any party to terminate mediation unilaterally at any time after the first session. Like other leading rules, they also permit the mediator to conclude the process if the mediator perceives that continuation of the process would not be useful.

In addition, it is often appropriate to provide for a reasonable time limit on the process. Any such time limit may be extended by mutual agreement.

1.7

If the contractual dispute resolution provision does not provide for mediation, how do parties arrange for it after disputes have arisen?

If the parties have not included a provision calling for mediation of disputes in their business agreement, they may agree to mediate after a dispute has arisen. One party may persuade another party to mediate an active dispute by explaining mediation's potential benefits.[26] One particularly effective approach, say some business persons, is to show great flexibility in the selection of a mediator (even to the point of giving the other party the primary role in selection) and in the handling of mediation-related costs.

---

24. *See* CPR Institute, *supra* note 16, at 3.
25. *See id.* at 4.
26. *See* CPR INSTITUTE FOR DISPUTE RESOLUTION, MEDIATION PROCEDURE, Commentary at 25–26 (1998).

Sometimes, the most effective catalyst for mediation is the urging of an independent third party. At pre-arbitration conferences, arbitrators may encourage the parties to consider mediating if the parties have not already done so. Rule 18 of the CPR Non-Administered Arbitration Rules (CPR Arbitration Rules) provides that either party or the arbitration tribunal may propose settlement negotiations, and that "[w]ith the consent of the parties, the Tribunal at any stage of proceedings may arrange for mediation . . . by a mediator acceptable to the parties."[27]

1.8

What role(s) can mediators play in setting the stage for arbitration?

Where mediation is not immediately successful in resolving all or some of the issues between the parties, the question may arise whether mediators should assist the parties in preparing for arbitration.

1. Preliminary questions

In making this determination, four preliminary questions should be addressed:

(1) What, if any, administrative framework already exists for the appointment of arbitrators and for conduct of the arbitration process? (It may make mediator efforts superfluous or counterproductive.)

(2) If such a framework already exists, does it fully meet the parties' needs, or can it be improved with the mediator's assistance?

(3) Have arbitrators already been appointed? (If so, it may be necessary to defer procedural matters to the arbitrators. In any event, the mediator must avoid undermining the authority of the arbitrator.)

(4) What limits, if any, have been placed on the mediator by the agreement of the parties?

2. Possible assistance by mediator

If, after considering the foregoing questions, a mediator determines that such action would be reasonable and appropriate under the circumstances, a mediator (with the approval of the parties) may:

---

27. CPR Institute for Dispute Resolution, Rules for Non-Administered Arbitration, Rule 18.2 (Rev. 2000) [hereinafter CPR Arbitration Rules].

(1) facilitate agreement on exchange of documents and other information;

(2) help to determine which issues have been resolved in mediation, and to identify or frame issues to be arbitrated;

(3) assist in the selection of an arbitrator or arbitrators;

(4) help the parties define or refine arbitration procedures; and

(5) remain "on call" during arbitration to help resolve issues informally at the request of the parties.

3. Facilitating arbitration procedures in the large, complex dispute

Commission member Tom Arnold points out that at the time a commercial contract is entered into and before a dispute has arisen, businesses often do not have a specific understanding of their ultimate dispute resolution needs.[28] There are many elements of choice that may affect the effectiveness of arbitration; yet, parties may be unaware of these or unable to appreciate what choices make sense in their specific circumstances. Particularly in large, complex disputes, mediators may help the parties to make process choices in arbitration by considering, among other things:

- the complexity or value of the ultimate dispute, the need for discovery, and the appropriate level of resources to devote to the dispute;
- the need for a quick decision;
- the pluses and minuses of one versus three arbitrators;
- the desirability of various experiential or professional qualifications (such as having some arbitrators who are non-lawyers with a technical background in the subject industry);
- the pros and cons of using party-appointed arbitrators (who may be deemed to be predisposed toward their appointing party) as opposed to arbitrators appointed by a third party;
- the pluses and minuses of various arbitration institutions or of "ad hoc" arbitration in lieu of "administered" arbitration;
- the differences among various arbitration rules and the significance of those differences;
- the advantages and disadvantages of including findings of fact or rationales as a part of arbitration awards;
- the pros and cons of explicit time or scope limits on discovery or on party presentations in arbitration hearings;
- the value of commitments by all participants to completing arbitration by a particular date;

---

28. *See generally* Tom Arnold, MEDALOA, The Dispute Resolution Process of Choice (Dec. 27, 1996).

- the value of explicit arbitrator authority to reject evidence deemed prejudicial, redundant and/or immaterial without risking a court setting the award aside for refusal to consider evidence;
- what appellate review, if any, the parties contemplate.[29]

Mediation should provide both the parties and the mediator with a better understanding of the issues, enhancing the parties' ability to structure an arbitration closely tailored to their specific needs. In such situations the mediator may play a particularly important role in setting the stage for arbitration by helping the parties tailor an arbitration process to the now-well-understood dispute and circumstance[s].[30]

1.9
Is it appropriate for a person to play the role of mediator and arbitrator in the same dispute?

1. "Not as a rule"

There has long been a debate as to whether mediators should assume the role of arbitrator in the event mediation does not resolve all of the issues in dispute.[31] Consistent with the traditional view, Commission members generally oppose arrangements by which it is agreed in advance that a single individual will function as a mediator and an arbitrator in the same dispute, because these roles are not only very different in focus but in some respects mutually incompatible.

Those who support the concept that a neutral third party should be able to function as a mediator and, if necessary, an arbitrator in the same dispute—an approach often referred to as "med-arb," perceive at least two major benefits of the mixing of roles in a single individual:

(1) *Increased efficiency.* Having a single neutral serve in both roles permits the parties to avoid having to educate two separate neutrals, with attendant savings of time and cost.

---

29. *Id.* at 3–4.
30. *See id.* at 2.
31. *See* Barry C. Bartel, *Comment, Med-Arb as a Distinct Method of Dispute Resolution: History, Analysis, and Potential*, 27 WILLAMETTE L. REV. 661 (1991) (good history and thoughtful analysis of issues and options); David C. Elliott, *Med/Arb: Fraught with Danger or Ripe with Opportunity?*, 34 ALBERTA L. REV. 163 (1995)(discussing developments in Canada, Australia, and Singapore); Richard P. Flake, *Nuances of Med/Arb: A Neutral's Perspective*, ADR CURRENTS, June 1998, at 8 (considering pros and cons, providing general guidelines); Karen L. Henry, *Note, Med-Arb: An Alternative to Interest Arbitration in the Resolution of Contract Negotiation Disputes*, 3 OHIO ST. J. ON DISPUTE RESOLUTION 385 (1988); James T. Peter, *Note & Comment: Med-Arb in International Arbitration*, 8 AM. J. INT'L ARB. 83 (1997)(analysis of commercial med-arb and its variants); Irene C. Warshauer, *The Neutral in Multiple Roles: Practical and Ethical Issues*, ARBITRATION: PREPARING FOR THE 21ST CENTURY 794 (1998).

(2) *Greater impetus to settle—the "big stick."* If the parties are aware that their mediator will render a final and binding decision in the absence of a settlement, they may be more encouraged to settle their disputes in mediation. In other words, the mediator's ultimate arbitral authority functions as a "big stick" to settle the case.[32]

Today, a few neutrals regularly employ this approach to resolve commercial disputes.[33] Some leading institutional sponsors of ADR are now offering "med-arb" procedures.[34] Nevertheless, significant concerns remain.

2. Concerns regarding "med-arb"

The weight of opinion generally—and among members of the CPR Commission—disfavors a mixing of roles.[35] There are a number of reasons for this traditional antipathy toward "med-arb":

(1) *Fundamental incompatibility of mediative and arbitral roles.* The mediative and arbitral roles are in a sense diametrically opposed, since the arbitrator's interaction with the parties is confined to adversary hearings in which parties present evidence and contest opposing evidence, while mediation usually involves extensive ex parte communications with individual parties.

(2) *Coercion.* Some fear that the "big stick" wielded by a mediator-arbitrator will undermine party self-determination and prevent a negotiated settlement from truly representing the will of the parties. This is particularly true if the neutral "telegraphs" a personal perspective on the issues.

(3) *Less candid communications.* Parties who know a mediator reserves the arbitral role should mediation fail may be less forthcoming in their discussions with the mediator, thereby compromising the ability of the mediator to serve the parties effectively. One Commissioner relates:

> I went through a thirteen-session mediation where the neutral was supposed to fill a dual role, first mediating and, if that didn't work, acting as a special master who would make findings of fact for the court. What ended up happening in the mediation was that both parties were putting on a performance of sorts to shape his view as

---

32. *See* Bartel, *supra* note 31 (discussing empirical studies on med-arb).

33. *See, e.g.,* Flake, *supra* note 31, at 8.

34. *See, e.g.,* JAMS, Rules and Procedures for Mediation/Arbitration of Employment Disputes (1999).

35. Perhaps the most articulate critic of the process is Lon Fuller, who addressed med-arb in the context of collective bargaining agreements. *See* Lon Fuller, *Collective Bargaining and the Arbitrator, in* Proc. of the Fifteenth Ann. Meeting of the Nat'l Acad. of Arb. 8, 29–31 (1962).

the ultimate fact finder. Wearing multiple hats can produce a very murky process where roles are unclear, and people are dancing around and posturing. It's very risky.

(4) *Due process concerns.*   Mediation usually involves extensive confidential ex parte communications between the mediator and individual parties. If mediation is unsuccessful, there is always the possibility that the mediator-turned-arbitrator's view of the issues has been affected by information shared in ex parte discussions. This may include information which is not directly relevant to the issues contested in arbitration, and is never tested by cross-examination or rebuttal in the arbitration hearing—but which nevertheless colors a neutral's view of the parties or their positions on the issues in conflict. Such concerns moved one Commissioner to query:

> How can a mediator turned arbitrator purge his mind of acts and positions learned in confidence? I don't believe it can be done!

(5) *Potential defenses to arbitration award.*   Parties who want a neutral to serve in mixed roles must be very clear about the resolution of the foregoing issues and should address pertinent waiver issues (such as parties' waiver of the right to challenge any resulting arbitration award on grounds of ex parte contact). Otherwise, the arrangement may set the stage for a motion to disqualify an arbitrator or vacate a resulting arbitration award.

For all of these reasons, a majority of Commission members generally discourage parties from entering into pre-dispute or even post-dispute arrangements before a mediation in which the same individual is assigned the roles of mediator and arbitrator.[36]

3. Guidelines for situations where parties desire a mediator to assume the role of arbitrator

Having said all of the above, there may be situations in which mediation has been unsuccessful in resolving all of the issues between the parties and the parties desire the mediator to arbitrate those issues. In such circumstances, some attorneys and business persons may find that the prospective benefits of such a procedure outweigh the risks.

At or near the end of mediation, the parties and the mediator may be in a good position to appraise the mediator's suitability as a decisionmaker. Their decision to continue on with the same neutral for the arbitration phase repre-

---

36. *Cf.* CPR Arbitration Rules, *supra* note 27, Rule 18.2 (noting that where arbitrators arrange for mediation during the proceedings, the "[m]ediator shall be a person other than a member of the Tribunal . . . Tribunal."); Rule 18.3 ("The Tribunal will not be informed of any settlement offers or other statements made during settlement negotiations or a mediation between the parties, unless both parties consent.").

sents their vote of confidence in the neutral's objectivity and in the process. Similarly, the mediator invited to assume the role of arbitrator will be in a position to make an independent determination regarding the appropriateness of assuming that role. With proper precautions, approaching the question late in mediation honors the autonomy of the parties and preserves the integrity of the mediation process.[37]

Ultimately, the success of such arrangements depends upon (1) the ability of parties to understand the concerns associated with mixed roles and then to use the process constructively, and (2) the involvement of a sophisticated neutral qualified to handle the dual role.[38] Here is a set of guidelines for parties and mediators considering if the mediator should serve as arbitrator.[39]

(1) *The parties should make an informed decision regarding the mediator's continued service in the role of arbitrator, and confirm their agreement in writing.* The agreement should include an appropriate waiver of grounds for disqualifying the arbitrator or challenging the arbitration award. Parties considering the use of med-arb should address the foregoing concerns before agreeing to the process. They may wish to refer questions regarding the process to the institution sponsoring their conflict resolution procedures, if any.

When a mediator is invited to continue service in the role of arbitrator, she should make reasonable efforts to ensure that the parties are making an informed decision regarding the process and her own qualifications to serve. The mediator may discuss potential advantages and disadvantages of the arrangement as well as other alternatives to this course of action. In no event, however, should parties be requested to make a decision regarding choice of process or of the neutral's appointment in the presence of the neutral.

The agreement regarding the mediator's continued service as arbitrator should be clearly and carefully drafted. Among other things, the parties should determine the scope of the evidentiary hearing in arbitration. They should also agree that the neutral's participation in prior settlement discussions will not be asserted by any party as grounds for challenging any arbitration award rendered by the neutral.

(2) *A mediator taking on the role of arbitrator should be fully qualified for both roles.* The roles of mediator and arbitrator demand very different skills; a fully qualified arbitrator may or may not be an effective mediator, and vice versa. Prior to appointing a neutral to a dual role, therefore, the parties should make certain that the neutral is fully qualified in both roles.

---

37. *See* Peter, *supra* note 31, at 98.

38. *See* Bartel, *supra* note 31, at 675, quoting Herman Torosian, *Interest Arbitration Laws in Wisconsin*, in TRUTH, LIE DETECTORS, AND OTHER PROBLEMS IN LABOR ARBITRATION: PROC. OF THE THIRTY-FIRST ANN. MEETING OF THE NAT'L ACAD. OF ARB. 342, 346-50 (J. Stern & B. Dennis, eds. 1979).

39. These guidelines are based in part on David W. Plant, Draft Protocol for Arbitrators Who Participate in Settlement Discussions (Feb. 2, 1999).

A neutral invited to serve in a dual role should make reasonable efforts to ensure that the parties are making an informed decision regarding the neutral's qualifications.

(3) ***The mediator invited to serve as arbitrator should strive to avoid perceptions that the parties are being coerced to settle the dispute.*** In no case should a mediator solicit a dual role or put pressure on the parties to employ the mediator in a dual role. If one party raises the possibility of the mediator's continuing service as an arbitrator, the mediator should respond that the matter is properly one for joint agreement by the parties, and defer further discussion of the matter unless and until the matter is raised by all parties jointly.

(4) ***A mediator-turned-arbitrator should respect the confidentiality of settlement communications, and should be capable of deciding issues on the formal record.*** Documents, statements, and conduct during the settlement discussions are confidential and are usually protected by statutory rules of evidence as well as contractual provisions. A mediator-turned-arbitrator should respect these strictures and take care to decide issues on the record in the arbitration hearing.

After mediating, a neutral may determine that as a result of being exposed to certain confidential information conveyed ex parte or under other circumstances the neutral is unable to render an impartial decision on the record presented at the arbitration hearing. In such circumstances, the neutral has an obligation to recuse herself from the role of arbitrator.[40]

1.10

What are some variations on mediation-followed-by-arbitration?

There is, of course, no requirement that mediation and arbitration always follow a particular format. The following variations have all been employed in commercial conflict resolution. Unless otherwise noted, the following discussion assumes that different individuals will serve as mediator and arbitrator(s); those considering having a single individual serve in dual roles should first consider the concerns mentioned previously.

---

40. *See id.*

1. MEDALOA[41]

MEDALOA is an acronym for MEDiation And Last Offer Arbitration. It involves traditional mediation followed by a process in which each party submits a written final or "last offer" to the arbitrator. The arbitrator proceeds to pick the last offer he considers most equitable, or most appropriate under the standards established by the parties.[42]

In some cases MEDALOA is a means of breaking an impasse in a mediation, particularly where there is relatively little at risk or where the parties are not so far apart as to justify a full-fledged arbitration, and where the parties repose great trust in the mediator. In such cases, usually, the mediator becomes the arbitrator; after hearing short, trial-type summations of the parties' cases, the mediator-turned-arbitrator chooses the "last offer" which he regards as most just. That choice becomes the basis of an arbitration award. A Commissioner reports:

> I was recently involved in a multi-million dollar corporate dispute which had been in the court system for several years. When it became apparent that both parties were unwilling to make further concessions, the mediator suggested to the parties that since they were so sure of their respective positions, they might consider submitting the issue to last offer arbitration. Facing the prospect of a trial and a likely appeal, the parties discussed the idea and agreed to a timetable for last offer arbitration. They approached the mediator about serving as arbitrator, agreed on a procedure for submission of written materials to the latter, established a short form for the arbitrator's final award, arranged to have the award incorporated in a stipulated order of the court, and set an expedited timetable for the process. Within a matter of weeks, an award was rendered and the issue was finally resolved.

A variation would be where the parties exchange written last offers. The numbers are not disclosed to the arbitrator. The arbitrator makes his ruling. The parties agree that the award will be the offer closest to the arbitrator's number.

A second variation would be where the parties exchange written last offers, but do not disclose the offers to the arbitrator. The arbitrator makes his ruling. If the ruling is between the two offers, the arbitrator's number becomes the award. If the arbitrator's ruling is below the low offer, the low offer becomes the award. If the arbitrator's number is above the high offer, the high offer becomes the award.

---

41. *See generally* Tom Arnold, *supra* note 28 (detailed monograph by well-known arbitrator with considerable experience in the intellectual property field).

42. A Wisconsin labor statute provides for a form of MEDALOA where other processes have failed. *See* WIS. STAT. ANN. § 111.70(4)(cm)(6)(b) (West 1988), discussed in Bartel, *supra* note 31, at 668.

Table 1.B

MEDALOA

Potential Advantages	*Concerns*
The approach provides a relatively quick way of breaking an impasse in mediation and finally disposing of disputes.	Where a single individual serves as mediator and arbitrator, although the arbitral authority is limited there are still potential concerns about reliance on facts learned in confidential discussions in making a final award.
Knowing that the arbitrator must choose between high and low "last offers" encourages parties to move closer together.	The approach may be problematic where there are multiple issues, including non-monetary matters, on the table. The format may also limit the ability of the arbitrator to tailor the most appropriate resolution.
The approach limits the authority of the arbitrator and the commensurate risks of the parties.	

2. Simultaneous mediation and arbitration

Another possibility is to appoint different individuals as mediator and arbitrator(s), having both neutrals present at a fact-finding hearing, with mediated sessions during or after the close of hearings. If mediated negotiation does not resolve the dispute, the arbitrator(s) renders an award.[43]

A variant of this approach involves "mediation windows in arbitration," in which a mediator remains "on call" during the course of an arbitration but does not sit in on the hearing. Mediation may be conducted at any mutually convenient time and address the merits as well as procedural issues.

---

43. *See* Peter, *supra* note 31, at 101. *See also* Christian Buhring-Uhle, *Co-Med-Arb Technique Holds Promise for Getting Best of Both Worlds*, 3(1) WORLD ARB. & MEDIATION REP. 21 (1992).

Table 1.C

Simultaneous Mediation and Arbitration

Potential Advantages	*Concerns*
The joint session permits a thorough airing of the legal and factual issues for dual purposes; if the subsequent mediation fails, an arbitration award may be rendered quickly.	Significant efficiency concerns are raised by requiring the mediator to sit through days or weeks of formal presentations. The parties may end up spending much more time and money than they would if they used simple mediation.
Since the arbitrator and the mediator are different individuals, there is no concern that the arbitration award will be tainted by ex parte communications.	After arbitration has commenced, the parties may become more fixed in their positions and less willing to engage in collaborative problem-solving.

1.11

What other forms of third-party intervention may help facilitate settlement of business disputes?

Although mediation is the most popular form of third party intervention aimed at facilitating settlement of business disputes, there are other alternatives which may be appropriate in certain circumstances. These include mini-trial, non-binding abbreviated arbitration, and early neutral evaluation. All of these alternatives are described in the Glossary.

While an extensive treatment is beyond the scope of this book, special recognition should be given to the growing use of neutral evaluation processes in commercial disputes. Such approaches are founded on the notion that sometimes the best way of resolving a dispute is to garner an objective opinion on the subject. In some cases, the benefit of an "outside view" may be greatest during the first days or weeks after issues arise, before positions have hardened. One variant of neutral evaluation is the dispute review board (DRB).[44] DRBs typically are panels of technical experts who render advisory opinions on issues arising on a construction site; in many situations their opinions have settled conflicts and avoided the need for further adjudication.

---

44. *See supra* note 7, at 358–63 (1998).

Mini-trial is another approach in which abbreviated presentations precede independent advisory opinions and settlement negotiations. A Commissioner relates an experience in which mini-trial formed the first stage in an innovative ADR process:

> Some years ago, one of our coal producing clients was sued in state court by a number of its purchasers, all of whom were local utilities. The amount in dispute was approximately $200 million. It was agreed to divert the case to a private mini-trial, with party representatives and a former judge hearing the case over a two-day period, then deliberating in an effort to settle. Although the mini-trial failed to settle the case, it successfully reduced the issues in dispute to two. The parties subsequently agreed to try those issues in a one-day baseball arbitration in which the arbitrator (the same former judge as in the mini-trial) would have to pick the proposal of one of the two parties. In this way, the dispute was resolved within seven months, with fees and expenses, including expert fees, for both sides totaling around $3 million. At about the same time, the press carried accounts of a substantially similar case that was litigated in the courts at a cost of more than $20 million.

1.12
What roles may arbitrators play in settlement negotiations or mediation during arbitration?

1. Arbitrators and settlement

The arbitrator is empowered by the parties to decide the case. Facilitation of settlement is at best peripheral to the arbitrator's adjudicative function, but it is appropriate for an arbitrator to inquire whether the parties have attempted to settle their differences, and to take certain other limited measures to encourage settlement efforts.

(1) *Preliminary inquiries.* At the preliminary hearing or at some other point early in the proceedings, an arbitrator may make a general inquiry regarding settlement efforts, including mediated settlement efforts. The arbitrator should explain that she is not seeking specific information regarding the nature or content of settlement discussions.

(2) *Later inquiries.* Later in the arbitration, after there has been some clarification of the issues, or where the arbitration has been bifurcated and certain issues decided in a partial award, it may be appropriate to

make further inquiries regarding settlement efforts. Inquiry regarding the possibility of mediation may be particularly appropriate if the parties have identified certain underlying issues which are not within the remedial authority of the arbitrators.

CPR Rule 18 envisions a flexible role for arbitral tribunals based on the needs of the parties in the individual case:

> The Tribunal may suggest that the parties explore settlement at such times as the Tribunal may deem appropriate.[45] . . . With the consent of the parties, the Tribunal at any stage of the proceeding may arrange for mediation of the claims asserted in the arbitration by a mediator acceptable to the parties.[46]

2. The arbitrator as mediator in the same matter

As previously discussed in connection with "med-arb," there are legitimate concerns regarding the intermingling of the roles of mediator and arbitrator. Many adhere to the rule that a third party appointed as an arbitrator with respect to certain issues should not mediate those same issues. The CPR Rules anticipate that where the arbitrators arrange for mediation with the consent of the parties, "[t]he mediator shall be a person other than a member of the Tribunal."[47]

Some of the special concerns associated with mixed roles have been discussed previously in the context of med-arb. Commissioner David Plant developed a set of guidelines for parties considering having an arbitrator assume a mediative role (see Appendix 1.1).

If mediation is successful in resolving all of the issues, or focuses only on issues which are not intertwined with the other issues to be arbitrated, all may work out well. One Commissioner relates:

> I was appointed to arbitrate various issues associated with the breakup of a corporation. After discussions with the parties, the arbitration was bifurcated into two parts dealing with separate and distinct issues: (a) the valuation of shares in the business, and (b) allegations of self-dealing by officers of the company. The plan was for me to render an award on the first set of issues before conducting hearings on the second. Midway through the first set of hearings, the parties attempted to negotiate a resolution of the valuation issue. When unassisted negotiations reached a roadblock, they asked me to mediate the issue. After discussing the pros and cons of such an

---

45. CPR ARBITRATION RULES, *supra* note 27, Rule 18.1.
46. *Id.* Rule 18.2.
47. *See id.*

approach with the parties and their attorneys, and giving them an opportunity to reconsider their suggestion, we proceeded to mediate, and the matter was resolved informally. I subsequently arbitrated the claims of self-dealing, but because they were totally separate issues there did not appear to be a problem with my resuming the arbitral role.

The key question is: if an arbitrator attempts to mediate disputes and mediation fails, can even a highly skilled arbitrator resume the role of a truly neutral and impartial arbitrator to his own satisfaction and to the satisfaction of the parties? We believe the answer is likely to be in the affirmative if (a) the arbitrator, acting as mediator, did not provide the parties with an evaluation of the dispute, however informal or elliptical, and gave the parties no clue as to his views on any of the issues; and (b) if he did not caucus separately with either party and did not receive information from either party that was not shared with the other.

The answer to the question becomes much more problematic if the arbitrator/mediator caucused separately with the parties and/or received confidential information from either party. The Plant protocol states:

> In the event the arbitrator must resume the role of arbitrator after participating in settlement discussions, the arbitrator must undertake to decide the remaining issues only on the merits and only on the formal record. The arbitrator must take especial care not to add subconsciously to the record as a result of information acquired informally and off the record during settlement discussions.

To follow Plant's prescription may be challenging even for a highly sophisticated arbitrator. Moreover, although the parties' attorneys will have given their "informed consent" to the mediation process in advance, they and their clients may well develop doubts as to the arbitrator's ability to live up to Plant's ground rules. In particular, the losing party may suspect that its loss was attributable to off-the-record information obtained by the arbitrator during the mediation process.

Mediators commonly find caucusing with the parties to be an important, often critical aspect of mediation. We cannot say in the abstract to what extent the mediator's effectiveness would be impaired in a given case by declining to caucus, but we can say that holding caucuses is likely to complicate shifting back to the arbitral role, should that become necessary.

Despite these concerns, some neutrals will believe that they are capable of serving in dual roles and some commercial parties will be willing to experiment with such processes. Commission members urge all participants to consider the foregoing, and proceed with caution.

Appendix 1.1
Draft Protocol for Arbitrators Who Participate in Settlement Discussions

David W. Plant, Esq.
Draft of February, 2000

Introduction

Under appropriate circumstances arbitrators should participate in settlement discussions. Such circumstances must be clearly understood. This DRAFT Protocol, which is an amalgam of rules I proposed about 18 months ago and Professor Hal Abramson's excellent original thinking, is meant to assist arbitrators, counsel, and parties in identifying those situations in which the participation of an arbitrator in settlement discussion might be useful, as well as alerting all concerned to rules that ought to be given serious consideration. (I have noted with initials the source of each protocol below.)

An important predicate for implementation of this draft protocol is fully informed consent on the parts of all parties, all counsel, and all arbitrators. That is, not only must all concerned understand the events that may unfold as an arbitrator transforms into a participant in settlement discussion, and perhaps re-transforms into an arbitrator, but all concerned must be aware of the consequences of revealing different information under the different circumstances of arbitration and settlement discussions.

Another important predicate is that the arbitrator-turned-settlement-participant avoid an evaluative role. An evaluation at the settlement discussion stage may be materially inconsistent with the later view of the retransformed arbitrator—leading to dismay (at minimum) on the part of at least one party and its counsel.

Obviously, I hold the view that all neutrals' antennae should always be tuned to ways to assist the parties in finding their own solution to their problem, if such a possibility might be more efficacious, durable, and inexpensive than litigation. Thus, I believe that neutrals and ADR institutions should not, where appropriate, let finely honed rules foreclose creative, practical approaches to dispute resolution. [Such a protocol] may inspire some otherwise reluctant neutrals (usually, arbitrators) to seize an opportunity to assist the parties and save them time, money, and emotional stress—even in "commercial" disputes.

Protocol

1. The neutral should be trained in both arbitration and in settlement facilitation. (HA (1))

2. The parties plus their counsel must be fully informed as to the proposed procedure and its implications, and must agree expressly, specifically, and in writing as to the role of the arbitrator[1] in settlement discussions. (DWP; HA (11))

3. The arbitrator must agree to participate in settlement discussions (a) only with the foregoing express written agreement, and (b) only in accordance with the specific terms and conditions of such agreement. All concerned should be aware that settlement discussions are fluid, non-dimensional phenomena, and that amendments to the original agreement may be appropriate and may be made. (HA (2); DWP)

4. The arbitrator must respect the principle of party self-determination. (This may turn out to be a pithy summary of 2. and 3. above.) (HA (3))

5. Senior members of parties' management must be present with full authority to settle and bind the party. (This may require modification in re organizations managed by committee or consensus.) (HA (4))

6. Documents, statements, and conduct during the settlement discussions are confidential and subject to Rule 408 kinds of protections. (HA (5); DWP Fifth adds: "unless the parties and the arbitrator expressly agree otherwise in writing;" in HA (7), the arbitrator is forbidden to caucus privately, unless the parties agree otherwise.)

7. In the event the arbitrator must resume the role of arbitrator after participating in settlement discussions, the arbitrator must undertake to decide the remaining issues only on the merits and only on the formal record. The arbitrator must take especial care not to add subconsciously to the record as a result of information acquired informally and off the record during settlement discussions. (DWP, cf. HA (9))

8. The parties and their counsel must agree expressly in writing or on the record that the arbitrator's participation in settlement discussions will not be asserted by any party as grounds for disqualifying the arbitrator or for challenging any award rendered by the arbitrator (unless, for example, on its face it is apparent that the award is based prima facie in material part on information outside the record and learned by the arbitrator during settlement discussions). (DWP; cf. HA (10))

9. During settlement discussions, the arbitrator will not hint at the arbitrator's view of the evidence or the likely outcome on the merits if the arbitration goes forward, and will attempt to avoid a feeling of coercion on the part of any party. (DWP; cf. HA (6))

---

1. "Arbitrator" in the singular is intended to include arbitral panels comprising more than one arbitrator. Nice questions arise as to the role of a party appointed arbitrator and the role of a presiding arbitrator. In any event, I assume in this draft that all arbitrators, whether party appointed or otherwise, are neutral, impartial, and independent—and eligible to participate in settlement discussions.

10. The parties may/must agree to reconfigure the arbitral panel to suit the settlement process. (HA (8))

11. The arbitrator must not judge the credibility of any witness on the basis of (a) the witness's having been a party representative during settlement discussions or (b) anything said by, attributed to, or about the witness during settlement discussions—including apparent inconsistencies between a statement on the record and a statement off the record. This applies whether the witness appears, or files a statement, on the record before the settlement discussions or after such discussions. (DWP)

12. The arbitrator must not judge a party's case in light of an intractable position of the party during settlement discussions—especially where the arbitrator perceives an apparently valid, objective basis for resolving the parties' differences. (DWP; cf. HA (9))

Dispute Resolution Provisions

Chapter Summary

Dispute Resolution Provisions

2.5 **What are the other principal issues the drafter of an arbitration clause should address?.....................** **45**

Beyond the question of administration, the content of an arbitration agreement and the selection of appropriate arbitration procedures hinges on a number of key questions, including the following:

(1) How will arbitration dovetail with prior steps in dispute resolution?

(2) Will the parties arbitrate all disputes arising out of the agreement, or only certain types of issues?

(3) Will there be one arbitrator or three, or will the number depend on the amount in dispute? Should they have special qualifications?

(4) Where will the arbitration take place?

(5) Should the arbitration clause authorize the arbitrator(s) to rule on jurisdictional issues?

(6) What statute of limitations will apply? Who will rule on the issue?

(7) Should the arbitration clause specify the scope of discovery?

(8) Should the arbitration clause authorize the arbitrator(s) to grant interim relief?

(9) What law will govern?

(10) Must the arbitrator(s) follow the law?

(11) Should the arbitrator award be "bare" or "reasoned"?

(12) Should the arbitration clause establish time limits?

(13) What remedies should the arbitrator(s) be empowered to award?

(14) How final will the award be?

(15) Will the award be enforceable?

(16) What level of confidentiality is desired?

(17) Should performance under the contract continue?

(18) Should the arbitration clause survive termination of the contract?

Dispute Resolution Provisions

2.1

What is the significance of a model dispute resolution procedure for business agreements?

Over 90 percent of commercial arbitrations in the U.S. take place pursuant to clauses in business agreements that require the parties to submit disputes arising out of the agreement to binding arbitration. Mediations also are more likely to take place when the parties have made a pre-dispute commitment to mediate. Once a dispute has arisen, parties have difficulty agreeing about anything, and a proposal by either party to arbitrate or mediate is likely to be viewed with skepticism by the other. Properly drafted arbitration agreements generally are enforceable in U.S. courts and in the courts of many other nations. While the case law is not extensive, there is also authority to the effect that agreements to mediate are enforceable.[1]

Increasingly, the boilerplate arbitration clause is giving way to more sophisticated dispute resolution provisions encompassing multiple intervention strategies. Building upon our discussion in Chapter 1, the Commission proposes a three-step approach beginning with unassisted negotiation, followed if necessary by mediated negotiation and, ultimately, binding arbitration. The following drafting considerations and model language are offered as a starting point. As explained in Chapter 1, business parties and counsel should carefully evaluate this and any other proposed models for suitability to their own needs.

2.2

What specific steps should precede arbitration?

As discussed in Chapter 1, the Commission believes that binding arbitration normally should be the final step in a dispute resolution process, to be preceded by direct negotiations between executives, and, if such negotiations do not resolve the matter, by mediation. The Commission recommends a three-step dispute resolution approach calling for negotiation, mediation, and, if need be, arbitration. The following forms may provide useful templates for the drafting of provisions suitable for specific business relationships.

---

1. *See, e.g.,* DeValk Lincoln Mercury, Inc. v. Ford Motor Co., 811 F.2d 326, 335–37 (7th Cir. 1987); Haertl Wolff Parker, Inc. v. Howard S. Wright Construction Co., 1989 U.S. Dist. LEXIS 14756 (Civ. No. 89-1033-FR, DC Or. Dec. 4, 1989); AMF Inc. v. Brunswick Corp., 621 F. Supp. 456 (E.D.N.Y. 1985), Citibank N.A. v. Bankers Trust Co., 633 N.Y.S.2d 314 (N.Y. App. Div., 1st Dep't, 1995); Annapolis Professional Firefighters Local v. City of Annapolis, 642 A.2d 889 (Ct. Of Special MD App., 1994) (1994 MD App. LEXIS 101). *See also* James H. Carter, *Enforcing an Obligation to Mediate or Negotiate,* ADR Currents, June 1999.

1. Provision for good faith negotiation

A short-form provision

A pre-dispute agreement for negotiation between responsible representatives of the parties is preferable to leaving such negotiations to chance after a dispute has arisen. A basic negotiation clause, suitable for a simple standard form agreement, might provide:

> The parties shall attempt to resolve any dispute arising out of or relating to this Agreement promptly by good faith negotiation between executives with authority to settle the dispute.[2]

A more detailed provision

Some business parties, particularly those negotiating a contract covering a more complex subject matter or contemplating an ongoing relationship, may desire a more detailed clause along the lines of the following:

> The parties shall attempt to resolve any dispute arising out of or relating to this Agreement or the termination, breach, or validity of the Agreement, promptly by good faith negotiation between executives who have authority to resolve the controversy and who are at a higher level of management than the persons with direct responsibility for administration of this contract. Any party may give the other party written notice of any dispute not resolved in the normal course of business. Within [15] days after delivery of the notice, the receiving party shall submit to the other a written response. The notice and the response shall include (a) a statement of the party's concerns and perspectives on the issues in dispute, a summary of supporting facts and circumstances, and (b) the name and the title of the executive who will represent that party and of any other person who will accompany the executive. Within [30] days after delivery of the original notice, the executives of both parties shall meet at a mutually acceptable time and place, and thereafter as often as they reasonably deem necessary, to attempt to resolve the dispute. [All reasonable requests for information made by one party to the other will be honored.]

> All negotiations pursuant to this clause are confidential and shall be treated as compromise and settlement negotiations for purposes of applicable rules of evidence.[3]

---

2. CPR Dispute Resolution Clauses—Abbreviated Clauses for Business Agreements—Negotiation Clauses.

3. CPR Dispute Resolution Clauses—Detailed ADR Clauses for Business Agreements—Negotiation Clauses.

2. Mediation provision

The business agreement should require the parties to mediate if direct negotiations do not resolve their dispute within a specified period of time. Although mediation is an informal and flexible process, CPR, AAA, JAMS, and other organizations have developed mediation procedures that reflect the advice of leading mediators and that provide useful ground rules. Such procedures typically address matters such as:

- selection of the mediator,
- handling of costs,
- pre-mediation memoranda,
- exchange of documents,
- the conduct of mediation sessions, and
- how mediation may be terminated.

The mediation clause should incorporate a mediation procedure by reference.

The CPR Mediation Procedure provides for self-administration by the mediator and the parties.[4] The AAA and JAMS procedures provide for administered mediation. (The question of whether administrative services are appropriate in a given situation is discussed in Section 2.4 below.) A comparison chart of mediation procedures is included as Rules Appendix R.4.

The Commission suggests the following "model" mediation clause, to follow a negotiation clause:

> If the dispute has not been resolved by negotiation within [45] days of the disputing party's notice, or if the parties failed to meet within [20] days of such notice, the parties shall try in good faith to resolve the dispute by mediation under the then current [Mediation Procedure] before resorting to arbitration [litigation].[5]

"The clause may also address the qualifications of mediators, method of payment, locale of meetings, and any other items of concern to the parties."[6] Those desiring more extensive drafting recommendations should consult CPR's Mediation Procedure and related commentary.[7]

---

4. *See generally* CPR INSTITUTE FOR DISPUTE RESOLUTION, MEDIATION PROCEDURE (1998) [hereinafter CPR MEDIATION PROCEDURE].

5. Based on CPR Dispute Resolution Clauses.

6. *See* AMERICAN ARBITRATION ASSOCIATION, COMMERCIAL DISPUTE RESOLUTION PROCEDURES 4 (Jan. 1, 1999)[hereinafter AAA COMMERCIAL PROCEDURES].

7. *See* CPR MEDIATION PROCEDURE, *supra* note 4.

2.3

What should be the starting point for drafting a pre-dispute arbitration provision?

The AAA states in the Introduction to its Commercial Dispute Resolution Procedures:

> The parties can provide for arbitration of future disputes by inserting the following clause into their contracts:
>
> > Any controversy or claim arising out of or relating to this contract, or the breach thereof, shall be settled by arbitration administered by the American Arbitration Association under its Commercial Arbitration Rules, and judgment on the award rendered by the arbitrator(s) may be entered in any court having jurisdiction thereof.[8]

This clause or a similar one has been included in innumerable contracts. Its simplicity gives it appeal. A clause of this kind is generally satisfactory for many forms of simple agreement, whether the rules incorporated by reference are those of the AAA or another organization. The key, ultimately, is whether the basic arbitration clause and any incorporated rules provide a satisfactory framework for the arbitration process. Arbitration is a creature of contract, and the nature of the arbitration experience is directly dependent upon choices made by the parties in contract drafting.

The Commission believes that in drafting an arbitration clause for inclusion in a sophisticated business agreement attorneys should consider a number of key issues and discuss them with the client. The relatively harmonious atmosphere that typically prevails when a business deal is entered into provides the best opportunity to agree on sensible arbitration ground rules.

Numerous checklists of arbitration issues have been prepared. The most complete, to our knowledge, is an unpublished list of forty-seven issues compiled by Tom Arnold of the Houston firm of Arnold, White & Durkee, a member of the Commission.

Even if it were practical, business persons and attorneys rarely have to address forty-seven issues related to arbitration when drafting arbitration agreements. CPR, AAA, and other organizations have promulgated well-thought-out arbitration rules, amended periodically, that address many of the critical issues.[9] Well-drafted arbitration clauses do not "reinvent the wheel" but incorporate the rules of a respected organization by reference.

---

8. AAA COMMERCIAL PROCEDURES, *supra* note 6, at 1–2.
9. *See* recently revised CPR INSTITUTE FOR DISPUTE RESOLUTION, RULES FOR NON-ADMINISTERED ARBITRATION (Rev. 2000) [hereinafter CPR ARBITRATION RULES]; AAA COMMERCIAL PROCEDURES, *supra* note 6.

At the same time, however, both AAA and CPR encourage custom drafting and modification of standard rules to meet the specific needs of the contracting parties. Both organizations promulgate drafting aids for custom drafting and industry-oriented drafting. The AAA has published a valuable, comprehensive booklet entitled *Drafting Dispute Resolution Clauses—A Practical Guide.*[10] Among the many helpful resources produced by CPR for commercial practitioners and business persons are the *CPR Model ADR Procedures and Practice (MAPP) series*[11] and *A Drafter's Guide to CPR Dispute Resolution Clauses.*[12]

There are significant differences between the rules of various organizations. A comparison of the CPR and AAA rules appears in Rules Appendix R.5. A fundamental difference, however, is that the CPR Arbitration Rules call for non-administered arbitration after appointment of the arbitrator(s). The AAA Rules, and most (if not all) other domestic arbitration rules, provide for administered arbitration. Which rules the parties will choose may well depend on whether they prefer administered or non-administered arbitration.

2.4

Should we provide for administered or non-administered proceedings?

1. Scope and nature of administrative services

The principal functions normally performed by an organization administering arbitration proceedings are to:

- provide a set of rules which the parties can adopt in a pre-dispute agreement or for an existing dispute;
- provide administrative staff to render impartial case-handling services and to insulate arbitrators from parties;
- provide lists of potential arbitrators;
- appoint the arbitrator(s) if necessary;
- decide arbitrator conflict-of-interest challenges if necessary;
- determine arbitrator fees and bill the parties for such fees;
- schedule hearings and send notices of hearings;
- provide hearing rooms; and
- distribute documents and awards.

---

10. AMERICAN ARBITRATION ASSOCIATION, DRAFTING DISPUTE RESOLUTION CLAUSES—A PRACTICAL GUIDE (1998).
11. *See, e.g.,* CPR MAPP Series (2000).
12. A DRAFTER'S GUIDE to CPR DISPUTE RESOLUTION CLAUSES (2000).

The charges of administering organizations typically are related to the amount in dispute, but rates vary.

The AAA Commercial Arbitration Rules, like other aspects of the AAA Commercial Dispute Resolution Procedures,[13] provide for proceedings administered by AAA. The CPR Arbitration Rules are entitled "CPR Rules for Non-Administered Arbitration"[14]; "semi-administered" may be a more accurate term, as CPR will assist the parties in the selection of arbitrators.[15] However, once arbitrators have been selected, they assume responsibility for administrative matters. The UNCITRAL Rules, widely used in international arbitration, call for non-administered arbitration.[16]

2. Factors in determining whether to opt for administered or non-administered arbitration

The primary factors in determining whether and to what extent an administrator or administering organization is needed are the relative sophistication and working relationship of the parties and their counsel. Participants with less arbitration experience are likely to derive a wider range of benefits from administrative support, which provides a source of information and direction at various stages of the arbitration. More experienced parties or counsel may opt for less extensive administration (or no administration) on the ground that some or all of those functions may be unnecessary, or will be assumed by the arbitrators. In cases where the parties' sophistication and bargaining power are markedly different, administration may provide the weaker, less sophisticated party with information and guidance that will help the arbitration run smoothly and fairly.

Where there is a modicum of trust between key players, it may be possible to dispense with some or all third party administration of a case. Where a relationship of trust is lacking, on the other hand, the administrative framework may provide a buffer between the parties.

In non-administered arbitration, the selection of an experienced single arbitrator, or panel chair, is particularly important, since this individual also assumes administrative responsibilities.

In international arbitration, and perhaps also to some extent in domestic arbitration, the name and imprimatur of the institution under whose aegis the arbitration was conducted may carry weight if judicial enforcement of the award becomes necessary.

---

13. *See* AAA COMMERCIAL PROCEDURES, *supra* note 6.

14. CPR ARBITRATION RULES, *supra* note 9.

15. CPR publishes a list of neutrals who will serve as mediators or arbitrators. CPR will appoint mediators or arbitrators if the parties so request or if the parties' contractual procedures fail to result in an appointment. CPR will also determine challenges to arbitrators.

16. G.A. Ros. 31/98, UNCITRAL, 9th Sess., Supp. No. 17, U.N. Doc. A/31/17, chap. V, sect. C (1976).

2.5

What are the other principal issues the drafter of an arbitration clause should address?

In addition to the question of whether to opt for administered or non-administered arbitration, drafters of arbitration agreements should consider a number of key issues affecting the arbitration process. Their answers to these questions may help the parties to determine which arbitration rules to incorporate in their agreement, as well as what, if any, modifications of those rules should be reflected in their agreement. Although many of the following issues are addressed at greater length in other chapters, here is a brief treatment of the salient questions for drafters. A model arbitration provision is included as Appendix 2.1.

1. Dovetailing arbitration with prior steps in dispute resolution

Because the Commission views arbitration as the final step in a three-step process, drafters should consider how and when mediation (or other non-binding settlement-oriented process) concludes and arbitration begins. In particular, the Commission recommends that the agreement avoid undue delays to dispute resolution by setting outside time limits on mediation, after which either party may file a demand for arbitration. Pertinent language is suggested in the Model Arbitration Provision below.

As noted in Chapter 1, moreover, some arbitration procedures envision a continuing role for arbitral tribunals in promoting settlement discussions[17] and/or mediation.[18]

2. Arbitration of all disputes vs. only certain types of issues

The provision above calling for arbitration of "any dispute arising out of or relating to this Agreement or the breach, termination or validity of the Agreement" reflects the common tendency of drafters to use language of extreme breadth in describing the scope of the arbitration agreement. Such a broad provision minimizes the likelihood of disputes over arbitrability, especially since

---

17. CPR ARBITRATION RULES, *supra* note 9, Rule 18.1.
18. *See id.* Rule 18.2.

the courts enforcing arbitration provisions under the Federal Arbitration Act ("FAA") and similar state arbitration statutes interpret such terms with great liberality.[19]

In some situations, however, business parties may have sound reasons for limiting arbitrability to specific issues (which should be defined with care), or to establish a dollar limit on claims subject to arbitration. Clauses that provide for arbitration of some types of disputes and not others frequently lead to disputes about whether the dispute that has arisen is arbitrable,[20] and should be used with caution.

3. Number of arbitrators

As explained in Chapter 3, the arbitrator is in many respects the key to the process. The proceeding is likely to be considerably more expeditious and economical if conducted by a single experienced arbitrator of proven ability. In order to enhance the likelihood of securing an individual with the desired qualifications, the parties may want to specify that the single arbitrator:

- shall be an attorney with at least ___ years' experience as a litigator, or
- shall have served as an arbitrator in a certain number of commercial arbitrations, or in arbitrations dealing with a particular kind of dispute, or
- shall have expertise in the subject matter of the dispute.

In some cases, business parties may deem it necessary or appropriate to have a panel of three arbitrators. If there are to be three arbitrators, the Commission recommends that all three be selected in a manner to assure they will be truly neutral. In Chapter 3 we discuss issues related to arbitrator selection, including the drawbacks of providing for party-appointed arbitrators. Again, the parties may want to consider setting forth specific qualifications for panelists where it is possible to anticipate what sorts of skills or experiences will prove valuable.

4. Place of arbitration

The parties should select the place of arbitration in their agreement. If no place is designated in the contract, and the parties cannot agree on a place once a dis-

---

19. *See generally* Ian R. Macneil, Richard E. Speidel & Thomas J. Stipanowich, I Federal Arbitration Law: Agreements, Awards & Remedies Under the Federal Arbitration Act § 15.1.5 (1994) [hereinafter Macneil et al.].

20. *See id.* at § 7.20.3.

pute has arisen, the place of arbitration will be fixed by the arbitrator(s) under the CPR Arbitration Rules[21] and by AAA under its rules.[22]

5. Authorizing the arbitrator(s) to rule on jurisdictional issues

Under the Federal Arbitration Act and prevailing state arbitration law, in the absence of an agreement to the contrary, courts address defenses to agreements to arbitrate.[23] Likewise, issues of "substantive arbitrability"—that is, the question of whether a dispute is within the scope of an agreement to arbitrate— traditionally have been for courts to decide.[24] Such issues are thereby distinguished from matters of "procedural arbitrability"—time limits on the filing of claims, compliance with notice provisions, laches, estoppel, and the like— which are typically handled by arbitrators.[25]

In *First Options of Chicago, Inc. v. Kaplan*,[26] the U.S. Supreme Court held that clear language in the agreement could authorize arbitrators to rule on issues relating to their own jurisdiction—including defenses to the arbitration agreement and matters of substantive arbitrability. Today, leading arbitration procedures give arbitrators explicit authority over such issues. An example of such a provision is CPR Rule 8, which provides in part:

> 8.1 The Tribunal shall have the power to hear and determine challenges to its jurisdiction.
>
> 8.2 The Tribunal shall have the power to determine the existence, validity or scope of the contract of which an arbitration clause forms a part, and/or of the arbitration clause itself. For the purposes of challenges to the jurisdiction of the Tribunal, the arbitration clause shall be considered as separable from any contract of which it forms a part.

Section R-8 of the AAA Commercial Procedures is to similar effect.[27]

Such provisions dramatically decrease the likelihood that a court will entertain jurisdictional defenses, thereby minimizing the probability of a pre-arbitration delaying action in the courts. On the other hand, such clauses give plenary authority over all conceivable challenges to arbitration to the arbitrators themselves; as explained in Chapter 7, their determinations will be subject to only limited review by the courts.

---

21. CPR ARBITRATION RULES, *supra* note 9, Rule 9.6.
22. AAA COMMERCIAL PROCEDURES, *supra* note 3, § R-11.
23. *See* MACNEIL ET AL., *supra* note 19, § 7.15.1.
24. *Id. See also* National Conference of Commissioners on Uniform State Laws, Uniform Arbitration Act (2000), § 6, Reporter's Commentary.
25. *See* MACNEIL ET AL., *supra* note 19, § 7.15.1.
26. First Options of Chicago, Inc. v. Kaplan, 514 U.S. 938 (1995). *See* MACNEIL ET AL., *supra* note 19, § 4.10.
27. AAA COMMERCIAL PROCEDURES, *supra* note 6, § R-8.

6. The statute of limitations will apply

Statutes of limitations typically relate to the commencement of actions in court. Most arbitration clauses do not specify what statute of limitation applies, on the assumption that the law specified as the governing law will determine what statute of limitation applies. To ensure predictability, the parties can provide that the statute of limitation of the governing substantive law will apply, exclusive of its conflict-of-laws rule, or they can establish a specific time limitation, which may be shorter than the statutory period, as follows:

> Any claim by either party shall be time-barred unless the asserting party commences an arbitration proceeding with respect to such claim within one year after the claim arose [OR, ALTERNATIVELY, within one year after the basis for such claim became known to the asserting party]. This time limit shall be tolled during any negotiation or mediation under the terms of this Article.

It is important to keep in mind that in the absence of a clear agreement to the contrary, issues relating to the timeliness of a claim, like other so-called procedural issues, are usually not decided by courts, but are referred to arbitration.[28] Under the typical broad-form clause, described above, this means that allegations that a claim was not filed within a limitations period will not normally prevent the arbitration provision from being enforced and the issue from going to arbitration.[29] This is particularly true under provisions such as CPR Rule 8[30] and § R-8 of the AAA Commercial Procedures[31] which authorize arbitrators to address all jurisdictional issues.

7. The scope of discovery

As discussed at greater length in Chapter 4, the ability to obtain adequate discovery is of concern to many parties when they consider arbitration. Rule 11 of the CPR Arbitration Rules provides:

> The Tribunal may require and facilitate such discovery as it shall determine is appropriate in the circumstances, taking into account the needs of the parties and the desirability of making discovery expeditious and cost-effective. The Tribunal may issue orders to protect the confidentiality of proprietary information, trade secrets and other sensitive information disclosed in discovery.[32]

---

28. *See* MACNEIL ET AL., *supra* note 19, § 7.15.2.
29. *Id.*
30. CPR ARBITRATION RULES, *supra* note 9, Rule 8.
31. AAA COMMERCIAL PROCEDURES, *supra* note 6, § R-8.
32. CPR ARBITRATION RULES, *supra* note 9, Rule 11.

The Commission believes the above provision adequately protects the interests of the parties and that the basic arbitration clause need not deal with discovery if the CPR Rules are incorporated by reference.

Rule 23(a) of the AAA Commercial Procedures is somewhat more limited, providing:

> At the request of any party or at the discretion of the arbitrator, consistent with the expedited nature of arbitration, the arbitrator may direct (i) the production of documents and other information, and (ii) the identification of any witnesses to be called.[33]

Sections L-4 and L-5 of the AAA Optional Procedures for Large, Complex Commercial Disputes are more detailed.[34]

The parties may want to provide that each party will produce early in the arbitration all documents it intends to rely upon, or may rely upon, in the arbitration. As discussed in Chapter 4, however, such issues will in many cases be addressed by the arbitrators at a pre-hearing conference.

8. Authorizing the arbitrator(s) to grant interim relief

Rule 13 of the CPR Arbitration Rules (a) empowers the arbitrator(s) to take interim measures that are deemed necessary, including measures for the preservation of assets, and (b) provides that a request to a court for interim measures shall not be deemed incompatible with an agreement to arbitrate or as a waiver of such an agreement.[35] The AAA Commercial Procedures are to the same effect and specifically authorize injunctive relief and measures for the conservation of property.[36]

Moreover, the AAA has promulgated Optional Rules for Emergency Measures of Protection.[37] When the parties have agreed to adopt such rules, relief may be granted by an "emergency arbitrator" or by a special panel before the regular arbitration panel is constituted.

If the parties incorporate the CPR Arbitration Rules or the AAA Commercial Procedures by reference, usually their agreement need not deal expressly with the subject of interim relief, unless in the case of an AAA arbitration they wish to adopt the Optional Rules referred to above.

The granting of interim relief by arbitrators is discussed in Chapter 4.

---

33. AAA COMMERCIAL PROCEDURES, *supra* note 6, § R-23(a).
34. *See id.* §§ L-4, L-5.
35. *See* CPR ARBITRATION RULES, *supra* note 9, Rule 13.
36. *See* AAA COMMERCIAL PROCEDURES, *supra* note 6, §§ R-36, R-45(a), (b).
37. *See id.* §§ O-1–O-8.

9. Governing law

Business parties typically provide in their agreement that the law of a particular jurisdiction, inclusive or exclusive of its conflict-of-laws rules, shall govern as to the merits of contract disputes. The picture is a bit more complicated when the parties agree to arbitration, because there is a body of federal and state law governing the enforcement of arbitration agreements and awards which must be considered separately from the normal choice-of-law issue.

Federal and state arbitration statutes and related law

Modern arbitration statutes—the FAA,[38] state enactments based on the Uniform Arbitration Act,[39] and similar statutes—establish a broad legal framework for the enforcement of arbitration agreements and arbitration awards. Such statutes typically:

- provide for the specific enforcement of arbitration agreements, subject to contract defenses aimed at the agreement to arbitrate;[40]
- authorize courts to stay pending litigation of disputes subject to arbitration, and to compel parties to arbitrate;[41]
- give courts authority to appoint arbitrators if the agreement fails to establish a method for appointment or there is a failure of the agreed-upon mechanism;[42]
- establish a mechanism for judicial enforcement of arbitral subpoenas;[43]
- provide for judicial confirmation, vacatur, or modification of arbitration awards.[44]

Arbitration statutes exist to facilitate the use of arbitration through private agreements. Although they provide a necessary judicial backdrop for such arrangements, they should *never* be considered a substitute for effective contract planning and should not be relied upon to fill in the specific details of arbitration procedure where the parties have failed to do so.

For most commercial parties, the FAA is the primary source of law respecting their arbitration agreement. The FAA governs arbitration agreements in contracts involving interstate or international commerce and supplies various rules for arbitration proceedings unless the parties specify otherwise. Although the FAA does not itself establish subject matter jurisdiction in any court for the

---

38. Federal Arbitration Act, 9 U.S.C. § 1-1 (West Supp. 1994) [hereinafter FAA].
39. 7 Uniform Laws Annotated 4 (1978).
40. *See, e.g.,* FAA, *supra* note 38.
41. *Id.*
42. *Id.*
43. *Id.*
44. *Id.*

purpose of enforcing arbitration agreements, the U.S. Supreme Court has identified the FAA as the source of a federal substantive law governing the enforcement of arbitration agreements—a body of law which preempts contrary state
law in federal or state court.[45] Since the Court has broadly interpreted the reach
of the FAA under the Commerce Clause,[46] arbitration agreements in most commercial transactions are likely to be subject to the FAA. Although in many cases
it makes little or no difference whether the FAA or state arbitration law controls,
there are circumstances where state arbitration law would dictate a different
result, as made clear below.

The extent of FAA preemption of state arbitration law is a subject of considerable debate.[47] The issue is complicated by *Volt Information Sciences, Inc. v.
Board of Trustees of the Leland Stanford Jr. University*,[48] in which Court held that
the FAA did not preempt application of contrary provisions of state arbitration
law where the parties' agreement expressly incorporated the laws of California.
Therefore, the Court ruled that it was appropriate for a court to apply a provision of the California arbitration statute empowering the court to stay arbitration in the context of a multiparty dispute pending judicial resolution of the
dispute—a result contrary to that which would otherwise obtain under the pro-
arbitration dictates of the FAA.

Commercial counsel are strongly advised to familiarize themselves with
potentially applicable statutory law, including the FAA and state statutes, and
court decisions interpreting them. This is particularly important in light of
anticipated revisions to the Uniform Arbitration Act, which is the template for
state arbitration law in the great majority of states.[49] Under most circumstances,
the Commission considers it advisable for a commercial arbitration agreement
to be governed by the FAA in order to ensure a measure of uniformity and
predictability in the enforcement of the arbitration agreement. To ensure that
the FAA will apply, regardless of the law which the parties have specified to govern on substantive issues, the arbitration clause should provide that the arbitration will be conducted under the FAA, to the exclusion of state laws inconsistent
therewith or which would produce a different result.

General choice of law clauses governing other aspects of the contract

As long as it is made clear that the arbitration agreement will be subject to the
FAA, the Commission favors the incorporation of a choice-of-law clause to govern interpretation and enforcement of the remainder of a commercial contract.

---

45. *See* Southland Corp. v. Keating, 465 U.S. 1, 104 S. Ct. 852, 79 L. Ed. 1 (1984). *See* MACNEIL ET AL., *supra* note 19, § 10.6.
46. *See* Allied-Bruce Terminix Cos. v. Dobson, 513 U.S. 1140 (1994). *See also* MACNEIL ET AL., *supra* note 19, § 14.8.
47. *See generally* MACNEIL ET AL., *supra* note 19, ch. 14.
48. 489 U.S. 468 (1989).
49. *See supra* note 24.

10. Following the law

As explained in Chapter 7, modern arbitration law and arbitration rules recognize broad authority on the part of arbitrators to conduct hearings and structure appropriate remedies. The AAA Commercial Procedures and the CPR Arbitration Rules, like many other commercial arbitration procedures, do not by their terms explicitly authorize arbitrators to disregard applicable law, but they also do not specifically require the arbitrator(s) to follow the law. Many attorneys and business persons regard such arbitral flexibility as a desirable feature of arbitration.

If, however, parties want to have disputes decided according to the law and reduce the likelihood of a "compromise award," they may state that "the arbitrator(s) shall decide in compliance with the applicable law and not *ex aequo et bono* or as *amiable compositeurs.*" While this language may affect the conduct of arbitrators, existing limits on judicial review of arbitration awards make it unlikely that an arbitration award will be reversed for errors of law, save in extreme cases involving "manifest disregard of the law." These issues are treated in Chapter 7.

11. "Bare" vs. "reasoned" awards

Rule 14.2 of the CPR Rules requires the arbitrator(s) to "state the reasons on which the award rests unless the parties agree otherwise."[50] On the other hand, § R-44(b) of the AAA Commercial Procedures provides for a bare award, unless the parties request an explanation of the award or the arbitrator(s) determines that an explanation is appropriate.[51] The rationale for "reasoned" awards is that (a) the parties want to know the basis for the decision, and (b) this requirement reduces the risk of an arbitrary or capricious decision. Some believe that such an award is more vulnerable to attack. If the parties were to provide for an expanded right of appeal, an explanation of the award would be an essential requirement. The pros and cons of "bare" and "reasoned" awards are discussed further in Section 7.5.

12. Time limits

Arbitration clauses sometimes specify time limits on completion of the arbitration, on certain phases of the arbitration, or on rendering of an award. While such time limits may be appealing, it is difficult to set realistic limits in a pre-

---

50. CPR Arbitration Rules, *supra* note 9, Rule 14.2.
51. AAA Commercial Procedures, *supra* note 6, § R-32(b).

dispute agreement, when the complexity and magnitude of the dispute are not known. It is suggested that if such limits are specified, the consequences of a failure to complete the specified activity by the time limit should be made clear. For example, under many standard rules, a failure to respond to an arbitration demand is specifically treated as a denial of the allegations in the demand.[52] Where parties agree to overall time limits on the completion of arbitration hearings or the rendition of an award, it is probably best to make clear that the intent is for the parties or arbitrators to use their best efforts to comply with the time limit, but that the failure to so comply will not abort the arbitration or cause the arbitrators to lose their jurisdiction.

The CPR Arbitration Rules empower the Tribunal to impose time limits on each phase of the proceeding, including party presentations at hearings.[53] Furthermore, CPR Rule 14.7 provides:

> The dispute should in most circumstances be submitted to the Tribunal for decision within six months after the initial pre-hearing conference required by Rule 9.3. The final award should in most circumstances be rendered within one month thereafter. The parties and the arbitrators shall use their best efforts to comply with this schedule.[54]

The AAA Commercial Procedures give arbitrators broad authority over the hearing, including the setting of time limits on presentation time.[55] AAA Commercial Procedures § R-43 requires submission of the award within thirty days from the closing of hearings, or, if the parties have waived oral hearings, thirty days from the AAA's final transmittal of the final statements and proofs to the arbitrators(s).[56]

While time limits may be of some assistance in ensuring that arbitration is not unduly delayed, the best assurance of an expeditious proceeding is the selection of an experienced arbitrator or panel chair who is able and determined to conduct the proceeding with a firm hand. The importance of process management is discussed in Chapters 4 and 5.

13. Limits on remedies

As explained in Section 7.1, some arbitration rules, including the AAA Commercial Procedures, empower the arbitrator(s) to grant any remedy or relief which they deem "just and equitable."[57] The recently revised CPR Arbitration Rules state that the "Tribunal shall apply the substantive law(s) or rules of law

---

52. *Id.* at § R-4 (c).
53. CPR ARBITRATION RULES, *supra* note 9, Rule 9.2.
54. *Id.* Rule 14.7.
55. See AAA COMMERCIAL PROCEDURES, *supra* note 3, § R-32(b).
56. *Id.* § R-43.
57. *See, e.g., id.* at § R-45(a).

designated by the parties as applicable to the dispute. Failing such a designation by the parties, the Tribunal shall apply such law(s) or rules of law as it determines to be appropriate."[58] Such provisions reinforce the general principle of arbitration law that in the absence of contrary agreement arbitrators have remedial authority commensurate with the nature and scope of the issues before them.

Punitive or exemplary damages; limits on damages

As indicated in Section 7.2, there is a strong trend in the United States toward recognizing the authority of arbitrators to award punitive damages when the parties' agreement permits such an award or is silent on the issue.[59] Consequently, if the parties do not wish to empower the arbitrator(s) to award punitive damages, or other damages in excess of compensatory damages, they are well advised to state this. An agreement to that effect does not necessarily mean that the parties have waived the ability to obtain punitive damages in court. Although commercial contracts sometimes incorporate terms that prospectively waive claims for punitive damages, the enforceability of such provisions is not free from doubt.

Section 7.5 also discusses general contractual limits on monetary awards. For example, parties sometimes restrict the discretion of arbitrators by establishing caps on monetary relief, or by agreeing (at the time of submitting a dispute to arbitration or even during the proceeding) to a dollar range within which the award must be rendered. One increasingly popular option is "last offer" or "baseball" arbitration, in which each party must submit a proposed award, and the arbitrator's power is limited to deciding between the parties' proposals.

Equitable relief

The CPR Arbitration Rules and AAA Commercial Procedures expressly empower arbitrators to order specific performance.[60] As previously noted, this includes the authority to grant interim relief such as orders for the preservation of goods or other property pending a final resolution on the merits.[61]

If the parties wish to empower the arbitrators to award only monetary damages, they should make their intentions explicit. To the extent that they intend to reserve the right to seek equitable relief in court, this should also be made plain.

---

58. CPR Arbitration Rules, *supra* note 9, Rule 10.1.
59. *See* Macneil et al., *supra* note 19, § 36.3.4.
60. *See* CPR Arbitration Rules, *supra* note 9, Rule 10.3; AAA Commercial Procedures, *supra* note 6, § R-45(a).
61. *See supra* text accompanying notes 36 and 37.

Interest

As explained in Section 7.1, some commercial arbitration rules empower the arbitrator(s) to award interest, including pre-award interest.[62] Some parties, however, may wish to provide more specific guidance regarding pre-award interest, including the applicable rate of interest.

Attorney's fees

As discussed in Section 7.3, the handling of attorney's fees varies under leading commercial rules. Under the CPR Arbitration Rules, arbitrators are specifically empowered to award "costs for legal representation and assistance" along with other costs,[63] while the AAA Commercial Procedures make no provision for arbitral awards of attorney's fees.[64] Under the latter rules, parties who wish arbitrators to have such authority must make certain that the agreement contains a specific provision to that effect.

14. Finality of the award

As discussed in Section 7.6, the grounds for vacation of an arbitration award under § 10 of the FAA and state counterparts are limited to arbitrator misconduct, partiality, corruption, and other grounds relating primarily to the fairness of the process. Although the law regarding judicial review of arbitration awards is uncertain, it may be said that courts rarely inquire into the merits of a commercial award.

Some business parties have sought to expand the scope of judicial review by so providing in their arbitration agreement. Chapter 7 discusses the pros and cons of such arrangements and explains why Commission members tend to discourage them.

For those desiring some oversight of arbitral awards, another approach is to arrange for review by a private appellate panel of arbitrators. CPR and JAMS have developed procedures for private appeals to a special panel of arbitrators.[65] Such procedures are also described in Chapter 7.

15. Enforceability of award

Modern arbitration statutes typically include provisions for enforcement of arbitration awards along the lines of § 9 of the FAA, which states:

> If the parties in their agreement have agreed that a judgment of the court shall be entered upon the award made pursuant to the arbitration, and shall

---

62. AAA COMMERCIAL PROCEDURES, *supra* note 6, § R-45(d).
63. *See* CPR ARBITRATION RULES, *supra* note 9, Rule 16.2(d).
64. *See generally* AAA COMMERCIAL PROCEDURES, *supra* note 6.
65. *See, e.g.*, CPR INSTITUTE FOR DISPUTE RESOLUTION, CPR ARBITRATION APPEAL PROCEDURE (1999).

specify the court, then at any time within one year after the award is made any party to the arbitration may apply to the court so specified for an order confirming the award, and thereupon the court must grant such an order unless the award is vacated, modified, or corrected as prescribed in sections 10 and 11 of this title. If no court is specified in the agreement of the parties, then such application may be made to the United States court in and for the district within which such award was made.[66]

Courts have refused to enforce arbitration awards when the arbitration agreement pursuant to which the award was rendered has not indicated the parties' intention that a court can enter judgment on the award.[67] Courts have found the necessary intent when the arbitration clause (1) states that judgment can be entered on the award, or (2) describes the award as "final" or "final and binding," or (3) incorporates rules such as the CPR and AAA Rules that contain such provisions.[68]

To avoid any doubt about the enforceability of an arbitration award under the FAA, parties should state in their arbitration clause that "the award rendered by the arbitrator(s) shall be final and binding and judgment upon the award may be entered by any court having jurisdiction thereof."

16. Level of confidentiality

Protecting confidentiality is important to many arbitration users. Chapter 6 discusses protection of the confidentiality of arbitration proceedings through arbitration rules and through supplementary agreements between the parties, with arbitrators and even with witnesses.

17. Performance of the contract

The parties may want to provide that performance of the contract will continue while negotiations, mediation, and arbitration are pending. The following language is suggested:

> Each party is required to continue to perform its obligations under this contract pending final resolution of any dispute arising out of or relating to this contract, [unless to do so would be impossible or impracticable under the circumstances].[69]

The parties also may want to confirm that pendency of the contemplated procedures "shall not be deemed a waiver of any right of termination under the contract."[70]

---

66. FAA, *supra* note 38, § 9.
67. *See* MACNEIL ET AL., *supra* note 19, § 38.2.
68. *Id.* § 15.2.
69. CPR Dispute Resolution Clauses.
70. *Id.*

18. Survival beyond the contract

As noted in Section 4.4 and as made explicit in CPR Rule 8[71] and some other commercial arbitration procedures, pre-dispute arbitration clauses generally are deemed separable from the contract of which they form a part, and therefore survive the expiration or termination of the contract of which they formed a part.[72] However, the cautious attorney can include a statement to that effect in the clause.

2.6

What provisions should be made for arbitration in multiparty agreements?

If a business agreement is among more than two independent parties whose interests may diverge, the agreement may nevertheless provide for arbitration of any disputes among all or certain of the parties, but the arbitration provision should differ in some respects from those suggested in the preceding sections. In particular, a provision calling for a three arbitrator tribunal, with two arbitrators to be appointed unilaterally by the parties, is likely to prove impractical when there are more than two parties with divergent interests. We recommend that, if the parties see a need for three arbitrators, the clause provide that all three shall be truly neutral and selected by agreement among all parties to the arbitration, and failing such agreement, by a neutral organization such as CPR or AAA.

2.7

Can third parties be included in the arbitration?

Some contractual disputes cannot be fully resolved without the inclusion of a third party that is not a party to the contract in dispute. In litigation such a third party usually can be made a co-defendant or third-party defendant, subject to possible jurisdictional barriers. Arbitration, however, is different in that (1) no one can be required to arbitrate unless they are bound by an agreement to arbitrate, and (2) where related transactions involve more than one contract, each

---

71. *See* CPR ARBITRATION RULES, *supra* note 9, Rule 8.
72. *See* MACNEIL ET AL., *supra* note 19, § 15.1.

of which has its own arbitration agreement, and multiple arbitrations arise from the same dispute but under different agreements, there may be a problem getting all of the parties into a single forum.[73] Thus, parties in the middle of a web of related commercial contracts may find themselves in multiple proceedings with attendant delays, additional costs, and perhaps even inconsistent results. Although some courts have ordered consolidated arbitration hearings pursuant to arbitration agreements in different contracts in multiparty disputes, others (including most courts which have addressed the issue under the FAA) have refused to order consolidated hearings in the absence of express agreements permitting it.[74]

The lesson for parties engaged in transactions involving multiple parties and multiple contracts: take into account the possibility of multiparty disputes in drafting an arbitration agreement. Parties wishing to preclude consolidation without party consent can include a statement to that effect in the arbitration clause. On the other hand, parties who enter into contracts with multiple parties, like owners of construction projects, may seek to avoid the prospect of multiple proceedings and potentially inconsistent results by including complementary provisions in all the arbitration agreements for consolidated hearings involving all parties in the event of a multiparty dispute. Such provisions must be drafted with particular care to ensure a workable and fair arbitrator selection procedure. One possibility would be to provide that if all parties cannot agree on an arbitrator or panel, a neutral organization should be authorized to make the appointment(s). The place of arbitration and governing law should be specified, subject to later agreement on another place or law.

2.8

Should we provide for an expedited procedure?

The AAA, JAMS, and certain other organizations have adopted expedited or fast-track procedures for cases of modest size. In the case of AAA, the procedure applies where no claims or counter-claims exceed $75,000, or by party agreement as to larger cases.[75] JAMS offers streamlined procedures for cases in which no disputed claim or counterclaim exceeds $250,000, excluding interest.[76] Such procedures feature short time limits, abbreviated arbitrator selection procedures, and hearings which are often limited to a submission of documents.

---

73. *See generally* MACNEIL ET AL., *supra* note 19, ch. 33.
74. *Id.*
75. *See* AAA COMMERCIAL PROCEDURES, *supra* note 6, § E-1*ff.*
76. *See* JAMS STREAMLINED ARBITRATION RULES AND PROCEDURES (1999).

The parties could provide in their arbitration clause that if such a case should arise, it will be arbitrated under the AAA or another expedited procedure. Absent a provision to that effect, if such a dispute arises, the parties may agree to expedited arbitration at that juncture.

2.9

What if we wish to provide for an expert determination?

In certain types of business transactions the parties can anticipate a dispute that is best resolved through a binding independent appraisal or other expert determination. The parties can provide for this contingency in different ways. Depending on the approach the parties take, the expert determination may be deemed (1) an arbitration award, enforceable as a court judgment, or (2) something other than an arbitration award, perhaps enforceable under other contract principles.

Modern arbitration statutes provide for judicial enforcement of arbitration agreements and awards and facilitate arbitration in a number of ways, including, for example, judicial appointment of arbitrators and enforcement of arbitrator-issued subpoenas. If a procedure involving a "binding" determination by a third party does not fall under the statute, the handling of such matters may be significantly less straightforward. While some courts will apply arbitration statutes to procedures which, while not labeled "arbitration," are functionally comparable (as where parties in dispute choose a judge to render a final and binding decision on the merits of the controversy and on the basis of proofs presented by the parties"[77]), others will not. Therefore, it is important for parties to make clear whether a procedure for binding determination by a third party is or is not "arbitration" within the meaning of the FAA or applicable state statutes.[78]

A clause envisaging an expert determination raises issues the parties should address, such as the following:

- How do the parties communicate with the expert?
- Does the expert have to hold hearings?
- Can parties present their own expert witnesses?
- Can parties or their experts examine and cross-examine (a) the expert and (b) other witnesses?
- Can experts do independent research or must they rely on data supplied by the parties?

---

77. *See* Francis Kellor, American Arbitration 5 (1948).
78. *See generally* Macneil et al., *supra* note 19, § 2.3.

- How can a party enforce an expert's decision?
- Do expert decisions enjoy any statutory or treaty protection?

Here are some of the options available to parties contemplating an expert determination in their contract:

(1) ***Treat the expert determination as an arbitration.***   The parties could provide for a binding determination by an expert and add that the determination is to be treated as an arbitration award for various purposes. The chances that a court would comply with the parties' "boot-strapping" language are uncertain but would be improved if an adversary procedure, including presentation of evidence and briefs, were prescribed.

(2) ***Place an expert on the arbitration panel.***   The parties could adopt a regular arbitration clause but require that one arbitrator be an expert in the subject matter of the dispute. Such an expert may not be comfortable presiding at oral hearings. The parties could waive evidentiary hearings and provide for submission of evidence in written form.

(3) ***Expert advisor in arbitration.***   The parties could use an arbitration clause and provide that in certain types of disputes one or more neutral experts will be appointed by agreement of the parties, and failing agreement, by the arbitrator(s). The expert's role would be to assist the arbitrator(s), who would make the ultimate decision. This approach is useful if the dispute is likely to involve contract interpretation or other issues not within the expert's orbit.

Appendix 2.1
Model Arbitration Provision

The following "model" arbitration provision, which would be incorporated in the dispute resolution provisions of a contract following good faith negotiation and mediation clauses, is offered as a starting point for drafting. This general template, which sets out a few of the more likely options for business parties, should be carefully reviewed and modified as appropriate after consideration of the issues raised in the foregoing pages. *(Note: The precise form and content of the basic arbitration provision may vary greatly depending upon the scope and detail of the incorporated arbitration procedures. It may also be necessary to provide that in the event of conflict between the contractual arbitration provision and the incorporated procedures, the former shall govern.)*

Article __ Dispute Resolution

__.3   Binding Arbitration

__.3.1 Any dispute arising out of or relating to this Agreement or the breach, termination, or validity of the Agreement which has not been resolved by mediation within __ days of the initiation of such procedure, or which has not been resolved prior to the termination of mediation, shall be resolved by arbitration in accordance with the [Arbitration Rules] in effect on the date of this Agreement. [If either party fails to participate in mediation, the other may initiate arbitration before expiration of the above period.]

__.3.2 Arbitration shall be before

[a sole arbitrator] OR

[three independent and impartial arbitrators, all of whom shall be appointed by agreement of the parties or by the administering authority in accordance with its rules] OR

[three independent and impartial arbitrators, of whom each party shall appoint one].

__.3.3 The place of arbitration shall be _____.

__.3.4 [The arbitrator(s) [are] [are not] empowered to award damages in excess of compensatory damages.]

OR

[The arbitrator(s) may award punitive damages or other exemplary relief if such an award is authorized by law in a civil action involving the same subject matter. The arbitrator shall specify the amount of the punitive damages or exemplary relief and the basis in law for such relief in the award.]

[NOTE: SEE DISCUSSION OF ARBITRAL REMEDIES FOR DISCUSSION OF ATTORNEY'S FEES AND OTHER RELIEF.]

__.3.5 The award rendered by the arbitrator(s) shall be final and binding, and judgment upon the award may be entered by any court having jurisdiction thereof.

__.3.6 All matters relating to the enforceability of this arbitration agreement and any award rendered pursuant to this agreement shall be governed by the Federal Arbitration Act, 9 U.S.C. § 1–16. The arbitrator(s) shall apply the substantive law of the State of _____, exclusive of any conflict of law rules.

__.3.7 Each party is required to continue to perform its obligations under this contract pending final resolution of any dispute arising out of or relating to this contract, [unless to do so would be impossible or impracticable under the circumstances].

__.3.8 [Any claim by either party shall be time-barred unless the asserting party commences an arbitration proceeding with respect to such claim within one year after the claim arose [OR, ALTERNATIVELY, within one year after the basis for such claim became known to the asserting party]. This time limit shall be tolled during any negotiation or mediation under the terms of this Article.]

OR

[The statute of limitations of the State of _____ applicable to the commencement of a lawsuit, exclusive of its conflict of laws rules, shall apply to the commencement of an arbitration hereunder, except that the statute of limitations shall be tolled during any negotiation or mediation called for by this Article.]

All issues relating to the timeliness of claims shall be resolved by the arbitrator(s).

Finding the Right Arbitrators

Chapter Summary

Finding the Right Arbitrators

Finding the Right Arbitrators

3.1

Why is the selection of a highly competent arbitrator or arbitration tribunal of overriding importance?

1. The arbitrator is the key to the process

The essence of arbitration—that which distinguishes the process from court adjudication—is freedom of choice. Private parties enjoy considerable autonomy in agreeing upon their own process and selecting their own decision-maker(s).

Choosing an arbitrator or arbitration tribunal is the most important decision facing parties in commercial arbitration, because in many respects, the arbitrator is the key to the arbitration process.[1] It is not enough to say that arbitrators combine the functions of judge and jury; under modern law and practice arbitrators have plenary authority regarding procedural as well as substantive matters in arbitration. They enjoy great leeway in interpreting and applying the rules governing the arbitration, judging the merits, and tailoring appropriate remedies. Judicial review of arbitrators' decisions is severely restricted under current federal and state statutory schemes.

In addition to acting as quasi-judicial officers with broad authority, arbitrators are usually expected to serve as "expediters" to ensure that the arbitration is as speedy and efficient as possible. In many cases, they are also expected to bring a degree of relevant commercial and/or legal knowledge, training, and experience to the table. Because arbitration proceedings are normally regarded as private proceedings, arbitrators must act to preserve the privacy of the hearings.

Despite the foregoing, parties often choose, or agree to the appointment of, arbitrators about whom they know very little. This is unfortunate because arbitrator performance is often critical to the arbitration experience.

2. Concerns regarding arbitrators

In light of the critical nature of the arbitral role and the varied expectations of parties in the high-stakes arena of commercial arbitration, it is not surprising that concerns regarding commercial arbitration often focus on perceived shortcomings of arbitrators and their decisions. A recent survey of leading U.S. cor-

---

1. *See generally* IAN R. MACNEIL, RICHARD E. SPEIDEL & THOMAS J. STIPANOWICH, III FEDERAL ARBITRATION LAW: AGREEMENTS, AWARDS & REMEDIES UNDER THE FEDERAL ARBITRATION ACT, at ch. 26 (1994) [hereinafter MACNEIL ET AL.].

porations[2] reported a wide range of experiences with and perceptions of commercial arbitrators.[3] More than a quarter of corporate respondents saw a *lack of qualified arbitrators* as a barrier to the use of arbitration.[4] *Nearly half* said that a *lack of confidence in arbitrators* was a deterrent. Related concerns include:

- arbitrator failure to conduct an expeditious, efficient process;[5]
- "compromise" awards;[6]
- "irrational awards" and limited grounds for appeal.[7]

While Commission members understand and acknowledge concerns regarding arbitrator quality and the possibility of poorly reasoned awards, their experiences with arbitrators in major commercial cases have been *generally very positive*, and provide a basis for helpful guideposts for arbitrator qualification and selection. We will discuss these in the remainder of this chapter. (We will return to the subject of arbitration awards in Chapter 7.) Special attention will be given to the unique concerns associated with tripartite panels involving arbitrators appointed by, and sometimes affiliated with, a single party.

3.2

What are the key attributes of effective arbitrators?

Is it possible to identify attributes of the ideal commercial arbitrator or arbitration tribunal? Clearly, different circumstances demand somewhat different arbitrator strengths and talents. Nevertheless, a Commission working group comprised of experienced users of arbitration, many of whom have served as arbitrators in major cases, identified the following as necessary characteristics of effective arbitrators.

---

2. David B. Lipsky & Ronald L. Seeber, The Appropriate Resolution of Corporate Disputes: A Report on the Growing Use of ADR by U.S. Corporations, Cornell/PERC Institute on Conflict Resolution (1998).
    3. *Id*. at 28–29.
    4. *Id*.
    5. Many businesses are looking to arbitration and other forms of alternative dispute resolution (ADR) as a means of reducing legal transaction costs and avoiding a legal system with which they have grown increasingly frustrated. *Id*. at 20–21. Conversely, perceptions that arbitration is "too costly" apparently deter some companies from using it. In light of the significant managerial role played by arbitrators, the choice of arbitrator is directly linked to perceptions of the process. *Id*. at 28–29.
    6. Many respondents, including a third of "frequent users," expressed concerns regarding the perceived tendency of arbitrators to render "compromise awards." *Id*.
    7. Many, including almost half of self-described "frequent users" of arbitration, expressed concerns regarding the difficulty of appeal of arbitration awards. This reflects a lack of confidence in the ability of arbitrators to produce rational, predictable results. *Id*.

1. Fairness, objectivity, open-mindedness

Fairness, objectivity, and the ability to keep an open mind are the most prized of arbitrator attributes. The reality and perception of a fair, just, and expeditious process is essential to the effectiveness of arbitration. Effective arbitrators thus conduct themselves in a manner which reveals no bias, preconception, or particular sympathy for either party, and avoid statements or actions which convey a sense that the outcome of the proceeding has been decided.[8] The concept of "fundamental fairness" at the hands of an independent, impartial arbitrator is embodied in laws governing arbitration, standard arbitration procedures, and the Code of Ethics for Arbitrators in Commercial Disputes.[9] Each of these will be considered in the following pages.

2. Diligence, efficiency, and decisiveness

Almost as important as fairness in an arbitrator is the ability to conduct proceedings efficiently and diligently, and, where necessary, to act decisively. Experience running an arbitration, a no-nonsense approach to case management, and personal availability for an expeditious hearing schedule all contribute to the orderliness, speed, and efficiency that so many business users regard as a major benefit of arbitration.[10] Says one commercial lawyer:

> My clients demand at the outset that an arbitrator be willing to take affirmative steps toward initiating [movement toward] the arbitration hearing, set a preliminary hearing, issue a written pre-arbitration order, abide by the terms of that order and require the parties to abide by that order, and keep the process moving fairly and efficiently. At the hearing, my clients want attention to the presentation, familiarity with pre-filed materials, rulings that take into account the evidence submitted, courtesy to all persons present, a clear ruling on deadlines for actions by the parties' representatives, as well as a clear deadline for the final award. Post-hearing, they demand a well-written decision covering all issues raised, issued by the announced date.[11]

---

8. AMERICAN ARBITRATION ASSOCIATION DEPARTMENT OF NEUTRALS' EDUCATION & DEVELOPMENT, ROLE OF THE PANEL CHAIR: UNDERSTANDING PANEL DYNAMICS 5–6 (1999)[hereinafter ROLE OF THE PANEL CHAIR].

9. AMERICAN ARBITRATION ASSOCIATION/AMERICAN BAR ASSOCIATION, CODE OF ETHICS FOR ARBITRATORS IN COMMERCIAL DISPUTES (1977). The Code is currently being revised through the efforts of the Arbitration Committee of the ABA Section on Dispute Resolution with the assistance of the American Arbitration Association, CPR, and other groups.

10. These conclusions are consistent with the observation by one recent commentator that in national and international ADR, "impartiality" and "authority" are key attributes of third party neutrals. Carole Silver, *Models of Quality for Third Parties in Alternative Dispute Resolution*, 12 OHIO ST. J. ON DISP. RES. 37, 45 (1996). *See also* ROLE OF THE PANEL CHAIR, *supra* note 8, at 6.

11. E-mail from Paul Keeper to Thomas J. Stipanowich, Professor, University of Kentucky College of Law, Jan. 7, 1999.

Arbitrators who are perceived as effective also demonstrate the ability to act decisively at appropriate times, whether in dealing with procedural rulings or in making a final award. As one guide for panel chairpersons explains, "Nothing undermines the authority of the panel as effectively as . . . backing down or equivocating after issuing a ruling or decision."[12] At the same time, however, the arbitrators must balance the need to act firmly and decisively with the requirements of fundamental fairness—a meaningful hearing before an open-minded decisionmaker.

To Commission members, many of whom frequently are involved in the resolution of large or complex commercial disputes, the desire for strong case management skills often means an arbitrator who is a member of the bar with extensive experience as an arbitration advocate, arbitrator, or judge. Because lawyers and judges vary greatly in ability and temperament, however, selections must be made with care.

3. Ability to get to "the truth of the matter"

An arbitrator needs the capability to get to "the truth of the matter." One guide for commercial arbitrators encourages arbitrators to maintain a healthy skepticism:

> It is rare indeed for parties and their counsel to incur the expense of bringing a dispute to arbitration without there being at least one difficult issue for the neutral to resolve. There may be uncertainty over the correct application of the law, over the relevant facts, or a conflict between the equities and the law which bring the parties to arbitration. No experienced . . . [arbitrator] should be gulled into believing early on that a case is a slam-dunk for one side or the other. The skeptical mind reserves judgment.[13]

Effective arbitrators exhibit not only personal discernment, but the ability and willingness to ask the right questions of witnesses or of counsel when it is critical to a full appreciation of the issues. In the view of some parties, it may also require an arbitrator with subject matter expertise.

In short, Commission members desire fair, open-minded, dependable arbitrators with experience handling and managing cases—neutrals who are dedicated to the process, to its expeditious, efficient execution, and to a just result. Beyond this, the appropriate blend of knowledge, experience, and personality traits hinges largely on the circumstances of the particular case.

Multi-member arbitration panels avoid the need to find all of the desired qualities in a single arbitrator. On a three-member panel the chair might be an arbitration process/legal expert and the "wing" arbitrators might be business or

---

12.   ROLE OF THE PANEL CHAIR, *supra* note 8, at 6.
13.   *Id.* at 5.

technical experts. The rationale for and dynamics of arbitration panels are discussed below.

How does one find arbitrators with the desired attributes?

Sometimes arbitrators can be chosen on the basis of personal acquaintance or professional reputation. Selecting an arbitrator with whom the parties or attorneys are familiar, through business or professional contacts, including bar associations or business or trade groups, may generate added confidence in the process and enhance the acceptability of the final award. The extent to which personal or professional relationships raise disclosure obligations on the part of arbitrators, and the risk that such relationships may occasionally lead to challenges to an arbitrator's appointment on grounds of partiality will be discussed below.

Consistent with the model described above, the tradition in this country has been for parties to draw arbitrators on a case-by-case basis from the ranks of active professionals or business persons; and commercial arbitration has not generally been viewed as a professional calling. Now, however, a growing number of people are marketing their services as commercial dispute resolution professionals. Most of them rely heavily upon word-of-mouth for referrals.[14] A number of national organizations also maintain lists of individuals available to serve as arbitrators. Some organizations publish these lists, but others do not. In addition, some law firms and business associations are beginning to advertise their members' services as arbitrators on a regional or national basis. At a time when arbitrating parties often know little or nothing about prospective arbitrators, there remains considerable variance in the qualifications and suitability of commercial arbitrators.

Arbitrating parties are therefore well advised to obtain information regarding prospective arbitrators with an eye to answering the following questions:

(1) Is the arbitrator capable of acting fairly and with an open mind?
(2) What are the arbitrator's professional or experiential qualifications?
(3) Has the arbitrator received pertinent education and training?
(4) Does the arbitrator have pertinent experience in an arbitrator's role? Has there been feedback on the arbitrator's performance?
(5) What are the arbitrator's fees? Is the arbitrator "reasonably available"?

---

14. *See* Silver, *supra* note 10, at 46.

The choice of arbitrators is often made more difficult by the fact that an arbitration agreement usually is entered into at the time a business relationship is created and prior to the emergence of disputes. The parties may not be sure of the kinds of commercial or legal expertise that may be appropriate for the arbitrator(s) of their dispute (or even whether they will need a single arbitrator or a panel). Parties intending to arbitrate in accordance with the rules of a particular arbitral organization should inquire regarding the general qualifications of arbitrators in the designated organization's commercial pool(s). A number of organizations make great efforts to develop and maintain high-quality panels of arbitrators by employing rigorous standards for the selection and training of candidates; others do not. As a rule, therefore, arbitrating parties should make a point of finding out what criteria, if any, are used by a sponsoring organization in choosing and training panelists.

A list of specific questions for provider organizations and prospective arbitrators is set forth in the Appendix 3.1.

1. Ability to act fairly and with an open mind

An independent, impartial decisionmaker is critical to the reality and perception of due process; for this reason, a party cannot judge his or her own dispute. Federal and state laws governing binding arbitration recognize that arbitrating parties have the right to be judged impartially and independently.[15] Thus, the Federal Arbitration Act (FAA), which among other things governs arbitration agreements in transactions involving interstate commerce, provides that an arbitration award may be vacated (undone) by a court "[w]here there was evident partiality or corruption in the arbitrators, or either of them,"[16] and most state arbitration laws contain similar language.[17] This basic tenet of procedural fairness assumes even greater significance in light of the strict limits on judicial review of arbitration awards.[18]

---

15. MACNEIL ET AL., *supra* note 1, § 28.2.1.

16. Federal Arbitration Act, 9 U.S.C. § 10(a)(2) (West Supp. 1994) [hereinafter FAA].

17. The Uniform Arbitration Act, adopted by most states, provides that an award may be vacated where "there was evident partiality by an arbitrator appointed as a neutral or corruption in any of the arbitrators or misconduct prejudicing the rights of any party." UNIF. ARB. ACT, § 12(a)(4) (1955).

18. *See* Drinane v. State Farm Mut. Auto Ins. Co., 153 Ill. 2d 207, 212, 606 N.E.2d 1181, 1183, 180 Ill. Dec. 104, 106 (1992) ("Because courts have given arbitration such a presumption of validity once the proceeding has begun, it is essential that the process by which the arbitrator is selected be certain as to the impartiality of the arbitrator."); *see also* Dowd v. First Omaha Securities Corp., 242 Neb. 347, 495 N.W.2d 36 (1993) (noting legal and practical limits on review of arbitration awards).

The tension between party choice, arbitrator expertise and impartiality

The problem of arbitrator partiality is a thorny one because consensual arbitration involves a tension between abstract concepts of impartial justice and the notion that parties are entitled to a decision maker of their own choosing, including an expert with the biases resulting from particular career experience.[19] As discussed below, arbitrating parties frequently choose arbitrators on the basis of prior professional or business associations or pertinent commercial expertise. In many commercial communities and legal specialties such associations are virtually impossible to avoid.

How, then, is the balance to be struck between a fair process and arbitrator "connectedness" to the participants or the issues? The answer is *arbitrator disclosure*. The idea, which runs through applicable law, commercial arbitration rules, and ethical standards, is that by giving parties timely information about a prospective arbitrator's past or present connections with those involved in the case and the disputed issues, the parties will be in a good position to decide whether the candidate is acceptable.[20]

Arbitrator disclosure and the law

Although the Federal Arbitration Act and most state arbitration statutes do not expressly require arbitrators to disclose potential conflicts of interest, the principle is well recognized by court decisions. The principle that questions of arbitrator partiality are best consigned to parties after due disclosure by arbitrators was expounded in the seminal case of *Commonwealth Coatings Corporation v. Continental Casualty Co.* (1968),[21] a decision under the FAA. In that case, the Supreme Court held that an undisclosed business relationship between an arbitrator and one of the parties constituted "evident partiality" requiring vacation of the award. Members of the Court differed, however, on the standards for disclosure. Justice Black, writing for a four-judge plurality, concluded that non-disclosure of "any dealings that might create an impression of possible bias" or creating "even an appearance of bias" would amount to evident partiality.[22] Justice White, while supporting the holding, argued for a more limited test which would require disclosure of "a substantial interest in a firm which has done more than trivial business with a party."[23] What is most significant about *Commonwealth Coatings* is the notion that an arbitrator's failure to disclose certain facts may itself be sufficient to strike down an award—even without proof of actual prejudice to a party.

---

19. *See* Merit Ins. Co. v. Leatherby Ins. Co., 714 F.2d 673, 679 (7th Cir. 1983), *cert. denied,* 464 U.S. 1009, 104 S. Ct. 529, 78 L. Ed. 2d 711, *modified,* 728 F.2d 943 (7th Cir. 1984) (applying FAA); Perl v. General Fire & Cas. Co., 34 A.D.2d 748, 310 N.Y.S.2d 196 (1970).

20. Burlington N. R.R. Co. v. Tuco Inc., 1997 WL 336314, *6 (Tex.).

21. 393 U.S. 145, 89 S. Ct. 337, 21 L. Ed. 2d 301 (1968).

22. 393 U.S. at 149, 89 S. Ct. at 339, 21 L. Ed. 2d at 305.

23. 393 U.S. at 150, 89 S. Ct. at 340, 21 L. Ed. 2d at 306. Three dissenting justices favored an approach under which an arbitrator's failure to disclose certain relationships established a rebuttable presumption of partiality.

The split of opinion in *Commonwealth Coatings* is reflected in many subsequent decisions addressing motions to vacate awards on grounds of "evident partiality" under federal and state law. A number of decisions have applied tests akin to Justice Black's "appearance of bias" test;[24] some courts have introduced an objective element by viewing the facts from the standpoint of a reasonable person apprised of all the circumstances.[25] A greater number of other courts, mindful of the tradeoff between impartiality and expertise inherent in arbitration, have placed a higher burden on those seeking to vacate awards on grounds of arbitrator interests or relationships.[26]

A few states have addressed the disclosure issue legislatively. In California, the arbitration statute establishes stringent disclosure standards for neutral arbitrators. Neutral arbitrators are required to disqualify themselves on grounds specified for disqualification of judges,[27] and failure to properly self-disqualify on receipt of a timely demand is a ground for vacation of the award.[28] Neutral arbitrators are also required to disclose information regarding prior arbitrations involving the same parties or attorneys.[29] Yet another provision on judicial appointment of arbitrators requires arbitrators to make a disclosure of a range of specified information "which might cause their impartiality to be questioned."[30]

In view of the critical importance of arbitrator disclosure to party choice and perceptions of fairness and the need for more consistent standards in this vital

---

24. *See, e.g.*, S.S. Co. v. Cook Indus., Inc., 495 F.2d 1260, 1263 (2d Cir. 1973) (applying FAA; failure to disclose relationships that "might create an impression of possible bias"); Weinger v. State Farm Fire & Cas. Co., 620 So. 2d 1298, 1299 (Fla. Ct. App. 1993) (arbitrator has affirmative duty to disclose any dealings that might create an impression of possible bias); Northwest Mech., Inc. v. Public Utilities Comm. of City of Virginia, 283 N.W.2d 522, 524 (Minn. 1979) (applying FAA; even if not producing actual prejudice, undisclosed dealings that might create an impression of possible bias mandate vacation of award). *See also* Drinane v. State Farm Mut. Auto Ins. Co., 153 Ill. 2d 207, 214–16, 606 N.E.2d 1181, 1184–85, 180 Ill. Dec. 104, 107–08 (1992) (presumption of evident partiality arises as result of undisclosed dealings that might create an impression of possible bias).

25. *See, e.g.*, Ceriale v. AMCO Ins. Co., 48 Cal. App. 4th 500, 55 Cal. Rptr. 2d 685 (1996) (question is whether record reveals facts that might create an impression of possible bias in eyes of hypothetical, reasonable person); Burlington N. R.R. Co. v. Tuco Inc., 1997 WL 336314 (Tex.) (evident partiality demonstrated where arbitrator does not disclose facts that might create reasonable impression of partiality).

26. *See, e.g.*, Morelite Constr. Corp. v. New York City Dist. Council Carpenters Benefit Funds, 748 F.2d 79 (2d Cir. 1984) (applying Labor Management Relations Act; evident partiality existed where a reasonable person would have to conclude that arbitrator was partial); Merit Ins. Co. v. Leatherby Ins. Co., 714 F.2d 673, 681 (7th Cir. 1983), *cert. denied*, 464 U.S. 1009, 104 S. Ct. 529, 78 L. Ed. 2d 711, *modified*, 728 F.2d 943 (7th Cir. 1984) (applying FAA; circumstances must be "powerfully suggestive of bias"); Giraldi v. Morrell, 892 P.2d 422 (Colo. Ct. App. 1994) ("evident partiality" standard requires more than impression or appearance of possible bias); Artists & Craftsmen Builders, Ltd. v. Schapiro, 232 A.D.2d 265, 648 N.Y.S.2d 550 (1996) (though award may be overturned on proof of appearance of bias or partiality, party seeking to vacate has heavy burden and must show prejudice); DeVore v. IHC Hosp., Inc., 884 P.2d 1246, 1253–56 (Utah 1994) (vacation appropriate if a reasonable person would conclude that arbitrator showed partiality or was guilty of misconduct that prejudiced rights of any party); State of Wyoming Game & Fish Comm. v. Thorncock, 851 P.2d 1300 (Wyo. 1993) (showing of prejudice required). *See also* Parekh Constr., Inc. v. Pitt Constr. Corp., 31 Mass. App. Ct. 354, 360–61, 577 N.E.2d 632, 636–37 (1991) (party challenging award on grounds of facts indicating evident partiality must show circumstances likely to have impaired arbitrator's impartiality toward challenger).

27. Cal. Civ. Proc. Code § 1281.9(e)(West Supp. 1998), referring to Cal. Civ. Proc. Code § 170.1 (West Supp. 1996).

28. Cal. Civ. Proc. Code § 1281.9(a)(West Supp. 1998).

29. Cal. Civ. Proc. Code § 1281.9 (West Supp. 1998).

30. Cal. Civ. Proc. Code § 1281.6 (West Supp. 1998), referring to Cal. Civ. Proc. Code § 1297.121 (West Supp. 1996). *See also* Minn. Stat. Ann. § 572.10 (2) (1998)(establishing affirmative disclosure requirements for arbitrators).

area, the Uniform Arbitration Act was recently revised to include affirmative disclosure requirements for arbitrators.[31]

Although there is broad recognition that an arbitrator's failure to disclose may have legal implications, the law generally limits the remedies of aggrieved parties to setting aside the final arbitration award. A suit against the arbitrator will almost certainly be of no avail because the arbitrator enjoys quasi-judicial immunity (see Section 3.9.1).

To understand what this means, consider the situation where Company A and Company B are arbitrating a dispute, and B discovers that the arbitrator has a long business association with A. First of all, to avoid an argument that it waived such conflicts, B must make a timely objection to the arbitrator's continued service. At this point, unless (1) the arbitrator agrees to disqualify herself, or (2) Company A and Company B have an agreed method for resolving a challenge to an arbitrator, Company B will have to wait until the very end of the process to seek judicial relief on the basis of an arbitrator's failure to disclose critical information. Even then, vacatur of award will be the only remedy.

In light of these realities, arbitrating parties should establish specific requirements for disclosure, challenge, and disqualification or removal of arbitrators. Leading commercial dispute resolution rules typically contain such provisions.[32]

Arbitrator disclosure, challenge, and disqualification under commercial arbitration rules

An example of disclosure, challenge, and disqualification procedures is the American Arbitration Association Commercial Dispute Resolution Procedures (AAA Commercial Procedures).[33] They provide that, unless the parties specifically agree to the contrary, "[a]ny neutral arbitrator . . . shall be subject to disqualification" upon grounds of bias, interest, or relationship with the parties or representatives.[34] Persons appointed as neutral arbitrators are required to

> disclose to the AAA any circumstance likely to affect impartiality or independence, including any bias or any financial or personal interest in the result of the arbitration or any past or present relationship with the parties or their representatives.[35]

The AAA communicates such information (from the arbitrator and other sources) to the parties, and rules on any objections to the appointment or con-

---

31. *See* RUAA § 8 (Draft of October, 1999). *See* National Conference of Commissioners on Uniform State Laws, Uniform Arbitration Act (2000) § 12.

32. *See, e.g.*, Bernstein v. Gramercy Mills, Inc., 16 Mass. App. Ct. 403, 414, 452 N.E.2d 231, 238 (1983) (AAA rule incorporated by arbitration agreement helps to describe level of non-disclosure that can lead to invalidation of award).

33. *See generally* AMERICAN ARBITRATION ASSOCIATION, COMMERCIAL DISPUTE RESOLUTION PROCEDURES (Jan. 1, 1999)[hereinafter AAA COMMERCIAL PROCEDURES].

34. *Id.* §§ R-12, R-19.

35. *Id.* § R-19.

tinued service of a challenged arbitrator. Such rulings, say the procedures, are "conclusive."[36]

The CPR Rules for Non-Administered Arbitration ("CPR Arbitration Rules") also contain provisions for disclosure and challenge.[37] Under these rules, "[a]ny arbitrator may be challenged if circumstances exist or arise that give rise to justifiable doubt regarding that arbitrator's independence or impartiality. . . . If neither agreed disqualification nor voluntary withdrawal occurs, the challenge shall be decided by CPR" in accordance with the CPR Challenge Protocol.[38]

Ethical standards governing arbitrator disclosure and recusal

The AAA/ABA Code of Ethics for Arbitrators in Commercial Disputes (AAA/ABA Code),[39] the most widely used ethical standard for commercial arbitrators, embodies the principle that "arbitrators should disclose the existence of any interests or relationships which are likely to affect their impartiality or which might reasonably create the appearance of partiality or bias." This broad disclosure requirement includes "direct or indirect financial or personal interest in the outcome of arbitration"[40] and

> any existing or past financial, business, professional, family or social relationships which are likely to affect impartiality or which might reasonably create an appearance of partiality or bias [including personal relationships with any party or its lawyer, or prospective witness, and including relationships involving family members or current employers, partners or business associates].[41]

Prospective arbitrators are admonished to "make a reasonable effort to inform themselves of [such] relationships"[42]; the disclosure obligation is a continuing one that extends throughout the period of appointment,[43] and extends to other arbitrators as well as the parties.[44] Arbitrators are required to withdraw upon request of all parties.[45] In other cases where a challenge is made on grounds of partiality or bias, arbitrators are required to withdraw unless they conclude, after careful consideration, that (1) "the reason for the challenge is not substantial," (2) the arbitrator "can act and decide the case impartially and fairly," and (3) "withdrawal would cause unfair delay or expense to another party or would be contrary to

---

36. *See id.*
37. CPR INSTITUTE FOR DISPUTE RESOLUTION, RULES FOR NON-ADMINISTERED ARBITRATION (Rev. 2000), RULE 7 [hereinafter CPR ARBITRATION RULES].
38. *Id.* Rules 7.5, 7.8.
39. AMERICAN ARBITRATION ASSOCIATION/AMERICAN BAR ASSOCIATION, CODE OF ETHICS FOR ARBITRATORS IN COMMERCIAL DISPUTES (1977).
40. *Id.* Canon II.A.(1).
41. *Id.* Canon II.A.(2).
42. *Id.* Canon II.B.
43. *Id.* Canon II.C.
44. *Id.* Canon II.D.
45. *Id.* Canon II.E.

the ends of justice."[46] If the parties have agreed that a third party will rule on challenges, arbitrators are bound by the third-party determinations made in accordance with the parties' agreement (as under the AAA or CPR rules).

The disclosure provisions of the AAA/ABA Code are sometimes cited by courts addressing disclosure issues,[47] and have been formally adopted by at least one state court.[48] Otherwise, the Code has no legal consequences, and parties have no formal mechanism to register complaints regarding an arbitrator's failure to live up to its standards. In extreme cases such behavior might lead an ADR organization which requires its arbitrators to adhere to the Code to remove an arbitrator from its roster.

Party-arbitrators

Some cases are arbitrated by tripartite panels involving one arbitrator appointed directly by each of the arbitrating parties and a third arbitrator jointly selected by the party-appointed arbitrators.[49] The legal and ethical standards for disclosure by party-arbitrators are discussed below.

2. The arbitrator's personal and experiential qualifications

Pertinent business or technical expertise

Arbitrator expertise in the subject-matter is often cited as a *sine qua non* of arbitration. Pertinent expertise of the arbitrator may save time and expense at the hearing stage and produce a result more in keeping with the parties' particular expectations. One experienced corporate counsel reported that in one very complex commercial case,

> [t]he fact that the [arbitrators] had professional backgrounds in the disciplines involved undoubtedly reduced the time needed for presentation of the technical testimony of both sides. In addition, the final result in the case was within the scope of a reasonably expectable outcome, given the practices and customs of the industries and professions involved. A jury trial may not have produced a similar result.[50]

---

46. *Id.*
47. *See, e.g.*, William C. Vick Constr. Co. v. North Carolina Farm Bureau Fed., 123 N.C. App. 97, 100–01, 472 S.E.2d 346, 348 (1996).
48. *See* Safeco Ins. Co. of Am. v. Stariha, 346 N.W.2d 663, 666 (Minn. Ct. App. 1984). Substantially similar language is contained in disclosure requirements of widely used securities arbitration rules. *See, e.g.*, NASD CODE OF ARBITRATION PROCEDURE § 10312 (August 1996).
49. *See generally* III MACNEIL ET AL., *supra* note 1, § 28.4.
50. Robert H. Gorske, *An Arbitrator Looks at Expediting the Large, Complex Case*, 5 OHIO ST. J. ON DISP. RES. 381, 391 (1990).

For such reasons, business and technical persons sometimes contend that the involvement of "one of their own" as decisionmaker is central to the process. As one engineer/arbitrator recently argued:

> [B]usinessmen in specialist areas sometimes have greater comfort from the decision of a colleague, one of their peers, whom they know to have understood and appreciated their difficulties, than from a purely legal tribunal, simulating a court and operating with the remoteness that is necessary if respect for the legal process, and its different methods, is to be maintained.[51]

The notion of the subject matter expert/arbitrator remains intertwined with commercial arbitration in many minds.

Expert-arbitrators are usually individuals with established credentials in a particular professional or commercial arena and not simply dedicated neutrals. Thus, the AAA, CPR, and JAMS require prospective commercial arbitrators to have extensive business or professional experience to be eligible for appointment. Panels of some other institutional providers reflect similar credentials. Organizations like the AAA and CPR also maintain rosters of specialists in fields such as construction, patent law, employment, intellectual property, and the environment, as well as rosters of generalists, who have experience in a great variety of fields.

The flip side of the coin, some Commission members point out, is that arbitrator expertise raises issues of bias. With experience in a particular industry or trade come particular perspectives—some might say baggage—which are brought to the arbitrator's chair. One Commissioner warns: "What you have in the expert-as-arbitrator is an un-cross-examined witness whose expertise may be very critical where a case turns on custom and practice."

Experience trying or managing arbitrated cases

As we will see in Chapters 4 and 5, effective arbitrators manage proceedings with a firm hand.[52] Given the importance of case management skills, experience with the arbitral process and other kinds of adjudication is usually seen as extremely important. This is particularly true of chairpersons of arbitration tribunals or arbitrators appointed to act alone. Especially in large or complex commercial cases, Commission members tend to favor attorneys with considerable experience trying cases. The assumption is that such individuals are attuned to dealing with procedural issues and the nuances of process management needed to handle an arbitration fairly and efficiently. Specialized legal experience, like other professional or business expertise, may sharpen an arbitrator's ability to discern and focus on key issues and points of proof, thereby reducing hearing

51. *See* Geoffrey M. Beresford Hartwell, *The Relevance of Expertise in Commercial Arbitration*, Presentation to Working Group II, 14th ICCA Congress (May 5, 1998), <http://www.hartwell.demon.co.uk/Paris.htm>.
52. *See* ROLE OF THE PANEL CHAIR, *supra* note 8, at 15.

time and cost and permitting a more realistic assessment of the issues.[53] One Commissioner goes so far as to argue that "at least in complex cases, the day of not having a lawyer run the procedure is behind us."

Partly for this reason, most panelists on the rolls of the AAA and *all* of CPR's appointees are attorneys. For example, CPR's espoused aim is to select "the best of the bar" for its panels, which consist of carefully selected arbitrators and mediators with impressive professional or personal credentials. In addition to requiring panelists to have at least twelve to fifteen years of practice experience, the AAA screens prospective arbitrators with the assistance of regional advisory committees.

The need for efficient administration has also led some to seek arbitrators in the ranks of retired judges. The imprimatur of court service also brings with it a perceived mantle of objectivity and independence. In recent years, JAMS and some other providers have placed special emphasis on marketing the services of retired federal and state court judges as mediators and arbitrators, and some former judges have made a second career of serving as mediators and/or arbitrators. But a number of Commissioners urge caution, pointing out that some retired judges have traits that are not compatible with arbitration. As one Commission member put it:

> Despite the "judicial mystique," many practitioners find that habits carried over from the bench are not always helpful in arbitration. Some judges were good on the bench; others were not. Some don't work well on a panel, and insist on having their own way. Parties must look carefully at each potential arbitrator as an individual, and do background research on his or her predilections and capabilities.

The bottom line is that by itself, professional expertise of any kind is never a guarantee of an effective arbitrator—one must look at the individual.

Diversity issues

If parties anticipate the possibility of arbitrating a variety of legal, technical, and business issues, they may need access to a diverse multidisciplinary roster of panelists consisting of lawyers, business persons, and other professionals. In subject matters such as employment, race and gender may affect perceptions of neutrality, and so some provider organizations are attempting to further diversify their panels.

Special panels

Some arbitral providers earmark individuals with special abilities and experience in case management as chairpersons or sole arbitrators. In addition, some organizations advertise "blue ribbon" panels for large, complex cases. A few

---

53. In the international arena, when a particular technical or scientific institution is charged with the responsibility of selecting the arbitrator, there is a general presumption that the appointment will be of someone with the technical or scientific expertise represented by the appointing institution. *See id.* at 3.

institutions showcase the services of individuals with particular skills or credentials who devote most or all of their time to arbitration and other conflict resolution approaches.

3. Pertinent education and training

Formal training in arbitration procedures and skills may be of great value to commercial arbitrators. Particularly where the parties and their counsel do not know prospective arbitrators, assurance that the arbitrators have been trained in principles of case management under pertinent rules and procedures is important.

Despite the popular image of arbitration as a relatively simple, informal alternative to adjudication in the courtroom, commercial arbitrators need to be conversant with the application of a variety of rules and standards in real life situations. Among other things, arbitrators may have to do some or all of the following:

- deal with personal and professional conflicts of interest;
- address questions of arbitrability, including third-party claims;
- rule on dispositive motions;
- issue subpoenas (or summonses);
- order and/or supervise discovery;
- rule on evidentiary matters;
- provide interim relief to a party;
- treat requests for postponement of hearings;
- appoint experts;
- apply the applicable law to the facts of the dispute; and
- tailor remedies.

In each case, their actions may be affected by rules and procedures governing the arbitration hearing, ethical guidelines, and pertinent legal standards (including federal and state arbitration statutes and related case decisions). Competence in these areas can have a significant impact on the conduct of the arbitration and on the final award.

Some organizations require arbitrators on their commercial rosters to complete educational programs covering their own arbitration rules as well as other applicable norms. This may include continuing education courses to help arbitrators stay abreast on the status of applicable rules (including ethical rules) and case law affecting commercial arbitration. Periodic "retooling sessions" may also permit arbitrators to share experiences and raise questions regarding procedural, legal, practical, and ethical issues—an exercise which can benefit the sophisticated arbitrator as well as the novice.

Skills training is equally critical to an arbitrator's preparation. According to the director of training for a leading provider organization, most user complaints center on perceived inefficiencies in the process for which they tend to blame ineffective management by arbitrators. Organizational sponsors of arbitration are coming to understand that many arbitrators need training in case management, starting with the pre-hearing conference and ending with the writing of an award. The AAA's new Commercial Arbitrator Development Program, which combines rigorous selection requirements with a program of initial and continuing education, may not become the template for all institutional providers, it will undoubtedly raise the bar for arbitrator education generally.[54]

4. Pertinent experience in an arbitrator's role and feedback on the arbitrator's performance

In arbitration as in other domains, experience is the best teacher. While few commercial arbitrators devote the bulk of their time to serving in that capacity, regular participation is important.

From the user's standpoint, the more information one has about an arbitrator's experience in the hearing room, the better. The exact nature of that experience—the kinds of issues presented, the number of parties, and the like—may ultimately be of greater importance than the number of cases arbitrated. Arbitration experience may be more critical in the choice of an arbitrator who will act alone or who will chair an arbitration panel than in the selection of a "wing" panelist on a three-member panel.

Meaningful evaluation also plays an important part in professional development. Effective commercial arbitrators benefit from feedback on their performances, and some organizations providing arbitration services are considering ways of monitoring and evaluating the performance of panelists. CPR routinely requests attorneys representing parties in arbitrations or mediations to complete neutral evaluation questionnaires. Besides providing an opportunity to assess arbitrators' performance in the hearing room, periodic reviews also permit organizations to determine whether arbitrators have made reasonable

---

54. *See* AMERICAN ARBITRATION ASSOCIATION, COMMERCIAL ARBITRATOR DEVELOPMENT PROGRAM (1998). The program, which places primary emphasis on efficient case management, includes several key components:
- a 4-hour introduction to the fundamentals of the arbitration process, including applicable legal principles;
- a training course on fundamentals of arbitration and case management techniques, including 16 hours of classroom participation in a workshop setting;
- a 16-hour advanced practicum in case management techniques;
- an annual arbitrator update (covering changes in the AAA rules and procedures and important developments in state and federal law); and
- annual "continuing education" requirements on a variety of subjects.

The AAA anticipates that this extremely ambitious mandatory educational program will discourage some existing panelists from continuing as arbitrators. Poor students also will be weeded out.

efforts to be available for service. For example, the AAA established a policy under which members of their rosters must be reappointed every two years. To make the determination whether to reappoint, regional advisory committees are provided with case performance evaluations submitted by parties or counsel, information from AAA staffers, and other material.

Although such evaluative information might be of value to parties considering the appointment of a particular arbitrator, for a variety of reasons provider organizations may be unwilling or unable to share it. The possibility of obtaining names of parties or counsel who appeared before the arbitrator is discussed in Section 3.4.3.

5. Fees and availability

Fees and expenses

Because arbitrators' fees and expenses are usually paid by the parties, such matters may be of considerable importance in designating a particular arbitrator. As discussed in Section 3.8, arbitrator fees are usually assessed on an hourly or per diem basis, and vary considerably. As the stakes in the outcome grow, concerns over arbitrator fees may be overshadowed by the importance of getting the best arbitrator. In large, complex commercial cases, arbitrator fees are a relatively small expense compared to the amount in controversy, attorney's fees, and other costs. Some organizational providers charge an administrative fee based on the amount in dispute. Such charges may be quite substantial in a big case.

Geographic proximity

A related issue is the geographic proximity of the arbitrator to the parties and prospective hearing sites. Clearly, long-distance commuting raises cost and scheduling issues. Proximity concerns have caused a number of national organizations (including the AAA, CPR, JAMS, and others) to maintain regional rosters of panelists; in some cases, administration is also performed on a regional basis. (For example, although the AAA has recently begun to centralize administrative services from 36 regional offices into a small number of multistate centers, some functions such as the maintenance of advisory committees are still maintained on a regional basis.)

General availability

Another, often critical concern is the general availability of a prospective arbitrator. Efficiency, economy—and perhaps fundamental fairness—hinge on the ability of arbitrators to devote the necessary time and attention to the case from the time of their appointment to the rendition of a final award. In seeking a reasonable commitment from the arbitrator(s), however, arbitrating parties must offer a reasonable estimate of the requirements of the case—something they frequently fail to do. One Commission member relates:

> In one complex case, the parties told the prospective panelists that there would be a need for no more than ten days of hearings. After the ten days were exhausted, it was apparent to all that considerably more time would be necessary to conclude the hearings. Unfortunately, the chair of the arbitration panel reported that he would be out of the country and unavailable for approximately six months. The hearings were suspended during his absence.

This horror story might have been averted by more careful planning by the parties and the arbitrators. The importance of pre-hearing management is treated in Chapter 4.

In the interest of getting prospective arbitrators to address the matter of time commitment seriously, the CPR Arbitration Rules provide that

> [b]y accepting appointment, each arbitrator shall be deemed . . . to have represented that he or she has the time available to devote to the expeditious process contemplated by these Rules.[55]

Similarly, AAA arbitrators are advised to take account of parties' strong preference for consecutive hearing days, and to decline appointment if they are unable to accommodate the parties' wishes.[56]

3.4

Where may arbitrating parties find helpful information regarding prospective arbitrators?

In the absence of first-hand experience with a commercial arbitrator, parties must assemble information about a candidate from several sources.

1. Arbitrator bio and other information provided by arbitrators and sponsoring organizations

One source of information is the arbitrator's curriculum vitae or professional biography. Such information is routinely provided by the sponsoring organization, if any. As one Commission member put it, such information "is usually

---

55. CPR Arbitration Rules, *supra* note 37, Rule 7.2.
56. *See* Role of the Panel Chair, *supra* note 8, at 21.

helpful, but may not be sufficient" due to its relative brevity and because the form is prepared by the arbitrator. Generally, parties should seek other sources of information.

The Commission recommends that the biographical information for a prospective arbitrator include:

- contact information (name, address, phone number, fax number, etc.);
- positions held over the previous twenty years, together with a broad description of responsibilities in each position and particular expertise required;
- education, including academic honors and awards;
- professional licenses, certifications, bar admissions, and court admissions (as applicable);
- number of matters in which the candidate has served (a) as a sole arbitrator or panel chair, or (b) as a wing arbitrator;
- broad description (without violating confidences) of some of the matters on which the person served as arbitrator;
- publications relating to arbitration or other pertinent topics;
- pertinent speaking and teaching engagements;
- arbitrator training or education;
- other activities or honors, including any directly related to arbitration or other pertinent fields.

The biography should be of a recent date and state the date of submission. A short arbitrator biography is contained in Appendix 3.2.

2. Personal interview or queries

Unilateral personal interviews with nominees as sole arbitrators or chairpersons are rare. Direct questioning of a neutral arbitrator raises the concerns typically associated with direct communications with a judge outside the hearing room. However, queries may be made through the intermediary arbitration institution or by means of a joint interview by counsel. Consider the positive experience of one Commissioner:

> The matter was one in which the parties were not getting along very well, but we were able to use a joint interview process to choose our arbitrator. The parties and their lawyers sat in a conference room and talked to the leading candidate, who sat at the head of the table. We talked for an hour about how he believed arbitration should be run, and what the issues were. We discussed and cleared potential conflicts of interest right there and then. The parties then went off into separate rooms and discussed the candidate. Ultimately, each decided that this was somebody they could have confidence in, and they exchanged slips of paper which indicated their "yes" to the arbitrator.

A joint interview may be conducted in person or by phone. Fair subjects of inquiry include the arbitrator's general background, pertinent professional experience (including arbitration experience with a particular kind of dispute or with complex multi-party arbitration), current availability, and philosophy regarding case management and scheduling. See Appendix 3.1. for suggested questions. Candidates should use discretion in fielding such inquiries, and are well advised to fend off any attempt to get the candidate to take a position regarding the merits.

3. Discussions with third parties and counsel

Parties may also be able to obtain information regarding prospective arbitrators from others who know them or have appeared before them in arbitration. The problem is in obtaining the names of such sources.

Asking an arbitrator for a list of references presents a number of potential difficulties. First of all, the practice of obtaining references directly from the candidate would require the latter to solicit support from parties or counsel who appeared before the candidate at an earlier date; that would raise conflict of interest issues. Inquiries of fellow neutral arbitrators or of attorneys who have practiced with the candidate would present less of a problem.

Will provider organizations pass along prior evaluations of nominees or share the names of attorneys and parties from earlier cases? Again, there are practical and ethical problems. While institutions sponsoring arbitration services have a significant interest in collecting evaluative information from arbitrating parties for the purpose of monitoring arbitrator performance, sharing such sensitive information with other parties without the consent of the persons involved is likely to be seen as an impermissible intrusion into the privacy of the arbitration process.

Even sharing names of participants in prior cases presents problems for arbitration institutions. Attorneys and parties in prior cases may not want to have their names given as sources of information regarding arbitrators. Attorneys may feel a proprietary interest in shielding their clients from such commitments. If only one "side" agrees to be a source, parties seeking information about the arbitrator's performance may receive a less-than-balanced picture. In response to such concerns, the AAA is initiating a policy under which references from attorneys who previously appeared before the nominee now may be obtained by third parties only if all attorneys in the case consent to be listed as references. CPR has a similar policy.

4. The internet and other sources

Today, a good deal of information regarding prospective arbitrators may be gleaned from effective use of the internet and other sources. For example, CPR's entire roster of arbitrators is available on the internet, and parties may request CPR's assistance in obtaining additional information or may take the initiative to contact panel members directly. In addition, some arbitrators or provider organizations publish biographical information on their web sites, sometimes with links to publications by the arbitrator or programs in which the arbitrator is involved. A summary of some of the tools available to an internet searcher seeking information on arbitrators and dispute resolution programs may be found in Appendix 3.3.

The expanding use of lists published by professional, trade, and interest groups also provides a mechanism for vetting a potential arbitrator. Moreover, many Commissioners routinely receive and respond to inquiries from members of their firms about prospective neutrals via e-mail.

Using Lexis, Nexis, Westlaw, and computerized search tools may uncover information regarding cases in which a candidate or a candidate's company or firm was involved. Such searches may also find articles written by the candidate, as well as statements or interviews.

Finally, some publishers have recently produced directories of "leading arbitrators" or dispute resolution professionals; one example is the *Martindale-Hubbell Dispute Resolution Directory*.[57] The Directory contains the names of thousands of individuals and organizations offering conflict resolution services, grouped by geographic location, alphabetically, and by specialty. Individual entries include a variety of information.

Such directories are often useful starting points for identifying potential arbitrators, especially when one is needed in a particular locality or where specific language skills or professional qualifications are required, but inclusion in a directory open to anyone willing to pay for an entry is not the equivalent of a professional endorsement. Parties should take care in relying on information provided entirely by would-be arbitrators.

3.5

What are the advantages and disadvantages of different arbitrator selection processes?

Arbitrator selection processes must take into account transactional economics, client psychology, the relative expectations of parties, and the size and complexity of the conflict.

Institutions facilitating arbitrator selection should make the selection process(es) as transparent as possible. They should also encourage mutual agreement on the neutral.

---

57. Martindale-Hubbell Dispute Resolution Directory (1996).

Parties should be pro-active in the selection process. Even if the choice of arbitrator is left to an institution that is sponsoring the arbitration, the parties may have considerable impact on the choice of arbitrator by providing "specifications" for the neutral(s).

1. Designation of arbitrators in a pre-dispute arbitration agreement

Though not the prevailing model, designating one or more arbitrators in the pre-dispute arbitration agreement may make sense in certain commercial contexts. Such designations often make the arbitrator a "standing neutral" who will "remain on call" during the course of the contractual relationship. Unlike the typical arbitrator, who is appointed to resolve a specific dispute, the standing arbitrator is prospectively given jurisdiction over all issues arising during performance of the designated contract or project. Potential advantages include a reduction in start-up time and continuity in decision making. Such arrangements may be helpful in circumstances where there is a need for a "close-to-the-ground" neutral who can step in within days or weeks of the emergence of a dispute.

The "standing neutral" approach is typically applied in the context of post-closing adjustments in business combinations, real estate development, and construction contracts. It may also be of value when parties see a potential need for the equivalent of a temporary restraining order or preliminary injunction against a partner pending a full hearing on the merits: as, for example, where a company depends heavily on continuing shipments under a long-term supply contract and cannot afford a suspension of deliveries while arbitrating.

In the construction context, the "standing neutral" concept is often applied to third parties who mediate or render non-binding decisions on matters in dispute after an abbreviated hearing (sometimes without the presence of attorneys). Although either party may seek a de novo hearing in court or arbitration, advisory opinions by standing neutrals are markedly successful in encouraging early settlement. A variant of the "standing neutral" concept, the dispute review board (a panel of arbitrators who render a decision—typically advisory—on disputes), has been successfully employed on many construction projects, including the mammoth Boston Central Artery/Tunnel Project.

A downside of pre-designating arbitrators is the possibility that the named neutral(s) will be unable to serve when the need arises. As one Commissioner relates:

> In one complex commercial case in which I'm involved, the parties designated an individual as arbitrator a decade ago. However capable he was then, he's no longer functioning very well.

Of course, death, incapacity, or changing circumstances are potential problems with any long-term arrangement involving arbitrators. If parties are contemplating the pre-designation of an arbitrator, they should also consider designating a back-up arbitrator or default selection plan.

Another concern is whether the named arbitrator(s) will be ideal for every possible dispute. A panel of three blue-ribbon arbitrators may represent "overkill" for a minor claim or controversy.

2. Post-dispute joint selection of arbitrators without outside assistance

On its face, mutual selection of the arbitrator(s) without the intervention of third parties is an appealing prospect. The problem is that parties are often ill-disposed to mutual agreement in the wake of conflict. There is always the strong possibility that the efforts to name a mutually acceptable arbitrator will reach an impasse, stymy the process, and perhaps require judicial intervention. As a Commission member puts it:

> You know, it's pretty easy for me to predict whether someone is going to be a good arbitrator in terms of coming up with a result I'm going to like. But selling the other party on that person is a very different thing!

Another laments:

> I've never had a case where parties in the middle of a dispute could sit down and agree on an arbitrator between themselves. The problem is that whenever I [as counsel for a party] propose someone, the other side naturally thinks that that person is in my pocket somehow. Another problem is that trying to find a mutually acceptable arbitrator just leads to too much delay.

Unassisted selection processes require mutual trust and cooperation between the parties and their attorneys. At contract time, anticipating whether such trust will prevail later, at the critical moment, is difficult. Parties are well advised to establish a default procedure for arbitrator selection in case they fail to agree on an arbitrator.[58] (Some possibilities are discussed below.) The parties should establish specific time frames for efforts to arrive at a mutual agreement; the selection process should not be permitted to drag on for months. Similar considerations should be given to the handling of vacancies due to arbitrator incapacity or resignation.[59]

One Commission member successfully employed the technique of providing the opposing party with a list of acceptable candidates and offering the other party a choice of arbitrator—an ingenious variant on the "I slice the cake, you pick the piece" concept.

---

58. The alternative would normally be resort to court under federal or state law.
59. *See* John Wilkinson, *When Arbitrator Vacancies Arise*, 2 ADR Currents No. 4, Fall 1997, at 20.

3. Assisted selection: List selection processes

Parties arbitrating in the United States often select arbitrators by the "list selection" procedure, in which the parties attempt to select mutually acceptable arbitrators from a list presented by an independent organization. If the parties are not able to agree on panelists, the organization makes the appointment. List selection offers the advantage of a perceptually fair selection method with relatively low transaction costs. It is also a straightforward way of addressing the "default" situation where the parties are unable to agree on a mutually acceptable arbitrator or panel. One Commissioner reports:

> What I do is to agree that a neutral party (such as CPR or some other forum) will generate a list of, say, twenty-five potential panelists if we need a three-person panel. (It could be far less if only one arbitrator is to be appointed.) Then the parties are required to rank some minimum percentage of those listed—say, sixty or seventy percent. It's pretty likely that you are going to end up with at least five or six potential arbitrators that both sides have confidence in, subject, of course, to challenges for good cause (such as conflicts of interest). So far, it's worked for my clients. I'm in a case right now where we ended up with five potential arbitrators—all of whom we have confidence in; ultimately, that's what we all wanted.

Another concurs, noting:

> I have never had a situation involving the selection of a single arbitrator where we have not been able to reach agreement on at least two or three candidates from a list of eight to ten.

List selection processes have become the predominant method of appointing arbitrators in commercial arbitration in the U.S.

CPR's arbitrator selection procedure provides an illustration of the list selection approach. When parties request CPR's assistance in the selection of arbitrators, a professional staff member first discusses with the parties the nature of the case and the qualifications they seek in an arbitrator. CPR then submits to the parties a short list of candidates after screening them for possible conflicts and availability. CPR also advises the parties of each candidate's current compensation rate. The parties are urged to agree on one of the candidates. If they do not agree, they are required to rank the listed candidates in order of their preference. The candidate with the lowest combined score is selected as arbitrator. CPR reports a high level of user satisfaction with these procedures.

In the words of one Commission member, list selection is an acceptable default in which both parties have equal input into the selection of the arbitrator(s). Of course, the list selection method is only as good as the list of prospective arbitrators and the quality of information provided to the parties regarding those candidates. Where the parties fail to identify any mutually acceptable candidates, most procedures permit the sponsoring organization to select the arbitrator(s).

4. Unilateral selection by a third party

General concerns

As one Commission member explained, leaving the choice of arbitrator entirely to the discretion of a third party is often "scary," and sometimes provides a strong incentive to agree on a mutual choice with one's opponent.

The attention given to arbitrator selection by provider organizations varies considerably. While some organizations providing arbitration services exercise great care in making unilateral selections, it is critical for parties to communicate as much information as possible regarding desired qualifications and experience.

Judicial appointment

Occasionally, arbitration agreements provide for appointment of arbitrators by federal or state judges. In addition, courts may be called upon to appoint an arbitrator pursuant to federal or state law when the selection mechanism chosen by the parties fails for some reason.[60]

In either case, parties must keep in mind that the court is not in the business of selecting arbitrators and is highly unlikely to have a list of qualified individuals at hand for the purpose. Although in the normal case the court will seek recommendations and other forms of guidance from the parties regarding the selection, the result of an unassisted selection may not be what either party would have anticipated. One Commission member relates:

> In a matter involving an option for the purchase of a large plant complex involving hundreds of millions of dollars, the agreement called for a single arbitrator to be chosen by the local state court. Not knowing any experienced arbitrators, the judge looked to his list of court-appointed neutrals— who were of course mediators. His eventual choice was an individual who was a good mediator but who had never arbitrated a case—and here he was arbitrating one of the big ones! He was uncomfortable the whole time and had difficulty managing hearings. After many months, when the hearings were nearly over, he tried to persuade the parties to let him mediate!

5. Party-arbitrators

Although tripartite panels with party-appointed arbitrators represent the model of choice in the international arena, their use in U.S. commercial arbitration has frequently created problems where the party-appointed arbitrators are deemed to be "less than neutral"; the approach sometimes results in litigation. The issues raised by the use of party-arbitrators are discussed below.

---

60. *See* FAA, *supra* note 16, § 5. Unif. Arb. Act § 3 (1955). *See generally* III Macneil et al., *supra* note 1, ch. 29.

3.6

When is a three-arbitrator panel preferable to a single arbitrator?

1. Rationale for, dynamics of a panel

Commercial arbitrations are usually conducted by a lone arbitrator or a three-member panel. Two-member panels are a rarity because of the worry that the arbitrators will be unable to agree on an award and there will be no way of breaking the deadlock.

Opinions vary on when a three-member arbitration panel is preferable to a single arbitrator. Some experienced users of arbitration typically rely on a sole arbitrator; others strongly favor the use of panels. When the parties agree, their agreement virtually always will be given effect.

As a rule, cost and scheduling concerns militate against the use of panels in small cases. This reality is reflected in many leading commercial rules. For example, cases under the AAA Commercial Procedures may be heard by a panel of three where the parties so agree, or the AAA determines that a panel should be employed (the wishes of each party being a primary concern).[61] Under the CPR Arbitration Rules, as under the AAA's Optional Procedures for Large, Complex Commercial Disputes, the presumption is a three-member panel.[62] For reasons of cost or schedule, a growing number of parties whose contract calls for three arbitrators will agree on a single arbitrator as long as they have confidence in the individual.

Where cost and scheduling concerns are not controlling, however, there may be good reasons to employ a panel. A multimember tribunal may afford the parties a mix of professional or commercial perspectives, and gives panel members an opportunity to test their perceptions and ideas on fellow arbitrators.

A Commissioner writes:

> Arbitrators are charged with the obligation of confidentiality and have the responsibility of reaching their decisions and preparing their awards without the assistance of third parties. The effect of these principles is that each member of a three-person tribunal can consult with his colleagues with respect to problems but that a sole arbitrator can properly consult only with himself. This places an enormous burden on a sole arbitrator. Unlike a judge who, even if he is sitting alone, has all of his colleagues available to discuss the matter before him, the sole arbitrator has no one. I have sat as chairman or co-arbitrator in several difficult cases, where the opportunity to discuss issues and problems with colleagues was of enormous assistance.

---

61. AAA Commercial Procedures, *supra* note 33, § R-17.
62. *Id.* § L-3; CPR Arbitration Rules, *supra* note 37, Rule 5.1.

In major cases, the added cost of two additional arbitrators is a small price to pay for the advantage of having three arbitrators available to analyze, consult and decide critical issues.

A Commissioner with considerable construction experience relates:

> A great strength of arbitration in construction cases is the mix of disciplines reflected in the makeup of the typical panel. As an advocate and as an arbitrator, I've appreciated the way arbitrators with different backgrounds complement each other. Construction professionals understand the way things go together, the dynamics of the job site, and relevant cost implications. Experienced construction lawyers place these realities in the legal framework of statute, common law and contract. In the best case, each arbitrator brings something to the table, and relies on the other arbitrators.

There are other positive dynamics involved in the panel approach. Parties are generally more accepting of an adverse award that is the unanimous conclusion of three arbitrators as opposed to one. From the practical perspective of counsel, as one Commission member explained, "it is easier to explain a loss at the hands of a three-member panel." In such cases, clients are more likely to accept the judgment and avoid an appeal. Similarly, it is generally felt that the risk of an irrational or "runaway" award is much smaller with a panel. The AAA, CPR, and other organizations find that for big cases a three-person panel is usually preferred, especially if technical or industry expertise is needed.

2. The panel chair

Role of the chair

One important consideration in panel selection is the identification of a chair. As presiding officer, the chair speaks for the arbitration panel and has primary responsibility for managing the arbitration and directing the proceedings toward a final award.[63] Effective panel chairs personify the desired characteristics of even-handedness, decisiveness, and skepticism, and encourage fellow panelists to cooperate in facilitating a fair, efficient process.[64] Chairs play a variety of roles during the course of arbitration, including the following.

> (1) ***Managing the interaction of the panel.*** Effective chairs provide leadership for the arbitration panel. They encourage orderly communications among panelists and facilitate "a spirit of constructiveness and teamwork."[65] They assign responsibilities among panelists in a just man-

---

63. *See generally* ROLE OF THE PANEL CHAIR, *supra* note 8.
64. *See id.* at 5–7.
65. *See id.* at 12.

ner, "consistent with the special skills and capacities of each."[66] (Thus, for example, an arbitrator who is a CPA might be charged with analyzing financial spreadsheets, or an arbitrator who is an experienced contractor might determine the reasonableness of a construction bid.) The chair establishes a consensus regarding panelists' roles at the hearing (including an understanding regarding rulings on procedural issues and objections), and encourages the panel to convey a united front in the hearing room.[67]

(2) ***Presiding over the arbitration process.***   As the presiding officer, the chair plays the key role in managing the arbitration process. Effective chairs are well-prepared for the hearing, having familiarized themselves with the governing arbitration procedures and having at hand hearing transcripts, exhibits, and other core documents.[68] In some cases they may also be responsible for making arrangements for the hearing room and other logistics. If the parties so agree, moreover, the chair may conduct some or all pre-hearing conferences without the assistance of the other arbitrators. Good chairs guide the panel to adapt a style of management to fit the needs of the case, and, with the explicit or implicit concurrence of their colleagues, often take the lead in dealing with procedural issues,[69] discovery disputes,[70] and evidentiary objections.[71]

(3) ***Guiding panel deliberations and the writing of a final award.***
Effective chairs encourage discussions among panelists on important issues as the case progresses, all the while bearing in mind that a final determination should await the conclusion of proofs and arguments. At the final determination, they facilitate full and frank discussions among panelists and seek wherever reasonable to achieve consensus. Some have found that a useful technique for achieving such consensus is to assign each panelist to draft a portion of the preliminary award for discussion by the panel.[72]

(4) ***Serving as liaison to the arbitration institution.***   The chair may also serve as the point of contact between the arbitration tribunal and the administering institution. Under AAA procedures, for example, the chair is encouraged to contact the case administrator for the purpose of coordinating interaction, and is expected to be in regular communication with the case administrator respecting issues such as fee deposits, scheduling, hearing location, physical surroundings, availability of equipment, storage of documents, and the like.[73] The AAA also requires

---

66. *Id.*
67. *Id.* at 6–7.
68. *Id.* at 5.
69. *See id.* at 15–16.
70. *See id.* at 22.
71. *See id.* at 24–25.
72. *See id.* at 25–26.
73. *See id.* at 10–11.

chairs to monitor and guide the ethical conduct of wing panelists and report breaches of the Code of Ethics, and to prepare evaluations of the other panelists at the conclusion of the proceeding.[74]

Selecting the chair

In some cases panel chairs are selected by the administering institution. In other cases, the chair is selected by agreement of the arbitrators. Where the arbitration agreement provides for direct appointment of a wing panelist by each party, the party appointees normally select a mutually acceptable chair. Some organizations provide special training for panel chairs.[75]

The important thing is that there is agreement regarding the means of choosing a chair. One Commission member cautions:

> There is no more awkward moment than when arbitrators get together with the parties for the first conference (sometimes by telephone), and no chair has been appointed. It isn't much better when an arbitrator who wants to be chair calls the other arbitrators before the first conference with the parties in order to achieve "concurrence" on his appointment. I really believe that arbitration institutions should solicit agreement of the parties on who should be the chair and if agreement cannot be achieved, the institution should simply appoint the chair on the basis of its knowledge of the panelists.

3.7

When, if ever, is it appropriate to employ a "tripartite" panel in which each party chooses an arbitrator? Should such arbitrators be neutral?

1. The problem with party-arbitrators

Tripartite panels involving party-appointed arbitrators, long the norm in international arbitration, are also a common feature of commercial arbitration between U.S. parties.

One reason for the popularity of this approach is its apparent simplicity. Each party picks its own arbitrator, and the party-arbitrators pick a third, sometimes referred to as the umpire, who chairs the panel. This notion of balanced unilateral choices (with a third, mutually acceptable chair) is straightforward,

---

74. *See id.* at 7–10.
75. *See id.* at 7.

and thus may hold particular appeal for parties engaged in an ad hoc arbitration unassisted by a provider organization.

Such mechanisms may be unavoidable in international arbitration, where differing legal and cultural perspectives raise special concerns regarding the makeup of panels. The same concerns are not present in disputes among U.S. parties. In U.S. commercial arbitration, significant offsetting concerns should cause parties to avoid using party-appointed arbitrators or at least to employ measures designed to avoid the abuses associated with tripartite panels.

The basic problem with tripartite panels lies in the tension between the expectation of open-mindedness and independence, which is central to the arbitrator's role, and each party's desire to have a "friendly" arbitrator on the panel. With the power to appoint an arbitrator come certain expectations. At the least the appointing party expects that the appointee will listen with an open mind, give due deference to the appointing party's arguments, and reach a rational decision. Often, the expectations are greater: that the appointee will forcefully advocate the appointing party's concerns and arguments to the rest of the panel. In some cases, the party-arbitrator may work in other ways to protect the appointing party's interests—even to the point of delaying the selection of a third arbitrator, disrupting hearings, or resigning in the face of an adverse award. While such activities may be violations of ethical responsibilities and may justify court intervention, they are nevertheless part of the reality of tripartite arbitration in the U.S.

Although many party-appointed arbitrators act as neutrals, as in the international arena, or because the agreement of the parties or applicable arbitration rules directed them to do so, most pertinent case law and leading ethical standards acknowledge that in the absence of contrary understandings, a party-arbitrator will be something less than neutral—not close-minded, but predisposed toward the appointing party. The model usually works to the extent that the structure of the panel—two party-appointees and a neutral third arbitrator— imparts a rough balance in decision making. Unfortunately, a lack of clarity in the role of party-arbitrators, the possibility of ex parte contacts between a party and its arbitrator, limited disclosure requirements, and, above all, the difficulty of policing party-appointed arbitrators' mental processes in the conceptual no-man's land between neutrality and advocacy create potential problems at various stages of the arbitration process.

Most party-arbitrators behave with integrity, but exceptions to this rule have been noted. In one case, a party was powerless to challenge the opposing party's appointment of a former business partner as his party-arbitrator even though the latter was under a federal drug indictment; midway through the hearings, the appointee had to be replaced after pleading *nolo contendere* to the charges. In another situation, a party-arbitrator who promised to remain independent and open-minded announced at the final deliberations that his long acquaintance with his appointing party persuaded him of the truth of the appointing party's testimony and the preponderance of every element of his case.

Published decisions testify to the various ways in which the less-than-neutral stance of party-arbitrators hurts the arbitration process and inhibits the development of collegiality or cooperation among panel members. In one extreme case, pre-hearing discovery revealed that one party-arbitrator's engineering firm was assisting the appointing party in the preparation of witnesses and of exhibits and other aspects of the case—activities not revealed to the other party or its arbitrator at the beginning of the process.

CPR has long discouraged tripartite panels with "predisposed" party-arbi-trators. CPR's rules[76] require party-appointed arbitrators to be neutral. The Commission endorses this approach. The AAA also disfavors non-neutral party-arbitrators, although AAA Commercial Procedures § R-12(b) states that "[u]nless the parties agree otherwise, an arbitrator selected unilaterally by one party is a party-appointed arbitrator and is not subject to disqualification [because of relationships with the parties or the case]."

One Commissioner summed up the prevailing attitude of Commission members regarding party-arbitrators in U.S. arbitration as follows:

> The classic American model of the party-arbitrator as a sort of inside partisan is becoming increasingly disreputable to people who practice arbitration. Advocates don't like the arrangement, the neutral arbitrator doesn't like it, and often, the people designated as party-arbitrators don't like it. And when the decision of the panel is unanimous, the losing party may feel let down by its party-arbitrator, and end up particularly disappointed. It's a very uncomfortable role fraught with ethical problems.

Another Commissioner reports:

> Working as the neutral chair of a tripartite panel with party-arbitrators is like having two arbitrations. The chair faces the prospect of managing the arbitration hearings and then listening to the same arguments all over again during the arbitrators' deliberations. Some time ago I vowed never to agree to work with non-neutral party-arbitrators. I think that the system is an old one that is rarely used now, at least in the [western] part of the country.

It is the consensus of Commission members that *all* arbitrators, no matter how they are chosen, should have *aspirations* of neutrality and should behave accordingly. What is ethically appropriate also makes good sense from a practical point of view: the experience of Commission members indicates that a party is usually best served by appointing an arbitrator who conveys a sense of reasonableness and open-mindedness rather than a down-the-line advocate. Partisan attitudes, on the other hand, tend to undermine an arbitrator's credibility and minimize that individual's influence on the arbitration panel.

Although the assumption under federal arbitration law and that of most states is that party-appointed arbitrators will be less than neutral,[77] parties often agree to the contrary, and many arbitrators insist on acting impartially and independently regardless of the manner of their appointment. Today many parties whose contracts provide for such a method of selection opt for a fully neutral panel instead.

---

76. CPR ARBITRATION RULES, *supra* note 37, Rule 7.1.
77. *See generally* III MACNEIL ET AL., *supra* note 1, § 28.4.

2. Screened selection of arbitrators

Parties who are concerned about the ability of party-arbitrators to act independently and impartially but who still want sole control over the choice of one panelist may employ an "indirect" or "screened" selection procedure. The approach has been successfully employed in ad hoc proceedings, as related by one Commission member:

> In a complex construction dispute, the parties arranged for a knowledgeable neutral third party to assemble a list of potential panelists with specialized expertise in construction law or mechanical specialties. Each party selected one candidate for the arbitration panel, but left it to the third party to notify the selectee and to handle billing arrangements with the arbitrators. There was no direct ex parte communication between the parties and the arbitrators, and the latter never knew the source of their appointment.

The recently revised CPR Arbitration Rules offer a "screened" arbitrator selection option in Rule 5.4. Under the process, CPR provides each party with a copy of the CPR Panels of Distinguished Neutrals list. Each party designates three candidates in order of preference and provides their choices to CPR and the other party. After CPR conducts a conflicts inquiry for each party's first choice candidate, those candidates are appointed assuming no conflicts exist or successful challenge is made. Otherwise the procedure is repeated for the next candidate preference list. The chair of the tribunal is appointed by CPR in consultation with the parties and a list selection process. Compensation matters are administered by the chair. Under the "screened" process, neither CPR nor the parties "shall advise or otherwise provide any information or indication to any arbitrator candidate or arbitrator as to which party selected either of the party-designated arbitrators. No party or anyone acting on its behalf shall have any *ex parte* communications relating to the case with any arbitrator or arbitrator candidate designated or appointed" under this process.[78]

3. Ex parte communications

Although in some proceedings the participants understand that the party-arbitrators will communicate with their respective appointing parties during the hearings, the Commission disfavors such conduct. As a rule, parties adopting a tripartite panel are better off adhering to the model embraced by some domestic and international rules which limits direct communication with a potential appointee to discussing the general nature of the case and the candidate's qualifications.[79] Ex parte communications should cease upon appointment. Although some procedures contemplate communications between party-appointees and appointing parties regarding the selection of a third arbitrator to chair the panel, it should be clearly understood that such discussions should be limited to that subject.

---

78. CPR ARBITRATION RULES, *supra* note 37, Rule 5.4.
79. *See, e.g.*, INTERNATIONAL CHAMBER OF COMMERCE, ICC RULES OF CONCILIATION AND ARBITRATION, art. 7 §§ 2, 3 (1998).

4. Disclosures

Departing to some extent from the model implicit in existing case law and ethical rules, the Commission supports a "full disclosure" model for party-appointed arbitrators. That is, party-arbitrators should be subject to the same disclosure obligations as neutral arbitrators. Although party-appointed arbitrators would not be subject to challenge by an opposing party on the grounds of bias or partiality in the absence of contrary agreement, full disclosure (including disclosure of ex parte discussions with the appointing party, if any) would permit all parties, including the other arbitrators, to make a better assessment of their impartiality and independence. Such a rule should also help to moderate choices. CPR Rule 7.3 requires full disclosure by all arbitrators, including party-appointed arbitrators.

Currently, the AAA/ABA Code requires non-neutral party-arbitrators to "describe the general nature and scope of any interest or relationship" with participants or the case, but does not require them to reveal "detailed information as is expected from neutral arbitrators."[80] Of course, nothing prevents parties from agreeing to more detailed disclosures. (The draft revised version of the Code of Ethics has broadened the requirements for disclosure of party-arbitrators' interests and relationships.)

Whether or not the applicable rules call for full disclosure, panel chairs serving on tripartite panels are well advised to

> ascertain from the party-appointed arbitrators the nature and extent of any relationship between that party and the party that appointed the arbitrator, and whether there will be any direct communication between [them].[81]

3.8
How are arbitrators compensated?

1. From pro bono servant to hired neutral

In the past it was common for arbitrators of commercial disputes to serve *pro bono*. For that matter, many arbitrators were laymen—often business persons who regarded the role as a form of service to their industry or trade—and the time an arbitrator spent on a case tended to be relatively brief.

Today, things have changed. Commercial arbitrations often involve greater expenditures of time, and a higher percentage of commercial arbitrators are

---

80. *See* AAA/ABA CODE OF ETHICS, *supra* note 39, Canon VII.B.(1).
81. *See* AMERICAN ARBITRATION ASSOCIATION, A GUIDE FOR COMMERCIAL ARBITRATORS 2 (1997).

practicing attorneys. Outside of trade associations, virtually all commercial arbitrators expect to be compensated for their services. Typically, compensation is by the hour or day. Rates vary substantially, depending on the arbitrator's stature and experience, prevailing rates in the locality, and whether the arbitrator is required to share the fee with a provider organization. Parties can expect to be informed of a candidate's rates before making a selection. Many arbitrators expect to be compensated for study time; some require a stipend for the time required for travel to and from hearings.

Other expenses include arbitrators' travel-related costs, as well as the costs of experts and other witnesses. Such fees and expenses may be apportioned at the discretion of the arbitrators under most state arbitration statutes,[82] although in light of the absence of clear authority under federal law parties should address the matter in the arbitration agreement.[83] The apportionment of arbitration costs and attorney fees in awards is treated in Chapter 7.

2. Fees and costs in administered arbitration

When proceedings are administered, as by AAA or JAMS, the organization acts as a conduit for fees from the parties to the arbitrators. The AAA also assesses administrative fees based upon a sliding fee schedule; the minimum fee for any case involving three or more arbitrators is $2,000.[84]

Initially, arbitrator fees and expenses are evenly divided between the parties, except in the rare instance in which the parties have agreed otherwise. Eventually, the award may apportion such costs on a different basis.[85]

3. Fees and costs in non-administered arbitration

In non-administered arbitrations, the arrangements vary depending on the agreement of the parties, or as arranged between parties and arbitrators. Under the CPR Arbitration Rules, the arbitrator will invoice the parties directly at the pre-agreed rate.[86] Ultimately, the costs of arbitration, broadly defined to include costs for legal representation, are to be apportioned by the arbitration tribunal in its award.[87] CPR receives no part of the arbitrators' fees; only when CPR is

---

82. *See* UNIF. ARB. ACT § 10.
83. *See* III MACNEIL ET AL., *supra* note 1, § 31.2.4.
84. AAA COMMERCIAL PROCEDURES, *supra* note 33, at 46.
85. *Id.* § R-45.
86. CPR ARBITRATION RULES, *supra* note 37, Rule 16.1.
87. *Id.* Rules 16.2, 16.3.

asked to assist in the selection process does it charge a service fee, which is not related to the size of the case.

While the fees charged by the chair may be larger than those charged by wing arbitrators, it may be divisive for the wing arbitrators to be compensated at different rates. Moreover, direct discussions regarding compensation between an arbitrator and a single party go against the principle that neutral arbitrators should avoid ex parte discussions with parties, and raise ethical and, potentially, legal concerns.[88] As the AAA/ABA Code admonishes, one-on-one discussion should be avoided wherever possible in favor of discussions regarding compensation for all panelists in the presence of all parties.[89] Sometimes, the chair handles billing matters for all three arbitrators. The fees of party-arbitrators—arbitrators appointed by individual parties who may act in a less-than-neutral fashion—are often paid directly by the appointing parties. Those desiring independent and impartial arbitrators should avoid this practice, as noted in Section 3.7.2.

4. Problems with payment of arbitrator fees

Entitlement to payment

Arbitrators sometimes experience difficulties in collecting fees, particularly after an award has been handed down. From time to time, a published court opinion reaffirms the right of arbitrators to enforce a compensation agreement against a party who refuses to pay.[90] In the absence of an explicit agreement, a number of decisions under federal and state law recognize an implied agreement by the parties to reimburse reasonable arbitrator fees and expenses.[91]

Deposits

To avoid post-award payment problems, some arbitrators require payment to be deposited at the outset of the proceeding, or, in any event, prior to the award. The rules of leading sponsor organizations now follow this practice.[92] Under the CPR Arbitration Rules, for example, the arbitration panel may require each party to deposit an appropriate amount for arbitrator fees, expenses, and other costs, and may request supplementary deposits during the proceeding.[93]

---

88.   *See* III MACNEIL ET AL., *supra* note 1, § 31.2.2.3.
89.   AAA/ABA CODE OF ETHICS, *supra* note 39, Canon VI.D.
90.   *See, e.g.,* Hunt v. Mobil Oil Corp., 654 F. Supp. 1487, 1507–1511 (S.D.N.Y. 1987).
91.   *See* III MACNEIL ET AL., *supra* note 1, § 31.2.2.2.
92.   *See, e.g.,* AAA COMMERCIAL PROCEDURES, *supra* note 33, § R-54.
93.   CPR ARBITRATION RULES, *supra* note 37, Rule 16.4.

3.9

What legal or ethical standards govern the actions of arbitrators? What are the consequences of an arbitrator's failure to abide by such standards?

As explained above in connection with arbitrator disclosure obligations, standards governing the activities of arbitrators derive from three general sources: most enforceable (1) federal and state laws governing arbitrations and (2) the agreement of the parties and incorporated commercial arbitration rules, if any, and, less enforceable, (3) applicable ethical rules, such as the AAA/ABA Code of Ethics. These standards provide an array of interlocking, often mutually supporting guideposts for arbitrator behavior. In some cases the breach of a standard will give rise to a remedy—nearly always in the form of a vacatur or undoing of all or part of the arbitration award. [94] More rarely, the result is some form of judicial action, such as the removal of an arbitrator, prior to award.[95] Arbitrators are not liable, as a rule, in damages for their failure to fulfill duties and obligations within the scope of their arbitral role; the principle of arbitrator immunity will be briefly treated before consideration of the range of arbitral duties and obligations.

1. Arbitrator immunity

The immunity of arbitrators from liability in the performance of activities within the scope of the arbitral role is well-established under federal and state law.[96] The principle finds justification in the functional comparability of arbitrators to judges, whose immunity is founded upon the need to protect their impartiality, independence, and freedom from undue influence. In the arbitral arena, immunity of the decisionmaker reinforces the limited role of courts in overseeing arbitrations, usually cabined within the confines of statutory vacatur provisions.[97] The cloak of immunity has been extended to institutions sponsoring arbitration.[98] It is often reinforced by standard commercial arbitration rules, such as CPR Rule 19, which provides that:

> Neither CPR nor any arbitrator shall be liable to any party for any act or omission in connection with any arbitration conducted under these Rules.[99]

---

94. *See* FAA, *supra* note 16, § 10, UNIF. ARB. ACT § 12 (1955).
95. *See generally* III MACNEIL ET AL., *supra* note 1, § 28.3.3.
96. *See id.* § 31.3.
97. *See id.*
98. *See id.* § 31.3.2.
99. CPR ARBITRATION RULES, *supra* note 37, Rule 19.

2. Requirements of arbitration law

Under modern federal and state arbitration laws, arbitrator duties and obligations are derived chiefly from statutory standards for vacatur of award.[100] These standards, which are discussed in Chapter 7, have important implications for all aspects of arbitrator performance from initial appointment to rendition of the final award. Although very few awards are vacated under the FAA and analogous state statutes, the mere possibility of judicial vacatur makes arbitrators more cautious, particularly when asked to deny admission of evidence.

In a few states, arbitrators' obligations are underlined by oaths of office which arbitrators are required to take at the time of appointment. In New York, for example, arbitrators swear to "faithfully and fully hear and examine the matters in controversy and . . . make a just award . . . ."[101]

3. Commercial arbitration rules

In most commercial arbitrations, statutory standards and powers of arbitrators are reinforced and fleshed out by commercial arbitration rules the parties have selected to govern the proceedings. For example, the CPR Arbitration Rules set forth a host of arbitral powers and commensurate duties, including:

- disclosing potential conflicts of interest;
- appointing a third arbitrator;
- deciding challenges to the jurisdiction of the panel;
- managing the proceedings expeditiously;
- scheduling, order of proof, narrowing of issues, etc.;
- avoiding ex parte communications;
- conducting a pre-hearing conference;
- overseeing discovery;
- encouraging settlement negotiations;
- entertaining motions for pre-hearing orders;
- fixing the place of arbitration;
- ruling on evidentiary matters;
- taking interim measures for the protection of property, etc.;
- rendering final, interim, interlocutory, or partial awards;
- fixing and allocating costs, and
- preserving confidentiality.

---

100. FAA, *supra* note 16, § 10.
101. *See* N.Y. C.P.L.R. § 7506 (1998).

When incorporated in the agreement of arbitrating parties, rules containing such provisions often not only establish the most helpful single source of standards for arbitrator performance, but also the source for specific application of the broad judicial standards of vacatur. They are typically reinforced by oaths of office required by the sponsoring organization.

4. Ethical standards

In 1977, the Code of Ethics for Arbitrators in Commercial Disputes was developed by a joint committee of representatives of the American Arbitration Association and the American Bar Association, and subsequently approved by both organizations. The Code is now employed by AAA and a number of other organizations sponsoring arbitration. It has been cited as the authoritative source of ethical guidance for arbitrators in a number of court opinions and in other sources.

The Code provides specific guideposts for arbitrators under several general headings, or Canons:

Canon I.   An Arbitrator Should Uphold the Integrity and Fairness of the Arbitration Process

Canon II.   An Arbitrator Should Disclose Any Interest or Relationship Likely to Affect Impartiality or Which Might Create an Appearance of Partiality or Bias

Canon III.   An Arbitrator in Communicating with the Parties Should Avoid Impropriety or the Appearance of Impropriety

Canon IV.   An Arbitrator Should Conduct the Proceedings Fairly and Diligently

Canon V.   An Arbitrator Should Make Decisions in a Just, Independent and Deliberate Manner

Canon VI.   An Arbitrator Should Be Faithful to the Relationship of Trust and Confidentiality Inherent in That Office.

A seventh Canon addresses the special concerns associated with tripartite panels involving party-arbitrators. (See above.)

The Code of Ethics contains the most detailed standards governing arbitrator behavior, and reinforces statutory and contractual performance standards. The full text of the Code of Ethics may be found in Appendix 3.4.

The Arbitration Committee of the ABA Section of Dispute Resolution recently initiated an effort to revise the 1977 Code with input from the American Arbitration Association, CPR, the International Law and Practice Section of the ABA, and other groups. That effort is underway at this time.

The Commission on Ethics and Standards in ADR sponsored by CPR and Georgetown University has drafted a proposed new Model Rule of Professional Conduct for the Lawyer as Third Party Neutral. The proposed Rule addresses the ethical responsibilities of lawyers serving as neutrals in arbitration, mediation, and other ADR fora. The proposed Rule, with commentary, may be found in Appendix 3.6.

3.10

Is it advisable to employ full-time "professional" arbitrators?

Traditionally, the majority of commercial arbitrators were business persons or professionals who had established a reputation in a separate professional or business setting and who did not depend on arbitration for a livelihood. In recent years, however, the growing use of mediation and other forms of ADR has produced a profusion of full-time neutrals who market arbitration services along with other dispute resolution services, as well as individuals who devote a substantial portion of their time and derive a substantial portion of their income from such services.

The trend toward more "professional" neutrals may result in more experienced, more capable arbitrators. Such neutrals may also offer a more extensive "track record" for review by arbitrating parties.

On the other hand, some argue that dependency on arbitration for fees might lead some to curry favor with likely repeat players[102] or to prolong hearings unnecessarily. Others spurn such reasoning; one Commissioner flatly declared:

> Such conclusions unnecessarily impugn the integrity of fine people. I have never seen people who exhibit such behavior.

Whatever the realities of the marketplace, it is likely that present trends will continue. Meanwhile, we have seen ways that organizations sponsoring arbitration services can enhance the qualifications of their arbitrators and provide the necessary quality control for the bulk of commercial cases.

---

102. *See* Silver, *supra* note 10, at 47 (discussing the relationship between arbitrators' personal authority and perceived independence).

Appendix 3.1
Disclosure Questions in Arbitrator Screening and Selection
A Supplement to Harry Mazadoorian's *Disclosure Questions ADR Counsel Should Ask When Screening and Selecting a Neutral*[1]

Thomas J. Stipanowich

Introduction

The following guidelines were developed as a supplement to Harry Mazadoorian's article on screening and selecting provider organizations and individual neutrals, *Disclosure Questions ADR Counsel Should Ask When Screening and Selecting a Neutral*. Prompted by the author's involvement with a working group of the CPR Commission on Ethics and Standards of Dispute Resolution Practice, these materials are intended to provide specific guidelines for individuals seeking arbitration services, or those representing such parties. This is, of course, a two-step problem since the provider organization is most often identified in an arbitration or ADR agreement contained in a commercial contract (or, increasingly, a public contract); the individual neutral or arbitration panel is chosen when disputes arise and are submitted to arbitration.

Modern arbitration statutes typically establish no prerequisites for appointment of arbitrators other than the disclosure of relationships or interests raising partiality concerns. Initially, therefore, acceptability to the parties is the chief qualification for arbitrators. The arbitrator selection method chosen by the parties should be identified with the goal of producing arbitrators with the desired characteristics.

Parties usually agree to arbitration at the time they enter into a contract, prior to the emergence of disputes. The arbitration agreement rarely identifies arbitrators by name, but typically incorporates selection procedures to be employed in the event of resort to arbitration. The procedures are often those of a provider organization which may also assist in the selection of arbitrators and administer other aspects of the process. The quality of support provided may enhance or diminish parties' satisfaction with arbitration.

We will first consider factors pertinent to screening and selecting a provider organization—usually a matter for discussion when entering into a contract.

---

1. Harry N. Mazadoorian, *Disclosure Questions ADR Counsel Should Ask When Screening and Selecting a Neutral*, 14 ALTERNATIVES 63 (Sept. 1996).

105

We will then address screening and selection of individual candidates, and, finally, focus on special concerns associated with tripartite panels involving party-arbitrators.

A final caveat: The following guidelines are intended primarily for parties in business-to-business disputes. Additional considerations may arise in the context of individual contracts of employment or standardized consumer agreements, including the even-handedness of arbitrator selection mechanisms and other due process concerns.

Screening and Selecting Provider Organizations

Background: General Considerations

Generally.   Organizations providing support for binding arbitration offer one or more of the following: (1) panels of arbitrators; (2) arbitration rules; and (3) administrative services. Some also are able to provide considerable assistance in the design of customized conflict resolution systems. Initially, a decision must be made regarding the desired scope of services. While some parties will require a "full service" organization, others may prefer more limited services on the basis of cost or perceived needs.

Relationship of provider to parties.   Providers of arbitration services range from non-profit or commercial organizations which contract with arbitrating parties to in-house programs sponsored by large corporations or associations. In many transactional contexts, some prior connections are inevitable—particularly in the case of major national providers. Moreover, many kinds of relationships are innocuous and should not be grounds for concern. Particularly where arbitration is made a condition of employment or of doing business with another party, however, it is appropriate to scrutinize the relationship of the provider to that party and ascertain whether or not there are reasonable grounds for concern regarding partiality of administrators or arbitrators. Although too-close relationships may ultimately establish a basis for vacation of award, there is also the possibility that a failure to make a timely objection to contractual arbitration procedures will be deemed a waiver of the right to object at a later time.

Availability of other ADR services.   Increasingly, parties seeking arbitration services are likely to view arbitration as the final step in a more comprehensive managed conflict resolution process which may involve one or more of the following: facilitation, counseling, unassisted negotiation, mediation, or non-binding evaluation. In this regard, Harry Mazadoorian's *Disclosure Questions ADR Counsel Should Ask When Screening and Selecting a Neutral* may be of assistance.

A growing number of organizations also provide, for a fee, consulting services aimed at developing conflict resolution programs aimed at particular transactional settings. Relatively few, however, are likely to combine competent advice with the administrative services to support the designed program. Before contracting for such front-end services (which is often partly a business-getting device, like "financial counseling" in which an insurance salesperson peddles his product), references should be sought and checked.

Arbitrator pools.   A traditional hallmark of binding arbitration is expertise in the adjudicator. The arbitrator pools, or "panels," of provider organizations vary greatly in terms of qualifications, training requirements, arbitration experience, and administrative oversight. Moreover, some providers offer small national cadres of "blue ribbon" neutrals, while others serve various regional and localities through much more extensive national networks. Fee structures also vary considerably; generally speaking, however, the day of the "volunteer arbitrator" is past.

Rules.   Arbitrating parties usually need a good set of arbitration rules to govern the process from the filing of a demand or submission to rendition of award (and, in some cases, beyond). On one extreme are organizations which publish rules for different transactional settings (and in some cases establish different "tracks" for cases of varying size and complexity); on the other end of the spectrum are programs which provide no governing rules. In the latter case, parties should furnish their own rules (a potentially daunting task) or run the risk of having arbitration delayed or disrupted by non-cooperative parties or arbitrator death or incapacity. Because the need for arbitrator impartiality is critical to the process, parties should normally agree to a procedure for disclosure of relationships and interests raising partiality issues at the time of appointment, and a mechanism for challenging appointments on partiality grounds.

Concerns regarding arbitration which is required as a condition of employment or of doing business have spurred a number of efforts to consider a "floor of expectations" for parties entering into such contracts. Among these efforts are the *Due Process Protocol for Mediation and Arbitration of Statutory Disputes Arising Out of the Employment Relationship (1995)* and other protocols addressing the needs of consumer contracts. It may be appropriate to compare proposed arbitration procedures against the "due process" afforded by this and other standards.

In some cases, parties may wish to adopt the rules of a particular organization but decline administrative assistance.

Scope of administration.   Provider organizations offer a variety of administrative support services to arbitrating parties, including assistance with arbitrator selection, scheduling and coordination of sessions, supervision of arbitrator fee arrangements and payment, and channeling of communications between parties and arbitrators.

Despite these potential advantages, third party administration occasionally has downsides. An overburdened administrator may find it difficult to meet prescribed timetables for arbitrator selection or commencement of hearings. Moreover, an administrator charged with selecting an arbitrator for the parties may have insufficient information or experience to identify the qualifications necessary for arbitration of a particular case.

Some organizations, while providing arbitration rules or panels of arbitrators, offer no other administrative services. In such cases, arbitrators are likely to have greater responsibility for administrative matters—a reality that should be taken into account at the time of arbitrator selection.

Inquiries of Provider Organizations
Relationship of Provider Organization to Parties, Counsel

- Extent of past or present relationship of provider and its arbitrator pool to parties or counsel, including prior or current use of services of the provider organization, roles of parties or counsel as neutrals for the provider, etc.

Range of ADR Services

- Availability of mediation, non-binding evaluation, and other third-party-assisted conflict resolution services.
- Availability of competent ADR system design services (Get references!)

Arbitrators

- Mechanism(s) for selecting arbitrators.
- Minimum qualifications (education, experiential, professional) for panelists.
- Arbitration training requirements, including continuing education.
- Availability of experienced arbitrators in the locality or region. [Ask for examples.]
- Mechanisms for evaluation and oversight of panelists.
- Scope of information provided to parties regarding prospective arbitrators. [Ask to inspect examples of arbitrator bios.]
- Where necessary, ability of parties to provide technical or experiential criteria for selection of arbitrators by administrator.
- Mechanism(s) for establishing fees; fee ranges.
- Provider fee for administering arbitrator selection only.

Rules   [A copy of the current rules should be requested and reviewed prior to incorporating them in an arbitration agreement.]

- Availability of rules pertinent to the transactional setting.
- Flexibility of rules to address disputes of different kinds, levels of complexity.
- Nature of default arbitrator selection process.

- Mechanism for challenging arbitrators on the basis of disclosed relationships or interests;
- Ability of rules to address contingencies such as refusal of party to cooperate, arbitrator death or incapacity, multiparty disputes, etc.
- Other "due process" elements (such as ability of parties to be represented by spokespersons of their own choosing, availability of pre-arbitration discovery, authority of arbitrator to run hearing and to render relief, form of award)
- Cost of using rules without other provider administrative services.

Administrative services

- Scope of services, including:
  - arbitrator selection (including assuring arbitrator impartiality);
  - arranging location of hearings;
  - scheduling, making arrangements for conferences, hearings;
  - handling payment and reimbursement of administrative fees and arbitrator fees and expenses;
  - serving as a buffer between parties and arbitrators, and conduit through which communications can be made outside of hearings;
  - providing counsel to arbitrators and parties concerning interpretation of rules, procedural matters.
- Administrative personnel:
  - qualifications, training requirements for case administrators;
  - role of case administrators in arbitrator selection, choice of hearing location, etc.;
  - case-load of case administrators.
- Administrative fees:
  - up-front fees, recurring fees;
  - ability of arbitrator(s) to allocate fees in award;
  - refunds in the event of settlement.

Selecting the Neutral Arbitrator(s)

Background; General Considerations

Requirement of impartiality.   Arbitrators are quasi-judicial officers. As such, they should possess a judicial temperament and be capable of producing a fair decision. Arbitral integrity and fairmindedness are critical to the working of the process and to parties' perceptions of arbitration. As a rule, arbitrators are legally and ethically required to disclose certain relationships with the parties or the dispute which raises questions of partiality. (Under the Federal Arbitration

Act, "evident partiality" of an arbitrator is a ground for vacation of award. Case decisions under the statute have established that proof of undisclosed relationships which create inferences of partiality may require an award to be vacated.)

Experiential qualifications.   Professional, technical, or commercial arbitrator expertise may be the most important potential advantage of arbitration. Expert arbitrators can deal more capably with factual issues, including evaluation of expert testimony, and should require less educating on technical matters. Their awards may also be more responsive to business reality and hence, more "just" in a commercial sense. The potential benefits of expertise must be weighed against the biases that come with experience, and the cost of attracting busy professionals and businesspersons. What kind of expertise is deemed appropriate will depend upon the parties and the issues presented.

Particularly in larger, complex cases, it is important that an arbitrator (or the chair of an arbitration panel) be skilled in managing hearing procedures. In some cases parties will seek a reasoned opinion, and will desire arbitrators who are comfortable preparing that form of award. Often, an effort will be made to secure a multi-member (usually three member) panel with a mixture of expertise or background. Multiple arbitrators cost more, of course, and make it more difficult to scheduling hearings.

Fees, availability.   If the arbitrator's fees vary from schedules established by the providing organization, they should be established at the outset, along with billing and payment procedures. If possible, billing and remuneration should be handled in such a manner as to avoid perceptions of partiality.

Because speed and efficiency of proceedings is usually a goal of arbitrating parties, care should be taken in determining the availability of a prospective arbitrator for the requisite number of hearings. Parties should be forthright in assessing their scheduling needs, and arbitrators their availability during the pertinent period.

Limitations on direct inquiries.   In many cases there will be no opportunity under the provider organization's rules for direct communication with the candidate. Much, if not all, of the information provided by the organization will be supplied by the candidate. In such cases it may be necessary to ask the administering organization for additional information regarding the candidate, perhaps by propounding questions through the administrator.

Inquiries of Candidates for Neutral Arbitrator
Impartiality

- Arbitrator's financial, business, professional, or personal relationships with the appointing party or that party's counsel.
- Arbitrator's interest in the matters in dispute or the underlying transaction.

Pertinent professional, commercial or technical experience

Arbitration experience   (Range of inquiry will depend on nature of disputes)

- Prior experience in binding arbitration

    - approximate number of arbitration experiences;
    - nature of disputes arbitrated (examples to illustrate the range may be sufficient);
    - relative complexity (examples may be sufficient).

- Experiences as panelist or chair of an arbitration panel
- Training, familiarity with rules of provider organization, and AAA/ABA Code of Ethics for Commercial Arbitrators
- Names, addresses of parties to prior arbitrations.

Writings, published opinions

Fees

Schedule, availability of arbitrator

Party-Arbitrator(s)

Background; General Considerations

One of the most confounding issues affecting binding arbitration involves the practice of arbitrators appointed by a single party to the dispute, which we shall refer to as "party-arbitrators." Party-arbitrators are normally utilized on tripartite arbitration panels in which each party is afforded the right to appoint an arbitrator; the two initial appointees then agree upon a third arbitrator. The process is routinely employed in international arbitration and frequently used in U.S. commercial arbitration.

Intended role of party-arbitrators.   Under prevailing international arbitration rules and practice, the "party-arbitrator" is expected to function independently and impartially. In the United States, however, the expectation is very different. According to the weight of judicial opinion under federal and state arbitration law, prevailing arbitration rules, and ethics rules, in the absence of contrary agreement the expectation is that the party-arbitrator will be predisposed toward the appointing party. In many cases, it is clear that the parties expect their appointees to function as advocates.

Theoretically, the tripartite panel is "neutral" because the party appointees serve as counterweights to one another, with the third, truly neutral arbitrator as the fulcrum. This assumes, of course, that both party-arbitrators understand

and fulfill their roles in similar fashion. If one party-arbitrator is decidedly more the advocate, it may tip the scales unfairly. To the extent possible, therefore, the parties must agree upon and seek to ensure that the party-arbitrators function in the same manner. (This is easier said than done, however, since policing "neutrality" in party-appointees is extremely difficult.)

Scope of mutual disclosures.   Non-neutral party-arbitrators are not typically required to withdraw if requested to do so by a party other than the appointing party. They are, however, required to disclose at least general information regarding the nature and scope of any interest or relationship which might raise questions of bias for the benefit of other parties and arbitrators. It is particularly important for other arbitrators to have this information, since it may have an impact on their expectations of and communications with that party-arbitrator. Neutral party-appointed arbitrators have the same disclosure obligations as any neutral arbitrators.

Whatever role is envisioned for party-arbitrators, it is advisable for the parties to agree beforehand on the precise scope of disclosure obligations. In addition, they may wish to place certain limits on the appointment of even non-neutral arbitrators (i.e. no family members or current business partners, persons under indictment, etc.)

Handling of ex parte communications.   Unlike neutral arbitrators, non-neutral party-arbitrators may communicate with their appointing party prior to and during arbitration. Ethical rules require them to disclose the fact that such communications have taken place, but not their substance.

On the other hand, neutral party-appointed arbitrators must generally avoid ex parte communications. Since many parties communicate with their arbitrators during the appointment process, however, some may take advantage of the ex parte contact to make factual or legal arguments to the arbitrator. This possibility should be anticipated and addressed prior to arbitrator selection; some parties may desire to go so far as to have a third party or organization supervise arbitrator selection so as to avoid direct communications. If direct contact cannot be avoided, a neutral party appointed arbitrator should be required to make specific disclosures regarding the substance of pre-arbitration ex parte communications.

Payment of fees.   Non-neutral party-arbitrators may receive payment directly from the appointing party. In the case of neutral party-appointees, of course, direct payment by the appointing party is another source of concern. What expectations, stated or unstated, arise with the "direct hire" relationship? What sense of obligation, however subtle, may accompany the mere knowledge that an arbitrator owes her appointment to a particular party? (The latter may have an insidious impact, particularly when the arbitration presents close questions.) Again, when the parties profess expectations of neutrality it may be desirable to employ mechanisms to avoid the "direct hire" approach, perhaps through the use of a third party or organization. Such indirect methods of payment may be appropriate for employer-sponsored arbitration programs and other programs in which one party "subsidizes" arbitration by paying most or all of the arbitrator's fee.

Contingencies; default rules.   As many reported decisions attest, cases involving tripartite panels are sometimes beset by problems associated with a lack of cooperation by parties or their appointees. A party may delay in appointing an arbitrator. The party-arbitrators may be unable to agree on a third arbitrator. Midway through the arbitration, a party arbitrator may resign. Such contingencies should be anticipated, and appropriate default rules structured.

With all of this in mind, the following list of areas of inquiry may serve as a guide for parties considering the use of tripartite panels.

Inquiries of Non-Neutral Party-Arbitrator
Relationships with parties, attorneys, arbitrators

- Arbitrator's financial, business, professional, or personal relationships with the appointing party or that party's counsel. (Parties may desire somewhat less specificity than in the case of a neutral party-appointee.)
- Arbitrator's interest in the matters in dispute or the underlying transaction.
- Relationships with candidates for third, neutral arbitrator.
- Communications with the appointing party or that party's counsel. (There should at least be disclosure of the fact that a communication has occurred, as soon after the communication as possible.)

Previous work as party-arbitrator

- Arbitrator's prior appointments (within reasonable period prior to the arbitration) as a non-neutral party-arbitrator, with names and addresses of parties.

Understanding of role, payment

- The arbitrator's understanding of the role of party-arbitrator. (This might take the form of a written agreement or affirmation. For example, each party arbitrator might be called upon to sign a specific statement delineating the nature of the role, including rules regarding communications and payment.)

Inquiries of "Neutral" Party-Appointed Arbitrator
Relationships with parties, attorneys, arbitrators

- Arbitrator's financial, business, professional, or personal relationships with the appointing party or that party's counsel. (In the case of a neutral

party appointee, the disclosures should be as specific as reasonably possible, and include all relationships which might reasonably create the appearance of partiality.)
- Arbitrator's interest in the matters in dispute or the underlying transaction.
- Relationships with candidates for third, neutral arbitrator.
- Communications with the appointing party or that party's counsel. (The scope and nature of ex parte communications, if any, at the time of appointment should be disclosed. Further ex parte contact should be avoided.)

Previous work as party-appointed arbitrator

- Arbitrator's prior appointments (within reasonable period prior to the arbitration) as a neutral party-appointed arbitrator, with names and addresses of parties.

Understanding of role

- The arbitrator's understanding of the role of a neutral arbitrator. (This might take the form of a written agreement or affirmation. For example, each party appointed arbitrator might be called upon to sign a specific statement delineating the nature of the role, including rules regarding communications and payment, and a promise to adhere to the rules for neutral arbitrators under the AAA/ABA Code of Ethics for Commercial Arbitrators.)

Writings, published opinions

Fees

Schedule, availability of arbitrator

Appendix 3.2
Sample Arbitrator Short Biography

Hon. Joseph W. Morris
Gable & Gotwals

Professional Experience

Judge Morris has been a member of the law firm of Gable & Gotwals since 1984. Until 1984 he was Vice President and General Counsel of Shell Oil Company, Houston, Texas. Prior to that, he served as the Chief Judge of the United States District Court for the Eastern District of Oklahoma, until he resigned from the bench in 1978. He is also the former General Counsel of Amerada Petroleum Corporation and Dean of the College of Law at the University of Tulsa.

Primary Practice Areas

Commercial Litigation and ADR

Dispute Resolution Experience and Training

He has spent 90% of his time on business ADR matters during the past 15 years, serving as an arbitrator, mediator and neutral advisor in more than 50 domestic and international cases, including arbitrations in London, England, Melbourne, Australia and the United Arab Emirates. In more than 2/3 of his arbitrations, he has been Chairman of the Panel or the sole arbitrator. In 1991, he taught alternative dispute resolution at the International Development Law Institute, Rome, Italy, and serves now as Special Master by appointment of the United States District Court for the District of Wyoming in the *In re: Copley Pharmaceutical, Inc. "Albuterol" Products Liability Litigation* class action.

Selected Honors, Awards, Publications, and/or Professional and Civic Associations

He is a member of the Advisory Board of the Institute for Transnational Arbitration of the Southwestern Legal Foundation, an emeritus member of The Rand Corporation's Board of Overseers of the Institute for Civil Justice, a life member of the American Law Institute, former Chairman of the Natural Resources Law

Section of the ABA, former State Regent of Higher Education for the State of Oklahoma, Master Emeritus of the Council Oak Chapter of the American Inns of Court Foundation and Past President, Tulsa County Bar Association.

Education
A.B., Washburn University, 1943; J.D., Washburn University, 1947; LL.M., University of Michigan, 1948; S.J.D., University of Michigan, 1955. The Order of the Coif.

Contact Information
1100 ONEOK Plaza
100 West Fifth Street
Tulsa, Oklahoma 74103-4217
Phone: (918) 595-4800
Fax: (918) 595-4990
Email: jmorris@gablelaw.com
Web site: www.gablelaw.com

Appendix 3.3
Searching for Potential Arbitrators on the Internet

Carroll E. Neesemann
Jennifer K. Kim and
*Sonna Moon**

I. Introduction

The Internet can be a great resource for parties searching for an arbitrator or neutral. Parties to alternative dispute resolution (ADR) may have traditionally turned to organized ADR providers to locate arbitrators for them, but now, parties may choose to locate arbitrators on their own by using one of a number of ADR-related web sites on the Internet.

There are a vast number of web sites on the Internet dedicated to arbitration and/or ADR in general. There are also a number of attorney locators maintained by law and government related directories that allow parties to search for attorneys with arbitration expertise. What we have complied here is a list of those major Arbitration and/or ADR-related web sites that we believe would offer especially useful starting points for a person hoping to use the Internet as an aid in locating an arbitrator/neutral through the Internet or procuring information about a potential arbitrator being considered. Admittedly what follows is only a representative list and by no means comprehensive. While we have endeavored to include most major academic, professional and non-profit organizations and institutes dedicated to Arbitration, we do not pretend completeness. We have found that, for the most part, the sites listed are a good point of departure for web-based research. In addition, most of the web sites listed contain related links to other sites, which should further assist in the research process. Many also offer extensive, searchable archives to aid in more directed research.

It should be noted that this work is intended as a general guide—web surfers with greater Internet expertise or those with especially pointed research objectives are advised to fashion their queries accordingly. One

*Carroll E. Neesemann is a partner at Morrison & Foerster LLP in New York City; Jennifer K. Kim is an associate with the firm; and Sonna Moon is a former summer associate with the firm.

final, important note: because there is not, as yet, a uniform, universally accepted standard of arbitrator/neutral certification or qualification, it is largely incumbent upon the party or parties that appoint an arbitrator to satisfy themselves that a candidate is qualified and appropriate. We cannot attest to the suitability of any of the arbitrators located through research conducted according to this guide, nor can we confirm the accuracy of the information found within the web sites we have noted. Such is the hazard of Internet-based research.

II. Finding Arbitration Resources on the Internet: Search Engines, Meta-Search Engines, and Directories

A. AltaVista <http://www.altavista.com>

Founded in 1995, AltaVista is probably one of the largest search engines on the Internet today. Pioneered by the company as the "first full-text search service in the world," their "search technology has consistently been the Internet's performance leader."

AltaVista tends to be over-inclusive in its search results, but is, on the other hand, extremely comprehensive. The broad scope of AltaVista's coverage can yield less accurate findings but may also allow the researcher to find sites that do not appear in other fora and thus justify the sacrifice of a highly "discriminating" search for a more "extensive" one.

B. Ask Jeeves <http://www.askjeeves.com>

Ask Jeeves is a natural language search service. Incorporated in 1996, Ask Jeeves combines its search technology with "the cognitive strengths and capabilities of human editors."

Online researchers may pose questions rather than search terms and Ask Jeeves directs you to the most relevant web sites based on a combination of the work of human editors and their patented popularity technology. This technology analyzes the previous searches of Internet users to determine the most relevant results for a query. If no match is found in its own database, Ask Jeeves will provide links to web pages found by other search engines.

C. Excite <http://www.excite.com>

Excite was launched in 1995, and is one of the more popular search engines around, even though it remains relatively small. Excite retrieves sites based on a "related concepts" structure in order to maximize results, however, Boolean searching (i.e., "and" "or") may be used for more precise research. Excite Precision Search was introduced in June 2000 for more precise searching "with less clutter."

D. FAST Search <http://www.alltheweb.com>

Fast Search and Transfer ASA (FAST) was established in 1997, and is currently the world's largest search engine service. It has "over 575 million full text web documents" and "provides users with highly accurate and relevant results" by "crawling and examining over 1.5 billion web documents," the most of any search engine today. FAST's goal is to index the entire web and, thus, its strength is the size of its index.

E. Google <http://www.google.com>

Google is a privately held company that launched in 1999. This search engine aims to search the World Wide Web quickly and efficiently and to bring the online researcher the most relevant results by employing a user voting system. Google's "PageRank" technology combines both popularity and relevance factors to match searches with results. "Important, high-quality sites receive a higher PageRank, which Google remembers each time it conducts a search." This is combined with "a sophisticated text-matching technique" to ensure relevance and importance to the query.

F. HotBot <http://www.hotbot.lycos.com>

This sophisticated search engine is a hit with "serious researchers" because it uses a very large database supported by Direct Hit and Inktomi. HotBot launched in 1996 and was bought out by Lycos in 1998.

G. Northern Light <http://www.northernlight.com>

Northern Light launched in 1997, to address what the founders perceived to be "shortcomings of traditional search engines, including the lack of organization and quality information." While Northern Light is not the most well-known of the search engines, it does have a very large index of the web and the ability to cluster search results by topic.

H. Yahoo <http://www.yahoo.com>

Yahoo has one of the largest directory databases on the Internet. Established in 1994, it is the oldest and the most well-known subject directory around. Yahoo has developed a reputation for smart categorization and ease of use, which has made it popular with Internet users.

I. Additional Search Engines, Meta-Search Engines and Directories
1. AOL Search <http://search.aol.com>
2. Direct Hit <http://www.directhit.com>
3. Go/Infoseek <http://www.go.com>
4. GoTo <http://www.goto.com>
5. IWon <http://www.iwon.com>

6. LookSmart <http://www.looksmart.com>
7. Lycos <http://www.lycos.com>
8. Metacrawler <http://www.metacrawler.com>
9. MSN Search <http://search.msn.com>
10. Netscape Search <http://search.netscope.com>
11. Open Directory <http://dmoz.org>
12. Snap <http://www.nbci.com>
13. Dogpile <http://www.dogpile.com>
14. Ixquick <http://www.ixquick.com>
15. Quick Browse <http://www.qbsearch.com>
16. Search.com <http://www.search.com>
17. Inference Find <http://www.infind.com>
18. ProFusion <http://www.profusion.com>
19. C4 <http://www.c4.com>
20. InfoGrid <http://www.infogrid.com>
21. Surfwax.com <http://www.surfwax.com/servlet/home>
22. Try9 <http://www.try9.com>

III. Major Public, Private and Governmental ADR Organizations and ADR Resources on the Internet

Search Engines are popular and useful tools for conducting Internet-based research. However, while the submission of a keyword term into a search engine query box will almost invariably yield many *potentially* useful web site links—and thus offer the online researcher innumerable opportunities and directions in which to pursue further investigation—often the greatest difficulty confronting online researchers is in effectively discriminating between these countless choices. In locating good sources of information about arbitration and, more particularly, in locating arbitrators online, professional, governmental and educational institutes and organizations devoted to the development of ADR systems may provide better, more nuanced lists of arbitration-related web sites and potential service providers.

A. ADRWorld.com <http://www.adrworld.com>

ADRWorld.com is an "independent source on the World Wide Web for up-to the minute news on arbitration, mediation and all forms of alternative dispute resolution." This site tracks recent developments in ADR in "all 50 states and the federal government," and provides "important court opinions, and a comprehensive library of statutes, court rules and policy documents."

ADRWorld.com also has a searchable online roster of ADR neutrals, service providers, attorney/advocates, trainers and education providers. ADRWorld.com's "ADR Exchange features advanced search capabilities and detailed profiles of ADR neutrals and service providers, offering disputing parties and the business community a powerful tool for finding ADR services that meet their needs."

B. **American Arbitration Association (AAA) <http://www.adr.org>**

Founded in 1926, the American Arbitration Association is the nation's leading full service ADR provider. In 1999 alone, it resolved "more than 140,000 cases through mediation or arbitration, [or] less formal methods of dispute resolution—such as fact-finding, mini-trial and partnering." The AAA "provides a forum for the hearing of disputes through 37 offices nationwide, tested rules and procedures that have broad acceptance, and a roster of nearly 12,000 impartial experts to hear and resolve cases."

AAA neutrals are well respected for their "expertise, integrity and dispute resolution skills." They must be elected to the National Roster of Arbitrators and Mediators of the American Arbitration Association and are "guided by the Association's *Code of Ethics* prepared by a Joint Committee of the American Arbitration Association and the American Bar Association, and the *Model Standards of Mediators*, developed by the American Arbitration Association, the American Bar Association and the Society of Professionals in Dispute Resolution." The AAA also aids in the publication of The Martindale-Hubbell Dispute Resolution Directory.

C. **American Bar Association <http://www.abanet.org/dispute>**

The Dispute Resolution Section of the American Bar Association is one of the ABA's newest and fastest growing sections with over 6,300 members. The Section's self-described objectives include: maintaining the ABA's national leadership role in the dispute resolution field; providing information and technical assistance to members, legislators, government departments and the general public on all aspects of dispute resolution; studying existing methods of the prompt and effective resolution of disputes; adapting current legal procedures to accommodate court-annexed and court-directed dispute resolution processes; activating state and local bar involvement, conducting public and professional education programs and conducting programs of research.

Within the Dispute Resolution Section of the ABA web site is a list of links to various other ADR entities. Although this is by no means an exhaustive list and is not annotated, the site does contain links to some major ADR providers such as the American Arbitration Association and the CPR Institute for Dispute Resolution. For individuals who may be seeking authoritative background information about arbitration and ADR, the links are a convenient segue to the next step of locating/choosing a neutral.

D. Better Business Bureau (BBB) <http://www.bbb.org>

The Better Business Bureau is a nonprofit organization supported by local businesses. Local BBBs can assist in the resolution of disputes between businesses and its customers. The BBB has "a national reputation for fairness because they remain neutral in a dispute. They do not take sides but work to get the problem settled as quickly as possible."

BBB arbitrators are volunteer neutrals who have been approved by the local BBB. They have, however, been "properly trained to listen to both sides, weigh the evidence, and to render a decision."

E. CPR Institute for Dispute Resolution <http://www.cpradr.org>

The CPR Institute for Dispute Resolution is an alliance of global corporations, leading law firms, legal academics and selected public institutions who's "mission is to install ADR into the mainstream of corporate law departments and law firm practice." About 4,000 operating companies have subscribed to the "CPR Corporate Policy Statement on Alternatives to Litigation, which obligates them to explore the use of ADR in disputes with other signers."

CPR also maintains a roster of neutrals comprised of "nearly 700 nationally and internationally prominent attorneys, former judges, academics and legally-trained executives," with specialization in over 30 practice areas and industries. Parties may contact CPR neutrals on their own from the CPR Panels of Distinguished Neutrals, or they may request assistance from the organization to select a neutral for them. The Panels are available for online viewing.

F. Hieros Gamos <http://www.hg.org/adr.html>

Self-titled "The Comprehensive Law and Government Portal," Hieros Gamos provides numerous links to ADR and Arbitration resources. The site not only contains general guides to ADR, it maintains a searchable database of arbitrators and mediators, and offers a list of major ADR providers.

G. JAMS/Endispute <http://www.jams-endispute.com>

Formed in 1994, through the merger of two of the largest private ADR providers in the United States, JAMS/Endispute seeks to "provide the highest-quality ADR services to our clients and to our local, national and global communities." The firm has 20 locations in the United States. Each JAMS/Endispute office has Judicial Panels composed of retired and former federal and state court judges specially selected for their experience, reputation and settlement-related abilities. The organization also has a staff of attorney-neutrals who work as arbitrators, mediators, and consensus builders. JAMS/Endispute offers its clients a free Case Coordination Service in which an Account

Representative assists clients, among other things, in the selection of the most appropriate neutral.

The JAMS/Endispute web site is well organized and basic. The site features links to office locations, each of which is linked to a city-specific roster of Judicial Panelists. Clicking the name of each panelist links the viewer to a brief resume of that candidate.

H. National Arbitration Forum <http://www.arb-forum.com>

Established in 1986, the National Arbitration Forum is a nationwide network of former judges, litigators, and law professors who "share the Forum principle that disputes should be decided according to established legal principles." The Forum conducts arbitration under the Forum Code of Procedure—a copy of which is available through its web site. By following strict guidelines, the Forum aims to produce more consistent results.

The Forum tries to distinguish itself from other ADR providers, stating that "unlike other arbitration systems, Forum arbitrators are not permitted to ignore the law and make decisions based solely on 'equity.'" Each Forum arbitrator is described as having "more than 15 years legal experience." The Forum web site also features an online filing system—allowing prospective clients the opportunity to file their claims through the Internet.

I. The Society of Professionals In Dispute Resolution (SPIDR) <http://www.spidr.org>

The Society of Professionals in Dispute Resolution was organized in 1972, "growing out of the labor-management mediation and arbitration movement." SPIDR's goal is to expand the use of ADR and to provide a forum where ADR practitioners could "discuss the latest innovations in the field" with other colleagues.

SPIDR has over 3,600 professional members and the organization maintains a directory. While the directory is not accessible online, the directory and other publications may be ordered by contacting the organization.

J. Additional ADR Resources

1. Apriori <http://adrr.com/apriori>
2. ADR Resources <http://www.adrr.com>
3. Construction Mediation Inc. <http://www.cmino.com>
4. Claim Resolution Forum <http://users.javanet.com/~ndarragn>
5. Dispute Resolution Specialists <http://www.mediates.com>
6. Federal Mediation and Conciliation Service <http://www.fmcs.gov>
7. Findlaw.com <http://www.findlaw.com>

8. Just Resolutions <http://www.justresolutions.com>
9. Massachusetts Dispute Resolution Services
   <http://www.mdrs.com>
10. Mediation Information & Resource Center
    <http://www.mediate.com>
11. National Mediation Board
    <http://www.nmb.gov/arbitration/amenu.html>
12. Online Resolution <http://www.onlineresolution.com>
13. Private Judging <http://www.privatejudgesla.com>
14. Securities Arbitration Center
    <http://www.seclaw.com/centers/arbcent.shtml>
15. The Resolution Center <http://www.alaska.net/~cdre>
16. The Justice Center of Atlanta <http://www.justicecenter.org>
17. United States Arbitration & Mediation
    <http://usam.com/services/arbitration.shtml>
18. World Intellectual Property Organization, Arbitration and
    Mediation Center <http://www.arbiter.wipo.int>

IV. Some Academic ADR-Related Web Sites

A. University of Colorado—Conflict Research Consortium
    <http://www.colorado.edu/conflict>
B. Cornell/PERC (The Foundation for the Prevention and Early
    Resolution of Conflict)—Institute on Conflict Resolution
    <http://www.ilr.cornell.edu/depts/icr>
C. City University of New York—Dispute Resolution Consortium
    <http://web.jjay.cuny.edu>
D. Duke University School of Law—The Private Adjudication Center
    <http://www.law.duke.edu/pac/index.html>
E. Emory University Legal Focal Points—Alternative Dispute
    Resolution Links <http://www.law.emory.edu/FOCAL/adr.html>
F. Fresno Pacific University—Center for Peacemaking and Conflict
    Studies <http://www.fresno.edu/pacs>
G. George Mason University—Institute for Conflict Analysis and
    Resolution <http://web.gmu.edu/departments/ICAR>
H. Hamline University School of Law—Dispute Resolution Institute
    <http://www.hamline.edu/law/adr/index.html>
I. Harvard Law School—Program on Negotiation
    <http://www.pon.harvard.edu>
J. Humboldt State University—Institute for Study of Dispute
    Resolution <www.humboldt.edu/~isadr>
K. University of Massachusetts, Amherst—
    Center for Information Technology and Dispute Resolution
    <http://www.aaron.sbs.umass.edu/center>

L. University of Missouri, Columbia School of Law—Center for the Study of Dispute Resolution <http://www.law.missouri.edu/csdr>

M. Nova Southeastern University of Florida—Institute for Conflict Resolution <http://www.nova.edu>

N. Ohio State College of Law—Program on Dispute Resolution, (accessible from) <http://www.osu.edu/units/law> and Ohio State Journal on Dispute Resolution <http://www.osu.edu/units/law/jdr>

O. Pepperdine University School of Law—The Strauss Institute for Dispute Resolution <http://law-www.pepperdine.edu/straus>

P. Quinnipiac University School of Law—Center on Dispute Resolution <http://www.quinnipiac.edu/academics/lawcenters/dispute_resolution>

Q. Rutgers, The State University of New Jersey— The Center for Negotiation and Conflict Resolution <http://policy.rutgers.edu/CNCR>

R. Stanford Law School—Gould Center for Conflict Resolution <http://www.law.stanford.edu/programs/gould>

S. Stetson University College of Law—Center for Dispute Resolution <http://www.law.stetson.edu/clinics/adr>

T. University of Texas School of Law— Center for Public Policy Dispute Resolution <http://www.utexas.edu/law/acadprogs/cppdr/index.html>

U. Willamette University College of Law—Dispute Resolution <http://www.willamette.edu/wucl/wlo/dis-res/home.htm>

V. Attorney Search Directories

In locating background information about a particular arbitrator, there are several possible avenues of exploration available to the online researcher. In investigating those individuals who are members of dispute resolution organizations, many of those organizations do provide brief resumes and bibliographic information through their organization web site. This is, of course, a very convenient way of beginning background research. However, to conduct more substantive review, it is possible to search the LEXIS and Westlaw commercial databases for possible recent publications by a potential candidate. Additionally, if a bibliographic cite is known, the LEXIS and Westlaw databases might contain a full text version of the said article/publication. Suggested database files/sources include: for LEXIS, in the library for secondary sources, the files ALLABA (ABA publications), ALLREV (the law review database) and ALLPLI (PLI publications); and for Westlaw, the database TP-ALL (all periodicals).

If the commercial database searches do not prove fruitful, another avenue of exploration might be to try a keyword query (using the name of the prospective neutral) on some of the search engines mentioned above in Section II. While this approach is admittedly haphazard, it may yield results missed by more directed methods of research. A word of caution to the online researcher: often names must be entered with great precision, as even slight derivations of names will not yield identical results. To conduct a comprehensive search of a search engine database, it may be necessary to use several forms of an individual's name, noting that seemingly minor distinctions—such as the inclusion or exclusion of middle names, the use of initials or the use of shortened forms of names—could potentially result in widely divergent findings.

A. Martindale-Hubbell <http://www.lawyers.com>

Martindale-Hubbell is the most comprehensive web site for locating lawyers and law firms. The service is also accessible through the Lexis site at <http://www.lexis.com>.

B. West Legal Directory <http://www.lawoffice.com>

The West Legal Directory is not as comprehensive as Martindale-Hubbell but includes all lawyers who subscribe to Westlaw. It is also available through the Westlaw research site at <http://www.westlaw.com>.

Both Martindale-Hubbell and the West Legal Directory have basic search features geared towards consumers looking for an attorney referral by practice area, city and state. Both also include advanced searches for fields such as firm name, country, and language(s) spoken.

C. Additional Attorney Search Directories

1. Law Research <http://www.lawresearch.com/v2/firms/lfarib.htm>
2. Attorney Locate
   <http://www.attorneylocate.com/html/arbitration_area.htm>
3. Arbitration.com
   <http://www.gama.com/HTML/arbitration/arb.html>

Appendix 3.4
The Code of Ethics for Arbitrators in Commercial Disputes (1977)

The Code of Ethics for Arbitrators in Commercial Disputes was prepared in 1977 by a joint committee consisting of a special committee of the American Arbitration Association and a special committee of the American Bar Association. It has been approved and recommended by both organizations.

Preamble

The use of commercial arbitration to resolve a wide variety of disputes has grown extensively and forms a significant part of the system of justice on which our society relies for fair determination of legal rights. Persons who act as commercial arbitrators therefore undertake serious responsibilities to the public as well as to the parties. Those responsibilities include important ethical obligations.

Few cases of unethical behavior by commercial arbitrators have arisen. Nevertheless, the American Bar Association and the American Arbitration Association believe that it is in the public interest to set forth generally accepted standards of ethical conduct for guidance of arbitrators and parties in commercial disputes. By establishing this code, the sponsors hope to contribute to the maintenance of high standards and continued confidence in the process of arbitration.

There are many different types of commercial arbitration. Some cases are conducted under arbitration rules established by various organizations and trade associations, while others are conducted without such rules. Although most cases are arbitrated pursuant to voluntary agreement of the parties, certain types of dispute are submitted to arbitration by reason of particular laws. This code is intended to apply to all such proceedings in which disputes or claims are submitted for decision to one or more arbitrators appointed in a manner provided by an agreement of the parties, by applicable arbitration rules, or by law. In all such cases, the persons who have the power to decide should observe fundamental standards of ethical conduct. In this code all such persons are called "arbitrators" although, in some types of case, they might be called "umpires" or have some other title.

Various aspects of the conduct of arbitrators, including some matters covered by this code, may be governed by agreements of the parties, by arbitration rules to which the parties have agreed, or by applicable law. This code does not take the place of or supersede such agreements, rules, or laws and does not establish new or additional grounds for judicial review of arbitration awards.

While this code is intended to provide ethical guidelines in many types of arbitration, it does not form a part of the arbitration rules of the American Arbitration

Association or of any other organization, nor is it intended to apply to mediation or conciliation. Labor arbitration is governed by the Code of Professional Responsibility for Arbitrators of Labor-Management Disputes, not by this code.

Arbitrators, like judges, have the power to decide cases. However, unlike full-time judges, arbitrators are usually engaged in other occupations before, during, and after the time that they serve as arbitrators. Often, arbitrators are purposely chosen from the same trade or industry as the parties in order to bring special knowledge to the task of deciding. This code recognizes these fundamental differences between arbitrators and judges.

In some types of arbitration, there are three or more arbitrators. In such cases, it is sometimes the practice for each party, acting alone, to appoint one arbitrator and for the other arbitrators to be designated by those two, by the parties, or by an independent institution or individual. The sponsors of this code believe that it is preferable for parties to agree that all arbitrators should comply with the same ethical standards. However, it is recognized that there is a long-established practice in some types of arbitration for the arbitrators who are appointed by one party, acting alone, to be governed by special ethical considerations. Those special considerations are set forth in the last section of the code, headed "Ethical Considerations Relating to Arbitrators Appointed by One Party."

Although this code is sponsored by the American Arbitration Association and the American Bar Association, its use is not limited to arbitrations administered by the AAA or to cases in which the arbitrators are lawyers. Rather, it is presented as a public service to provide guidance in all types of commercial arbitration.

CANON I.

An arbitrator should uphold the integrity and fairness of the arbitration process.

A. Fair and just processes for resolving disputes are indispensable in our society. Commercial arbitration is an important method for deciding many types of disputes. In order for commercial arbitration to be effective, there must be broad public confidence in the integrity and fairness of the process. Therefore, an arbitrator has a responsibility not only to the parties but also to the process of arbitration itself, and must observe high standards of conduct so that the integrity and fairness of the process will be preserved. Accordingly, an arbitrator should recognize a responsibility to the public, to the parties whose rights will be decided, and to all other participants in the proceeding. The provisions of this code should be construed and applied to further these objectives.

B. It is inconsistent with the integrity of the arbitration process for persons to solicit appointment for themselves. However, a person may indicate a general willingness to serve as an arbitrator.

C. Persons should accept appointment as arbitrators only if they believe that they can be available to conduct the arbitration promptly.

D. After accepting appointment and while serving as an arbitrator, a person should avoid entering into any financial, business, professional, family or social relationship, or acquiring any financial or personal interest, which is likely to affect impartiality or which might reasonably create the appearance of partiality or bias. For a reasonable period of time after the decision of a case, persons who have served as arbitrators should avoid entering into any such relationship, or acquiring any such interest, in circumstances which might reasonably create the appearance that they had been influenced in the arbitration by the anticipation or expectation of the relationship or interest.

E. Arbitrators should conduct themselves in a way that is fair to all parties and should not be swayed by outside pressure, by public clamor, by fear of criticism or by self-interest.

F. When an arbitrator's authority is derived from an agreement of the parties, the arbitrator should neither exceed that authority nor do less than is required to exercise that authority completely. Where the agreement of the parties sets forth procedures to be followed in conducting the arbitration or refers to rules to be followed, it is the obligation of the arbitrator to comply with such procedures or rules.

G. An arbitrator should make all reasonable efforts to prevent delaying tactics, harassment of parties or other participants, or other abuse or disruption of the arbitration process.

H. The ethical obligations of an arbitrator begin upon acceptance of the appointment and continue throughout all stages of the proceeding. In addition, wherever specifically set forth in this code, certain ethical obligations begin as soon as a person is requested to serve as an arbitrator and certain ethical obligations continue even after the decision in the case has been given to the parties.

CANON II

An arbitrator should disclose any interest or relationship likely to affect impartiality or which might create an appearance of partiality or bias.

Introductory Note

This code reflects the prevailing principle that arbitrators should disclose the existence of interests or relationships that are likely to affect their impartiality or that might reasonably create an appearance that they are biased against one party or favorable to another. These provisions of the code are intended to be applied realistically so that the burden of detailed disclosure does not become so great that it is impractical for persons in the business world to be arbitrators, thereby depriving parties of the services of those who might be best informed and qualified to decide particular types of case. *See Footnote.*

This code does not limit the freedom of parties to agree on whomever they choose as an arbitrator. When parties, with knowledge of a person's interests and relationships, nevertheless desire that individual to serve as an arbitrator, that person may properly serve.

Disclosure

A.   Persons who are requested to serve as arbitrators should, before accepting, disclose

1.   any direct or indirect financial or personal interest in the outcome of the arbitration;

2.   any existing or past financial, business, professional, family or social relationships which are likely to affect impartiality or which might reasonably create an appearance of partiality or bias. Persons requested to serve as arbitrators should disclose any such relationships which they personally have with any party or its lawyer, or with any individual whom they have been told will be a witness. They should also disclose any such relationships involving members of their families or their current employers, partners or business associates.

B.   Persons who are requested to accept appointment as arbitrators should make a reasonable effort to inform themselves of any interests or relationships described in the preceding paragraph A.

C.   The obligation to disclose interests or relationships described in the preceding paragraph A is a continuing duty which requires a person who accepts appointment as an arbitrator to disclose, at any stage of the arbitration, any such interests or relationships which may arise, or which are recalled or discovered.

D.   Disclosure should be made to all parties unless other procedures for disclosure are provided in the rules or practices of an institution which is administering the arbitration. Where more than one arbitrator has been appointed, each should inform the others of the interests and relationships which have been disclosed.

E.   In the event that an arbitrator is requested by all parties to withdraw, the arbitrator should do so. In the event that an arbitrator is requested to withdraw by less than all of the parties because of alleged partiality or bias, the arbitrator should withdraw unless either of the following circumstances exists.

1.   If an agreement of the parties, or arbitration rules agreed to by the parties, establishes procedures for determining challenges to arbitrators, then those procedures should be followed; or,

2.   if the arbitrator, after carefully considering the matter, determines that the reason for the challenge is not substantial, and that he or she can nevertheless act and decide the case impartially and fairly, and that withdrawal would cause unfair delay or expense to another party or would be contrary to the ends of justice.

CANON III

An arbitrator in communicating with the parties should avoid impropriety or the appearance of impropriety.

A. If an agreement of the parties or applicable arbitration rules referred to in that agreement, establishes the manner or content of communications between the arbitrator and the parties, the arbitrator should follow those procedures notwithstanding any contrary provision of the following paragraphs B and C.

B. Unless otherwise provided in applicable arbitration rules or in an agreement of the parties, arbitrators should not discuss a case with any party in the absence of each other party, except in any of the following circumstances.

   1. Discussions may be had with a party concerning such matters as setting the time and place of hearings or making other arrangements for the conduct of the proceedings. However, the arbitrator should promptly inform each other party of the discussion and should not make any final determination concerning the matter discussed before giving each absent party an opportunity to express its views.
   2. If a party fails to be present at a hearing after having been given due notice, the arbitrator may discuss the case with any party who is present.
   3. If all parties request or consent to it, such discussion may take place.

C. Unless otherwise provided in applicable arbitration rules or in an agreement of the parties, whenever an arbitrator communicates in writing with one party, the arbitrator should at the same time send a copy of the communication to each other party. Whenever the arbitrator receives any written communication concerning the case from one party which has not already been sent to each other party, the arbitrator should do so.

CANON IV.

An arbitrator should conduct the proceedings fairly and diligently.

A. An arbitrator should conduct the proceedings in an evenhanded manner and treat all parties with equality and fairness at all stages of the proceedings.

B. An arbitrator should perform duties diligently and conclude the case as promptly as the circumstances reasonably permit.

C. An arbitrator should be patient and courteous to the parties, to their lawyers and to the witnesses and should encourage similar conduct by all participants in the proceedings.

D. Unless otherwise agreed by the parties or provided in arbitration rules agreed to by the parties, an arbitrator should accord to all parties the right to appear in person and to be heard after due notice of the time and place of hearing.

E. An arbitrator should not deny any party the opportunity to be represented by counsel.

F. If a party fails to appear after due notice, an arbitrator should proceed with the arbitration when authorized to do so by the agreement of the parties, the rules agreed to by the parties or by law. However, an arbitrator should do so only after receiving assurance that notice has been given to the absent party.

G. When an arbitrator determines that more information than has been presented by the parties is required to decide the case, it is not improper for the arbitrator to ask questions, call witnesses, and request documents or other evidence.

H. It is not improper for an arbitrator to suggest to the parties that they discuss the possibility of settlement of the case. However, an arbitrator should not be present or otherwise participate in the settlement discussions unless requested to do so by all parties. An arbitrator should not exert pressure on any party to settle.

I. Nothing in this code is intended to prevent a person from acting as a mediator or conciliator of a dispute in which he or she has been appointed as arbitrator, if requested to do so by all parties or where authorized or required to do so by applicable laws or rules.

J. When there is more than one arbitrator, the arbitrators should afford each other the full opportunity to participate in all aspects of the proceedings.

CANON V.

An arbitrator should make decisions in a just, independent and deliberate manner.

A. An arbitrator should, after careful deliberation, decide all issues submitted for determination. An arbitrator should decide no other issues.

B. An arbitrator should decide all matters justly, exercising independent judgment, and should not permit outside pressure to affect the decision.

C. An arbitrator should not delegate the duty to decide to any other person.

D. In the event that all parties agree upon a settlement of issues in dispute and request an arbitrator to embody that agreement in an award, an arbitrator may do so, but is not required to do so unless satisfied with the propriety of the terms of settlement. Whenever an arbitrator embodies a settlement by the parties in an award, the arbitrator should state in the award that it is based on an agreement of the parties.

CANON VI.

An arbitrator should be faithful to the relationship of trust and confidentiality inherent in that office.

A. An arbitrator is in a relationship of trust to the parties and should not, at any time, use confidential information acquired during the arbitration proceeding to gain personal advantage or advantage for others, or to affect adversely the interest of another.

B. Unless otherwise agreed by the parties, or required by applicable rules or law, an arbitrator should keep confidential all matters relating to the arbitration proceedings and decision.

C. It is not proper at any time for an arbitrator to inform anyone of the decision in advance of the time it is given to all parties. In a case in which there is more than one arbitrator, it is not proper at any time for an arbitrator to inform anyone concerning the deliberations of the arbitrators. After an arbitration award has been made, it is not proper for an arbitrator to assist in post-arbitral proceedings, except as is required by law.

D. In many types of arbitration it is customary practice for the arbitrators to serve without pay. However, in some types of cases it is customary for arbitrators to receive compensation for their services and reimbursement for their expenses. In cases in which any such payments are to be made, all persons who are requested to serve, or who are serving as arbitrators, should be governed by the same high standards of integrity and fairness as apply to their other activities in the case. Accordingly, such persons should scrupulously avoid bargaining with parties over the amount of payments or engaging in any communications concerning payments which would create an appearance of coercion or other impropriety. In the absence of governing provisions in the agreement of the parties or in rules agreed to by the parties or in applicable law, certain practices relating to payments are generally recognized as being preferable in order to preserve the integrity and fairness of the arbitration process. These practices include the following.

   1. It is preferable that before the arbitrator finally accepts appointment the basis of payment be established and that all parties be informed thereof in writing.

   2. In cases conducted under the rules or administration of an institution that is available to assist in making arrangements for payments, the payments should be arranged by the institution to avoid the necessity for communication by the arbitrators directly with the parties concerning the subject.

   3. In cases where no institution is available to assist in making arrangement for payments, it is preferable that any discussions with arbitrators concerning payments should take place in the presence of all parties.

CANON VII.

Ethical considerations relating to arbitrators appointed by one party.

Introductory Note

In some types of arbitration in which there are three arbitrators, it is customary for each party, acting alone, to appoint one arbitrator. The third arbitrator is then appointed by agreement either of the parties or of the two arbitrators, or, failing such agreement, by an independent institution or individual. In some of these types of arbitration, all three arbitrators are customarily considered to be neutral and are expected to observe the same standards of ethical conduct. However, there are also many types of tripartite arbitration in which it has been the practice that the two arbitrators appointed by the parties are not considered to be neutral and are expected to observe many but not all of the same ethical standards as the neutral third arbitrator. For the purposes of this code, an arbitrator appointed by one party who is not expected to observe all of the same standards as the third arbitrator is called a "nonneutral arbitrator." This Canon VII describes the ethical obligations that nonneutral party-appointed arbitrators should observe and those that are not applicable to them.

In all arbitrations in which there are two or more party-appointed arbitrators, it is important for everyone concerned to know from the start whether the party-appointed arbitrators are expected to be neutrals or nonneutrals. In such arbitrations, the two party-appointed arbitrators should be considered nonneutrals unless both parties inform the arbitrators that all three arbitrators are to be neutral or unless the contract, the applicable arbitration rules, or any governing law requires that all three arbitrators be neutral.

It should be noted that, in cases conducted outside the United States, the applicable law might require that all arbitrators be neutral. Accordingly, in such cases, the governing law should be considered before applying any of the following provisions relating to nonneutral party-appointed arbitrators.

A. *Obligations under Canon I*

Nonneutral party-appointed arbitrators should observe all of the obligations of Canon I to uphold the integrity and fairness of the arbitration process, subject only to the following provisions.

1. Nonneutral arbitrators may be predisposed toward the party who appointed them but in all other respects are obligated to act in good faith and with integrity and fairness. For example, nonneutral arbitrators should not engage in delaying tactics or harassment of any party or witness and should not knowingly make untrue or misleading statements to the other arbitrators.

2. The provisions of Canon I.D relating to relationships and interests are not applicable to nonneutral arbitrators.

B. *Obligations under Canon II*

Nonneutral party-appointed arbitrators should disclose to all parties, and to the other arbitrators, all interests and relationships which Canon II requires be disclosed. Disclosure as required by Canon II is for the benefit not only of the party who appointed the nonneutral arbitrator, but also for the benefit of the other parties and arbitrators so that they may know of any bias which may exist or appear to exist. However, this obligation is subject to the following provisions.

1. Disclosure by nonneutral arbitrators should be sufficient to describe the general nature and scope of any interest or relationship, but need not include as detailed information as is expected from persons appointed as neutral arbitrators.
2. Nonneutral arbitrators are not obliged to withdraw if requested to do so by the party who did not appoint them, notwithstanding the provisions of Canon II.E.

C. *Obligations under Canon III*

Nonneutral party-appointed arbitrators should observe all of the obligations of Canon III concerning communications with the parties, subject only to the following provisions.

1. In an arbitration in which the two party-appointed arbitrators are expected to appoint the third arbitrator, nonneutral arbitrators may consult with the party who appointed them concerning the acceptability of persons under consideration for appointment as the third arbitrator.
2. Nonneutral arbitrators may communicate with the party who appointed them concerning any other aspect of the case, provided they first inform the other arbitrators and the parties that they intend to do so. If such communication occurred prior to the time the person was appointed as arbitrator, or prior to the first hearing or other meeting of the parties with the arbitrators, the nonneutral arbitrator should, at the first hearing or meeting, disclose the fact that such communication has taken place. In complying with the provisions of this paragraph, it is sufficient that there be disclosure of the fact that such communication has occurred without disclosing the content of the communication. It is also sufficient to disclose at any time the intention to follow the procedure of having such communications in the future and there is no requirement thereafter that there be disclosure before each separate occasion on which such a communication occurs.
3. When nonneutral arbitrators communicate in writing with the party who appointed them concerning any matter as to which communication is permitted under this code, they are not required to send copies of any such written communication to any other party or arbitrator.

D. Obligations under Canon IV

Nonneutral party-appointed arbitrators should observe all of the obligations of Canon IV to conduct the proceedings fairly and diligently.

E. Obligations under Canon V

Nonneutral party-appointed arbitrators should observe all of the obligations of Canon V concerning making decisions, subject only to the following provision.

1.   Nonneutral arbitrators are permitted to be predisposed toward deciding in favor of the party who appointed them.

F. Obligations under Canon VI

Nonneutral party-appointed arbitrators should observe all of the obligations of Canon VI to be faithful to the relationship of trust inherent in the office of arbitrator, subject only to the following provision.

1.   Nonneutral arbitrators are not subject to the provisions of Canon VI.D with respect to any payments by the party who appointed them.

Annotations

1.   In applying the provisions of this code relating to disclosure, it might be helpful to recall the words of the concurring opinion, in a case decided by the U.S. Supreme Court, that arbitrators "should err on the side of disclosure" because "it is better that the relationship be disclosed at the outset when the parties are free to reject the arbitrator or accept him with knowledge of the relationship." At the same time, it must be recognized that "an arbitrator's business relationships may be diverse indeed, involving more or less remote commercial connections with great numbers of people." Accordingly, an arbitrator "cannot be expected to provide the parties with his complete and unexpurgated business biography," nor is an arbitrator called on to disclose interests or relationships that are merely "trivial" (a concurring opinion in *Commonwealth Coatings Corp. v. Continental Casualty Co.*, 393 U.S. 145, 151–152, 1968).

Appendix 3.5
CPR Model Agreement for Parties and Arbitrator*

Agreement made _____, _____
                          (date)

between_____

represented by_____

and_____

represented by_____

and_____
                  (the Arbitrator)

A dispute has arisen between the parties (the "Dispute"). The parties have agreed to participate in an arbitration proceeding (the "Proceeding") under the CPR Rules for Non-Administered Arbitration (Revised and Effective September 15, 2000), as modified by mutual agreement (the "Procedure"). The parties have chosen the Arbitrator for the Proceeding. The parties and the Arbitrator agree as follows:

A. Duties and Obligations
   1. The Arbitrator and each of the parties agree to be bound by and to comply faithfully with the Procedure.
   2. The Arbitrator has no previous commitments that may significantly delay the expeditious conduct of the Proceeding and will not make any such commitments.

B. Disclosure of Prior and Existing Relationships
   1. The Arbitrator has made a reasonable effort to learn and has disclosed to the parties in writing (a) all business or professional relationships the

---

*The form assumes that the arbitrator is affiliated with a law firm. If that is not the case, delete D.2. and references to the arbitrator's firm in paras. B.1 and C.

137

Arbitrator and/or the Arbitrator's firm have had with the parties or their law firms within the past five years, including all instances in which the Arbitrator or the Arbitrator's firm served as an attorney for any party or adverse to any party or in which the Arbitrator served as an arbitrator or mediator in a matter involving any party; (b) any financial interest the Arbitrator has in any party; (c) any significant social, business or professional relationship the Arbitrator has had with an officer or employee of a party or with an individual representing a party in the Proceeding; and (d) any other circumstances that may give rise to justifiable doubt regarding the Arbitrator's independence or impartiality in the Proceeding.

2. Each party and its law firm has made a reasonable effort to learn and has disclosed to every other party and the Arbitrator in writing any relationships of a nature described in paragraph B.1. not previously identified and disclosed by the Arbitrator.

3. The parties and the Arbitrator are satisfied that any relationships disclosed pursuant to paragraphs B.1. and B.2. will not affect the Arbitrator's independence or impartiality. Notwithstanding such relationships or others the Arbitrator and the parties did not discover despite good faith efforts, the parties wish the Arbitrator to serve in the Proceeding, waiving any claim based on said relationships, and the Arbitrator agrees to so serve.

4. The disclosure obligations in paragraphs B.1. and B.2. are continuing until the Proceeding is concluded. The ability of the Arbitrator to continue serving in this capacity shall be explored with each such disclosure.

C. Future Relationships

[NOTE: The circumstances under which the arbitrator or the arbitrator's law firm, exclusive of the arbitrator, should be permitted to represent a party to the arbitration in the future on matters unrelated to the arbitration is a subject of debate and does not appear suitable for inclusion in a form of model agreement. However, the parties and the arbitrator may be well advised to include a section dealing with this subject in their agreement.]

D. Compensation

1. The Arbitrator shall be compensated for all time expended in connection with the Proceeding at the rate of $_____, (per hour, per day, flat fee) plus reasonable travel and other out-of-pocket expenses. The Arbitrator's fee shall be shared equally by the parties, subject to Rule 16.3 of the Procedure.

2. The Arbitrator may utilize members and employees of the firm to assist in connection with the Proceeding and may bill the parties for the time expended by any such persons, to the extent and at a rate agreed upon in advance by the parties.

E. Confidentiality
  1. The Arbitrator and each of the parties agree to be bound by and to comply faithfully with Rule 16 of the Procedure relating to confidentiality.
  2. The Arbitrator shall be disqualified a witness, consultant or expert in any pending or future action relating to the subject matter of the arbitration, including actions between persons not parties to the arbitration.
  3. Whenever a party or the Arbitrator, or their agents, employees, experts or attorneys, is requested, pursuant to a subpoena, a request for production of documents or things or other legal process, to disclose to persons or entities not party to this arbitration, any information regarding the process, including any transcripts, documents, things or testimony, prior to responding thereto such party or Arbitrator shall immediately notify the other party, or in the case of the Arbitrator, both parties, of the existence and terms of such request.
  [4. Within [x] days after termination of the arbitration, each party and the Arbitrator shall, at the election of the party furnishing the same, destroy or return all documents, transcripts or other things, and any copies thereof, as well as all summaries or other materials containing or disclosing information contained in, or directly related to, such documents, transcripts or things. Each party and the Arbitrator shall so certify under oath.]
  [5. The parties and the Arbitrator agree that damages are not adequate, and no adequate remedy at law exists for any threatened or actual disclosure or use of information in violation of this Section E of this Agreement. Accordingly, each consents to the entry of an injunction against threatened or actual disclosure or use of the information in violation of this Section E of this Agreement.]

F. Immunity
  The Arbitrator shall not be liable to any party for any act or omission in connection with any arbitration conducted under the Procedure.

_____   _____
Party   Party

by _____   by _____
  Party's Attorney   Party's Attorney

            _____
                   Arbitrator

Appendix 3.6

CPR-Georgetown Commision on Ethics and Standards in ADR
Proposed Model Rule of Professional Conduct for the Lawyer as Third Party Neutral[1]

Draft for Comment (April 1999)

Reported by
Prof. Carrie Menkel-Meadow
Chair, CPR-Georgetown Commission on Ethics and Standards in ADR
and
Elizabeth Plapinger
Staff Director, CPR-Georgetown Commission on Ethics and Standards in ADR

The Commission on Ethics and Standards in ADR (sponsored by Georgetown University and CPR Institute for Dispute Resolution) has drafted this proposed Rule for adoption into the Model Rules of Professional Conduct.[2] We offer here a framework or architecture for consideration by the appropriate bodies of the American Bar Association and any state agency or legislature charged with drafting lawyer ethics rules. The proposed Rule is in progress.

The proposed Model Rule addresses the ethical responsibilities of lawyers serving as third party neutrals, in a variety of Alternative Dispute Resolution (ADR) fora (arbitration, mediation, early neutral evaluation, etc.). As an initial jurisdictional matter, the proposed Rule does not address the ethical requirements of non-

---

1. The Proposed Model Rule of Professional Conduct for the Lawyer as Third Party Neutral has been prepared by the CPR-Georgetown Commission on Ethics and Standards in ADR, sponsored by CPR Institute for Dispute Resolution and Georgetown University Law Center, with support from the William and Flora Hewlett Foundation.

The drafters of this proposed rule are members of the Drafting Committee of the CPR-Georgetown Commission on Ethics and Standards in ADR. The committee is part of the CPR-Georgetown's Commission's Working Group on ADR and Law Practice. The Drafting Committee includes the Honorable Jerome Simandle, the Honorable Edmund Spaeth, John Bickerman, Esq., Lawrence Fox, Esq., Duane Krohnke, Esq., Bruce Meyerson, Esq., Professor Nancy Rogers, Elizabeth Plapinger, Esq. and Prof. Carrie Menkel-Meadow. Professor Geoffrey Hazard has served as a consultant and commentator for the group.

2. There have been several earlier efforts and suggestions for rules in the ADR area to be added to the Model Rules, *see, e.g.,* Judith Maute, *Public Values and Private Justice: A Case For Mediator Accountability,* 4 GEO. J. LEG. ETHICS 503 (1991). For a good review of ethical issues facing mediators, *see* Robert A. Baruch-Bush, *The Dilemmas of Mediation Practice: A Study of Ethical Dilemmas and Policy Implications,* 1 J. DISP. RESOL. 1, 3 (1994), reprinted in Dwight Golann, *Mediating Legal Disputes: Effective Strategies for Lawyers and Mediators,* ch. 14, ETHICAL DILEMMAS (Little Brown & Co., 1996).

The CPR-Georgetown effort attempts to remedy some of the inadequacies of transdisciplinary ethical code drafting, *see, e.g.,* the American Arbitration Association (AAA), the American Bar Association (ABA) and the Society of Professionals in Dispute Resolution (SPIDR), Model Standards of Conduct for Mediators (adopted in 1994 by the AAA, SPIDR, and the ABA Section of Dispute Resolution, but not ratified to date by the ABA Board of Governors), as well as the silences of current legal ethics formulations. For a discussion of the failure of the forthcoming Restatement of the Law Governing Lawyers to deal with the ethical issues raised by ADR practice, see Carrie Menkel-Meadow, *The Silences of the Restatement of the Law Governing Lawyers: Lawyering as Only Adversary Practice,* 10 GEO. J. LEGAL ETHICS 631 (Summer 1997).

lawyers performing these duties[3] or the ethical duties of lawyers acting in Alternative Dispute Resolution proceedings as representatives or advocates.[4]

Proposed New Model Rule of Professional Conduct Rule 4.5 for the Lawyer as Third Party Neutral[5]

Preamble

As client representatives, public citizens and professionals committed to justice and fair and efficient legal process, lawyers should help clients and others with legal matters pursue the most effective resolution of legal problems. This obligation should include pursuing methods and outcomes that cause the least harm to all parties, that resolve matters amicably where possible, and that promote harmonious relations. Modern lawyers serve these values of justice, fairness, efficiency and harmony as partisan representatives and as third-party neutrals.

This Rule applies to the lawyer who acts as third party neutral to help represented or unrepresented parties resolve disputes or arrange transactions among each other. When lawyers act in neutral, non-representative capacities, they have different duties and obligations in the areas addressed by this Rule than lawyers acting in a representative capacity. The current Model Rules are silent on lawyer roles as third party neutrals, which are different from the representational functions addressed by the Model Rules of Professional Conduct and judicial functions governed by the Judicial Code of Conduct.[6]

Contemporary law practice involves lawyers in a variety of new roles within the traditional boundaries of counselors, advocates and advisors in the legal system. Lawyers now commonly serve as third party neutrals, either as facilitators to settle disputes or plan transactions, as in mediation, or as third party decision makers, as in arbitration.[7] Such proceedings, including mediation, arbitration and other hybrid forms of settlement or decision-making, occur both as adjuncts to the litigation process (either through a court referral or court-based

---

3. The proposed rule is designed to be incorporated in lawyer ethical codes. The question of what other agencies may promulgate transdisciplinary rules (such as the AAA/ABA/SPIDR Model Standards of Conduct for Mediators, or state statutes governing all mediators, for example) is not addressed.

4. This rule attempts to regulate solely the ethical responsibilities of lawyers serving as neutrals and does not deal with other issues such as the potentially different duties of lawyers as representatives or advocates within ADR settings. For an overview of these issues, see Carrie Menkel-Meadow, *Ethics in Mediation Representation*, DISPUTE RESOLUTION MAGAZINE 3 (Winter 1997). For a summary of current efforts to address ethics issues of ADR representatives, *see* note 18 *infra*.

5. The proposed rule is numbered Rule 4.5 (contemplating an addition to the Model Rules section on "Transactions with Persons Other Than Clients" in simple numerical order). Ideally, the Lawyer as Third Party Neutral would be a new Rule 4, with the other current rules simply dropping down a number.

Where possible, we use language, definitions, standards and formulations consistent with the current Model Rules. We also take note, where pertinent, of the ongoing work of the Ethics 2000 Commission of the American Bar Association, which is proposing revisions to the Model Rules of Professional Conduct, and the forthcoming Restatement of the Law Governing Lawyers.

6. *See* Carrie Menkel-Meadow, *Ethics in Alternative Dispute Resolution: New Issues, No Answers From the Adversary Conception of Lawyers' Responsibilities*, 38 SO. TEXAS L. REV. 407 (1997); *see also*, Menkel-Meadow, *The Silences of the Restatement*, *supra* note 2.

7. For definitions of these processes, see text below at *Definitions*.

program, or by agreement of the parties) and outside litigation via private agreement. These proceedings are commonly known as "ADR" processes.[8] Some state ethics codes, statutes or court rules now require or strongly suggest that lawyers have a duty to counsel their clients regarding ADR means.[9]

When lawyers serve as ADR neutrals they do not have partisan "clients," as contemplated in much of the Model Rules, but rather serve all of the parties. Lawyer neutrals do not "represent" parties, but have a duty to be fair to all participants in the process and to execute different obligations and responsibilities with respect to the parties and to the process.[10] Nor do the rules which apply to judges, such as the Judicial Code of Conduct, adequately deal with many issues that confront lawyer neutrals. For example, lawyers who act as third party neutrals in one case may serve as representational counsel in other matters and thus confront special conflicts of interest, appearance of impropriety, and confidentiality issues as they switch roles. *See Poly Software International, Inc. v. Su*, 880 F. Supp. 1487 (D. Utah, 1995). Unlike the judge or arbitrator who remains at "arms-length" distance from the parties and who hears information usually when only both parties are present, mediators have different ethical issues to contend with as they hear private, proprietary facts from both sides, in caucuses and ex parte communications. *See Cho v. Superior Court*, 45 Cal. Rptr. 2d 863 (1995).[11]

While there continues to be some controversy about whether serving as a mediator or arbitrator is the practice of law or may be covered by the ancillary practice Rule 5.7,[12] it is clear that lawyers serving as third party neutrals need

---

8. The term ADR is used here to connote "appropriate dispute resolution," suggesting a choice of methods to be used to fit the matter. In more common parlance, ADR is used to connote "*alternative* dispute resolution" processes, where the processes are seen as alternatives to more conventional trial or litigation methods.

9. *See, e.g.*, Marshall Breger, *Should an Attorney be Required to Advise a Client on ADR Options?*, Discussion Paper Prepared for the ABA Section of Dispute Resolution and distributed at ABA Annual Meeting (1998), including listing of relevant statutes, court rules and ethical provisions; *see also* Colorado Rule of Professional Conduct 2.1; Georgia Rules of Civil Procedure, EC 7-5 (1996).

10. While the third party neutral does not represent or advocate for any of the parties to an ADR proceeding, in some circumstances, the third party neutral may provide information or advice to the parties without establishing a representational relationship. *See infra*, notes 12 and 13.

11. The Judicial Code may also need revision to take account of new roles undertaken by judges in the use of ADR, such as referral to ADR processes, ex parte communications with parties, and third party neutrals, as well as judicial roles in settlement conferences. *See* Carrie Menkel-Meadow, *Ex Parte Talks with Neutrals: ADR Hazards*, 12 ALTERNATIVES 209 (September 1994); Carrie Menkel-Meadow, *Judicial Referral to ADR: Issues & Problems Faced by Judges*, 7 F.J.C. DIRECTIONS 8 (1994); *see also Cho v. Superior Court*, 45 Cal. Rptr. 2d 863 (1995).

See also Rule 4.5.2, Confidentiality, and Rule 4.5.4., Conflicts of Interest, *infra*, for discussion in text and comment of the special ethical issues in these areas facing lawyer neutrals.

12. In 1994, Professor Geoffrey Hazard opined that activities in ADR can be considered "ancillary" functions of the lawyer, under current Rule 5.7, making the Model Rules applicable to lawyers serving in ADR situations. *See* Geoffrey C. Hazard, Jr., *When ADR is Ancillary to a Legal Practice, Law Firms Must Confront Conflicts Issues*, 12 ALTERNATIVES 147 (1994). We believe that subsequent analysis and case law support the need for the new rule proposed here. *See* Menkel-Meadow, *Ethics in Alternative Dispute Resolution, supra* note 6; Menkel-Meadow, *The Silences of the Restatement, supra* note 2; and *Poly Software International, Inc. v. Su*, 880 F. Supp. 1487 (D. Utah, 1995); *Cho v. Superior Court*, 45 Cal. Rptr. 2d 863 (1995).

For commentary on the debate over whether mediation constitutes the practice of law, see Carrie Menkel-Meadow, *Is Mediation the Practice of Law*, 14 ALTERNATIVES, May 1996 at 57; Bruce Meyerson, *Lawyers Who Mediate Are Not Practicing Law*, 14 ALTERNATIVES, June 1996 at 74; Symposium, *Is Mediation the Practice of Law*, NIDR FORUM, June 1997; Geetha Ravindra, *When Mediation Becomes the Unauthorized Practice of Law*, 15 ALTERNATIVES, July-August 1997, at 94; Carrie Menkel-Meadow, *To the Editors: Is Mediation the Practice of Law? Redux*, NIDR NEWS, Nov.-Dec. 1997, Jan. 1998, at 2; *NJ Panel Finds ADR is Part of Law Practice*, 12 ALTERNATIVES, July 1994, at 87.

ethical guidance from the Model Rules with respect to their dual roles as partisan representatives and as neutrals. The drafters believe that it is especially important to develop clear ethical rules when the lawyer, commonly conceived of as a "partisan" representative, takes on the different role of "neutral" problem-solver, facilitator or decision-maker.

Lawyers may be disciplined for any violation of the Model Rules or misconduct, regardless of whether they are formally found to be serving in lawyer-like roles. Accordingly, while other associations provide guidance within specific contexts, see, e.g., the Code of Ethics for Arbitrators in Commercial Disputes (American Arbitration Association (AAA)-American Bar Association (ABA), 1977), when lawyers serve as mediators or arbitrators their ethical duties and discipline under the Model Rules of Professional Conduct may be implicated. For these reasons, this proposed Rule is submitted to provide guidance for lawyers who serve as third party neutrals, and to advise judicial officers and state discipline counsel who enforce lawyer ethical or disciplinary standards.[13]

Scope of the Model Rule

The proposed Model Rule is drafted to govern lawyers serving in the full variety of ADR neutral roles, as arbitrators, mediators, evaluators and in other hybrid processes. (See definitions which follow.) The Drafting Committee believes that a general rule governing lawyers serving in all third party neutral roles is appropriate because the proposed Rule addresses core ethical duties that apply to virtually all neutral roles. Where different neutral roles give rise to different duties and obligations, the proposed Rule so provides in text or comment.[14] A single rule is also consistent with the generally transsubstantive approach of the Model Rules. As the Model Rules recognize increasing diversity of lawyer roles, see Rule 3.8, Special Responsibilities of Lawyer as Prosecutor; Rule 2.1, Lawyer as Advisor; Rule 1.13, Organization as Client, separate rules for lawyers as mediators or arbitrators may be appropriate in the future.

The proposed Rule applies only to lawyers serving as third party neutrals.[15] Many other professionals now serve as arbitrators, mediators, conciliators, evaluators or ombuds, and other bodies have promulgated transdisciplinary ethical

---

13. Whether third party neutrals will be liable in malpractice or on other legal theories to parties to an ADR is a question of state law.
14. *See, e.g.,* treatment of "partisan," party-appointed arbitrators in this Rule 4.5.4, Conflicts of Interest. In facilitating dispute resolution and transaction planning in a variety of different ways, neutrals may have different obligations with respect to confidentiality (where ex parte or caucus sessions are used), conflicts of interests (multiple use of single neutral by one party) and other issues depending on the role intended, agreement of the parties, or the law or regulation in the relevant jurisdiction.
15. This Rule also governs mainly issues of individual ethical responsibility, rather than organizational duties. In the conflicts area, however, both individual and organizational responsibilities are stated in the imputation and screening rule, *see* Rule 4.5.4 (b). Other rules, standards and bodies of law may regulate the organizational or associational providers of ADR services. For example, the CPR-Georgetown Commission of Ethics and Standards in ADR is developing Principles for ADR Provider Organizations. This document will be released in draft for public comment by the Drafting Committee in 1999. For more information, contact Elizabeth Plapinger. *See also* NY disciplinary rules on law firm conduct; Ted Schneyer, *Law Firm Discipline*, 77 CORNELL L. REV. 1 (1991).

rules relating to those services.[16] When a lawyer serves as a third party neutral in a capacity governed by multiple sets of ethical standards, the lawyer must note that the Model Rules of Professional Conduct govern his/her duties as a lawyer-neutral and that discipline *as a lawyer* will be governed by the Model Rules.[17] Nor does the Rule govern lawyers in their capacity as representatives or advocates within ADR proceedings. When a lawyer serves as an advocate, representative or counselor to a party in an ADR proceeding, he or she is governed by such other rules as are applicable to lawyer conduct, either before tribunals (Rule 3.3) or in relation to all other third parties (Rule 4.1).[18]

The proposed Rule, where possible, uses the same language and definitions of other lawyer and judicial standards, including formulations from the Model Rules of Professional Conduct,[19] the Judicial Code of Conduct, the Code of Ethics for Arbitrators in Commercial Disputes (American Arbitration Association-American Bar Association, 1997),[20] and the forthcoming Restatement of the Law Governing Lawyers.[21] As the Preamble to the Model Rules states, these rules are not to be used as liability standards for malpractice or other purposes. On the other hand, the forthcoming Restatement of the Law Governing Lawyers recognizes that ethical rules and standards are often used for civil liability, as well as for discipline, and this proposed Rule has been drafted accordingly.

---

16. *See, e.g.,* the ABA-AAA-SPIDR Model Standards for Mediators *supra* note 2; Society of Professionals in Dispute Resolution, *Ethical Standards of Professional Responsibility for the Society of Professionals in Dispute Resolution*, 1986; Academy of Family Mediators, *Model Standards of Practice for Family and Divorce Mediation*, 1984.

17. This Rule distinguishes the lawyer's role as neutral from the lawyer who may serve as an "intermediary" under Rule 2.2 and who therefore "represents" several clients in an "intermediation" of their relationship such as a partnership, joint venture, or in some cases, divorce proceedings. The Model Rules are currently being examined and proposals for revision developed by the American Bar Association's Ethics 2000 Commission. A current Ethics 2000 Commission proposal calls for the elimination of Rule 2.2.

18. A joint initiative of the CPR-Georgetown Commission and the ABA Dispute Resolution Section Ethics Committee is proposing amendments to the text and comments of existing Model Rules to address these issues. For more information about this effort, known as the Joint Initiative on the Ethics of Lawyer Representatives, please contact Elizabeth Plapinger at CPR.

Among the issues being addressed by the Joint Initiative is the meaning and scope of the term "tribunal" in the Model Rules. The term "tribunal" in the Model Rules has been interpreted to apply to adjudicative or trial-type hearings, thereby arguably excluding facilitative-type processes. The Joint Initiative drafters believe that the term should be clarified to include "ADR" proceedings which are not adjudicative, but held pursuant to court rules and regulations, within the courthouse or not.

The Joint Initiative, the Ethics 2000 Commission, and other groups are also considering current proposals to redraft Model Rules 3.3 and 4.1 for possible increased duties of candor to tribunals, to clients and to other third parties (such as in the rectification of fraud). In addition, some of the rules which apply to the lawyer's role as counselor (Rules 2.1–2.3) and general rules of lawyer-client relations (such as confidentiality, Rule 1.6) might also need to be supplemented or amended to take account of lawyers' different ethical responsibilities in different kinds of settings, *see, e.g.,* the Ethics 2000 Commission's current proposed drafts of Rule 1.6, 3.3. Some have also suggested that the duty of candor and good faith participation should perhaps be greater in some forms of ADR proceedings, *see, e.g.,* Kimberlee Kovach, *Lawyer Ethics in Mediation: Time for a Requirement of Good Faith*, 4 DISP. RES. MAG. 9 (1997); *see generally*, Symposium, *Focus on Ethics in Representation in Mediation*, 4 DISP. RES. MAG. (Winter 1997).

19. As noted above in note 5, the Model Rules are currently being examined and proposals for revision developed by the ABA's Ethics 2000 Commission.

20. These rules are currently being revised by Ad Hoc Committee on the Code of Ethics for Arbitrators in Commercial Disputes Convened by the Arbitration Committee, Section of Dispute Resolution, American Bar Association.

21. For commentary on the Restatement's failure to address lawyering issues raised by ADR practice, see Menkel-Meadow, *The Silences of the Restatement, supra* note 2; Geoffrey Hazard, Jr., *Non-Silences of Professor Hazard on "The Silences of the Restatement": A Response to Professor Menkel-Meadow*, 10 GEO. J. LEGAL ETHICS 671 (Summer 1997).

Definitions

This Rule is intended to be applied to the duties and responsibilities of lawyers who act as third party neutrals in the following processes:

I.   Adjudicative

Arbitration—A procedure in which each party presents its position and evidence before a single neutral third party or a panel, who is empowered to render a resolution of the matter between the parties. Arbitrators may be chosen jointly by all parties, by contractual arrangements, under court or other rules, and in some cases, may be chosen specifically by each side. Arbitrators chosen separately by each party to a dispute may be considered "partisan" arbitrators or "neutral" arbitrators, depending on the rules governing the arbitration. If the parties agree in advance, or applicable law provides, the award is binding and is enforceable in the same manner as any contractual obligation or under applicable statute (such as the Federal Arbitration Act or state equivalents). Agreements by the parties or applicable law may provide rules for whether the award must be in writing and what recourse the parties may have when the arbitration is not binding.

II.   Evaluative

Neutral Evaluation—A procedure in which a third-party neutral provides an assessment of the positions of the parties. In a neutral evaluation process, lawyers and/or parties present summaries of the facts, evidence and legal principles applicable to their cases to a single neutral or a panel of neutral evaluators who then provide(s) an assessment of the strengths, weaknesses and potential value of the case to all sides. By agreement of the parties or by applicable law, such evaluations are usually non-binding and offered to facilitate settlement. By agreement of the parties or by applicable law or practice, if the matter does not reach a settlement, the neutral evaluator may also provide other services such as case planning guidance, discovery scheduling, or other settlement assistance. By agreement of the parties or applicable law, the neutral evaluator(s) may issue fact-finding, discovery and other reports or recommendations.

Mediation—A procedure in which a third party neutral facilitates communications and negotiations among the parties to effect resolution of the matter by agreement of the parties. Although often considered a facilitative process (see below) in which a third party neutral facilitates communication and party negotiation, in some forms of mediation, the third party neutral may engage in evaluative tasks, such as providing legal information, helping parties and their counsel assess likely outcomes and inquiring into the legal and factual strengths and weaknesses of the problems presented. By agreement of the parties or applicable law, mediators may sometimes be called on to act as evaluators or special discovery masters, or to perform other third party neutral roles.

III. Facilitative

Mediation—A procedure in which a neutral third party facilitates communication and negotiations among the parties to seek resolution of issues between the parties. Mediation is non-binding and does not, unless otherwise agreed to by the parties, authorize the third party neutral to evaluate (see above), decide or otherwise offer a judgment on the issues between the parties. If the mediation concludes in an agreement, that agreement, if it meets otherwise applicable law concerning the enforceability of contracts, is enforceable as a contractual agreement. Where authorized by applicable law, mediation agreements achieved during pending litigation may be entered as court judgments.

IV. Hybrid Processes

Minitrial—A procedure in which parties and their counsel present their matter, which may include evidence, legal arguments, documents and other summaries of their case, before a neutral third party and representatives of all parties, for the purpose of defining issues, pursuing settlement negotiations or otherwise sharing information. A neutral third party, usually at the parties' request, may issue an advisory opinion, which is non-binding, unless the parties agree otherwise.

Med-arb—A procedure in which the parties initially seek mediation of their dispute before a third party neutral, but if they reach impasse, may convert the proceeding into an arbitration in which the third party neutral renders an award. This process may also occur in reverse in which during a contested arbitration proceeding, the parties may agree to seek facilitation of a settlement (mediation) from the third party neutral. In some cases, these third party neutral functions may be divided between two separate individuals or panels of individuals.

Other—Parties by agreement, or pursuant to court rules and regulations, may create and utilize other dispute resolution processes before third party neutral(s) in order to facilitate settlement, manage or plan discovery and other case issues, seek fact-finding or conciliation services, improve communication, simplify or settle parts of cases, arrange transactions or for other reasons. Such processes may be decisional (adjudicative) or facilitative or a hybrid of the two, and they may be binding or non-binding as party agreements or court rules or statutes provide.

Lawyers who provide neutral services as described above shall be subject to the duties, and obligations as specified below.

Rule 4.5.1   Diligence and Competence

(a)   **A lawyer serving as a third party neutral should act diligently, efficiently and promptly, subject to the standard of care owed the parties as required by applicable law or contract.**

(b)   **A lawyer serving as a third party neutral should decline to serve in those matters in which the lawyer is not competent to serve.**

Comment

Diligence

[1]   Like its equivalent in representational work (see Model Rule 1.3, discussing diligence in the lawyer-client relationship), this Rule requires the ADR neutral to act diligently, efficiently and promptly, subject to the duty of care owed the parties by applicable law or contract. Other rules or specifications of timeliness and standards of care may be specified in agreements of the parties, rules provided by relevant organizations or by applicable case law dealing with mediator or arbitrator civil liability. The standard of care to be applied to the work of mediators and arbitrators is currently evolving in practice and case law.

[2]   The lawyer-neutral should commit the time necessary to promote prompt resolution of the dispute and should not let other matters interfere with the timely and efficient completion of the matter. If a lawyer-neutral cannot meet the parties' expectations for prompt, diligent and efficient resolution of the dispute, the lawyer neutral should decline to serve.

[3]   While settlement or resolution is the goal of most ADR processes, the primary responsibility for the resolution of the dispute and the shaping of a settlement in mediation and evaluation rests with the parties. Accordingly, when serving in a facilitative or evaluative process (see definitions), the lawyer-neutral should not coerce or improperly influence a party to make a decision, to continue participating in the process, or to reach settlement or agreement. *See* Proposed Florida Rules for Certified and Court-Appointed Mediators, Rule 10.031.

[4]   When serving in an adjudicative or evaluative capacity, the lawyer-neutral should decide all matters justly, exercising independent judgment, without permitting outside pressure to affect the decision. The lawyer-neutral serving in adjudicative or evaluative roles should be guided by judicial standards of diligence and competence, *see* Model Code of Judicial Conduct, Canon 3B, and other concurrent ethical standards, *see, e.g.*, Code of Ethics for Arbitrators in Commercial Disputes (AAA-ABA, 1977) (currently under revision).

Competence

[5]   A lawyer should decline appointment as a neutral when such appointment is beyond the lawyer's competence. A lawyer-neutral should serve "only

in cases where the neutral has sufficient knowledge [and skill] regarding the process and subject matter to be effective." *Ethical Standards of Professional Responsibility for the Society of Professionals in Dispute Resolution*, adopted June 2, 1986.

[6]   In determining whether a lawyer-neutral has the requisite knowledge and skill to serve as neutral in a particular matter and process, relevant factors may include: the parties' reasonable expectations regarding the ADR process and the neutral's role, the procedural and substantive complexity of the matter and process, the lawyer-neutral's general ADR experience and training, legal experience, subject matter expertise, the preparation the lawyer-neutral is able to give to the matter, and the feasibility of employing experts or co-neutrals with required substantive or process expertise. In many instances, a lawyer-neutral may accept a neutral assignment where the requisite level of competence can be achieved by reasonable preparation.

Rule 4.5.2   Confidentiality

(a)   A lawyer serving as a third party neutral shall maintain the confidentiality of all information acquired in the course of serving as a third party neutral, unless the third party neutral is required or permitted by law or agreement of all the parties to disclose or use any otherwise confidential information.

   (1)   A third party neutral should discuss confidentiality rules and requirements with the parties at the beginning of any proceeding and obtain party consent with respect to any ex parte communication or practice.

   (2)   As between the parties, the third party neutral shall maintain confidentiality for all information disclosed to the third party neutral in confidence by a party, unless the party agrees or specifies otherwise.

   (3)   A lawyer who has served as a third party neutral shall not thereafter use information acquired in the ADR proceeding to the disadvantage of any party to the ADR proceeding, except when the information has become publicly known or the parties have agreed otherwise or except when necessary under (b) below or to defend the neutral from a charge of misconduct.

(b)   A third party neutral may use or disclose confidential information obtained during a proceeding when and to the extent the third party believes necessary to prevent:

   (1)   death or serious bodily injury from occurring; or

   (2)   substantial financial loss from occurring in the matter at hand as the result of a crime or fraud that a party has committed or intends to commit.

(c) **Before using or disclosing information pursuant to section (b), if not otherwise required to be disclosed, the third party neutral must, if feasible, make a good faith effort to persuade the party's counsel or the party, if the party is unrepresented, either not to act or to warn those who might be harmed by the party's action.**

Comment

[1]   ADR confidentiality is distinctly different from lawyer-client confidentiality, which is defeated when adverse parties reveal information to each other or in the presence of a third party. The extent of ADR confidentiality protections can be determined by contract, court rules, statutes or other professional norms or rules. This Rule addresses the confidentiality responsibilities of the lawyer-neutral and delineates the neutral's duties to the parties, the process, and the public. *See Poly Software International, Inc. v. Su*, 880 F. Supp. 1487, 1494; *Cho v. Superior Court*, 45 Cal. Rptr. 2d 863 (1995); Symposium, *Confidentiality in Mediation*, DISPUTE RESOLUTION MAGAZINE (Winter 1999).

[2]   Principles of confidentiality are given effect in the laws of evidence (which govern evidentiary uses, restrictions and privileges) and in ethics rules (which establish professional ethical obligations). Privileges apply in judicial and other proceedings in which the lawyer neutral may be called as a witness or otherwise required to produce evidence regarding an ADR process. The rule of confidentiality in professional ethics applies in situations other than those where evidence is sought from the lawyer-neutral through compulsion of law. This Rule is intended to provide the ADR neutral and parties with confidentiality protections for ADR processes, where privacy of the process and unguarded, candid communications are central to their use and effectiveness.

[3]   Since there is no attorney-client relationship between parties and lawyer neutrals, and because most disclosures of information in most forms of ADR occur in the presence of the other party, the confidentiality protection guaranteed to clients by their representational lawyers by Rule 1.6 (as well as the evidentiary privilege of attorney-client) does not apply in most ADR settings.

[4]   The general rule that lawyers may divulge confidences to facilitate law practice within the firm is not applicable in ADR confidentiality, especially mediation. "Since the essence of mediation is the preservation of confidential communications, most lawyer-mediators are scrupulous not to disclose such confidential information to anyone, even attorneys in their own firm. Mediators may discuss fact patterns or mediation issues with other mediators within the firm or the community of mediators. As a matter of routine, most mediators will screen such comments to ensure that they never reveal names or confidential information." James E. McGuire, *Conflicts in Subsequent Representation*, DISPUTE RESOLUTION MAGAZINE 4 (Spring 1996).

[5]   This rule imposes an ethical duty of confidentiality on the ADR neutral to protect the ADR process and the parties. The rule's confidentiality standards can be altered by agreement of all parties or applicable law.

Many jurisdictions and courts provide confidentiality protections to parties and ADR neutrals as a matter of law. While some statutes are narrowly evidentiary in nature (and govern only the use of information in a court proceeding), other mediation confidentiality provisions include both evidentiary restrictions and broader prohibitions against disclosure. *See* Nancy Rogers and Craig McEwen, *Mediation: Law, Policy and Practice* (Clark, Boardman & Callaghan, 2nd ed., 1994 (state legislatures have enacted over 200 mediation statutes); Elizabeth Plapinger and Donna Stienstra, *ADR and Settlement in the Federal District Courts: A Sourcebook for Judges and Lawyers* (Federal Judicial Center and CPR Institute for Dispute Resolution, 1996) (federal district courts provide for confidentiality of ADR processes by local rule or court orders). Additionally, confidentiality is often provided by contract among parties and neutrals in private forums. *See, e.g., CPR Mediation Procedure*, confidentiality provision at para. 9, in CPR MAPP Series, 1998; *CPR Model Confidentiality Agreement*, in CPR MAPP Series, Confidentiality, 1998.

[6]   Since ADR confidentiality can be governed by different and sometimes conflicting sources of law and ethical duties, it is important that the parties and the neutral understand the extent and uncertainties of the ADR confidentiality protections. Accordingly, section (1) requires the third party neutral to discuss the applicable confidentiality rules with the parties and counsel at the beginning of the process.

Statutory or common law privileges, evidence codes, protective orders issued by courts under discovery or other statutes, as well as party contracts and court rules all can affect the scope of confidentiality for the parties, the third party neutral and others outside of the particular matter. See Rogers and McEwen, *supra*, at ch.8, Confidentiality. Some states, for example, require mediators to disclose certain information, like the occurrence of child abuse or domestic violence. *See, e.g.*, Cal. Penal Code section 11164. Additionally this Rule, like the ABA's Ethics 2000 Commission's proposed revision of Model Rule 1.6 and the forthcoming Restatement of the Law Governing Lawyers section 117, permits disclosure of information to prevent imminent bodily harm or substantial financial loss. *See* Comment [10] below.

[7]   In addition to advising the parties about the scope of confidentiality protections under law and applicable agreement, section (1) also requires the neutral to discuss and obtain party consent regarding the nature of ex parte communications, if any, contemplated by the process. In some mediation processes, for example, parties meet separately with the mediator and share information confidentially. In arbitration processes, ex-parte communications with partisan arbitrators may be permitted under certain rules and prohibited under others. *See, e.g.*, Code of Ethics for Arbitrators in Commercial Disputes

(AAA-ABA, 1977) (Canon VII.C(2), permitting ex-parte communications between the non-neutral arbitrator and the party who appointed them); *cf. CPR Rules for Non-Administered Arbitration,* Rule 9.3, in CPR MAPP Series, Arbitration, 1998 (prohibiting ex-parte communications with neutral or party-appointed arbitrators).

[8]   Given the extensive use in mediation of separate, ex parte meetings or caucuses with the mediator, parties and their lawyers may reveal information in caucus that is not to be disclosed to the other party without permission. Section (2) establishes that the neutral shall maintain the confidentiality of all information disclosed to the third party in confidence, unless the party agrees or specifies otherwise. In effect, all information revealed in confidence in ex-parte sessions or through other confidential means, is to be considered confidential, absent a specific statement or agreement by the party otherwise.

[9]   Section (3) prohibits the use by the neutral of any information acquired in the ADR proceeding to the disadvantage of any party, subject to the exceptions stated in the rule. This formulation tracks the current Model Rule 1.9(c)(1) for conflicts of interest for representational attorneys and former clients. Particularly in mediation or other ADR fora where ex parte sessions are used, the third-party neutral may hear information or settlement facts that may not be legally relevant but that are highly sensitive or proprietary. Under this rule, the lawyer-neutral is prohibited from using this information in subsequent neutral or representational work to the disadvantage of the former ADR party.

[10] Like the ABA's Ethics 2000 Commission's proposed version of Model Rule 1.6 and the forthcoming Restatement of the Law Governing Lawyers section 117, this rule permits disclosure by the neutral third party of information to prevent death or serious bodily harm to anyone on the basis of any information learned, and disclosure to prevent substantial financial loss from occurring in the manner at hand, as a result of a crime or fraud one of the parties has committed or intends to commit. Several states, notably New Jersey and Florida, require (not just permit) lawyers to reveal information to prevent death or serious bodily harm, as well as to avoid some criminal acts or fraud on the tribunal, even when learned in an otherwise confidentially-protected situation. *See, e.g.,* N.J. Rule of Professional Conduct 1.6.

In many jurisdictions, third party neutrals are already under an obligation to reveal such information under separate statutes or case law, *see, e.g.,* Cal. Penal Code sec 11164 (West 1992) (requiring child abuse to be reported); Idaho Rules of Evid. Section 507(4) (West 1998) (child abuse learned about in mediation is not a protected confidence); *cf. Tarasoff v. The Regents of the*

University of California, 17 Cal. 3d 425 (1976) (placing an affirmative duty on psychologist to inform patient's intended victim of danger).

Rule 4.5.3   Impartiality

(a)   A lawyer who serves as a third party neutral should be impartial with respect to the issues and the parties in the matter.

    (1)   A lawyer who serves as a third party neutral should conduct all proceedings in an impartial, unbiased and evenhanded manner, treating all parties with fairness and respect. If at any time the lawyer is unable to conduct the process in an impartial manner, the lawyer shall withdraw, unless prohibited from doing so by applicable law.

    (2)   A lawyer serving in a third party neutral capacity should not allow other matters to interfere with the lawyer's impartiality.

    (3)   When serving in an adjudicative capacity, the lawyer shall decide all matters fairly, with impartiality, exercising independent judgment and without any improper outside influence.

(b)   A lawyer who serves as a third party neutral should:

    (1)   Disclose to the parties all circumstances, reasonably known to the lawyer, why the lawyer might not be perceived to be impartial. These circumstances include (i) any financial or personal interest in the outcome, (ii) any existing or past financial, business, professional, family or social relationship with any of the parties, including, but not limited to any prior representation of any of the parties, their counsel and witnesses, or service as an ADR neutral for any of the parties, (iii) any other source of bias or prejudice concerning a person or institution which is likely to affect impartiality or which might reasonably create an appearance of partiality or bias, and (iv) any other disclosures required of the lawyer by law or contract.

    (2)   Conduct a reasonable inquiry and effort to determine if any interests or biases described in section (b)(1) exist, and maintain a continuing obligation to disclose any such interests or potential biases which may arise during the proceedings,

    (3)   Decline to participate as a third party neutral unless all parties choose to retain the neutral, following all such disclosures, unless contract or applicable law require participation. If, however, the lawyer believes that the matters disclosed would inhibit the lawyer's impartiality, the lawyer should decline to proceed;

(c)   All disclosures under (b) extend to those of the lawyer, members of his or her family, his or her current employer, partners or business associates.

(d)   After accepting appointment and while serving as a neutral, a lawyer shall not enter into any financial, business, professional, family or social

relationship or acquire any financial or personal interest which is likely to affect impartiality or which might reasonably create the appearance of partiality or bias, without disclosure and consent of all parties.

Comment

Impartiality

[1]   Impartiality means freedom from favoritism or bias either by word or action, and a commitment to serve the process and all parties equally. Section (a) codifies established concepts of neutrality and neutral conduct.

Disclosure

[2]   Understanding that absolute neutrality is unobtainable even under the best circumstances, this rule establishes a broad and continuing standard of disclosure by lawyer-neutrals with the possibility of waiver by the parties. The rule describes the circumstances which should be disclosed in determining whether the neutral third party is without impermissible partiality and bias to serve in the particular matter. This form of disclosure is accepted practice in ADR proceedings, including both arbitration and mediation.

A lawyer, as prospective neutral, should err on the side of disclosure because it is better that the relationship or other matter be disclosed at the outset when the parties are free to reject the prospective neutral or to accept the person with knowledge of the relationship. *See Commonwealth Coatings Corp. v. Continental Co.*, 393 U.S. 145, 151–52 (1968) (concurring opinion). While there is often disagreement over what may reasonably constitute a potential conflict, the growing acceptance of the principle of disclosure acts as some reassurance that potentially disadvantaged parties will be given an opportunity to object or at least investigate further. *See* Christopher Honeyman, *Patterns of Bias in Mediation*, J. Disp. Resol. 141 (1985). Conversely, it allows all parties to select a neutral after full disclosure, where the parties knowingly decide to go forward.

[3]   Where possible, best practices suggest that the disclosures should be in writing, as should any subsequent waivers or consents. While the ABA's Ethics 2000 Commission revision of MRPC 1.7 currently requires written disclosures of all representational conflicts and waivers, this section advises, but does not require, the preparation of written disclosures and consents. *Cf.* Calif. arbitration statute, Cal. Code Civ. Proc. section 1281.9 (requires all conflicts disclosures in writing).

[4]   What constitutes reasonable inquiry and effort by the lawyer neutral to uncover interests or relationships requiring disclosure depends on the circumstances. Typically, in matters where the parties are represented, this will involve the prospective lawyer-neutral obtaining from the parties a complete identification of the parties, their representatives, insurers, lawyers, witnesses and attendees at the ADR process and submitting that list to the prospective

neutral's conflicts system. *See Al-Harbi v. Citibank*, 85 F.3d 680, 681–683 (D.C. Cir. 1996). We note that there may be a tension under the law between the duty to disclose prior matters, clients, financial holdings etc., and the confidentiality required to be maintained with respect to on-going or concluded representations and ADR proceedings.

The rule defines the scope of required disclosure to include immediate family members and business partners and associates as defined in Model Rule of Professional Conduct 1.8 (I).[22] It also follows Rule 1.10 and Restatement of the Law Governing Lawyers section 203 for definitions of business associations and law firm associations.[23] The rule does not follow the Judicial Code of Conduct Canon 3(E)(1)(d).

[5]   Where a lawyer-neutral volunteers to act as a neutral at the request of a court, public agency or other group for a de minimis period and pro bono publico, section (b)(2) recognizes that there may not be opportunity for full inquiry, disclosure or disqualification challenge. In such circumstances, a third party neutral may have to proceed with the minimal inquiry and disclosure which may be reasonable under the circumstances. If the lawyer from memory recognizes an interest or relationship relevant to the case, the lawyer should identify that interest or relationship. Otherwise the lawyer should disclose the general nature of the lawyer-neutral's practice and affiliations with law firms or other associations, or other known disqualifying circumstances. *See also* Rule 4.5. 4 (b).

[6]   In general, parties may elect to retain a lawyer as neutral after the latter's disclosure of reasons why the lawyer reasonably might be perceived not to be neutral. However, section (b)(3) imposes on the lawyer-neutral the obligation to decline to serve if the lawyer-neutral believes that the matters disclosed or other circumstances would inhibit the lawyer's impartiality or otherwise impugn the integrity of the process. In such instances, the lawyer neutral should decline to serve even if the parties consent to the lawyer's retention as a neutral.

[7]   Section (d) tracks language from the Code of Ethics for Arbitrators in Commercial Disputes (AAA-ABA, 1977) (currently under revision) and is intended to prevent partiality from developing through the acquisition of future business during the pendency of an ADR proceeding. The parties may consent to waive this provision. The consent provision may prevent difficulties for third party neutrals engaged to mediate or arbitrate a number of disputes with the same party, either through contractual appointment pre-dispute or through multiple, simultaneous appointments or appointments during the pendency of a particular case.

---

22. We note that the ABA's Ethics 2000 Commission is currently considering changes to this Model Rule of Professional Conduct.
    23. Restatement of the Law Governing Lawyers, Proposed Final Draft No. 2 (1998).

Rule 4.5.4   Conflicts of Interest

(a) Disqualification of Individual Third Party Neutrals

  (1) A lawyer who is serving as a third party neutral shall not, during the course of an ADR proceeding, seek to establish any financial, business, representational, neutral or personal relationship with or acquire an interest in, any party, entity or counsel who is involved in the matter in which the lawyer is participating as a neutral, unless all parties consent after full disclosure.

  (2) A lawyer who has served as a third party neutral shall not subsequently represent any party to the ADR proceeding (in which the third party neutral served as neutral) in the same or a substantially related matter, unless all parties consent after full disclosure.

  (3) A lawyer who has served as a third party neutral shall not subsequently represent a party adverse to a former ADR party where the lawyer-neutral has acquired information protected by confidentiality under this Rule, without the consent of the former ADR party.

  (4) Where the circumstances might reasonably create the appearance that the neutral had been influenced in the ADR process by the anticipation or expectation of a subsequent relationship or interest, a lawyer who has served as a third party neutral shall not subsequently acquire an interest in or represent a party to the ADR proceeding in a substantially unrelated matter for a period of one year or other reasonable period of time under the circumstances, unless all parties consent after full disclosure.

(b) Imputation of Conflicts to Affiliated Lawyers and Removing Imputation

  (1) If a lawyer is disqualified by section (a), no lawyer who is affiliated with that lawyer may knowingly undertake or continue representation in any substantially related or unrelated matter unless the personally disqualified lawyer is adequately screened from any participation in the matter, is apportioned no fee from the matter and timely and adequate notice of the screening has been provided to all affected parties and tribunals, provided that no material confidential information about any of the parties to the ADR proceeding has been communicated by the personally disqualified lawyer to the affiliated lawyer or that lawyer's firm.

(c) A lawyer selected as a partisan arbitrator of a party in a multi-member arbitration panel is not prohibited from subsequently representing that party, nor are any affiliated lawyers.

(d) If a lawyer serves as a neutral at the request of a court, public agency or other group for a *de minimis* period and *pro bono publico*, the firm with which the lawyer is associated is not subject to imputation under 4.5.4(b).

Comment

Conflicts

[1]   ADR conflicts policy, like all conflicts regulation, has two main objectives: to protect the parties from actual harm suffered by conflicts of interest, and to protect the process, the public, and the parties from the "appearance" of improper influences. In the ADR context, it is essential that conflicts rules protect against both actual harm and the appearance of self-interest.

Modern law practice is increasingly characterized by lawyer mobility, both externally where lawyers move among law firms and organizations, and internally where lawyers on a case-by-case basis move from representative to neutral roles within their law firm and through association with other private or public organizations (such as court or bar volunteer ADR programs). This Rule strives to protect against both actual harm from lawyer role changes,[24] and to protect the ADR processes, the lawyer neutrals, the parties and the public against the corrosive but less tangible "appearance of impropriety" or "public" harms which threaten the integrity of these processes, the neutrality of the lawyer neutrals, and the public's confidence in these dispute resolution procedures.[25]

[2]   Section (a)(1) governs conflicts which may arise during the pendency of an ADR process and is intended to be a bar against using the ADR process to obtain additional employment or other benefit. Conflicts arising under this section can be consented by all parties after full disclosure.

[3]   Section (a)(2) prohibits future representational roles by lawyer-neutrals in the same or substantially related matters, absent disclosure and consent by all parties. This section codifies the rule established in *Poly Software*: "Where a mediator has received confidential information in the course of a mediation, that mediator should not thereafter represent anyone in connection with the same or a substantially factually related matter unless all parties to the mediation consent after disclosure." *Poly Software*, 880 F. Supp. at 1495. We believe that the logic behind *Poly Software*'s prohibition of future representational relationships in the same or substantially related cases also applies to adjudicative processes such as arbitration. Accordingly, under this Rule, a

---

24. *See Poly Software International, Inc. v. Su, supra* (The court disqualified a lawyer-mediator from representing a litigant in a subsequent matter related to an earlier case in which the mediator had received confidences from the parties) and *Cho v. Superior Court of Los Angeles*, 45 Cal. Rptr. 2d 863 (The court disqualified the law firm as counsel after the firm hired the retired judge who had previously presided over the action and had participated in settlement conferences with the parties. The court also rejected the use of Rule 1.12 for screening of a former judge or arbitrator, *see infra*, note 25).

25. *See, e.g., Cho, supra* (Although the firm had established a screening process to shield the former judge from the case and the judge stated that he had no recall of the settlement conferences, the court stated that "no one could have confidence in the integrity of a legal process" where the former judge who had received ex parte revelations from one of the parties joins the law firm of opposing counsel.)

neutral arbitrator is subject to the same restrictions as a mediator, although a partisan arbitrator is excepted from these restrictions by Rules 4.5. 4(c).

[4]   Conflicts may exist when lawyer-neutrals, who have facilitated disputes and learned confidential and proprietary information about the disputing parties, are asked to represent a party adverse to a former ADR party. When trying to facilitate solutions, third-party neutrals may learn significant "settlement facts"—proprietary information about entities or individuals learned within the neutral setting that may not be legally relevant but that affect the possibility of settlement. *See* Menkel-Meadow, *The Silences of the Restatement, supra*, note 2. In this situation, the conflicts issue is whether an ADR neutral who learned facts (e.g., about financial solvency, human relations, product development, acquisitions or entity future plans) during the ADR would or could use those facts against the former ADR party in the subsequent representation. Section (a)(3) addresses this situation by prohibiting a lawyer-neutral from representing a party adverse to a former ADR party where the lawyer-neutral has acquired settlement facts or other information protected by this rule's confidentiality provision, Rule 4.5.2, absent consent by the former ADR party.

[5]   Section (a)(4) addresses potential future representational or other relationships between the lawyer neutral and a party to the prior ADR in unrelated cases. These relationships are often referred to by the bar as "downstream conflicts." The section is designed to protect against the appearance or the actuality that an expectation of a beneficial future relationship or interest has influenced the neutral's conduct in the preceding ADR process. The language in this section is derived from Canon I.D. of the Code of Ethics for Arbitrators in Commercial Disputes (AAA-ABA, 1977) (currently under revision).[26]

Imputation and Screening

[6]   This rule follows the trend of the Restatement of the Law Governing Lawyers and the draft revisions by the Ethics 2000 Commission to Rule 1.10 to provide for screening of lawyer-neutrals disqualified under section (a) in unrelated or substantially-related matters. This formulation continues to impute disqualification to the whole firm for the same matter, *see Cho*, (screening not sufficient to defeat law firm's disqualification when the judge who heard the action and presided over confidential, ex parte settlement conferences joined

---

26. This Rule provides for a presumptive one-year period of disqualification, but also provides flexibility to shorten or lengthen the disqualification period as circumstances require. Although the Model Rules of Professional Conduct prefer general and not time-based rules, the Drafting Committee and consulting member Professor Geoffrey Hazard believe that a presumptive one-year safe-harbor period is preferable to a general rule of reasonableness, given the substantial need among lawyers and law firms for a clearly defined rule. Understanding that the time-based rule will not be appropriate in all circumstances, a rule of reasonableness is also included.

the opposing party's law firm). This rule is premised, in part, on the different confidentiality obligations of third party neutrals and lawyer representatives. Unlike lawyers representing clients, lawyer neutrals generally should not share information with other lawyers in their firm, and thus are particularly well-suited for screening. *See* Comment [4] to Rule 4.5.2, Confidentiality, *supra*.

An alternative formulation, which the Drafting Committee rejected, would apply the current non-screen, imputation formulation of Model Rule 1.10. This rule would read: "Unless all affected parties consent after disclosure, in any matter where a lawyer would be disqualified under section (a), the restrictions imposed therein also restrict all other lawyers who are affiliated with that lawyer under Rule 1.10." We believe that a no-screen imputation rule is contrary to the trend in the law, as noted above, and would inappropriately limit the growth of mixed neutral and representational roles for lawyers, with its attendant benefits to both the practice and the public.

[7]   Screening in the ADR context involves the same actions as screening in other contexts. *See, e.g.,* Model Rule of Professional Conduct 1.11(a)(1), which permits the law firm of a former government lawyer to undertake or continue representation in a matter in which the former government lawyer participated personally and substantially if the lawyer is screened from further participation in it, including receipt of fees from it; *see also* Restatement of the Law Governing Lawyers. The Annotated Model Rule 1.11 states that: "An effective screen commonly includes the following factors: (1) the disqualified lawyer does not participate in the matter, (2) the disqualified lawyer does not discuss the matter with any member of the firm, (3) the disqualified lawyer represents through sworn testimony that he or she had not imparted any confidential information to the firm, (4) the disqualified lawyer does not have access to any files or documents relating to the matter; and (5) the disqualified lawyer does not share in any of the fees from the matter." *Annotated Model Rules of Professional Conduct* at 186 (3rd ed.). In addition, under the proposed rule, notice of the screening must be provided to all affected parties and tribunals.

[8]   Section (c) excepts partisan, party-appointed arbitrators from the restrictions on future representational work under section (a), and from imputation and screening under section (b). We note, however, the lack of consensus regarding the role and practices of partisan arbitrators, and suggest that if "partisan" arbitrators become more like neutral arbitrators, section (c) will need to be amended.

[9]   Section (d) excepts lawyer neutrals and their affiliated lawyers from the imputation and screening rule when the lawyer neutral volunteers his or her services at the request of a court, other public agency, or institution and serves for a de minimis period.

Rule 4.5.5   Fees

(a) Before or within a reasonable time after being retained as a third party neutral, a lawyer should communicate to the parties, in writing, the basis or rate and allocation of the fee for service, unless the third party neutral is serving in a no-fee or pro bono capacity.

(b) A third party neutral who withdraws from a case should return any unearned fee to the parties.

(c) A third party neutral who charges a fee contingent on the settlement or other specific resolution of the matter should explain to the parties that such an arrangement gives the third party neutral a direct financial interest in settlement that may conflict with the parties' possible interest in terminating the proceedings without reaching settlement. The third party neutral should consider whether such a fee arrangement creates an appearance or actuality of partiality, inconsistent with the requirements of Rule 4.5.3.

Comment

[1]   This rule requires a written communication specifying the basis, rate and allocation of fees to all parties, unless the third party neutral is serving in a no-fee or pro bono capacity.

[2]   It has become relatively common to use contingent fee or bonus compensation schemes to provide an incentive to participate in ADR or to reward the achievement of an effective settlement. Section (3) of the rule does not prohibit contingent fees (which some jurisdictions or provider organizations do) but requires the third party neutral to explain what the effects of such a fee arrangement may be, including conflicts of interest. This rule imposes two obligations on the neutral. The lawyer neutral is required to assess the possible conflicts attendant to use of contingent fees and whether the appearance or actuality of partiality prohibits its use under Rule 4.5.3, Impartiality. If use of the compensation arrangements is not prohibited under that standard, the neutral is required to disclose the possible consequences of this fee arrangement to the parties.

Rule 4.5.6.   Fairness and Integrity of the Process

(a) The lawyer serving as third party neutral should make reasonable efforts to determine that the ADR proceedings utilized are explained to the parties and their counsel, and that the parties knowingly consent to the process being used and the neutral selected (unless applicable law or contract requires use of a particular process or third party neutral).

(b) The third party neutral should not engage in any process or procedure not consented to by the parties (unless required by applicable law or contract).

(c)   **The third party neutral should use all reasonable efforts to conduct the process with fairness to all parties. The third party neutral should be especially diligent that parties who are not represented have adequate opportunities to be heard and involved in any ADR proceedings.**

(d)   **The third party neutral should make reasonable efforts to prevent misconduct that would invalidate any settlement. The third party neutral should also make reasonable efforts to determine that the parties have reached agreement of their own volition and knowingly consent to any settlement.**

Comment

[1]   While ethical rules cannot guarantee the specific procedures or fairness of a process, this rule is intended to require third party neutrals to be attentive to the basic values and goals informing fair dispute resolution. These values include party autonomy; party choice of process (to the extent permitted by law or contract); party choice of and consent to the choice of the third party neutral (to the extent permitted by law or contract); and fairness of the conduct of the process itself. This rule is concerned not only with specific harms to particular participating parties but with the appearance of the integrity of the process to the public and other possible users of these processes.[27]

[2]   This section requires third party neutrals to make reasonable efforts to determine that the parties have reached an agreement of their own volition, one which is not coerced. While some have suggested that third party neutrals should bear some moral accountability or legal responsibility for the agreements they help facilitate, *see* Lawrence Susskind, *Environmental Mediation and the Accountability Problem*, 9 Vt. L. Rev. 1 (Spring 1981), these Rules do not make the third party neutral the guarantor of a fair or just result. (The Kutak Commission rejected an earlier effort to prevent lawyers

---

27.   The proposed Rule articulates a preferred rule of party choice and autonomy, about the type of process (including whether mediation is facilitative or evaluative), whether caucuses are to be used or not, and the selection of the neutral. This may not be possible in situations where processes are mandated, either by contract (adhesion or freely negotiated) or by court rules and requirements. The questions implicated in the fairness and integrity of the process are very controversial at the present time (including legal challenges to compulsory arbitration clauses in some contracts) and thus, we (or the appropriate ABA ethics body) might conclude that such a matter is too "substantive" or too unsettled for rule-making at this time.

As we write this, the case law is rapidly changing. The United States Supreme Court recently held that an arbitration clause in a collective bargaining agreement must clearly and unmistakably state that federal anti-discrimination claims are subject to arbitration, *Wright v. Universal Maritime Service Corp*, 119 S. Ct. 391 (Nov. 16, 1998). Similarly, the 9th Circuit has refused to enforce arbitration in several employment cases where the plaintiffs did not knowingly agree to arbitrate statutory discrimination claims, *see Duffield v. Richardson Stephens & Co.*, 144 F. 3d 1182 (9th Cir. 1998), *cert. denied*, 119 S. Ct. 465 (date), *Renteria v. Prudential Ins. Co. of Am.*, 113 F.3d 1104 (9th Cir. 1997); and *Nelson v. Cyprus Bagdad Copper Corp.*, 119 F.3d 756 (9th Cir. 1997). The California Supreme Court also raised serious questions about the fairness and enforceability of Kaiser's contractual mandatory medical malpractice arbitration, *see Engalla v. Kaiser Permanente Medical Group, Inc.*, 64 Cal. Rptr. 2d 843 (1997). The *Engalla* case has lead to a comprehensive assessment and restructuring of the Kaiser arbitration process by outside experts. *See* The Blue Ribbon Advisory Panel on Kaiser Permanente Arbitration, *The Kaiser Permanente Arbitration System: A Review and Recommendations for Improvement*, January 5, 1998.

from facilitating negotiated agreements which would be held unconscionable as a matter of law, see Proposed Rule 4.3, Draft Model Rules, 1980).

[3]   This section of the Rule is designed to prevent harm not only to parties engaged in dispute resolution processes, but to the appearances presented to the general public of how legal processes are conducted. Although this section of the Rule may suffer from the same complaints about vagueness as the former Canon 9 "appearance of impropriety" did under the old structure of the Code of Professional Conduct, the drafters believe that where lawyers "switch" sides and roles, from partisan to neutral, it is important to provide for basic criteria of fairness to be monitored in the process for the acceptability and legitimacy of the process and the lawyers within it.

CPR—Georgetown Commission on Ethics and Standards of Practice in ADR

Chair
Prof. Carrie Menkel-Meadow
Georgetown University Law Center
Washington, DC

Prof. Marjorie Corman Aaron
University of Cincinnati College of Law
Cincinnati, OH

Hon. Arlin M. Adams
Schnader, Harrison, Segal & Lewis
Philadelphia, PA

Howard J. Aibel
LeBoeuf, Lamb, Greene & MacRae
New York, NY

Tom Arnold
Arnold, White & Durkee
Houston, TX

Jonathan D. Asher
Legal Aid Society of Metropolitan Denver
Denver, CO

Hon. Nancy F. Atlas
U.S. District Court
Houston, TX

Richard W. Austin
Pretzel & Stouffer
Chicago, IL

Margery F. Baker
Resolution Resources Inc.
Potomac, MD

Fred Baron
Baron & Budd
Dallas, TX

Howard S. Bellman
Madison, WI

John Bickerman
Bickerman Dispute Resolution Group
Washington, DC

Sheila L. Birnbaum
Skadden, Arps, Slate, Meagher & Flom
New York, NY

Hon. Wayne D. Brazil
U.S. District Court
Oakland, CA

William H. Champlin III
Tyler Cooper & Alcorn
Hartford, CT

Richard Chernick
Los Angeles, CA

Hon. Kenneth Conboy
Latham & Watkins
New York, NY

Frederick K. Conover II
The Faegre Group
Denver, CO

Hon. Mario M. Cuomo
Willkie Farr & Gallagher
New York, NY

John J. Curtin, Jr.
Bingham, Dana & Gould
Boston, MA

Dean John D. Feerick
Fordham University Law School
New York, NY

Lawrence J. Fox
Drinker, Biddle & Reath
Philadelphia, PA

Howard Gadlin
National Institute of Health
Bethesda, MD

Bryant Garth
American Bar Foundation
Chicago, IL

Shelby R. Grubbs
Miller & Martin
Chattanooga, TN

Prof. Geoffrey C. Hazard, Jr.
University of Pennsylvania
Philadelphia, PA

H. Roderic Heard
Wildman, Harrold, Allen & Dixon
Chicago, IL

James F. Henry
CPR Institute for Dispute Resolution
New York, NY

Christopher Honeyman
Madison, WI

J. Michael Keating, Jr.
Chris Little & Associates
Providence, RI

Judith Korchin
Holland & Knight
Miami, FL

Duane W. Krohnke
Faegre & Benson
Minneapolis, MN

Frederick B. Lacey
LeBoeuf, Lamb, Greene & MacRae
Newark, NJ

Prof. Homer LaRue
Howard University School of Law
Washington, DC

Michael K. Lewis
ADR Associates, L.L.C.
Washington, DC

Deborah Masucci
JAMS
New York, NY

Prof. Harry N. Mazadoorian
Quinnipiac Law School
Hamden, CT

Prof. Barbara McAdoo
University of Missouri-Columbia
    School of Law
Columbia, MO

Bruce Meyerson
Steptoe & Johnson
Phoenix, AZ

Hon. Milton Mollen
Graubard Mollen Horowitz
Pomeranz & Shapiro
New York, NY

Jean S. Moore
Hogan & Hartson
Washington, DC

Robert C. Mussehl
Mussehl & Rosenberg
Seattle, WA

John E. Nolan, Jr.
Steptoe & Johnson
Washington, DC

Melinda Ostermeyer
Washington, DC

Wayne N. Outten
Lankenau Kovner & Kurtz
New York, NY

Charles Pou
Mediation Consortium
Washington, DC

Sharon Press
Supreme Court of Florida
Tallahassee, FL

Charles B. Renfrew
Law Offices of Charles B. Renfrew
San Francisco, CA

Prof. Nancy Rogers
Ohio State University
Columbus, OH

Prof. Frank E. A. Sander
Harvard Law School
Cambridge, MA

Robert N. Sayler
Covington & Burling
Washington, DC

Hon. William W. Schwarzer
U.S. District Court
San Francisco, CA

Kathleen Severens
U.S. Department of Justice
Washington, DC

Margaret L. Shaw
ADR Associates, L.L.C.
New York, NY

Hon. Jerome B. Simandle
U.S. District Court
Camden, NJ

William K. Slate
American Arbitration Association
New York, NY

Stephanie Smith
Hewlett Foundation
Menlo Park, CA

Larry S. Stewart
Stewart Tilghman Fox & Bianchi
Miami, FL

Prof. Thomas J. Stipanowich
University of Kentucky
College of Law
Lexington, KY

Harry P. Trueheart III
Nixon, Hargrave, Devans & Doyle
Rochester, NY

Hon. John J. Upchurch
CCB Mediation, Inc.
Daytona Beach, FL

Alvora Varin-Hommen
U.S. Arb. & Mediation Service
Bensalem, PA

Hon. John L. Wagner
Irell & Manella
Newport Beach, CA

Hon. William H. Webster
Milbank, Tweed, Hadley & McCloy
Washington, DC

John W. Weiser
Bechtel Group, Inc.
San Francisco, CA

Michael D. Young
JAMS
New York, NY

CPR Staff

Elizabeth Plapinger
CPR Institute for Dispute Resolution
New York, NY

Kathleen Scanlon
Vice President
CPR Institute for Dispute Resolution
New York, NY

CHAPTER **4**

Preparing for the Hearing

Chapter Summary

4.1 How can we avoid delay and enhance the speed, efficiency, and fairness of arbitration prior to the hearing? . . 173

In achieving the proper balance between efficiency and fairness, the pre-hearing period is critical. It is then that the procedural framework is refined, a timetable established, and the precise character of arbitration determined.

4.2 What are the priorities for pre-hearing case management? . . 174

Pre-hearing case management often includes:

(1) Promoting dialogue between participants through pre-hearing conferences or conference calls
(2) Addressing jurisdictional issues
(3) Developing a timetable or framework for the arbitration
(4) Addressing requests for interim relief
(5) Facilitating information exchange and discovery
(6) Addressing dispositive motions
(7) Planning the hearings
(8) Planning the form of the final award

4.3 Should there be pre-hearing meetings or conference calls to promote dialogue between the participants?. 176

Pre-hearing conferences are a primary tool for effective management. They are a useful vehicle for setting the tone for arbitration, understanding and refining the issues, encouraging settlement, creating a timetable, and clarifying procedures. Pre-hearing conferences provide the foundation for the development of case management orders.

Preparing for the Hearing

Preparing for the Hearing

Preparing for the Hearing

4.1

How can we avoid delay and enhance the speed, efficiency, and fairness of arbitration prior to the hearing?

Among the primary reasons business parties use arbitration are the *speed* and *efficiency* of the process relative to court trial. A Commissioner observes:

> The corporate head of litigation is concerned about resolving the dispute as quickly as possible. The need is for someone to grab hold of it and get it tried. In such cases arbitration can be of great benefit.

Evidence from the field indicates that in most cases commercial disputes *are* resolved more quickly by arbitration than by jury trial or bench trial,[1] especially where the disputes involve relatively small amounts of money. This is often attributed to the absence of extensive pre-trial practice in commercial arbitration.[2] In addition to avoiding often-crowded court dockets, arbitration usually involves a streamlining of the procedures associated with litigation, including abbreviated discovery and motion practice.

With the benefits of streamlined process, however, come tradeoffs—and concerns regarding the *fundamental fairness* of arbitration procedures.[3] The larger the stakes and the more complex the case, the greater the tension between expeditious resolution and the perceived need for procedural fairness. A satisfactory arbitration process depends upon successfully balancing the worth of speed and efficiency against expectations of due process and the requirements of fundamental fairness. The precise balance depends upon the circumstances of the case and, ultimately, upon the needs and expectations of the arbitrating parties. Surveys of users indicate that in large commercial cases speed may not be a paramount priority.[4] On the other hand, unless great care is taken in the management of the process, "big case" arbitrations have the potential to become "monuments to delay."[5]

In meeting the expectations of arbitrating parties regarding speed and efficiency, and in striking the proper balance between these values and those of procedural fairness, the period prior to hearings on the merits of the dispute is in many ways the most critical stage of the process. No set of commercial arbitration procedures, however comprehensive, provides a precise blueprint for

---

1. *See* Thomas J. Stipanowich, *Rethinking American Arbitration*, 63 IND. L.J. 425, 460 (1988).
2. *See id.* at 474, citing S. LAZARUS ET AL., RESOLVING BUSINESS DISPUTES: THE POTENTIAL OF COMMERCIAL ARBITRATION 105–06 (1965).
3. For a discussion of the legal standards for fundamental fairness in arbitration, *see generally* IAN R. MACNEIL, RICHARD E. SPEIDEL & THOMAS J. STIPANOWICH, FEDERAL ARBITRATION LAW: AGREEMENTS, AWARDS AND REMEDIES UNDER THE FEDERAL ARBITRATION ACT § 32.3.1 (1994) [hereinafter MACNEIL ET AL.].
4. *See id.*
5. *See* Stipanowich, *supra* note 1, at 450–51.

conducting an arbitration. Even if such detail were possible, it would not be desirable in light of the wide range of claims, controversies, and circumstances with which arbitrators are presented. It is during the pre-hearing process that the often sketchy procedural framework established by the arbitration agreement is refined. It is here, in the creation of an arbitration timetable, the handling of discovery and of other procedural issues, and setting the stage for hearings, that the participants often determine the precise character of their arbitration experience.

In fleshing out the bare bones of the arbitration agreement, arbitrators typically enjoy considerable leeway.[6] Leading commercial arbitration rules reinforce the well-recognized broad discretion of arbitrators to manage virtually all aspects of the arbitration.[7] At the same time, effective arbitrators recognize that all participants usually are best served by striving for party consensus, and by reserving unilateral arbitrator rulings for when consensus cannot be achieved.

4.2

What are the priorities for pre-hearing case management?

In the simplest commercial arbitrations, there may be little or no need for active pre-hearing management by the arbitrator. Standard fast-track rules place a premium on getting the dispute resolved with minimal process.[8] As the stakes grow or the issues become more complex, it becomes increasingly important for the arbitrator to take a more active role in managing the process with the involvement, and, hopefully, the cooperation of the parties.

1. Guidelines for managing the arbitration process

In light of the variety of management issues that may arise in the course of arbitration, participants are well advised to consult appropriate guidelines. Applicable arbitration procedures may provide guidelines for the pre-hearing

---

6. *See* MACNEIL ET AL., *supra* note 3, § 32.1.2.
7. *See id.* § 32.1.3.
8. *See, e.g.*, AMERICAN ARBITRATION ASSOCIATION, COMMERCIAL DISPUTE RESOLUTION PROCEDURES §§ E-1–E-10 (Jan. 1, 1999) [hereinafter AAA COMMERCIAL PROCEDURES]. *See also* Thomas J. Stipanowich, *At the Cutting Edge: Conflict Avoidance and Resolution in the Construction Industry, in* ADR & THE LAW 65, 68–70 (1997) (discussing features of AAA Fast Track procedures for construction cases).

stage. For example, Rule 9.3 of the CPR Rules for Non-Administered Arbitration (CPR Arbitration Rules) directs the arbitrators to hold a "pre-hearing conference for the planning and scheduling of the proceeding."[9] The purpose of the conference is "to discuss all elements of the arbitration with a view to planning for its future conduct."[10] Another possible "template" for case management in arbitration is the UNCITRAL Notes on Organizing Arbitral Proceedings developed in 1996.[11]

Although the precise needs of arbitrating parties will vary with the circumstances, the Commission offers the following list of priorities for pre-hearing case management.

Table 5. A
Priorities for Pre-Hearing Case Management

Elements that can have a significant impact on the arbitration experience

1. Promoting dialogue between participants through pre-hearing conferences or conference calls
2. Addressing jurisdictional issues
3. Developing a timetable and management plan for the arbitration
4. Addressing requests for interim relief
5. Facilitating information exchange and discovery
6. Addressing dispositive motions
7. Planning the hearings
8. Planning the form of the final award

Other matters that may need to be addressed

1. Rules for arbitration
2. Place of arbitration
3. Language of arbitration
4. Administrative services
5. Deposits for fees and costs
6. Confidentiality
7. Routing of written communications
8. Fax, e-mail and other electronic forms of communication

Let us consider each element of the checklist above in turn, beginning with what are likely to be the most important issues.

---

9. CPR Institute for Dispute Resolution, Rules for Non-Administered Arbitration, Rule 9.3 (Rev. 2000) [hereinafter CPR Arbitration Rules].

10. *Id.*

11. *See generally* United Nations Commission on International Trade Law, *UNCITRAL Notes on Organizing Arbitral Proceedings* (June 14, 1996) <http://www.transdata.ro/drept/uncitral/arbnotes.htm>. *See also* Tom Arnold, Setting up the Preliminary Administration Conference, The First Arbitrator-Party Communications (1999)(describing one experienced arbitrator's preparations for and conduct of pre-hearing conferences, including preliminary letter sent to counsel).

4.3

Should there be pre-hearing meetings or conference calls to promote dialogue between the participants?

1. Pre-hearing conferences are a primary tool for effective management

As discussed at length in Chapter 5, members of the Commission concur that effective arbitrators guide proceedings with a firm hand. Effective management of the arbitration requires early communication between the duly appointed arbitrator(s) and the parties. This process often begins with conferences where the arbitrators first discuss case particulars with the parties, ascertain the needs and expectations of the participants, and, thereafter, explain their own expectations and ground rules.[12] Such pre-hearing conferences (sometimes called "pre-liminary hearings") are critical to achieving the proper balance between speed, efficiency, and due process. Reflecting upon his role as arbitrator in a particularly large, complex case, an experienced corporate counsel reports:

> Prehearing conferences are indispensable in large cases. Because hearing procedures in arbitration are not as rigid and prescribed as are court pro-ceedings, it is essential for the arbitrator and the parties to arrive at a mutual understanding of the rules of the game early in the case. . . . The participants should leave the pre-hearing conference with a clear understanding of what is expected of them and how the overall case will be presented.[13]

Most experienced attorneys agree.[14]

Pre-hearing conferences can lay the groundwork for arbitration in several important ways.

(1) *Setting the proper tone.* Pre-hearing conferences give arbitrators the first, and best opportunity to establish the proper atmosphere for a suc-cessful arbitration: impartiality, fairness, and firmness on the part of the tribunal; civility and cooperation on the part of the parties. The initial meeting is the time to convey by word and action that the arbitrators are

---

12. Allen Poppleton, *The Arbitrator's Role in Expediting the Large and Complex Commercial Case*, 36 ARB. J., Dec. 1981, at 6, 7. Experienced arbitrator Tom Arnold sets the stage for pre-hearing conferences with an extensive letter to counsel. *See generally* Arnold, *supra* note 11.

13. *See* Robert H. Gorske, *An Arbitrator Looks at Expediting the Large, Complex Case*, 5 OHIO ST. J. ON DISPUTE RESOLUTION 381, 396 (1990).

14. In one extensive survey on commercial arbitration, nine-tenths of responding attorneys acknowl-edged that pre-hearing conferences were often helpful. Respondents cited their value in arranging for discov-ery, narrowing factual and legal issues, familiarizing the parties with the panel, and discussing hearing proce-dures. *See* Stipanowich, *supra* note 1, at 463.

independent neutrals who will approach all matters evenhandedly.[15] Effective arbitrators also make clear they are in charge, and that they expect the full cooperation of the parties and their attorneys in moving forward with resolution. A Commission member with extensive judicial and arbitral experience offers a memorable metaphor:

> [Just as] . . . the teacher on the first day of school sets the tone of the class, the arbitrator must assert early control. It is not acceptable to let the parties proceed as they wish. Many lawyers dislike arbitration and approach it half-heartedly, and will fall into the old patterns of litigation if they are allowed to. They must be quickly brought to realize that they are in a firmly controlled and expeditious proceeding, and that they jeopardize their client's position by anything less than serious and full participation in the matter.

Similarly, a member of the panel that arbitrated a massive dispute involving seventeen multinational oil companies reported that pre-hearing conferences were critical in taking firm control of the proceeding, carefully structuring the arbitration and the procedures to be followed, gaining credibility with the parties, and giving the parties confidence in in the process.[16]

Good arbitrators encourage the parties to cooperate with one another in resolving procedural issues, but they remain ready to resolve matters by order when necessary.

(2) *Understanding, refining the issues.*   A thorough understanding of the issues is the necessary first step in planning their resolution. Often, a claimant's initial demand for arbitration and the respondent's answer (if any answer is provided) will contain only the barest details of the case. Pre-hearing conferences permit parties to begin filling in the details, elaborating on some issues and narrowing the focus in other ways. An appreciation of the issues may be helpful in establishing the sequence in which issues are addressed at the hearings, the order of proof and the format(s) for presentation. Sometimes it is advantageous to bifurcate hearings so that liability issues may be resolved prior to presentations on damages. The process sometimes reveals that a single crucial issue should be decided before the rest of the matter proceeds.

Closely tied to the issues in dispute is the question of the appropriate remedies. Arbitrators have considerable discretion in tailoring relief to the circumstances before them. Effective arbitrators, however, often seek clear indications from the parties regarding what they regard as appropriate relief. The subject of remedies is generally discussed in Chapter 7.

---

15. *See* MACNEIL ET AL., *supra* note 3, § 32.2.

16. *See* Richard J. Medalie, *Developing Innovative Procedures in a Complex Multiparty Arbitration, in* AMERICAN ARBITRATION ASSOCIATION, COMMERCIAL ARBITRATION FOR THE 1990s, 56, 59 (1991).

In some cases, a party may want to discuss matters that require immediate attention, such as a motion to dismiss or a request for interim or provisional relief. Because of the importance of these issues at the pre-hearing stage, they are discussed at length later in this chapter.

(3) *Encouraging settlement.* As explained in Chapter 1, binding arbitration should be the *final* resort for parties seeking to resolve business disputes. Often, however, parties have not explored settlement possibilities prior to arbitration. Pre-hearing conferences provide an opportunity for arbitrators, if they deem it appropriate, to encourage the parties to consider the possibility of settlement, and to resolve their issues by less formal means such as mediated negotiation.

(4) *Creating the timetable.* Pre-hearing conferences provide an invaluable mechanism for establishing and refining the timetable for the entire process from preliminary exchange of information to rendition of award. The arbitration timetable or management plan is discussed below.

(5) *Clarifying procedures.* Pre-hearing conferences facilitate the "fleshing out" of the arbitration, from the handling of preliminary matters such as discovery, interim relief, and dispositive motions (discussed in Sections 4.7–4.9), to the admissibility of evidence at the hearing (treated in Chapter 5).

2. Formats for pre-hearing conferences

The pre-hearing conference is now an established feature of leading arbitration rules. The CPR Arbitration Rules have mandated a pre-hearing conference since their adoption in 1989. CPR's Rule 9.3 provides:

> The Tribunal shall hold an initial pre-hearing conference for the planning and scheduling of the proceeding. Such conference shall be held promptly after the constitution of the Tribunal, unless the Tribunal is of the view that further submissions from the parties are appropriate prior to such conference. The objective of this conference shall be to discuss all elements of the arbitration with a view to planning for its future conduct. Matters to be considered in the initial pre-hearing conference may include, *inter alia*, the following:
>
> (a) Procedural matters (such as setting specific time limits for, and manner of, any required discovery; the desirability of bifurcation or other separation of the issues in the arbitration; the desirability and practicability of consolidating the arbitration with any other proceeding; the scheduling of conferences and hearings; the scheduling of pre-hearing memoranda; the need for and type of record of conferences and hearings, including the need for transcripts; the amount of time allotted to each party for presentation of its case and for rebuttal; the mode, manner and order for presenting proof; the need for expert witnesses and how expert testimony should be presented; and the necessity for any on-site inspection by the Tribunal);

(b) The early indentification and narrowing of the issues in the arbitration;

(c) The possibility of stipulations of fact and admissions by the parties solely for purposes of the arbitration, as well as simplification of document authentication;

(d) The possibility of appointment of an independent expert by the Tribunal; and

(e) The possibility of the parties engaging in settlement negotiations, with or without the assistance of a mediator.

After the initial conference, further pre-hearing or other conferences may be held as the Tribunal deems appropriate.[17]

AAA Commercial Procedures § R-22 authorizes arbitrators to schedule a

preliminary hearing with the parties and/or their representatives . . . at the request of any party or at the discretion of any arbitrator or the AAA . . . as soon as practicable . . . [to] discuss the future conduct of the case, including clarification of the issues and claims, a schedule for the hearings and any other preliminary matters.[18]

Arbitrators have discretion to conduct the hearing by telephone. In cases under the AAA Procedures for Large, Complex Disputes, a prompt preliminary hearing is mandated with guidelines similar to CPR Rule 9.3.[19]

In major cases, arbitrators often find it necessary or appropriate to conduct a series of pre-hearing conferences, facilitating effective management of the process through periodic interaction of parties and arbitrators.[20] "Milestone" conferences (or conference calls) are useful for charting and maintaining the progress of information exchange and other preparations for arbitration hearings, and help to address pending problems and nip emerging conflicts in the bud.

In the interest of efficiency or economy, parties sometimes agree to confer authority on the chair of the arbitration panel alone to conduct such conferences, particularly when a tripartite panel with party-arbitrators is engaged.[21]

3. Development of pre-hearing case management orders

Pre-hearing conferences or conference calls provide the foundation for the arbitrators to develop pre-hearing case management orders which set forth the framework for arbitration. These subjects are discussed in more detail under the heading "What should be included in the pre-hearing timetable and case management plan for arbitration?"

---

17. CPR ARBITRATION RULES, *supra* note 9, Rule 9.3.
18. AAA COMMERCIAL PROCEDURES, *supra* note 8, § R-22 .
19. *Id.* § L-4.
20. *See* CPR ARBITRATION RULES, *supra* note 9, Commentary to Rule 9.
21. *See, e.g.,* AAA COMMERCIAL PROCEDURES, *supra* note 8, § L-4.

4.4

How are jurisdictional issues—questions regarding the arbitrator's authority to decide the issues—appropriately addressed?

1. Handling jurisdictional issues

Because arbitration is a creature of contract, a valid and enforceable agreement to arbitrate is a fundamental prerequisite to an arbitrator's jurisdiction.[22] Usually, there is no question that the parties have agreed to arbitrate the issues, and there is no threshold question of jurisdiction. When, however, a party challenges an arbitrator's jurisdiction on the basis that it is not bound by a valid arbitration agreement, or that the arbitration agreement does not cover the matters at issue, there may be a question whether the jurisdictional issue should be resolved by the arbitrator or by a court. The answer depends, first and foremost, upon the agreement of the parties.

Approach of leading arbitration rules

If the parties have agreed that arbitration shall be governed by arbitration procedures such as the CPR Arbitration Rules or AAA Commercial Procedures, the authority of arbitrators to address jurisdictional issues will be clear. CPR Rule 8 provides:

> The Tribunal shall have the power to hear and determine challenges to its jurisdiction... [It] shall have the power to determine the existence, validity or scope of the contract of which an arbitration clause forms a part, and/or of the arbitration clause itself ....[23]

AAA Commercial Procedures § R-8 contains substantially similar language.[24]

Under the foregoing provisions, a party to a contract that incorporates the CPR or AAA procedures has agreed to consign virtually all questions touching upon the arbitrator's authority to the arbitrator. The policy behind provisions like CPR Rule 8 and AAA Commercial Procedures § R-8 is to discourage resort to the courts, an approach that often delays and disrupts the arbitration. In the face of such clear language, courts acting under the Federal Arbitration Act (FAA)[25] and, most likely, those acting under state arbitration law, will defer pre-arbitration jurisdictional questions to the arbitrators, and will limit their post-award review of such determinations to the limited grounds that normally

---

22. *See* MACNEIL ET AL., *supra* note 3, § 17.3.
23. CPR ARBITRATION RULES, *supra* note 9, Rule 8.
24. AAA COMMERCIAL PROCEDURES, *supra* note 8, § R-8.
25. *See* First Options of Chicago, Inc. v. Kaplan, 514 U.S. 938 (1995) (applying the FAA). *See also* MACNEIL ET AL., *supra* note 3, § 14.10.1.

confine such review.[26] Standards for judicial review of awards are discussed in Chapter 7.

The goals of speed and efficiency are further served by provisions that require those asserting jurisdictional challenges to act promptly or be deemed to have waived the right to challenge. CPR Rule 8 states:

> Any challenges to the jurisdiction of the Tribunal, except challenges based on the award itself, shall be made not later than the notice of defense or, with respect to a counterclaim, with reply to the counterclaim. . . .[27]

To similar effect, see AAA Commercial Procedures § R-8(c).[28]

Court determination of arbitrability

With regard to agreements governed by the FAA, the U.S. Supreme Court has said, "Courts should not assume that the parties agreed to arbitrate arbitrability unless there is 'clear and unmistakable' evidence that they did so."[29] In the absence of a clear agreement that gives the arbitrator power to decide whether an agreement to arbitrate is valid or whether a controversy is subject to the agreement, federal arbitration law and prevailing state arbitration law put those matters in the hands of the courts.[30] An arbitration provision that incorporates the CPR Arbitration Rules or the AAA Commercial Procedures constitutes "clear and unmistakable" evidence that the parties want the arbitrators to determine jurisdictional questions.

The effect of delay.   A party desiring to raise the question of arbitrability in court must act promptly to avoid allegations of waiver.[31] The present practice of some arbitration institutions is that if either party raises the existence of a valid arbitration clause or other arbitrability issues in a court proceeding after arbitrators have been appointed, the arbitrators in their discretion may continue the arbitration unless the court issues an order to stay the arbitration or makes a final determination that the matter is not arbitrable.[32]

Separability of defenses and issues.   A generally recognized limitation on the authority of courts to consider the enforceability of arbitration agreements under federal or state law is the "separability doctrine." The leading statement of this limitation is *Prima Paint Corp. v. Flood & Conklin Mfg. Co.*,[33] which involved an attempt to avoid arbitration of disputes under an agreement of purchase of a business on the ground that the purchase agreement had been induced by the

---

26. *See* MACNEIL ET AL., *supra* note 3, § 14.10.

27. CPR ARBITRATION RULES, *supra* note 9, Rule 8.

28. AAA COMMERCIAL PROCEDURES, *supra* note 8, § R-8(c).

29. *First Options, supra* note 25, 514 U.S. at 944.

30. *See* National Conference of Commissioners on Uniform State Laws, Uniform Arbitration Act (2000) [hereinafter Revised UAA], § 6, Reporter's Commentary.

31. *See also* MACNEIL ET AL., *supra* note 3, §§ 21.3.

32. *See supra* note 30.

33. 388 U.S. 395 (1967).

fraud. Applying the FAA, the Supreme Court determined that in the absence of a clear agreement to the contrary, an allegation that an arbitration provision was itself induced by fraud is for the court to consider. Under a broadly-worded arbitration agreement, however, challenges to the enforceability of the underlying contract based on fraud, illegality, mutual mistake, duress, unconscionability, and other defenses are for the arbitrators to decide.[34] In other words, most states recognize some form of the separability doctrine under their state arbitration laws. As recently revised, the Uniform Arbitration Act incorporates the separability principle.[35]

The "separability" principle is reinforced by CPR Rule 8.2, which provides that "[f]or the purposes of challenges to the jurisdiction of the Tribunal, the arbitration clause shall be considered as separable from any contract of which it forms a part." Similar language is contained in AAA Commercial Procedures § R-8(b).

A Commission member offers the following perspective on the practical impact of the separability principle:

> There was a time not so long ago when courts would single out a clause of a business contract calling for arbitration of any disputes under that contract for the specific purpose of striking the arbitration clause down. Now, the tables have effectively turned: courts will enforce a commercial arbitration agreement under federal or state law even if there are allegations that the contract of which it is a part is unenforceable, so long as there are no valid defenses to the arbitration agreement itself (such as a misrepresentation of the nature or content of that arbitration agreement, or unconscionable arbitration procedures). That's a relatively rare case in the commercial world.
>
> Under the typical broadly-framed arbitration provision (such as one calling for arbitration of "disputes arising under or relating to the contract or the breach thereof"), virtually any defense relating to the overall contract—material breach, mutual mistake, fraud—you name it—is a matter for the arbitrators to decide. Some people have problems with the separability concept because it means that arbitrators determine the viability and enforceability of the contract under which they are empowered. On the other hand, the separability principle substantially reduces the likelihood of a party running to court to challenge an arbitration agreement on the eve of arbitration. And now that the AAA, CPR and others are recognizing the authority of arbitrators to handle defenses to the arbitration agreement itself, there is substantially less reason than ever for judicial involvement prior to arbitration.

Procedural issues are for the arbitrator.   Issues regarding the enforceability of the arbitration agreement should be distinguished from the procedural questions that are normally the province of arbitrators in the absence of a con-

---

34. *See* MACNEIL ET AL., *supra* note 3, §§ 15.2–15.3.
35. *See* Revised UAA, *supra* note 30, § 6.

trary agreement.[36] For example, if an agreement provides that an arbitration demand must be filed within thirty days of a certain event, issues regarding the timeliness of a filing will normally be a question for the arbitrator(s) under the usual broad arbitration clause.[37] This approach is consistent with the general principle of liberal enforceability of arbitration agreements under federal and state law, and the principle that arbitrators normally enjoy plenary authority over procedural matters.[38]

Issues relating to third parties

Occasionally, arbitrators are confronted with issues involving third parties who are not signatories to the arbitration agreement under which the arbitrators derive their authority.[39] In the absence of a contractual agreement, the arbitrators have no jurisdiction. With the consent of the parties to the arbitration agreement as well as the third party, the third party may be joined. At the pre-hearing conference, the arbitrators may entertain discussion of:

- the treatment of third parties who want to become part of the arbitration;
- the possibility of consolidating arbitration hearings in a dispute that involves more than one contract;
- the possibility that the arbitrators' lack of jurisdiction over third parties may result in an award that fails to accord meaningful relief;
- the problem of subpoenaing third-party witnesses, especially outside the jurisdiction. (See discussion in Section 4.7.2.)

4.5

What should be included in the timetable and case management plan for arbitration?

By means of pre-hearing conferences or other discussions and the development of pre-hearing orders, effective arbitrators establish a timetable and framework for arbitration. The following discussion treats various key elements of forward planning.

---

36. *See* MACNEIL ET AL., *supra* note 3, §§ 15.1.3–15.1.4.2.
37. *Id.* § 15.1.4.2.
38. *Id.*
39. For a thoughtful discussion of some of these issues, see John M. Townsend, *Nonsignatories and Arbitration: Agency, Alter Ego and Other Identity Issues*, 3 ADR CURRENTS, Sept. 1998, at 19.

1. Setting a timetable

There are several potential benefits associated with the early creation and subsequent maintenance of a schedule for the arbitration.

(1) *A conceptual framework.*   Fixing hearing dates helps to focus attention on the ensuing process of arbitration and its eventual endpoint—the award—which establishes a framework for the activities of the participants.

(2) *A critical path to the award.*   The timetable serves as a critical path that guides the parties' preparation for hearings. Among other things, it sets deadlines for the sharing of statements of position, information exchange and discovery, and any procedural motions.

(3) *A spur to settlement.*   Setting dates for the events of arbitration frequently encourages talk of settlement. As counsel contemplates the possibility of preparing for discovery or presenting the case to the arbitrators, there is often simultaneous consideration of a negotiated alternative. As one Commission member is fond of saying, "Setting tight time limits helps to get rid of cases." Another member echoes this perception:

> Although lawyers don't like to hear it, sometimes the best thing a judge or arbitrator can do is to set a trial date. It really fixes the mind on the realities of the case—what it's going to take to prove your case—and the possibilities of settlement. It also discourages the tendencies of some lawyers to "over-practice" a case—that is, over-doing discovery and other elements of case preparation.

(4) *An opportunity to schedule hearing dates.*   Setting hearing dates at the outset often permits the arbitrators, the parties, and counsel to avoid serious scheduling conflicts and arrange more consecutive or otherwise advantageous hearing dates.

Pre-set time limits

Default limits in commercial rules.   Arbitration procedures sometimes incorporate time limits for the submission of initiating documents and pleadings, the selection of arbitrators, and other activities. Such limits, coupled with default procedures that take over if a party fails to act within the set time, are important to ensure that parties do not unduly delay the process. Under fast track or expedited procedures, the entire arbitration may be conducted in accordance with a fixed timetable.[40]

Problems with unrealistic pre-dispute time limits.   Arbitrating parties sometimes set their own parameters for the rendition of awards (e.g., "Awards must be

---

40. *See, e.g.*, AAA Commercial Procedures, *supra* note 8, §§ E-1–E-10.

rendered within 120 days of the arbitrator's appointment.") One Commission member contends that overall time limits should be negotiated in the original contract, since the requisite cooperation may be lacking in the wake of conflict:

> After a dispute arises, the parties are much less malleable than they are in a pre-dispute setting. Therefore, I encourage parties to include in their contractual pre-dispute arbitration clause an agreement that arbitration awards will be rendered within a certain number of months after the demand is filed, and that they will work with the arbitrators to achieve that goal. That kind of time limit is difficult to negotiate once you have a dispute.

However, pre-arranged time limits sometimes prove unrealistic in light of the circumstances, as exemplified by one Commission member's experience:

> My corporation was party to an $850 million insurance contract which had an arbitration clause that had a neat little provision that any dispute would be arbitrated in 30 days. Now, you can complain that arbitration is supposed to be quick and cheap, but there is no way you're going to decide an $850 million dispute in 30 days! We simply could not enforce the clause as written.

Another Commissioner points out that in addition to raising practical problems, too-short time limits raise potential legal issues:

> If the agreement provides that an arbitration award shall be rendered by such and such a date and it isn't, the argument may be made that the arbitration panel becomes functus officio—essentially, without authority—after that date and no longer has jurisdiction to render an award.[41]

Confronted with these concerns, in one case, parties with an unrealistic contractual time limit found it necessary to renegotiate their whole dispute resolution agreement:

> Prior to commencing a large public construction project, the owner and contractor agreed that arbitration of any disputes would occur within a week after their emergence. When disputes did occur, it became obvious to both parties that their ambitious arrangement was fraught with problems and totally unrealistic. With the assistance of a mediator, they ultimately modified the agreement. The parties' desire for dealing promptly with conflicts arising on the job site was addressed by an arrangement involving periodic mediated discussions regarding job problems. In those situations where a party wished to arbitrate, the parties agreed to establish hearing schedules appropriate to the case.

Where, despite such concerns, the parties decide to establish timetables prior to the emergence of disputes, they should seriously consider giving the arbitra-

---

41. *See* MACNEIL ET AL., *supra* note 3, § 30.3.2 (discussing doctrine of functus officio and termination of arbitrator authority through failure to meet time deadlines).

tor(s) authority to grant extensions of time for good cause. Another alternative is to provide that the parties should use their best efforts to meet an award deadline, but to avoid making the deadline absolute.

Establishing timetables through pre-hearing discussions and orders

Except for the time limits on specified activities in leading arbitration rules, parties usually eschew the use of rigid pre-set timetables in favor of flexible arrangements in which schedules are established by agreement of the parties or at the discretion of the arbitrators.[42]

The key, say many, is to get the arbitrator on board, to broach the subject during the earliest discussions (such as a conference call or pre-hearing conference), discuss the needs of the parties and the special circumstances of the case, and seek consensus on a time frame. In the absence of an agreed-upon time frame, the arbitrators may set deadlines (at least for the specified stages of the case up to and including the hearings). The AAA Commercial Procedures, for example, contemplate that the arbitrators will establish the schedule after discussing the case with the parties, and that the parties will "respond to requests for hearing dates, be cooperative in scheduling . . . and adhere to the schedule."[43] Similarly, CPR Tribunals are "empowered to impose time limits . . . on each phase of the proceeding" after discussing planning and scheduling issues with the parties at pre-hearing conference(s).[44]

A Commission member and frequent arbitrator describes his typical approach:

> In small or medium-sized commercial cases where I am the only arbitrator (other than cases which are already on a fast-track) I often find it appropriate to conduct a conference call with counsel for all parties to discuss the conduct of the arbitration and to make a preliminary schedule for the process. I explain that the best approach is for them to reach mutual consensus on timing issues, as on other procedural matters, but that I will render a decision if necessary. Usually, we are able to work out hearing dates as well as interim milestones. Sometimes we start by discussing prospective hearing dates; other times we begin by talking about how long it will take to conduct discovery. Either way, we discuss where we want to end up, and how we get there. Before concluding the call, I make arrangements for a follow-up call for the purpose of monitoring progress toward the hearing and addressing any problems that may have arisen.

One often-effective case management technique involves setting hearing dates—or even a date for the final award—and then working backwards to

---

42. *See* Stipanowich, *supra* note 1, at 466.
43. AAA COMMERCIAL PROCEDURES, *supra* note 8, §§ R-22, R-24.
44. CPR ARBITRATION RULES, *supra* note 9, Rules 9.2, 9.3.

establish interim milestones.[45] The scheduling of arbitration hearings is treated in greater detail in Chapter 5.

2. Developing a case management plan

The pre-hearing conference should also address a number of management issues for the arbitration process. Clarifying these procedures during the planning stage will give the parties guidelines for preparing materials and help the arbitration process move smoothly.

Written submissions; pre-hearing memoranda

A critical part of arbitration planning involves the scope and timing of pre-hearing briefs and other written submissions. Preliminary memoranda on the legal and factual issues in a case are often of great value to arbitrators in organizing hearing procedures and acting upon discovery issues and other procedural motions.[46] Many arbitrators also emphasize the importance of a pre-hearing exchange of damages calculations and detailed information supporting their request(s) for relief. Two-thirds of those responding to one recent arbitrator survey indicated that they usually order an exchange of detailed claims statements and rebuttals.[47] Most attorneys understand the value of such requirements.[48]

CPR Rule 12.1 sets forth specific guidelines for pre-hearing memoranda covering asserted facts and claims, applicable law and other authorities, requested relief (including the basis for any damages claimed), and statements of the nature and manner of presentation of the evidence, including name, capacity, and subject of testimony of any witnesses to be called and a time estimate for each witness's direct testimony. Arbitrators may alter the format of the presentation as the circumstances dictate.[49]

Among other things, the participants should discuss whether the submissions will be sequential or simultaneous, whether rebuttals will be permitted, and page and format limitations. For example, it may be possible to reduce preparation time and cost by permitting written presentations in an outline format.

Information exchange; discovery

Information exchange is normally an important pre-hearing activity, and arbitrators sometimes facilitate or supervise discovery. The subject of arbitration-related discovery is discussed in Section 4.8 below.

---

45. Gorske, *supra* note 13, at 396.
46. *See id.* at 392.
47. *See* Dean B. Thomson, *Arbitration Theory and Practice: A Survey of AAA Construction Arbitrators*, 23 HOFSTRA L. REV. 137, 142 (1994).
48. More than three-quarters of the attorneys responding to a survey by the ABA Forum on the Construction Industry thought that parties should be required to file detailed pre-hearing statements of claim in cases involving more than $250,000. *See* Stipanowich, *supra* note 1, at 465.
49. CPR ARBITRATION RULES, *supra* note 9, Rule 12.1.

Factual stipulations

Effective arbitrators place great importance on narrowing the issues in dispute. Stipulations of fact and admissions should be strongly encouraged at the pre-hearing stage.[50]

Preliminary motions

Occasionally an arbitrating party will present a request for preliminary relief, such as a motion for a preliminary injunction, or will seek a summary dismissal of claims based on pleadings or other information. Action on such motions may obviate the need for full-blown hearings on the merits and may dictate the pace or scope of discovery. The treatment of preliminary motions is explored in separate sections later in this chapter.

Exhibits

Preparation and exchange of exhibits is a central element of arbitration planning. Considerations may include:

- the time limits for submission of exhibits (which, most Commission members believe, should be several days or weeks prior to the start of hearings);
- the marking or numbering of exhibits (including the possibility of chronological numbering), and the number of copies to be prepared;
- the possibility of joint submissions (which some Commission members find to be a useful way of saving time at the hearing and also a means of encouraging the parties to work together to avoid deluging each other, and the panel, with useless documents);
- the use of photocopies, and the extent to which it may be possible to regard documents as "self-authenticating" and avoid or limit challenges to the authenticity or correctness of photocopies and other documents;
- the consequences of late submission;
- the possibility of reducing voluminous evidence through written summaries, charts, samples, or extracts; and
- the preferred methods of presentation, such as tabbed notebooks.[51]

One Commission member finds it useful to have the parties identify which witness(es) will address each exhibit. Exhibits are treated more extensively in Chapter 5.

---

50. CPR Arbitration Rules, *supra* note 9, Rule 9.3(c).

51. *See* Thomson, *supra* note 47, at 143. Sixty-eight percent of arbitrators responding to a recent survey said they preferred to receive arbitration notebooks, including exhibits, from the parties prior to the hearing.

Inspections or tests

A thorough evidence-taking may require inspections (such as site investigations or inspections of goods) or tests. Discussions at the pre-hearing conference may treat questions of scope and timing as well as initial responsibility for related costs. Such matters are treated more fully in Chapter 5.

Fact witnesses; use of affidavits

Arrangements should be made for the parties to provide advance notice regarding the names of prospective witnesses, the scope of their testimony, and the likely order of their appearance. It should be clarified whether witnesses may remain in the room when not testifying.

The parties might also discuss the use of depositions or affidavits in lieu of live testimony and the arbitrators' treatment of such evidence. See Chapter 5.

Expert witnesses, including panel-appointed experts

Expert witnesses are a common feature of commercial arbitration. See Chapter 5. Pertinent questions for the pre-hearing conference include:

- whether or not the parties intend to call expert witnesses, arrangements for advance notice of the experts' names, and the scope of their testimony;
- whether or not the experts' written report or findings will be introduced into evidence, and, if so, when they will be made available to the other party;
- special arrangements for expert testimony, including the possibility of simultaneous questioning of opposing experts; and
- the appropriateness of arbitrator-appointed experts, the terms of their employment, and the ability of the parties to cross-examine them or challenge their findings.

Conduct of hearings

The arbitration hearing is usually a primary focus of the pre-hearing conference. See Chapter 5 for a treatment of topics relating to hearings. Questions for discussion may include:

- the scheduling of hearings and the parties' reasonable expectations and requirements for speed;
- the sequence in which issues will be addressed and the order of proof;
- the possibility of bifurcation of hearings on liability and damages;
- the scope of opening and closing arguments, including written briefs or memos;
- evidentiary issues, such as whether and to what extent direct testimony may be submitted in writing in lieu of live testimony subject to cross-examination at the hearing and how hearsay evidence will be handled; and
- whether there will be a record of the hearing and, if so, what kind and at whose expense.

Award

Issues that parties may want to discuss relating to the final award include:

- whether the award should contain a breakdown of individual issues; and
- whether the award should include a rationale or explanation.

These issues are discussed at length in Chapter 7.

4.6

Is it possible to obtain interim relief pending the final arbitration award?

It is a truism that "justice delayed is justice denied." Denial of justice occurs when a party is irreparably harmed or loses an effective remedy before a case can come to trial.

Consider the example of a business that depends on a long-term supply contract for all of its fuel requirements, and that is faced with a sudden cutoff of deliveries. Failing other sources of supply, the economic consequences may be dire unless it can force its original supplier to continue to perform pending a trial on the merits. To prevent such irreparable injury, courts sometimes grant preliminary injunctions. Other forms of interim or "provisional" relief include orders attaching assets, imposing liens on property, and directing the submission of a bond for security purposes.[52] All of these approaches may represent critical elements of fairness to those whose rights and remedies are affected.

But what if the agreement contains an arbitration clause? What role, if any, is there for arbitrators in protecting the rights and remedies of a party until a final decision can be reached in arbitration? What role, if any, remains for the courts?

As explained below, arbitrators as well as courts may play a role in structuring provisional relief pending an arbitration award. Generally speaking, arbitrators' ability to grant such relief is a facet of their broad authority to tailor remedies appropriate to the circumstances.[53] To the extent courts intervene to grant provisional relief, it is usually to facilitate and protect the integrity of the arbitration process.[54]

---

52. *See* MACNEIL ET AL., *supra* note 3, ch. 25.
53. *See id.* § 25.3.
54. *See id.*

1. The role of arbitrators

Commercial arbitration rules

Very often, contractual arbitration procedures recognize the authority of arbitrators to render equitable relief.[55] Standard commercial arbitration rules specifically empower arbitrators to render preliminary injunctions and other interim relief. CPR Rule 13 is explicit, for example:

> 13.1 At the request of a party, the Tribunal may take such interim measures as it deems necessary, including measures for the preservation of assets, the conservation of goods or the sale of perishable goods. The Tribunal may require appropriate security as a condition of ordering such measures.

> 13.2 A request for interim measures by a party to a court shall not be deemed incompatible with the agreement to arbitrate or a waiver of that agreement.[56]

AAA Commercial Procedures § R-36 contains very similar language, and also makes clear that the arbitrators may cast such measures in the form of an award.[57]

The AAA Commercial Procedures also incorporate Optional Rules for Emergency Measures of Protection.[58] Such procedures, where adopted by the agreement of the parties, provide an expedited procedure for the appointment of a single emergency arbitrator, a quick hearing, and possible emergency relief in the form of an interim arbitration award pending the constitution of an arbitration panel.

In the absence of explicit provisions

The FAA and state arbitration statutes generally are silent on interim remedies, but standard broad-form commercial arbitration agreements put requests for interim relief within the arbitrators' jurisdiction. This is because, within the scope of the arbitration agreement, arbitrators have plenary power to decide the merits of disputes and fashion appropriate remedies.[59] Therefore, they have inherent authority to issue a preliminary award or order in the nature of a preliminary injunction, order of attachment or other protective order, even if the rules under which the arbitration is conducted are not explicit.[60] See Chapter 7. For example, arbitrators have:

- directed a coal supplier to continue deliveries to a municipal customer pending a final decision as to whether they had a binding contract;[61]
- directed the posting of a bond as security for claims;[62]

55. *See id.*, citing Island Creek Coal Sales Co. v. City of Gainesville, 729 F.2d 1046 (6th Cir. 1984).
56. CPR ARBITRATION RULES, *supra* note 9, Rule 13.
57. *See* AAA COMMERCIAL PROCEDURES, *supra* note 8, § R-36.
58. *Id.* §§ O-1–O-8.
59. *See* MACNEIL ET AL., *supra* note 3, § 36.1.1.
60. *See id.* at § 36.6.1, citing Merrill Lynch, Pierce, Fenner & Smith v. Dutton, 844 F.2d 726 (10th Cir. 1988).
61. Island Creek Coal Sales Co. v. City of Gainesville, 729 F.2d 1046 (6th Cir. 1984).
62. Compania Chilena de Navegacion Interoceania, S.A. v. Norton, Lilly & Co., 652 F. Supp. 1512 (S.D.N.Y. 1987).

- ordered the creation of an escrow account;[63] and
- ordered a reduction in a ship charterer's lien where the underlying claim was clearly overstated and the vessel owner's financial viability was threatened.[64]

2. The role of courts

The role of the courts in granting provisional relief to a party to an arbitration agreement is very limited. Such intervention is viewed as a derogation of the authority of the arbitrator, who is normally in the best position to weigh the need for interim relief against the potential harm to other parties and to the arbitration process. A related concern is that resort to a court may delay arbitration.[65]

Reasons for judicial involvement

Judicial involvement in provisional relief may be necessary or appropriate for one or more of the following reasons:[66]

(1) *Some forms of relief cannot wait for the appointment of arbitrators.* In some situations the need for an immediate order preserving assets or directing continued performance cannot await the appointment of arbitrators. On the other hand, a court may be reluctant to act in the face of an agreement for expedited arbitration.[67] Such concerns are addressed by the AAA Optional Rules for Emergency Measures of Protection, discussed above in Section 4.7.1. Use of these rules, however, requires a special agreement by the parties.

(2) *The law sometimes requires judicial intervention.* In some cases, the law requires resort to the court system for the preservation or vindication of rights and remedies. Examples include filings in bankruptcy, actions to preserve and protect lien rights, and priorities and other rights in collateral.[68]

(3) *The effectiveness of arbitrator-ordered interim relief often depends upon judicial enforcement.* Arbitrators lack the judicial contempt power. An arbitrator's order directing the preservation of assets or

---

63. Pacific Reins. Mgmt. Corp. v. Ohio Reins. Corp., 935 F.2d 1019 (9th Cir. 1991).
64. Southern Seas Navigation, Ltd. v. Petroleos Mexicanos, 606 F. Supp. 692, 694 (S.D.N.Y. 1985).
65. *See id.* at § 36.6.1, 36:56.
66. *See* Macneil et al., *supra* note 3, ch. 25.
67. *See, e.g.*, UPS (New York), Inc. v. Local 804, 698 F.2d 100 (2d Cir. 1983)(case involving collective bargaining agreement).
68. *See* Donald Lee Rome, *A New Approach to ADR for the Financial Services Industry*, 54 Secured Lender, May/June 1998, at 22, 24, 30.

requiring continuing performance pending a final award may be ineffective in the absence of court enforcement of that order.[69]

Limits on judicial grants of provisional relief

Courts are often reluctant to grant interim relief to parties to arbitration agreements for fear of preempting the arbitrators' decision on the merits. But there may be situations where the court's failure to grant interim relief will render any subsequent arbitration award valueless.[70] Despite the silence of the FAA and state arbitration statutes and concerns about court intervention in the arbitration process, there is substantial authority for judicial issuance of preliminary injunctions in appropriate cases,[71] as well as some authority for judicial orders of attachment and other kinds of provisional relief,[72] subject to the standards normally imposed on grants of such relief in court. Respect for the authority of the arbitral tribunal may cause a court to stay its hand where the tribunal could address the request for interim relief. Where the arbitrators have denied such relief, it is extremely unlikely that a court would step in.[73]

Where there is likely to be a need for court-ordered provisional relief in aid of arbitration, it is appropriate to address such issues in the arbitration provision.[74] See Chapter 2.

The concern that an application to court for interim relief might be viewed as a waiver of the right to arbitrate has prompted provisions in standard arbitration rules making clear that such applications should not be so characterized.[75]

Enforcement of arbitral awards granting interim relief

Arbitrators can impose various sanctions, but they lack contempt power. They can enjoin a competitor from soliciting clients from a stolen customer's list, but they cannot police the infraction by sending the wrongdoer to jail.

When arbitrators grant a preliminary injunction or other interim relief and court enforcement is deemed necessary, the arbitrators' order should be presented to the court as an interim award subject to confirmation under applicable federal or state arbitration law.[76]

---

69. *See* Island Creek Coal Sales, *supra* note 61.
70. *See* MACNEIL ET AL., *supra* note 3, §§ 25.1, 25.2.
71. *See* MACNEIL ET AL., *supra* note 3, §§ 25.4.2, 25.5.
72. *See, e.g.*, BancAmerica Commercial Corp. v. Brown, 806 P.2d 897 (Ariz. Ct. App. 1991) (writ of attachment in order to secure a settlement agreement between debtor and creditor); Hughley v. Rocky Mountain Health Maintenance Organization, Inc., 927 P.2d 1325 (Colo. 1996) (preliminary injunction directing HMO to continue chemotherapy treatment pending arbitration award); Salvucci v. Sheehan, 212 N.E.2d 243 (Mass. 1965) (TRO to prevent defendant from conveying or encumbering property pending arbitration). *See generally* MACNEIL ET AL., *supra* note 3, at §§ 25.4.3, 25.5.
73. *See id.* at § 25.1 (discussing factors affecting availability of interim remedies in court).
74. *See* Rome, *supra* note 68.
75. *See, e.g.*, AAA COMMERCIAL PROCEDURES, *supra* note 8, § R-36(c); CPR ARBITRATION RULES, *supra* note 9, Rule 13.2.
76. *See* MACNEIL ET AL., *supra* note 3, § 36.6.1, at 36:55.

Pending revisions to the Uniform Arbitration Act

Pending revisions to the Uniform Arbitration Act (UAA), which is in effect in most states, specifically address some of the foregoing issues. Proposed Section 8 provides that:

(a) Before an arbitrator is appointed and is authorized and able to act, the court, upon motion of a party to an arbitration proceeding and for good cause shown, may enter an order for provisional remedies to protect the effectiveness of the arbitration proceeding to the same extent and under the same conditions as if the controversy were the subject of a civil action.

(b) After an arbitrator is appointed and is authorized and able to act, the arbitrator may issue such orders for provisional remedies, including interim awards, as the arbitrator finds necessary to protect the effectiveness of the arbitration proceeding and to promote the fair and expeditious resolution of the controversy, to the same extent and under the same conditions as if the controversy were the subject of a civil action. After an arbitrator is appointed and is authorized and able to act, a party to an arbitration proceeding may move the court for a provisional remedy only if the matter is urgent and the arbitrator cannot act timely or if the arbitrator cannot provide an adequate remedy.

(c) A motion to a court for a provisional remedy under subsection (a) or (b) does not waive any right of arbitration.[77]

4.7

Is discovery available in arbitration?

The popular understanding once was that there was "no discovery in arbitration." Now, although limitations on discovery still set arbitration apart from court trial, parties will often be granted some discovery in the interest of fairness and efficiency. Rules of leading arbitration institutions and some state statutes governing arbitration make specific reference to discovery. In large, complex commercial cases, discovery is virtually inevitable.

Given that lawyers as well as business persons often associate pre-trial discovery abuse with many of the problems of litigation, why is some discovery frequently permitted in arbitration?

(1) ***Fundamental fairness often requires a sharing of information.*** A party may not possess all of the information necessary to have a complete

---

77. *See* Revised UAA, *supra* note 30, § 8(c).

appreciation of the issues in dispute, or to persuade an arbitrator of the soundness of its position. Although it will often be in the mutual interest of parties to exchange information, one or both may refuse to divulge critical information. Cross-examination of an opponent at the arbitration hearing is a time-consuming and often unsatisfactory substitute.

In the court system, modern discovery rules reflect the rationale that parties should have access to as much information as possible to ensure a fair and informed judgment. Although in arbitration these concerns must be carefully weighed against the important goals of economy, speed, and efficiency, they provide a basis for limited discovery.

(2) ***It is generally fairer and more efficient to conduct discovery prior to hearings.*** The absence of any pre-hearing discovery often has the unintended effect of prolonging hearings. Lacking some of the information in the hands of an adversary, attorneys may conduct long, drawn-out cross-examination. Upon identifying information that may be advantageous to their case, they may ask the arbitrator(s) to order disclosure of the underlying information, and to postpone further proceedings pending that discovery. Thus, carefully supervised, limited discovery may result in more efficiency at the hearing stage. While in some cases discovery still occurs during the course of hearings,[78] it is much more common for arbitrators to direct at least some pre-hearing discovery.

There are substantial differences, however, between pre-trial discovery and discovery in arbitration. In court litigation, discovery is viewed as a wide-ranging sharing of information of various kinds which leads to the uncovering of evidence material to the controversy. In arbitration, the focus is on categories of information—usually documents—that relate to important issues in dispute. A Commission member explains:

> One of the intuitions that underlies the growth of arbitration is that courts have gone way overboard in following the principle of full disclosure, and that there are significant costs associated with obtaining information which is frequently not essential to proving or defending a case.

As the commentary accompanying the CPR Arbitration Rules so aptly explains, "Arbitration is not for the litigator who will 'leave no stone unturned.'"[79] Most arbitrators emphasize document discovery and limit other forms of discovery. (As noted in the following pages, this practice varies with the arbitrator and with the commercial circumstances.)

---

78. *See* Gorske, *supra* note 13, at 394.
79. *See* CPR ARBITRATION RULES, *supra* note 9, Commentary to Rule 11.

1. The role of arbitrators in discovery, document production, and evidence

Provisions of leading arbitration procedures

Leading arbitration rules envision a role for arbitrators in facilitating the exchange of information among arbitrating parties, including some authority to direct production of relevant evidence. CPR Rule 11 states:

> The Tribunal may require and facilitate such discovery as it shall determine is appropriate to the circumstances, taking into account the needs of the parties and the desirability of making discovery expeditious and cost-effective.[80]

AAA Commercial Procedures § R-23 provides:

> (a) At the request of any party or at the discretion of the arbitrator, consistent with the expedited nature of arbitration, the arbitrator may direct (i) the production of documents and other information . . . .
> (b) The arbitrator is authorized to resolve any disputes concerning the exchange of information.[81]

Furthermore, AAA Commercial Procedures § R-33 directs the parties to "produce such evidence as the arbitrator may deem necessary to an understanding and determination of the dispute";[82] arbitrators and other persons authorized by law may "subpoena witnesses or documents . . . upon the request of any party or independently."[83]

The AAA Large, Complex Case Procedures are even more explicit regarding the role of arbitrators in discovery matters, calling for the parties to

> cooperate in the exchange of documents, exhibits and information within [their] control if the arbitrator(s) consider such production to be consistent with the goal of achieving a just, speedy and cost-effective resolution.[84]

The Procedures also authorize arbitrators to direct document discovery, "for good cause shown and consistent with the expedited nature of arbitration," if the parties cannot agree.[85] In appropriate cases, the arbitrators may also direct the taking of depositions or the propounding of interrogatories.

Although parties are free to agree to federal or state court procedures governing discovery, and sometimes do, most Commissioners believe that discovery should be left to the discretion of the arbitrator after consideration of the parties' needs.

A Commission member points out that where discovery is wrongfully withheld, the arbitrator can draw an adverse inference from the withheld information. Often, the threat of such an inference is enough to induce compliance.

---

80. *Id.* Rule 11.
81. AAA Commercial Procedures, *supra* note 8, § R-23.
82. *Id.* § R-33(a).
83. *Id.* § R-33(d).
84. *Id.* § L-5(b).
85. *Id.* § L-5(b).

Authority of arbitrators under federal and state arbitration law

Although the FAA and most state statutes do not contain provisions directly addressing the subject of discovery, under FAA § 7 and its state counterparts, arbitrators have the authority to issue summonses or subpoenas to parties or third parties.[86] FAA § 7 authorizes arbitrators to "summon in writing any person to attend before them or any of them as a witness and in a proper case to bring with him or them any book, record, document, or paper which may be deemed material as evidence in the case." Similarly, UAA § 7 authorizes the issuance of "subpoenas for the attendance of witnesses and for the production of books, records, documents and other evidence . . . ." Nearly two-thirds of arbitrators responding to a recent survey indicated that they "regularly grant parties subpoenas requiring other parties to produce documents."[87]

A few state arbitration statutes specifically authorize arbitrators to subpoena witnesses for a pre-hearing deposition[88] or acknowledge broader discovery powers.[89] As discussed below, however, the FAA and most state statutes are unclear on the subject of subpoenas for depositions, thereby raising a question whether arbitrators can use the subpoena mechanism to direct the production of evidence prior to hearings. As we will see, some court decisions have concluded that there is statutory authority for subpoena depositions. Moreover, there are practical ways of addressing some of these concerns.

Authority of arbitrators regarding information in the hands of third parties

Arbitrators can issue subpoenas for third parties as well as parties to appear at the hearing for the purpose of testifying or presenting needed documentation.[90] Under FAA § 7 and state arbitration law, the arbitral subpoena power is backed by the enforcement authority of courts, subject to a judicial determination that the information sought is relevant and material.[91] Special problems arise as the result of territorial limitations on the arbitral subpoena power, a subject discussed below.

If a third party is directly under the control of a party or closely tied to a party, there are other, more direct ways of encouraging cooperation. One Commission member explains:

> I think I have the power to compel a corporate party to produce an employee. Their investment banker is not in the same position but, being in the ambit of their influence, may be persuaded to give testimony. I think it is appropriate in the latter circumstance to say, as arbitrator, that if you don't produce the investment banker I will have to draw an adverse conclusion.[92]

---

86. Federal Arbitration Act, 9 U.S.C. § 7 (West Supp. 1994) [hereinafter FAA].
87. *See* Thomson, *supra* note 47, at 147–48.
88. *See, e.g.,* CAL. CIV. PROC. CODE §§ 1283, 1282.6 (West 1998).
89. *See* GA. CODE ANN. § 9-9-9(b) (1988).
90. *See* Gorske, *supra* note 13, at 395.
91. *See* MACNEIL ET AL., *supra* note 3, § 34.2.1.2.
92. *See id.* § 34.2.1.6.

2. Depositions of witnesses

Rationales for depositions in arbitration

Despite the general presumption in favor of limited discovery and the general emphasis on document discovery, parties sometimes find it advantageous to conduct a limited number of depositions for the purpose of preserving testimony or saving time at the hearing. Sometimes arbitrators permit a limited number of depositions to give parties early access to key opposing witnesses and to avoid wasting time with "fishing expeditions" at the hearing. One arbitrator recalls that

> [w]hile prehearing discovery depositions are quite unusual (and even unwelcome) in the usual arbitration proceeding, they can be quite useful in the large, complex case. . . . [In one big case of mine] the discovery depositions were helpful in eliminating certain areas of inquiry which would have taken considerable hearing time had the hearing been the only means available for . . . discovery.[93]

Depositions may also help to resolve disputes informally, prior to the arbitration hearing. For that reason, the Commission cautions against pre-dispute agreement to procedural rules that expressly deny arbitrators discretion to order depositions as appropriate. Generally, however, arbitrators should require parties to justify the need for depositions before ordering them.

Provisions in leading arbitration procedures

As discussed above, some standard arbitration procedures explicitly authorize the taking of depositions prior to arbitration, or at least give arbitrators discretion to order depositions. For example, the AAA Optional Procedures for Large, Complex Commercial Disputes state that arbitrators may "upon good cause shown, . . . order the conduct of the deposition of . . . such persons who may possess information . . . necessary to determination of [the case]."[94] Some practitioners interpret this or similar language in an arbitration agreement to authorize arbitrators to issue deposition subpoenas to third parties as well as parties.[95] Others question whether the parties' agreement may give arbitrators subpoena power over non-parties beyond the authority granted them by applicable arbitration statutes.

---

93. *See* Gorske, *supra* note 13, at 395.
94. *See*, e.g., AAA COMMERCIAL PROCEDURES, *supra* note 8, § L-5.
95. *See* Paul M. Lurie, *Arbitral Subpoena Powers and Prehearing Discovery*, ADR CURRENTS, Dec. 1999, at 18, 19 (discussing breadth of subpoena power under AAA Commercial Procedures and other rules). *See also* Amgen, Inc. v. Kidney Center of Delaware Cty., Ltd., 879 F. Supp. 878 (N.D. Ill. 1995) (arbitrator subpoena to third party under arbitration agreement incorporating Federal Rules of Civil Procedure not enforceable beyond territorial limits of district court, though attorney could subpoena third party in another jurisdiction); *dismissed*, 101 F.3d 110; *remanded*, 95 F.3d 562 (7th Cir. 1996).

Authority under arbitration statutes

Because the FAA and most state arbitration statutes do not explicitly authorize arbitrators to subpoena a person to appear at a deposition and because often the statutes imply that arbitrators' subpoena power applies only to an appearance before one or more of the arbitrators, there is doubt about the ability of arbitrators to issue deposition subpoenas to parties or non-parties.[96] Although there is some authority under the FAA enforcing deposition subpoenas[97]—a helpful conclusion from the standpoint of arbitrators trying to manage a large and complex case—there is also authority to the contrary.[98] In *COMSAT Corporation v. National Science Foundation*,[99] for example, the U.S. Court of Appeals for the Fourth Circuit reversed a lower court order directing a non-party to comply with pre-hearing subpoenas ordering it to produce certain documents and the testimony of employees. Said the court:

> Nowhere does the FAA grant an arbitrator the authority to order non-parties to appear at depositions, or the authority to demand that non-parties provide the litigating parties with documents during prehearing discovery. By its own terms, the FAA's subpoena authority is defined as the power of the arbitration panel to compel non-parties to appear "before them;" that is, to compel testimony by non-parties at the arbitration hearing.[100]

The court acknowledged, however, that a federal court might compel a third party to comply with an arbitrator subpoena in circumstances of "particular need or hardship."[101]

Even without issuing a deposition subpoena, arbitrators may be able to accomplish the same objective indirectly by summoning a party or third party to appear, with or without documents, at a scheduled arbitration hearing. If necessary, the hearings might be continued for a time sufficient to permit counsel to review the documents and other information thus produced.[102] Although this approach (which was the traditional one in the pre-discovery days of arbitration) entails a cost to efficiency, the understanding that an arbitrator is prepared to take it may convince parties and non-parties to agree to pre-hearing production.

One experienced arbitrator suggests that:

> [the arbitrators can sometimes facilitate] what amounts to a pre-hearing deposition [of a third party] by use of a subpoena directed to the third party and returnable at his own business location, with attendance of the arbitrator if necessary. Experience shows that parties are often willing

96. *See* MACNEIL ET AL., *supra* note 3, § 34.2.1.5.
97. *See, e.g.*, Meadows Indemnity Co. v. Nutmeg Insur. Co., 157 F.R.D. 45 (M.D. Tenn. 1994); Stanton v. Paine Webber Jackson & Curtis, Inc., 685 F. Supp. 1241 (S.D. Fla. 1985).
98. *See, e.g.*, COMSAT Corp. v. National Science Foundation, 190 F.3d 269 (4th Cir. 1999); Integrated Insur. Co. v. American Centennial Insur., 885 F. Supp. 69 (S.D.N.Y. 1995).
99. 190 F.3d 269 (4th Cir. 1999).
100. *Id.* at 275.
101. *Id.* at 276, 278.
102. *See id.*

to substitute this approach for attendance at the hearing itself, which would perhaps be a less convenient time and location for the third party. Compensation of the third party may be warranted under certain circumstances.[103]

Territorial limits on arbitrator subpoenas; the problem of third parties

Federal and state law typically express territorial limits on arbitral subpoenas. FAA § 7, for example, requires arbitrator-issued subpoenas to be directed and served "in the same manner as subpoenas to appear and testify before the court." At least one court has determined that this makes the arbitral subpoena power coterminous with that of the federal district court for the jurisdiction in which the arbitration is taking place.[104] District court subpoenas to non-parties are subject to geographical limitations set out in Federal Rule of Civil Procedure 45.[105]

How, if at all, may parties to arbitration effectively enforce subpoenas for non-parties outside such territorial limits? Were the action in federal court, there would be the option of filing for a deposition subpoena in the federal district court where the party is to be found, and taking the deposition there.[106] (Similar arrangements may be made in state court actions.) One federal court concluded that there is no equivalent procedure for arbitral subpoenas for extra-territorial depositions under the FAA.[107]

What are concerned parties to do? One long-time observer of commercial arbitration insists that in the majority of cases, those who receive subpoenas—including distant third parties—comply.[108] As previously mentioned, if a distant witness is under the control of a party, it may be possible for the arbitrator to encourage cooperation by threatening to draw adverse inferences from the witness' unwillingness to appear at a hearing or deposition. Some experienced arbitrators suggest that where there is a critical need to acquire information in the hands of a distant third party, the arbitrators may consider temporarily moving the hearing to the jurisdiction where the party resides.

Recent revisions to the UAA address these and other concerns respecting discovery in arbitration by specific provisions for arbitrator-supervised discovery, including depositions.[109]

---

103. *See* Gorske, *supra* note 13, at 395.
104. *See* Commercial Solvents Corp. v. Louisiana Liquid Fertilizer Co., 20 F.R.D. 359 (S.D.N.Y. 1957), discussed in MACNEIL ET AL., *supra* note 3, § 34.2.1.6. *See also Amgen, supra* note 95, at 882.
105. *See* FED. R. CIV. PROC. 45(c)(3)(A)(ii); 45(e).
106. *See* JACK H. FRIEDENTHAL ET AL., CIVIL PROCEDURE § 7.7 n.26 (2d ed. 1993).
107. *See Amgen, supra* note 95.
108. *See* William Slate, President, American Arbitration Association, Letter to Thomas J. Stipanowich, Nov. 5, 1999.
109. *See* Revised UAA, *supra* note 30, § 17.

Flexibility in deposition formats

Special, expedited deposition formats may be useful for particular purposes. One experienced arbitrator finds it advantageous to follow submission of expert reports with depositions. Others place limits on the number of depositions or the time allotted for depositions, or make specific arrangements for the use of depositions in the hearing. See Chapter 5.

3. The role of courts in arbitration-related discovery

The primary role for courts in arbitration-related discovery is in enforcing arbitral subpoenas. In the absence of voluntary compliance, only a court can enforce compliance—and it has some independent discretion in that role.[110]

On the other hand, courts are properly reluctant to initiate discovery in arbitration, viewing judicial action as an invasion of the proper province of the arbitrator.[111] Courts generally initiate discovery only in exceptional circumstances involving potential loss of evidence,[112] or with regard to issues specifically within the purview of the courts such as the enforceability of arbitration agreements and awards.[113]

4. Balancing the parties' need for information and the desire for efficiency and economy

Information exchange in arbitration is complicated by parties' varying discovery needs, and by the tension between the need to ensure fundamental fairness through a sharing of information and the desire for an expeditious, cost-effective pre-hearing process. Although the general expectation is that pre-hearing discovery will be much more limited than in court, every case presents somewhat different requirements for information exchange.

One long-time arbitrator and corporate general counsel speaks of his own experience:

> In a typical case, either the parties have little or no need for discovery, or they informally agree to the necessary exchanges, leaving only a few disputes to be resolved by the arbitrators. In the less typical case, extensive discovery requests may be clearly out of line, and can be refused by the arbitrators without hesitation. [In a particularly large, complicated case, however] the board made an early decision to be liberal on the matter of

---

110. *See* MACNEIL ET AL., *supra* note 3, §§ 34.2.1.2, 34.2.1.3.
111. *See id.* § 34.3.
112. *See id.* § 34.3.2.
113. *See id.* § 34.3.3.

discovery [while closely supervising the process]. . . [since i]f discovery had been more restricted, the hearing would have inevitably been prolonged.[114]

A general approach to information exchange and discovery

Many experienced arbitrators follow a general approach similar to the following.

1. ***Explain the "presumption against extensive discovery."*** Most business parties and arbitrators come to arbitration with a presumption that there will be less discovery—perhaps much less discovery—than in court litigation. This principle is often made manifest by the arbitrators, who place the burden on the parties to provide cogent arguments for obtaining particular information.

   Whatever ground rules arbitrators believe appropriate (within the limits of the parties' agreement and the circumstances) should be clearly conveyed to the parties early on. One Commissioner cautions:

   > At the first pre-hearing conference, my experience is that arbitrators usually set dates for document requests, objections to requests, negotiation of objections between the parties and presentation of unresolved discovery disputes to the arbitrators. When the latter are ultimately put before the arbitrators, however, it is not unusual to find one side thinking it is entitled to document production under the Federal Rules, while the other side thinks it is required to produce only the contract on which the claim is based. The waste of time that can result from such confusion is enormous. It saves a lot of time down the road to delineate at the first pre-hearing conference precisely what the standards are going to be for the scope of document production. Personally, I apply a standard far more confined than the Federal Rules and generally limit production to documents which are directly relevant to a significant issue in the case.

2. ***Seek consensus.*** It is best if the parties can agree on the nature and scope of discovery rather than submitting such issues to the arbitrators.[115] In many cases the parties will have relatively few discovery needs, or may be able to agree to exchange information informally. As a result, usually there are relatively few discovery issues for the arbitrators to resolve.

3. ***Emphasize document discovery.*** Many arbitrators believe that as a general principle, arbitrator-ordered information exchange should be limited to document discovery.[116] Many commercial arbitrators see no useful function for interrogatories and are reluctant to order depositions. As

---

114. *See* Gorske, *supra* note 13, at 391.
115. Poppleton, *supra* note 12, at 7.
116. A survey of hundreds of arbitrators of construction disputes revealed that while 74% of those responding usually ordered exchanges of project-related documents, only about one-third thought other types of discovery were helpful or appropriate. *See* Thomson, *supra* note 47, at 142–43. Similar results were obtained in an earlier survey of attorneys with arbitration experience. *See* Stipanowich, *supra* note 1, at 465.

explained above, however, other arbitrators find that limited use of depositions can be effective in saving time at the hearing or preserving testimony.

4. ***Set tight time limits, adhere to a schedule.***   As noted throughout this chapter and in Chapter 5, it is critically important for arbitrators to set and keep time limits. Nowhere is this more crucial than in the context of discovery. There should be an overall time limit for information exchange, with a deadline some time before the hearing. Regular conference calls provide a good mechanism for supervising discovery.

4.8

Are claims ever summarily dismissed in arbitration?

Arbitration commences with very general pleadings offering little detail regarding the issues in dispute or the positions of the parties. As a rule, therefore, dismissal of claims on the pleadings will be inappropriate in arbitration. As the parties exchange information and develop more detailed positions, however, there may be some point at which issues have ripened sufficiently for arbitrators to act knowledgeably upon a motion for summary judgment. At such time it may be possible to determine that a party will be unable to bear the burden of proving a case in the arbitration hearing, and to render an award in favor of the opposing party.[117]

Provisions of leading arbitration rules

AAA Commercial Procedures § R-32, while not addressing dispositive motions specifically, permits arbitrators to "direct the parties to focus their presentations on issues the decision of which could dispose of all or part of the case."[118] More explicit treatment of dispositive motions may be found in AAA Construction Industry Dispute Resolution Procedures § R-29, which provides:

> The arbitrator shall entertain motions, including motions that dispose of all or part of a claim, or that may expedite the proceedings, and may also make preliminary rulings and enter interlocutory orders.[119]

Rule 16 of the JAMS Comprehensive Arbitration Rules and Procedures is direct, stating that "[t]he Arbitrator(s) may hear and determine a Motion for Summary

---

117. *Cf.* Celotex Corp. v. Catrett, 477 U.S. 317, 317 (1986) (interpreting Federal Rule of Civil Procedure 56).
118. AAA COMMERCIAL PROCEDURES, *supra* note 8, § R-32.
119. AMERICAN ARBITRATION ASSOCIATION, CONSTRUCTION INDUSTRY DISPUTE RESOLUTION PROCEDURES, § R-29 (Jan. 1, 1999).

Disposition of a particular claim or issue, either by agreement of all interested Parties or at the request of one Party, provided other interested Parties have reasonable notice to respond to the Request."[120] The rule sets parameters for the establishment of a briefing schedule and record, stating that "[o]rdinarily, oral argument will not be allowed, unless all Parties or the Arbitrator(s) so request."[121]

In the absence of explicit provisions

Although some arbitration rules do not specifically address the authority of arbitrators to dispose of claims summarily, such authority is consistent with the broad discretion accorded arbitrators by prevailing arbitration law. A number of courts have upheld arbitrators' summary disposition of cases even though federal and state arbitration laws do not specifically address the subject.[122]

Many arbitrators, however, are reluctant to dispose summarily of some or all of the issues in a case without granting the parties an opportunity to present live evidence—in some cases, their entire case. This reluctance may be founded on a sense that the parties are entitled to their "day in court" coupled with a concern that arbitrators should not make a definitive ruling without hearing all the evidence.

If a dispositive ruling is challenged in court, the standard of judicial review will probably be FAA § 10(c), which provides for the vacating of an award where the arbitrator was "guilty of misconduct . . . in refusing to hear evidence pertinent and material to the controversy," or its state counterparts.[123] While such challenges are rarely granted, decisions under the FAA indicate that the ultimate question for the court is whether the challenging party received a "fundamentally fair hearing"[124]—that is, whether there has been adequate "notice, opportunity to be heard and to present relevant and material evidence and argument before the decision makers."[125] Similar standards will apply under state law. Whether or not an award based on the submission of briefs, on oral argument, affidavits, or live testimony stands or falls depends on meeting these fundamental requisites.

In one much-publicized decision, a California appellate court upheld an arbitrator's granting of a motion for summary adjudication on a question of contract interpretation.[126] The court found that although neither the California arbitration statute nor the applicable arbitration rules explicitly authorized summary adjudication, the arbitrator had implicit authority to rule on such

---

120. JAMS COMPREHENSIVE ARBITRATION RULES AND PROCEDURES, Rule 16 (1999).

121. *Id.*

122. *See, e.g.*, Intercarbon Bermuda, Ltd. v. Caltex Trading & Transp. Corp., 146 F.R.D. 64 (S.D.N.Y. 1993); Schlessinger v. Rosenfeld, Meyer & Susman, 47 Cal. Rptr. 2d 650 (Cal. Ct. App. 1995); Stifler v. Seymour & Weiner, 488 A.2d 192 (1985); Pegasus Constr. Corp. v. Turner Constr. Co., 929 P.2d 1200 (1997).

123. FAA, *supra* note 86, § 10; *see also* MACNEIL ET AL., *supra* note 3, § 8.3.5.

124. *See* MACNEIL ET AL., *supra* note 3, ch. 8.

125. Prudential Securities, Inc. v. Dalton, 929 F. Supp. 1411, 1417 (N.D. Okla. 1996), citing Robbins v. Day, 954 F.2d 679, 685 (11th Cir.), *cert. denied*, 506 U.S. 870 (1992).

126. Schlessinger v. Rosenfeld, Meyer & Susman, 47 Cal. Rptr. 2d 650 (Cal. Ct. App. 1995).

motions. Furthermore, although arbitrating parties are entitled to a "hearing," this does not necessarily include an oral presentation or live testimony, or an opportunity to cross-examine witnesses—merely an opportunity to present one's case. Said the court, "In a case where a legal issue or defense could possibly be resolved on undisputed facts, the purpose of the arbitration process would be defeated by precluding a summary judgment or summary adjudication motion and instead requiring a lengthy trial."[127] Under the circumstances, the court found that the arbitrators had provided an adequate hearing (which, in the case of a question of law, was accomplished by permitting briefings and argument on points of law). Although the court urged caution in the use of summary procedures in arbitration, it concluded that the propriety of such action "depend[s] upon a variety of factors, including the nature of claims and defenses, the provisions of the arbitration agreement, the rules governing arbitration, the availability of discovery, and the opportunity to conduct adequate discovery before making or opposing a motion."[128]

In another case, however, an award summarily dismissing a securities broker's claim of fraud against his former employer was vacated on fairness grounds.[129] The reviewing court found that the arbitrators had rejected the claim on its face despite the fact that the claimant had raised factual issues, and had denied the claimant an opportunity to present evidence supporting the allegations he raised or to compel production of documents relevant to the issues.

Although the decisions encourage caution in the summary adjudication of issues, arbitrators should not shy from addressing clearly dispositive issues upon a proper motion. For example, there may be procedural or jurisdictional issues or a clear statute of limitations that, if applicable, would dispose of a case (or part of a case) without the necessity of a full-blown presentation on the merits.

Recent revisions to the Uniform Arbitration Act

Recent revisions to the UAA specifically treat the subject of summary adjudication by arbitrators:

> An arbitrator may decide a request for summary disposition of a claim or particular issue by agreement of all interested parties or upon request of one party to the arbitration proceeding if that party gives notice to all other parties to the arbitration proceeding and the other parties have a reasonable opportunity to respond.[130]

The proposed language has been the focus of much debate. Some argue that the provision will encourage unhelpful motion practice and is unnecessary in light of the fact that arbitration is already a relatively speedy alternative to court hearings and that all parties should have the ability to present their cases on the merits. Others counter that summary adjudication procedures may avoid

127. *Id.* at 656.
128. *See id.* at 660.
129. *See* Prudential Securities, Inc. v. Dalton, 929 F. Supp. 1411 (N.D. Okla. 1996).
130. *See* Revised UAA, *supra* note 30, § 15(b).

unwarranted delay or expense by making evidentiary hearings unnecessary. This is most important, they argue, in complex cases that involve significant pre-hearing discovery.[131]

4.9
How should hearings be organized?

Arbitrators are given a high degree of discretion in organizing and managing hearings under both arbitration law and institutional rules. Experienced arbitrators agree that the parties' satisfaction with the process is dependent upon good planning and ongoing management by the arbitrators. The organization and management of arbitration hearings is given detailed treatment in Chapter 5.

4.10
What should be the format of the arbitration award?

Arbitrators have the authority to tailor remedies suitable to the situation. Unless there are agreements to the contrary, arbitrators generally have as much leeway as a court in granting relief. Chapter 7 covers the subject of arbitration awards in further detail.

4.11
What other matters may need to be addressed during the pre-hearing process?

1. Rules for arbitration

Arbitration usually occurs pursuant to a pre-dispute arbitration clause that incorporates institutional arbitration rules. In the rare event that the parties have not agreed upon such arbitration rules, the source and nature of governing proce-

---

131. *See id.*, Reporter's Comments.

dures must be discussed. If nothing else, the parties and the arbitrators should discuss the authority of the arbitrators to establish basic rules for the hearing.

In the more likely event that the parties' agreement incorporates standard arbitration rules, there may still be good reason to discuss them. The parties should consider whether to modify or waive certain standard provisions in the interest of better serving their specific needs.[132]

2. Place of arbitration

If the parties have not already agreed upon a location for the hearings or assigned that determination to an arbitration institution, they will need to address the matter at the pre-hearing conference. The parties may also wish to consider special arrangements for site visits and other meetings outside the place designated for arbitration.

One Commission member uses information technology to conduct what he describes as a "placeless" arbitration—one which takes place over electronic media and not in a hearing room. The scenario may raise questions about what is the place of the arbitration for legal purposes—which is an important question because the prevailing law may provide important interstitial rules. This is becoming an issue in international arbitration because the *lex loci fori* is important for choice of law purposes and for the purpose of enforcing awards under the 1958 New York Convention on Enforcement of Foreign Arbitral Awards.[133] One possibility is for the parties to provide that for such purposes, the place of arbitration shall be deemed to be where the arbitrator resides or some other specified location.

3. Language of arbitration; interpreter

Although the issue is much less likely to arise in an arbitration within the U.S. than in an arbitration outside the U.S., there may be a need to agree upon the language in which the arbitration will be conducted. It may also be necessary to deal with the selection and cost of an interpreter.

4. Administrative or ancillary services

Arrangements to use the services of an arbitration institution, if any, are normally made prior to the appointment of arbitrators. Even in such cases, however, it

---

132. *See* Tom Arnold, Arbitration Clause Checklist of Considerations (Apr. 18, 1998).

133. The New York Convention applies to arbitral awards "made only in the territory of another [state adopting the Convention]." United Nations Convention on the Recognition and Enforcement of Arbitral Awards, U.N. Doc. E/Conf. 26/9 Rev. 6/10 Article I (1958).

may be necessary or appropriate to discuss the role of the institution in facilitating the arbitration process (for example, arranging conference calls, procuring meeting facilities, conveying correspondence among the parties and the arbitrators, and handling fees and expenses). Often, such matters will be discussed with the arbitration institution's representatives prior to pre-hearing conferences.

5. Deposits for fees and costs

Under the rules of some arbitration institutions, arrangements regarding arbitration-related fees and expenses are handled by an institutional representative and not by the arbitrators. In other cases, the payment of fees and costs should be addressed. The discussion should include a decision on the amounts to be deposited, an understanding regarding their management (such as arrangements for an escrow account) and the possibility of supplementary deposits. See Chapter 3.

6. Confidentiality

Discussions at the pre-hearing conference should include which individuals will be permitted in the hearing room, and whether witnesses will be required to stay outside the hearing room before testifying. Such rules may not make much sense given the current state of technology which permits full transcripts within hours of the hearing, unless the arbitrator imposes limits on the use of the transcript. Privacy concerns may necessitate an agreement respecting the confidentiality of certain evidence or of the proceedings. See Chapter 6.

7. Routing of written communications among the parties and the arbitrators

The rules of some arbitration institutions provide for written communications among the parties to be channeled through a case manager or case administrator in the interest of minimizing ex parte communications. Sometimes, participants agree to eliminate this intermediate step in the interest of efficiency, provided that all parties receive the correspondence.

Under some commercial arbitration rules, parties are required to file materials with the arbitration institution, which then forwards them to the arbitrators.[134] The purpose of such "screened communications" is to eliminate direct contact between individual parties and the arbitrators outside the hearing

---

134. *See, e.g.,* AAA COMMERCIAL PROCEDURES, *supra* note 8, § R-20(a).

room. As one experienced arbitrator notes, however, "In a large, complex case, this approach simply does not work."[135] Often, the parties agree to file papers directly with the arbitrator(s) (frequently by fax or overnight mail) while simultaneously serving copies on the other party.

Commission members raise a note of caution regarding the practice of direct communications between parties and arbitrators. No ex parte oral communication should occur and both parties should receive copies of any written communications at roughly the same time. Where there are party-appointed arbitrators (treated in Chapter 3), it may be critical to prohibit unilateral communications between a party and a party-appointed arbitrator.[136]

8. Fax, e-mail, and other electronic forms of communication

Today, it is essential to consider the developing possibilities of telephonically transmitted facsimiles (fax), e-mail, magnetic or optical disks, and other forms of electronic communication. Such mechanisms may substantially reduce communication time and/or cost.

Purely electronic forms of communication may also reduce the volume of paper with which parties and arbitrators must contend. However, most participants are likely to insist upon a paper "backup" for electronic documentation. The parties should discuss these matters with the arbitrators.

---

135. Gorske, *supra* note 13, at 393.
136. *See, e.g.,* AAA COMMERCIAL PROCEDURES, *supra* note 8, § R-20(b).

The Hearing

CHAPTER **5**

Chapter Summary

Effective arbitrators actively manage hearings and function as role models for other participants. They make expectations clear at the outset and simplify, clarify, and prioritize issues.

Effective parties and advocates appreciate the differences between arbitration and court trial, including the relatively broad authority and expertise of arbitrators. They are well prepared, act civilly and cooperatively, are not overly argumentative, and tailor their case presentation to the arbitrators' expertise.

Forward planning and careful ongoing management are critical to establishing and maintaining a schedule for arbitration. Arbitration hearings should be scheduled with as few interruptions as possible. Arbitrators should mix firmness with reasonable flexibility in scheduling. Where possible, they should anticipate potential problems and seek creative solutions so that delays due to changing circumstances can be minimized. The absence of a party does not mandate canceling a hearing (and declaring a party in default), but if a party fails to attend without good cause after due notice the arbitrator and remaining party(ies) may proceed with the hearing.

The Hearing

5.1

What roles can arbitrators play in assuring that hearings will be conducted fairly, efficiently, and civilly?

In arbitration, evidentiary hearings represent the "main event." The presentation of the case before the arbitration tribunal is the central focus of participants' energies and, for most, the primary determinant of their perspective of the arbitration experience.

As stated in Chapter 4, while substantial evidence suggests that most users perceive of arbitration as a relatively speedy and efficient path to justice, many parties still voice complaints about what they view as unnecessary delays.[1] During hearings, as in the pre-hearing period, concerns about scheduling delays, disruptions, and procedural inefficiencies must be balanced against fairness concerns—which federal and state statutes guarantee.[2]

The law governing arbitration provides only the most general parameters for the conduct of hearings.[3] Even leading arbitration rules, while more specific than applicable statutes and their judicial interpretations, leave considerable discretion to arbitrators and, often, room for choice by participants.

1. Active management

Effective arbitrators actively manage the hearing

Just as the judge is the manager of proceedings in court, the arbitrator controls the arbitration hearing. In some respects, given the degree of discretion accorded them under arbitration law and leading institutional rules, arbitrators enjoy even greater authority than judges over hearings. Commission members agree that the experience of arbitrating parties' satisfaction with the process directly depends upon the willingness of arbitrators to use their authority effectively.

A frequently cited article aimed at arbitrators in large, complex commercial cases advises that to achieve the goals of "expeditious, economical, and just determination of disputes, . . . arbitrators should not be passive, but rather should manage the conduct of proceedings with a firm hand."[4] Even in arbitra-

---

1. *See, e.g.*, Michael Segalla, *Survey: The Speed and Cost of Complex Commercial Arbitrations*, 46 ARB. J. 12, 14–15 (1991).

2. *See generally* IAN R. MACNEIL, RICHARD E. SPEIDEL & THOMAS J. STIPANOWICH, FEDERAL ARBITRATION LAW: AGREEMENTS, AWARDS & REMEDIES UNDER THE FEDERAL ARBITRATION ACT chs. 32–37 (1994) [hereinafter MACNEIL ET AL.].

3. *See id.*

4. Allen Poppleton, *The Arbitrator's Role in Expediting the Large and Complex Commercial Case*, 36 ARB. J. 6, 7 (1981). *See also* William L. D. Barrett, *Arbitration of a Complex Commercial Case: Practical Guidelines for Arbitrators and Counsel*, 41 ARB. J. 15 (1986).

tion, the author explains, parties do not have an absolute right to present their cases in whatever manner they please, with the arbitrator as a mere umpire.[5] Many Commission members echo this view, including one arbitrator with considerable experience on the bench:

> The arbitration process needs to be managed. One of the advantages of arbitration is informality, but "informal" does not mean out of control. Arbitration has been criticized [in cases where] ... the hearings took too long because the arbitrators didn't enforce starting times, length of recesses and adjournments. The hearing itself, like all other aspects of the process, should be disciplined. I don't mean arbitrary or autocratic. The arbitrators should control the hearings, insist on starting at the agreed time and put in full days.

In the words of another Commissioner:

> I have not had problems with "civility" among lawyers or parties in arbitration. Part of the reason, I believe, is that I have always considered it my job (whether acting alone or with other panel members) to "grab the bull by the horns" immediately and keep control of events. After all, an arbitration typically carries with it all of the "baggage" of litigation, namely, strong-willed parties and lawyers, strong desires to win and all of the elements involved in sometimes nasty disputes. My experience is that parties (and their lawyers) expect arbitrators to act with authority and professionalism.

These realities are reflected in the AAA Commercial Dispute Resolution Procedures, which state:

> Arbitrators shall take such steps as they may deem necessary or desirable to avoid delay and to achieve a just, speedy and cost-effective resolution of Large, Complex Commercial Cases.[6]

Similarly, the CPR Non-Administered Arbitration Rules provide that "the Tribunal may conduct the arbitration in such manner as it shall deem appropriate"[7] and they empower arbitrators to ensure that proceedings are conducted "as economically and expeditiously as possible."[8]

Although effective management is most critical in big cases, it is also important in the broad run of commercial arbitrations.[9] As discussed in Chapter 4, active management begins well before the first hearing, with the creation of an arbitration timetable, facilitation of information exchange, and other events that help set the stage for hearings. As explained further below, "active" arbitra-

---

5. *See* Poppleton, *supra* note 4, at 7.

6. AMERICAN ARBITRATION ASSOCIATION, COMMERCIAL DISPUTE RESOLUTION PROCEDURES, § L-5 (Jan. 1, 1999) [hereinafter AAA COMMERCIAL PROCEDURES].

7. CPR INSTITUTE FOR DISPUTE RESOLUTION, RULES FOR NON-ADMINISTERED ARBITRATION, Rule 9.1 (Rev. 2000) [hereinafter CPR ARBITRATION RULES].

8. *Id.* Rule 9.2.

9. *See* AAA COMMERCIAL PROCEDURES, *supra* note 6, § R-32 (describing managerial role of arbitrators in proceedings under standard arbitration rules).

tors schedule hearings for the presentation of evidence in the manner most conducive to efficiency as well as fairness. They establish the order of presentation and encourage the use of presentation formats (including those incorporating new technologies) that aid in the meaningful presentation of the case in the shortest possible time.

At the same time, effective arbitrators remain vigilant for and do their best to anticipate emerging problems. They also help arrange creative solutions that avoid unnecessary disruptions to the hearing schedule. For example, becoming aware that a witness may be unavailable for an afternoon session, an arbitrator may seek the parties' assistance in developing a contingency plan that involves taking a witness out of order or tending to other business. Other examples are provided in the following pages.

Effective arbitrators do not simply act as passive receptacles for the receipt of evidence, to avoid having to deal with evidentiary objections. Rather, they explain their guidelines for the admission of evidence—along with the rationale for those guidelines. Specific examples are discussed below.

Effective arbitrators also recognize that in the interest of gaining a complete understanding of the issues and the facts, it may be appropriate for the arbitrator to put questions to witnesses after the advocates have finished their questioning. Such actions can help arbitrators clarify points and alert the parties to their questions and concerns.[10]

Finally, most commercial parties and attorneys are aware that bad behavior during a hearing is counterproductive and most Commission members have had little difficulty maintaining civility in the hearing room. Nevertheless, arbitrators must take great care to deal decisively with disruptive or discourteous behavior and not to let things get out of control. This can happen fairly quickly: if it is perceived that one party "got away" with certain behavior, the other party may feel obliged to reciprocate, and will be sensitive to what is perceived as unequal treatment. Such behavior should be stopped immediately with a rule equally and emphatically enforced. ("There shall be no cross-talk; all remarks shall be directed to the tribunal.") In rare cases, the arbitrator may have to adjourn the hearing and call in counsel. (In one case, where the parties were putting pressure on the lawyers to "be tough," with consequent frequent disruptions in the hearing, an experienced arbitrator recalls summoning the lawyers and threatening to resign if they did not modify their behavior. They complied.) In extreme cases, a party's lack of cooperation may justify some form of sanction. Such options, which include cost-shifting, are discussed below.

Arbitrators as role models

As the foregoing discussion indicates, leadership flows from the arbitrator. In many cases, respect for the arbitrator goes a long way toward establishing standards for cooperation in the hearing room. In the case of a three-member panel,

10. *See* Barrett, *supra* note 4, at 20.

much depends upon the character and qualifications of the chair. CPR Rule 9.1 makes the chair "responsible for the organization of the arbitral conferences and hearings and arrangements with respect to the functioning of the Tribunal."[11] The CPR Commentary acknowledges that

> [t]he efficiency of the proceeding will depend in large part on the chair's taking the lead in asserting the Tribunal's control over critical aspects of the procedure, including the setting of time limits as authorized by Rule 9.2.[12]

An arbitrator's actions often speak louder than words. If the arbitrator regularly emphasizes the prime importance of maintaining hearing schedules and backs that up by consistent action, such as starting hearings on time and extending hearings into the evening when necessary to conclude the examination of a witness, other participants will often adopt a similar attitude. If, on the other hand, an arbitrator routinely starts hearings late or ends them early to attend to other business, the parties and their attorneys are likely to conclude that such behavior is acceptable and follow suit.

The parties' most basic expectation is that the arbitrator will be fair and impartial in the conduct of the case. Perceptions of fairness and impartiality hinge primarily on the statements, actions, and demeanor of arbitrators during the hearing. Leading commercial arbitration rules make explicit the notion that ex parte contact between arbitrators and parties should be avoided,[13] but arbitrators must be engaged in the proceedings and must listen actively and respectfully to the parties' presentations. Although awards are rarely reversed because of arbitrator inattention or disrespectful attitude toward parties or witnesses,[14] such behavior can undermine parties' respect for the process and the award.

As discussed in Chapter 3, many Commission members have concerns regarding selection procedures in which the parties appoint two members of a three person arbitration panel.[15] Although many of these "party-arbitrators" attempt to fulfill their arbitral office with integrity, many situations arise in which party-arbitrators' relationship with the affiliated party has a negative impact on the arbitration. In Chapter 3, proposals are advanced for addressing these concerns by limiting ex parte contact between party-arbitrators and their appointing parties after the beginning of arbitration, or even by setting up "screened" appointment procedures in which the arbitrators are unaware of who appointed them. In the absence of such safeguards, the participants must be aware of the potential pitfalls of "partisan" party-arbitrators and should commit to avoiding them. At the very least, the chair of the arbitration panel should seek commitment from both party-arbitrators to cooperate in setting and maintaining the hearing schedule, maintaining decorum in the hearing

---

11. CPR ARBITRATION RULES, *supra* note 7, Rule 9.1.
12. *Id.* Commentary to Rule 9.
13. AAA COMMERCIAL PROCEDURES, *supra* note 6, § R-20; CPR ARBITRATION RULES, *supra* note 7, Rule 7.4.
14. *See* MACNEIL ET AL., *supra* note 2, § 32.3.1.
15. *See id.* § 28.4.

room, and exhibiting civility toward other arbitrators and participants. (Such expectations are consistent with the Code of Ethics for Arbitrators in Commercial Disputes and prevailing arbitration law.[16])

2. Making expectations clear

From the earliest contact with the parties, as explained in Chapter 4, effective commercial arbitrators make deliberate efforts to communicate to the parties their mutual expectations of the arbitration process. Because most commercial arbitration procedures leave considerable room for arbitral judgment (informed in many cases by discussion among the participants), there is a need for clarification on various points of procedure, such as the handling of hearsay, burdens of proof,[17] the arbitrator's role in questioning, and other evidentiary matters.

3. Maintaining the focus

Although the pre-hearing process may help to simplify, clarify, and prioritize the issues in dispute, effective arbitrators keep the participants focused on the issues during evidentiary hearings:

> The arbitrator must . . . direct the parties to the real issues and each party's position with respect to them. The arbitrator must ensure that the parties do not become sidetracked on minor or irrelevant issues which will not materially influence the outcome of the proceeding.[18]

Arbitrators may keep the parties focused by utilizing techniques such as periodic summations, pointed questions to counsel or witnesses, and other techniques discussed in Section 5.4.

4. A subject for training

Commission members generally concur that issues related to controlling the hearing should be a regular part of the training of commercial arbitrators.

---

16. *See id.* § 28.4.5.
17. *See* Robert C. Field & Robert W. Robertson, *The Hearing, in* THE ALTERNATIVE DISPUTE RESOLUTION PRACTICE GUIDE, § 12.17, at 23 (Bette J. Roth et al., eds., 1993).
18. *See* James J. Myers, *10 Techniques for Managing Arbitration Hearings*, 51 DISPUTE RES. J. 28 (1996).

Case Study
An Arbitrator's Guideposts for Effective Case Management[19]

In one multi-million-dollar case, the parties estimated that more than 110 hearing days over a two-year period would be required to present their case. The arbitrators insisted on time-saving procedures, and as a result the case was heard in nine hearing days and the award was rendered within eight months of the panel's appointment. An arbitrator in the case attributed the results to a number of actions by the arbitrators, including:

1. Calling a pre-hearing conference immediately after appointment and establishing ground rules for the hearing.
2. Explaining to the parties that cooperation in the exchange of information would be expected, and that the arbitrators would immediately resolve conflicts regarding production upon request.
3. Rigorously scheduling continuous, uninterrupted hearings over a designated period of days.
4. Insisting on long hearing days.
5. Requiring the parties to submit a detailed factual brief or synopsis of claims or defenses in advance of hearing.
6. Arranging the self-authentication of documents wherever possible.
7. Requiring parties to provide each other with a list of witnesses to be called, in order of expected presentation, with a synopsis of issues on which each will testify.
8. Permitting testimony from "secondary" witnesses to come in through depositions or affidavits, subject to the right of cross-examination.
9. Requiring the parties to pre-submit written biographies of witnesses to avoid live examination of background information.
10. Encouraging the parties to use charts, graphs, and other summaries.
11. Warning against and cutting off repetitive or cumulative testimony and cross-examination.
12. Restricting argument to designated periods, such as the post-hearing briefs.

---

19. *See generally* Poppleton, *supra* note 4.

5.2

How can parties and advocates function most effectively in arbitration hearings?

1. Appreciating the realities of arbitration

Surveys of commercial arbitrators, lawyers, and business participants often reflect dissatisfaction with what they perceive to be inappropriate courtroom tactics in arbitration—tactics they see as a leading cause of delay or disruption.[20] Skillful advocates and perceptive clients understand that effective representation in arbitration requires sensitivity to the following realities of out-of-court adjudication:

(1) arbitration is *not* court trial, and assumptions and expectations brought from the courtroom may be misplaced in arbitration;

(2) under applicable law and the rules governing the hearing, arbitrators have considerable flexibility in handling evidentiary objections and making other rulings; and

(3) the tribunal often includes laymen, not necessarily attorneys, who may have pertinent expertise and bring with them particular perspectives on the issues in dispute.

2. Effective and ineffective arbitration techniques

Dean Thomson conducted a survey of arbitrators regarding their experiences and attitudes about advocacy that resulted in some useful guideposts for advocates in arbitration.[21] The arbitrators were asked to describe the attributes of an effective advocate in arbitration, and then to describe those of an ineffective advocate.[22] Table 5.A lists the characteristics they most often mentioned.

---

20. *See* Thomas J. Stipanowich, *Rethinking American Arbitration*, 63 IND. L.J. 425, 473 (1988)(citing several studies).

21. *See* Dean B. Thomson, *Arbitration Theory and Practice: A Survey of AAA Construction Arbitrators*, 23 HOFSTRA L. REV. 137 (1994).

22. *See generally id.*

Table 5.A
Characteristics of Effective and Ineffective Advocates

Effective advocates are:	Ineffective advocates are:
Brief and concise	Verbose and redundant
Well-prepared	Unprepared and disorganized
Organized	
Knowledgeable about the law	Ignorant of the facts of the case
and the facts	Ignorant of pertinent commercial
	norms or practices
	Unfamiliar with arbitration
Clear and simple in their presentations	
Honest in their assessments of the	Likely to ignore harmful facts or not to
strengths and weaknesses of the case	admit fault
Able to focus on key issues	Too quick to make legal or technical
	objections
Calm, professional, and courteous	Loud, offensive, combative, and uncivil

Table 5.B
Effective and Ineffective Advocacy Techniques

Effective techniques	Ineffective techniques
Focusing on facts through witness testimony	
Clear, orderly, well organized, logical and easy-to-follow presentations	Excessive repetition of testimony
	Unprepared attorneys and witnesses
	Argumentative exchanges
	Irrelevant testimony or focus
Use of photos, pictures, or videos	Too many exhibits and too much
Use of graphics and other visual aids	information with inadequate
	organization
Simple, direct, straightforward	Emotional, theatrical presentations
presentation with little embellishment	Distorted or biased presentations
or artifice	of facts
	Harrassing, abusive, or hostile cross-examination
Brief and concise presentations	Rambling, disorganized presentations
Distribution of notebooks with exhibits well organized, tabbed, and easily accessible during testimony	
Written or oral summaries at the opening of the hearing	

The arbitrators were also asked to identify advocacy techniques which they viewed as particularly effective or ineffective.[23] Their responses (shown in Table 5.B) echo their earlier answers.

As the foregoing suggests, the preparation, strategies, and demeanor of attorneys can have a major impact on the response of the arbitration tribunal. Further thoughts on effective case presentation, offered by Commission members, are detailed in the sections that follow.

Being prepared

In arbitration as in court, there is no substitute for effective preparation. Effective preparation means not only having a thorough understanding of all aspects of the case, factual and legal, but also considering how to make the clearest and most meaningful presentation to the arbitrators. The latter often includes a well-organized "arbitration notebook" which serves as the framework for presentation at the hearing—a subject which is discussed below.

On the other hand, some advocates make the mistake of believing that because arbitration is less formal than the courtroom, it is unnecessary to "sweat the details" in preparing for the arbitration hearing—that they can rely on seat-of-the-pants advocacy to prevail. This can lead to particularly embarrassing results, as reflected in the following anecdote:

> The party presented a rather extensive claim for allegedly defective work and assured the arbitration panel that the claim would be amply supported by testimony from the president of the company performing corrective work. When the latter testified, however, his rather vague statements failed to provide detailed support for the claim. When, after cross-examination, he was pressed by the arbitration panel to give more information, he turned to counsel for the claimant and inquired, "Shall I tell the arbitrators about the letter I sent you that you told me not to tell them about?" He then proceeded to explain that he had informed counsel in writing that their client's claim was dramatically overblown—testimony that was, of course, devastating to the claim.

In the days when pre-hearing discovery was relatively rare, one might understand an advocate's expectation that case preparation would be completed as information spilled (or dribbled) out during the hearings. As arbitrators increasingly exercise their authority under current arbitration rules to direct pre-hearing exchanges of information, there is much less reason for such a state of affairs.

---

23. *See id.* at 160–62.

Nevertheless, arbitration continues to present some special challenges for advocates. The pre-hearing process still tends to be much shorter than corresponding preparatory times in litigation.[24] During hearings, advocates may be required to deal with:

- lengthy hearings that make witness preparation and other forward planning more difficult;
- the need to arrange contingency plans to make good use of the time when witnesses fail to show up, including taking witnesses out of order (and perhaps shuttling a particular witness on and off the stand); and
- the likelihood that witnesses will be subject to questioning by arbitrators as well as by opposing counsel.

Civility, cordiality and cooperation

Just as parties expect arbitrators to listen carefully and respectfully to their presentations, arbitrators anticipate courtesy among participants in the hearing room and cooperation in planning and conducting hearings. As we saw in Chapter 4, effective pre-hearing management begins with a search for consensus; the same principle governs the handling of procedures throughout the hearing. The General Commentary to the CPR Arbitration Rules makes clear that "[c]ounsel are expected to cooperate fully with the Tribunal and with each other to assure that the proceeding will be conducted with civility in an efficient, expeditious and economical manner" and cautions that in some cases a lack of cooperation may result in sanctions.[25]

The need to avoid being overly argumentative

Although the rules of evidence are a familiar tool of trial lawyers, they are not applicable in arbitration unless required by the agreement of the parties.[26] Section R-33 of the AAA Commercial Procedures makes explicit the traditional principle that the arbitrator shall be the judge of the admissibility, relevancy, and materiality of evidence offered, and that conformity to legal rules of evidence shall not be required.[27] This is not to say that no objection should ever be made to the admissibility of evidence;[28] the rationale for many modern exclusionary rules may be a helpful guide to the arbitrators in admitting or weighing the probativeness of evidence.[29]

Advocates should be aware that many arbitrators discount evidentiary objections in making their decisions, and that such objections may be perceived as an unnecessary irritant by one or more members of the tribunal.[30] Although

---

24. *See* Barrett, *supra* note 4, at 18.
25. *See* CPR ARBITRATION RULES, *supra* note 7, General Commentary.
26. *See* MACNEIL ET AL., *supra* note 2, § 35.1.2.1.
27. *See id.*
28. *See* Field & Robertson, *supra* note 17, § 12.5, at 8.
29. *See id., quoting* Robert Coulson, *Business Arbitration: What You Need to Know* 22 (American Arbitration Association, 4th ed. 1991). For a discussion of specific evidentiary issues, *see generally* MACNEIL ET AL., *supra* note 2, § 35.3.
30. *See* Thomson, *supra* note 21, at 148–49; Barrett, *supra* note 4, at 20.

other arbitrators may appreciate the rationale for objections, moderation is advised. In the event there are non-lawyer arbitrators on the panel, it may be appropriate to explain in straightforward terms the rationale of the pertinent evidentiary rule if that can be done without appearing condescending.

At all times, effective advocates avoid engaging in unnecessary arguments with opposing counsel or witnesses. As one Commission member explains, "Arbitration is not a forum where histrionics produce benefits." Another confides:

> Some of my fellow attorneys believe that "zealous advocacy" means never conceding a point, no matter how dubious, and debating every point of procedure or substance. Frankly, I've learned from sitting as an arbitrator that these tactics can backfire. The arbitrator may come to resent unrelenting argument, and will certainly tend to discount what the attorney has to say.

Another way of testing the patience of arbitrators is by repeating previously offered evidence, seeking to counter evidence of little value to the case,[31] or asking a witness variants of the same question over and over. Although effective arbitrators will be unlikely to put up with such tactics for long, they sometimes consume significant hearing time to the detriment of the questioner. A Commissioner recalls a particularly irritating round of questioning that ended as follows:

> *Arbitrator:* Mr. _____, how many times are you going to ask the witness the same question?
> *Counsel:* I will keep asking the question until I get the right answer! (Whereupon he stopped.)

Yet another risky practice is failing to cooperate in the exchange of information. Such tactics may cause the arbitrators to order a postponement of hearings until the information can be received and assimilated by the other party.[32] A continuing refusal or failure to produce may result in some form of sanction, as discussed in Section 5.6.

Considering the arbitrators' expertise

Many arbitrators believe that attorneys or their clients waste time by failing to recognize and take advantage of arbitrator expertise.[33] Arbitrators frequently complain that advocates take too long to present their case, are needlessly repetitive, and often lay needless foundations.[34] A realistic assessment of the arbitrators' capabilities may permit advocates to take shortcuts that reduce presentation time.

> The parties should be reminded that the arbitrator is knowledgeable in the industry. Therefore, they should be advised to prepare, and try, their cases

---

31. *See* Field & Robertson, *supra* note 17, § 12.15, at 21.
32. *See* Barrett, *supra* note 4, at 19.
33. *See* Thompson, *supra* note 21, at 150.
34. *See id.*

with that level of competence in mind, and not expend time and costs at the evidentiary hearing "educating" the arbitrator unnecessarily.[35]

In the case of a panel, of course, such options may be limited by the varied expertise of the members. Some panelists may consider a legal or technical discussion superfluous while others find it enlightening. Moreover, counsel may be unfamiliar with an arbitrator and have little knowledge of the arbitrator's expertise.

The fact of arbitrator expertise may be critical in the preparation of experts and other witnesses. Effective advocates recognize that, from the standpoint of the arbitrators, the most important interrogation may come at the hands of the arbitrators themselves—especially where the latter bring to the questioning pertinent knowledge or experience.

In developing final arguments and briefs, the best advocates pay close attention to the questions arbitrators have raised to the attorneys or to various witnesses during the hearing.[36]

5.3

What are effective ways of scheduling hearings and establishing time limits?

Scheduling is a critical element of hearing management. Some years ago, a survey of advocates revealed that half of all commercial arbitrations involving more than $250,000 involved at least five days of hearings, while a quarter of those arbitrations required more than thirteen hearing days.[37] (The average number of hearing days for the latter group of cases was forty-five days.) In half of the reported cases, more than seven months elapsed between the first hearing and the arbitration award; one-fourth of the time it took 11.7 months or more to reach an award.[38] If these statistics do not convey the importance of managing hearing schedules, it should be noted that forty percent of less experienced advocates (those who had participated in five or fewer large, complex cases) and seventy-four percent with more experience reported encountering unnecessary delays.[39]

---

35. Poppleton, *supra* note 4, at 9.
36. *See* Field & Robertson, *supra* note 17, § 12.15, at 21.
37. *See* Segalla, *supra* note 1, at 14, 16.
38. *See id.* at 16.
39. *See id.* at 20.

1. The importance of forward planning and continuous management of the hearing schedule

As discussed in Chapter 4, in most cases the initial blueprint for the arbitration is established prior to hearings on the merits, through pre-hearing conferences or other communications. At that time, the participants should be prepared to discuss and establish the schedule of hearings, including time parameters for case presentation. Proper forward planning will make it more likely that the arbitration timetable—including anticipated hearing dates—reflects the perceived needs of the parties and the case and are not simply the odd open dates remaining on participants' schedules. During the remainder of the pre-hearing and hearing period, the schedule may be refined and revisited to accommodate changing needs and circumstances.

AAA Commercial Procedures § R-32(b) recognizes that "[t]he arbitrator, exercising his or her discretion, shall conduct the proceedings with a view to expediting the resolution of the dispute . . ."[40] Similar wide latitude in scheduling proceedings is accorded arbitrators by CPR Rule 9, which provides that in the interest of expediting hearings:

> [t]he Tribunal is empowered to impose time limits it considers reasonable on each phase of the proceeding, including without limitation the time allotted to each party for presentation of its case and for rebuttal. In setting time limits, the Tribunal should bear in mind its obligation to manage the proceeding firmly in order to complete proceedings as economically and expeditiously as possible.[41]

Such provisions reinforce the broad discretion arbitrators enjoy under federal and state arbitration law.[42]

2. The goal of minimizing interruptions

Should arbitration hearings be scheduled back-to-back, without intervening breaks? Commercial parties and their counsel often complain about the prejudicial impact of interruptions in the hearing schedule. The longer and more frequent the breaks, the greater the potential for stalling tactics,[43] for the loss of momentum, and for forfeiture of a "sense of the whole."

---

40. AAA Commercial Procedures, *supra* note 6, § R-32(b).
41. CPR Arbitration Rules, *supra* note 7, Rule 9.2.
42. *See* Macneil et al., *supra* note 2, §§ 32.9, 35.2.
43. *See* Stipanowich, *supra* note 20, at 466.

With this in mind, one noted commentator argues strongly for an approach aimed at achieving a continuous hearing schedule.[44] He explains that in particular,

> "big case[s]"... should not be scheduled only during the gaps in someone's busy schedule. Rather, other matters should be scheduled around it.[45]

There is also support for uninterrupted hearings among Commission members. One member with extensive bench and bar experience argues:

> The arbitration hearings should be scheduled without interruption. As a practitioner, one of the disadvantages of arbitrations from my point of view, was the inability to get the parties and the arbitrators to adjust schedules so that a continuous hearing could take place. Hearings that are broken up are wasteful. As an arbitrator, therefore, I encourage parties to commit a time period that is sufficient to conclude the matter. During the arbitrator selection process, moreover, parties should get commitments from prospective panelists to devote necessary time to the matter to hear the complete case without interruption.

Under the Procedures for Large, Complex Commercial Disputes of the AAA Commercial Dispute Resolution Procedures, uninterrupted hearings are not just an aspiration, but an expectation. Section L-5 provides that "[g]enerally hearings will be scheduled on consecutive days or in blocks of consecutive days in order to maximize efficiency and minimize costs."[46] The commentary to the CPR Arbitration Rules also recognizes that "[t]he efficiency of the proceeding will be enhanced substantially if hearings are held consecutively."[47]

Some arbitrators will achieve the goal of uninterrupted hearings by

> insisting that the evidentiary hearing be conducted in a specific, finite number of hearing days, with X days allowed to the claimant and Y days allowed the respondent, ... in one continuous session ....[48]

> After receiving the parties' estimates of hearing days needed and their advice as to schedule conflicts, the arbitrator should make a considered judgment of the number of days each party will require, assign that number of days to each party, place that total number of days in the schedule of the parties where it is least objectionable, announce that decision, and remain firm.[49]

As noted above, arbitral orders establishing time limits on case presentations are specifically authorized under CPR Rule 9.2.[50] Furthermore, the CPR Commen-

---

44. *See* Poppleton, *supra* note 4, at 9.
45. *See id.* at 10.
46. AAA Commercial Procedures, *supra* note 6, § L-5.
47. CPR Arbitration Rules, *supra* note 7, Commentary to Rule 12.
48. *See* Poppleton, *supra* note 4, at 9.
49. *See id.*
50. CPR Arbitration Rules, *supra* note 7, Rule 9.2.

tary cautions that "[i]f the Tribunal heeds every schedule conflict claim and adjournment request by either counsel, the hearings may drag on quite unnecessarily."[51] One Commissioner relates:

> I was a sole arbitrator in a vigorously contested arbitration among three parties that was conducted under the CPR Rules. The parties had agreed that the case would be heard and concluded in four continuous weeks. Those weeks were set aside and blocked out. At the end of the first week, two of the parties filed a motion stating that the arbitration could not be concluded in the time frame unless I imposed time limits on each party. The third party vigorously contested the motion. After hearing their respective positions, I used my authority under CPR Rule 9 to allocate a set number of hours to each party and had an associate who was assisting me keep the time. Each morning counsel would inquire how much time he had used and how much he had left. The plan worked well, and the arbitration was completed a day and one-half early. I am satisfied that the imposition of time limits was an important factor which brought about an early conclusion of the arbitration.

In the name of speed and efficiency, and believing that counsel tend to use whatever time is allotted them, some arbitrators attempt to compress rigorously the number of hearing days—by imposing strict schedules through a unilateral order.[52] The Commission urges arbitrators to mingle firmness with reasonable flexibility in scheduling.

The need for firmness with reasonable flexibility

While arbitrators should continuously explore every avenue for making the process shorter and more efficient, they also have an obligation to make reasonable allowances for legitimate conflicts and good faith concerns regarding scheduling or presentation time on the part of other participants. Most arbitrators act in the awareness that an arbitrator's failure to postpone hearings for good cause may amount to prejudicial misconduct sufficient to overturn or vacate the arbitrator's award.[53]

The role of consensus.   As explained in Chapter 4, arbitrators should emphasize consensus in establishing hearing schedules. In many cases, early schedule-setting will permit participants to have the pick of hearing dates several months hence and avoid significant controversy over dates or the duration of hearings.

Where an arbitrator considers counsels' estimates of presentation time to be excessive, a draconian order slashing the allotted time may not be the proper course. Although in some cases high stakes or strategic considerations may moti-

---

51. *Id.* Commentary to Rule 12.
52. *See id.*
53. *See id.*; *see also* MACNEIL ET AL., *supra* note 2, § 35.2.

vate inflated estimates, many disputes are inherently complex.[54] A classic example is the construction claim involving a lengthy course of performance and numerous incidents allegedly contributing to project delay and disruption—the kind of controversy which regularly confounds efforts at truncated presentation. Since arbitrators rarely have detailed information regarding the substance of claims and defenses when the initial arbitration timetable is established, second-guessing the estimates of counsel is risky. As the parties prepare for their case and exchange information, a more realistic determination of the schedule may be possible. One Commission member suggests the following approach:

> When I explore scheduling needs with the parties, they often end up in the same ballpark in estimating days of hearing, and we use that as the basis for initial scheduling. If there is a great disparity in their perceptions, we may discuss the matter and arrive at a reasonable compromise for scheduling purposes. As we get closer to the hearing, we use periodic conference calls to fine-tune hearing plans and make necessary adjustments.

In the final analysis, there are few if any absolute rules. As always, much depends upon the circumstances:

> While my goal is to move the arbitration along [says another Commission member], I have a serious concern about failing to finish in the time initially set aside. In one of my first arbitrations, the attorneys dramatically underestimated the time it would take to resolve the case; after exhausting the planned ten days of hearing, the parties had to wait six months before all of the arbitrators were again available! Based on this experience, I encourage parties to be realistic about the time it will take to present the case. In some cases, if the additional time and expense is not a factor, it may mean going five days instead of four. (I would rather we have that extra day on the calendar from the beginning even if we never need it—and sometimes we don't—than running out of time and having to schedule more hearings weeks or months later).
>
> In other cases, we accomplish the same goal by arranging to go late one or two evenings if necessary. As arbitrator, I habitually try to make myself available for long sessions if the parties are willing. Sometimes we find it advantageous to take lunch in the hearing room and avoid a mid-day adjournment.

Dealing with changing circumstances

Firmness and reasonable flexibility are appropriate in dealing with the inevitable changed circumstances.[55] The arbitrator's authority respecting hearing schedules includes discretion to "postpone any hearing upon agreement of the parties,

---

54. *See* Barrett, *supra* note 4, at 16.
55. *See* MACNEIL ET AL., *supra* note 2, § 32.9.1.1.

upon request of a party for good cause shown, or upon the arbitrator's own initiative."[56] According to Thomson's survey, commercial arbitrators often postpone hearings where, among other things, a party is confronted with a new claim (sixty-six percent), or a party has failed to provide pertinent documents (fifty-one percent), or a party has failed to provide enough information regarding asserted claims (thirty-nine percent).[57]

Sometimes it may be possible to avoid or minimize the effect of a change of plan. If, for example, an attorney is called away to attend to an emergency hearing, it may be possible for the assisting attorney, if any, to fill in during the absence.[58]

A Commission member offers the following example of an arbitrator maintaining control of the hearing schedule by anticipating problems and "going with the flow":

> Most problems that come up during arbitration hearings can be dealt with by a combination of good housekeeping and a bit of ingenuity. As arbitrator, my custom is to begin and end each segment of the hearing (morning and afternoon) by attending to various details of the hearing. I ask the attorneys about their plans for the next segment and for the following days. I inquire about the availability of witnesses and any anticipated scheduling problems, and I encourage them to be ready with a backup plan if things go amiss.
>
> Of course, there are some things you just can't anticipate. In those situations you do the best you can to accomplish your goals. Once, a key non-party witness contacted the lawyer who was presenting his testimony on the morning he was to appear. He and his family had been threatened with bodily injury if he testified, and he had never left his home out of state. The arbitrators were fearful of losing the witness' testimony. After brief discussion with all participants, the arbitrators proposed to take his testimony over the phone—a plan with which the parties and the witness agreed.

Hearings in the absence of a party

Under prevailing arbitration law in the U.S., the absence of a party from hearings does not mandate canceling the hearing (and declaring the absent party in default).[59] Assuming that party has received due notice and has failed to appear at the hearing without good cause, the arbitrator and remaining party or parties may proceed with the hearing.

Clearly, the better practice in the case of a non-appearance is to require the party present to go forward with its case and to render the award that is most appropriate in terms of the record before the arbitrator. Under both the CPR

56. AAA COMMERCIAL PROCEDURES, *supra* note 6, § R-30.
57. *See* Thomson, *supra* note 21, at 143–44.
58. *See* Poppleton, *supra* note 4, at 10.
59. *See* Field & Robertson, *supra* note 17, § 12.1, at 4.

Arbitration Rules and AAA Commercial Procedures, the present party must submit evidence sufficient for the arbitrator to make an award in its favor.[60] A Commissioner describes the treatment of one such scenario:

> The defendant company could not be reached by anyone, even its attorney. The panel directed the case administrator to make a record of efforts to contact the party at the last known address. After being satisfied that reasonable efforts were made to notify the defendant, we heard the claimant's case at a hearing on the record. The panel members each asked a number of questions in the course of satisfying themselves regarding the proof presented. We then deliberated and rendered an award.

5.4

What are effective ways of organizing the presentation of evidence and arguments?

1. Order of proof

AAA Commercial Procedures § R-32(a) summarizes the normal expectations of parties regarding order of presentation in the routine case: "The claimant shall present evidence to support its claim. The respondent shall then present evidence to support its defense."[61]

In a variety of circumstances the order of proof is varied by agreement of the parties or arbitral order. "With a view to expediting the resolution of the dispute," AAA Commercial Procedures § R-32(b) recognizes arbitrators' discretion to "direct the order of proof, bifurcate proceedings and direct the parties to focus their presentations on issues the decision of which could dispose of part or all of the case."[62] In a similar vein, CPR Rule 12.1 states that "[t]he Tribunal shall determine the manner in which the parties shall present their cases";[63] Rule 9.3 contemplates that specifics such as "the desirability of bifurcation or other separation of the issues" shall be considered during pre-hearing planning.[64]

Serial treatment of claims or issues

In some cases the claimant should not present its entire case prior to the presentation of the defense. A common example is the complex construction case

---

60. CPR Arbitration Rules, *supra* note 7, Rule 15; AAA Commercial Procedures, *supra* note 6, § 31.
61. AAA Commercial Procedures, *supra* note 6, § R-32(a).
62. *Id.* § R-32(b).
63. CPR Arbitration Rules, *supra* note 7, Rule 12.1.
64. *Id.* Rule 9.3.

involving many and varied claims that may take weeks or months to present. Such cases are often best approached by a presentation of both sides of each issue in turn. The arrangement may be tailored to accommodate the schedules of particular witnesses, as the following anecdote by a Commission member illustrates:

> Among the hundreds of disputes we were required to arbitrate were dozens of minor alleged changes which had never been resolved between the contractor and the owner. After some informal discussion, it was agreed that the latter could be presented in narrative form by key representatives of the two parties, with limited testimony by subcontractor representatives. Claims involving each of the subcontractors were grouped together so the witnesses would not have to shuttle in and out.

A Commission member describes another situation in which the order of proof was varied to fit the circumstances:

> In the arbitration of a "corporate divorce," the parties wished to address the issue of valuation of shares prior to dealing with claims and counterclaims for breach of contract. It also became apparent that the resolution of the first issue might stimulate settlement, and all regarded it as appropriate to delay the second round of hearings for a couple of months. As it happened, the first matter was successfully mediated and issues narrowed for the later round of hearings.

Bifurcation of liability and damages

In most commercial arbitrations, parties tend to present evidence regarding liability and damages at the same time.[65] In cases that will require considerable time to present proof of damages—participants should consider postponing such proof pending an award on the preliminary issue of liability. Where, for example, the liability can be determined relatively quickly but damages cannot, a rational balance may be struck in favor of separating proof of the two issues.[66]

2. Framing the presentation: statements and briefs

Statements of claim or briefs

In Chapter 4 we discussed the likelihood that parties will be required to file some form of pre-hearing statement detailing claims or defenses. Although there is no set form for such a statement, they will often explain the factual predicate for the party's position on the issues and, perhaps, address legal issues.

---

65. *See* Robert H. Gorske, *An Arbitrator Looks at Expediting the Large, Complex Case*, 5 OHIO ST. J. ON DISPUTE RESOLUTION 381, 393 (1990).

66. *See* Myers, *supra* note 18, at 29; CPR ARBITRATION RULES, *supra* note 7, at 25.

Either here or at the beginning of the hearing, summaries of damages and requested relief should be presented.[67] CPR Rule 12.1 requires that the presentation of a party's case shall include a pre-hearing memorandum with a prescribed content.[68]

Opening statements

Ninety-seven percent of the arbitrators responding to Thomson's survey found the use of opening statements helpful.[69] A Commission member with considerable experience as a judge and arbitrator says:

> I like opening statements at the hearing, even if there have been preliminary submissions in writing. Opening statements with the client present are usually helpful to the arbitrator and focus and clarify the issues.

The opening statement provides an opportunity, in tandem with the pre-hearing statement or brief, to begin educating the arbitrator about the issues in the case and to reinforce the particular perspectives and positions of the presenting party. Says another Commission member:

> Arbitrators, like judges, are usually looking for a road map for resolution of the dispute. The best advocates are the ones who respond to that need by laying out the road map from the beginning, from clear positions on the issues to a clear summary of the relief sought.

The opening statement is, in essence, the outline of a "road map" for resolution of the issues and rendition of a full and final award. As noted above, arbitrators are interested in a thoughtful, concise, and dispassionate treatment of the case and not a lengthy partisan harangue.[70]

Periodic summations

One experienced commentator suggests that, where it would be helpful to focus presentations, arbitrators should ask the party presenting a witness to summarize the testimony of that witness and explain its relevance to the issues in the case at the outset.[71]

In cases involving many days of hearings, it may be helpful to supplement the usual opening and closing summaries with periodic summations at the end of presentations on specific claims or issues. As a Commissioner explains:

> I often find in a long, complex arbitration that the evidence tends to meander to the edge and often beyond the edge of relevance, causing everyone to lose sight of the issues. As an arbitrator, one thing I have done which seems to help

---

67. *See* John J. Fitzpatrick, Jr., *Preparing for the Hearing*, *in* The Alternative Dispute Resolution Practice Guide, § 11.10, at 13 (Bette J. Roth et al. eds., 1993).

68. CPR Arbitration Rules, *supra* note 7, Rule 12.1.

69. *See* Thompson, *supra* note 21, at 151.

70. *See* Fitzpatrick, *supra* note 67, at 13; Barrett, *supra* note 4, at 20.

71. *See* Myers, *supra* note 18, at 29.

in this regard is to have counsel "sum up" for a half hour or 45 minutes each week as to what they have accomplished during the week and where they are headed in the future. In the course of these summations, it often becomes apparent (even to counsel presenting the evidence) that much of the week's proof was not particularly relevant. Also, the summations provide a good setting for the arbitrators to give direction as to what they see as relevant and how marginal evidence might be curtailed in the future. I have found such summations tend to refocus attention on the issues and can save significant amounts of hearing time.

Another long-time arbitrator suggests that, where appropriate, the arbitrator should ask the party presenting a witness to summarize the evidence of the witness in writing after the conclusion of the witness's testimony.[72] Some Commissioners point out, however, that such a practice may be of limited usefulness in light of the tendency of some attorneys to put "spin" on the testimony in summarizing, and the practice of some arbitrators or panel chairs to rely on the transcript or, in the absence of a transcript, to prepare their own summaries of testimony. One Commissioner suggested that summaries by counsel might be helpful where there is no transcript and where opposing counsel is permitted to review and comment on the summary.

Closing statements

Although the subject is nowhere addressed in leading arbitration procedures, eighty-three percent of the commercial arbitrators responding to Thomson's survey found closing statements beneficial.[73] As at the beginning of the hearing, the effective advocate addresses the issues in calm and dispassionate fashion. At the end of the hearing, the arbitrator has heard all of the evidence, and counsel should have some sense of what issues and questions are important to the arbitrator. It is time to finish the "road map" to an award.

Post-hearing briefs

Although the AAA Commercial Procedures and some other commercial arbitration rules contemplate the possibility of filing post-hearing briefs, only about one-third of the commercial arbitrators responding to Thomson's survey typically order submission of post-hearing briefs.[74] This may be because such briefs often rehash earlier written and oral arguments which unduly postpone the final award.[75] Properly focused briefs, however, can effectively address critical legal questions which may remain in the arbitrator's mind. Focused briefing during the hearings may accomplish the same purpose. In large, complex cases, post-hearing briefs may be the best mechanism for pulling together vast amounts of

---

72. *See id.*
73. *See* Thomson, *supra* note 21, at 152.
74. *See id.*
75. *See* Field & Robertson, *supra* note 17, § 12.19, at 25.

information in transcripts and written documents. Arbitrators should provide clear guidelines for the scope and coverage of briefs so they can be sure to receive information helpful to their decisions. They may also set page limits on briefs.

3. Streamlining testimony

In commercial arbitration, the emphasis is not on technical conformity to formal rules of evidence but on obtaining relevant and material evidence that the arbitrators regard as helpful in reaching a decision. Hence, AAA Commercial Procedures § R-33 provides:

> The parties may offer such evidence as is relevant and material to the dispute and shall produce such evidence as the arbitrator may deem necessary to an understanding and determination of the dispute. Conformity to legal rules of evidence shall not be necessary [although principles underlying legal privileges such as the attorney-client privilege should be taken into account]. . . .
>
> The arbitrator [has discretion regarding] . . . admissibility, relevance and materiality of the evidence offered and may exclude evidence deemed by the arbitrator to be cumulative or irrelevant.[76]

CPR Rule 12 contains substantially similar language, and provides, furthermore, that the arbitrators "shall determine the manner in which witnesses are to be examined."[77]

While arbitration seldom completely abandons the procedure of the courtroom, it affords many opportunities for shortcutting and for deformalizing the handling of evidence. One Commission member with experience on the bench relates:

> It is the essence of arbitration that it be less formal and more free-wheeling than a regular trial, and if parties contract for the equivalent of judicial rules of evidence that advantage is lost.

There are a number of ways, detailed in the sections which follow, in which participants in arbitration can streamline the testimony of witnesses.

Substitutes for live testimony

Biographical information and written summaries.   Arbitrators often advise parties to provide written biographical information on each witness who will present testimony, thus obviating the need to devote hearing time to topics such as the witness's identity, education, and work experience.[78]

---

76. AAA Commercial Procedures, *supra* note 6, § R-33.
77. CPR Arbitration Rules, *supra* note 7, Rule 12.4.
78. *See* Barrett, *supra* note 4, at 21; Poppleton, *supra* note 4, at 8.

At least in the case of "secondary" witnesses who support the testimony of others or whose testimony is less central to the issues in dispute, it is possible to accept sworn testimony in writing if the parties agree. In one complicated case scenario involving delays to a construction project, the arbitration panel went a step further, proposing a format similar to that used by many regulatory agencies: direct testimony and exhibits would be pre-filed in written form two weeks before hearing, thus helping to reduce hearing time. Direct testimony of most fact witnesses was limited to one hour each; there were no time limitations on the testimony of outside experts, or on cross-examination.[79]

Affidavits.   Although arbitrators will sometimes accept affidavits in lieu of live testimony, their value may be minimal unless the author is made available for cross-examination.[80] Some experienced arbitrators and counsel often seek to reduce hearing time by using affidavits in lieu of direct examination while permitting cross-examination of the witness.[81] Some, however, express the concern that this approach can make it more difficult for arbitrators to judge the credibility of the witness, and suggested that such concerns might be addressed by permitting limited direct exam.

A CPR advisory group addressing arbitration of patent and trade secret disputes described a novel practice involving extensive use of affidavits:

> The entirety of both parties' case in chief is presented first by affidavit evidence submitted a good while before the hearing. The parties then designate which of the other party's witnesses' affidavits they accept without cross-examination and which of those witnesses they wish to cross-examine, who are produced at the hearing for cross-examination.
>
> Without sacrificing the values of needed cross-examination, this practice avoids calling unnecessary witnesses live while receiving their proofs in the most efficient form and thereby shortening the hearing, which can in part be an efficient narrative restatement of affidavit testimony followed by cross-examination of witnesses from whom cross-examination is sought.[82]

Depositions.   Another substitute for live testimony is the introduction of all or portions of a deposition. Introduction of a deposition may be the only alternative in situations where a witness is unable to attend a hearing. As one Commission member points out, however, the typical deposition format is very different from a presentation at a hearing:

> Where testimony is given in a deposition, the direct examination is usually akin to cross-examination, being conducted by a hostile attorney, and the cross-examination is usually conducted by a friendly attorney. These nuances may impact on the arbitrator.

---

79. *See* Gorske, *supra* note 65, at 383.
80. *See* AAA COMMERCIAL PROCEDURES, *supra* note 6, § R-34.
81. *See* Poppleton, *supra* note 4, at 8.
82. CPR INSTITUTE FOR DISPUTE RESOLUTION, RULES FOR NON-ADMINISTERED ARBITRATION OF PATENT AND TRADE SECRET DISPUTES, Commentary to Rule 11.

Although videotaped depositions offer the advantage of permitting arbitrators to observe witness demeanor, their viewing may consume considerable hearing time.

Evidentiary objections

As previously mentioned, court evidentiary rules are seldom strictly applied in arbitration, although their rationale may be considered important when arbitrators consider the admissibility or weight of evidence.[83] Moreover, it is appropriate for arbitrators to make clear what, if any, general guidelines they intend to follow for the admission of evidence.

One Commission member advises:

> What arbitrators generally do, in my experience, is to be at least as liberal as a judge would be in admitting evidence in a bench trial, and usually they are more liberal than that.

Another Commission member explains the need to give guidance to the parties regarding standards for admissibility:

> A very real problem can arise from the fact that there is no uniform rule in arbitration with regard to hearsay, and standard arbitration rules rarely address the subject in detail. Standards may vary from arbitrator to arbitrator. This can lead to serious unfairness, where, for example, a party is surprised to learn in the midst of the hearing that an arbitrator is going to exclude a large portion of his case on hearsay grounds. For this reason, I like to tell the parties at the pre-hearing conference what the hearsay standard is going to be. For what it's worth, my own standard in arbitration is to accept hearsay if it is not particularly important. If it is important, however, I will generally not take it unless it can be established that the declarant cannot be produced to testify. If this is shown, I generally take hearsay, but will give it much less weight than I would to live testimony.

Although many arbitrators are reluctant to impose court evidentiary rules in arbitration, one Commissioner reports success with the following approach to admissibility issues:

(1) Reject no evidence on relevancy grounds alone, unless it appears that one side is introducing a lot of useless information. (If relevancy is challenged, however, have the offering party explain the relevancy of the challenged testimony.)
(2) Follow the Federal Rules of Evidence (unless the parties agree otherwise). If you make an exception, explain to the parties why you are doing so, in order not to open the door for future misunderstandings or abuse.

---

83. *See* CPR ARBITRATION RULES, *supra* note 7, Rule 12.2; AAA COMMERCIAL PROCEDURES, *supra* note 6, § R-33.

(3) Follow hearsay rules (which were developed for good reasons), again making exceptions only for specific reasons which are explained to the parties, along with an indication of the weight you intend to give the hearsay. I have been told by counsel that this procedure made it much easier for them to evaluate where they were in their case presentation, and whether or not to try to rebut admitted hearsay.

Questions often arise regarding admissibility of information that might fall within the scope of a legal privilege such as attorney/client communications, attorney work product, and statements made during the course of settlement discussions. Leading commercial procedures now encourage arbitrators to consider the policies behind legal limitations on the admissibility of evidence in treating objections. The CPR Arbitration Rules require the Tribunal to "apply the lawyer-client privilege and the work product immunity."[84]

Follow-up questions by arbitrators

Another difference between the arbitration hearing and the courtroom is the more inquisitorial nature of the former. Arbitrators sometimes augment the direct and cross-examination of witnesses with their own queries—a straightforward means of providing additional clarification for the arbitrators while informing the parties of the arbitrator's concerns.[85] CPR Rule 12.3 states, "The Tribunal, in its discretion, may require the parties to produce evidence in addition to that initially offered."[86] Similarly, AAA Commercial Procedures § 33 provides that "parties . . . shall produce such evidence as the arbitrator may deem necessary to an understanding and determination of the dispute" and authorizes arbitrators to "subpoena witnesses or documents . . . independently."[87]

A Commission member describes his normal approach:

As an arbitrator, I routinely wait until the completion of direct and cross-examination (and re-cross and re-direct) to ask questions, because effective counsel often raise the questions I have in my own mind and it is appropriate to defer initially to them. However, I often find that following up with a question or two directly to the witness will help clarify matters in my own mind, and sometimes provides critical additional information.

Another Commissioner emphasizes the importance of direct arbitrator feedback to the parties:

As an arbitrator, I always try to give the parties feedback about whether their efforts to explain things are getting across and I don't hesitate to ask

---

84. *See* CPR Arbitration Rules, *supra* note 7, Rule 12.2; AAA Commercial Procedures, *supra* note 6, § R-33(c).
85. *See* Macneil et al., *supra* note 2, § 35.4.5.
86. CPR Arbitration Rules, *supra* note 7, Rule 12.3.
87. AAA Commercial Procedures, *supra* note 6, § 33.

questions which may sound primitive or make me look not too bright. One of the beauties of arbitration is that arbitrators can do this without the fear of looking "non-judicial."

4. Handling of exhibits, summaries, and graphic elements

Self-authenticating documents

Parties often agree that documents (and copies) will be self-authenticating and presumed genuine if no specific challenge is raised to their authenticity.[88] A Commissioner, who is a former judge, concludes:

> The best rule on admissibility of documents is that anything referred to by a witness is automatically admitted without the usual formal motion. All documents are deemed genuine unless specifically challenged.

Trial notebook; summaries

Sixty-eight percent of the respondents to Thomson's survey indicated that they like to be provided with an arbitration notebook containing exhibits and other information, in advance of hearings.[89] A Commission member tellingly observes:

> While it might sound like a mundane thing, it can save immense amounts of time if each side numbers and arranges its exhibits (other than those to be used on cross-examination) in tabbed binders prior to the hearing. This enables everyone to focus on a document in seconds and averts having everyone wait while a document is located, marked, distributed and reviewed for possible objections.

Another member puts it even more strongly:

> When properly prepared, arbitration notebooks are an immensely powerful advocacy tool—particularly in complex cases. The best ones often contain a narrative of the party's position on each claim or dispute, pertinent time lines where appropriate, and supporting documentation (including invoices and other materials supporting damages), as well as a summary of all claims concluding with a total dollar figure which is the basis of the party's position or request for relief. If being an effective advocate consists of knowing how to "tell the best story," this is a wonderful way to accomplish the goal. The well-prepared notebook often becomes the "script" for the entire hearing—with everybody (even the other side) constantly referring to it and relying upon it.

---

88. *See* Gorske, *supra* note 65, at 384.
89. *See* Thomson, *supra* note 21, at 143.

Some arbitrators encourage or require parties to submit a joint set of numbered exhibits,[90] or, in cases involving great volumes of documents, to maintain a library of exhibits in the hearing room for easy access during hearings.

Charts, graphic presentations

When asked whether graphics and other forms of demonstrative evidence assisted them in arriving at an appropriate award, arbitrators in Thomson's survey overwhelmingly answered "yes" (eighty-seven percent).[91] Consider the thoughts of one Commission member:

> Well-prepared charts, summaries and other demonstrative exhibits can be among the most effective tools in a party's arsenal. Almost without fail, arbitrators tend to devote a disproportionate amount of attention to such exhibits, whether a critical path analysis of delays to a construction project, a year-by-year comparison of costs or cash flow, a summary of damages, a time line pulling together related events or documentation, or a three-dimensional model or drawing.

Two things are critical. First, the party should thoroughly consider what it wishes to convey, and the best, most straightforward way of communicating the desired information. Second, and just as important, the party must construct the exhibit from existing evidence—evidence which should be readily available at the hearing. The Commission member continues:

> Nothing is more frustrating than a chart or summary which cannot be supported by reference to the underlying evidence—or which utilizes information so selectively that it severely skews the truth. As an arbitrator I expect parties to take me through backup documentation so that I can see for myself how the exhibit was prepared and, if necessary, recreate the process on my own. Sloppily prepared demonstrative exhibits can severely undermine the credibility of counsel and damage the party's case.

Another Commissioner adds:

> Charts, summaries and the like must be based on evidence in the record. If they are not they should not be received in evidence.

5. Use of experts

Summaries, reports

Before the hearing, arbitrators often require parties calling experts to provide the other party with summaries of the experts' qualifications and the substance of the proposed testimony, along with some details supporting the experts' conclusions. Such information may eliminate the need to take hearing time to

---

90. See Barrett, *supra* note 4, at 21.
91. See Thomson, *supra* note 21, at 164.

establish the expert's qualifications and permits the opposing party to prepare in advance for cross-examination.

"Dueling experts"

In arbitration, as in other adversarial fora, users sometimes complain that opposing experts often present diametrically-opposed points of view, and leave the decisionmaker with little basis upon which to assess the validity of one or the other viewpoint. With this in mind, a number of commercial arbitrators have experimented with the concept of simultaneously placing opposing experts on the stand and asking them each to answer the same questions, or even allowing them to question each other. Some arbitrators report that the procedure has been successful in eliminating some points of apparent disagreement between the experts, and occasionally causes one expert to reconsider certain aspects of his or her testimony.

Arbitrator-appointed experts

Arbitration panels sometimes encourage parties to consent to the appointment of neutral experts by the arbitrators. Such arrangements avoid the cost of multiple experts and the conflicting loyalties which sometimes skew party-appointed experts' views. In the interest of fairness, all parties must have access to the neutral expert's report and have an opportunity to examine the expert. CPR Rule 12.3 provides that the Tribunal "may . . . appoint neutral experts whose testimony shall be subject to cross-examination and rebuttal."[92] The accompanying Commentary explains:

> CPR expects this power to be exercised sparingly, and only following consultation with the parties as to the need for a neutral expert, the scope of the assignment, and identification of well-qualified candidates. It is not intended that the expert give advice to the Tribunal *ex parte*; indeed, the Rule entitles the parties to cross-examine and to rebut the expert.[93]

A Commission member describes an exercise of the authority to appoint an independent expert:

> In an arbitration involving numerous claims and counterclaims regarding the construction of a plant, many issues centered around alleged defects in construction. There was much contradictory evidence on the subject, and the panel eventually decided to order an independent investigation by an engineering firm. The parties were permitted to be present when the latter made its investigation. After the firm issued its final report to all parties, the parties were allowed to cross-examine the inspectors, and to introduce evidence rebutting elements of the final report. Although the arbitrators directed the parties to split the firm's expenses pending a resolution of the issues, they retained authority to allocate those expenses as they saw fit in the final award.

---

92. CPR ARBITRATION RULES, *supra* note 7, Rule 12.3.
93. CPR ARBITRATION RULES, *supra* note 7, Commentary to Rule 12.3.

6. Site inspections, investigations

Site inspections and other investigations often play an important role in commercial arbitration. In construction cases, for example, a visit to the work site may help an arbitrator visualize in three dimensions the locus of controversy. For this reason, it may be appropriate to schedule the visit early in the hearings.[94]

Under the AAA Commercial Procedures § R-35, arbitrators are specifically authorized to make a site inspection or investigation. Under the CPR Arbitration Rules, the necessity for any on-site inspection by the Tribunal is a subject to be addressed at the initial pre-hearing conference.[95] Fairness requires that parties be given notice of any planned inspection or investigation by the arbitrator and have the chance to be present.

5.5

How can developing technology be effectively employed in arbitration?

New technologies have dramatically changed the nature of litigation and arbitration over the past decade, and the trend continues unabated. Arbitration has two advantages over traditional litigation in the use of new technology.

First, arbitrators have greater leeway than judges in establishing the procedural rules governing the arbitration. Because they are not bound by the rigid framework of the rules of civil procedure, arbitrators are free to tailor the proposed use of new technology to the circumstances of the proceeding before them.

Second, arbitration proceedings are largely free from the dangers of prejudice and confusion particular to jury trials. As a result, arbitrators can deal flexibly with problems that are troubling in a courtroom, such as unexpected electronic failures or allegations that high-tech evidence is misleading or prejudicial.

Arbitrators have a substantially greater ability than judges to innovate with new technology to achieve the traditional goals of arbitration. Parties and arbitrators should make use of these opportunities where appropriate.

The CPR Commission did not evaluate any particular new technology for use in arbitration proceedings, nor does it minimize the difficulties involved in using some new technologies efficiently. The Commission recognizes that these new technologies have the *potential* of making arbitration proceedings less time consuming, less expensive, and less burdensome. Accordingly, parties and arbitrators should make all reasonable efforts to encourage the use of new technologies to these ends. Some examples of possible applications follow.

---

94. Field & Robertson, *supra* note 17, § 12.15, at 22.
95. AAA COMMERCIAL PROCEDURES, *supra* note 6, § R-35; CPR Arbitration Rules, *supra* note 7, Rule 9.3.

1. Document management and retrieval

In complex cases, new technologies are used to manage numerous documents for trial preparation by imaging the documents (for retrieval by category index) or by OCR scanning (for retrieval by index or full text search). Documents organized in this manner are stored on CD-ROM and may be called up during the hearing on video displays. Some systems permit enlargement of portions of documents, side-by-side comparisons, and electronic highlighting or "writing" on the images.

2. Display of visual materials

Virtually all of the visual materials traditionally presented by lawyers can now be generated or captured by computerized systems, stored electronically, and called up during the hearing on video displays. These include charts, graphs, flow diagrams, photographs, chronologies, timelines, diagrams, illustrations, and electronic slide shows. High quality computer animations can be presented either directly under computer control or by videotape.

3. Presentation of testimony

Videotape has long been used in hearings, either to present impeaching material from depositions, or (where appropriate) to present the full testimony of a witness not available for trial. With recent advances, video conferencing can now present "live" witnesses who are unable to appear in person at the hearing.

Some commentators question the benefits of the foregoing developments. They suggest that problems inherent in the new technologies make them inappropriate or inefficient for use in the courtroom or in arbitration proceedings. For example, some technology for the display of documents has poor legibility. Other technology depends on the (often limited) computer capabilities of arbitrators or attorneys representing the parties. Computer-generated re-enactments or other animations are potentially misleading. Although some critics argue that much of the new technology is inconsistent with the arbitral goals of efficiency and economy, one California trial judge credits the use of new technology for reducing the trial of a complex case by about seven days, and he believes that even more time could have been saved.[96] The experimental, high-tech "Courtroom 21" project at the William & Mary School of Law also supports the view that the use of computer-based systems for the display of visual evidence and for document management and retrieval improves the speed and efficiency of trial.[97]

---

96. Kissane-Gaisford, *The Case for Disc-Based Litigation: Technology of the Cyber Courtroom*, 8 HARVARD J. L. & TECH. 471, 479 (1995).

97. *See* Lederer, "An Introduction to Augmented Litigation" (visited Sept. 7, 2000) <http://www.courtroom21.net/auglit.html>; Lederer, "Courtroom Technology from the Judges' Perspective" (visited Sept. 7, 2000) <http://www.courtroom21.net/judicial.html>.

4. Transcript of hearings

Modern technology also permits rapid creation and dissemination of transcripts, electronic searches of the record for key words or phrases, and quick indexing of testimony.

Audio-taping or videotaping proceedings provides a relatively low-cost means of creating a record if stenographic means are deemed too costly. Under AAA Commercial Procedures § L-5(f) "the arbitrator(s) may direct the recording of the hearings [in large, complex cases], the cost of which shall be borne equally by the parties."[98] As one Commissioner explains, however, such recordings present a number of potential drawbacks:

> Use of audio or videotape to create a record is a terrible idea for several reasons. First, search-and-retrieving relevant passages is a nightmare. Second, storage and cataloging of tapes for a lengthy hearing can be a major problem. Third, I have never had the benefit of a high quality tape recording in a contested matter; invariably, people talk over others, and it is difficult for reviewers (especially those who were not present) to distinguish among speakers. Last, videotaping a hearing presents tremendous logistical difficulties, such as determining what views are prime, how to trigger microphones, etc.

Another Commission member reflects:

> At the request of one of the parties, the arbitration panel agreed to permit the hearings to be videotaped. Unfortunately, without a full-time operator it was impossible for any of the participants to give sufficient attention to the camera, and on several occasions the tape ended without anyone noticing it. The record was far from complete.

5.6

When, if ever, may arbitrators sanction parties or counsel?

The use of arbitral sanctions to police delaying or disruptive conduct evokes mixed responses among members of the Commission, many of whom have experienced few serious problems with civility or lack of cooperation in the hearing room.

---

98. AAA COMMERCIAL PROCEDURES, *supra* note 6, § L-5(f).

Where a party asserts a frivolous claim or defense, seeks to delay or disrupt hearings, or materially fails to cooperate in discovery, many arbitrators consider the imposition of sanctions. CPR Rule 15 states:

> Whenever a party fails to comply with these Rules, or any order of the Tribunal pursuant to these Rules, in a manner deemed material by the Tribunal, the Tribunal shall fix a reasonable period of time for compliance and, if the party does not comply within said period, the Tribunal may impose a remedy it deems just, including an award on default. Prior to entering an award on default, the Tribunal shall require the non-defaulting party to produce evidence and legal argument in support of its contentions as the Tribunal may deem appropriate. The Tribunal may receive such evidence and argument without the defaulting party's presence or participation.[99]

The CPR Commentary states:

> [The broad power of arbitrators to apportion costs] is intended to permit the arbitrators to apportion a greater share of costs than they otherwise might to a party which has employed tactics the arbitrators consider dilatory, or in other ways has failed to cooperate in assuring the efficient conduct of the proceeding.[100]

Some Commission members are comfortable with sanctions, such as drawing adverse inferences when a party fails to present requested documentation or testimony, but they are skeptical of other sanctions, such as awards of attorney's fees. Other Commission members argue that arbitrators deal with lack of cooperation without sanctions because parties will rarely push an arbitrator "too far" in the face of arbitral firmness. Still other Commission members support the ability of arbitrators to award costs and attorney's fees in appropriate cases. They point out that international arbitration rules tend to permit awards of attorney's fees.[101] Awards of costs and fees are discussed in Chapter 7.

---

99. CPR ARBITRATION RULES, *supra* note 7, Rule 15.
100. *Id.* General Commentary.
101. *See, e.g.,* INTERNATIONAL CHAMBER OF COMMERCE, ICC RULES OF ARBITRATION, Art. 31 (Jan. 1, 1998). In a mid-1980s survey regarding commercial arbitration, two-thirds of responding attorneys thought that arbitrators should have discretion to award attorney's fees. *See* Stipanowich, *supra* note 20, at 467.

CHAPTER **6**

Preserving Confidentiality

Preserving Confidentiality

6.1

How can confidentiality be assured in arbitration?

1. Issues regarding disclosure of testimony and other information

For many parties privacy and confidentiality are important factors favoring arbitration over litigation.

Arbitration is by its very nature a private proceeding. There is no public record. The media and others having no legitimate reason to attend can be excluded from hearings. As a rule, arbitration awards are not published.

Nevertheless, issues sometimes emerge regarding the possible disclosure of documents, testimony, and material from an arbitration proceeding: transcripts, the contents of an award, or possibly even the very existence or subject matter of the proceeding. Moreover, the desire to protect trade secrets, attorney work product, and other privileged information from another party or from third parties may raise special issues at the discovery stage as well as during hearings.

2. Absence of specific statutory treatment

Neither the Federal Arbitration Act (FAA) nor state arbitration laws specifically address the subject of confidentiality of arbitration proceedings or the protection of proprietary or privileged information in arbitration.[1] No specific bar exists against communication to or discovery by third parties regarding arbitration documents and other information relating to the arbitration, although, as discussed in Section 6.2, strong public policies generally protect arbitrators from being deposed or testifying about the arbitral process.

A growing number of jurisdictions have laws or rules of court protecting information revealed in certain non-binding ADR processes, notably mediation and court-annexed non-binding arbitration.[2] Such laws and rules, which are intended to foster candid communications among participants in settlement negotiations, do not apply to communications made or information revealed in the course of binding arbitration hearings.

In the absence of statutory protections, it is incumbent upon arbitrating parties to consider confidentiality issues when adopting arbitration rules and

---

1. *See* Ian R. Macneil, Richard E. Speidel & Thomas J. Stipanowich, Federal Arbitration Law: Agreements, Awards, and Remedies under the Federal Arbitration Act, § 32.6 (1994) [hereinafter Macneil et al.].

2. *See, e.g.,* Cal. Evid. Code §§ 1115, 1119 (West 1998); Ohio Rev. Code Ann. § 2317.023 (Baldwin 1998).

tailoring an arbitration agreement to their own needs. They may also wish to take practical steps to enhance the privacy of arbitration. While absolute protection of confidentiality cannot be assured, risks of disclosure of confidential information can be reduced substantially through the approaches described below.

6.2
How can the privacy of hearings be maintained?

The level of privacy experienced by arbitrating parties depends primarily upon the measures they have taken to ensure their specific expectations. The latter often include an expectation that access to the hearing room will be limited, and that non-essential persons will be excluded. Sometimes privacy concerns focus on participants' communications with third parties regarding the arbitration. A related concern involves the ability of third parties to subpoena arbitrators or discover arbitration-related information. We will consider how each of these privacy concerns may be addressed.

1. Restricting access to the hearing room

The AAA Commercial Dispute Resolution Procedures provide:

> The arbitrator and the AAA shall maintain the privacy of the hearings unless the law provides to the contrary. Any person having a direct interest in the arbitration is entitled to attend hearings. The arbitrator shall otherwise have the power to require the exclusion of any witness, other than a party or essential person, during the testimony of any other witness. It shall be discretionary with the arbitrator to determine the propriety of the attendance of any other person other than a party and its representatives.[3]

The AAA provision specifically authorizes arbitrators to limit access to the hearing room to parties, their representatives, and others whom that arbitrator deems to have a "direct interest."[4]

---

3. AMERICAN ARBITRATION ASSOCIATION, COMMERCIAL DISPUTE RESOLUTION PROCEDURES, § R-25 (Jan. 1, 1999) [hereinafter AAA COMMERCIAL PROCEDURES].
   4. *Id.*

The section also provides for separation of witnesses,[5] as do the CPR Arbitration Rules.[6] As in the court system, such provisions are intended to diminish the likelihood that a witness, having heard another's testimony, will shape his or her own testimony to complement or rebut the former. Of course, the benefits of witness separation may be substantially reduced where witnesses have access to transcripts or summaries of earlier testimony prior to giving evidence.

2. Limits on communication of information by participants

Restrictions on arbitrator communications

According to the AAA Commercial Procedures, "[t]he arbitrator and the AAA shall maintain the privacy of the hearings unless the law provides to the contrary."[7] This provision appears to restate and reinforce a primary ethical standard for commercial arbitrators. The AAA/ABA Code of Ethics for Arbitrators of Commercial Disputes provides in Canon VI.B:

> Unless otherwise agreed by the parties, or required by applicable rules or law, an arbitrator should keep confidential all matters relating to the arbitration proceedings and decision.[8]

Canon VI.B, like the AAA Commercial Procedures, offers assurance that arbitrators will respect the confidentiality of the process. Occasionally, arbitrators are required to execute more specific confidentiality agreements at the time of their appointment.

Such strictures are reinforced by judicial precedents protecting the arbitrator from being deposed or testifying about the arbitral process or the bases of their awards, except to allow arbitrators to defend themselves on charges of misconduct.[9] The general basis for these opinions is that arbitrators are "judges" chosen by the parties and serve in quasi-judicial capacities.[10]

Of course, the foregoing standards are applicable to arbitrators only. They do not prohibit parties and other participants from communicating arbitration-related information with third parties, or protect them from third party discovery. Parties wishing to limit such communications must address the matter specifically in their agreement or incorporate procedures which do so.

---

5. *Id.*

6. *See* CPR INSTITUTE FOR DISPUTE RESOLUTION, RULES FOR NON-ADMINISTERED ARBITRATION, Rule 2.4 (Rev. 2000) [hereinafter CPR ARBITRATION RULES].

7. AAA COMMERCIAL PROCEDURES, *supra* note 3, § 25.

8. AMERICAN ARBITRATION ASSOCIATION/AMERICAN BAR ASSOCIATION CODE OF ETHICS FOR ARBITRATORS IN COMMERCIAL DISPUTES, Canon VI.B (1977).

9. MACNEIL ET AL., *supra* note 1, § 38.5.

10. *See, e.g.,* Gramling v. Food Machinery & Chemical Corp., 151 F. Supp. 853 (W.D.S.C. 1957).

Restrictions on communications by parties and other participants

Besides placing limitations on arbitrators, some commercial arbitration procedures restrict outside communications by the parties. For example, the CPR Arbitration Rules state:

> Unless the parties agree otherwise, the parties, the arbitrators and CPR shall treat the proceedings, any related discovery and the decisions of the Tribunal, as confidential, except in connection with judicial proceedings ancillary to the arbitration, such as a judicial challenge to, or enforcement of, an award, and unless otherwise required by law or to protect a legal right of a party. To the extent possible, any specific issues of confidentiality should be raised with and resolved by the Tribunal.[11]

Some procedures are broader—covering not only arbitrators and parties but other participants—and contain a variety of specific directives for the maintenance of confidentiality. An example is the CPR Rules for Non-Administered Arbitration of Patent and Trade Secret Disputes, drafted by and for patent attorneys; this standard is addressed below in our discussion of the treatment of proprietary information (Section 6.3.3).

Some parties may find it beneficial to have witnesses and experts sign a confidentiality agreement before participating in the arbitration. They may also weigh the need to provide for specific enforcement of the terms of the confidentiality agreement by the arbitrator or by a court, or specify remedies for breach of the agreement. Some confidentiality agreements establish specific guidelines for the handling of certain documents, including limitations on copying and arrangements for documents to be returned to the originating party at the conclusion of arbitration.

Practical steps: limiting the record

Parties may also place limitations on the taking or preservation of the record of hearings. The maintenance of a record of arbitration proceedings is not required by law or by any of the leading arbitration rules—it is strictly a matter for agreement between the parties. There are cogent reasons for having transcripts of hearings, particularly in long, complex cases. However, from the viewpoint of maintaining confidentiality, the use of transcripts can have serious drawbacks. A leading treatise on arbitration gives some practical advice:

> In addition to reducing the cost of arbitration, the absence of transcripts or other records enhances the privacy and confidentiality of the process. It also contributes, for better or worse, to the finality of the award. While a verbatim record is not a prerequisite to a motion for vacation of award under FAA § 10 the lack of a record may be a formidable obstacle to successful challenges based upon acts or omissions of the arbitrators or other participants during the hearings.[12]

---

11. CPR Arbitration Rules, *supra* note 6, Rule 17.
12. Macneil et al., *supra* note 1, § 32.7.3.

When records are created, parties can take precautions to prevent access by third parties by restricting access to a limited number of people; and agreeing as part of their procedures to notify the parties in interest if access to material is requested.

Sample agreements respecting confidentiality appear in Appendix 6.1.

3. Protection against third party discovery

Arbitration law of limited relevance

Federal and state arbitration law imposes no specific bar on discovery by third parties of documents and other arbitration-related information. Requests for discovery are evaluated under traditional standards applicable to civil litigation. For example, in one case a general contractor seeking damages against a medical center for breach of their construction contract successfully sought a court order directing the medical center to produce transcripts from an earlier arbitration proceeding involving the center and another general contractor on the same project.[13] On appeal, the medical center argued that "[e]ven absent evidence of a stipulation of confidentiality, . . . [an order] tending to expose normally relaxed arbitration proceedings to public scrutiny . . . [would] cause parties to such proceedings to become circumspect and overly litigious and thus chill the informal process."[14] The court disagreed, pointing to the fact that neither the parties' agreement, incorporated arbitration rules, nor applicable arbitration law required strict confidentiality. Concerns regarding the revelations of attorney opinions and other work product of the medical center's attorneys were resolved by permitting the center to excise such portions of the transcript.[15]

As previously noted, for public policy reasons arbitrators are largely immune from testifying or being deposed regarding their awards. Such protections do not extend to arbitrating parties, however.

Agreements

The best course for parties seeking to protect arbitration-related information from disclosure is to incorporate in their agreement not only a statement of their intention to keep information confidential, but specific steps designed to minimize the likelihood of disclosure. These will be addressed below in the context of concerns associated with proprietary information.

---

13. Industrotech Constructors, Inc. v. Duke Univ., 314 S.E.2d 272 (N.C. App. 1984). *Cf.* Milone v. General Motors Corp., 446 N.Y.S.2d 650 (N.Y. App. Div. 1981).

14. *Id.* at 274.

15. *Id.* at 275.

6.3

How can privileged or proprietary information be maintained?

1. Privileged communications and attorney work product

To ensure the confidentiality of communications made within certain relationships, the law recognizes testimonial privileges of witnesses not to testify in civil proceedings regarding such communications.[16] The CPR Arbitration Rules require the arbitrator to apply the lawyer-client privilege and the work product immunity.[17] The AAA Commercial Procedures state: "The arbitrator shall take into account applicable principles of legal privilege, such as those involving confidentiality of communications between lawyer and client."[18]

There are strong arguments that arbitrators should honor privileges even in the absence of such explicit language in the parties' agreement or incorporated rules. As one Commissioner elsewhere observed,

> Legal privileges are . . . grounded on rights. Privileges such as those protecting attorney-client, doctor-patient, husband-wife, priest-penitent and other types of communications are based on public policies intended to encourage and protect communications in situations where the law deems freedom to engage in them more important than a party's right to intrude on them for purposes of discovery and use in litigation or arbitration. This is an area of law quite different from evidentiary rules intended to protect jurors. There is no reason why respect for privileges or the scope of privileges should [not be as important] . . . in arbitration [as in litigation].[19]

Several courts have recognized that privileges are applicable in arbitration.[20] In at least one case, the failure to honor a privilege was raised as a ground for vacatur of an arbitration award.[21]

Experienced commercial arbitrators, like judges, tend to recognize the importance of privileges. Some go out of their way to avoid breaching a privilege in discovery orders as well as rulings on admissibility of evidence.

The most difficult problems involve complicated privilege issues relating to substantial numbers of documents—as where a defense is based in whole or in part on advice provided by counsel. The arbitrators may be confronted with the immense practical problem of reviewing volumes of paper in order to determine the applicability of the privilege. Although it may be possible to address

---

16. *See, e.g.,* FED. R. EVID. 501; see also MACNEIL ET AL., *supra* note 1, § 35.3.4.
17. CPR ARBITRATION RULES, *supra* note 6, Rule 12.2.
18. AAA COMMERCIAL PROCEDURES, *supra* note 3, § R-33(c).
19. James H. Carter, *The Attorney-Client Privilege in Arbitration,* ADR CURRENTS, Winter 1996/1997, at 1, 16.
20. *See id.* at 17.
21. *See* Fahnestock & Co. v. Waltman, 1990 U.S. Dist. LEXIS 11024 (S.D.N.Y. Aug. 23, 1990)(holding arbitrators properly applied privilege), *aff'd*, 935 F.2d 512 (2d Cir.), *cert. denied*, 502 U.S. 942 (1991).

the problem by reviewing a schedule of allegedly privileged documents with the attorney asserting the privilege, one set of international arbitration rules authorizes arbitrators to appoint an independent expert to conduct a privilege review and allocate the resulting costs.[22]

There are also practical steps that may assist arbitrators in addressing privilege issues. When preparing for arbitration, for example, attorneys should prepare materials as if for litigation and carefully label information as work product where appropriate.

2. Settlement offers and related discussions

Judicial evidentiary rules limit the admissibility of conduct or statements made in compromise negotiations.[23] They serve to promote and encourage candor in such discussions, and at the same time recognize that settlement positions are often influenced by factors other than the merits of the dispute. The same considerations make it appropriate for arbitrators to bar or limit evidence of settlement offers and related communications.[24]

The AAA Commercial Procedures do not address the subject of settlement discussions, although the AAA's *Guide for Commercial Arbitrators* cautions arbitrators to be "sensitive" to the policies underlying judicial limits on admissibility.[25] The CPR Arbitration Rules explicitly address settlement and mediation. The Tribunal may suggest or either party may propose exploration of settlement. Moreover, with the consent of the parties, the Tribunal "at any stage of the proceeding may arrange for mediation of the claims . . . by a mediator acceptable to the parties. The mediator shall be a person other than a member of the Tribunal." The Rules further provide that the "Tribunal will not be informed of any settlement offers or other statements made during settlement negotiations or a mediation between the parties, unless both parties consent."[26]

While the admission of settlement communications might constitute arbitral misconduct or an act exceeding the arbitrator's authority warranting vacatur of award under federal or state arbitration law, those seeking vacatur will have a difficult burden.[27] In one decision, the Tenth Circuit Court of Appeals held that an attempt by a prevailing party's attorney to influence an arbitral award by repeatedly communicating to the panel the terms of the other party's offer of settlement did not require vacatur of the award under the FAA.[28] While acknowl-

---

22. *See* Standard Rules of Evidence, Mediterranean and Middle East Institute of Arbitration, Article 5 (1987); Carter, *supra* note 19, at 16, 18.
23. *See, e.g.,* FED. R. EVID. 408.
24. *See, e.g.,* Wayne Insul. Co. v. Hex Corp., 534 A.2d 1279, 1281 (D.C. App. 1987)(arbitrator, while not bound by evidentiary rules, was free to apply limits on offers of compromise to encourage "unfettered dialogue in negotiations"). See generally MACNEIL ET AL., *supra* note 1, § 35.3.5.
25. *See* AMERICAN ARBITRATION ASSOCIATION, A GUIDE FOR COMMERCIAL ARBITRATORS 18 (1997).
26. CPR ARBITRATION RULES, *supra* note 6, Rule 18.
27. *See supra* note 15.
28. *See* Bowles Fin. Grp., Inc. v. Stifel, Nicolaus & Co., Inc., 22 F.3d 1010 (10th Cir. 1994).

edging that its ruling might well discourage parties from communicating settlement offers prior to or during arbitration, the court observed that "the rules of arbitration agreed to by the parties [did] . . . not explicitly condemn the communication of settlement offers to the arbitrators."[29] Moreover, the arbitrators stated that they would not be influenced by knowledge of the settlement offer in making their decision, and there was no evidence to the contrary.

3. Proprietary information

In the course of arbitration proceedings it may become necessary for a party to disclose trade secrets or other proprietary information to another party. Certainly, any such information should be clearly identified and marked as proprietary. It may be possible to obtain confirmation from the receiving party of the proprietary nature of the information.

It may well be advisable to request the arbitrator to issue an order protecting specific information before the same is disclosed. The CPR Arbitration Rules provide:

> The Tribunal may issue orders to protect the confidentiality of proprietary information, trade secrets and other sensitive information disclosed in discovery.[30]

The AAA Commercial Procedures do not contain such express authority, but the authority may well be implied. An order of this nature is likely to be helpful, inter alia, in resisting efforts by third parties to discover the proprietary information.

Disputes about intellectual property rights may require special measures to ensure confidentiality. Some years ago, a leading corporation and one of its investment consultants settled a trade secret suit by entering into a stipulated order which established an arbitration panel to resolve future disputes between the parties.[31] Among other things, the order provided for

(1) initial referral of disputes to designated executives for "consideration and solution," followed by binding arbitration where necessary;

(2) arbitral awards enjoining the consultant from disclosing proprietary information and taking other necessary steps to protect such information;

(3) where the agreement was breached by disclosure, arbitral awards of actual and punitive damages (with actual damages being defined as the sum of (i) "three times the value of the protected information disclosed" and (ii) the greater of the consultant's unjust profits or the protected party's lost profits;

---

29. *Id.* at 1013.

30. CPR ARBITRATION RULES, *supra* note 6, Rule 11. The issues relating to protection of trade secrets and other confidential business information in arbitration are similar to those confronting participants in litigation. For a helpful discussion of the latter, see William L. Schaller, *Protecting Trade Secrets during Litigation: Policies and Procedures*, 88 ILL. BAR J., May 2000, at 260.

31. *IBM & Gartner Group Settle Trade Secret Suit by Creating Future Arbitration Panel*, 2 ALTERNATIVES TO THE HIGH COST OF LITIGATION, Sept. 1984, at 8.

(4) a confidentiality requirement binding all participants in the arbitration;

(5) limits on the selection and qualification of independent experts to ensure non-disclosure.

Rule 17 of the CPR Rules for Non-Administered Arbitration of Patent and Trade Secret Disputes, drafted by and for patent attorneys, offers a variety of protections for parties disputing intellectual property rights.

RULE 17.   CONFIDENTIALITY

17.1   All transcripts, documents, things and other information of the furnishing party produced and the testimony given in or attendant to the arbitration shall be maintained in confidence by the receiving party and the Tribunal, and shall be used only for purposes of this arbitration. The parties will insure that their respective agents, employees, attorneys and experts agree in writing to be bound by the confidentiality provisions of this Rule 17.

17.2   The obligations of Rule 17.1 hereof shall terminate with respect to any particular portion of the confidential information when a receiving party (including an arbitrator) can document that such portion:

(a) is in the public domain through no fault of the receiving party,

(b) was in the receiving party's possession free of any obligation of confidence at the time of its communication thereof,

(c) was rightfully communicated to the receiving party free of any obligation of confidence subsequent to the time it was communicated by the party to this proceeding,

(d) was developed by employees or agents of the receiving party independently of and without reference to any information that was disclosed in confidence by the other party, or

(e) when it is communicated by the transmitting party to a third party free of any obligation of confidence.

17.3   Whenever a party, arbitrator, expert witness or other person bound by the confidentiality provisions of this Rule 17 is requested pursuant to a subpoena, request for production of documents or things, civil investigative demand or other legal process, or is otherwise required by law to disclose to persons or entities not a party to this arbitration any confidential transcripts, documents, things or testimony in this arbitration, prior to responding thereto such person shall notify the parties and third persons who produced confidential information for purposes of the arbitration, if such confidential information is requested, of the existence and terms of such request. If a response to such request is due in 10 days or less, such notice shall be given within 24 hours after receipt of such request.

17.4   Within 30 days after entry of judgment of confirmation, or within 120 days after issuance of the award where judicial confirmation is not sought, each party and each arbitrator, at the election of the party furnishing the same, shall destroy or return all documents, transcripts or other things, and any copies thereof, as well as all summaries or other materials containing or disclosing information contained in, or directly related to, such documents, transcripts or things; provided, however, that counsel for the receiving party shall not be required to destroy or return its own work product which includes any of the aforesaid materials. Each party and each arbitrator shall certify under oath compliance with the above requirement.

17.5   The confidentiality provisions of this Rule 17 shall survive the arbitration proceeding, subject to the provisions of Rule 17.2 hereof.

17.6   The Tribunal may issue such orders as it deems necessary to protect any trade secrets or proprietary information that might be disclosed during the proceeding.

17.7   Damages are not adequate, and the parties otherwise would be without an adequate remedy at law for any threatened or actual disclosure or use of information in violation of Rule 17. Accordingly, an injunction may be entered against any threatened or actual disclosure or use of the information in violation of Rule 17 or any protective order issued by the Tribunal.[32]

4. Conclusion

In conclusion, arbitration is indeed a private process. Among the parties, the arbitrator, and witnesses a strong assurance of confidentiality is attainable through a combination of

- adoption of rules that include confidentiality provisions;
- signing of appropriate agreements; and
- certain practical steps.

Protection against discovery by third parties cannot be assured. It can be pointed out, as a minimum, that it will be substantially more difficult for a third party to obtain information developed in an arbitration proceeding than if the same information had been developed in a court proceeding.

Finally, a party that may need to seek protection of materials it provided in an arbitration should take care to comply fully with all confidentiality restrictions, lest it be accused later of having waived the same.

---

32. CPR INSTITUTE FOR DISPUTE RESOLUTION, RULES FOR NON-ADMINISTERED ARBITRATION OF PATENT AND TRADE SECRET DISPUTES, Rule 17 (1993).

Appendix 6.1
CPR Model Arbitration Confidentiality Agreement

AGREEMENT made _____, _____ between _____
of _____ represented by _____
and _____ of _____
represented by _____; and _____.
(the Arbitrator)

A dispute has arisen between the parties. The parties have agreed to attempt to resolve their dispute through arbitration under the CPR Rules for Non-Administered Arbitration (the "Rules"). The parties have chosen the Arbitrator to arbitrate their dispute. The parties and the Arbitrator wish to protect the confidentiality of the arbitration process.

Accordingly, the parties and the Arbitrator agree as follows:

1. Scope

The Arbitrator and each of the parties agree to comply faithfully with Rule 16 of the Rules, which provides:

> The parties and the arbitrators shall treat the proceedings, any related discovery and the decisions of the Tribunal, as confidential, except in connection with a judicial challenge to, or enforcement of, an award, and unless otherwise required by law.

All transcripts, documents, things and other information produced and the testimony given in or attendant to the arbitration shall be maintained in confidence by the parties and the Arbitrator and shall be used only for purposes of the arbitration. The parties will insure that their respective agents, employees, attorneys and experts agree in writing to be bound by the provisions of this Agreement.

2. Termination

The obligations of paragraph 2 hereof shall terminate with respect to any particular portion of the confidential information when a receiving party (including the Arbitrator) can document that such portion

(a) was in the public domain at the time of its communication thereof to such party,

(b) entered the public domain through no fault of the receiving party subsequent to the time of communication thereof,

(c) was in the receiving party's possession free of any obligation of confidence at the time of its communication thereof,

(d) was rightfully communicated to the receiving party free of any obligation of confidence subsequent to the time it was communicated by the party to this proceeding;

(e) was developed by employees or agents of the receiving party, independently of and without reference to any information that was disclosed in confidence by the other party;

(f) when it is communicated by the transmitting party to a third party free of any obligation of confidence by the other party; or,

(g) in any event, [   ] years after termination of the arbitration.

3. Disqualification of Arbitrator as Witness

The Arbitrator shall be disqualified as witness, consultant or expert in any pending or future action relating to the subject matter of the arbitration, including actions between persons not parties to the arbitration.

4. Third Party Requests for Disclosure

Whenever a party or the Arbitrator, or their agents, employees, experts or attorneys, is requested, pursuant to a subpoena, a request for production of documents or things or other legal process, to disclose to persons or entities not party to this arbitration, any information regarding the process, including any transcripts, documents, things or testimony, prior to responding thereto such party or Arbitrator shall immediately notify the other party, or in the case of the Arbitrator, both parties, of the existence and terms of such request.

5. Return of Materials

Within 30 days after termination of the arbitration, each party and the Arbitrator shall, at the election of the party furnishing the same, destroy or return all documents, transcripts or other things, and any copies thereof, as well as all summaries or other materials containing or disclosing information contained in, or directly related to, such documents, transcripts or things. Each party and the Arbitrator shall so certify under oath.

6. Survival

This Agreement shall survive the termination of the arbitration, subject to the provisions of paragraphs 1 and 2 hereof.

7. Enforcement

The parties and the Arbitrator agree that damages are not adequate, and no adequate remedy at law exists for any threatened or actual disclosure or use of information in violation of the provisions of this Agreement. Accordingly, each consents to the entry of an injunction against threatened or actual disclosure or use of the information in violation of any provision of this Agreement.

IN WITNESS WHEREOF, the parties by their attorneys have executed this Agreement as of the date first above written.

_____
Party

by:_____
Party's Attorney

_____
Party

by:_____
Party's Attorney

_____
Arbitrator

CPR MODEL NON-PARTY CONFIDENTIALITY AGREEMENT

I have received a copy and have read the Confidentiality portion, Section E, of the Agreement for Parties and Arbitrator ("Agreement") dated _____, between _____ and _____. I agree that I am fully bound by all provisions of Section E (Confidentiality) of that Agreement and that I will not violate any of such provisions. I agree that I will be subject to the same penalties as all other signatories to the Agreement or those represented by them, should I violate any of the Section E Agreement provisions. I further understand that any violation of the Section E Agreement provisions by me may subject any attorney or party hereto who has requested me to attend the arbitration proceedings to the same sanctions and penalties as if the violations had been committed by those attorneys or parties.

Name   Affiliation

_____

The Arbitration Award: Finality versus Reviewability

CHAPTER **7**

Chapter Summary

The Arbitration Award:
Finality versus Reviewability

To increase the likelihood that arbitration awards are well reasoned and consistent with the norms or standards the parties deem important, parties should consider:

(1) choosing capable arbitrators;
(2) setting clear, specific standards for the arbitrators' decision;
(3) placing limits on awards of damages or on the kinds of relief arbitrators may grant;
(4) requiring that arbitrators include a statement of reasons for their award; and
(5) providing for expanded judicial review or private review of the award (although this is a very controversial option which should be very carefully considered).

Modern laws governing binding arbitration set forth limited grounds for vacating (overturning) all or part of an arbitration award. These grounds tend to be aimed at ensuring a fundamentally fair process, consistent with the parties' bargain. They do not authorize judicial review of the merits of arbitrators' awards, but maximize the likelihood that the award will be the final resolution of the conflict, without second-guessing by courts. In addition, courts have enunciated a number of additional grounds for vacatur of awards. None of the latter have resulted in the vacatur of significant numbers of awards, but they have increased the confusion and uncertainty surrounding judicial review.

The Arbitration Award: Finality versus Reviewability

7.1

How much discretion do arbitrators have in rendering an award?

Two traditional values of arbitration are speed and finality of award. These values are closely intertwined, since the ability of arbitration to produce a speedy resolution of conflict is partly a result of courts having very limited authority under the law to review arbitrators' awards. Arbitrators typically have not been required to give reasons for their awards, which reinforces the finality of awards and contributes to the speedy resolution of disputes.

These realities are reinforced by another important traditional value of arbitration—autonomy in the choice of decisionmaker(s). As explained in Chapter 3, business persons often look for arbitrators with real world experience in the substance of the matter in dispute, be they other business persons, lawyers, or other professionals with pertinent backgrounds. The premise is that such expertise may enable the arbitrators to better understand and decide the issues in dispute—issues that may hinge more on commercial customs and usages or technical principles than on application of the law. The principle of party autonomy in choosing the decisionmaker(s) and the understanding that arbitrators often bring special expertise to adjudication reinforce the principle that the arbitrators' award should be final. Decisions under modern arbitration statutes tend to give arbitrators relatively free rein in the kinds of decisions they render—a flexibility often enhanced by the rules agreed upon for the conduct of the arbitration.

Speed, finality of award, autonomy in the choice of decisionmaker and arbitrator expertise are compelling values supporting both the flexibility of arbitrators to render awards and the related limitations on judicial oversight of commercial arbitration awards. However, some attorneys and business users of arbitration bemoan their inability to appeal what they view as bad awards—results that are difficult to explain. In some instances, they complain that the arbitral award is utterly irrational or appears to be the result of "splitting the baby," rather than a good faith effort to fairly judge the case under the facts and the law.

In this chapter we will consider key questions respecting the making of awards and the process of appealing an award to a court. In the course of the discussion we will explore the various options available to business parties for obtaining satisfactory arbitral awards, including:

- standards for the making of awards,
- limits on arbitral remedies,
- standards for review of arbitration awards by courts, and
- the possibility of "private appeal"—that is, review of the award by an appellate arbitration panel.

We will examine the possible benefits—and the costs—of each of these alternatives.

It should be noted that some Commission members voiced the concern that our extensive treatment of agreements to expand judicial review was inappropriate in light of the strong policies supporting finality of award and the related fear that expanded judicial review will eliminate a primary distinction between arbitration and litigation. Nevertheless, the Commission recognized that some business parties and counsel are now seriously considering provisions for expanded judicial review and needed to be made aware of the many practical and legal concerns associated with such arrangements. The depth of the discussion reflects the important and complex issues associated with such choices, *not* an endorsement of the concept of more judicial review. As explained below, those desiring some oversight of awards may be better served by a private appeal process.

1. Arbitrators enjoy considerable discretion in rendering an award and tailoring relief appropriate to the circumstances

Under modern arbitration law, arbitrators have considerable discretion in fashioning remedies. Generally speaking, in the absence of contrary agreement, they have at least as much authority as a court to tailor relief, including damages, temporary and permanent injunctive relief, an accounting of a business, and a declaration of parties' rights and obligations under a contract.[1] On occasion, courts have acknowledged that arbitrators' remedy-making authority may be even broader than that of judges![2] In one case, for example, a court upheld an arbitrator's order to a contractor to complete the building of a house even though such an order would have been beyond the authority of a court.[3] Although such awards are highly unusual, the case illustrates how much leeway the law grants arbitrators.

2. Broad arbitration provisions and broad remedies clauses reinforce arbitrators' remedy-making power

Arbitrators enjoy the greatest range of discretion under broad arbitration agreements, like those encompassing "all disputes arising under or relating to this

---

1. There may be some limited exceptions. For example, there is authority in California that only a court may appoint a receiver. *See* Marsch v. Williams, 28 Cal. Rptr. 2d 402, 407 (1994).

2. Ian R. Macneil, Richard E. Speidel & Thomas J. Stipanowich, Federal Arbitration Law: Agreements, Awards & Remedies under the Federal Arbitration Act, § 36.1 (1994) [hereinafter Macneil et al.].

3. *See* Bradigan v. Bishop Homes, Inc., 20 A.D.2d 966, 249 N.Y.S.2d 1018 (1964). *See generally* Macneil et al., *supra* note 2, at § 36.5.3. *See also* David Co. v. Jim Miller Construction, Inc., 444 N.W.2d 836 (Minn. 1989) (builder of defective housing units required to buy project and property from owner, although this involved relief unknown at law or in equity), *discussed in* Macneil et al., *supra* note 2, § 36.1.2.

agreement, or the breach thereof." This is especially so when such provisions are accompanied by express recognition of commensurate power to fashion remedies, as is the case when the parties agree to incorporate leading commercial arbitration rules. AAA § R-45 empowers the arbitrator(s) to "grant any remedy that the arbitrator deems just and equitable and within the scope of the agreement of the parties . . . ."[4] Whether or not it makes a difference in practice, some arbitrators conclude that the authority to grant "just and equitable" relief also empowers them to arrive at a decision they consider just and equitable, whether or not the decision is in compliance with the law. CPR Rule 10.3 provides that the "Tribunal may grant any remedy or relief, including but not limited to specific performance of a contract, which is within the scope of the agreement of the parties and permissible under the law(s) or rules of law applicable to the dispute." CPR Rule 10.1 further provides that the "Tribunal shall apply the substantive law(s) or rules of law designated by the parties as applicable to the dispute. Failing such a designation by the parties, the Tribunal shall apply such law(s) or rules of law as it determines to be appropriate."[5] If the parties wish to require the arbitrator(s) to adhere to applicable law, they would be well advised to include a statement to that effect in their arbitration agreement.

3. Limitations on judicial review are also an important factor

Broad arbitrator discretion in structuring remedies is strongly buttressed by limitations on the scope of judicial review of arbitration awards, a subject discussed below. As we will see, even a requirement that the arbitrators "follow the law" or similar restrictions on arbitral discretion may be insufficient to trigger judicial review of the merits of the award. Even if courts wished to exercise greater scrutiny, their efforts would be stymied by the absence of a record of hearings or a rationale accompanying the award.

---

4. AMERICAN ARBITRATION ASSOCIATION, COMMERCIAL DISPUTE RESOLUTION PROCEDURES, § R-45 (Jan. 1, 1999) [hereinafter AAA COMMERCIAL PROCEDURES].

5. CPR INSTITUTE FOR DISPUTE RESOLUTION, RULES FOR NON-ADMINISTERED ARBITRATION, Rules 10.3, 10.1 (Rev. 2000) [hereinafter CPR ARBITRATION RULES].

7.2

May arbitrators award punitive damages?

1. Unless otherwise agreed, arbitrators may award punitive damages

Because arbitration is a creature of contract and arbitrators act at the will of private parties, it may come as a surprise that under prevailing law in the United States arbitrators are empowered to award punitive damages when authorized by applicable law.[6] Under broad arbitration agreements arbitrators are called upon to handle all manner of contract-related claims, including tort claims and statutory causes of action where courts may impose punitive damages. It is generally recognized that arbitrators may also do so unless the parties agree to the contrary.

This has been the strong trend of judicial decisions under the Federal Arbitration Act (FAA),[7] which is likely to govern arbitrator remedies in transactions involving interstate commerce. Even New York state, long the leading opponent of punitive damages in arbitration,[8] appears to have joined the trend.[9]

---

6. *See generally* MACNEIL ET AL., *supra* note 2, § 36.3.2.1.

7. 9 U.S.C. § 1 *et seq.* (1998).

8. *See* Garrity v. Lyle Stuart, Inc., 40 N.Y.2d 354 (N.Y. 1976).

9. In Mastrobuono v. Shearson Lehman Hutton, 514 U.S. 52 (1995), the Supreme Court held that a New York choice of law clause, in and of itself, was not an indication that a customer outside New York in an NASD arbitration had intended to agree to the application of the rule in the *Garrity* case.

Mastrobuono seemingly left open the issue of whether *Garrity* was still good law in New York for New York residents who would in general expect to be governed by New York law, particularly if New York law was chosen in the agreement. And *Mastrobuono* was a case decided by looking to the intent of the parties. It did not expressly invoke preemption under the FAA.

Any doubt that *Mastrobuono* applies in New York has been eliminated by a string of appellate division cases upholding the right of arbitrators to award punitive damages wherever the parties may live. Kidder, Peabody & Co. v. Fisch, 661 N.Y.S.2d 31 (2d Dep't), *appeal denied*, 667 N.Y.S.2d 682 (1997); Americorp Sec., Inc. v. Sager, 656 N.Y.S.2d 762 (1st Dep't 1996); Merrill Lynch, Pierce, Fenner & Smith, Inc. v. Adler, 651 N.Y.S.2d 38 (1st Dep't 1996); Hamershlag, Kempner & Co. v. Oestrich, 651 N.Y.S.2d 489 (1st Dep't 1996); R.C. Layne v. Stratton Oakmont, Inc., 651 N.Y.S.2d 973 (1st Dep't 1996); Mulder v. Donaldson, Lufkin & Jenrette, 648 N.Y.S.2d 535, 538 (1st Dep't 1996). These cases assume that *Garrity* has been preempted and apply the rule that arbitrators may award punitive damages unless "the parties have unequivocally agreed otherwise." *Mulder*, 648 N.Y.S.2d at 538; *see Mastrobuono*, 514 U.S. at 58.

This view is further strengthened by a case in the New York Court of Appeals that, although not itself a punitive damages case, has broad language that arguably covers them. *See* Smith Barney Shearson, Inc. v. Sacharow, 91 N.Y.2d 39, 49 (1997) (New York choice of law clause should be read "to encompass substantive principles that New York courts would apply, but not to include special rules limiting the authority of arbitrators"). The federal cases in the Second Circuit are in accord. Paine Webber v. Richardson, 94 Civ. 3104, 1995 U.S. Dist. LEXIS 5317 (S.D.N.Y. Apr. 20, 1995); Kidder, Peabody & Co. v. Marriner, 961 F. Supp. 50 (S.D.N.Y. 1997); Oldroyd v. Elmira Savs. Bank, 956 F. Supp. 393 (W.D.N.Y. 1997); A.S. Goldmen & Co. v. Bochner, 96 Civ. 1285, 1996 U.S. Dist. LEXIS 10373 (S.D.N.Y. July 24, 1996); Cowen & Co. v. Tecnoconsult, 96 Civ. 3748, 1996 U.S. Dist. LEXIS 9763 (S.D.N.Y. July 11, 1996).

2. Such awards are rare in commercial arbitration

Having the power to award punitive damages and using it are two different things. The experience of most Commission members is that commercial arbitrators in the U.S. tend not to award punitive damages.[10] (In international arbitration, discussed in Chapter 8, punitive damages are even less likely since they are unavailable in most legal systems and would be contrary to public policy in many countries.) Nevertheless, some business parties may decide that they would rather include a provision in the arbitration agreement restricting arbitrators' ability to render punitive awards. While such an agreement will definitely take punitive damages off the table in arbitration, there is still the possibility that a party might seek punitive remedies in court.

7.3

May arbitrators award attorney's fees?

1. In some cases, arbitrators may award attorney's fees

Under the "American rule," attorney's fees are not to be awarded by courts in the United States, unless

(1) the parties have agreed that they may be awarded (as, for example, through a contract provision calling for an award of attorney's fees if a party is required to go to court to enforce rights or obligations under the contract),[11]
(2) a statute provides for an award of attorney's fees,[12] or
(3) there has been misconduct in the proceedings.[13]

Awards of attorney's fees are also exceptional in commercial arbitration. Under both the FAA, applicable to transactions involving interstate commerce, and state arbitration law, arbitrators, like courts, may award attorney's fees if the

---

10. Even in the consumer arena, there appear to be relatively few punitive awards. Statistics on arbitration awards in customer-broker disputes suggest that only 2.1% of awards contain an identified punitive element. See Thomas J. Stipanowich, *Punitive Damages and the Consumerization of Arbitration*, 92 Nw. U. L. Rev. 1, 38 (1997).

11. An agreement may be found to exist when both sides ask for attorney's fees. See First Interregional Equity Corp. v. Haughton, 842 F. Supp. 105 (S.D.N.Y. 1994); U.S. Offshore, Inc. v. Seabulk Offshore, Ltd., 753 F. Supp. 86, 92 (S.D.N.Y. 1990); Wing v. J.C. Bradford & Co., Index #16833/91 (N.Y. Sup. Ct. Apr. 6, 1992); CS First Boston v. Schuman, N.Y.L.J. Feb. 10, 1997 at 28 (N.Y. Sup. Ct.); Spector v. Torenberg, 852 F. Supp. 201, 210 (S.D.N.Y. 1994); Berman v. Stratton Oakmont, Inc., N.Y.L.J. Oct. 18, 1996 at 34 (N.Y. Sup. Ct.).

12. Dan B. Dobbs, Law of Remedies § 3.10 (1) (2d ed. 1993).

13. See Alyeska Pipeline Serv. Co. v. Wilderness Soc'y, 421 U.S. 240, 247, 258 (1975).

parties so agree.[14] Courts applying the FAA have also enforced awards of fees pursuant to a statute[15] or where there was a frivolous claim or defense.[16] Although the Uniform Arbitration Act (UAA), which is the model for most state arbitration statutes, appears to require an agreement of the parties on attorney's fees,[17] the recently revised version of the UAA, in the absence of contrary agreement, empowers arbitrators to award attorney's fees "if such an award is authorized by law in a civil action involving the same claim or by the agreement of the parties to the arbitration proceeding."[18]

2. The handling of attorney's fees varies under leading commercial arbitration rules

Under the CPR Arbitration Rules, arbitrators are specifically empowered to "fix" and apportion the "costs of arbitration," including "costs for legal representation and assistance."[19] The Commentary notes that in making awards of fees and other costs the arbitrators "may take into account tactics by either party that unreasonably interfered with the expeditious conduct of the proceeding."[20]

The AAA Commercial Procedures permit an award of attorney's fees only "if all parties have requested such an award or it is authorized by law or their arbitration agreement."[21] AAA arbitrators are authorized to assess and apportion among the parties administrative fees, expenses, and compensation as deemed

---

14. *See* MACNEIL ET AL., *supra* note 2, § 36.8.3.
15. *See, e.g.,* Kamakazi Music Corp. v. Robbins Music Corp., 684 F.2d 228 (2d Cir. 1982). *See generally* MACNEIL ET AL., *supra* note 2, § 36.8.2.
16. *See, e.g.,* Todd Shipyards Corp. v. Cunard Line, Ltd., 943 F.2d 1056 (9th Cir. 1991). *See generally* MACNEIL ET AL., *supra* note 2, § 36.8.4.
17. § 10 of the Uniform Arbitration Act (1997) states:

> Unless otherwise provided in the agreement to arbitrate, the arbitrators' expenses and fees, together with other expenses, not including counsel fees, incurred in the conduct of the arbitration, shall be paid as provided in the award.

UNIF. ARBITRATION ACT § 10, 7 U.L.A. 131 (1985). *Cf.* New York CPLR § 7513 (1998).
18. *See* National Conference of Commissioners on Uniform State Laws, Uniform Arbitration Act (2000) § 21(b) [hereinafter Revised UAA]. In any event, as in all issues respecting arbitrator remedies, the FAA has an influence over whether arbitrators can award attorney's fees. A number of cases have held that under federal law, they can be awarded by arbitrators regardless of state law. A.S. Goldmen & Co., Inc. v. Bochner, 96 Civ. 1285, 1996 U.S. Dist. LEXIS 10373, at *4 (S.D.N.Y. July 24, 1996); Cowen & Co. v. Technoconsult Holdings Ltd., 96 Civ. 3748, 1996 U.S. Dist. LEXIS 9753, at *16–17 (S.D.N.Y. July 11, 1996); Merrill Lynch, Pierce, Fenner & Smith v. Adler, 651 N.Y.S.2d 38 (1st Dep't 1996); Merrill Lynch, Pierce, Fenner & Smith, Inc. v. Dreissens, N.Y.L.J. Oct. 23, 1996, at 1 (N.Y. Sup. Ct.); Lester Schwab Katz & Dwyer v. Yukevich, 641 N.Y.S.2d 505, 506 (Sup. Ct. 1996). But the cases are not as consistently supportive of arbitrator power, regardless of state law, as in the case of punitive damages. *See* Paine Webber, Inc. v. Richardson, 94 Civ. 3104, 1995 U.S. Dist. LEXIS 5317, at *3 (S.D.N.Y. Apr. 21, 1995); Merrill Lynch, Pierce, Fenner & Smith, Inc. v. Cornell, N.Y.L.J. Feb. 15, 1996 at 25 (N.Y. Sup. Ct.); Stratton Oakmont, Inc. v. Fairbank, Index no. 105127/96 (N.Y. Sup. Ct. May 13, 1996); Merrill Lynch, Pierce, Fenner & Smith, Inc. v. Levine, N.Y.L.J. July 5, 1995 at 26 (N.Y. Sup. Ct.); and Lybrand v. Merrill Lynch, Pierce, Fenner & Smith, Inc., 467 S.E.2d 745, 747 (S.C. Ct. App. 1996). On the other hand, under a broad arbitration clause, the parties' choice for arbitrators to decide if attorney's fees may be awarded overrides state law to the contrary. Paine Webber, Inc. v. Bybyk, 81 F.3d 1193 (2d Cir. 1996).
19. CPR ARBITRATION RULES, *supra* note 5, Rules 16.2.–16.3.
20. *Id.* Commentary to Rule 16.
21. AAA COMMERCIAL PROCEDURES, *supra* note 4, § R-45(d).

appropriate.[22] "Expenses" is defined as "expenses of witnesses for either side" and "other expenses . . . including travel and other expenses of the arbitrator, AAA representatives, and any witness...."[23]

7.4

Are abuses of arbitral discretion—irrational or unacceptable compromise awards—a problem?

1. Commission members' perspectives

Complaints are heard regarding arbitration awards that a party views as exceptionally unsound or unfair. Because court review of arbitration awards is very limited, a frustrated party may have no outlet other than to complain. It is important to note, however, that as a rule Commission members have been reasonably satisfied with awards rendered by commercial arbitrators. In their experience, the "irrational" award is an exceptional event.

Commission members associate several factors with satisfactory awards. Selection of the right arbitrator(s) is far and away the most important factor in getting an acceptable result. This subject is treated briefly below, and at greater length in Chapter 3.

Another part of the prescription for obtaining a satisfactory result is to establish clear standards for decisionmaking, such as a particular body of law, commercial norms, or technical standards. These requirements may be set out in the original arbitration agreement. The importance of adhering to the standards may be reinforced at the pre-arbitration conference and during the hearing, and in briefs filed on behalf of the parties. See Sections 7.5 and 7.6.

For a variety of reasons, it may be advantageous to require the arbitrators to publish a statement of the rationale supporting their award. As discussed below, this is especially true in high-stakes disputes and other cases where the additional cost of preparing a written opinion is offset by the perceived benefits of having the arbitrators explain their reasoning.

In some cases, Commission members have found it useful to limit the scope of the arbitrators' authority regarding awards, as in "baseball" or "last offer" arbitration. These approaches are discussed in Section 7.5.

Finally, there is the possibility of agreeing to a more extensive judicial review of an arbitration award—a controversial approach upon which Commission members differ greatly, and which must be approached with considerable caution. Related questions and concerns are discussed at some length in the following pages, as is the alternative of submitting arbitration awards to a private appellate panel—in essence, appellate arbitration.

---

22. *Id.* § R-45(c).
23. *See id.* § R-52.

2. The perception that arbitration awards often represent an inappropriate compromise—and some likely explanations

Complaints about arbitration awards are often based on the perception that arbitrators have—in the vernacular of lawyers and business persons, "split the baby"—that is, rendered an award that represents a mere compromise of the positions espoused by the parties. Complaining parties often attribute "splitting the baby" to

- the inability or unwillingness of arbitrators to decide close issues one way or the other;
- the arbitrators' desire not to offend either party by giving something to everyone; or
- an averaging of the positions of individual members of an arbitration panel.

While any of these concerns may be justified in a particular case, it is likely that the tendency of arbitrators to compromise is overstated.[24] What some call "splitting the baby" may also be the product of a rational decision. Consider that in arbitration:

- there will often be a number of claims asserted—sometimes dozens—and it is reasonable to assume that some will prevail while others will not;
- there will often be counterclaims on various issues that may partially off-set awards on successful claims;
- the arbitrators may find it necessary to modify one or more elements of the damages calculations based upon their own view of the proof; or
- the arbitrators may believe it appropriate to reduce an award to reflect a claimant's own partial responsibility for damages (as where, in a construction arbitration, it is proven that both owner and contractor caused delays during a particular time period for which the owner claims delay damages).

In many cases a judge might have arrived at a similar result. The difference is that arbitrators are often not required to explain their decision. Moreover, there generally is little a court can do to overturn an award even if it suspects that the award is illogical or not in conformance with the facts or with applicable law.

---

24. In 1986, the AAA conducted a study of 100 randomly selected cases concluded that year. In over half of those cases, arbitrators awarded more than 60% of the amount claimed; in another 34% of the cases, they awarded less than 40%. Only 13% of the awards were within the range of 40–60% of the amount claimed. American Arbitration Association, Case Administration—Update, Press Release (July 25, 1986). Although this may not prove that arbitrators do not compromise, it is clear that they do not routinely "split things down the middle."

7.5

How can parties lower the risk of unacceptable compromise awards or other abuses of arbitral discretion?

There are a number of things business parties can do to try to ensure that arbitration awards are well reasoned and consistent with the norms the parties consider important. These options include:

(1) choose capable arbitrator(s),
(2) set clear, specific standards for the arbitrators' decision,
(3) place limits on awards of damages or on the kinds of relief that arbitrators may grant,
(4) require that the arbitrators include a statement of reasons for their award, and
(5) provide for expanded judicial review or private review of the award.

Parties are free to exercise any and all of these choices in structuring their own arbitration. As discussed above, some of these options have been regularly and successfully employed by members of the Commission. Other options—such as agreements for expanded judicial review of arbitration awards—are much more controversial, and involve potentially significant additional costs to arbitrating parties. Review may also undermine other traditional values of arbitration, such as speed and finality.

With that caution in mind, let us consider each of the options in turn.

1. Choose capable arbitrator(s)

Commission members agree that the best way to eliminate the likelihood of unsatisfactory awards is to select arbitrators who are likely to make a sound award. (Arbitrator selection is discussed at length in Chapter 3.)

2. Set clear and specific standards for the arbitrators' decision

The second most important factor in ensuring an award that meets expectations is to make certain those expectations are clearly communicated to the arbitrators.

Identify appropriate standards in the agreement.   First of all, parties may specify in their agreement the standards to be used by the arbitrator in rendering a decision, such as the law of a particular state, norms of an industry (including, for example, commercial grades or standards of quality), or technical requirements. At the same time, they might make clear that it is these standards and not the arbitrators' own sense of justice or fair play that should control the decision. (In the international arena, as we will see in Chapter 8, the parties would explain that the arbitrators could not act as an *amiable compositeur* or *ex aequo et bono*.)

Reinforce expectations at the pre-arbitration conference(s) and the hearing.   The expectation that arbitrators will render an award in accordance with certain standards may be reinforced by discussions at the pre-arbitration conference(s) and at the arbitration hearings. Responsive decisions may also be encouraged by written arguments or briefs filed by the parties during or after the hearings—the most obvious kind of example being a legal brief citing pertinent law on the issues in dispute.

3. Place limits on awards of damages or on the kinds of relief that arbitrators may grant

It is also possible for parties to agree to limit the range of damages that arbitrators may award, or to preclude them from granting certain kinds of relief. The main problems with this approach are that (1) it may be impossible or impractical to identify appropriate limitations when the parties are writing their predispute arbitration agreement into their contract, and (2) the necessary consensus may be lacking after disputes arise. Nevertheless, there are circumstances in which the parties may agree to one of the following options.

Place limits on damages awards.   By placing limits on awards of monetary damages, the parties may limit the upside or downside risk. Thus, for example, parties who concur that Party A owes Party B a certain amount of money but differ as to the appropriate amount might establish a dollar range within which the arbitrator(s) could render an award. One Commissioner reports:

> A common scenario for "high/low" arbitration is the situation where an insurance company trades out a questionable argument of "no liability" for a low maximum limit of damages.

Another approach is to set forth standards for the imposition of damages in the arbitration award: for example, "Extended home office overhead shall be calculated in accordance with the Eichleay method."

Give the arbitrator an "either/or" choice: last offer arbitration, baseball arbitration.   Even less arbitrator discretion is involved in procedures such as "last offer" arbitration or "baseball" arbitration in which the decisionmaker must make an award based on the offer of one party or the other. Let's consider the pros and cons:

Pros
- The parties have a high degree of control over the result, since the arbitration award is limited to as few as two options, and the options are identified by the parties themselves.
- There is no possibility of an inappropriate compromise award.
- Requiring an arbitrator to pick one of several tendered proposals forces the parties to be realistic, so that often there is little difference between their proposals, inducing party compliance with the award.

Cons
- All of the foregoing is gained at the almost total loss of arbitral flexibility—there is no ability to acknowledge a reality other than the positions stated by the parties.

Preclude awards of certain kinds of relief, such as punitive damages. Some arbitration agreements preclude arbitrators from making awards of punitive damages, or damages in excess of actual damages proven.

Pros
- If the parties agree to limited remedies or otherwise limit the arbitrators' discretion, there may be less likelihood of an award that shocks one side, and more likelihood of satisfaction with the arbitration and voluntary compliance with the award. This is particularly true in the case of punitive damages, where (unless the award is based on a statutory formula such as "treble damages") there is no way of predicting the amount of the eventual award.

Cons
- If arbitrators cannot police extreme behavior by awarding punitive damages in appropriate cases, then arbitration may be a haven for bad actors.
- It is possible that preventing arbitrators from awarding punitive damages will only divert such issues into the court system, where a jury may decide the matter. Due to public policy concerns, punitive damages may not be waivable by pre-dispute agreement.

4. Require that the arbitrators include a statement of reasons for their award

Traditionally, commercial arbitrators were discouraged from including a rationale with their award on the basis that offering a statement of reasons would only encourage a party to seek further judicial scrutiny. Today, however, many commercial arbitration agreements in major business contracts call for arbitrators to provide a statement of reasons supporting the arbitration award. For example, the CPR Rules provide that "[a]ll awards shall be in writing and shall state the reasoning on which the award rests unless the parties agree otherwise."[25] The AAA Commercial Dispute Resolution Procedures do not expressly call for a statement of rationale. What are the pros and cons of a requirement that the award include a statement of reasons?

Pros

- The requirement of providing reasons sometimes helps the arbitrator(s) analyze the problems fully and consider all relevant evidence and arguments. As one scholar notes:

    The requirement of a statement of reasons for the award [(1)] provide[s] notice to the arbitrator that parties expect the resolution of their dispute to be founded on careful, thoughtful efforts, . . . [(2)]propel[s] advocates to frame their cases-in-chief and arguments in a manner that facilitates methodical analysis by the arbitrator . . . and . . . [(3)] will oblige arbitrators to pay careful attention and remain fully engaged throughout the proceedings.[26]

- Obvious errors may be brought to the attention of the arbitrator(s) and corrected.
- It may make voluntary compliance with an award more likely, and discourage the further expense of litigation to confirm or challenge the award, because the parties will have a better sense that they have had their "day in court" and their positions have been considered.
- As several scholars have noted, the absence of written opinions can be an insurmountable hurdle for parties seeking judicial review.[27]

Cons

- A published rationale may give disgruntled parties more of a "target" for appeal of the award, and may make a challenge to the award even more likely. Some argue that a written decision may encourage attorneys to pursue appeal and to articulate additional reasons for vacatur of the award.
- Requiring reasons adds to the cost of arbitration, particularly when there are three arbitrators, because the arbitrators work longer and charge more to ren-

---

25. CPR ARBITRATION RULES, *supra* note 5, Rule 14.2.

26. Stephen L. Hayford, *A New Paradigm for Commercial Arbitration: Rethinking the Relationship Between Reasoned Awards and the Judicial Standards for Vacatur*, 66 GEO. WASH. L. REV. 443, 501 (1998).

27. No matter how much intellectual energy judges expend in trying to set down clear standards for reviewing the merits of challenged arbitration awards, the absence of any indicia of the arbitrator's mode of decision prevents the judges from reliably ascertaining whether the type or degree of purported arbitral error in a given case warrants vacatur. Because arbitral error can be judicially divined only from the award's face, the thresholds for this inference must be set so high that the promise of meaningful review is rendered illusory, leaving the parties with no guarantee of accurate and correct results. *Id.* at 499.

der their reasoned award. One Commissioner notes that "three arbitrators can spend prodigious amounts of time revising each other's draft award."

For such reasons, the AAA discourages the use of such opinions in the absence of specific agreement by the parties. (Since the AAA procedures do not provide for a written statement of rationale, if the parties desire an opinion they should require one in their contract or so agree at the beginning of the arbitration.) By contrast, CPR Arbitration Rule 14 requires all awards to be reasoned, unless the parties agree otherwise. As explained in the Commentary to Rule 14, CPR considers it good discipline for arbitrators to require them to spell out their reasoning and restrains any tendency on the part of arbitrators to reach compromise awards.

5. Provide for expanded judicial review or private review of the award

The final options—expanded judicial review of arbitration awards, or appeal of awards to another private panel—are also the most controversial. Although both choices may provide additional insurance against irrational arbitration awards, they also carry costs and other burdens of their own that may or may not be justified by the perceived benefits.

Because an understanding of these options requires an appreciation of the present state of law and practice, and because each option actually encompasses a number of choices, the remainder of this chapter is devoted to their treatment.

7.6

What are the standards for judicial review of arbitration awards under present law?

Arbitration awards are subject to relatively limited judicial review under existing legal standards. These standards derive from two sources: federal and state statutes (such as the standards set forth in § 10 of the FAA[28] and judicial decisions.[29] Under the statutes, arbitrators have broad authority to conduct the

---

28. 9 U.S.C. § 1 *et. seq.* (1998).
29. For a more thorough discussion *see* MACNEIL ET AL., *supra* note 2, ch. 40. *See also* Stephen L. Hayford, *Law in Disarray: Judicial Standards for Vacatur of Arbitration Awards*, 30 GA. L. REV. 731 (1996).

process, to examine evidence and hear arguments, and to resolve factual and legal issues (including issues of contract interpretation).[30] Had the parties wanted court due process and a determination under the law by judge or jury, the argument goes, they would not have agreed to arbitrate. The limited grounds for overturning an award under modern arbitration statutes reflect the strong policy supporting finality of arbitration awards and minimal judicial interference with the judgments of arbitrators. From time to time federal and state courts have announced additional grounds for overturning awards to avoid what they view as gross injustice or a violation of law or public policy. Even so, commercial arbitration awards tend to be significantly more "bulletproof" than court judgments. Courts tend to confirm and enforce awards absent "clear evidence of gross impropriety."[31]

1. Statutory standards for review

Modern laws governing binding arbitration set forth limited grounds for vacating (overturning) all or part of an arbitration award. These grounds tend to be aimed at ensuring a fundamentally fair process rather than reviewing the merits of the arbitrators' decision. For example, § 10 of the FAA[32] empowers courts to vacate an award

- where the award was procured by corruption, fraud, or undue means;
- where there was evident partiality or corruption in one or more arbitrators;
- where the arbitrators were guilty of misconduct in refusing to postpone the hearing upon sufficient cause shown, or in refusing to hear evidence pertinent and material to the controversy, or of any other misbehavior by which the rights of any party have been prejudiced, or
- where the arbitrators exceeded their powers, or so imperfectly executed them, that a mutual, final, and definite award upon the subject matter was not made.

Nearly all of these grounds concern the fairness of the hearing and the presiding arbitrators; the last also ensures that the arbitrators act within their jurisdiction as defined by the parties' agreement and submissions.[33] There is no provision permitting vacatur for misapplication of the law or for errors of fact, no matter how obvious. For this reason, some courts have gone so far as to say that perhaps judicial action under these standards "ought not be called review at all."[34]

---

30. *See* MACNEIL ET AL., *supra* note 2, § 40.6.1.
31. *Id.* at § 40.1.4 (discussing judicial decisions under the FAA).
32. 9 U.S.C. § 10 (1998).
33. Still, the strong federal policy favoring arbitration causes courts to accord the "narrowest of readings" to the "exceeded their powers" standard. *See, e.g.,* Davis v. Chevy Chase Finance Ltd., 667 F.2d 160, 164–65 (D.C. Cir. 1981). *See generally* MACNEIL ET AL., *supra* note 2, § 40.5.3.
34. *See* UHC Management Co. v Computer Services Corp., 148 F.3d 992 (1998).

The rationale behind the statutory schemes is simple:

(1) make sure that parties have a fair process, consistent with their bargain, and
(2) maximize the likelihood that the award will be the final resolution of the conflict, without second-guessing by courts.

2. "Non-statutory" standards for vacatur of award

Over time, federal and state courts have announced additional standards for review and vacatur of arbitration awards.[35] These "non-statutory" standards vary from jurisdiction to jurisdiction. For example, although the U.S. Court of Appeals for the Fourth Circuit rejects all such grounds for review,[36] the remaining federal appellate courts recognize at least one of the following bases for vacating an award under federal arbitration law:

- the award was rendered in manifest disregard of the law;[37]
- the award was arbitrary and capricious;[38]
- the award was completely irrational;[39]
- the award was in violation of public policy;[40] or
- the award fails to draw its essence from the parties' underlying contract.[41]

Such standards evolved to protect parties against awards that seem contrary to law, reason, or prevailing public policy. Although often described as independent of statutory grounds, they are sometimes viewed as particular interpretations or definitions of the statutory authority to vacate when arbitrators "exceed their powers."[42] Whatever their genesis, for reasons of policy and practicality they are seldom employed to vacate awards.

A brief discussion of each of these standards will suffice:

(1) ***The award was rendered in manifest disregard of the law.*** It has been said that the standard of "manifest disregard" offers protection in those relatively rare instances where an arbitrator understands and correctly states the law, but then disregards the law when rendering an award.[43] In

---

35. *See* Comment, Bret F. Randall, *The History, Application and Policy of the Judicially Created Standards of Review for Arbitration Awards*, 1992 B.Y.U. L. Rev. 759 (1992).
36. Hayford, *supra* note 29, at 731.
37. *See* Wilko v. Swan, 346 U.S. 427, 436–37 (1953).
38. *See, e.g.*, Ainsworth v. Skurnick, 960 F.2d 939, 941 (11th Cir. 1992).
39. *See* Swift Indust. v. Botany Indust., 466 F.2d 1125 (3rd Cir. 1972).
40. *See, e.g.*, Seymour v. Blue Cross/Blue Shield, 988 F.2d 1020, 1023 (10th Cir. 1993).
41. *See, e.g.*, Anderman/Smith Operating Co. v. Tennessee Gas Pipeline Co., 918 F.2d 1215 (5th Cir. 1990).
42. *See* Macneil et al., *supra* note 2, §§ 40.1.3.2, 40.5.1.
43. *See* Advest, Inc. v. McCarthy, 914 F.2d 6, 9 (1st Cir. 1990); Siegel v. Titan Indus. Corp., 779 F.2d 891, 892–93 (2d Cir. 1985). *See generally* Macneil et al., *supra* note 2, § 40.7.

one widely cited decision, however, the standard was recently used to overturn an award in an employment case where the absence of a statement of reasons accompanying the award reinforced the court's conclusion that the arbitrators manifestly disregarded the law.[44]

(2) ***The award is arbitrary and capricious; the award is completely irrational.*** Such standards, among others, are used to describe circumstances in which arbitrators go "flat out" against the terms of the contract.[45] Courts reaching such conclusions often explain that "the arbitrator's decision cannot be inferred from the facts of the case,"[46] or "the award cannot be rationally derived from the agreement or the facts surrounding the dispute."[47] When one allows for the broad authority of arbitrators to interpret the contract, the law and other norms, to oversee the taking of evidence, and to find facts, however, it is understandable why vacatur on such grounds is rare. (These standards are treated more extensively below among possible options for those agreeing to enhanced review.)

(3) ***The award is against public policy.*** It is also possible, although highly unusual, for courts to vacate an award as contrary to federal or state public policy. Normally, however, vacatur is limited to circumstances where a well-defined and dominant public policy is violated; it may even be necessary for the award to compel a violation of positive law.[48] At least under federal arbitration law, therefore, the public policy defense is dead in the absence of a clear expression of Congressional intent to limit arbitral authority.[49] (In the international realm, the U.N. Convention on the Recognition and Enforcement of Foreign Arbitral Awards makes public policy a ground for non-enforcement of an award. See Chapter 8.)

(4) ***The award fails to draw its essence from the agreement.*** This standard is a questionable borrowing from decisions involving collective bargaining agreements; it is sometimes used vigorously to "rein in" labor arbitrators.[50] It is rarely used in the commercial context.[51]

Although none of the foregoing standards has resulted in the vacatur of significant numbers of arbitration awards, they have increased the confusion and uncertainty surrounding judicial review. At the same time, they have not meaningfully enhanced judicial oversight of awards for those parties desiring such oversight. (We will return to these concerns in the context of options for those agreeing to enhanced judicial review.)

---

44. Halligan v. Piper Jaffray, Inc., 148 F.3d 197 (2d Cir. 1998).
45. *See* Macneil et al., *supra* note 2, § 40.6.1.
46. *See* Ainsworth v. Skurnick, 960 F.2d 939 (11th Cir. 1992).
47. Swift Indust. v. Botany Indust., 466 F.2d 1125 (1972).
48. Stroh Container Co. v. Delphi Indus., Inc., 783 F.2d 743 (8th Cir. 1986).
49. *See* Macneil et al., *supra* note 2, § 40.8.1.1.
50. *Id.* § 40.6.1.
51. Anderman/Smith Operating Co. v. Tennessee Gas Pipeline Co., 918 F.2d 1215 (5th Cir. 1990).

3. Practical limitations on judicial review

Whatever the standard of judicial review of arbitration awards, court oversight may be significantly limited by lack of information about how arbitrators reach their decisions. The frequent absence of a record of the arbitration proceedings and the want of a rationale accompanying the arbitration award, deprive courts of the tools necessary to scrutinize arbitral judgments. In the absence of information to the contrary, for example, courts will generally assume that the arbitrators have not exceeded their powers.[52] (See the discussion of the pros and cons of a statement of reasons above.)

The publication of a statement of reasons for the award is no guarantee that the parties will have a clear understanding of the factual and legal predicates for the decision. There is a big difference between a three-sentence explanation and a multi-page compendium with a treatment of legal sources, findings of fact, and conclusions of law. As discussed below, in the interest of making judicial review meaningful a New Jersey statute authorizing parties to "opt into" enhanced judicial review of arbitration awards requires arbitrators to make "findings of all relevant material facts, and . . . all applicable determinations of law."[53]

7.7

Can the parties agree to expand the standards of judicial review for arbitration awards? When, if ever, is such a course advisable? What standards should be applied?

1. The current debate over the enforceability of agreements to expand judicial review of arbitration awards

Conflicting precedents

Agreements to expand or enhance judicial review of arbitration awards are a fairly recent phenomenon and have engendered much debate.[54] Because court

---

52. *See* Barbier v. Shearson Lehman Hutton Inc., 948 F.2d 117, 121 (2d Cir. 1991).

53. New Jersey Alternative Dispute Resolution Act, N.J. STAT. ANN. 2A, §§ 23A–12 (1999).

54. *See* Hans Smit, *Contractual Modification of the Scope of Judicial Review of Arbitral Awards*, 8 AM. REV. INT'L ARB. 147 (1997); Alan Scott Rau, *Contracting out of the Arbitration Act*, 8 AM. REV. OF INT'L ARB. 225 (1997); Andrea F. Lowenfeld, *Can Arbitration Coexist with Judicial Review?*, ADR CURRENTS, Sept. 1998 at 1; Stephen P. Younger, *Agreements to Expand the Scope of Judicial Review of Arbitration Awards*, 63 ALB. L. REV. 241 (1999); Carroll E. Neeseman, *Party-Chosen Arbitral Review Standards Can Inspire Confidence in the Process, and Is Good for Arbitration*, 5 DISP. RES. MAG., Fall 1998, 18; Stanley McDermott, III, *Expanded Judicial Review of Arbitration Awards Is a Mixed Blessing That Raises Serious Questions*, 5 DISP. RES. MAG., Fall 1998, 18. At least one special arbitration statute, a California enactment setting up a special arbitration procedure for public contracts disputes, incorporates a provision calling for judicial review of awards for factual or legal errors, permitting vacatur if the award "is not supported by substantial evidence . . . or is not decided under or in accordance with the laws of [California]." *See* CAL. PUB. CON. CODE § 10240.12 (1999).

decisions conflict regarding the ability of parties to confer greater authority on reviewing courts,[55] parties wishing to incorporate such provisions in their agreement to arbitrate must proceed with caution. The current trend, however, appears to be in favor of the enforceability of agreements to expanded judicial review (at least so long as the agreed standard of review does not impose an undue burden upon the court).[56] This position is consistent with the general principle that arbitration is, first and foremost, a creature of contract, and that it affords parties considerable flexibility in tailoring their dispute resolution process to their own particular needs.

A primary argument against privately expanded review is founded on the notion that the "jurisdiction" of a federal court cannot be conferred by agreement. For example, some courts have concluded that allowing parties to contract for expanded judicial review under federal arbitration law would illegally allow parties to create federal court jurisdiction in violation of Article III of the Constitution.[57]

Those disagreeing with this conclusion question the underlying assumption that the courts would not otherwise have jurisdiction to review the matter under modern arbitration law. They point out that this assumption ignores the fact that the FAA and parallel state arbitration statutes neither confer nor remove jurisdiction, but serve only to facilitate and vindicate agreements to arbitrate.[58] Courts must have independent subject matter jurisdiction to review the award of an arbitrator.[59] Parties do not create jurisdiction in the courts by allowing them to review a matter over which they already had jurisdiction. The statutory limits on judicial review of arbitration awards are no more than a "default rule" reflecting traditional views on the binding effect of awards, and can be varied at will by the parties.[60]

"Jurisdiction" is, however, often loosely used to describe more than the subject matter jurisdiction of the courts. In this context expressed concern about "jurisdiction" might in fact reflect the view of some that a statutory standard of review cannot be expanded by private agreement because to do so would conflict with the legislature's reasons for specifying the standard. Thus, for instance, if the standards of review in the FAA were animated in part by a desire to divert business from the federal courts, it might be thought inconsistent with

---

55. Decisions supporting the enforceability of such agreements include Syncor Int'l Corp. v. McLeland, No. 96-2261, 1997 U.S. App. LEXIS 21248 (4th Cir. Aug. 11, 1997); Gateway Tech., Inc. v. MCI Telecomm. Corp., 64 F.3d 993 (5th Cir. 1995); Lapine Tech. Corp. v. Kyocera Corp., 130 F.3d 884 (9th Cir. 1997); and Fils Et Cables D'Acier De Lens v. Midland Metals Corp., 584 F. Supp. 240 (S.D.N.Y. 1984). Those opposed include Chicago Typographical Union v. Chicago-Sun Times, Inc., 935 F.2d 1501 (7th Cir. 1991); UHC Management Co. v. Computer Sciences Inc., 148 F.3d 992 (8th Cir. 1998). *See also Kyocera*, 130 F.3d at 891 (Mayer, J., dissenting).

56. *See* James M. Ringer & Martin L. Seidel, *Judicial Review Clauses in Transnational Arbitration Agreements*, 12 No. 5 INSIDE LITIG. 6, 9 (1998).

57. *See Chicago Typographical Union, supra* note 55, 935 F.2d at 1505; *UHC Management, supra* note 55, 148 F.3d at 998.

58. *See Kyocera, supra* note 55, 130 F.3d at 890.

59. *See id.* at 889, citing Moses H. Cone Mem'l. Hosp. v. Mercury Constr. Corp., 460 U.S. 1, 25 n.32 (1983).

60. *See* Rau, *supra* note 54, at 231.

legislative intent to permit expansion of those standards by private agreement. Moreover, some standards, such as those specified in a treaty, may be deemed non-derogable for other reasons.[61] Professor Rau argues, however, that under modern arbitration law the preeminent policy is to "rigorously enforce agreements to arbitrate"—a policy that trumps public or private interests in speed and economy; in this light, limitations on judicial review are not meant to be a straitjacket.[62]

Whether the issue is defined as conferring jurisdiction by contract, or simply intrusion by private parties into court procedure and administration, the propriety of enhanced judicial review of arbitration awards will be the subject of continuing debate until resolved at the highest judicial level or through statutory amendment. Until such time, there will be the danger in many jurisdictions that an agreement for enhanced judicial review will be collaterally attacked, delaying final resolution of the underlying dispute.

Statutory reform

The growing interest in agreements to expand judicial review of arbitration awards and the ensuing debate over their enforceability has already inspired attempts at statutory reform.

Thus far, the only state which has enacted a general statute providing for enhanced judicial review of arbitration awards is New Jersey. Under New Jersey law, parties may contractually agree that their arbitration is to be governed by the New Jersey Alternative Procedure for Dispute Resolution (New Jersey APDRA).[63] Under the APDRA, arbitrator's awards are subject to judicial review (and potential vacatur) for, among other things, "committing prejudicial error by erroneously applying law to the issues and the facts."[64] In addition, the statute requires a written award which states "findings of all relevant material facts" and makes "all applicable determinations of law . . . in accordance with applicable principles of substantive law."[65] It also provides that "a decision of the [arbitrator] . . . on the facts shall be final if there is substantial evidence to support that decision."[66] Furthermore, the act states that, upon a determination that the arbitrator committed prejudicial error in applying applicable law, the reviewing court shall vacate or modify the award and "appropriately set forth the applicable law and arrive at an appropriate determina-

---

61.· As some scholars have argued, another way to look at enhanced review is to see such agreements as placing certain acts—such as errors of law—beyond the scope of the arbitrator's authority; judicial review for such errors may then be appropriate under the terms of FAA § 10(a)(4) and its state counterparts. *See* Thomas J. Stipanowich, *Rethinking American Arbitration*, 63 IND. L.J. 425, 486 n.339 (1988); Rau, *supra* note 54, at 238–39.

62. *See* Rau, *supra* note 54, at 245.

63. New Jersey Arbitration Act, N.J. STAT. ANN. §§ 2A:24-1, *et. seq.* (1999); New Jersey Alternate Procedure for Dispute Resolution, N.J. STAT. ANN. 2A, §§ 23A-1, *et. seq.* (1999). As explained in note 54 *supra*, at least one state has a special arbitration statute providing for more searching review of arbitration awards rendered in public contracts disputes.

64. N.J. STAT. ANN. 2A, § 23A-13c.(5) (1999).

65. N.J. STAT. ANN. 2A, § 23A-12 (1999).

66. N.J. STAT. ANN. 2A, § 23A-13b. (1999).

tion under the applicable facts . . . ."[67] In other cases, the court may order a rehearing before the same or another arbitrator.[68] Finally, the APDRA attempts to substantially shorten the duration of appeals by precluding review of arbitration awards beyond the Chancery Division of the Superior Court.[69]

While the New Jersey APDRA is a creative response to the perceived need for an option for enhanced judicial review, it also points up the number of pre- and post-award procedural issues which are implicated in structuring such review. In other words, agreeing to enhanced judicial review involves much more than setting the appropriate standard. In the case of an implementing statute like the APDRA, many of these issues can be addressed by law.[70] Where, as in most places, there is no implementing statute, it is up to the parties to address relevant procedural issues in their agreement.

More recently, a drafting committee of the National Conference of Commissioners on State Laws (NCCUSL) revising the Uniform Arbitration Act, the model for state arbitration law in most jurisdictions, submitted alternative draft provisions permitting parties to opt into enhanced judicial review for consideration by NCCUSL.[71] After much debate, NCCUSL voted down the proposed provisions for enhanced judicial review.

2. Other considerations for those contemplating enhanced review

Perceived benefits of expanded review

Corporate philosophy, bad experiences with arbitration, or extremely high stakes may encourage a party to seek what they perceive as insurance of enhanced judicial oversight. According to a recent survey of more than 600 Fortune 1,000 corporations, many U.S. businesses regard the relative lack of appeal from an arbitration award as a major drawback of arbitration.[72] Some of these companies may prefer the "full process" of litigation in the court system. Others may seek contractually-expanded judicial review of the arbitration award.

By heightening judicial scrutiny of arbitration awards, it is reasoned, there will be more of a chance that bad awards will be undone, and arbitrators, mindful of the possibility of reversal on appeal, will be more judicious and more temperate in their deliberations. In addition to providing more protection against clear error, some argue, increased judicial involvement may add legitimacy to the arbitration process and encourage more individuals to experiment with arbitration.

67. N.J. Stat. Ann. 2A, § 23A-13f. (1999).
68. N.J. Stat. Ann. 2A, § 23A-14 (1999).
69. N.J. Stat. Ann. 2A, § 23A-12 (1999).
70. The New Jersey APDRA does not limit the flexibility of parties to craft their own modifications to its terms. *See* Mt. Hope Devel. Assoc. v. Mt. Hope Waterpower Project, L.P., 712 A.2d 180 (1998).
71. *See* Revised Uniform Arbitration Act, *supra* note 18, § 23, Reporter's Notes.
72. *See* David B. Lipsky & Ronald L. Seeber, The Appropriate Resolution of Corporate Disputes: A Report on the Growing Use of ADR by U.S. Corporations, Cornell/PERC Institute on Conflict Resolution 28 (1998).

Concerns regarding expanded review

The members of the Commission are not of one mind on the issue of permitting expanded judicial review as a matter of policy. One member writes:

> While I understand the problems which lead people to wish for some review mechanism, on balance, I do not favor enhanced judicial review. Arbitration is already taking on too many trappings from the court system. If we add enhanced judicial review, we destroy much of the reason for arbitration. In my judgment, the problems which lead to the desire for an appeal process can be largely addressed by better management of the arbitrational process.

It is widely assumed that appellate review gives a greater assurance of justice. At least one member of the Commission questions this assumption. He points out that the original tribunal will have devoted much more time to pondering the case than an appellate tribunal is able to do. This is likely to result in a fair and practical award, even if arguably an award not in strict compliance with applicable law.

Parties planning an expanded role for courts in overseeing arbitration awards are advised to proceed with great caution.

Need for a record, statement of reasons.   The tradeoff between enhanced process and loss of efficiency and cost-saving begins at the hearing. If meaningful judicial review is to occur, an adequate record and a statement of reasons accompanying the award are usually considered critical. Both entail additional costs and potential concerns.

Procedural realities of enhanced review.   Once a court is committed to close scrutiny of a decision, any hope of a speedy resolution of conflict may be dashed by the realities of court docketing. The starkest possibilities inherent in expanded judicial review are exemplified by the very case that gave rise to the leading decision supporting the concept: *Lapine Technology Corp. v. Kyocera Corp.*[73] The parties to an international joint venture had agreed to arbitrate under the ICC Rules, but also agreed that the arbitration panel was to include "detailed findings of fact and conclusions of law" with the award. They further provided that the reviewing court could vacate, modify, or correct on the grounds specified in the FAA, or "where the arbitrators' findings of fact are not supported by substantial evidence, or . . . where the arbitrators' conclusions of law are erroneous."[74] When complex disputes arose, the parties engaged in an arbitration which produced a record of more than 15,000 pages of transcript and 72 boxes of documents, and, ultimately, an award containing "hundreds of findings of fact and conclusions."[75] When the award was challenged, the district

---

73. *See* 130 F.3d 884 (9th Cir. 1997).
74. *See* Rau, *supra* note 54, at 225.
75. *See id.* at 248.

court refused to scrutinize the arbitrators' findings of fact or conclusions of law.[76] Reversing the lower court ruling, the Ninth Circuit remanded the case "for review of the [award] . . . by use of the agreed-to standard."[77] Although, as one judge observed, the district court's task in review is less onerous than that imposed on the arbitration panel[78] (presumably, even under a "substantial evidence" standard, it will not be reviewing the entire 72 boxes of evidence but that which is brought to their attention by the parties[79]), there is no doubt that the effort will require many months and postpone significantly final disposition of the disputes. Ironically, the company which originally urged incorporation of the review provision now challenges its enforceability.

Concerns regarding over-use of appellate option.   Another concern with establishing a practice of contractually enhancing judicial review has to do with the tendencies of some legal counsel to view the choice of added process as a mandate. Although some experienced attorneys will assuredly weigh the advantages and disadvantages of enhanced review on a case-by-case basis, other attorneys may deem the failure to opt for more judicial review as tantamount to malpractice. Once the enhanced review procedure is in place, the AAA states in its literature, "[p]roviding a mechanism for such an appeal assures that the losing party will use it."[80] On the other hand, some recent experience with private appeal systems suggests that use of the mechanism is not inevitable. (Private appeal processes are discussed below.)

Impact on arbitrator remedy-making.   Finally, there is concern that enhanced judicial scrutiny, with all of its attendant procedural trappings, may discourage arbitrators from fashioning creative solutions to the problems before them. Where such flexibility is of high priority to the parties, enhanced review may undermine the parties' goals.

Many of the foregoing concerns surfaced during the annual meeting of the National Conference of Commissioners on Uniform State Laws (NCCUSL), which debated whether the Uniform Arbitration Act should be amended to incorporate a provision specifically authorizing agreements for expanded judicial review of awards.[81] As mentioned above, the group decided against such action.

The Supreme Court of New Jersey summed up the attitude of many members of the bench and bar most pointedly:

> [F]or those who think parties are entitled to a share of justice, and that such justice exists only in the care of the court, [we] hold that parties

---

76. *See* Lapine Technology Corp. v. Kyocera Corp., 909 F. Supp. 697 (N.D. Cal. 1995).

77. 130 F.3d 884, 891 (9th Cir. 1997).

78. 130 F.3d at 891 (Kozinski, J., concurring).

79. *See* Rau, *supra* note 54, at 249, *citing* LOUIS L. JAFFE, JUDICIAL CONTROL OF ADMINISTRATIVE ACTION 602 (abridged ed. 1965).

80. American Arbitration Association, *Drafting Dispute Resolution Clauses—A Practical Guide*, 770 PLI/COMM. 19, 52 (Jan. 1998)[hereinafter *Drafting Dispute Resolution Clauses*].

81. *See* note 71, *supra.*

are free to expand the scope of judicial review . . . [of arbitration awards] by contract . . . . I doubt that many will. And if they do, they should abandon arbitration and go directly to the courts.[82]

Ultimately, a matter of party choice

When all is said and done, there will be business persons and counsel who believe that providing enhanced review is important as a "relief valve" to protect the legitimate expectations of parties in big cases. Some parties may demand the "insurance" of enhanced judicial oversight before arbitration becomes an attractive option. It all comes down to a fundamental question, as a member of the CPR Commission explains:

> I just helped draft a contract for a very sophisticated international company with considerable arbitration experience which contained a provision for enhanced judicial review of the award. The company's view was that you should only use such a provision in a "bet the company" case because it comes down to a tradeoff. First of all, in going to court you risk whether it's going to be enforceable. Ultimately, you really have to think about whether you want to sacrifice the speed and economy of arbitration for a better quality award, because you'll have an arbitrator who'll be thinking about an appellate court reviewing the award. As a client explained, "Even if I had Judge Cardozo on my panel, there might be mistakes. We all make mistakes." The question is, is the opportunity for review worth the time and expense?

3. Standards for Enhanced Judicial Review

Those who conclude, despite all the drawbacks, that enhanced judicial review may be beneficial must ultimately settle upon a standard. Given the lack of guidance on this issue, the selection of the standard of review involves the parties' careful consideration of their goals and reasonable expectations for the dispute resolution process. If parties value efficiency and finality more than the presumed "perfect award," common sense would dictate the selection of a standard affording the utmost deference to the arbitrator's decisions. This would decrease the likelihood of vacatur and should decrease the incentive of the parties to seek judicial review. If parties are concerned with proper application of the law and are seeking judicial review to enforce this expectation on the arbitrator, they might opt for a more searching inquiry respecting legal issues under a less deferential standard of review.

---

82. Tretina Printing Co. v. Fitzpatrick & Assoc., Inc., 640 A.2d 788, 793 (N.J. 1994).

In the interest of providing basic guidance for those providing for enhanced judicial review, several options are outlined below. To one degree or another, they reflect the historical distinctions between "law" and "fact" that permeate appellate review in the courts. They also bring with them, for better or worse, the baggage of years of application in the judicial realm; they often provide rather vague and variable guideposts for post-award judicial intervention.

De novo review for errors of law

In appellate review of judicial decisions, the greatest scrutiny is reserved for errors of law. The appellate court will decide questions of law de novo.[83] In such circumstances, the argument goes, "[t]he appellate court actually is in as good a position as the trial court to decide those legal questions and, indeed, ruling on questions of law is one if its functions in guiding the lower courts."[84] (Factual determinations are subject to less searching review, as discussed below.)

For those who, as a result of philosophy or circumstance, believe arbitration is strengthened by promoting adherence to the rule of law, this approach may have some merit. In the words of one federal court of appeals, limiting the substance of review to legal errors would be "clearly far less searching and time consuming . . . than a full trial."[85]

There are, however, several disadvantages to this type of review. It may force a strict application of the law in cases where commercial circumstances would have warranted otherwise. For one who choses arbitration to avoid the "rough edges of the law," it may undermine the primary benefits of the process. Because the review for legal error is similar to that undertaken in the court system, moreover, additional costs and delays will take the place of quick and convenient justice. As in the public justice arena, distinguishing mixed questions of law and fact, which are subject to the de novo standard, from purely factual questions, which are not, may produce complex analyses since factual and legal issues are often closely intertwined.[86]

In considering whether to incorporate a provision specifically authorizing parties to opt into an "error of law" standard of judicial review, the NCCUSL drafting committee revising the Uniform Arbitration Act (UAA) expressed serious concerns regarding the difficulty of devising "an unambiguous, bright line test for application of . . . [a] standard that would not lead to significant variance across the states . . . [,] a goal that has to date eluded the federal and state courts."[87] NCCUSL has since voted down proposals for "opt-in" provisions in the revised UAA.

If, despite these concerns, the parties still wish to incorporate an "error of law" standard for review of arbitration awards, it is appropriate if not necessary to make clear that to justify vacatur the error of law must be one that results in prejudice to a party, as in the New Jersey APDRA.[88]

---

83. *See* Jack H. Friedenthal, Mary Kay Kane & Arthur R. Miller, Civil Procedure §13.4 (2d ed. 1993).
84. *See id.* at 604.
85. Flexible Manuf. Sys. v. Super Products Corp., 86 F.3d 96, 100 (7th Cir. 1996).
86. *See* Friedenthal et al., *supra* note 83, at 605–06.
87. *See* note 71, *supra.*
88. N.J. Stat. Ann. 2A, § 23A-13c(5) (1999).

The clearly erroneous standard

Within the judicial system, the "clearly erroneous" standard of review is typically used to evaluate the factual determinations reached by trial courts.[89] The Supreme Court stated: "A finding is 'clearly erroneous' when although there is evidence to support it, the reviewing court on the entire evidence is left with the definite and firm conviction that a mistake has been committed."[90] One federal court of appeals went so far as to conclude that "under the 'clearly erroneous' review a court may substitute its judgment for that of the trial court and upset findings which are unreasonable."[91]

Attempts to adopt the "clearly erroneous" standard for review of agency findings of fact under the Administrative Procedure Act (APA) have been rigorously opposed on the basis that it would permit courts to substitute their own views for those of expert administrators and result in delay and inefficiency, in addition to problems derived when a case is remanded after the arbitrator(s) may have lost jurisdiction.

In the arbitration arena, judicial review to determine whether the evidence supports the fact findings is a substantial step beyond review for errors of law (although practically speaking, issues of law and fact are often "inextricably intertwined"[92]):

> Here the power of the arbitrators to make binding determinations with respect to the merits of the dispute has been drastically truncated; although there is an initial adjudication by the arbitrators, the court remains the ultimate repository of decision making authority. In so structuring their agreement , the parties have not only required the creation of a record—they have also imposed on a . . . court the obligation to examine it, and test the arbitrators' findings against it.[93]

For most, searching review of the factual basis of arbitration awards is an option to be avoided because of its effect on the finality of the arbitrator's decision and the efficiency of the process.

The substantial evidence standard

The "substantial evidence" standard evolved in the context of appellate court review of jury verdicts to distinguish their treatment from the "clearly erroneous" standard then applicable to findings of judges sitting without juries.[94] The standard is now applied by the APA to review of agency findings of fact adopted through formal rulemaking or formal, on-the-record adjudication.[95] As

89. FED. R. CIV. P. 52(a). See FRIEDENTHAL ET AL., supra note 83, at 604–05; BERNARD SCHWARTZ, ADMINISTRATIVE LAW § 10.11 (3rd ed. 1991).
90. United States v. Gypsum Co., 333 U.S. 364, 395 (1948).
91. Ethyl Corp. v. EPA, 541 F.2d 1, 35 n.74 (D.C. Cir. 1976).
92. See Rau, supra note 54, at 248.
93. Id. (discussing application of the "substantial evidence" standard of review).
94. See KENNETH CULP DAVIS & RICHARD J. PIERCE, JR., ADMINISTRATIVE LAW TREATISE § 11.2, 174 (1994).
95. 5 U.S.C. § 706(2)(E). See generally DAVIS & PIERCE, supra note 94, § 11.2.

explained by a leading commentator, "the test is whether a reasonable person could draw the conclusion reached."[96] In the words of the Supreme Court:

> Substantial evidence is more than a scintilla, and must do more than create a suspicion of the existence of a fact to be established. It means such relevant evidence as a reasonable mind might accept as adequate to support a conclusion, . . . and it must be enough to justify, if the trial were to a jury, a refusal to direct a verdict when the conclusion sought to be drawn from it is one of fact for the jury.[97]

Fundamentally, the standard is one of *reasonableness*.[98] Since a finding of fact can be wrong and still admit of a reasonable explanation, the standard is theoretically more deferential than "clearly erroneous" (but there are those who question whether practical differentiations can be made between the standards[99]). It is theoretically less deferential than the "arbitrary and capricious" test[100]—although, as suggested below, courts have little guidance for distinguishing the two tests and there may be little or no practical difference in their application to findings of fact.

In the administrative context, the Supreme Court has explained that "the substantiality of evidence must take into account whatever in the record fairly detracts from its weight . . . [and this is why the APA requires courts to] consider the whole record."[101] On the other hand, according to the Supreme Court, "the possibility of drawing two inconsistent conclusions from the evidence does not prevent [a] . . . finding from being supported by substantial evidence."[102] An extensive treatment of judicial applications of the "substantial evidence" standard in administrative settings is contained in the Davis & Pierce treatise.[103]

Like the "clearly erroneous" standard, the "substantial evidence" standard is only appropriate in circumstances where the parties desire more than minimal judicial oversight of arbitrator fact findings. Again, "the court remains the ultimate repository of decisionmaking authority"; there must be a record against which to examine and test the arbitrators' findings.[104]

The arbitrary and capricious standard

Borrowing both from judicially created standards of review and administrative law, parties could choose to adopt a standard whereby awards are vacated only when they are deemed "arbitrary" or "capricious." The Administrative Procedure Act requires courts to apply the "arbitrary and capricious" test to

---

96. *See* DAVIS & PIERCE, *supra* note 94, § 11.2, *citing* Stern, *Review of Findings of Administrators, Judges and Juries: A Comparative Analysis*, 58 HARV. L. REV. 70, 84 (1944).

97. NLRB v. Columbian E. & S. Co., 306 U.S. 292, 300 (1939).

98. *See* SCHWARTZ, *supra* note 89, § 10.13.

99. *See, e.g.*, Rau, *supra* note 54, at 249.

100. *See* Abbott Laboratories, Inc. v. Gardner, 387 U.S. 136, 143 (1967).

101. Universal Camera Corp. v. NLRB, 340 U.S. 474, 488 (1951).

102. Consolo v. Federal Maritime Commission, 383 U.S. 607, 619–21 (1966).

103. *See generally* DAVIS & PIERCE, *supra* note 94, § 11.2. *See also* Schwartz, *supra* note 89, §§ 10.7–10.12.

104. *See supra* note 93.

agency acts in the context of informal adjudication—essentially, without a formal hearing on the record, or informal rulemaking.[105]

Although courts have defined "arbitrary and capricious" in various ways, the Eleventh Circuit (which adopted the standard ex cathedra as a ground for vacatur of award) stated that the standard requires vacatur when "the ground for the arbitrator's decision cannot be inferred from the facts of the case."[106] This standard resembles the "completely irrational" standard described below in its attempt to accord considerable deference to the decisions of arbitrators. Long ago, the Supreme Court said that in applying the standard in the review of agency factfindings:

> [i]f any state of facts can be conceived that would sustain [the agency order], there is a presumption of the existence of the state of facts, and one who assails [the presumption] must carry the burden of showing . . . that the action is arbitrary.[107]

As one leading treatise on administrative law explains, such a test "demands virtually nothing . . . except a lawyer with enough creativity to identify a plausible justification for the [challenged action] . . . based on a plausible pattern of facts."[108]

Courts which have applied the "arbitrary and capricious" standard to arbitration awards have tended to employ a strong presumption that the arbitration award is correct. Practically speaking, therefore, "arbitrary and capricious" is "a very difficult standard for the party contesting (an) arbitration award to overcome. Indeed, the award is presumptively correct, and will be vacated only if there is no ground whatsoever for the (arbitrator's) decision."[109] Mere legal error, for example, may not be a sufficient basis for vacatur under this standard of review.[110] Thus understood, the "arbitrary or capricious" standard would best be invoked in agreements between parties whose priorities are efficiency and finality, but who want a limited opportunity to seek non-statutory review in extraordinary circumstances.

One further note of caution: application of the "arbitrary and capricious" standard may be complicated by a line of cases dealing with findings of fact made by federal agencies whose actions are subject to statutory judicial review—a body of precedent which is much less deferential to the agency than traditional "arbitrary and capricious" applications. The leading decision in this vein is *Citizens to Preserve Overton Park v. Volpe*,[111] in which the Court stated that the "arbitrary and capricious" test demands "searching and careful" inquiry into the factual bases of

---

105. The Administrative Procedure Act requires courts to "hold unlawful and set aside agency action" that is "arbitrary, capricious, an abuse of discretion . . ." 5 U.S.C. § 706(2)(A) (1998).

106. Ainsworth v. Skurnick, 960 F.2d 939, 941 (11th Cir. 1992).

107. Pacific States Box & Basket Co. v. White, 296 U.S. 176, 186 (1935). Put another way, in some administrative contexts the test is passed if an agency action "has any chance of furthering a legitimate goal based on any plausible state of facts." *See* DAVIS & PIERCE, *supra* note 94, § 7.4, 311, *citing* Allied Stores v. Bowers, 358 U.S. 522, 530 (1959).

108. DAVIS & PIERCE, *supra* note 94, at 311.

109. Lifecare, Inc. v. CD Medical, Inc., 68 F.3d 429, 435 (11th Cir. 1995).

110. *See, e.g.*, Plaza Bank of West Port v. Board of Governors of Federal Reserve System, 575 F.2d 1248 (8th Cir. 1990); Hurley v. U.S. 575 F.2d 792 (10th Cir. 1992).

111. 401 U.S. 402 (1971).

the agency's decision.[112] Although *Overton Park* and its progeny have been much criticized, they have provided a vehicle for manipulating the "arbitrary and capricious" test to permit judicial reversal of agency rulings with which courts disagree.[113] Moreover, although the Court has often stated that the substantial evidence test requires more stringent judicial review than "arbitrary and capricious," the Court has never explained the difference between the two standards.[114]

In light of the possible confusion resulting from the *Overton Park* gloss and other questions arising from judicial precedent, parties considering the use of the "arbitrary and capricious" standard should probably define specifically what they intend by incorporating that standard, or come up with different terms to achieve the same end. (See, for example, the standard incorporated in the CPR Arbitration Appeal Procedure, Appendix 7.1.)

The abuse of discretion standard

Although often overlooked by commentators, control of discretionary power is a matter separate and apart from issues of law or fact. Under APA § 706, for example, agency actions must satisfy the requirement of reasoned decision making independent of the question of evidentiary support for its findings.

The "abuse of discretion" standard is yet another possible alternative for parties seeking expanded judicial review of arbitration awards. This standard of review, not unlike the "completely irrational" and "arbitrary and capricious" standards mentioned above, embodies a strong presumption in favor of affirming an arbitrator's award. Because this standard is highly deferential, however, the likelihood of success on appeal would be very limited. Those parties wanting only very limited opportunity for judicial review may consider this standard as a viable supplement to those contained in § 10 of the FAA. In reality, the abuse of discretion standard may not provide any more meaningful review than the "exceeded their powers" provision of § 10 of the FAA.

The complete irrationality standard

Another standard only permits vacatur where the arbitrator's decision is found to be "completely irrational."[115] This minimal threshold accords extreme deference to arbitrators' decisions, but preserves an opportunity for vacatur for awards that severely frustrate the expectations of the parties.[116] It may, however, provide too little protection for parties who seek meaningful protection from misapplications of the law and too little guidance for the judges charged with applying it.

---

112. *Id.* at 416.
113. *See* DAVIS & PIERCE, *supra* note 94, § 11.4.
114. *See id.* at 202.
115. *See* Swift Industries v. Botany Industries, 466 F.2d 1125 (3rd Cir. 1972).
116. It has been argued that:

    [s]uch a minimal requirement does not inflict judicial intermeddling in the arbitral process. . . . Any party agreeing to arbitrate disputes with another implicitly expects the arbitrator to resolve the conflict reasonably. Such a party may bargain for simplicity and informality, but no one bargains for the abdication of reason.

Kenneth R. Davis, *When Ignorance of the Law Is No Excuse: Judicial Review of Arbitration Awards*, 45 BUFF. L. REV. 101–02 (1997).

4. Other matters to consider in drafting provisions for enhanced review

As previously mentioned in connection with the drafting of statutory provisions for enhanced judicial review of arbitration awards, settling upon an acceptable standard of review is only one aspect of the problem. Those drafting contract provisions for enhanced review should consider a number of pre- and post-award process issues. These include:

- dollar limits or subject matter limits on enhanced review (e.g., "Where the matter in controversy submitted to arbitration exceeds $100,000");
- the nature of the record of the arbitration hearing;
- the nature and contents of the award, including findings of fact or conclusions of law;
- requirements for notifying other parties of intent to seek enhanced review;
- the possibility of remand to the original panel, who likely have lost jurisdiction, or to another arbitration panel; and
- allocation of costs of appellate procedure; possible reimbursement of appellee's costs, expenses, and fees if the appeal is unsuccessful.

A Commission working group developed a model provision for enhanced judicial review of awards that addresses such issues.

Many of the same issues are discussed below in the context of private appeal processes. An example of a private appeal process, the CPR Arbitration Appeal Procedure, is contained in Appendix 7.1.

5. A blueprint for contractually enhanced judicial review

(1) The array of potential standards for enhanced judical review of arbitration awards offers parties a variety of choices. Because of the great potential for undermining the goals of finality and efficiency that are so often paramount to commercial parties, contractual provisions for enhanced review should be approached with the greatest care. Such provisions are most likely to be perceived as beneficial in "big" or "bet the company" cases. (Of course, the stakes may not always be apparent when the original pre-dispute arbitration clause is drafted.)

(2) Based on experience to date, parties desiring enhanced judicial review usually want review for error of law. Such review is appropriate where legal issues are likely to play a prominent part in controversies between the parties, as is often the case in large, complex disputes.

(3) Parties should make a separate determination regarding the appropriateness of a review of findings of fact. Although, practically speaking, it may not always be easy to differentiate factual and legal issues, standards

that permit courts to review the whole record (clear error of fact, substantial evidence) repose ultimate discretion in the courts as opposed to the arbitrators. Although those seeking greater deference to arbitrator findings of fact may opt for an "arbitrary and capricious" standard, the varying applications of that and other standards by courts may lead to confusion. Parties are urged to consider the possibility of defining the standard they intend to use, perhaps by incorporating one of the frequently cited judicial definitions.

(4) In the course of selecting a standard of review, the parties must consider what pre- and post-award procedures must be put in place to implement the standard in a meaningful way.

7.8

Can the parties agree to a private appellate process? Should they?

What if commercial parties desire some form of review to address irrational awards, but have concerns regarding review in the courts? Some will address the problem by a private appellate mechanism—in effect, a second tier of arbitration—to permit oversight of the initial award.

1. Existing appellate arbitration procedures and programs

Although they are the exception rather than the rule, provisions for appellate arbitration may be found in a variety of commercial arbitration procedures.[117] They have been incorporated in the arbitration rules of some trade associations,[118] various international arbitration procedures,[119] and a process crafted under the collective bargaining agreement between the National Basketball Association and the National Basketball Players Association.

---

117. *See generally* MACNEIL ET AL., *supra* note 2, § 37.7.

118. NATIONAL GRAIN AND FEED ASS'N (NGFA) ARBITRATION RULES, Section 9 (Apr. 9, 1998); AMERICAN SPICE TRADE ASS'N (ASTA) ARBITRATION RULES, Section H (May 1989).

119. One example is the INTERNATIONAL CENTRE FOR SETTLEMENT OF INVESTMENT DISPUTES (ICSID) ARBITRATION RULES, CONVENTION ON THE SETTLEMENT OF INVESTMENT DISPUTES BETWEEN STATES AND NATIONALS OF OTHER STATES, Art. 52 (1966); *see also* ICSID Rules of Procedure for Arbitration Proceedings, Rule 52 (1968).

Another appellate procedure is tied to the World Trade Organization's Dispute Settlement system, which addresses disputes among national parties to WTO agreements. *See* <http://www.wto.org/wto/about/dispute1.htm>.

Since 1995, JAMS has offered an optional appeal procedure.[120] The procedure is adopted as a part of consensual arbitration procedures in about ten percent of cases filed (although it is actually resorted to in very few cases). CPR promulgated an Arbitration Appeal Procedure in mid-1999.[121] In its most recent guidelines for drafters of arbitration provisions, moreover, the American Arbitration Association endorsed the concept of private appeal and set forth proposed language for drafters.[122] A handful of published opinions make reference to appellate arbitration procedures.[123]

2. The debate over private appeal

The evidence suggests that more and more parties are considering the use of such "internal" appeal mechanisms in lieu of or in addition to judicial review. Those favoring private appeal may view it as a salutary alternative to judicial review, both in terms of cost- and time-saving and meaningful oversight of the arbitral award. Some believe private procedures can alleviate the need to challenge an award in court while enhancing confidence in the arbitration process.

Others argue that appeal to a private arbitration panel may only add to the time and expense of finally resolving a dispute. A party might continue to contest an award in court even after private appeal, either by bringing a motion to vacate or forcing an opponent to seek confirmation of award and execution upon the resulting judgment. Better, some say, to concentrate on finding sound arbitrators for the original arbitration hearing and "getting it right the first time around."[124]

On the other hand, arbitrating parties may feel the need for a second look, particularly when the stakes are very high, or when outsiders are concerned about procedural due process.[125] But an appeal procedure may only be practical in cases involving large amounts of money or other significant interests, where

---

120. JAMS COMPREHENSIVE ARBITRATION RULES AND PROCEDURES, Rule 32 (revised June 2000) <http://www.jamsadr.com/comprehensive_arb_rules.asp>.

121.   *See* CPR ARBITRATION APPEAL PROCEDURE (1999), reproduced in Appendix 7.1.

122.   *See Drafting Dispute Resolution Clauses, supra* note 80, at 30–31 (the guidelines were prepared by a committee including CPR Commission members James Carter, Dana Freyer, and John Wilkinson). Yet another proposed template, intended for "commercial arbitration agreements between parties with equal bargaining power" is provided by New York attorney and arbitrator Stephen Hochman. *See* Stephen A. Hochman, *Model Dispute Resolution Provisions for Use in Commercial Agreements Between Parties with Equal Bargaining Power, in* ALI-ABA COURSE OF STUDY MATERIALS, ALTERNATIVE DISPUTE RESOLUTION: HOW TO USE IT TO YOUR ADVANTAGE! (Mar. 19, 1998).

123.   *See, e.g.,* Coast Trading Co. v. Pacific Molasses Co., 681 F.2d 1195, 1197 (9th Cir. 1982)(arbitration appeals committee of Pacific Northwest Pea Growers and Dealers Ass'n); Tamari v. Bache Halsey Stuart Inc., 619 F.2d 1196, 1202–1203 (7th Cir. 1980)(Committee of Appeals of Chicago Board of Trade); Cofinco, Inc. v. Bakrie & Bros., N.V., 395 F. Supp. 613 (S.D.N.Y. 1975)(appellate procedures of Rules of Green Coffee Ass'n).

124.   For example, one Oregon attorney with considerable arbitration experience, who successfully challenged an appellate award in court, suggests that in most commercial cases a second tier of arbitration is superfluous. He urges parties to find good arbitrators and good procedures in the first instance, get a decision, and be done with it.

125.   For example, the Chair of the American Spice Trade Association (ASTA) Arbitration Supervision Board says that ASTA's appellate procedures were developed partly in response to the concerns of foreign merchants. Interview with Walter Weening (Oct. 2, 1998).

process cost is not a significant issue.[126] It should not be used where people are most concerned about process cost or speed.

The finality of arbitration awards may well lead parties to opt for litigation in high stakes cases. A private appeal procedure offers insurance against an aberrant award that may induce such parties to arbitrate rather than litigate. However, the appeal procedure is likely to be invoked rarely. This assumption is confirmed by the experience of JAMS, which reports that parties that have agreed to incorporate its appellate procedure rarely use it.[127]

On balance, it appears that there is a place for well-crafted, carefully tailored appellate arbitration procedures in commercial arbitration. Leading institutional providers of arbitration services (including CPR and JAMS) have acknowledged that in some cases a private appellate option may be desired by arbitrating parties, and it is possible to structure the appeals option as a pre-dispute or post-dispute election.

3. Issues associated with appellate arbitration

Those weighing the possibility of a private appellate process should consider each of the following issues.

Limitations on scope

In agreeing to a private appeal process, parties often establish certain limits on the kinds of disputes that may be submitted for review. For example, some trade association programs exempt from appeal arbitrator determinations regarding the quality of goods.[128]

As noted above, cost considerations are likely to induce some parties to limit review to cases involving large amounts of money. According to one major institutional provider, parties sometimes delay the decision to employ an appellate procedure until a dispute has arisen and an arbitration demand has been filed.[129] At this time, the parties will be in the best position to decide whether or

---

126. David Barrett, Counsel for Public Affairs of the National Grain and Feed Association (NGFA) points out that the kinds of cases that get appealed are the big dollar cases where parties feel strongly. Interview with David Barrett (Oct. 2, 1998). In the NGFA system, "test" appeals are sometimes used to predict the likely outcome of similar cases in the system, thus avoiding extended process in other cases. NGFA Trade Rules and Arbitration Rules Booklet, Arbitration Rules § 9 (1998) [hereafter NGFA Rules].

Dariush Etemad-Moghadam of JAMS strongly concurs. He believes that the appellate procedures provided by JAMS are a "great option" for large cases. He offers the example of a huge, complex environmental dispute in which the parties would probably not have elected arbitration at all but for the option of private appeal. In the event, they were not able to settle the dispute until they had exhausted the appellate procedure. Interview with Dariush Etemad-Moghadam, Senior Project Manager, JAMS (Oct. 2, 1998).

127. *Id.*

128. Walter Weening of the American Spice Trade Association (ASTA) Arbitration Supervision Board points out that quality determinations—a highly discretionary arbitral function—are not subject to review in the ASTA system. (It should be noted, however, that disputes sometimes arise about whether a particular issue is one of quality.) Interview with Walter Weening, *supra* note 125.

129. Interview with JAMS, n.126 *supra.*

not the "extra process" might be justified. CPR suggests that the parties stipulate a monetary threshold for the appellate process. See Appendix 7.1.

Procedural requirements

Some programs establish filing requirements and other hurdles for appealing parties. These may include additional filing fees, or a requirement that sums representing all or part of any adverse arbitration award be placed in escrow pending appeal. Such requirements may have a significant impact on the use of the appellate process.[130]

JAMS charges a filing fee for appeals comparable to the fee for the initial filing of an arbitration.[131] Parties opt to include the appellate procedure in their arbitration agreement in approximately one in ten cases. The parties' mutual decision to incorporate the procedure typically occurs after the filing of a demand and prior to the commencement of arbitration hearings, and usually arises in the context of relatively large, complex disputes.

Time limits on the appeal process

Although they vary in detail, private appeal procedures typically include specific time limits within which key events must occur. Some even establish an overall time limit for the private appeal.[132] The common aim is avoidance of undue delay in finalization of the arbitration award.

Special qualifications for arbitrators

As we have seen, picking the right arbitrator is critical to a satisfactory process. This is no less true in appellate arbitration.[133]

Appellate arbitration procedures often establish special qualifications for arbitrators at the appellate level. The CPR Arbitration Appeal Panel, for example, consists exclusively of former federal judges.[134] In light of the con-

---

130. For example, the ASTA procedures require appealing parties to pay 50% of any adverse monetary arbitration award into escrow at the time they file an appeal. Arbitration Supervision Board Chair Walter Weening observes that, apparently as a consequence of this rule, appeals are very rare. *Id.* According to an ASTA staff member, there is no record of any appeal being filed since the escrow requirement was established some years ago. Interview with Gerri Critantiello (Oct. 2, 1998).

Similarly, the NGFA Rules require appellants to submit a filing fee for appeal. David Barrett notes that the motivating principle was to avoid unnecessary delays in payment of awards. The NGFA requirements do not seem to have eliminated appeals; however, they occur in less than 20% of arbitrated cases according to Barrett. Interview with David Barrett, *supra* note 126.

131. Interview with Dariush Etemad-Moghadam, *supra* note 126.

132. *See* Collective Bargaining Agreement, National Basketball Association and National Basketball Players Ass'n, Art. XXXII, Sec. 6 (Sept. 1995).

133. Efficiency may be promoted by selection of the right appellate arbitrators. For example, David Barrett, Counsel for Public Affairs of the National Grain and Feed Association (NGFA) observes that because they are comprised of experienced business persons, NGFA appellate panels typically act very quickly. Interview with David Barrett, *supra* note 126.

134. ASTA's supervisory board selects a special panel of arbitrators with input from the parties. NGFA has a standing Arbitration Appeals Panel of twelve people, five of whom (including the Panel's chair) sit on any particular appeal; according to David Barrett, all are well respected in the industry, and experienced arbitrators. *Id.*

tentious atmosphere which may surround appellate arbitrator selection, more-over, parties are well-advised to have a mutually acceptable "default" selection method.[135] Most institutional appeal procedures provide for such a method.

Standard(s) of review

The most important (and arguably the most difficult) question for those consider-ing a private appellate process is the appropriate standard of review. Some private appellate procedures provide no standards for review. This is a serious mistake.

A spectrum of possible choices from the court and administrative law spheres is set forth above in the discussion of contractual agreements to enhance judicial review; such considerations also arise in the context of private appeal. In structuring its Arbitration Appeal Procedure, CPR concluded that the appel-late tribunal should be required to accord a high level of deference to the origi-nal arbitration award. Thus, the procedure permits vacatur or modification only on the grounds specified in § 10 of the Federal Arbitration Act, or where the appeals panel determines:

> (i) the Original Award contains one or more material and prejudicial errors of law of such a nature that the Original Award does not rest on any appropriate legal basis, or (ii) that it is based upon factual findings clearly unsupported by the record.[136]

The NBA's procedure incorporates standards of review employed by the Second Circuit Court of Appeals. ICSID's grounds for "annulment" are similar to grounds for judicial vacation of award under leading arbitration statutes.[137]

At least one set of rules limits each party to one appeal per case.

Record of arbitration proceedings

As previously noted, meaningful appellate review may not be possible without an adequate record of the arbitration proceedings. Therefore, most existing appellate rules establish certain requirements for the development of a record to facilitate review. At least one set of rules provides a mechanism for the admin-istering institution to "assemble" the record in preparation for review.[138]

---

135. JAMS does not have a special panel of appellate arbitrators. It does, however, encourage parties to attempt to reach agreement on very basic qualifications for arbitrators (e.g., that they be former federal judges, or be from a particular location). Dariush Etemad-Moghadam reports that appealing parties are often par-ticularly concerned about having appellate arbitrators who do not have connections to the original arbitra-tor(s). Interview with Dariush Etemad-Moghadam, *supra* note 126.

136. *See* CPR ARBITRATION APPEAL PROCEDURE, *supra* note 121, Rule 8.2.

137. In the 1980s, four appeals in the ICSID process provoked substantial critical commentary. However, according to Antonio Parra, Legal Adviser to ICSID, despite a "phenomenal" growth in the ICSID caseload since the 1980s, no parties have employed the annulment process. Maybe, suggests Parra, the process has had an in terrorem effect on arbitrators. Interview with Antonio Parra (Oct. 2, 1998).

138. The NGFA Rules provide that the Secretary of the Association will assemble the arbitration record with the assistance of the parties. *See generally* NGFA Rules, *supra* note 126.

Written opinion accompanying the award

For similar reasons, rules providing for private appeal also require the original arbitrators to prepare a written award with a statement of reasons and/or findings of fact and conclusions of law. At least one set of rules contemplates the possibility that the original arbitrator will be invited to the appellate session.[139]

Opportunity for oral argument

Most private appeal procedures contemplate oral arguments, although some leave it to the option of the parties.[140] Under the CPR Arbitration Appellate Procedure, for example, either party or the appellate tribunal may require an oral hearing. Although it is theoretically possible for an appellate arbitration procedure to consist of "paper hearings," this is unlikely in large, complex cases that will probably be the staple of private appeal.

Remanding the award to the original panel or a different panel

The procedural alternatives available to appellate arbitration panels, including remand to the original panel or to a new arbitration panel, should be established with some clarity. The failure to set forth such alternatives clearly may result in surprise and confusion at the appellate level.[141]

CPR recognized that remand to the original panel is problematic because that panel loses its authority upon rendering its decision under the CPR Arbitration Rules. It was also decided that creation of a new panel would be cumbersome and cause substantial additional delay. The CPR Arbitration Appellate Procedure therefore empowers the appellate tribunal to reopen the record if that is deemed necessary, but does not empower the tribunal to remand the case. See Appendix 7.1.

Shifting of costs

Some have expressed the concern that appellate processes may simply compound the costs and delays of getting a dispute resolved. There is also concern that recalcitrant parties may pursue an appeal in court once internal appellate procedures are exhausted.[142]

---

139. AMERICAN SPICE TRADE ASSOCIATION, ARBITRATION BOOKLET NO. 5 § H (1989).

140. David Barrett says that oral arguments are rare in the NGFA system, which tends to rely heavily on paper submissions at all levels. Interview with David Barrett, *supra* note 126.

141. One lawyer who successfully challenged a determination by an appellate panel of a trade association in federal court complained that the rules of that organization were flawed in not making clear the options available to an appeals panel. This can result in considerable confusion, particularly where the appellate panel is comprised of non-lawyers. Interview with Harvey A. Strickton, Esq. (Oct. 2, 1998).

142. According to an attorney for the NBA, during several seasons of operation there were no efforts to challenge in court private appellate determinations under the NBA/Player's Association provisions. Interview with Howard Ganz, Esq. (Oct. 2, 1998).

Within commercial communities, pressures may develop to encourage parties to comply with appellate arbitration awards.[143] In the absence, or in addition to, such pressures, parties may agree to cost-shifting measures in the event of an unsuccessful appeal, such as those specified in the CPR Arbitration Appeal Procedure.

The CPR procedure requires the unsuccessful arbitration appellant to reimburse the appellee's legal fees and other expenses incurred in connection with the appeal, unless the appellate tribunal rules otherwise. Should there be a petition for judicial review of the appellate award that is unsuccessful, the same cost-shifting rule applies.[144]

In the Commentary to the CPR Appeal Procedure, CPR suggests that parties may wish to provide in their arbitration agreement that by filing an appeal from the original arbitration award the appellant waives the right to vacatur under § 10 of the FAA or state counterparts. However, CPR explains that it is unclear whether such a waiver would be enforceable. See Appendix 7.1.

Separate appellate arbitration systems

When private appeal procedures are linked to particular arbitration rules, the initial arbitration process can be set up to accommodate the requirements of the appellate process (including the establishment of a record, a more complete award, and the like). However, an appellate option also can be developed with sufficient flexibility to accommodate arbitrations under rules not linked to the appellate procedure.

For example, the CPR Arbitration Appeal Procedure is free-standing and may be invoked following an arbitration conducted under CPR's arbitration rules or under other rules, provided that certain pre-conditions with respect to the award and the record are met.

The appellate option need not be incorporated in a pre-dispute agreement; it can be addressed by agreement of the parties after a demand for arbitration is filed and the precise parameters of the conflict are understood.

---

143. For example, David Barrett of NGFA says that members can be expelled from the Association if they do not comply with an arbitration award or refuse to participate in arbitration. Judicial appeals are consequently very rare. Interview with David Barrett, *supra* note 126.

144. *See* CPR ARBITRATION APPEAL PROCEDURE, *supra* note 121, Rules 12, 14.

Appendix 7.1
CPR Arbitration Appeal Procedure (1999)

CPR Institute for Dispute Resolution

I. Appeal Clause

It is suggested that parties wishing to authorize an appeal to the CPR Arbitration Appeal Tribunal under the Rules of Procedure set forth below include the following language in their arbitration clauses. The appeal provision should in most circumstances appear in the basic agreement between the parties. A similar clause can also be inserted in a post-dispute arbitration agreement.

> An appeal may be taken under the CPR Arbitration Appeal Procedure from any final award of an arbitral panel in any arbitration arising out of or related to this agreement that is conducted in accordance with the requirements of such Procedure. Unless otherwise agreed by the parties and the appeal tribunal, the appeal shall be conducted at the place of the original arbitration.

II. Rules of Procedure

A. General and Introductory Rules

Rule 1. Scope of Application

1.1. The parties to any binding arbitration conducted in the United States, pursuant to CPR Rules or otherwise, may agree in writing that a party may file an appeal (the "Appeal") under the CPR Arbitration Appeal Procedure (the "Procedure") from an arbitration award (the "Original Award").

1.2 The appeal shall be to a CPR Arbitration Appeal Tribunal (the "Tribunal") chosen from the panel constituted by CPR to hear Appeals (the "Panel"), consisting of former Federal judges.

1.3 No appeal may be filed hereunder, unless:

(a) the arbitrator(s) (was) (were) required to reach a decision in compliance with the applicable law and rendered a written decision setting forth the factual and legal bases of the award; and

(b) there is a record (the "Record") that includes all hearings and all evidence (including exhibits, deposition transcripts, affidavits, etc. admitted into evidence) in the arbitration proceeding from which the appeal is taken.

Rule 2. Commencement of Appeal

2.1   An Appeal shall be commenced by written notice to the opposing party(ies) and to CPR (attention: Panel Management Group), given within thirty days of the date on which the Original Award was received but the parties, unless the parties agree on a different period. The notice shall set forth the agreement in writing providing for the appeal, shall state the elements of the Original Award that are being appealed and the basis for the Appeal and shall transmit that portion of the Record that the appellant deems relevant to the Appeal.

2.2   The opposing party(ies) may serve a cross-appeal by notice in writing to the appellant(s) and to CPR (attention: Panel Management Group) within fourteen days of receipt of the notice of appeal. The notice shall state the elements of the Original Award that are being appealed and the basis for the Appeal. The appellee shall transmit any portion of the Record deemed relevant by the appellee that was not transmitted by the appellant.

2.3   Once an Appeal has been timely filed, the Original Award shall not be considered final for purposes of seeking judicial confirmation, enforcement, vacation or modification. If the Tribunal affirms the Original Award, it shall be deemed final as of the date of the Tribunal's affirmance. If the Tribunal does not affirm the Original Award, its award on appeal (the "Appellate Award") shall be deemed the final award in the arbitration, in lieu of the Original Award. If the Appeal is withdrawn for any reason (other than a settlement), the Original Award shall be deemed final as of the date of such withdrawal.

2.4   By agreeing to become a party to an Appeal under these Rules, each party (a) irrevocably waives the right to initiate court action to seek to confirm, enforce, vacate or modify the Original Award until the appeal process has been completed, and (b) agrees that any statutory time period for the commencement of court actions to confirm, enforce, vacate or modify arbitral awards shall be tolled for the period beginning with the commencement of the appeal and ending with the decision on the appeal under these Rules. Subject to these Rules of Procedure, each party may request the Tribunal to affirm, vacate or modify the Original Award on any of the grounds specified in Rule 8.2 hereof.

Rule 3. Notices

The provisions of Rule 2 of the CPR Rules for Non-Administered Arbitration (Rev. 2000) (the "CPR Arbitration Rules") shall apply to all proceedings pursuant to these Rules.

B. Rules with Respect to the Tribunal

Rule 4. Selection of Appeal Tribunal

4.1   The Tribunal shall consist of three members of the Panel, unless the parties agree that it shall consist of one Panel member.

4.2   After CPR has received the notice of appeal and any notice of cross-appeal, it shall promptly submit to the parties a list of not less than seven candidates from the Panel (or not less than three candidates if one is to be chosen) who have been pre-screened for possible conflicts and availability. The list shall be accompanied by each candidate's biographic information and compensation rate. The parties shall attempt to agree on the required number of candidates from the list. They shall promptly inform CPR of any candidates on whom they have agreed. Failing complete agreement within ten days, the parties shall submit the list to CPR within an additional five days, rank ordering the candidates on whom they did not agree. Thereupon, the required number of candidates receiving the lowest combined score shall be chosen by CPR, which shall also break any tie. Any party failing without good cause to return a rank-ordered-candidate list within the prescribed time shall be deemed to have assented to all candidates on the list.

4.3   If the Tribunal is composed of three members, they shall select one of their number as the chair (the "Chair"). The Chair shall be responsible for the expeditious conduct of the proceedings and for administrative matters, but shall be equal in voting and all other respects.

Rule 5. Qualifications, Challenges and Replacement of Arbitrator

Rule 7 of the CPR Arbitration Rules shall apply to the qualifications of, challenges to and replacement of members of Tribunals selected pursuant to these Rules.

Rule 6. Challenge to the Jurisdiction of the Tribunal

Rule 8 of the CPR Arbitration Rules shall apply to any challenge to the jurisdiction of the Tribunal.

C. Rules with Respect to the Conduct of the Appeal

Rule 7. General Provisions

7.1   Rules 9.1 and 9.2 of the CPR Arbitration Rules shall apply to the conduct of any appeal under these Rules.

7.2   The appellant(s) shall be allowed one opening brief and one response brief. The appellee(s) shall be allowed one brief, except that an appellee who is also a cross-appellant shall be allowed two briefs. Briefs or memoranda previously submitted may be used. The Chair shall request the parties to agree on a briefing schedule. Failing prompt agreement, the Chair shall set the schedule. The Tribunal may request the parties to submit such further briefs or other materials as it may deem appropriate.

7.3   The Tribunal may request the parties to supplement the Record initially submitted by the parties as it may deem appropriate in order to fulfill its functions under Rule 8.

7.4   Oral argument shall be held at the request of a party or if the Tribunal sees a need therefor. The Tribunal shall set the date, duration and place for oral argument in consultation with the parties. If the appellant alleges one or more of the grounds for vacating the Original Award set forth in Section 10 of the Federal Arbitration Act, the Tribunal may take evidence supporting and rebutting such an allegation.

Rule 8. The Decision

8.1   If the Tribunal finds that it does not have appellate jurisdiction, it shall forthwith dismiss the Appeal and the Original Award will thereupon be final.

8.2   If the Tribunal hears the Appeal, it may issue an Appellate Award modifying or setting aside the Original Award, but only on the following grounds:

    a.   That the Original Award (i) contains material and prejudicial errors of law of such a nature that it does not rest upon any appropriate legal basis, or (ii) is based upon factual findings clearly unsupported by the record; or

    b.   That the Original Award is subject to one or more of the grounds set forth in Section 10 of the Federal Arbitration Act for vacating an award.*

The Tribunal does not have the power to remand the award.

8.3   If the Tribunal does not modify or set aside the Original Award pursuant to Rule 8.2 above, it shall issue an Appellate Award approving the Original Award and the Original Award shall be final as provided in Rule 8.6 below.

8.4   A three member Tribunal shall make its decision by majority vote. The decision shall be set forth in an Appellate Award in writing and shall include a concise written explanation, unless all parties agree otherwise. A member who does not join the decision may file a dissenting opinion, which shall not constitute part of the Appellate Award.

---

*These grounds are the following:

1. Whether the award was procured by corruption, fraud or undue means.
2. Where there was evident partiality or corruption in the arbitrators, or any of them.
3. Where the arbitrators were guilty of misconduct in refusing to postpone the hearing, upon sufficient cause shown, or in refusing to hear evidence pertinent and material to the controversy; or of any other misbehavior by which the rights of any party have been prejudiced.
4. Where the arbitrators exceeded their powers, or so imperfectly executed them that a mutual, final, and definite award upon the subject matter submitted was not made.

8.5   If a party refuses to participate in an Appeal after having agreed to do so, the Tribunal shall maintain jurisdiction over the Appeal, including authority to make an Appellate Award.

8.6   The Chair shall cause the Tribunal's Appellate Award and any dissenting opinion to be mailed to the parties. The Appellate Award or the Original Award, as the case may be, shall be final upon receipt by the parties.

D. Miscellaneous Rules

Rule 9.   Use of Best Efforts to Avoid Delay

The parties and the Tribunal shall use their best efforts to avoid delay and to assure that the Appeal will be concluded within six months of its commencement.

Rule 10. Compensation of the Tribunal

Each member of a Tribunal shall be compensated at an hourly rate determined at the time of appointment for all time spent in connection with the proceeding and shall be reimbursed for any travel and other expenses.

Rule 11. Deposit of Costs

The Tribunal may require each party to deposit with the Chair an equal amount as an advance for the anticipated fees and expenses of its members. Any such funds shall be held and disbursed in such a manner as the Tribunal may deem appropriate. After the Appellate Award has been rendered, the Tribunal shall return any unexpended balance from deposits made to the parties. If the requested deposits are not paid in full within twenty days after receipt of the request, the Tribunal may so inform the parties in order that jointly or severally they may make the required payment. If such payment is not made, the Tribunal may suspend or terminate the proceedings.

Rule 12. Distribution of Costs

In the event that the Tribunal fully affirms the Original Award, the appellant(s) shall promptly reimburse the appellee(s) (a) the share of the costs of the Appeal theretofore expended by the appellee(s), and (b) the appellee's attorney fees and other out-of-pocket expenses related to the Appeal, unless the Tribunal orders otherwise. If the Tribunal modifies or reverses the Original Award, the Tribunal may apportion the parties' costs of the Appeal, attorney fees and other out-of-pocket expenses among the parties in such manner as it deems reasonable, taking into account the circumstances and result of the Appeal.

Rule 13. Confidentiality

The parties and the arbitrators shall treat the proceedings, including the Record, and the decision of the Tribunal as confidential, except in connection with a judicial challenge to, or enforcement of, the Original Award and the Appellate Award, and unless otherwise required by law.

Rule 14. Costs with Respect to Judicial Appeal

If following an Appellate Award, a party(ies) seeks judicial review (or opposes confirmation), that does not result in the vacation or substantial modification of the Original Award or the Appellate Award handed down by the Tribunal, that party(ies) shall promptly reimburse the opposing party(ies) legal fees and other out-of-pocket expenses incurred in connection with the judicial review.

Rule 15. Action Against CPR or Member of Tribunal

Neither CPR nor any member of a Tribunal shall be liable to any party for any act or omission in connection with any Appeal conducted under these Rules, except for wilful misconduct.

Commentary

Most parties who opt for arbitration, rather than litigation, find the finality of an arbitration award appealing. However, when the stakes may well be very large, some are concerned about the possibility of an irrational award and find that finality a deterrent.

The statutory grounds for vacating an arbitration award under Section 10 of the Federal Arbitration Act and state counterparts are limited to matters such as arbitrator corruption, fraud, evident partiality, misconduct and exceeding of powers. These grounds do not go to the merits of the award. Parties can agree that an arbitration award will be subject to judicial review on the merits, but it is uncertain whether a court will agree to hear such an appeal, and docket backlog may cause lengthy delays.

In the first instance arbitrations can and should be structured so as to minimize the risk of an erroneous award or an unjustified compromise award. The single most important factor is the selection of a highly qualified arbitrator or panel. Other suggestions appear below. Nevertheless, there are situations in which the parties wish to stipulate that an award the loser considers outlandish will be subject to appeal. CPR believes a well structured private appeal to a highly qualified tribunal is likely to be preferable to seeking judicial review with all the attendant uncertainties. Consequently, CPR is promulgating the CPR Arbitration Appeal Procedure (the "Procedure"), which was developed with the advice of several leading arbitrators and scholars of arbitration. Special thanks are due Robert B. von Mehren of Debevoise & Plimpton and Dean Paul R. Verkuil of Benjamin N. Cardozo School of Law, who participated actively in drafting the Procedure.

Highlights of the Procedure

- CPR has organized an appeal panel consisting exclusively of former federal judges who are also experienced arbitrators. [The roster is available on the Web at www.cpradr.org.]
- The Procedure is "free standing." It may be invoked whether or not the original arbitration was conducted under CPR Rules.
- The tribunal for the individual case will consist of three members of the appeal panel, selected in accordance with the Procedure, unless the parties agree to present the appeal to a single arbitrator.
- Pre-conditions for an appeal are that the arbitrators in the original proceeding be required to apply the law, a record of the original proceeding and a written award stating findings of fact and conclusions of law.
- A cross-appeal may be filed.
- An oral hearing will not be held, unless requested by either party or the tribunal.
- The tribunal may affirm, modify or set aside the original award, but it may not remand the case.
- The grounds for modification or setting aside the award are:

    a. that the Original Award (i) contains one or more material and prejudicial errors of law of such a nature that it does not rest upon any appropriate legal basis, or (ii) that it is based upon factual findings clearly unsupported by the record; or
    b. that the Original Award is subject to one or more of the grounds set forth in Section 10 of the Federal Arbitration Act for vacating an award.

- If the original award is fully affirmed on appeal, the appellant will bear the entire cost of the appeal, including the appellee's legal fees and other expenses, unless the tribunal orders otherwise. If the award is not fully affirmed, the tribunal is empowered to allocate all such costs.
- If, following the appeal process, a party seeks to have the award vacated in court and is unsuccessful, that party shall bear the opponent's costs related to the court proceeding.
- The appeal procedure is confidential.
- The parties can agree on the Procedure as part of a pre-dispute arbitration agreement or after a dispute has arisen.

CPR's Rationale

On the one hand, CPR wishes to allay the concerns of attorneys and clients regarding the rare arbitration award that blatantly fails to apply the law or for which there is scant support in the record. On the other hand, CPR does not wish to encourage widespread appeals from arbitration awards. With both objectives in mind, CPR has established relatively narrow grounds for setting aside the original award, beyond the statutory grounds for vacatur under Section 10 of the Federal Arbitration Act and state counterparts.

In addition, the CPR Procedure has built-in financial disincentives to appeal by requiring a record of the original proceeding, a significant expense, and by requiring an unsuccessful appellant to reimburse the legal fees, arbitrator fees and other costs the appellee incurred in connection with the appeal, unless the tribunal orders otherwise.

The Procedure is intended primarily to serve the interests of a party against which a large sum has been awarded, and that, based on careful professional analysis, concludes that it is the victim of a gross injustice.

Inability to appeal an arbitration award frequently leads parties in larger cases to opt for a panel of three arbitrators, resulting in substantial additional cost and often delay. If parties have the safeguard of an appeal, they may see less need for three arbitrators. Moreover, if a private appeal is available, the losing party may be less inclined to seek review in court even on statutory grounds.

Party Modifications of CPR Procedure

a. Monetary Threshold

The Procedure does not set a monetary threshold for appeals. If the parties wish, they may specify in their arbitration agreement that only a monetary award exceeding a certain amount will be appealable. If it is clear at the outset of an arbitration that the monetary award, if any, will be below the specified amount, compliance with the pre-conditions to an appeal set forth in Rule 1.3 will not be necessary.

b. Unanimous Award by Three Arbitrators

The parties can provide that the appeal procedure will not apply to an original award rendered unanimously by a panel of three arbitrators

c. Waiver of Statutory Vacatur

The Procedure does not preclude an unsuccessful appellant from seeking judicial review of the appellate award on statutory grounds. The parties may provide in their arbitration agreement that by filing an appeal from the original arbitration award under the Procedure the appellant waives the right to vacatur under Section 10 of the FAA or state counterparts. However, CPR cannot give assurance that such a waiver would be enforceable.

d. Escrow Deposit

As an additional disincentive, the parties' agreement may require that the appellant deposit all or a part of any monetary award in the original proceeding in escrow pending the outcome of the appeal.

Other Approaches

In addition to assuring the appointment of a highly qualified arbitrator or panel, ways to minimize the risk of a irrational award include:

- require a "reasoned" award;
- require the arbitrator(s) to apply the substantive law of a specific jurisdiction;
- prohibit an award exceeding compensatory damages;
- require the parties to submit final offers to the arbitrator(s), who will approve the offer they consider the more reasonable, commonly called "baseball arbitration;"
- the parties can agree in advance on a range that the award may not exceed on the high or low side.

CHAPTER **8**

International Arbitration

Chapter Summary

International Arbitration

8.1

Are there special reasons to use ADR in the international realm?

No modern treatment of commercial arbitration can ignore the increasing globalization of world markets and the growing importance of international commercial transactions. Concurrently, there has been a spectacular increase in the number of international commercial arbitration cases worldwide. Between 1976 and 1987, for example, the International Chamber of Commerce (ICC) averaged slightly fewer than 300 new cases annually. In 1998, however, 466 new requests for arbitration were filed with the ICC. Those requests involved 1,151 parties from over 100 countries. In more than half of the new cases, the amount in dispute exceeded $1 million U.S. dollars. Similar increases in new filings were reported by other major arbitral institutions in the United States, Europe, and Asia.[1]

A single chapter can only highlight some of the special concerns and practical realities of conflict management in the international realm. The reader is strongly advised to consult other sources and materials on the subject, some of which are cited in this book, in order to understand the complex topic of international arbitration.

1. Conflict management in the international commercial realm

The realities underlying CPR's tenets of commercial conflict management set forth in Chapter 1 are magnified in international transactions—especially in long term commercial relationships.[2] A growing number of U.S. companies join in cross-border arrangements involving foreign partners, customers, and competitors—not to mention diverse cultures, practices, and ways of communicating.[3] These realities enhance the likelihood of disputes, as does the sheer size and complexity of many transnational business relationships, exemplified by long-term alliances for technological development.[4]

Given the compounding of risk factors often associated with cross-border relationships, appropriate structures for the management of conflict are critical. No written agreement, no matter how detailed or thoughtful, can anticipate or address all of the contingencies and risks that may arise over the duration of a business relationship. This is especially true if the business relationship involves

---

1. International Chamber of Commerce, *Facts and Figures on ICC Arbitration* <http://www.iccwbo.org>.
2. *See* CHRISTIAN BUHRING-UHLE, ARBITRATION AND MEDIATION IN INTERNATIONAL BUSINESS ch. 1, 3–37 (1996).
3. *Id.* at 4.
4. *Id.* at 5–7.

persons of different cultural and political backgrounds who may use different words, exhibit different behaviors, and harbor very different values and attitudes.[5] "In international business disputes," explains Professor Park, "the text of an international agreement is often less important than the context of its interpretation."[6] There is a need for governance structures—mechanisms which help to channel and manage the inevitable conflict—tailored to the particular realities of the commercial relationship and the business partners.[7]

Limitations of the courts

As mechanisms for the resolution of transnational commercial conflict, national courts leave much to be desired.[8] Logistical concerns, procedural differences among legal systems, and language barriers may be only part of the problem for a commercial party in a foreign court. In some settings, a party may fear the prospect of "home town justice" at the hands of a xenophobic tribunal and harbor legitimate concerns regarding the independence and impartiality of judges.[9] Enforcement of a foreign judgment often presents another set of problems.[10]

Role of binding arbitration

When it comes to submitting disputes to judgment by a third party, arbitration offers the most acceptable means of resolving disputes involving international transactions.[11] Arbitration under the provisions of a recognized arbitral institution keeps the parties out of each other's courts and allows them to select a neutral forum, in a mutually accessible location, with impartial decisionmakers and procedures designed to provide a fundamentally fair hearing. It also provides a binding award which is widely enforceable under the terms of international conventions. In the words of the U.S. Supreme Court, international arbitration clauses are "an almost indispensable precondition to achievement of the orderliness and predictability essential to any business transaction."[12]

As in the domestic sphere, however, arbitration has its costs and limitations. Particularly in a large, complex case, the cost of getting and enforcing an award may be great. Today, with a specialized arbitration bar heavily influencing the process, international commercial arbitration often bears the earmarks of com

---

5. *Id.* at 12–15.
6. William W. Park, *Introduction* to BUHRING-UHLE, *supra* note 1, at vii, viii. *See also* William W. Park, *When and Why Arbitration Matters, in* THE COMMERCIAL WAY TO JUSTICE 73 (G. Beresford Hartwell, ed., 1997).
7. BUHRING-UHLE, *supra* note 1, at 6–17. *Cf.* Thomas J. Stipanowich, *The Multi-Door Contract and Other Possibilities,* 13 OHIO ST. J. OF DISP. RES. 303, 328–336 (1998).
8. *Id.* at 17–36.
9. *See* Park, *supra* note 5.
10. *See* BUHRING-UHLE, *supra* note 1, 34–36. *See also* Laurence Craig, *Some Trends and Developments in the Laws and Practice of International Commercial Arbitration,* 30 TEX. INT'L. L.J. 1, 3 (1995).
11. *See* Laurence Craig, *Some Trends & Developments in the Laws and Practice of International Commercial Arbitration,* 30 TEX. INT'L L.J. 1, 2 (1995); Park, *supra* note 5, at vii, viii.
12. Scherk v. Alberto-Culver Co., 417 U.S. 506, 516 (1974). An excellent discussion of the culture of international arbitration is provided in Yves Dezalay & Bryant Garth, *Merchants of Law as Moral Entrepreneurs: Constructing International Justice from the Competition for Transnational Business Disputes,* 29 LAW & SOC. REV. 27 (1995).

plex litigation.[13] Like any approach that invests the authority to resolve conflict in a third party, moreover, arbitration may represent a lost opportunity for the parties to explore and settle upon mutually acceptable solutions, including creative options beyond the range of adjudicated solutions. A high percentage of civil lawsuits and claims submitted to arbitration are disposed of before hearings, mostly by settlement. See Chapter 1. For these reasons, CPR and some other institutions encourage parties to international agreements to consider the possibility of a negotiated settlement and strongly support the use of mediation and other approaches that facilitate settlement.[14] Although this chapter emphasizes issues relating to binding arbitration, it should be remembered that in the international realm, too, arbitration rarely stands alone.

2. Relevant standards and procedures

Conventions

Reference will be made to two international conventions governing international arbitration that are of particular relevance to U.S. parties: the 1958 Convention on the Recognition and Enforcement of Foreign Arbitral Awards (popularly known as the "New York Convention")[15] and the Inter-American Convention on International Commercial Arbitration (known as the "Panama Convention").[16] The New York Convention, which has now been ratified by more than 120 countries—including the United States, China, Russia, Japan, and most countries in Europe and Latin America—provides for broad international enforcement of arbitration agreements and ensuing awards with limited judicial intervention.[17] In the words of one leading commentator, the New York Convention is "the cornerstone of current international commercial arbitration."[18] The Panama Convention is a similar treaty focusing on enforcement of awards rendered in signatory nations in the Western Hemisphere.[19]

In the United States, both conventions have been implemented under the rubric of the Federal Arbitration Act (FAA).[20] The U.S. version of the New York Convention incorporates two permissive limitations contained in the Conven-

---

13. *See* BUHRING-UHLE, *supra* note 1, at 41–42, paraphrasing the remarks of Claude Raymond; Dezalay & Garth, *supra* note 11, at 55–58.

14. *See generally* CPR INSTITUTE FOR DISPUTE RESOLUTION, ADR PROCEDURES AND PRACTICE TOOLS, INTERNATIONAL ADR (CPR MAPP SERIES, 1998) [hereinafter INTERNATIONAL ADR].

15. Convention on the Recognition and Enforcement of Foreign Arbitral Awards, June 10, 1958, 21 UST 2517 [hereinafter New York Convention].

16. Inter-American Convention on International Commercial Arbitration, January 30, 1975, [hereinafter Panama Convention]. The Convention was adopted by the OAS in 1975 and by the U.S. in 9 U.S.C.A § 301 (1990).

17. *See generally* New York Convention, *supra* note 14.

18. ALBERT JAN VAN DEN BERG, THE NEW YORK ARBITRATION CONVENTION OF 1958: TOWARDS A UNIFORM JUDICIAL INTERPRETATION 1 (1981).

19. *Id.*

20. *See* 9 U.S.C. §§ 201–208, 301–307 (1990).

tion:[21] (1) it applies only to the recognition and enforcement of awards made in another signatory state, and (2) it is limited to "commercial" relationships (including those between U.S. citizens involving property, performance, or other connections with foreign states[22]). When both the New York Convention and Panama Convention are applicable, the former is deemed to control unless a majority of the parties to the arbitration agreement are citizens of states that have ratified the Panama Convention and are members of the Organization of American States.[23]

National statutes; U.S. state statutes

Even if a nation has acceded to a Convention, domestic arbitration law may still play a part in governing the conduct of international arbitration. It is important that the terms of an international arbitration agreement be consistent with the arbitration law of the place of arbitration. Parties should make certain that their arbitration clause reflects what procedures, if any, are mandated by applicable arbitration law.[24]

The FAA.   The U.S. version of the New York Convention specifically incorporates provisions of the domestic FAA.[25] A given arbitration agreement may also be subject to both the domestic and international provisions of the FAA.[26] For U.S. parties and their business partners, therefore, American arbitration law may be of great significance.[27] Under the FAA, as discussed in earlier chapters, arbitrating parties enjoy considerable flexibility in tailoring arbitration agreements; judicial oversight of the process and of arbitral awards is extremely limited.

State statutes.   A number of U.S. states[28] have adopted statutes covering international arbitration, some of which are at least partly modeled on the UNCITRAL Model Law on International Commercial Arbitration,[29] discussed below. As explained in Chapter 2, however, within its purview the FAA applies in both federal and state courts,[30] and preempts conflicting state law unless the parties have specifically agreed to the contrary.[31]

---

21. New York Convention, *supra* note 14, Art. I § 3.

22. 9 U.S.C. § 202.

23. *Id.* § 305.

24. *See generally* Debevoise & Plimpton, Annotated Model Arbitration Clause for International Contracts (1997).

25. 9 U.S.C. §§ 1–16 (1988). *See* IAN R. MACNEIL, RICHARD E. SPEIDEL & THOMAS J. STIPANOWICH, FEDERAL ARBITRATION LAW: AGREEMENTS, AWARDS & REMEDIES UNDER THE FEDERAL ARBITRATION ACT § 44.9.1.3 (1994) [hereinafter MACNEIL ET AL.].

26. *See* MACNEIL ET AL., *supra* note 24, § 44.9.1.7.

27. *See id.* § 44.8.2.1.

28. These include California, Florida, Texas, Connecticut, and Hawaii. *See* David Rivkin, *International Arbitration, in* COMMERCIAL ARBITRATION FOR THE 1990s (ABA Section of Litigation 1991).

29. UNITED NATIONS COMMISSION ON INTERNATIONAL TRADE LAWS, UNCITRAL MODEL LAW ON INTERNATIONAL COMMERCIAL ARBITRATION, 40 U.N. GAOR Supp.(No. 17), Annex 1 at 81–93, U.N. Doc. A/40/17 (1985) [hereinafter UNCITRAL MODEL LAW].

30. *See* Allied-Bruce Terminix Co. v. Dobson, 513 U.S. 265 (1995).

31. *See* Doctors Assoc., Inc. v. Casarotto, 116 S. Ct. 1652, 1656–57 (1996).

UNCITRAL

The United Nations Committee on International Trade Law (UNCITRAL) developed a model law on arbitration and rules for arbitration. The UNCITRAL Model Law on International Commercial Arbitration,[32] adopted by the United Nations General Assembly in 1985, generally parallels the New York Convention and is consistent with that convention. The UNCITRAL Model Law is more detailed, however, and fills some of the gaps left by the Convention's limited provisions.[33] A number of countries, primarily those whose arbitration law was not up to date, have adopted the UNCITRAL Model Law.[34] In addition, some U.S. states have enacted statutes based at least partly on the UNCITRAL Model Law. In jurisdictions subject to the U.N. Convention but not the UNCITRAL Model Law, the Convention may be supplemented by an agreement incorporating the UNCITRAL International Commercial Arbitration Rules.[35]

Administrative rules and procedures

A growing number of institutions sponsor international commercial arbitration or have published arbitration procedures.[36] These institutions, and considerations attending the use of institutional procedures, are discussed in the following section.

8.2

What issues should be considered in drafting provisions for international dispute resolution?

1. The starting point

The first consideration in drafting international dispute resolution clauses will be to determine the starting point for the parties' dispute resolution procedure. The clause may need to address the preliminary steps that would be taken before arbitration begins.

---

32. *See generally* UNCITRAL MODEL LAW, *supra* note 27.
33. *See generally* Craig, *supra* note 10, at 25–28.
34. *See* Rivkin, *supra* note 28.
35. UNITED NATIONS COMMISSION ON INTERNATIONAL TRADE LAWS, UNCITRAL ARBITRATION RULES, 31 U.N. GAOR Supp. (No. 17) at 34, U.N. Doc. A/31/17 (1976) [hereinafter UNCITRAL ARBITRATION RULES]. *See* MACNEIL ET AL., *supra* note 24, §§ 44.5.2.1, 44.5.2.2, 44.6.2.
36. *See* MACNEIL ET AL., *supra* note 24, § 44.6.

ADR prior to arbitration

Many U.S. companies are incorporating provisions in their international contracts stipulating that all disputes should be addressed through mediation, senior management review, mini-trial, or other amiable procedures in a good faith attempt to resolve the disputes short of arbitration. Since many cultures favor voluntary amicable discussions over litigation or arbitration, it is anticipated that provisions for mediation or other forms of ADR will find their way into international dispute resolution agreements. As explained in Chapter 2, such requirements may have an impact on the timing or scope of arbitration. While Commissioners see significant potential benefits in the use of mediation and other settlement-oriented approaches, they urge caution in the preparation of multistep dispute resolution clauses. One Commissioner explains,

> In the international arena, we have had a number of problems with parties represented by counsel who use mediation simply for strategic advantage. Also, in some cases it is very difficult to find a mediator who is acceptable to foreign parties.

Another reinforces a lesson from Chapter 2:

> In agreeing to a provision which calls for negotiations or mediation prior to arbitration, make sure that the provision includes reasonable, clear time limits for various phases. Then, in the "worst case" scenario where settlement efforts fail, there will not be undue delay in getting to arbitration.

The CPR Institute, among other organizations, now provides guidelines for drafters of international transactions who wish specifically to provide for mediation and other forms of dispute resolution in their agreements.[37]

Standard provisions of leading arbitration institutions; arbitration rules

No single arbitration provision is suitable for all international transactions. A good place for drafters to start, however, is the standard arbitration provisions used by recognized institutions administering international arbitrations. For example, the International Chamber of Commerce Rules of Arbitration (ICC Arbitration Rules) refer to that body's standard clause, which reads as follows:

> All disputes arising out of or in connection with the present contract shall be finally settled under the Rules of Arbitration of the International Chamber of Commerce by one or more arbitrators appointed in accordance with the said Rules.[38]

---

37. *See* INTERNATIONAL ADR, *supra* note 13.
38. INTERNATIONAL CHAMBER OF COMMERCE, ICC RULES OF ARBITRATION 8 (Jan. 1, 1998) [hereinafter ICC ARBITRATION RULES].

This provision, which is similar in general outline to provisions recommended by other leading institutions here and abroad,[39] accomplishes the same important things as an arbitration provision in a contract between U.S. parties:

(1) It demonstrates an intent to use arbitration rather than national court litigation to resolve disputes.
(2) It legally binds the parties to arbitration in most countries in the world.
(3) It references effective procedures for commencing the arbitration, for appointing arbitrators, and conducting the arbitration process, thus minimizing the need to negotiate procedural points.

In addition, arbitration provisions should provide a foundation for enforcement of the arbitration award. For example, the CPR Model International Arbitration Existing Dispute Submission Agreement provides the following:

> We [the parties] . . . shall abide by and perform any award rendered by the arbitrator(s). Judgment upon the award may be entered by any court having jurisdiction thereof.[40]

2. Procedures to be incorporated

As in the domestic arena, the initial issue for drafters is the choice of arbitration procedures and the related question of whether some level of third party administration is appropriate.

International arbitration institutions

Today, there are literally dozens of institutions ready and willing to assist parties to international arbitration agreements. Indeed, there are arbitral institutions in almost every leading trading country in the world. Many parties will initially suggest using their home country institution, if only for the sake of convenience. To avoid the dilemma of protracted negotiation over a particular administering institution, however, many agreements look to an institution that has the aura of neutrality and is not based in the home country of either party.[41] Moreover, some institutions offer significantly more experience and organizational expertise than others.[42]

International Chamber of Commerce. The Paris-based International Chamber of Commerce International Court of Arbitration is the oldest institu-

---

39. CPR Institute for Dispute Resolution, Rules for Non-Administered Arbitration of International Disputes (Rev. 2000) [hereinafter CPR Int'l Arbitration Rules].
40. *Id.*
41. *See* Craig, *supra* note 10, at 11–16 (discussing the need for neutrality in an arbitral forum).
42. *See* Debevoise & Plimpton, *supra* note 23, at 4.

tion devoted to administering international disputes without ties to any one country. The sixty-five-member ICC Court organizes and supervises arbitrations held under the ICC Arbitration Rules,[43] which are incorporated in many international commercial contracts. The ICC has administered arbitrations "in some 40 countries, in several languages and with arbitrators of some 60 different nationalities."[44]

London Court of International Arbitration.   The London Court of International Arbitration (LCIA) is a common choice for Americans doing business abroad. Although many LCIA arbitrators are British barristers, the organization has expanded its roll of arbitrators to include more neutrals from outside Great Britain.[45]

American Arbitration Association, CPR Institute for Dispute Resolution.
The American Arbitration Association (AAA) International Arbitration Rules and the CPR Institute for Dispute Resolution Rules for Non-Administered Arbitration of International Disputes are alternatives associated with U.S.-based institutions. The AAA recently established an International Center for Dispute Resolution to administer all international disputes filed with the Association; the AAA International Rules, based largely on the UNCITRAL International Commercial Arbitration Rules, were updated in 1997.[46]

The CPR Arbitration International Rules, like their domestic counterpart, call for a process primarily administered by the parties and their counsel. Institutional involvement by CPR or another designated Neutral Organization arises only when the parties request it in connection with arbitrator appointment issues and challenges. The CPR International Arbitration Rules have recently been updated in 2000, along with the CPR Arbitration Rules.[47]

Other institutions.   The Rules of the Arbitration Institute of the Stockholm Chamber of Commerce (SCC) are very often selected by U.S. companies in contracts with Chinese or Russian companies. The Commercial Arbitration and Mediation Center for the Americas (CAMCA)—established in 1996 by the AAA, the Mexico City Chamber of Commerce, and Canadian organizations—is intended to focus primarily on transactions involving parties in the Western Hemisphere.

Specialized fora.   Some institutions sponsor arbitration for specific kinds of disputes. For example, the 1965 Convention on the Settlement of Investment

---

43. ICC ARBITRATION RULES, *supra* note 37, at 6.
44. *Id. See* Jean-Francois Bourque, *More Self-Administration Seen in International Arbitration*, 15 ALTERNATIVES TO THE HIGH COST OF LITIGATION, Mar. 1997, 37 (discussing recent trends in ICC arbitration).
45. *See* Debevoise & Plimpton, *supra* note 23, Appendix 1, at 2.
46. *See generally* Michael F. Hoellering, *International Arbitration Agreements: A Look Behind the Scenes*, DISP. RES. J. 64 (Nov. 1998) (discussing AAA international program).
47. *See generally* CPR INT'L ARBITRATION RULES, *supra* note 38.

Disputes Between States and Nationals of Other States ("Washington Convention")[48] created an arbitral facility known as the International Centre for Settlement of Investment Disputes (ICSID). ICSID is intended to resolve legal disputes over investments between a contracting state (or its agencies) and a national of another contracting state.[49]

Nature, purpose of arbitration procedures

As in domestic arbitration, international arbitration procedures tell the parties and the arbitrators how the arbitration will proceed. The rules establish parameters for commencing the arbitration and for exchanging and presenting evidence. They provide methods for getting around potential impasses such as the failure of a party to appoint an arbitrator or the failure of party-appointed arbitrators to appoint a presiding arbitrator.

Generally speaking, international arbitration procedures describe a process which is more efficient and less formal than litigation. There are, however, considerable differences among arbitration procedures, some of which are discussed below. An extensive Chart Comparing International Commercial Arbitration Rules was published by the international law firm of Simpson Thacher & Bartlett in conjunction with Columbia University Law School.[50]

3. Choosing administered procedures or ad hoc international rules

At their best, arbitral institutions offer:

(1) well-understood rules that are thoughtfully drafted and time-tested;
(2) an advisory body of international experts who advise the institution on problems and keep the rules current and responsive to changing needs and realities;
(3) a full-time staff to answer questions and field complaints; and
(4) panels or lists of qualified international arbitrators.

The imprimatur of a prestigious international arbitration institution may also enhance the likelihood that an award will be enforced or complied with voluntarily. For example, one study suggests that more than ninety percent of ICC awards were the subject of voluntary compliance.[51]

---

48. Convention on the Settlement of Investment Disputes Between States and Nationals of Other States, October 14, 1966, 575 UNTS 159 [hereinafter Washington Convention].

49. INTERNATIONAL CENTRE FOR THE SETTLEMENT OF INVESTMENT DISPUTES, ICSID INSTITUTION RULES (*last modified* Feb. 26, 2000) <www.internationaladr.com>.

50. *See generally* SIMPSON THACHER & BARTLETT, A CHART COMPARING INTERNATIONAL COMMERCIAL ARBITRATION RULES (1998).

51. *See* Patrick Thieffry, *The Finality of Awards in International Arbitration*, 2 (3) J. INT'L ARB. 27, 29 n.3 (1985).

Some international arbitration institutions offer a range of administrative services for arbitrating parties, others provide little or no administrative support. As explained in Chapter 2, these options reflect the varying needs of commercial parties.[52]

Administered arbitration

Administrative services.   Organizations such as the ICC, LCIA, AAA, and SCC provide a range of administrative services for arbitrating parties, although the level of support varies. The ICC Arbitration Rules contemplate a relatively high level of institutional involvement throughout the process. For example, under the ICC Arbitration Rules, the Secretariat of the ICC handles pleadings and other written communications among the parties and arbitrators, is empowered to grant extensions of time for certain filings,[53] and handles the payment of administrative fees and expenses.[54] The ICC Court of Arbitration is authorized to make initial determinations regarding the existence of an arbitration agreement,[55] to fix the place of arbitration in the absence of agreement by the parties,[56] to approve the terms of reference where a party refuses to sign them,[57] consider various extensions of time for procedures,[58] and to approve the final award by the arbitration tribunal.[59] A lower level of institutional involvement is provided under the LCIA's Rules,[60] and under the AAA International Arbitration Rules.[61]

Administering institutions may play an important role in helping to overcome difficulties created by vague or ambiguous arbitration agreements, too-stringent timetables or conditions for arbitrator selection.[62] In recent years, each of these organizations modified its procedures to streamline the arbitration process; the changes reflect some borrowings from other institutions, resulting in greater similarities between the rules.[63]

Generally speaking, it is desirable to have arbitration rules which permit proceedings to go forward in the absence of a party in order to avoid the time and cost of judicial proceedings to compel attendance.[64]

Arbitral appointments and related functions.   Among the most important institutional roles are those having to do with the appointment and compensa-

---

52. *See generally* Gerald Aksen, *Ad Hoc Versus Institutional Arbitration*, 2 ICC Int'l Arb. Bulletin, 8 (1991). *See also* Eric A. Schwartz, *The Role of the Arbitral Institution in the New Millennium*, 65 Arbitration 321 (1999).
53. *See* ICC Arbitration Rules, *supra* note 37, Art. 5.
54. *See id.* Art. 30.
55. *See id.* Art. 6(2).
56. *See id.* Art. 14(1).
57. *See id.* Art. 18(3).
58. *See, e.g., id.* Art. 24(2).
59. *See id.* Art. 27.
60. *See generally* London Court of International Arbitration, LCIA Rules (1998) [hereinafter LCIA Rules].
61. *See* Hoellering, *supra* note 45, at 65–67.
62. *See id.,* at 66–67.
63. *See* Comment, *1997: A Year of Rules Changes*, [1998] Int'l Arbitration L. Rev. 91.
64. *See* Debevoise & Plimpton, *supra* note 23, at 4.

tion of arbitrators. Under the ICC Arbitration Rules, for example, the ICC Court of Arbitration is empowered to make appointments where the agreed selection method fails.[65] This is a significant role: in 1995, for example, the ICC Court appointed approximately more than a third of the arbitrators on ICC tribunals[66] and decided the number of arbitrators at least a quarter of the time.[67] The ICC Rules also provide a mechanism for arbitrator disclosure of potential conflicts of interest[68] and for administrative determination of challenges to appointments.[69] Finally, the ICC handles fee and cost issues,[70] thus avoiding direct negotiations between arbitrators and parties. Like many other institutions, the ICC provides education and training for arbitrators. Issues relating to arbitrator selection processes are discussed in Section 8.3.

In recent rules changes, the ICC, LCIA, and AAA each took steps to appoint the arbitration tribunal and begin proceedings more quickly than before.[71] Rules vary respecting the authority of the remaining arbitrators to continue with hearings or deliberations in the absence of a recalcitrant third panelist.[72] An alternative is to provide a mechanism for replacement of the absent arbitrator.[73]

Some appointing authorities are equipped only to appoint arbitrators from one country. Others are used to making appointments from around the world. Choosing the former type of appointing authority gives the parties a better idea of the probable language and background of any arbitrator the appointing authority is likely to select. The latter type of appointing authority assures the parties a wider range of available candidates. Some appointing authorities may also provide parties with a list of interpreters to assist in multilingual hearings.

As discussed below in this section, the CPR International Arbitration Rules also provide for institutional assistance when the parties reach an impasse in their selection process to enable the proceedings to be conducted expeditiously and to decide challenges.

Other ADR services.   In light of the growing importance of mediation and other intervention strategies aimed at helping parties to resolve conflict through negotiation, parties considering incorporating the rules of an institution sponsoring arbitration services should consider whether or not the institution offers services of those kinds. Many institutions currently offer mediation or conciliation procedures and lists of experienced neutrals.[74]

---

65. *See, e.g.*, ICC Arbitration Rules, *supra* note 37, Arts. 8(3), 8(4), 9.
66. Bourque, *supra* note 43.
67. *Id.*
68. *See* ICC Arbitration Rules, *supra* note 37, Art. 7.
69. *See id.* Art. 11.
70. *See, e.g., id.* Art. 30.
71. *See* Comment, *supra* note 62, at 91.
72. *Compare* American Arbitration Association, International Arbitration Rules (April 1, 1997) Art. 11 [hereinafter AAA Int'l Arbitration Rules] (remaining arbitrators may continue with hearings or deliberations) *with* ICC Arbitration Rules, *supra* note 37, Art. 12.5, *and* LCIA Rules, *supra* note 59, Art. 12 (permitting remaining arbitrators to act without third arbitrator only at the deliberation stage, after the close of hearings).
73. *See, e.g.*, ICC Arbitration Rules, *supra* note 37, Art. 12.2. *Cf.* CPR Int'l Arbitration Rules, *supra* note 38, Rules 7.8–7.10.
74. *See, e.g.*, ICC Rules of Conciliation (in force as from Jan. 1, 1988) (1997 rev.).

Fees.   Administering institutions typically charge fees for their services. Although these fees vary from organization to organization and may be sizable in a large or complex case, their method of computation varies. For example, although a number of organizations base administrative fees upon the amount in controversy, the LCIA bases fees on tasks performed.[75]

Non-administered arbitration: The UNCITRAL Model Clause for ad hoc proceedings

The UNCITRAL Arbitration Rules, promulgated in 1976, have worldwide application and significant use. The Model Arbitration Clause published by the United Nations Commission for International Trade Law (UNCITRAL) provides:

> Any dispute, controversy or claim arising out of or relating to this contract, or the breach, termination or invalidity thereof, shall be settled by arbitration in accordance with the UNCITRAL Arbitration Rules as at present in force.[76]

The referenced UNCITRAL Arbitration Rules[77] are commonly used in ad hoc arbitration that is conducted without the active involvement of an arbitral institution; UNCITRAL does not administer arbitrations or act as an appointing authority. UNCITRAL recognized that for its rules to be complete, however, someone needed to perform certain basic functions of an institution (1) to appoint arbitrators if the parties are unable to agree or (2) to consider challenges to arbitrators. UNCITRAL allows for the naming of an institution or a person to perform the role of an appointing authority.[78] Many international arbitral institutions have agreed to act as appointing authorities under UNCITRAL Rules. If parties who choose the UNCITRAL Rules fail to name an appointing authority in their arbitration clause, the rules provide that the Secretary General of the Permanent Court of Arbitration in The Hague will name an appointing authority if one becomes necessary.[79]

Non-administered arbitration under the CPR International Arbitration Rules

As discussed in Chapter 2, the CPR Institute for Dispute Resolution offers institutional support and assistance only when the parties request it. In the event that the parties need assistance in selecting the arbitral tribunal, CPR can provide such support as set forth in Rules 5 and 6 of the CPR International Arbitration Rules. CPR also will provide institutional support when an arbitrator is challenged by a party, by deciding the challenge.[80]

---

75. *See* Debevoise & Plimpton, *supra* note 23, Appendix 1, at 2.
76. UNCITRAL Arbitration Rules, *supra* note 34, at 6 n.1.
77. *See generally id.*
78. *Id.* at § II Art. 6.1(b).
79. *Id.* at § II Art. 7.2(b).
80. CPR Int'l Arbitration Rules, *supra* note 38, Rule 7.

Under the CPR International Arbitration Rules, CPR will act as the designated Neutral Organization to perform the functions specified in Rules 5, 6, and 7, unless the parties agree upon another Neutral Organization.[81] Numerous arbitral organizations outside the U.S. have agreed to act as a Neutral Organization under the CPR International Arbitration Rules.

As discussed in Chapters 1 and 2, CPR advocates and publishes procedures for mediation and other settlement-oriented processes. The latter include rules for international business transactions.[82] In fact, under the CPR International Arbitration Rules, a separate rule, Rule 18, is devoted to "Settlement and Mediation," which reminds the parties and Tribunal that settlement and mediation can be explored at any stage of the proceeding. The Rule provides that if mediation occurs, the "mediator shall be a person other than a member of the Tribunal."[83]

4. Other principal issues an international clause should address

Sophisticated drafters of international arbitration agreements go beyond merely incorporating a set of arbitration procedures.[84] For example, the ICC recommends that parties stipulate in the arbitration clause the law governing the contract, the number of arbitrators, the location of the arbitration, and the language of the hearing.[85] The AAA and CPR also recommend specific agreements on the number of arbitrators, place of arbitration, and language of the hearing.[86] Although these elements are particularly important, thoughtful drafters consider other issues as well.

The following outline is intended to provide some guidance for negotiating and drafting an appropriate agreement.[87] Although institutional procedures usually cover some or all of the following, parties should consider the advisability of tailoring provisions to better suit their needs. Agreements involving specialized areas of the law, such as patents, may require consultation with an attorney knowledgeable in the field.

Types of disputes covered
Scope of the arbitration agreement.   In most cases, business parties desire the arbitration provision to cover all disputes having anything to do with their

---

81. *Id.* Rule 6.1.
82. *See generally* CPR INT'L ARBITRATION RULES, *supra* note 38.
83. *Id.* Rule 18.2.
84. *See* Bourque, *supra* note 43 (noting propensity of many parties to contracts referencing ICC Arbitration Rules to address specific procedural matters by agreement).
85. ICC ARBITRATION RULES, *supra* note 37, at 8.
86. *See generally* AAA INT'L ARBITRATION RULES, *supra* note 71; CPR INT'L ARBITRATION RULES, *supra* note 38.
87. Another helpful guide for drafting was developed by the law firm of Debevoise and Plimpton. *See generally* Debevoise & Plimpton, *supra* note 23.

agreement. Limiting the differences that are subject to arbitration invites disputes over whether a claim falls within or outside the arbitrators' jurisdiction. Thus, provisions recommended by leading institutions usually include broad arbitrability provisions, such as language referring to arbitration "[a]ll disputes arising out of or in connection with the present contract."[88] One Commissioner points out that since the New York Convention uses the word "differences,"[89] it is a safe word to use as a synonym for disputes, to wit: "The parties agree to resolve all differences arising out of or relating to this agreement by arbitration."

If the parties desire a more narrowly tailored clause, the scope of arbitration should be very carefully described. Disputes over coverage may dramatically increase the length of time and the cost of conflict resolution.

Rulings on jurisdiction.   A related issue has to do with the authority of arbitrators to rule on issues of arbitrability and jurisdiction—to use the German phrase familiar to Europeans, "Kompetenz-Kompetenz."[90] Under the FAA, agreements to confer such authority on arbitrators must be clearly stated.[91] Such issues are discussed in Section 8.4.

Number of arbitrators, selection, qualifications

Given the importance of arbitrator selection, drafters should carefully review applicable provisions of incorporated institutional rules and determine whether or not they are acceptable in light of the needs of the parties. Relevant considerations are addressed in Section 8.3.

Place of arbitration

There are a number of issues to consider in determining the locale of international arbitration. The literature includes more extensive treatments of these issues, including helpful discussions of special considerations associated with various choices of locale.[92]

Strategic and logistical considerations.   The place chosen for arbitration should probably be a neutral site, as parties are often properly reluctant to arbitrate in the country of the other party, especially if the other party is a government or a governmental agency. The choice of location should also take into account ease of access, the appropriateness of meeting facilities, and the availability of qualified arbitrators.[93]

Conventions.   The seat of arbitration should be a country that is a signatory to the New York Convention or the Panama Convention so that the award is as broadly enforceable as possible. Enforceability issues are discussed in Section 8.7.

---

88. *See supra* note 37.
89. New York Convention, *supra* note 14, § 1.1.
90. *See* GARY D. BORN, INTERNATIONAL COMMERCIAL ARBITRATION IN THE UNITED STATES 54–55 (1994).
91. *See* text accompanying note 140 *infra*.
92. *See, e.g.*, Debevoise & Plimpton, *supra* note 23, Appendix 2 ("Choice of Arbitration Seats") at 5.
93. *See id.*

Impact of local law on arbitration.   A major concern regarding choice of locale involves the impact of local arbitration law. The latter may determine matters such as types of disputes excluded from arbitration, qualifications for persons who act as arbitrators, qualifications for counsel who can appear in arbitration, arbitrators' powers, the degree to which local courts can interfere with arbitration proceedings, and grounds for challenging an award.[94] It may be necessary to consult with local counsel regarding such issues. As noted below, in some cases it may be possible and desirable to limit judicial interference or oversight by an appropriate waiver.

Since the persons or organization appointing the presiding arbitrator often look for a resident of the place of arbitration, the place of arbitration may also determine whether the presiding arbitrator has a civil law or common law background and whether the presiding arbitrator's first language is the language of the arbitration.

Language

Particularly where the parties to an arbitration agreement speak different languages, it is important to specify the language of the arbitration. The latter should be one in which counsel, party-appointed arbitrator, and presiding arbitrator are completely fluent.

It is rarely advisable to agree to use more than one language in arbitration. It is dangerous to have a case decided on translations of briefs and interpretations of oral arguments and witnesses' testimony. Confirming the quality of written translations and oral interpretation is difficult. Using more than one language also creates special logistical issues: for example, deadlines for briefs and other written submissions must take into account the time necessary for translation. Finally, the use of multiple languages tends to increase the cost of the arbitration.

If a party insists on using more than one language, it is best to negotiate a place of arbitration and an appointing authority that will increase the likelihood that the presiding arbitrator's first language will be the preferred language of party and counsel.

In the absence of specific agreement by the parties, institutional rules vary concerning the language of the arbitration, but all place some degree of emphasis on the language of the arbitration agreement itself. The ICC Rules authorize the arbitrators to make the determination, with due regard to all circumstances "including the language of the contract."[95] The CPR Rules and the AAA Rules presume that the language of the "documents containing the arbitration agreement" will control, but give the arbitrators discretion to determine otherwise in appropriate circumstances.[96] The LCIA Rules are to similar effect.[97]

---

94. *See id.* at 5–12 (describing salient features of applicable law in a number of countries).

95. ICC ARBITRATION RULES, *supra* note 37, Art. 17.1.

96. *See* CPR INT'L ARBITRATION RULES, *supra* note 38, Rule 9.6; AAA INT'L ARBITRATION RULES, *supra* note 71, Art. 14.

97. *See* Francis J. Higgins et al., *Pitfalls in International Commercial Arbitration*, 35 BUS. LAW. 1035, (1980).

Governing law

It is also important to agree on the substantive law to govern the contract and the resolution of any dispute arising out of or relating to the contract.[98] The purpose of choosing a law to govern the contract and the arbitration of related disputes is to provide predictability. Choice of law has important implications for arbitrator selection and procedural matters as well as questions of the enforceability and interpretation of contracts, the effect of bankruptcy, and many other issues. The attorneys who are drafting the contract and those likely to handle any arbitration should be familiar with the governing law. It is generally advisable to exclude conflict of law rules that would call for application of the law of another jurisdiction. Often neither party will agree to use the law of the country of the other party, and it may be necessary to agree to employ the law of a third country. It is advisable to consult an attorney familiar with the latter to be sure that that law is a wise choice for the particular transaction.[99]

Waiver of sovereign immunity

If one or more of the contracting parties is a government or an agency of a government, the arbitration provision should include a waiver of sovereign immunity. The waiver should cover all defenses based on sovereignty to the arbitration, to judicial proceedings in aid of the arbitration, and to the enforcement of any award or judgment entered thereon.

Waiver of judicial recourse, review

In England and some other countries, courts have the authority to decide questions of law during arbitration and to review arbitral awards for errors of law. The advantages and disadvantages of including an express waiver of judicial review should be carefully considered, with particular attention to the law of the arbitral forum and the scope of the grounds for challenging such awards. This subject is discussed more fully in Section 8.7.

Discovery

The ability to obtain discovery is of concern to many parties when they consider international arbitration. Rights to obtain discovery under other countries' laws are generally vague, meager, or non-existent. Many practitioners find it helpful to provide specific language on discovery, and some (but not all) international rules contain relevant provisions. The subject is discussed in more detail in Section 8.4.

---

98. *Id.* at 1035, 1039 ("That this choice may be outcome determinative is obvious."). *See* Louise Barrington, *Law to Be Applied in International Arbitration, in* ARBITRATING INTERNATIONAL DISPUTES IN THE NEW MILLENNIUM, Center for Int'l Studies (visited Sept. 3, 2000) <http://www.arbitration2000.com>.

99. Other alternatives, such as making different parts of the contract subject to different laws, incorporating standards not tied to any particular legal system, such as "lex mercatoria," or ignoring choice of law altogether tend to be less satisfactory. *See* Barrington, *supra* note 97.

Rules of evidence

As of 1999, practitioners have the benefit of the International Bar Association Supplementary Rules Governing the Presentation and Reception of Evidence in Commercial Arbitration.[100] These rules can be specifically incorporated into the arbitration agreement and should be helpful in providing an international uniform framework for the efficient and economic manner of taking evidence in international commercial arbitrations. Although it is not necessary to include the IBA Rules in the contract since arbitral tribunals may adopt them on a case by case basis, they should nonetheless be considered as a guideline for contracting parties.

Parties usually avoid incorporating rules of civil procedure or evidence for litigation into the arbitration, but some problems have arisen with arbitrators ignoring legal privileges, such as the attorney-client privilege. Although they do not require a Tribunal to adhere to rules of evidence, the CPR International Rules specify that the arbitrators "shall determine the applicability of any privilege or immunity" in the course of admitting evidence;[101] the AAA International Arbitration Rules require arbitrators to "take into account principles of legal privileges, such as those involving the confidentiality of communications between a lawyer and a client."[102] Other sets of rules have no such express requirement. Parties that choose other rules may want to include a provision in their arbitration clause along these lines.

Other evidentiary issues are discussed in Section 8.5.

Time limits

Arbitration is supposed to provide expedition over national court proceedings. Many parties believe that international arbitration is too slow.[103] In order to assure prompt adjudication by international arbitrators, many agreements provide for time limits that are shorter or less flexible than those contained in arbitral rules. Three principal areas where time limits are found are (1) to conclude an ADR process prior to arbitration, (2) to appoint arbitrators, and (3) to render the final award. However, a Commission member, a veteran counsel and arbitrator, urges reasonableness in prospectively setting limits:

> As arbitrator in a $250 million international case, I was presented with a situation where the agreement called for an award to be rendered within 60 days of appointment. That was, of course, totally inadequate—particularly in an international case involving parties in different countries. Fortunately, we managed to get the parties to agree to an extension.

Time limits are discussed further in Sections 8.4 and 8.5.

---

100. INTERNATIONAL BAR ASSOCIATION SUPPLEMENTARY RULES GOVERNING THE PRESENTATION AND RECEPTION OF EVIDENCE IN COMMERCIAL ARBITRATION [hereinafter IBA RULES].
101. CPR INT'L ARBITRATION RULES, *supra* note 38, Rule 12.2.
102. AAA INT'L ARBITRATION RULES, *supra* note 71, Art. 20.2.
103. *See* Higgins et al., *supra* note 96, at 1038.

Specifying or limiting arbitral remedies; currency of the award

Normally, international arbitrators have broad authority to fashion any relief that is deemed appropriate and within the governing agreement or applicable rules. Sometimes, however, parties want to assure that the arbitrators have total freedom to award any relief deemed appropriate—that is, to act *ex aequo et bono*—and sometimes the parties want to limit the relief that arbitrators may grant. Common issues relating to arbitral remedies include the availability of an injunction or specific performance, punitive damages, an award of costs and pre-award interest, and the currency of the award. These and other issues relating to arbitral remedies are discussed in Section 8.7.

Date of rules

Arbitration institutions change their rules from time to time. Parties are faced with the question of whether they want to avail themselves of the rules that were effective on the date the contract was concluded or the date that the arbitration is commenced. The question is a timely one. Five of the arbitral institutions mentioned in this chapter have recently revised their international arbitration rules in a substantive manner.

Consolidation of multiple arbitrations

As explained in Chapter 2, a vexing problem in both domestic and international arbitration is whether the matter may be consolidated with related arbitrations under the same or other contracts.[104] The situation normally arises when a single venture or transaction involves multiple parties or more than one contract. A typical example is a large construction contract between an owner and design and construction professionals.

Drafting issues.   As a general rule, unless all the parties have agreed in the contract or contracts to consolidation, courts and arbitrators consider themselves without power to order consolidation.[105] Some countries and U.S. states have enacted legislation allowing consolidation of arbitrations that arise under separate contracts. If consolidation is important, to the extent possible, (1) where a single venture or transaction involves multiple parties, or (2) more than one contract is relevant, the drafters should seek to include language in the arbitration clauses that allows consolidation either by courts or an arbitral tribunal.

Drafting of appropriate language to permit consolidation is fairly difficult. However, the drafters must consider each of the following points: (1) who decides whether to consolidate (court or arbitral tribunal); (2) to which contracts consolidation applies; (3) how the arbitral tribunal is selected with mul-

---

104. As one commentator observed, were the volume of international arbitration to increase greatly, "the lack of effective multi-party procedures would be a very serious impediment to efficient disposal of disputes." JOHN UFF & ELIZABETH JONES, EDS., INTERNATIONAL AND ICC ARBITRATION 12 (1990).

105. *See* Debevoise & Plimpton, *supra* note 23, at 11.

tiple parties; (4) which rules apply; (5) impact of award on parties that do not participate in the consolidated arbitration; (6) possibility of inconsistent results if consolidation is denied; and (7) controlling arbitral procedures with multiple parties. These factors and other thorny issues make consolidation clauses a formidable challenge; nonetheless, they should be addressed in joint ventures and multiparty deals.

Institutional rules.   Some years ago, the French Court de Cassation found ICC procedures for appointing arbitrators in cases involving multiple claimants or respondents to violate public policy.[106] In the *Dutco* decision, the Court de Cassation overturned a Paris Court of Appeals decision that upheld the ICC practice of requiring multiple respondents to nominate, or have named on their behalf, a single arbitrator for a panel of three. The court was concerned that all parties have a right to equal treatment in the selection of arbitrators, and cannot renounce that right in advance under French law.

Recently, arbitration institutions such as the ICC, the LCIA, CPR, and the AAA have modified their rules to provide appointment procedures in multiparty disputes which respond to the concerns raised by the French Court in *Dutco*.[107] Each set of rules provides that where there are more than two claimants or respondents, the parties shall attempt to agree on a method for appointing an arbitral tribunal. Failing such agreement, the institution will appoint all three arbitrators.[108] Under such an approach, no party enjoys superior rights in selection; all are treated equally.

8.3

Is the selection of arbitrators more important in international dispute resolution?

In Chapter 3, it is noted that choosing an arbitrator is probably the most important decision facing a party to a commercial arbitration. For the purposes of this chapter, strike the word "probably": there is no more important step at the commencement of an international arbitration.[109] In most international arbitrations, moreover, that step must be taken twice. First, unilaterally, to name a party-selected arbitrator, and second, in conjunction with the adverse party and

---

106. BKMI Industrieanlagena against Dutco Construction Co. (Pvt.) Ltd., No. 89-28.708 Y; Siemens AG against Dutco Construction Co. (Pvt.) Ltd., No. 89-18.726 Y combined, Cour de Cassation 1st Civil Chamber; Jan. 7, 1992. *See* Stephen R. Bond & Christopher Seppala, *The New (1998) Rules of Arbitration of The International Chamber of Commerce,* 12 Mealey's International Arbitration Reports, May 1997.

107. *See* ICC Arbitration Rules, *supra* note 37, Art. 10; LCIA Rules, *supra* note 59, Art. 8; CPR Int'l Arbitration Rules, *supra* note 38, Rule 5.4; AAA Int'l Arbitration Rules, *supra* note 71, Art. 6.5.

108. *See id.*

109. *See* Higgins et al., *supra* note 96, 1043–1045 (discussing importance and realities of arbitrator selection).

the appointing authority, to name the presiding arbitrator. Each step is critically important, but different considerations apply to each.

While parties are generally free to select arbitrators in any manner they choose, some arbitration rules limit their selection to either one or three arbitrators; others apparently permit any number of arbitrators pursuant to the parties' agreement.[110] As discussed in Chapter 3, it is not advisable to have a panel with an even number of arbitrators given the danger of impasse. A panel of more than three arbitrators is cumbersome. Although one arbitrator is less expensive than three and scheduling problems are fewer with a single arbitrator, most people prefer three arbitrators when the arbitration is likely to involve large amounts of money or complex issues. Some contracts provide for one arbitrator if the amount in dispute is less than a certain amount and for three arbitrators if the amount in dispute is greater than that sum.

1. Party-selected arbitrators

Arbitrator selection procedures

Although some arbitration rules provide for the appointment of a single arbitrator in the absence of contrary agreement,[111] appointing bodies typically have discretion to have a three-member panel if appropriate due to the size or complexity of the dispute or the circumstances.[112] In addition, many international arbitration clauses specify a three-arbitrator panel.

In the three-arbitrator model, each side typically chooses one of the arbitrators.[113] As a leading commentary explains:

> The advantage to a party of being able to nominate an arbitrator is that it contributes to a feeling of confidence in the arbitration tribunal. This is particularly important in international arbitration where, in addition to the matters formally in issue, there may well be differences of legal practice, language, tradition and culture between the parties and, indeed, among the members of the arbitral tribunal themselves.[114]

---

110. *See* MACNEIL ET AL., *supra* note 24, § 44.27.1.2.

111. *See, e.g.,* UNCITRAL ARBITRATION RULES, *supra* note 34, Art. 5.

112. *See, e.g.,* ICC ARBITRATION RULES, *supra* note 37, Art. 8.2; AAA INT'L ARBITRATION RULES, *supra* note 71, Art. 5. According to one leading treatise:

> The LCIA has sometimes specified an arbitral tribunal of three arbitrators regardless of the amount in dispute in order to accommodate the twin objectives of having one arbitrator trained in the applicable law, whilst insuring that a majority of the members of the tribunal are of a nationality or nationalities different from that of the parties.

JAN PAULSSON, NIGEL RAWDING, LUCY REED, ERIC SCHWARTZ, THE FRESHFIELDS GUIDE TO ARBITRATION AND ADR: CLAUSES IN INTERNATIONAL CONTRACTS 67–68 (2d ed. 1999).

113. *See, e.g.,* ICC ARBITRATION RULES, *supra* note 37, Art. 8.4; UNCITRAL ARBITRATION RULES, *supra* note 34, Art. 7.1.

114. PAULSSON ET AL., *supra* note 111 at 69.

This model presupposes a two-party arbitration. The challenges to arbitrator selection posed by a multiparty international arbitration are beyond the scope of this discussion.[115] The third, who usually chairs the proceeding, is then chosen either by agreement of the parties, by the party-nominated arbitrators, or by an arbitral institution or appointing authority, depending on the clause, the rules, and the ability of the parties to work together. We return to the choice of the presiding arbitrator in the next section.

Most arbitration rules permit the parties to create their own procedures for appointing arbitrators. If the parties have not agreed on a procedure or if one or more of the parties fails to follow the procedure, the rules provide a default method of appointment.[116] Often, the agreement or incorporated rules provide that each party will name one arbitrator within a certain time limit and that the two party-appointed arbitrators will name the presiding arbitrator within another time limit. If either of the parties or the party-appointed arbitrators do not act within the prescribed time limits, the appointing authority makes the appointment(s).[117] Parties are well advised to check the applicable arbitration rules to see if the default method for appointing arbitrators is satisfactory.

Problems may arise when the arbitration is among more than two parties and the parties want three arbitrators. If the parties can group themselves into one group of claimants and one group of respondents, each group can agree on an arbitrator and the two party-appointed arbitrators can name the presiding arbitrator just as in a two-party arbitration. In a multiple-party arbitration where the parties cannot group themselves into one group of claimants with similar interests and one group of respondents with similar interests, the parties can agree that the appointing authority will appoint all three arbitrators and designate one of them to act as presiding arbitrator.

Independence and impartiality

Notice that we do not refer to the presiding arbitrator in this context as the "neutral" arbitrator, nor do we use the American term "party-arbitrator" to describe the arbitrators nominated by the parties. That is because the general understanding in most international arbitrations today is that all three arbitrators should be independent and impartial, even if two of them are chosen unilaterally by the parties.[118] In Europe, especially, this is a point of some sensitivity, and great offense can be given to the party-selected arbitrators by singling out only the presiding arbitrator as "neutral." Leading arbitration rules

---

115. *See* ICC ARBITRATION RULES, *supra* note 37, Art. 10.
116. *See, e.g.* ICC ARBITRATION RULES, *supra* note 37, Art. 8.4; AAA INT'L ARBITRATION RULES, *supra* note 71, Art. 6.3; LCIA RULES, *supra* note 59, Art. 7.2; CPR INT'L ARBITRATION RULES, *supra* note 38, Rule 6.
117. *See, e.g.*, ICC ARBITRATION RULES, *supra* note 37, Art. 8.4; AAA INT'L ARBITRATION RULES, *supra* note 71, Art. 6.5; LCIA RULES, *supra* note 60, Art. 7.2; CPR INT'L ARBITRATION RULES, *supra* note 38, Rule 6.
118. *See generally* MACNEIL ET AL., *supra* note 24, § 44.28; BORN, *supra* note 89, at 64.

provide for disclosure of conflicts of interest and challenges on such grounds;[119] uniform ethical standards for international arbitrators reinforce the obligation of independence and impartiality.[120]

That being said, however, a liberal grain of salt should be added. Any party who trusts entirely in the impartiality of the arbitrator nominated by the adverse party may as well be considered a potential buyer for the Brooklyn Bridge. Impartiality, as a concept applied to party-designated arbitrators in international arbitrations, should be understood to be, to some extent, aspirational. Everyone professes to believe in it, and arbitrators and parties are expected to behave (at least in public) as though the impartiality of all three arbitrators were unquestionable. But most participants occasionally encounter situations where their faith in the other side's adherence to this principle is strained. Some argue there is little difference between the realities of European and U.S. practice in terms of the independence and impartiality of party-selected arbitrators.[121]

As explained in Chapter 3, the nature and scope of communications between parties and appointee-arbitrators is central to the discussion of independence and partiality.[122] The CPR International Arbitration Rules prohibit parties and representatives from having

> [a]ny *ex parte* communications concerning any matter of substance relating to the proceeding with any arbitrator or arbitrator candidate, except that a party may advise a candidate for appointment as its party-appointed arbitrator of the general nature of the case and discuss the candidate's qualifications, availability, and independence and impartiality with respect to the parties, and a party may confer with its party-appointed arbitrator regarding the selection of the chair of the Tribunal.[123]

The AAA International Rules limits ex parte communications with prospective or current party-arbitrators to "the general nature of the controversy and of the anticipated proceedings . . . [,] the candidate's qualifications, availability or independence . . . , or . . . the suitability of candidates for selection as third arbitrator."[124] Parties and their representatives are also prohibited from ex parte communications with candidates for presiding arbitrator. The LCIA takes a different tack, forbidding arbitrators from advising "any party on the merits or outcome of the dispute" before or after appointment.[125]

---

119. *See, e.g.,* ICC ARBITRATION RULES, *supra* note 37, Arts. 7, 9, 11; AAA INT'L ARBITRATION RULES, *supra* note 71, Art. 7; UNCITRAL ARBITRATION RULES, *supra* note 34, Arts. 9–12; CPR INT'L ARBITRATION RULES, *supra* note 38, Rule 7.

120. *See* BORN, *supra* note 89, at 64 (discussing International Bar Association's Ethics for International Arbitrators (1987)). Unlike the prevailing American arbitrator ethics standards, the IBA Ethics rules forbid ex parte post-appointment communications between the arbitrator and the appointing party. This is, of course, essential to the preservation of independence and impartiality. *See id.*

121. *See id.* at 65. *See also* Higgins et al., *supra* note 96, at 1043–45.

122. *See* Andreas F. Lowenfeld, *The Party-Appointed Arbitrator in International Controversies: Some Reflections,* 30 TEX. INT'L L.J. 59, 64 (1995).

123. *See* CPR INT'L ARBITRATION RULES, *supra* note 38, Rule 7.4.

124. AAA INT'L ARBITRATION RULES, *supra* note 71, Art. 7.2.

125. LCIA RULES, *supra* note 59, Art. 5.2.

Selection strategies

How should one go about deciding whom to select as a party-nominated arbitrator? However an adversary may behave, counsel should take care not to expose a client to any imputation that it failed to respect the neutrality of the tribunal. At the same time, it is logical to exercise the choice of arbitrator in the manner most likely to help that party's chances of a favorable outcome.

Ability to communicate with and influence the presiding arbitrator. The first step is to define the characteristics the appointing party would like to see in an arbitrator, with an eye on how the presiding arbitrator is to be chosen and the characteristics that process is expected to produce. The nominee should be an individual who is likely to relate well to the presiding arbitrator, who will, realistically, be the one to make the ultimate decision. Thus, for example, if one anticipates that the process for selecting the presiding arbitrator is likely to result in the selection of a professor from the German-speaking cantons of Switzerland, a party's interests may be better served by selecting a German arbitrator, or at least a German-speaking arbitrator, than by selecting an arbitrator from its own country who may have more difficulty communicating with the presiding arbitrator.

Ideally, a party's nominee should be someone who understands the party's legal culture and perspectives as well as that of the presiding arbitrator. Such an individual may help the presiding arbitrator better understand legal arguments advanced by a party.[126] If one expects the presiding arbitrator to be a lawyer—and most international arbitrators are either lawyers or law professors—it may be important to make a reasoned guess about whether the presiding arbitrator is likely to come from a common-law or a civil-law background. (If the dispute is between an Australian company and an American company, and governed by English law, one will be able to predict with some confidence that the presiding arbitrator will be a native English speaker with common-law training. If the dispute is between an American company's French subsidiary and an Egyptian contractor, on the other hand, with no choice of law specified and Athens named as the place of arbitration, the prediction may be more difficult.) The effort to make the prediction is nevertheless worthwhile, because the civil law/common law divide is one of the great traps for the unwary in international arbitration. The differences between the two methods of procedure have been greatly reduced over the last twenty years by the emergence of a widespread consensus about how international arbitrations should be conducted, resulting in a hybrid combining elements of both systems. But it remains true that the processes of analysis, proof, and legal reasoning differ across the common law/civil law divide, and that it is often easier for those with common legal traditions to communicate. It may be enormously helpful in establishing good communications between the arbitrator appointed by a party and the presiding arbitrator that they both be comfortable with the same legal system.

---

126. *See* Lowenfeld, *supra* note 121, at 68.

Other qualifications.   One should also consider the kinds of professional or experiential qualifications that may give an arbitrator a helpful perspective on legal, business, or technical issues in dispute. For example, if there are concerns that an opposing party is trying to evade the clear intent of a contract on a technicality, it may be appropriate to select as arbitrator a business lawyer with experience negotiating contracts who will appreciate the critical elements of the transaction. If the dispute involves a software license, the best choice might be a lawyer who has computer experience, or one familiar with applicable licensing practices. Although there may be situations where the most effective party arbitrator would be a non-lawyer such as a chemical engineer or an accountant, the general practice in international arbitration is to appoint lawyer arbitrators.[127] In part, that is because of the different role played by experts in the international realm (discussed in Section 8.5 of this chapter); the primary reason, however, may be that the legal counsel making the choices tend to believe that because presiding arbitrators tend to be lawyers, having a lawyer as a party-selected arbitrator is likely to enhance communications between the two.

Finding a person with the desired qualifications

After one has identified the characteristics desired in a party-selected arbitrator, one must confront the problem of finding an individual who fits the bill. To some extent the process is the same as that discussed in Chapter 3, but at least two differences need to be borne in mind. The first is international attitudes about interviewing potential arbitrators, and the second is the need to decide whether to look for an arbitrator within or outside what is sometimes referred to as "The Club."

Interviews.   Twenty years ago, most well-known figures in international arbitration would have at least professed to be offended by a request that they submit to an interview by the party considering appointing them. Today it is more common for a potential arbitrator to agree to meet a party and to discuss the experience of the arbitrator and his or her preferences as to methods and procedures.[128] Nevertheless, all of the cautions expressed in Chapter 3 about preliminary discussions with an arbitrator apply with doubled force in the international arena.

"The Club."   The last of this abbreviated list of points to consider is whether to nominate an arbitrator from within "The Club."[129] It is a reluctantly acknowledged fact that the number of people who have served as arbitrators in a significant number of international cases has traditionally been very small, and most of them know each other. No judgment needs to be made as to whether this is a good or a bad thing (although the comments made in Chapter 3 about

---

127.   Paulsson et al., *supra* note 111 at 74–75.
128.   *Id.* at 60–62.
129.   *See generally* Dezalay & Garth, *supra* note 11.

"professional" arbitrators certainly apply), but it is a fact that one choosing an arbitrator must confront. The most practical way to approach it is to consider "membership" another factor in predicting how a nominee will relate to the likely presiding arbitrator. It may be that picking a member of "The Club" will improve the chances of the two communicating well, but doing so may also impair those chances, depending on the identity of the presiding arbitrator. This is simply another in the series of judgments that must be made on a case-by-case basis.

2. The presiding arbitrator

It is almost invariably better to reach agreement with an adversary on who the presiding arbitrator should be, if that is possible, than to leave the choice to an appointing authority (as under the UNCITRAL Arbitration Rules[130]) or an administering organization. This approach guarantees that one will have at least some input into the choice of an arbitrator.

The flexibility enjoyed by parties in arriving at a mutual choice will, however, be disciplined by the default provision provided in the arbitration agreement. For example, in the case of an ICC arbitration clause in a contract governed by French law between two non-French parties that provides for arbitration in Paris, one has a fairly precise idea of how the arbitrator will be chosen in the absence of mutual agreement: the ICC will ask its French National Committee to name an arbitrator.[131] If the contract also requires familiarity with one or more languages other than French and with some particular field of law, both sides will probably be able (if well advised) to assemble a mental list of half a dozen likely candidates, with some confidence that the presiding arbitrator will be among them. That mental list will probably be more agreeable to one side of the dispute than to the other, and will give the party who likes the mental list a clear advantage in negotiating who the presiding arbitrator will be, because it will be more willing to accept the outcome of an impasse. As a general rule, predicting the likely outcome of a default selection will define the qualities that a presiding arbitrator chosen by agreement is likely to have, even if the result (to continue the above example) is agreement on an individual who would not have been chosen by the French National Committee.

Candidates being considered as possible choices for the role of presiding arbitrator will not (and should not) normally agree to be interviewed by either party alone. It has become increasingly common for such candidates to be interviewed by both parties together, however. Such interviews, if properly conducted (to focus on qualifications, background, and process, rather than on the merits of the dispute) can be very helpful in giving both sides confidence that

---

130. UNCITRAL ARBITRATION RULES, *supra* note 34, Art. 7.2.
131. ICC ARBITRATION RULES, *supra* note 37, Art. 8.4.

they have chosen a presiding arbitrator capable of dealing with their particular arbitration. It is important to select a person who has the personality and the background that will allow him to develop a proper esprit de corps in the tribunal. This requires many qualities, among them presence, capacity to listen to others, and diplomacy.[132]

3. Agreed criteria

A final consideration involves agreements regarding the qualifications for one or all of the arbitrators. Commissioners offer a variety of observations:

> Sometimes it is helpful for the parties to agree upon criteria for the chair, or all panelists.

> Such agreements may not be necessary if you are dealing with one of the better institutions.

> Criteria sometimes create interpretational issues. For example, some contracts now provide that all arbitrators must be "fluent" in two languages; this raises the question of what "fluent" means.

> I have seen situations where parties boxed themselves in by agreeing to such stringent requirements that their universe was too small. In one insurance matter, the parties agreed that the arbitrator should be an insurance company executive; the universe of qualified persons was very small, and the difficulty of finding an arbitrator great.

8.4

Are special considerations necessary when preparing for an international hearing?

The variations in the expectations of parties and arbitrators introduced into international cases by diversity of custom, culture, language, and legal system come to a head in the preparation for and conduct of the hearings themselves. Much of the advice offered in prior chapters about these stages of an arbitral proceeding in a domestic case applies as well in an international dispute, but there are significant differences, too. Those differences can lay traps for the

---

132. For an experienced arbitrator's thoughtful, in-depth discussion of considerations in selecting chairs and the different roles chairs play in international arbitration, *see* Marc Blessing, *Selecting the Chair—and His Role, in* ARBITRATING INTERNATIONAL DISPUTES IN THE NEW MILLENNIUM, Center for Int'l Studies (visited Sept. 3, 2000) <http://www.arbitration2000.com>.

unwary, so the overarching consideration in preparing for and conducting an international arbitration hearing is to have on the team someone who is familiar with the idiosyncrasies of the forum in which the case is brought.

We assemble here some illustrations of the types of procedural variations that may be encountered. The catalog is suggestive, not exhaustive.

1. Terms of Reference

The wisdom of dynamic, continuing pre-hearing supervision by the arbitrators of the preparatory phase of a case does not lose its force in the international arena. It can, however, be harder to accomplish logistically, and quite different in style from domestic cases.

Certainly the most salient, formal feature of the post-pleading, pre-hearing phase of international cases is the requirement under the ICC Rules that the parties and arbitrators arrive at "Terms of Reference."[133]

There is a considerable literature on the history, techniques, requirements and, indeed, the value of the Terms of Reference,[134] and in an ICC proceeding that body of information must be understood. In its origin, the ICC requirement stems from a civil law tradition requiring a definition of the arbitrator's commission, after the dispute had arisen, with a degree of formal particularity.[135] Vestiges of that function are still found in some of the formal requirements prescribed by the ICC rules for the document, and in the fact that the final award in an ICC proceeding will be subject to scrutiny by the ICC Court for, among other things, its conformity to the mandate of the Terms of Reference.[136]

However formalistic its history may have been, in current practice, its utility derives principally from its value as a tool of pre-hearing preparation, much like the order that might emanate from a preliminary conference in a domestic case. Apart from the technical requirements of the ICC rule, the heart of the Terms of Reference is composed of matters familiar to domestic arbitrators: a description of the basic positions of the parties, a clear delineation of the tribunal's jurisdiction (or the issues to be decided about that subject), a focused description of the issues to be decided and the relief sought, and an outline of the method by which procedural decisions are to be made.

The process by which the Terms of Reference comes into being may vary widely depending on arbitrators' experience and custom, parties' (and their counsels') attitudes, geography, and the complexity of the matter. Much more often than not, the endeavor will consume some time and require considerable discussion between the parties in an attempt to agree on terms to submit to the

---

133. *Id.* Art. 18.
134. *See e.g.*, W. LAWRENCE CRAIG, WILLIAM W. PARK & JAN PAULSSON, INTERNATIONAL CHAMBER OF COMMERCE ARBITRATION § 15 (3d ed. 2000) [hereinafter CRAIG ET AL.].
135. *See id.* § 15.01.
136. ICC ARBITRATION RULES, *supra* note 37, Art. 27.

panel. Failing agreement, the tribunal will enter the discussions and may exercise decisive influence on resolution of disputed items, though in theory and largely in practice, the document is the parties' consensual charter for the reference to the tribunal of their dispute. In the dialog this entails, it is often possible to simplify issues, agree on procedures, and, not infrequently, to settle the case itself.

The Terms of Reference, as such, are a feature unique to ICC arbitration. Nevertheless, arbitrators experienced in international cases, when acting under other regimes, may well borrow concepts from the Terms of Reference and engage in a process similar to their formulation in "shaping up" a case for presentation. Such activities are anticipated by provisions in institutional rules calling for pre-hearing conferences to, in the words of the CPR International Rules, "discuss all elements of the arbitration with a view to planning for its future conduct."[137]

Many of the considerations faced at this point are the same in international and domestic cases: for example, whether there are challenges to arbitral jurisdiction and how they are to be resolved; what information exchange should occur; what timetable should be set for the hearings and for the submission of materials to the tribunal; what interim measures may be required and how they should be handled. In all of these matters, while the issues may be the same, the style of consideration and the outcome may be different from what develops in U.S. cases.

Moreover, other issues that arise less pressingly or not at all in domestic cases have to be addressed at the outset of international arbitrations. Examples include the following:

- What shall the language of the arbitration be? If it is not the common tongue of all the parties (or witnesses or documents) how shall translations be obtained that are agreed upon or are otherwise authenticated?
- Where will the hearings actually be held (as distinguished from their formal seat)? Particularly in non-administered cases, what are the arrangements for hearing facilities, communications and support facilities, interpreters, stenographers, hotel rooms, and the like at the proposed site?
- Is the proposed site hospitable to international arbitrations? That is, may counsel from other countries "appear" and "act" before an arbitral tribunal there or are those functions reserved to local lawyers? Can arbitrators act freely and with appropriate legal immunity there? Can the documents and other paraphernalia required for the hearings readily be transported there and pass unhindered through customs?
- In construction cases, are site visitations anticipated and, if so, what arrangements are needed for them?
- Are attorney's fees and costs of the arbitration to be awarded to the winning party, and if so in what manner, i.e., in the discretion of the arbitrators?

---

137. *See* CPR Int'l Arbitration Rules, *supra* note 38, Rule 9.3. *See also* AAA Int'l Arbitration Rules, *supra* note 71, Art. 16.2.

At the great arbitral centers, these and similar administrative matters have ready answers, but in less familiar locales such issues may well consume more effort than the substantive pre-hearing matters.

2. Jurisdictional challenges

The generally accepted rule in many European nations is that an arbitral tribunal may be vested with the authority to rule on its own jurisdiction (either by positive law or by agreement of the parties). This doctrine is referred to as that of "Kompetenz-Kompetenz" (or "compétence-compétence"; literally, "jurisdiction concerning jurisdiction").[138] This principle is sometimes viewed as fundamental in international law because the alternatives for dispute settlement among parties of differing nationality are very limited and often ineffectual. Applications of Kompetenz-Kompetenz notions may vary greatly from country to country. Under French law, for example, arbitrators have authority to decide jurisdictional questions as a preliminary matter; their determination is subject to review, although not until the conclusion of arbitration.[139] In Germany, on the other hand, there has been case authority for the proposition that arbitrators may be empowered to rule in a binding way on their own jurisdiction; Germany's recent adoption of the UNCITRAL Model Law, however, has cast doubt on the continuing validity of this principle.[140]

"Kompetenz-Kompetenz" is often reinforced by the rules of arbitral institutions. For example, the ICC Rules provide that "any decision as to the jurisdiction of the Arbitral Tribunal shall be taken by the Arbitral Tribunal itself."[141]

The precise extent to which the "Kompetenz-Kompetenz" doctrine is the law in the U.S. remains to be seen. Although the question whether the parties have agreed to arbitrate a particular dispute is normally a question for the courts under modern arbitration statutes, the Supreme Court held that a clearly expressed agreement to submit such issues to arbitration should be enforced by courts applying the FAA, and indicated in dicta that in such cases an arbitral tribunal's decision regarding its own jurisdiction may be entitled to judicial deference.[142] The precise effect of the Court's dicta remains to be seen.

---

138. *See* Born, *supra* note 89, at 54–55.

139. *See* William W. Park, *The Arbitrability Dicta in First Options v. Kaplan: What Sort of Kompetenz-Kompetenz Has Crossed the Atlantic?*, Mealey's Int'l Arb. Rep., Oct. 1996, at 136, 150; William W. Park, *Determining Arbitral Jurisdiction: Allocation of Tasks between Courts and Arbitrators*, 8 Am. Rev. Int'l Arb. 133 (1997).

140. Park, *The Arbitrability Dicta in First Options*, *supra* note 138, at 151.

141. ICC Arbitration Rules, *supra* note 37, Art. 6.2.

142. *See* First Options v. Kaplan, 115 S. Ct. 1920 (1995).

3. Particular requirements of the forum and state

In preparing for submission of the case to the tribunal it is vital to appreciate what particular procedural, substantive, or formal requirements may be imposed on the arbitral process, not only by the law of the forum, but also by the law of any state in which enforcement of the ultimate award may be sought. While the New York Convention and the Inter-American Convention prescribe limited grounds for refusing to enforce an award,[143] some relevant nations may not be signatories and even signatories may have parochial interpretations of the Conventions that require careful pre-hearing attention.

4. Provisional remedies, interim relief

Need for interim relief; arbitration law

As discussed in Chapter 4, there may be circumstances where it is necessary to petition a court for interim relief to preserve the status quo pending appointment of the arbitral tribunal. International arbitration rules often contain explicit provisions stating that application to a court in such circumstances is not inconsistent with or a waiver of the right to arbitrate.[144] Although the New York Convention does not appear to bar judicial action in such cases, U.S. courts are divided on whether they have authority to render provisional relief in international cases.[145] A Commission member reflects:

> The availability of interim relief at the hands of a court depends on the jurisdiction. My experience is that in places like New York, Geneva and London, it is possible to get fairly quick judicial relief. That may be one reason why international arbitration clusters in such places.

Institutional rules

A Commissioner states emphatically: "It is best to provide in the agreement that arbitrators can grant emergency interim relief." Although international arbitral tribunals probably have implicit authority to render interim relief, provisions in international arbitration rules often make their authority clear.[146] The ICC

---

143. *See* Park, *supra* note 138.

144. *See* ICC ARBITRATION RULES, *supra* note 37, Art. 23.2; LCIA RULES, *supra* note 59, Art. 25.3; CPR INT'L ARBITRATION RULES, *supra* note 38, Rule 13.2; AAA INT'L ARBITRATION RULES, *supra* note 71, Art. 21.3.

145. *Compare* McCreary Tire & Rubber Co. v. CEAT, SpA, 501 F.2d 1032, 1038 (3rd Cir. 1974) (denying provisional relief) *with* Borden, Inc. v. Meiji Milk Prods. Co., 919 F.2d 822, 826 (2d Cir. 1990) (permitting provisional relief). *See generally* Rivkin, *supra* note 28. For a discussion of pertinent law in some other countries, see Francois J. Knoepfler, *What Interim Measures Are Authorized and Are They Enforceable? in* ARBITRATING INTERNATIONAL DISPUTES IN THE NEW MILLENNIUM, Center for Int'l Studies (visited Sept. 3, 2000) <http://www.arbitration2000.com>.

146. *See, e.g.,* LCIA RULES, *supra* note 59, Art. 25; CPR INT'L ARBITRATION RULES, *supra* note 38, Rule 13.1; AAA INT'L ARBITRATION RULES, *supra* note 71, Art. 21.

Rules are silent as to arbitral interim relief, but ICC arbitrators have granted such relief on a number of occasions.[147] Rules of the ICC, LCIA, CPR, and AAA all contain provisions authorizing arbitrators to order interim remedies.[148] For example, the CPR International Arbitration Rules state:

> At the request of a party, the Tribunal may take such interim measures as it deems necessary, including measures for the preservation of assets, the conservation of goods or the sale of perishable goods. The Tribunal may require appropriate security as a condition of ordering such measures.[149]

In addition, the Rules state that a request for such relief from a court "shall not be deemed incompatible with the agreement to arbitrate or as a waiver of that agreement."[150]

Interim relief is increasingly sought in the context of disputes involving intellectual property. Recent revisions to the AAA International Rules, by referring to measures for the "protection" of property, were intended to make clear that interim relief may be directed toward intangibles as well as tangible assets.[151] Confidentiality measures are discussed in Section 8.6.

5. Discovery

Scope of discovery, impact of law

In general, discovery in international arbitration proceedings is more limited in scope than the expansive discovery common in U.S. litigation. A Commissioner observes: "While American lawyers love discovery, the word is anathema in some other parts of the world."

The nature and scope of discovery is influenced by the national law governing the site of arbitration as well as the national or legal background of the tribunal (i.e., civil or common law).[152] In the U.S., a number of jurisdictions have considered whether 28 U.S.C. § 1782, which authorizes a U.S. court to order a party to produce documents or testimony "for use in a proceeding with a foreign or international tribunal,"[153] may be used to obtain discovery from U.S. parties and non-parties in international arbitration, including foreign arbitrations. The issue has provoked conflicting rulings.[154]

---

147. David E. Wagoner, *Interim Relief in International Arbitration: Enforcement Is a Substantial Problem*, 51 Disp. Res. J., Oct. 1996, at 68, 72.

148. *See* ICC Arbitration Rules, *supra* note 37, Art. 23.1; LCIA Rules, *supra* note 59, Art. 25; CPR Int'l Arbitration Rules, *supra* note 38, Rule 13.1; AAA Int'l Arbitration Rules, *supra* note 71, Art. 21.

149. CPR Int'l Arbitration Rules, *supra* note 38, Rule 13.1.

150. *Id.* Rule 13.2.

151. AAA Int'l Arbitration Rules, *supra* note 71, Art. 21.1.

152. *See* Born, *supra* note 89, at 81–84.

153. 28 U.S.C. § 1782 (1996).

154. *Compare In re* Application of Alvaro Noboa, 1996 W. 648885 (D. Conn. Oct. 23, 1996) (granting discovery) *with In re* Honda American Motor Co., 1996 U.S. Dist. LEXIS 10357 at *8 (E.D. Pa. July 24, 1996); *In re* Wilander, 168 F.R.D. 535 (D. Md. 1996) (denying discovery).

International arbitration procedures.   Some leading international arbitration procedures include provisions dealing with discovery and production of documents, at least to the extent of empowering the tribunal to address such matters. For example, the CPR International Arbitration Rules provide:

> The Tribunal may require and facilitate such disclosure as it shall determine is appropriate in the circumstances, taking into account the needs of the parties and the desirability of making disclosure expeditious and cost-effective.[155]

As discussed below, depositions are rare in international arbitration, and other discovery generally is limited by the parties' agreement or the rulings of the arbitral tribunal.

Effect of national laws on the roles of arbitrators and courts

In the U.S. and some other countries, national law permits the parties to agree to the scope and manner of discovery in arbitration, affords arbitrators some ability to order the production of parties and documents (consistent with the agreement of the parties),[156] and ensures judicial assistance in forcing the disclosure of discovery or evidence.[157] In some civil law countries such as Germany, however, arbitrators are prohibited from ordering discovery and the parties must resort to the national courts for assistance.[158] In other countries, the arbitral tribunal may order discovery or disclosure of evidence, but the courts cannot aid the tribunal in the enforcement of its order.[159] Except to the extent permitted by applicable law, no arbitration agreement can empower arbitrators to order non-parties to participate in discovery.

Effect of the civil law tradition

The traditions and expectations of civil law practitioners are reflected in prevailing attitudes toward specific kinds of discovery.

Depositions.   Of all the differences between U.S. and international practice at the pre-hearing stage, the sharpest is the widespread rejection in the latter of oral depositions for discovery purposes.[160] While, as we have already noted, even in U.S. practice there is a general inhospitality to discovery depositions in arbi-

---

155. CPR INT'L ARBITRATION RULES, *supra* note 38, Rule 11.

156. BORN, *supra* note 89, at 82.

157. *Id.* at 826–31. Discovery under the FAA and U.S. commercial arbitration rules is discussed in Chapter 4, and in MACNEIL ET AL., *supra* note 24, Ch. 34. In one case under the New York Convention, a U.S. federal district court held that the arbitrator and not the court decides questions of discovery in arbitration, and that the court can enforce the discovery ruling of a foreign arbitrator, but should not order discovery independently. *In re* Technostroyexport, 853 F. Supp. 695 (S.D.N.Y. 1994).

158. *See* BORN, *supra* note 89, at 826–31.

159. *See id.* at 831–32. In 1990, England passed legislation restricting courts from aiding in the enforcement of arbitral discovery. Courts and Legal Serv. Act 1990 § 103.

160. *See* CRAIG ET AL., *supra* note 133, § 26.02.

tration, the presumption against their availability internationally is very strong indeed. Partly this results from the view, common elsewhere, that the facts needed to state and prove a case should be in hand before it is brought.[161] Partly it derives from the relative lack of emphasis on oral case presentation in the civil law system. In any event, it is a fact of international case preparation that deposition testimony for discovery purposes is very rarely available.

Document production. Document production is another matter. The pre-hearing conferences and arbitral orders will address what kind of documentary "discovery" can be had. There is widening recognition of the propriety of fairly comprehensive document exchanges as the size and complexity of international cases continues to grow. And there is a well-established international custom of heavy reliance on documentary evidence to establish a claim or defense.

Even here, however, the liberality of documentary discovery allowed under the federal and most state laws in U.S. courts, and reflected to a degree in domestic arbitration practice, simply is not found. The general expectation is that each party will voluntarily turn over to the other the transactional and related records that bear on either the claim or its defense, and that is the end of the matter. Lengthy, particularized (even more so, non-particularized) litanies of document discovery demands, with accompanying pages of "definitions" and "instructions" are likely to get short shrift from an international arbitral panel, and leave a bad impression besides. By the same token, suppression of relevant documents, formalistic or dilatory objections to production, or an obvious recalcitrance or failure to cooperate in what international arbitrators regard as an obvious duty to be forthcoming will likely damage the credibility of the offending side with the tribunal. In all of this, international arbitrators will expect—and demand—a higher degree of mutual cooperation between the parties in "getting the facts out" than is the current fashion in American courts, and both parties and counsel would be well advised to meet that expectation in good faith.

6. Experts

An early determination should be made regarding the use of expert testimony in the arbitration. Here the variety of methods for dealing with the question is very wide. For one thing, it is much more common in international practice than in domestic American arbitration for the Tribunal to appoint a neutral expert to report to it. The practice of civil law countries is reflected in some international arbitration rules.[162] In such cases, the ground rules for selection of the expert and the expert's method

---

161. *See, e.g.,* UNCITRAL ARBITRATION RULES, *supra* note 34, Art. 24 § 1 ("Each party shall have the burden of providing the facts relied upon to support its claim or defense.") *But see* ICC ARBITRATION RULES, *supra* note 37, Art. 20 § 1.

162. *See, e.g.,* ICC ARBITRATION RULES, *supra* note 37, Art. 20 § 4; UNCITRAL ARBITRATION RULES, *supra* note 34, Art. 27; CPR INT'L ARBITRATION RULES, *supra* note 38, Rule 12.3.

of operation, sources of information, availability for input from the parties, as well as the parties' opportunity and methods to comment on the report or question the expert, all must be considered and addressed early in the case.

Even where no neutral expertise is sought out by the tribunal, battles of forensic experts of the kind common in U.S. practice are unwelcome in international cases. Tribunals may take various approaches to this, including, for example, convening part of the hearing as a "seminar" in which the contending experts conduct a dialog on the question at hand among themselves and with the tribunal. Other panels have required a similar process—without the arbitrators' presence—as a pre-hearing step designed to forge a consensus or at least to narrow the matters in dispute. In the international arena, "expertise" connotes a degree of professional detachment from a partisan cause, and experts who do not evince this quality are unlikely to fare well.

In all of these examples, caveats and qualifications abound—as they do with the considerable number of other varietals that could have been, but have not been, discussed. The fundamental point is in the nature of a product safety warning: do not assume that familiarity with domestic pre-hearing practice in arbitration is an adequate preparation for conducting an international case.

8.5

How do arbitration hearings differ in the international and domestic arenas?

It is during the hearing itself that the more pronounced variations between international and domestic arbitrations, and even among international arbitrations conducted under different jurisdictional rules, become apparent. Some examples are given below.

1. The role of the chair

Normally, the chair of an international tribunal has greater autonomy to manage the hearing without interference by the other arbitrators than the chair of a domestic tribunal. The nationality of the chair as well as his or her own prior arbitral experiences should always be considered by the parties in approaching various management issues because various cultural differences become important. This is particularly true in comparing civil law and common law procedures. Most international arbitrators are lawyers and they will tend to follow the judicial procedures they know best and with which they are most comfortable. Thus, an arbitrator from a civil law country will be more likely to want to apply civil law procedures whereas an arbitrator from a common law country will tend to adopt procedures from that country.[163] In general, the chair in an international arbitration will expect to have the final say in matters of scheduling and procedures, so the chair's background and nationality may often be at least presumptively determinative on some of these issues.

Where there are Terms of Reference, such as required by the ICC,[164] many of these issues can be discussed and settled amicably by the parties and the tribunal before the hearing. If they are not, it will frequently be within the province of the chair to decide them using the input, if any, that is requested from the other members of the panel and the parties.

2. Hearing procedures

Control of the hearing; discretion in the receipt of evidence

International arbitrators are frequently of the belief that they are called upon to adopt whatever procedures they believe will assist them in resolving the dispute, and this concept is supported by the rules governing various international arbitrations. Arbitrators have considerable discretion in the receipt of evidence; for example, the ICC provides that arbitrators have the discretionary power to determine the facts "by all appropriate means."[165] This generally means that more formal evidentiary rules are not used and all evidence is accepted "for whatever weight it has." Exclusion of evidence also might lead to a challenge of the award for "refusal to hear evidence pertinent to the controversy." The tribunal can on its own determine that certain witnesses should be called to testify even if the parties would choose not to call that witness and may in appropriate cases allow the arbitrators to pursue a line of inquiry not presented by the parties.

While various international arbitration rules do provide some guidelines for the conduct of hearings, they focus primarily on guaranteeing each side a fair opportunity to be heard, and leave procedural details to the tribunal. The International Bar Association Supplementary Rules Governing the Presentation and Reception of Evidence in Commercial Arbitration[166] is a good source which sets forth widely accepted standards. Practitioners may want to incorporate these rules into the arbitration agreement in order to avoid subsequent conflicts over hearing procedures.[167]

As in the domestic sphere, rules of leading institutions now make clear that arbitrators have broad authority to conduct proceedings expeditiously and efficiently.[168] The CPR International Arbitration Rules, for example, plainly state

---

163. *See* BORN, *supra* note 89, at 87–93.
164. ICC ARBITRATION RULES, *supra* note 37, Art. 18.
165. *Id.* Art. 20.
166. *See generally* IBA RULES, *supra* note 98.
167. BORN, *supra* note 89, at 88.
168. LCIA RULES, *supra* note 59, Art. 14.1; AAA INT'L ARBITRATION RULES, *supra* note 71, Art. 16.

that arbitration "shall be conducted in an expeditious manner" and empower the tribunal to impose reasonable time limits on all phases of the hearing.[169]

Preference for submission of direct testimony in writing

Because of the strong influence of civil law on many international arbitrations, the tribunal will often have a strong preference for having all direct testimony submitted in writing and for curtailing attorney cross-examination in favor of questioning by the tribunal. Such cross-examination may be a poor substitute for the more rigorous cross-examination that is customary in common law jurisdictions. Impeachment of a witness's credibility can often be compromised by too heavy a reliance on written testimony, particularly when cross-examination is also curtailed, and counsel must be alert to raising this issue early on if credibility issues are considered important. The procedures for the handling of written testimony and limited cross-examination can become even more pertinent when a member of the tribunal is an American who is normally more accustomed to the oral style of presentation as a means of establishing the underlying facts, whereas continental lawyers are more accustomed to reviewing a written record and only utilizing oral testimony as a secondary source.

Timetables and logistics

Given the exigencies of international travel and the frequent need for translation services and other litigation aids, firm timetables and logistics take on increasing importance in international arbitration and as a result longer segments of consecutive daily hearings will often be appropriate. The importance of timetables is explicitly acknowledged by institutional procedure; for example, the ICC Arbitration Rules require the arbitration tribunal to establish a provisional timetable for the arbitration in the Terms of Reference.[170] This may be true even though under civil law procedures, the total time devoted to hearing oral testimony will generally be less than under the common law approach. In any event, to spare costs and inconvenience to the tribunal, parties, and witnesses alike, counsel should consider consenting to hearings in locales other than the "place of arbitration."

Written submissions, briefs

Brief writing is generally similar in both domestic and international arbitrations and is heavily dependent upon the particulars of the case. Because of the emphasis in civil law countries on written submissions, however, briefs or memoranda in arbitrations governed by civil law or where the arbitrators are from a civil law background tend to be more heavily focused upon a complete development of the facts, with attendant references to document exhibits. There is often less attention to legal precedents, except when the correct interpretation of a statute is an issue.

---

169. *See* CPR Int'l Arbitration Rules, *supra* note 38, Rule 9.2.
170. ICC Arbitration Rules, *supra* note 37, Art. 22.

Transcript of hearing

The issue of whether a verbatim transcript of the hearing is to be used should be settled early, as in many international arbitrations the preference is simply for the Chair to summarize the points covered at the close of each session. This method may or may not do justice to the proceedings, particularly when an issue develops in a later session which would have relevance to a matter discussed but not adequately recorded earlier.

Introduction of documentary evidence

The methods for the introduction and handling of documents to be used as exhibits is generally similar to methods used in domestic arbitration. "Bundling of documents," i.e., putting all exhibits in loose-leaf binders for review by the tribunal prior to the commencement of the hearing, is the preferred method. However, counsel would be well advised to clarify with the tribunal its views of the introduction of additional documents not in the original "bundles," i.e., what standard—good cause or some other—may be required to be satisfied for such introduction.

Expert testimony

Finally, as explained in Section 8.4 dealing with the pre-hearing stage, counsel needs to understand the tribunal's rules and expectations with respect to the use of experts. Variations run from the expert-assessor who is appointed by the tribunal and available to give advice directly to the tribunal, to the neutral expert appointed by the tribunal or the Court and responsible for preparing an expert report available to all parties, to party-appointed experts, each vying with the other in offering their expert opinions. Simply following the practices followed in domestic arbitrations may result in unfortunate surprises where the international tribunal determines to proceed in a very different way in utilizing expert witnesses.

8.6

How are the rules of privacy and confidentiality applied in international arbitration?

There is no international consensus regarding privacy and confidentiality in arbitration. While some element of privacy typically is assumed, there is disagreement over the extent to which one party should be permitted to deny another party the ability to rely on and use an arbitration award and/or at least some other materials from an arbitration. In practice, total secrecy rarely applies to the arbitration process. A party typically is free to lodge an award in a public court file as part of a proceeding to enforce or set aside the award, for example.

Courts may also allow discovery by third parties of others' arbitration files that may be relevant to a subsequent court proceeding; and non-party witnesses often are not restricted in what they may say about an arbitration proceeding. However, courts generally resist wholesale intrusion on the arbitral process.

1. National arbitration laws

The laws of most nations do not address the subject of confidentiality in arbitration, leaving that as a matter for agreement of the parties through the rules they select or otherwise.[171] Courts sometimes find an element of arbitral confidentiality implied in their national law, even if it is not expressed. As in the case of the rules that do address confidentiality, decisions based on such implied confidentiality typically recognize that there will be exceptions to confidentiality restrictions. These include disclosure required pursuant to judicial actions (including actions to enforce an award) and mandatory submissions to regulatory authorities. Some courts also recognize exceptions for the legitimate business interests that a party may have in making public the outcome of an arbitration.

There are two conflicting lines of international authority regarding the existence of a presumption of secrecy surrounding the arbitral proceedings. The courts of England, for example, recognize such an implied term in arbitration agreements calling for arbitration in England;[172] the courts of Australia, on the other hand, do not do so.[173] In a recent decision, a Swedish appellate court took a middle position, recognizing only a limited presumption of secrecy and focusing on the kind of information being made public.[174] The court held that, for example, "information touching on the operations of the parties or [the award's] explanation of the action in the arbitration dispute may normally be regarded as more worthy of protection than information that an arbitration dispute between the parties is in progress or information that concerns purely procedural issues of a general nature." The court also directed attention to the reason for the publicizing of an arbitration award and the extent, if any, to which the other party has been damaged. The court held that parties are not free to "neglect" the application of "discretion" with respect to disclosures of matters concerning arbitration proceedings.

---

171. *See* Richard H. Kreindler, *Arbitration Versus Litigation in Transnational Contracts: Recent Trends in the United States Relevant to Foreign Parties Faced with the Choice*, 2 INT'L BUS. J. 173, 175–176 (1998).

172. Dolling-Baker v. Merret [1990] 1 WLR 1205.

173. Esso Australia Resources Ltd. v. Plowman [1995] 128 ALR 391.

174. A. I. Trade Finance Inc. v. Bulgarian Foreign Trade Bank, Case No. 1092-98, SVEA App.(1999).

2. Provisions of leading arbitration procedures

Privacy of the hearing room

Most arbitration rules establish certain expectations of privacy with respect to hearings by limiting access to parties and other necessary participants.[175] The UNCITRAL Arbitration Rules provide for in camera hearings unless the parties agree otherwise.[176]

Obligations of, restrictions on participants

Some rules specify that the arbitrators or the arbitral institution have an obligation to maintain confidentiality concerning the arbitration, but do not place similar obligations on parties. For example, the ICC Rules of Arbitration establish the confidential character of the work of the ICC Court itself. Subject to the contrary agreement of the parties, the AAA International Arbitration Rules also subject arbitrators and administrators (but not parties) to a general confidentiality restriction on "all matters relating to the arbitration or the award."[177]

Other international arbitration rules extend various confidentiality obligations to parties and other participants. The UNCITRAL Arbitration Rules provide that the arbitration award may be made public only with the consent of both parties;[178] the AAA International Arbitration Rules state that an award may be made public "only with the consent of all parties or as required by law."[179] The CPR International Arbitration Rules provide that:

> Unless the parties agree otherwise, the parties, the arbitrators and the Neutral Organization shall treat the proceedings, any related disclosure and the decisions of the Tribunal, as confidential, except in connection with judicial proceedings ancillary to the arbitration, such as a judicial challenge to, or enforcement of, an award, and unless otherwise required by law or to protect a legal right of a party. To the extent possible, any specific issues of confidentiality should be raised with and resolved by the Tribunal.[180]

The LCIA Arbitration Rules are even more detailed, providing that, unless the parties expressly agree in writing to the contrary, they

> undertake as a general principle to keep confidential all awards in their arbitration, together with all materials in the proceedings created for the purpose of the arbitration and all other documents produced by another party in the proceedings not otherwise in the public domain.[181]

---

175. *See, e.g.*, ICC ARBITRATION RULES, *supra* note 37, Art. 21(3); AAA INT'L ARBITRATION RULES, *supra* note 71, Art. 20.4; CPR INT'L ARBITRATION RULES, *supra* note 38, Rule 17.
176. UNCITRAL ARBITRATION RULES, *supra* note 34, Art. 25.4.
177. AAA INT'L ARBITRATION RULES, *supra* note 71, Art. 34.
178. UNCITRAL ARBITRATION RULES, *supra* note 34, Art. 32.5.
179. AAA INT'L ARBITRATION RULES, *supra* note 71, Art. 27.4.
180. CPR INT'L ARBITRATION RULES, *supra* note 38, Rule 17.
181. LCIA RULES, *supra* note 59, Art. 30.1.

Like the CPR Rules, the LCIA Rules make exceptions

> to the extent that disclosure may be required of a party by legal duty, to protect or pursue a legal right or to enforce or challenge an award in bona fide legal proceedings before a state court or other judicial authority.[182]

The LCIA Rules also impose confidentiality obligations on the Tribunal and the LCIA Court.[183]

Not surprisingly given the sensitivity of the subject matter involved in intellectual property disputes, the World Intellectual Property Organization's (WIPO) Arbitration Rules on confidentiality are even more extensive, providing for the protection of trade secrets and other confidential information used in the arbitration,[184] confidentiality of the existence of the arbitration,[185] confidentiality of disclosures made during the arbitration,[186] confidentiality of the award,[187] and maintenance of confidentiality by the WIPO Center and the arbitrators.[188] Again, however, the confidentiality restrictions recognize the necessity of various exceptions such as court challenges to the arbitration, actions for enforcement of an award or when an award "must be disclosed in order to comply with the legal requirement imposed on a party or in order to establish or protect a party's legal rights against a third party."[189]

3. Protecting privileged or proprietary information

Some international arbitration rules specifically authorize arbitrators to take measures to protect trade secrets and confidential information.[190] For example, the CPR International Arbitration Rules, among others, provide that "[t]he Tribunal may issue orders to protect the confidentiality of proprietary information, trade secrets and other sensitive information disclosed."[191] The WIPO Arbitration Rules contain detailed provisions for protection of trade secrets and other sensitive information, including emergency arbitration procedures.[192]

---

182. *Id.*
183. *Id.* Arts. 30.2, 30.3.
184. World Intellectual Property Organization, WIPO Arbitration Rules, Art. 52 (1997) [hereinafter WIPO Arbitration Rules].
185. *Id.* Art. 73.
186. *Id.* Art. 74.
187. *Id.* Art. 75.
188. *Id.* Art. 76.
189. *Id.* Arts. 73, 75.
190. *See, e.g.,* ICC Arbitration Rules, *supra* note 37, Art. 20.7.
191. CPR Int'l Arbitration Rules, *supra* note 38, Rule 11.
192. WIPO Arbitration Rules, *supra* note 183, Art. 52.

4. Confidentiality agreements

In Chapter 6 we discuss the important role of confidentiality agreements between the parties in protecting the confidentiality of arbitration proceedings. Such agreements also can be useful in international arbitrations, particularly if the applicable law and rules are inadequate.

8.7

How do international practices affect the determination and enforceability of arbitral awards?

The authority of arbitrators to fashion relief and the enforceability of awards incorporating particular remedies are a function of the scope of the agreement of the parties and applicable substantive law. Not surprisingly, the picture is less straightforward than that presented in Chapter 7 with respect to domestic arbitration.

1. Arbitral remedies

Specific, non-monetary relief

Awards of specific performance and other non-monetary relief should be enforceable to the extent they are within the scope of the parties' agreement and not prohibited by applicable law. Parties foreseeing a potential need for such relief are well advised to address the issue by an explicit provision in their agreement. The CPR International Arbitration Rules explicitly authorize arbitrators to award such relief;[193] a number of other institutional rules do not. The subject of interim relief is discussed in Section 8.4 above.

Punitive or exemplary damages

As explained in Chapter 7, under the FAA and the weight of state arbitration law in the U.S., arbitrators have authority to award punitive or exemplary damages. Parties from other legal systems, especially those which regard such measures as contrary to public policy, tend to view such possibilities with alarm. For such reasons, parties to international commercial agreements may consider expressly

---

193. *See* CPR INT'L ARBITRATION RULES, *supra* note 38, Rule 10.4.

denying arbitrators the authority to make such awards, or even "waive" such relief entirely. Both the CPR International Arbitration Rules and the AAA International Rules have such provisions. For example, the AAA International Arbitration Rules provide that:

> Unless the parties agree otherwise, the parties expressly waive and forego any right to punitive, exemplary or similar damages unless a statute requires that compensatory damages be increased in a specified manner.[194]

As noted in Chapter 7, the enforceability of an outright pre-dispute waiver of punitive damages remains an open question, at least in the U.S. One commentator suggests that in light of this uncertainty, any language attempting to "waive" the punitive or exemplary damages should not be included in the arbitration provision, but in an independent provision. In such case, if for any reason the waiver is deemed ineffective, the party seeking punitive damages will be required to submit the issues to arbitration and not a court.[195]

Costs

Most international arbitral rules provide that the costs of the of the arbitration shall be allocated by the arbitral tribunal in the final award that is rendered.[196] The general rule—embodied in the LCIA Rules—is that costs follow the event.[197] This usually means that the losing party pays the costs. If parties are desirous of providing otherwise, that provision should be included in the arbitration clause. A usual provision is that the costs of arbitration shall be borne equally unless the tribunal in its discretion determines otherwise. The CPR International Rules contain a detailed description of what is entailed by "costs,"[198] and recognizes the authority of the Tribunal to require a deposit as an advance for anticipated costs.[199]

Pre-award interest

Pre-award interest on awarded damages may represent a significant sum; therefore, the awardability of interest should normally be addressed in the agreement. Some arbitration procedures, such as the CPR International Arbitration Rules and AAA International Rules, contain pertinent provisions.[200] If the parties do not address the point, the governing law may or may not be of help. Where the agreement is silent, arbitrators tend to find that pre-award interest is a matter within their discretion.

---

194. AAA INT'L ARBITRATION RULES, *supra* note 71, Art. 28.5; CPR INT'L ARBITRATION RULES, *supra* note 38, Rule 10.5

195. *See* Rivkin, *supra* note 28, at 129–130.

196. *See, e.g.,* ICC ARBITRATION RULES, *supra* note 37, Art. 31.3; CPR INT'L ARBITRATION RULES, *supra* note 38, Rule 16.2; AAA INT'L ARBITRATION RULES, *supra* note 71, Art. 31.

197. LCIA RULES, *supra* note 59, Art. 28.4.

198. *See* CPR INT'L ARBITRATION RULES, *supra* note 38, Rule 16.2.

199. *Id.* Rule 16.4.

200. *See* CPR INT'L ARBITRATION RULES, *supra* note 38, Rule 10.6; AAA INT'L ARBITRATION RULES, *supra* note 71, Art. 28.4.

2. Currency of the award

Due to the nature of international agreements, the currency of the award may be crucial. Currency fluctuations themselves are the cause of many disputes. Even though an agreement may be with a U.S. party and in the English language, there is no assurance that the award will be rendered in U.S. dollars. If the contract is silent, the arbitrators will decide the currency in which the award will be paid. Parties should consider specifying the currency of the award—especially in cases where the drafter's client is likely to be the claimant. It is best to specify a convertible currency, such as U.S. dollars. Some institutional rules address these issues. The CPR International Arbitration Rules state that "[a] monetary award shall be in the currency or currencies of the contract unless the Tribunal considers another currency more appropriate. . . ."[201]

3. Standards for decision-making

Under leading international arbitration rules, arbitrators typically are required to apply the law, and not their own concepts of equity or fairness (ex aequo et bono).[202] There are, however, instances in which the parties explicitly have given the arbitrators the power to disregard strict rules of law, e.g., to act as an amiable compositeur.[203] Such provisions are sometimes used in long-term commercial contracts, including reinsurance agreements.[204] In practical experience, even where no such power has been conferred on them, arbitration panels often believe they have the power to "do justice," and their decisions may appear based in whole or in part on considerations of fairness. Where the parties to the arbitration agreement prefer the panel to apply the law strictly, they should say so in the agreement.

4. Statements of rationale

Awards accompanied by a statement of reasons should be and generally are provided in international arbitral proceedings, although some attorneys believe that such statements may make awards more vulnerable to attack in subsequent proceedings. Under the rules of most international arbitral institutions, some form of accompanying statement of rationale is required unless the parties agree to the contrary.[205]

---

201. CPR INT'L ARBITRATION RULES, *supra* note 38, Rule 10.6.
202. *See, e.g.*, ICC ARBITRATION RULES, *supra* note 37, Art. 17.1; AAA INT'L ARBITRATION RULES, *supra* note 71, Art. 28; CPR INT'L ARBITRATION RULES, *supra* note 38, Rule 10.
203. *See, e.g.*, ICC ARBITRATION RULES, *supra* note 37, Art. 17.3.
204. *See* Debevoise & Plimpton, *supra* note 23, at 14–15.
205. *See, e.g.*, AAA INT'L ARBITRATION RULES, *supra* note 71, Art. 27.1; ICC ARBITRATION AWARDS, *supra* note 37, Art. 25; CPR INT'L ARBITRATION RULES, *supra* note 38, Rule 14.2.

5. Finality of international awards

International arbitration awards involve many of the same practical and legal considerations discussed in Chapter 7 with respect to the finality and review-ability of domestic awards.

The policy and practice of treating international awards as final and review-able only on narrow grounds have been enforced by courts in the U.S. and Europe—although precise standards vary. Most of the international arbitral institutions promoting international arbitration as the preferred method of resolving disputes emphasize the finality of proceedings conducted under their rules,[206] and the extremely limited scope of judicial review applicable to such awards.

6. Enforceability of foreign awards under the New York Convention

The enforceability of foreign arbitral awards is essentially a matter of international treaty. As explained in Section 8.1, the 1958 New York Convention[207] is the most significant of these treaties. It applies to awards made within the territory of a state other than the state in which recognition and enforcement is sought, and to "arbitral awards not considered as domestic awards in the state where the recognition and enforcement are sought."[208]

Under the Convention, prior judicial recognition of an award in the country where the award was rendered is not typically required for enforcement. Once the proponent of the award has produced the award and arbitral agreement under which it was granted,[209] the burden of proving the non-enforceability of an award is on the party "against whom it is invoked."[210]

Article V of the Convention sets forth a limited list of grounds upon which a country may refuse recognition or enforcement to an award. These include:

(1) invalidity of the arbitration agreement under applicable law (as specified in the agreement or, in the absence of specific provision, under the law of the country where the award was made);[211]
(2) lack of a fair opportunity to be heard;[212]
(3) an award outside the scope of the submission;[213]

---

206. *See, e.g.*, CPR INT'L ARBITRATION RULES, *supra* note 38, Art. 14.6.
207. New York Convention, *supra* note 14, § 8.1.
208. *Id.* Art. I § 1.
209. *Id.* Art. IV § 1.
210. *Id.* Art. V.
211. *Id.* Art. V. § 1(a).
212. *Id.* Art. V. § 1(b).
213. *Id.* Art. V. § 1(c).

(4) an arbitral authority or procedures not in accordance with the parties' agreement, or, in the absence of such agreement, the law of the country where the award was made;[214]

(5) lack of a final, binding award, as where an award "has been set aside or suspended by a competent authority of the country in which, or under the law of which, that award was made."[215]

These grounds tend to be narrowly construed.[216]

Enforcement of the award can also be resisted under the Convention on the basis that the subject matter of the dispute was not arbitrable under the law of the country in which enforcement is sought, or on the grounds that the public policy of that forum would be violated.[217] Again, however, such grounds are generally narrowly construed.[218]

Thus, any comprehensive assessment of the enforceability of an arbitral award must include an evaluation of the law, not only of the forum country (or country whose substantive law is applied by agreement), but also of the country where enforcement is sought. Generally speaking, the U.S. court decisions under the New York Convention have been very favorable toward enforceability of international arbitration awards.[219]

Enforcement and challenge in the courts of the country where the award is rendered

A number of questions regarding application of the New York Convention to the enforcement and vacatur of awards in the country where rendered have been addressed by judicial decisions.

Enforcement of non-domestic awards rendered in the U.S.   Courts have made clear that the Convention may apply to awards rendered in the U.S. in an arbitration in which some[220] or all[221] of the parties are foreign.

Law applicable to set-aside actions.   Article V(1)(e) of the Convention impliedly contemplates an action seeking to have the award vacated or set aside by the courts of the country of rendition. It does not, however, specify whether that country's domestic arbitration law is applicable to such actions. The question is very important since the domestic law of some countries provides

---

214. *Id.* Art. V. § 1(d).

215. *Id.* Art. V. § 1(e).

216. *See, e.g.*, Scherk v. Alberto-Culver Co., 417 U.S. 506, 520 n.15 (1974).

217. New York Convention, *supra* note 14, Art. V § 2.

218. *See* Rivkin, *supra* note 28, at 135.

219. *See* Gerald Aksen & Wendy S. Dorman, *Application of the New York Convention by United States Courts*, 2 AMER. REV. OF INT'L ARB. 65 (1991).

220. *See, e.g.*, Lander Co., Inc. v. MNP Investments, Inc., 107 F.3d 476 (7th Cir. 1997).

221. *See, e.g.*, Bergeson v. Joseph Muller Corp., 710 F.2d 928 (2d Cir. 1983); Transchemical Ltd. v. China Nat'l Machinery Import & Export Corp., 978 F. Supp. 266 (S.D. Tex. 1997).

grounds for vacatur beyond those set forth in Article V of the Convention, discussed above.[222]

In one recent decision, the U.S. Second Circuit Court of Appeals concluded that while a U.S. court could not refuse to enforce an award rendered in a foreign country on grounds other than those enumerated in Article V, the Convention authorized set-aside actions in the country of rendition, under the domestic law of that country.[223] Under this approach, "non-domestic awards" rendered in the U.S. (such as an award in an arbitration between two foreign parties or an arbitration between a domestic party and a foreign party) are subject to the grounds for the review of domestic awards under the Federal Arbitration Act (FAA) in addition to the grounds described in the Convention. Because it exposes international arbitration awards to the vagaries of local law, arguably undermining the intended goal of the Convention to provide uniform enforcement of such awards, this result has been criticized by a number of commentators.[224]

There is authority for the proposition that in the U.S. a party may raise defenses to enforcement under Article V of the New York Convention without moving to set aside the award.[225]

Impact of a set-aside on foreign enforcement.[226]   Article VII of the New York Convention states that "the provisions of the Convention shall not act to deprive any interested party of any right he may have to avail himself of an arbitral award in the manner and to the extent allowed by law . . . of the country where such award is sought to be relied upon."[227] Relying upon this language, and upon the fact that the Convention apparently gives courts discretion to refuse to enforce an award vacated in the country where rendered under Article V(1)(e), a U.S. federal district court in the *Chromalloy* decision denied res judicata effect to an Egyptian court decision nullifying an arbitration award on grounds of U.S. policy, and enforced the award under the FAA.[228] More recently, the Second Circuit refused to follow *Chromalloy* in a similar case, citing principles of comity and the impropriety of enforcing an award nullified in a proper set-aside action in a foreign court.[229] *Chromalloy* has engendered fierce debate between those who say it appropriately limits the ability of courts in the coun-

---

222.   *See* Hamid G. Gharavi, *Enforcing Set Aside Awards: France's Controversial Steps Beyond the New York Convention*, 6 J. Transnat'l L. & Pol'y 93, 99 (1996).

223.   *See* Yusuf Ahmed Alghanim & Sons, W.L.L. v. Toys "R" Us, 126 F.3d 15 (2d Cir. 1997).

224.   *See, e.g.*, Thomas Carbonneau, *Debating the Proper Role of National Law under the New York Convention*, 6 Tul. Int'l & Comp. L. 277 (1998).

225.   *See* Generica, Ltd. v. Pharmaceutical Basics, 1996 WL 535321 (N.D. Ill. 1996), *aff'd*, 125 F.3d 1123 (7th Cir. 1997).

226.   *See generally* William W. Park, *Duty and Discretion in International Arbitration*, 93 Am. J. Int'l L. 805 (1999).

227.   New York Convention, *supra* note 14, Art. VII.

228.   *See* Chromalloy Aeroservices v. Arab Republic of Egypt, 939 F. Supp. 907 (D.D.C. 1996).

229.   *See* Baker Marine (Nig.) Ltd. v. Chevron (Nig.) Ltd., Nos. 97-9615, 97-9617, 1999 WL 781594 (2d Cir., Aug. 13, 1999).

try of rendition to thwart enforcement abroad through set-aside actions[230] and those who believe it permits inconsistent treatment of set-aside awards.[231]

Strategic challenges.   Occasionally, awards are challenged in the country where rendered for strategic reasons. In certain circumstances, an award that is under attack in the courts of the country where it was rendered will not be enforced anywhere until the judicial challenge has been finally resolved, although there are notable exceptions to this principle.[232] In the jurisdiction where the challenge has been filed, a final resolution could take years. The prospect of delay may motivate a settlement of the dispute on terms different from those prescribed in the award.

Strategic challenges to arbitration awards are generally disfavored by established members of the international arbitration bar. Unless extraordinary error has obviously infected the arbitral proceedings, the presumption of and preference for finality in such awards is strong among lawyers who specialize in international arbitration. If a party believes that the arbitral panel has committed serious error, but finds that its counsel in the proceedings is unduly reluctant to consider any effort to challenge the award in judicial proceedings in the country where rendered, a second opinion from independent, qualified counsel may be desirable.

Waiver of the right to judicial recourse

Where applicable law permits resort to courts on points of law, concerns regarding the potential delays and costs associated with judicial intervention may motivate parties to seek to avoid such recourse. In England, for example, the courts traditionally had the power to decide all questions of law in arbitration, and parties often raised issues of law during arbitration and delayed the proceedings by asking a court to decide the issues. A party unhappy with an award could also challenge the award on the basis that the arbitrators had made a mistake of law. Over the years, various arbitration acts have given parties power to agree to limit the courts' monopoly on deciding questions of law. The English Arbitration Act of 1996 permits parties to waive their rights to bring questions of law to the courts during an arbitration and to challenge an award for a mistake of law.[233] Especially if the place of arbitration is England or a British Commonwealth country, parties may wish to include a provision in their arbitration clause waiving any right the parties may have to seek judicial rulings on issues of law during the arbitration and waiving any right to appeal the arbitral

---

230. *See* Gary H. Sampliner, *Enforcement of Foreign Arbitral Awards After Annulment in Their Country of Origin*, 11 MEALEY'S INT'L ARB. REP. 22, 28 (1996).

231. *See* Hamid G. Gharavi, *Chromalloy: Another View*, 12 MEALEY'S INT'L ARB. REP. 21, 23 (1997).

232. For a recent contrary authority, *see* Chromalloy AeroServices v. Egypt, 939 F. Supp. 907 (D.D.C. 1996) recognizing as enforceable in the U.S. an award annulled in Egypt because the annulment was found not entitled to *res judicata* effect and the award was decreed by the U. S. court to be proper under U. S. law. *See supra* text accompanying note 224.

233. English Arbitration Act 1996, Art. 69.1.

award based on errors of law. Some sets of arbitration rules, including the LCIA Rules and the Singapore International Arbitration Centre (SIAC) Rules, contain such waivers.[234] English courts have also held that a clause incorporating the ICC Arbitration Rules operate as a waiver of the right to seek judicial rulings on errors of law.[235]

Agreements to expand judicial review

As explained in Chapter 7, Commission members tend to have serious reservations about agreements to expand the scope of judicial review of arbitration awards. These attitudes are even stronger with respect to international arbitration awards.[236]

7. Appellate arbitration procedures

Experience with appellate arbitration procedures in the international arena is even more limited than in U.S. arbitration. Some years ago, however, the International Center for Investment Disputes (ICSID) established a procedure under which a party might seek to have an award annulled by a private review committee. Several awards were annulled, and new arbitration hearings were required. These events raised great concern in the international arbitration community, and memories of the ICSID experience may still reinforce the attitudes of some practitioners that appeal procedures of any kind should be avoided, or at least approached with great caution.[237]

8. Impact of growth of international arbitration

The explosive growth of international arbitral proceedings will undoubtedly produce new challenges and unexpected pressures on the doctrines that historically have insured the finality and enforceability of arbitration awards. The role of the courts in further defining these crucial doctrines deserves continuing careful scrutiny as international arbitration becomes a more frequent fact of life in the global economy.

---

234. *See, e.g.*, LCIA RULES, *supra* note 59, Art. 29.2.
235. *See generally* Debevoise & Plimpton, *supra* note 23, at 5.
236. *Cf.* Hoellering, *supra* note 45, at 67 (noting concerns of AAA about such provisions in the international sphere).
237. *See* Rivkin, *supra* note 28, at 128.

Appendix 8.1
National/International ADR Organizations

National

American Arbitration Association
335 Madison Avenue, 10th Floor
New York, NY 10017-4605
phone: 212/716-5800
fax: 212/716-5905
e-mail: aaaheadquarters@adr.org
web: www.adr.org

CPR Institute for Dispute Resolution
366 Madison Avenue
New York, NY 10017-3122
phone: 212/949-6490
fax: 212/949-8859
web: www.cpradr.org

JAMS
1101 17th Street, N.W., Suite 808
Washington, DC 20036
phone: 202/942-9180
fax: 202/942-9186
web: www.jamsadr.com

International

International Chamber of Commerce (ICC)
ICC International Secretariat
38, Cours Albert 1er
75008 Paris
France
phone: +33 1 49 53 28 28
fax: +33 1 49 53 29 42
web: www.iccwbo.org

London Court of International Arbitration (LCIA)
The International Dispute
Resolution Centre
8 Breams Building
Chancery Lane
London EC4A 1HP
England
phone: +44 020 7405 8008
fax: +44 020 7405 8009
web: www.lcia-arbitration.com

**International Centre for
Settlement of Investment
Disputes (ICSID)**
1818 H Street, N.W.
Washington, DC 20433
phone: 202/458-1534
fax: 202/522-2615
web: www.worldbank.org/icsid

**Arbitration and Mediation Center
World Intellectual Property
Organization(WIPO)**
34, Chemin des Colombettes
P.O. Box 18
1211 Geneva 20
Switzerland
phone: +41 22 338 9111
fax: +41 22 740 3700
web: www.arbiter.wipo.int

Rules Appendices

Appendix R.1
CPR Institute for Dispute Resolution Mediation Procedure

Revised and effective as of April 1, 1998

1. AGREEMENT TO MEDIATE

The CPR Mediation Procedure (the "Procedure") may be adopted by agreement of the parties, with or without modification, before or after a dispute has arisen. The following provisions are suggested:

A. Pre-dispute Clause

The parties shall attempt in good faith to resolve any dispute arising out of or relating to this Agreement promptly by confidential mediation under the [then current] CPR Mediation Procedure [in effect on the date of this Agreement], before resorting to arbitration or litigation.

B. Existing Dispute Submission Agreement

We hereby agree to submit to confidential mediation under the CPR Mediation Procedure the following controversy:

(Describe briefly)

2. SELECTING THE MEDIATOR

Unless the parties agree otherwise, the mediator shall be selected from the CPR Panels of Neutrals. If the parties cannot agree promptly on a mediator, they will notify CPR of their need for assistance in selecting a mediator, informing CPR of any preferences as to matters such as candidates' mediation style, subject matter expertise and geographic location. CPR will submit to the parties the names of not less than three candidates, with their resumes and hourly rates. If the parties are unable to agree on a candidate from the list within seven days following receipt of the list, each party will, within 15 days following receipt of the list, send to CPR the list of candidates ranked in descending order of preference. The candidate with the lowest combined score will be appointed as the mediator by CPR. CPR will break any tie.

Before proposing any mediator candidate, CPR will request the candidate to disclose any circumstances known to him or her that would cause reasonable doubt regarding the candidate's impartiality. If a clear conflict is disclosed, the individual will not be proposed. Other circumstances a candidate discloses to CPR will be disclosed to the parties. A party may challenge a mediator candidate if it knows of any circumstances giving rise to reasonable doubt regarding the candidate's impartiality.

The mediator's rate of compensation will be determined before appointment. Such compensation, and any other costs of the process, will be shared equally by the parties unless they otherwise agree. If a party withdraws from a multiparty mediation but the procedure continues, the withdrawing party will not be responsible for any costs incurred after it has notified the mediator and the other parties of its withdrawal.

Before appointment, the mediator will assure the parties of his or her availability to conduct the proceeding expeditiously. It is strongly advised that the parties and the mediator enter into a retention agreement. A model agreement is attached hereto as a Form.

3. GROUND RULES OF PROCEEDING

The following ground rules will apply, subject to any changes on which the parties and the mediator agree.

(a) The process is non-binding.
(b) Each party may withdraw at any time after attending the first session, and before execution of a written settlement agreement, by written notice to the mediator and the other party or parties.
(c) The mediator shall be neutral and impartial.
(d) The mediator shall control the procedural aspects of the mediation. The parties will cooperate fully with the mediator.

  i. The mediator is free to meet and communicate separately with each party.
  ii. The mediator will decide when to hold joint meetings with the parties and when to hold separate meetings. The mediator will fix the time and place of each session and its agenda in consultation with the parties. There will be no stenographic record of any meeting. Formal rules of evidence or procedure will not apply.

(e) Each party will be represented at each mediation conference by a business executive or other person authorized to negotiate a resolution of the dispute, unless excused by the mediator as to a particular conference. Each party may be represented by more than one person, e.g. a business executive and an attorney. The mediator may limit the number of persons representing each party.
(f) Each party will be represented by counsel to advise it in the mediation, whether or not such counsel is present at mediation conferences.

(g) The process will be conducted expeditiously. Each representative will make every effort to be available for meetings.

(h) The mediator will not transmit information received in confidence from any party to any other party or any third party unless authorized to do so by the party transmitting the information, or unless ordered to do so by a court of competent jurisdiction.

(i) Unless the parties agree otherwise, they will refrain from pursuing litigation or any administrative or judicial remedies during the mediation process or for a set period of time, insofar as they can do so without prejudicing their legal rights.

(j) Unless all parties and the mediator otherwise agree in writing, the mediator and any persons assisting the mediator will be disqualified as a witness, consultant or expert in any pending or future investigation, action or proceeding relating to the subject matter of the mediation (including any investigation, action or proceeding which involves persons not party to this mediation).

(k) If the dispute goes into arbitration, the mediator shall not serve as an arbitrator, unless the parties and the mediator otherwise agree in writing.

(l) The mediator may obtain assistance and independent expert advice, with the prior agreement of and at the expense of the parties. Any person proposed as an independent expert also will be required to disclose any circumstances known to him or her that would cause reasonable doubt regarding the candidate's impartiality.

(m) Neither CPR nor the mediator shall be liable for any act or omission in connection with the mediation, except for its/his/her own willful misconduct.

(n) The mediator may withdraw at any time by written notice to the parties (i) for serious personal reasons, (ii) if the mediator believes that a party is not acting in good faith, or (iii) if the mediator concludes that further mediation efforts would not be useful. If the mediator withdraws pursuant to (i) or (ii), he or she need not state the reason for withdrawal.

4. EXCHANGE OF INFORMATION

If any party has a substantial need for documents or other material in the possession of another party, or for other discovery that may facilitate a settlement, the parties shall attempt to agree thereon. Should they fail to agree, either party may request a joint consultation with the mediator who shall assist the parties in reaching agreement.

The parties shall exchange with each other, with a copy to the mediator, the names and job titles of all individuals who will attend the joint mediation session.

At the conclusion of the mediation process, upon the request of a party which provided documents or other material to one or more other parties, the recipients shall return the same to the originating party without retaining copies.

5. PRESENTATION TO THE MEDIATOR

Before dealing with the substance of the dispute, the parties and the mediator will discuss preliminary matters, such as possible modification of the procedure, place and time of meetings, and each party's need for documents or other information in the possession of the other.

At least 10 business days before the first substantive mediation conference, unless otherwise agreed, each party will submit to the mediator a written statement summarizing the background and present status of the dispute, including any settlement efforts that have occurred, and such other material and information as the mediator requests or the party deems helpful to familiarize the mediator with the dispute. It is desirable for the submission to include an analysis of the party's real interests and needs and of its litigation risks. The parties may agree to submit jointly certain records and other materials. The mediator may request any party to provide clarification and additional information.

The parties are encouraged to discuss the exchange of all or certain materials they submit to the mediator to further each party's understanding of the other party's viewpoints. The mediator may request the parties to submit a joint statement of facts. Except as the parties otherwise agree, the mediator shall keep confidential any written materials or information that are submitted to him or her. The parties and their representatives are not entitled to receive or review any materials or information submitted to the mediator by another party or representative without the concurrence of the latter. At the conclusion of the mediation process, upon request of a party, the mediator will return to that party all written materials and information which that party had provided to the mediator without retaining copies thereof or certify as to the destruction of such materials.

At the first substantive mediation conference each party will make an opening statement.

6. NEGOTIATIONS

The mediator may facilitate settlement in any manner the mediator believes is appropriate. The mediator will help the parties focus on their underlying interests and concerns, explore resolution alternatives and develop settlement options. The mediator will decide when to hold joint meetings, and when to confer separately with each party.

The parties are expected to initiate and convey to the mediator proposals for settlement. Each party shall provide a rationale for any settlement terms proposed.

Finally, if the parties fail to develop mutually acceptable settlement terms, before terminating the procedure, and only with the consent of the parties, (a) the mediator may submit to the parties a final settlement proposal; and (b) if the mediator believes he/she is qualified to do so, the mediator may give the parties an evaluation (which if all parties choose, and the mediator agrees, may be in writing) of the likely outcome of the case if it were tried to final judgment, subject to any limitations under any applicable mediation statutes/rules, court rules or ethical codes. Thereupon, the mediator may suggest further discussions to explore whether the mediator's evaluation or proposal may lead to a resolution.

Efforts to reach a settlement will continue until (a) a written settlement is reached, or (b) the mediator concludes and informs the parties that further efforts would not be useful, or (c) one of the parties or the mediator withdraws from the process. However, if there are more than two parties, the remaining parties may elect to continue following the withdrawal of a party.

7. SETTLEMENT

If a settlement is reached, a preliminary memorandum of understanding or term sheet normally will be prepared and signed or initialed before the parties separate. Thereafter, unless the mediator undertakes to do so, representatives of the parties will promptly draft a written settlement document incorporating all settlement terms. This draft will be circulated, amended as necessary, and formally executed. If litigation is pending, the settlement may provide that the parties will request dismissal of the case. The parties also may request the court to enter the settlement agreement as a consent judgment.

8. FAILURE TO AGREE

If a resolution is not reached, the mediator will discuss with the parties the possibility of their agreeing on advisory or binding arbitration, "last offer" arbitration or another form of ADR. If the parties agree in principle, the mediator may offer to assist them in structuring a procedure designed to result in a prompt, economical process. The mediator will not serve as arbitrator, unless all parties agree.

9. CONFIDENTIALITY

The entire mediation process is confidential. Unless agreed among all the parties or required to do so by law, the parties and the mediator shall not disclose to any person who is not associated with participants in the process, including any judicial officer, any information regarding the process (including pre-process exchanges and agreements), contents (including written and oral information), settlement terms or outcome of the proceeding. If litigation is pending, the participants may, however, advise the court of the schedule and overall status of the mediation for purposes of litigation management. Any written settlement agreement resulting from the mediation may be disclosed for purposes of enforcement.

Under this procedure, the entire process is a compromise negotiation subject to Federal Rule of Evidence 408 and all state counterparts, together with any applicable statute protecting the confidentiality of mediation. All offers, promises, conduct and statements, whether oral or written, made in the course of the proceeding by any of the parties, their agents, employees, experts and attorneys, and by the mediator are confidential. Such offers, promises, conduct and statements are privileged under any applicable mediation privilege and are inadmissible and not discoverable for any purpose, including impeachment, in litigation between the parties. However, evidence that is otherwise admissible or discoverable shall not be rendered inadmissible or non-discoverable solely as a result of its presentation or use during the mediation.

The exchange of any tangible material shall be without prejudice to any claim that such material is privileged or protected as work-product within the meaning of Federal Rule of Civil Procedure 26 and all state and local counterparts.

The mediator and any documents and information in the mediator's possession will not be subpoenaed in any such investigation, action or proceeding, and all parties will oppose any effort to have the mediator or documents subpoenaed. The mediator will promptly advise the parties of any attempt to compel him/her to divulge information received in mediation.

CPR MODEL AGREEMENT FOR PARTIES AND MEDIATOR*

Agreement made _____, _____
                                (date)

between_____

represented by_____

and_____

represented by_____

and_____
                        (the Mediator)

A dispute has arisen between the parties (the "Dispute"). The parties have agreed to participate in a mediation proceeding (the "Proceeding") under the CPR Mediation Procedure [, as modified by mutual agreement] (the "Procedure"). The parties have chosen the Mediator for the Proceeding. The parties and the Mediator agree as follows:

A. DUTIES AND OBLIGATIONS

1. The Mediator and each of the parties agree to be bound by and to comply faithfully with the Procedure, including without limitation the provisions regarding confidentiality.
2. The Mediator has no previous commitments that may significantly delay the expeditious conduct of the proceeding and will not make any such commitments.

---

*This form assumes that the mediator is affiliated with a firm. If that is not the case, delete paras. C.3., D.2. and references to the mediator's firm in paras. B.1. and C.1.

3. The Mediator, the CPR Institute for Dispute Resolution (CPR) and their employees, agents and partners shall not be liable for any act or omission in connection with the Proceeding, other than as a result of its/his/her own willful misconduct.

B. DISCLOSURE OF PRIOR RELATIONSHIPS

1. The Mediator has made a reasonable effort to learn and has disclosed to the parties in writing (a) all business or professional relationships the Mediator and/or the Mediator's firm have had with the parties or their law firms within the past five years, including all instances in which the Mediator or the Mediator's firm served as an attorney for any party or adverse to any party; (b) any financial interest the Mediator has in any party; (c) any significant social, business or professional relationship the Mediator has had with an officer or employee of a party or with an individual representing a party in the Proceeding; and (d) any other circumstances that may create doubt regarding the Mediator's impartiality in the Proceeding.
2. Each party and its law firm has made a reasonable effort to learn and has disclosed to every other party and the Mediator in writing any relationships of a nature described in paragraph B.1. not previously identified and disclosed by the Mediator.
3. The parties and the Mediator are satisfied that any relationships disclosed pursuant to paragraphs B.1. and B.2. will not affect the Mediator's independence or impartiality. Notwithstanding such relationships or others the Mediator and the parties did not discover despite good faith efforts, the parties wish the Mediator to serve in the Proceeding, waiving any claim based on said relationships, and the Mediator agrees to so serve.
4. The disclosure obligations in paragraphs B.1. and B.2. are continuing until the Proceeding is concluded. The ability of the Mediator to continue serving in this capacity shall be explored with each such disclosure.

C. FUTURE RELATIONSHIPS

1. Neither the Mediator nor the Mediator's firm shall undertake any work for or against a party regarding the Dispute.
2. Neither the Mediator nor any person assisting the Mediator with this Proceeding shall personally work on any matter for or against a party, regardless of specific subject matter, prior to six months following cessation of the Mediator's services in the Proceeding.
3. The Mediator's firm may work on matters for or against a party during the pendency of the Proceeding if such matters are unrelated to the Dispute. The Mediator shall establish appropriate safeguards to insure that other members and employees of the firm working on such matters unrelated to the Dispute do not have access to any confidential information obtained by the Mediator during the course of the Proceeding.

D. COMPENSATION

1. The Mediator shall be compensated for time expended in connection with the Proceeding at the rate of $_____, plus reasonable travel and other out-of-pocket expenses. The Mediator's fee shall be shared equally by the parties. No part of such fee shall accrue to CPR.

2. The Mediator may utilize members and employees of the firm to assist in connection with the Proceeding and may bill the parties for the time expended by any such persons, to the extent and at a rate agreed upon in advance by the parties.

_____   _____
Party   Party

by _____   by _____
Party's Attorney   Party's Attorney

_____
Mediator

Appendix R.2
CPR Institute for Dispute Resolution
Rules for Non-Administered Arbitration

Revised and effective September 15, 2000

REVISION HISTORY

1989   CPR published Rules and Commentary for Non-Traditional Arbitration for Business Disputes.

1993   Significant CPR revision of selected provisions of the Rules.

1994   New Title: Non-Administered Arbitration Rules & Commentary.

1995   Changes made to Rules 5.1, 6.4(b) and Commentary on Rule 5 regarding use of CPR Panels of Distinguished Neutrals.

1998   Bibliography updated.

2000   Significant CPR revision to Rules and Commentary. Bibliography updated.

STANDARD CONTRACTUAL PROVISIONS

The CPR Institute for Dispute Resolution Rules for Non-Administered Arbitration are intended in particular for use in complex commercial arbitrations and are designed to assure the expeditious and economical conduct of proceedings. The Rules may be adopted by parties wishing to do so by using one of the following standard provisions:

A. Pre-Dispute Clause

"Any dispute arising out of or relating to this contract, including the breach, termination or validity thereof, shall be finally resolved by arbitration in accordance with the CPR Institute for Dispute Resolution Rules for Non-Administered Arbitration by (a sole arbitrator) (three arbitrators, of whom each party shall appoint one) (three arbitrators, of whom each party shall designate one in accordance with the "screened" appointment procedure provided in Rule 5.4) (three arbitrators, none of whom shall be appointed by either party). The arbitration shall be governed by the Federal Arbitration Act, 9 U.S.C. §§ 1-16, and judgment upon the award rendered by the arbitrator(s) may be entered by any court having jurisdiction thereof. The place of the arbitration shall be (city, state)."

B. Existing Dispute Submission Agreement

"We, the undersigned parties, hereby agree to submit to arbitration in accordance with the CPR Institute for Dispute Resolution Rules for Non-Administered Arbitration (the "Rules") the following dispute: [Describe briefly]

We further agree that the above dispute shall be submitted to (a sole arbitrator) (three arbitrators, of whom each party shall appoint one) (three arbitrators, of whom each party shall designate one in accordance with the "screened" appointment procedure provided in Rule 5.4) (three arbitrators, none of whom shall be appointed by either party). We further agree that we shall faithfully observe this agreement and the Rules and that shall abide by and perform any award rendered by the arbitrator(s). The arbitration shall be governed by the Federal Arbitration Act, 9 U.S.C. §§ 1-16, and judgment upon the award may be entered by any court having jurisdiction thereof. The place of the arbitration shall be (city, state)."

RULES FOR NON-ADMINISTERED ARBITRATION

A. General and Introductory Rules

Rule 1: Scope of Application
Rule 2: Notices
Rule 3: Commencement of Arbitration
Rule 4: Representation

B. Rules with Respect to the Tribunal

Rule 5: Selection of Arbitrators by the Parties
Rule 6: Selection of Arbitrator(s) by CPR
Rule 7: Qualifications, Challenges and Replacement of Arbitrator(s)
Rule 8: Challenges to the Jurisdiction of the Tribunal

C. Rules with Respect to the Conduct of the Arbitral Proceedings

Rule 9: General Provisions
Rule 10: Applicable Law(s) and Remedies
Rule 11: Discovery
Rule 12: Evidence and Hearings
Rule 13: Interim Measures of Protection
Rule 14: The Award

D. Miscellaneous Rules

Rule 15: Failure to Comply with Rules
Rule 16: Costs
Rule 17: Confidentiality
Rule 18: Settlement and Mediation
Rule 19: Actions against CPR or Arbitrator(s)
Rule 20: Waiver

A. GENERAL AND INTRODUCTORY RULES

Rule 1:   Scope of Application

1.1   Where the parties to a contract have provided for arbitration under the CPR Institute for Dispute Resolution ("CPR") Rules for Non-Administered Arbitration (the "Rules"), or have provided for CPR arbitration without further specification, they shall be deemed to have made these Rules a part of their arbitration agreement, except to the extent that they have agreed in writing, or on the record during the course of the arbitral proceeding, to modify these Rules. Unless the parties otherwise agree, these Rules, and any amendment thereof adopted by CPR, shall apply in the form in effect at the time the arbitration is commenced.

1.2   These Rules shall govern the arbitration except that where any of these Rules is in conflict with a mandatory provision of applicable arbitration law, that provision of law shall prevail.

Rule 2:   Notices

2.1   Notices or other communications required under these Rules shall be in writing and delivered to the address specified in writing by the recipient or, if no address has been specified, to the last known business or residence address of the recipient. Notices and communications may be given by registered mail, courier, telex, facsimile transmission, or any other means of telecommunication that provides a record thereof. Notices and communications shall be deemed to be effective as of the date of receipt. Proof of transmission shall be deemed *prima facie* proof of receipt of any notice or communication given under these Rules.

2.2   Time periods specified by these Rules or established by the Arbitral Tribunal (the "Tribunal") shall start to run on the day following the day when a notice or communication is received, unless the Tribunal shall specifically provide otherwise. If the last day of such period is an official holiday or a non-business day at the place where the notice or communication is received, the period is extended until the first business day which follows. Official holidays and non-business days occurring during the running of the period of time are included in calculating the period.

Rule 3:   Commencement of Arbitration

3.1   The party commencing arbitration (the "Claimant") shall address to the other party (the "Respondent") a notice of arbitration.

3.2   The arbitration shall be deemed commenced as to any Respondent on the date on which the notice of arbitration is received by the Respondent.

3.3   The notice of arbitration shall include in the text or in attachments thereto:

    a. The full names, descriptions and addresses of the parties;
    b. A demand that the dispute be referred to arbitration pursuant to the Rules;

   c. The text of the arbitration clause or the separate arbitration agreement that is involved;
   d. A statement of the general nature of the Claimant's claim;
   e. The relief or remedy sought; and
   f. The name and address of the arbitrator appointed by the Claimant, unless the parties have agreed that neither shall appoint an arbitrator or that the party-appointed arbitrators shall be appointed as provided in Rule 5.4.

3.4   Within 20 days after receipt of the notice of arbitration, the Respondent shall deliver to the Claimant a notice of defense. Failure to deliver a notice of defense shall not delay the arbitration; in the event of such failure, all claims set forth in the demand shall be deemed denied. Failure to deliver a notice of defense shall not excuse the Respondent from notifying the Claimant in writing, within 20 days after receipt of the notice of arbitration, of the arbitrator appointed by the Respondent, unless the parties have agreed that neither shall appoint an arbitrator or that the party-appointed arbitrators shall be appointed as provided in Rule 5.4.

3.5   The notice of defense shall include:

   a. Any comment on items (a), (b), and (c) of the notice of arbitration that the Respondent may deem appropriate;
   b. A statement of the general nature of the Respondent's defense; and
   c. The name and address of the arbitrator appointed by the Respondent, unless the parties have agreed that neither shall appoint an arbitrator or that the party-appointed arbitrators shall be appointed as provided in Rule 5.4.

3.6   The Respondent may include in its notice of defense any counterclaim within the scope of the arbitration clause. If it does so, the counterclaim in the notice of defense shall include items (a), (b), (c), (d) and (e) of Rule 3.3.

3.7   If a counterclaim is asserted, within 20 days after receipt of the notice of defense, the Claimant shall deliver to the Respondent a reply to counterclaim which shall have the same elements as provided in Rule 3.5 for the notice of defense. Failure to deliver a reply to counterclaim shall not delay the arbitration; in the event of such failure, all counterclaims set forth in the notice of defense shall be deemed denied.

3.8   Claims or counterclaims within the scope of the arbitration clause may be freely added or amended prior to the establishment of the Tribunal and thereafter with the consent of the Tribunal. Notices of defense or replies to amended claims or counterclaims shall be delivered within 20 days after the addition or amendment.

3.9   If a dispute is submitted to arbitration pursuant to a submission agreement, this Rule 3 shall apply to the extent that it is not inconsistent with the submission agreement.

Rule 4:   Representation

4.1   The parties may be represented or assisted by persons of their choice.

4.2   Each party shall communicate the name, address and function of such persons in writing to the other party and to the Tribunal.

B. RULES WITH RESPECT TO THE TRIBUNAL

Rule 5:   Selection of Arbitrators by the Parties

5.1   Unless the parties have agreed in writing on a Tribunal consisting of a sole arbitrator or of three arbitrators not appointed by parties or appointed as provided in Rule 5.4, the Tribunal shall consist of two arbitrators, one appointed by each of the parties as provided in Rules 3.3 and 3.5, and a third arbitrator who shall chair the Tribunal, selected as provided in Rule 5.2. Unless otherwise agreed, any arbitrator not appointed by a party shall be a member of the CPR Panels of Distinguished Neutrals ("CPR Panels").

5.2   Within 30 days of the appointment of the second arbitrator, the two party-appointed arbitrators shall appoint a third arbitrator, who shall chair the Tribunal. In the event the party-appointed arbitrators are unable to agree on the third arbitrator, the third arbitrator shall be selected as provided in Rule 6.

5.3   If the parties have agreed on a Tribunal consisting of a sole arbitrator or of three arbitrators none of whom shall be appointed by either party, the parties shall attempt jointly to select such arbitrator(s) within 30 days after the notice of defense provided for in Rule 3.4 is due. The parties may extend their selection process until one or both of them have concluded that a deadlock has been reached. In this event, the arbitrator(s) shall be selected as provided in Rule 6.

5.4   If the parties have agreed on a Tribunal consisting of three arbitrators, two of whom are to be designated by the parties without knowing which party designated each of them, as provided in this Rule 5.4, either party, following the expiration of the time period for the notice of defense, may request CPR in writing, with a copy to the other party, to conduct a "screened" selection of party-designated arbitrators as follows:

   a. CPR will provide each party with a copy of its CPR Panels list. Within 15 days thereafter, each party shall designate three candidates, in order of preference, from the CPR Panels as candidates for its party-designated arbitrator, and so notify CPR and the other party in writing.
   b. CPR will ask the first candidate so designated by each party to confirm his or her availability to serve as arbitrator and to disclose in writing any circumstances that might give rise to justifiable doubt regarding the candidate's independence or impartiality, as provided in Rule 7. CPR will circulate to the parties each candidate's completed disclosure form. A party may object to the appointment of any candidate on

independent and impartial grounds by written and reasoned notice to CPR, with copy to the other party, within 10 days after receipt of that candidate's disclosure form. CPR shall decide the objection after providing the non-objecting party with an opportunity to comment on the objection. If there is no objection to the candidate, or if the objection is overruled by CPR, CPR shall appoint the candidate as arbitrator, and any subsequent challenges of that arbitrator, based on circumstances subsequently learned, shall be made and decided in accordance with the procedures set forth in Rules 7.6–7.8.

c. If the first candidate designated by a party is unavailable, or if his or her independence or impartiality is successfully challenged, CPR will repeat the process provided in Rule 5.4(b) as to the subsequent candidates designated by that party, in order of the party's indicated preference. A party may designate additional candidates if the three candidates designated by that party are unavailable or do not meet the requirements of Rule 7.

d. Neither CPR nor the parties shall advise or otherwise provide any information or indication to any arbitrator candidate or arbitrator as to which party selected either of the party-designated arbitrators. No party or anyone acting on its behalf shall have any ex parte communications relating to the case with any arbitrator or arbitrator candidate designated or appointed pursuant to this Rule 5.4.

e. The chair of the Tribunal will be appointed by CPR in accordance with the procedure set forth in Rule 6.4, which shall proceed concurrently with the procedure for appointing the party-designated arbitrators provided in subsections (a)–(d) above.

f. The compensation of all members of the Tribunal appointed pursuant to Rule 5.4 shall be administered by the chair of the Tribunal in accordance with Rule 16.

5.5   Where the arbitration agreement entitles each party to appoint an arbitrator but there is more than one Claimant or Respondent to the dispute, and either the multiple Claimants or the multiple Respondents do not jointly appoint an arbitrator, CPR shall appoint all of the arbitrators as provided in Rule 6.4.

Rule 6:   Selection of Arbitrator(s) by CPR

6.1   Whenever (i) a party has failed to appoint the arbitrator to be appointed by it; (ii) the parties have failed to appoint the arbitrator(s) to be appointed by them acting jointly; (iii) the party-appointed arbitrators have failed to appoint the third arbitrator; (iv) the parties have provided that one or more arbitrators shall be appointed by CPR; or (v) the multi-party nature of the dispute calls for CPR to appoint all members of a three-member Tribunal pursuant to Rule 5.5, the arbitrator(s) required to complete the Tribunal shall be selected as provided in this Rule 6, and either party may request CPR in writing, with copy to the other party, to proceed pursuant to this Rule 6.

6.2   The written request may be made as follows:

   a. If a party has failed to appoint the arbitrator to be appointed by it, or the parties have failed to appoint the arbitrator(s) to be appointed by them through agreement, at any time after such failure has occurred.
   b. If the party-appointed arbitrators have failed to appoint the third arbitrator, as soon as the procedure contemplated by Rule 5.2 has been completed.
   c. If the arbitrator(s) are to be appointed by CPR, as soon as the notice of defense is due.

6.3   The written request shall include complete copies of the notice of arbitration and the notice of defense or, if the dispute is submitted under a submission agreement, a copy of the agreement supplemented by the notice of arbitration and notice of defense if they are not part of the agreement.

6.4   Except where a party has failed to appoint the arbitrator to be appointed by it, CPR shall proceed as follows:

   a. Promptly following receipt by it of the request provided for in Rule 6.3, CPR shall convene the parties in person or by telephone to attempt to select the arbitrator(s) by agreement of the parties.
   b. If the procedure provided for in (a) does not result in the selection of the required number of arbitrators, CPR shall submit to the parties a list, from the CPR Panels, of not less than five candidates if one arbitrator remains to be selected, and of not less than seven candidates if two or three arbitrators are to be selected. Such list shall include a brief statement of each candidate's qualifications. Each party shall number the candidates in order of preference, shall note any objection it may have to any candidate, and shall deliver the list so marked to CPR and to the other party. Any party failing without good cause to return the candidate list so marked within 10 days after receipt shall be deemed to have assented to all candidates listed thereon. CPR shall designate as arbitrator(s) the nominee(s) willing to serve for whom the parties collectively have indicated the highest preference and who appear to meet the standards set forth in Rule 7. If a tie should result between two candidates, CPR may designate either candidate. If this procedure for any reason should fail to result in designation of the required number of arbitrators or if a party fails to participate in this procedure, CPR shall appoint a person or persons whom it deems qualified to fill any remaining vacancy.

6.5   Where a party has failed to appoint the arbitrator to be appointed by it, CPR shall appoint a person whom it deems qualified to serve as such arbitrator.

Rule 7:   Qualifications, Challenges and Replacement of Arbitrator(s)

7.1   Each arbitrator shall be independent and impartial.

7.2   By accepting appointment, each arbitrator shall be deemed to be bound by these Rules and any modification agreed to by the parties, and to have represented that he or she has the time available to devote to the expeditious process contemplated by these Rules.

7.3   Each arbitrator shall disclose in writing to the Tribunal and the parties at the time of his or her appointment and promptly upon their arising during the course of the arbitration any circumstances that might give rise to justifiable doubt regarding the arbitrator's independence or impartiality. Such circumstances include bias, interest in the result of the arbitration, and past or present relations with a party or its counsel.

7.4   No party or anyone acting on its behalf shall have any *ex parte* communications concerning any matter of substance relating to the proceeding with any arbitrator or arbitrator candidate, except that a party may advise a candidate for appointment as its party-appointed arbitrator of the general nature of the case and discuss the candidate's qualifications, availability, and independence and impartiality with respect to the parties, and a party may confer with its party-appointed arbitrator regarding the selection of the chair of the Tribunal. As provided in Rule 5.4(d), no party or anyone acting on its behalf shall have any *ex parte* communications relating to the case with any arbitrator or arbitrator candidate designated or appointed pursuant to Rule 5.4.

7.5   Any arbitrator may be challenged if circumstances exist or arise that give rise to justifiable doubt regarding that arbitrator's independence or impartiality, provided that a party may challenge an arbitrator whom it has appointed only for reasons of which it becomes aware after the appointment has been made.

7.6   A party may challenge an arbitrator only by a notice in writing to CPR, with copy to the Tribunal and the other party, given no later than 15 days after the challenging party (i) receives notification of the appointment of that arbitrator, or (ii) becomes aware of the circumstances specified in Rule 7.5, whichever shall last occur. The notice shall state the reasons for the challenge with specificity. The notice shall not be sent to the Tribunal when the challenged arbitrator is a party-designated arbitrator selected as provided in Rule 5.4; in that event, CPR may provide each member of the Tribunal with an opportunity to comment on the substance of the challenge without disclosing the identity of the challenging party.

7.7   When an arbitrator has been challenged by a party, the other party may agree to the challenge or the arbitrator may voluntarily withdraw. Neither of these actions implies acceptance of the validity of the challenge.

7.8   If neither agreed disqualification nor voluntary withdrawal occurs, the challenge shall be decided by CPR, after providing the non-challenging party and each member of the Tribunal with an opportunity to comment on the challenge.

7.9   In the event of death, resignation or successful challenge of an arbitrator not appointed by a party, a substitute arbitrator shall be selected pursuant to the procedure by which the arbitrator being replaced was selected. In the event of the death, resignation or successful challenge of an arbitrator appointed by a party, that party may appoint a substitute arbitrator; provided, however, that should that party fail to notify the Tribunal (or CPR, if the Tribunal has been constituted as provided in Rule 5.4) and the other party of the substitute appointment within 20 days from the date on which it becomes aware that the opening arose, that party's right of appointment shall lapse and the Tribunal shall promptly request CPR to appoint a substitute arbitrator forthwith.

7.10   In the event that an arbitrator fails to act or is *de jure* or *de facto* prevented from duly performing the functions of an arbitrator, the procedures provided in Rule 7.9 shall apply to the selection of a replacement. If the parties do not agree on whether the arbitrator has failed to act or is prevented from performing the functions of an arbitrator, either party may request CPR to make that determination forthwith.

7.11   If the sole arbitrator or the chair of the Tribunal is replaced, the successor shall decide the extent to which any hearings held previously shall be repeated. If any other arbitrator is replaced, the Tribunal in its discretion may require that some or all prior hearings be repeated.

Rule 8:   Challenges to the Jurisdiction of the Tribunal

8.1   The Tribunal shall have the power to hear and determine challenges to its jurisdiction, including any objections with respect to the existence, scope or validity of the arbitration agreement.

8.2   The Tribunal shall have the power to determine the existence, validity or scope of the contract of which an arbitration clause forms a part. For the purposes of challenges to the jurisdiction of the Tribunal, the arbitration clause shall be considered as separable from any contract of which it forms a part.

8.3   Any challenges to the jurisdiction of the Tribunal, except challenges based on the award itself, shall be made not later than the notice of defense or, with respect to a counterclaim, the reply to the counterclaim; provided, however, that if a claim or counterclaim is later added or amended such a challenge may be made not later than the response to such claim or counterclaim.

C. RULES WITH RESPECT TO THE CONDUCT OF THE ARBITRAL PROCEEDINGS

Rule 9:   General Provisions

9.1   Subject to these Rules, the Tribunal may conduct the arbitration in such manner as it shall deem appropriate. The chair shall be responsible for the organization of arbitral conferences and hearings and arrangements with respect to the functioning of the Tribunal.

9.2   The proceedings shall be conducted in an expeditious manner. The Tribunal is empowered to impose time limits it considers reasonable on each phase of the proceeding, including without limitation the time allotted to each party for presentation of its case and for rebuttal. In setting time limits, the Tribunal should bear in mind its obligation to manage the proceeding firmly in order to complete proceedings as economically and expeditiously as possible.

9.3   The Tribunal shall hold an initial pre-hearing conference for the planning and scheduling of the proceeding. Such conference shall be held promptly after the constitution of the Tribunal, unless the Tribunal is of the view that further submissions from the parties are appropriate prior to such conference. The objective of this conference shall be to discuss all elements of the arbitration with a view to planning for its future conduct. Matters to be considered in the initial pre-hearing conference may include, *inter alia*, the following:

   a. Procedural matters (such as setting specific time limits for, and manner of, any required discovery; the desirability of bifurcation or other separation of the issues in the arbitration; the desirability and practicability of consolidating the arbitration with any other proceeding; the scheduling of conferences and hearings; the scheduling of pre-hearing memoranda; the need for and type of record of conferences and hearings, including the need for transcripts; the amount of time allotted to each party for presentation of its case and for rebuttal; the mode, manner and order for presenting proof; the need for expert witnesses and how expert testimony should be presented; and the necessity for any on-site inspection by the Tribunal);
   b. The early identification and narrowing of the issues in the arbitration;
   c. The possibility of stipulations of fact and admissions by the parties solely for purposes of the arbitration, as well as simplification of document authentication;
   d. The possibility of appointment of a neutral expert by the Tribunal; and
   e. The possibility of the parties engaging in settlement negotiations, with or without the assistance of a mediator.

After the initial conference, further pre-hearing or other conferences may be held as the Tribunal deems appropriate.

9.4   In order to define the issues to be heard and determined, the Tribunal may, *inter alia*, make pre-hearing orders and instruct the parties to file more detailed statements of claim and of defense, and pre-hearing memoranda.

9.5   Unless the parties have agreed upon the place of arbitration, the Tribunal shall fix the place of arbitration based upon the contentions of the parties and the circumstances of the arbitration. The award shall be deemed made at such place. The Tribunal may schedule meetings and hold hearings wherever it deems appropriate.

Rule 10:   Applicable Law(s) and Remedies

10.1   The Tribunal shall apply the substantive law(s) or rules of law designated by the parties as applicable to the dispute. Failing such a designation by the parties, the Tribunal shall apply such law(s) or rules of law as it determines to be appropriate.

10.2   Subject to Rule 10.1, in arbitrations involving the application of contracts, the Tribunal shall decide in accordance with the terms of the contract and shall take into account usages of the trade applicable to the contract.

10.3   The Tribunal may grant any remedy or relief, including but not limited to specific performance of a contract, which is within the scope of the agreement of the parties and permissible under the law(s) or rules of law applicable to the dispute.

10.4   The Tribunal may award such pre-award and post-award interest, simple or compound, as it considers appropriate, taking into consideration the contract and applicable law.

Rule 11:   Discovery

The Tribunal may require and facilitate such discovery as it shall determine is appropriate in the circumstances, taking into account the needs of the parties and the desirability of making discovery expeditious and cost-effective. The Tribunal may issue orders to protect the confidentiality of proprietary information, trade secrets and other sensitive information disclosed in discovery.

Rule 12:   Evidence and Hearings

12.1   The Tribunal shall determine the manner in which the parties shall present their cases. Unless otherwise determined by the Tribunal or agreed by the parties, the presentation of a party's case shall include the submission of a pre-hearing memorandum including the following elements:

   a. A statement of facts;
   b. A statement of each claim being asserted;
   c. A statement of the applicable law and authorities upon which the party relies;
   d. A statement of the relief requested, including the basis for any damages claimed; and
   e. A statement of the nature and manner of presentation of the evidence, including the name, capacity and subject of testimony of any witnesses to be called and an estimate of the amount of time required for each witness's direct testimony.

12.2   If either party so requests or the Tribunal so directs, a hearing shall be held for the presentation of evidence and oral argument. Testimony may be presented in written and/or oral form as the Tribunal may determine is appropriate. The Tribunal is not required to apply the rules of evidence used in judicial proceedings, provided, however, that the Tribunal shall apply the lawyer-client privilege and the work product immunity. The Tribunal shall determine the applicability of any privilege or immunity and the admissibility, relevance, materiality and weight of the evidence offered.

12.3 The Tribunal, in its discretion, may require the parties to produce evidence in addition to that initially offered. It may also appoint neutral experts whose testimony shall be subject to cross-examination and rebuttal.

12.4 The Tribunal shall determine the manner in which witnesses are to be examined. The Tribunal shall have the right to exclude witnesses from hearings during the testimony of other witnesses.

Rule 13: Interim Measures of Protection

13.1 At the request of a party, the Tribunal may take such interim measures as it deems necessary, including measures for the preservation of assets, the conservation of goods or the sale of perishable goods. The Tribunal may require appropriate security as a condition of ordering such measures.

13.2 A request for interim measures by a party to a court shall not be deemed incompatible with the agreement to arbitrate or as a waiver of that agreement.

Rule 14: The Award

14.1 The Tribunal may make final, interim, interlocutory and partial awards. With respect to any interim, interlocutory or partial award, the Tribunal may state in its award whether or not it views the award as final for purposes of any judicial proceedings in connection therewith.

14.2 All awards shall be in writing and shall state the reasoning on which the award rests unless the parties agree otherwise. The award shall be deemed to be made at the seat of arbitration and shall contain the date on which the award was made. When there are three arbitrators, the award shall be made and signed by at least a majority of the arbitrators.

14.3 A member of the Tribunal who does not join in an award may file a dissenting opinion. Such opinion shall not constitute part of the award.

14.4 Executed copies of awards and of any dissenting opinion shall be delivered by the Tribunal to the parties.

14.5 Within 15 days after receipt of the award, either party, with notice to the other party, may request the Tribunal to interpret the award; to correct any clerical, typographical or computation errors, or any errors of a similar nature in the award; or to make an additional award as to claims or counterclaims presented in the arbitration but not determined in the award. The Tribunal shall make any interpretation, correction or additional award requested by either party that it deems justified within 30 days after receipt of such request. Within 15 days after delivery of the award to the parties or, if a party requests an interpretation, correction or additional award, within 30 days after receipt of such request, the Tribunal may make such corrections and additional awards on its own initiative as it deems appropriate. All interpretations, corrections, and additional awards shall be in writing, and the provisions of this Rule 14 shall apply to them.

14.6   The award shall be final and binding on the parties, and the parties will undertake to carry out the award without delay. If an interpretation, correction or additional award is requested by a party, or a correction or additional award is made by the Tribunal on its own initiative as provided in Rule 14.5, the award shall be final and binding on the parties when such interpretation, correction or additional award is made by the Tribunal or upon the expiration of the time periods provided in Rule 14.5 for such interpretation, correction or additional award to be made, whichever is earlier.

14.7   The dispute should in most circumstances be submitted to the Tribunal for decision within six months after the initial pre-hearing conference required by Rule 9.3. The final award should in most circumstances be rendered within one month thereafter. The parties and the Tribunal shall use their best efforts to comply with this schedule.

D. MISCELLANEOUS RULES

Rule 15:   Failure to Comply with Rules

Whenever a party fails to comply with these Rules, or any order of the Tribunal pursuant to these Rules, in a manner deemed material by the Tribunal, the Tribunal shall fix a reasonable period of time for compliance and, if the party does not comply within said period, the Tribunal may impose a remedy it deems just, including an award on default. Prior to entering an award on default, the Tribunal shall require the non-defaulting party to produce evidence and legal argument in support of its contentions as the Tribunal may deem appropriate. The Tribunal may receive such evidence and argument without the defaulting party's presence or participation.

Rule 16:   Costs

16.1   Each arbitrator shall be compensated on a reasonable basis determined at the time of appointment for serving as an arbitrator and shall be reimbursed for any reasonable travel and other expenses.

16.2   The Tribunal shall fix the costs of arbitration in its award. The costs of arbitration include:

    a.   The fees and expenses of members of the Tribunal;
    b.   The costs of expert advice and other assistance engaged by the Tribunal;
    c.   The travel and other expenses of witnesses to such extent as the Tribunal may deem appropriate;

    d. The costs for legal representation and assistance and experts incurred by a party to such extent as the Tribunal may deem appropriate;

    e. The charges and expenses of CPR with respect to the arbitration;

    f. The costs of a transcript; and

    g. The costs of meeting and hearing facilities.

16.3   Subject to any agreement between the parties to the contrary, the Tribunal may apportion the costs of arbitration between or among the parties in such manner as it deems reasonable, taking into account the circumstances of the case, the conduct of the parties during the proceeding, and the result of the arbitration.

16.4   The Tribunal may request each party to deposit an appropriate amount as an advance for the costs referred to in Rule 16.2, except those specified in sub-paragraph (d), and, during the course of the proceeding, it may request supplementary deposits from the parties. Any such funds shall be held and disbursed in such a manner as the Tribunal may deem appropriate.

16.5   If the requested deposits are not paid in full within 20 days after receipt of the request, the Tribunal shall so inform the parties in order that jointly or severally they may make the requested payment. If such payment is not made, the Tribunal may suspend or terminate the proceeding.

16.6   After the proceeding has been concluded, the Tribunal shall return any unexpended balance from deposits made to the parties as may be appropriate.

Rule 17:   Confidentiality

Unless the parties agree otherwise, the parties, the arbitrators and CPR shall treat the proceedings, any related discovery and the decisions of the Tribunal, as confidential, except in connection with judicial proceedings ancillary to the arbitration, such as a judicial challenge to, or enforcement of, an award, and unless otherwise required by law or to protect a legal right of a party. To the extent possible, any specific issues of confidentiality should be raised with and resolved by the Tribunal.

Rule 18:   Settlement and Mediation

18.1   Either party may propose settlement negotiations to the other party at any time. The Tribunal may suggest that the parties explore settlement at such times as the Tribunal may deem appropriate.

18.2   With the consent of the parties, the Tribunal at any stage of the proceeding may arrange for mediation of the claims asserted in the arbitration by a mediator acceptable to the parties. The mediator shall be a person other than a member of the Tribunal. Unless the parties agree otherwise, any such mediation shall be conducted under the CPR Mediation Procedure.

18.3   The Tribunal will not be informed of any settlement offers or other statements made during settlement negotiations or a mediation between the parties, unless both parties consent.

Rule 19:   Actions against CPR or Arbitrator(s)

Neither CPR nor any arbitrator shall be liable to any party for any act or omission in connection with any arbitration conducted under these Rules.

Rule 20:   Waiver

A party knowing of a failure to comply with any provision of these Rules, or any requirement of the arbitration agreement or any direction of the Tribunal, and neglecting to state its objections promptly, waives any objection thereto.

For the accompanying CPR Commentary, see <www.cpradr.org> (Procedures and Clauses).

Appendix R.3
American Arbitration Association
Commercial Dispute Resolution Procedures
(Including Mediation and Arbitration Rules)

As amended and effective on January 1, 1999
Mediation fee as amended and effective on November 1, 1999

Introduction

Each year, many millions of business transactions take place. Occasionally, disagreements develop over these business transactions. Many of these disputes are resolved by arbitration, the voluntary submission of a dispute to an impartial person or persons for final and binding determination. Arbitration has proven to be an effective way to resolve these disputes privately, promptly, and economically.

The American Arbitration Association (AAA), a public service, not-for-profit organization, offers a broad range of dispute resolution services to business executives, attorneys, individuals, trade associations, unions, management, consumers, families, communities, and all levels of government. Services are available through AAA headquarters in New York and through offices located in major cities throughout the United States. Hearings may be held at locations convenient for the parties and are not limited to cities with AAA offices. In addition, the AAA serves as a center for education and training, issues specialized publications, and conducts research on all forms of out-of-court dispute settlement.

Standard Arbitration Clause

The parties can provide for arbitration of future disputes by inserting the following clause into their contracts:

> Any controversy or claim arising out of or relating to this contract, or the breach thereof, shall be settled by arbitration administered by the American Arbitration Association under its Commercial Arbitration Rules, and judgment on the award rendered by the arbitrator(s) may be entered in any court having jurisdiction thereof.

Arbitration of existing disputes may be accomplished by use of the following:

> We, the undersigned parties, hereby agree to submit to arbitration administered by the American Arbitration Association under its Commercial Arbitration Rules the following controversy: (describe briefly). We further

agree that the above controversy be submitted to (one) (three) arbitrator(s). We further agree that we will faithfully observe this agreement and the rules, that we will abide by and perform any award rendered by the arbitrator(s), and that a judgment of any court having jurisdiction may be entered on the award.

In transactions likely to require emergency interim relief, the parties may wish to add to their clause the following language:

The parties also agree that the AAA Optional Rules for Emergency Measures of Protection shall apply to the proceedings.

These Optional Rules may be found at the end of this pamphlet.

The services of the AAA are generally concluded with the transmittal of the award. Although there is voluntary compliance with the majority of awards, judgment on the award can be entered in a court having appropriate jurisdiction if necessary.

Administrative Fees

The AAA's administrative fees are based on service charges. There is a filing fee based on the amount of the claim or counterclaim, ranging from $500 on claims below $10,000 to a negotiated amount for claims in excess of $5 million. In addition, there are service charges for hearings and postponements. This fee information, which is included with these rules, allows the parties to exercise control over their administrative fees.

The fees cover AAA administrative services; they do not cover arbitrator compensation or expenses, if any, reporting services, or any post-award charges incurred by the parties in enforcing the award.

Mediation

The parties might wish to submit their dispute to mediation prior to arbitration. In mediation, the neutral mediator assists the parties in reaching a settlement but does not have the authority to make a binding decision or award. Mediation is administered by the AAA in accordance with its Commercial Mediation Rules. There is no additional administrative fee where parties to a pending arbitration attempt to mediate their dispute under the AAA's auspices.

If the parties want to adopt mediation as a part of their contractual dispute settlement procedure, they can insert the following mediation clause into their contract in conjunction with a standard arbitration provision:

If a dispute arises out of or relates to this contract, or the breach thereof, and if the dispute cannot be settled through negotiation, the parties agree first to try in good faith to settle the dispute by mediation administered by the American Arbitration Association under its Commercial Mediation Rules before resorting to arbitration, litigation, or some other dispute resolution procedure.

If the parties want to use a mediator to resolve an existing dispute, they can enter into the following submission:

> The parties hereby submit the following dispute to mediation administered by the American Arbitration Association under its Commercial Mediation Rules. (The clause may also provide for the qualifications of the mediator(s), method of payment, locale of meetings, and any other item of concern to the parties.)

Large, Complex Cases

Unless the parties agree otherwise, the Optional Procedures for Large, Complex Commercial Disputes, which appear in this pamphlet, will be applied to all cases administered by the AAA under the Commercial Arbitration Rules in which the disclosed claim or counterclaim of any party is at least $1,000,000 exclusive of claimed interest, arbitration fees and costs, and in which either (1) all parties have elected to have the Procedures apply to the resolution of their dispute; or (2) a court or governmental agency of competent jurisdiction has determined that a dispute should be resolved before the AAA pursuant to the Procedures.

The key features of these Procedures include:

- a highly qualified, trained Roster of Neutrals;
- a mandatory preliminary hearing with the arbitrators, which may be conductedby teleconference;
- broad arbitrator authority to order and control discovery, including depositions;
- presumption that hearings will proceed on a consecutive or block basis.

Commercial Mediation Rules

M-1. Agreement of Parties

Whenever, by stipulation or in their contract, the parties have provided for mediation or conciliation of existing or future disputes under the auspices of the American Arbitration Association (AAA) or under these rules, they shall be deemed to have made these rules, as amended and in effect as of the date of the submission of the dispute, a part of their agreement.

M-2. Initiation of Mediation

Any party or parties to a dispute may initiate mediation by filing with the AAA a submission to mediation or a written request for mediation pursuant to these rules, together with the appropriate Filing Fee [page 78]. Where there is no submission to mediation or contract providing for mediation, a party may request the AAA to invite another party to join in a submission to mediation. Upon receipt of such a request, the AAA will contact the other parties involved in the dispute and attempt to obtain a submission to mediation.

M-3. Requests for Mediation

A request for mediation shall contain a brief statement of the nature of the dispute and the names, addresses, and telephone numbers of all parties to the dispute and those who will represent them, if any, in the mediation. The initiating party shall simultaneously file two copies of the request with the AAA and one copy with every other party to the dispute.

M-4. Appointment of the Mediator

Upon receipt of a request for mediation, the AAA will appoint a qualified mediator to serve. Normally, a single mediator will be appointed unless the parties agree otherwise or the AAA determines otherwise. If the agreement of the parties names a mediator or specifies a method of appointing a mediator, that designation or method shall be followed.

M-5. Qualifications of the Mediator

No person shall serve as a mediator in any dispute in which that person has any financial or personal interest in the result of the mediation, except by the written consent of all parties. Prior to accepting an appointment, the prospective mediator shall disclose any circumstance likely to create a presumption of bias or prevent a prompt meeting with the parties. Upon receipt of such information, the AAA shall either replace the mediator or immediately communicate the information to the parties for their comments. In the event that the parties disagree as to whether the mediator shall serve, the AAA will appoint another mediator. The AAA is authorized to appoint another mediator if the appointed mediator is unable to serve promptly.

M-6. Vacancies

If any mediator shall become unwilling or unable to serve, the AAA will appoint another mediator, unless the parties agree otherwise.

M-7. Representation

Any party may be represented by persons of the party's choice. The names and addresses of such persons shall be communicated in writing to all parties and to the AAA.

M-8. Date, Time, and Place of Mediation

The mediator shall fix the date and the time of each mediation session. The mediation shall be held at the appropriate regional office of the AAA, or at any other convenient location agreeable to the mediator and the parties, as the mediator shall determine.

M-9. Identification of Matters in Dispute

At least ten days prior to the first scheduled mediation session, each party shall provide the mediator with a brief memorandum setting forth its position with regard to the issues that need to be resolved. At the discretion of the mediator, such memoranda may be mutually exchanged by the parties.

At the first session, the parties will be expected to produce all information reasonably required for the mediator to understand the issues presented.

The mediator may require any party to supplement such information.

M-10. Authority of the Mediator

The mediator does not have the authority to impose a settlement on the parties but will attempt to help them reach a satisfactory resolution of their dispute. The mediator is authorized to conduct joint and separate meetings with the parties and to make oral and written recommendations for settlement. Whenever necessary, the mediator may also obtain expert advice concerning technical aspects of the dispute, provided that the parties agree and assume the expenses of obtaining such advice. Arrangements for obtaining such advice shall be made by the mediator or the parties, as the mediator shall determine.

The mediator is authorized to end the mediation whenever, in the judgment of the mediator, further efforts at mediation would not contribute to a resolution of the dispute between the parties.

M-11. Privacy

Mediation sessions are private. The parties and their representatives may attend mediation sessions. Other persons may attend only with the permission of the parties and with the consent of the mediator.

M-12. Confidentiality

Confidential information disclosed to a mediator by the parties or by witnesses in the course of the mediation shall not be divulged by the mediator. All records, reports, or other documents received by a mediator while serving in that capacity shall be confidential. The mediator shall not be compelled to divulge such records or to testify in regard to the mediation in any adversary proceeding or judicial forum.

The parties shall maintain the confidentiality of the mediation and shall not rely on, or introduce as evidence in any arbitral, judicial, or other proceeding:

(a) views expressed or suggestions made by another party with respect to a possible settlement of the dispute;
(b) admissions made by another party in the course of the mediation proceedings;
(c) proposals made or views expressed by the mediator; or
(d) the fact that another party had or had not indicated willingness to accept a proposal for settlement made by the mediator.

M-13. No Stenographic Record

There shall be no stenographic record of the mediation process.

M-14. Termination of Mediation

The mediation shall be terminated:

 (a) by the execution of a settlement agreement by the parties;
 (b) by a written declaration of the mediator to the effect that further efforts at mediation are no longer worthwhile; or
 (c) by a written declaration of a party or parties to the effect that the mediation proceedings are terminated.

M-15. Exclusion of Liability

Neither the AAA nor any mediator is a necessary party in judicial proceedings relating to the mediation. Neither the AAA nor any mediator shall be liable to any party for any act or omission in connection with any mediation conducted under these rules.

M-16. Interpretation and Application of Rules

The mediator shall interpret and apply these rules insofar as they relate to the mediator's duties and responsibilities. All other rules shall be interpreted and applied by the AAA.

M-17. Expenses

The expenses of witnesses for either side shall be paid by the party producing such witnesses. All other expenses of the mediation, including required traveling and other expenses of the mediator and representatives of the AAA, and the expenses of any witness and the cost of any proofs or expert advice produced at the direct request of the mediator, shall be borne equally by the parties unless they agree otherwise.

Administrative Fees

Mediation fees vary for each AAA office. Please check with your local AAA office for rates and mediator availability.

Commercial Arbitration Rules

R-1. Agreement of Parties*

The parties shall be deemed to have made these rules a part of their arbitration agreement whenever they have provided for arbitration by the American Arbi-

---

* A dispute arising out of an employment relationship will be administered under the AAA's National Rules for the Resolution of Employment Disputes, unless all parties agree otherwise after the commencement of AAA administration.

tration Association (hereinafter AAA) under its Commercial Arbitration Rules or for arbitration by the AAA of a domestic commercial dispute without specifying particular rules. These rules and any amendment of them shall apply in the form in effect at the time the demand for arbitration or submission agreement is received by the AAA. The parties, by written agreement, may vary the procedures set forth in these rules.

R-2. AAA and Delegation of Duties

When parties agree to arbitrate under these rules, or when they provide for arbitration by the AAA and an arbitration is initiated under these rules, they thereby authorize the AAA to administer the arbitration. The authority and duties of the AAA are prescribed in the agreement of the parties and in these rules, and may be carried out through such of the AAA's representatives as it may direct. The AAA may, in its discretion, assign the administration of an arbitration to any of its offices.

R-3. National Panel of Arbitrators

The AAA shall establish and maintain a National Panel of Commercial Arbitrators and shall appoint arbitrators as provided in these rules. The term "arbitrator" in these rules refers to the arbitration panel, whether composed of one or more arbitrators and whether the arbitrators are neutral or party-appointed.

R-4. Initiation under an Arbitration Provision in a Contract

(a) Arbitration under an arbitration provision in a contract shall be initiated in the following manner:

    i. The initiating party (the "claimant") shall, within the time period, if any, specified in the contract(s), give to the other party (the "respondent") written notice of its intention to arbitrate (the "demand"), which demand shall contain a statement setting forth the nature of the dispute, the names and addresses of all other parties, the amount involved, if any, the remedy sought, and the hearing locale requested.

    ii. The claimant shall file at any office of the AAA two copies of the demand and two copies of the arbitration provisions of the contract, together with the appropriate filing fee as provided in the schedule included with these rules.

    iii. The AAA shall confirm notice of such filing to the parties.

(b) A respondent may file an answering statement in duplicate with the AAA within 15 days after confirmation of notice of filing of the demand is sent by the AAA. The respondent shall, at the time of any such filing, send a copy of the answering statement to the claimant. If a counterclaim is asserted, it shall contain a statement setting forth the nature of the counterclaim, the amount involved, if any, and the remedy sought. If a counterclaim is made, the party making the counterclaim shall forward to the AAA with the answering statement the appropriate fee provided in the schedule included with these rules.

(c) If no answering statement is filed within the stated time, respondent will be deemed to deny the claim. Failure to file an answering statement shall not operate to delay the arbitration.

(d) When filing any statement pursuant to this section, the parties are encouraged to provide descriptions of their claims in sufficient detail to make the circumstances of the dispute clear to the arbitrator.

R-5. Initiation under a Submission

Parties to any existing dispute may commence an arbitration under these rules by filing at any office of the AAA two copies of a written submission to arbitrate under these rules, signed by the parties. It shall contain a statement of the nature of the dispute, the names and addresses of all parties, any claims and counterclaims, the amount involved, if any, the remedy sought, and the hearing locale requested, together with the appropriate filing fee as provided in the schedule included with these rules. Unless the parties state otherwise in the submission, all claims and counterclaims will be deemed to be denied by the other party.

R-6. Changes of Claim

After filing of a claim, if either party desires to make any new or different claim or counterclaim, it shall be made in writing and filed with the AAA. The party asserting such a claim or counterclaim shall provide a copy to the other party, who shall have 15 days from the date of such transmission within which to file an answering statement with the AAA. After the arbitrator is appointed, however, no new or different claim may be submitted except with the arbitrator's consent.

R-7. Applicable Procedures

Unless the parties or the AAA in its discretion determines otherwise, the Expedited Procedures shall be applied in any case where no disclosed claim or counterclaim exceeds $75,000, exclusive of interest and arbitration costs. Parties may also agree to use the Expedited Procedures in cases involving claims in excess of $75,000. The Expedited Procedures shall be applied as described in Sections E-1 through E-10 of these rules, in addition to any other portion of these rules that is not in conflict with the Expedited Procedures. All other cases shall be administered in accordance with Sections R-1 through R-56 of these rules.

R-8. Jurisdiction

(a) The arbitrator shall have the power to rule on his or her own jurisdiction, including any objections with respect to the existence, scope or validity of the arbitration agreement.

(b) The arbitrator shall have the power to determine the existence or validity of a contract of which an arbitration clause forms a part. Such an arbitration clause shall be treated as an agreement independent of the other terms of the contract. A decision by the arbitrator that the contract is null and void shall not for that reason alone render invalid the arbitration clause.

(c) A party must object to the jurisdiction of the arbitrator or to the arbitrability of a claim or counterclaim no later than the filing of the answering statement to the claim or counterclaim that gives rise to the objection. The arbitrator may rule on such objections as a preliminary matter or as part of the final award.

R-9. Mediation

At any stage of the proceedings, the parties may agree to conduct a mediation conference under the Commercial Mediation Rules in order to facilitate settlement. The mediator shall not be an arbitrator appointed to the case. Where the parties to a pending arbitration agree to mediate under the AAA's rules, no additional administrative fee is required to initiate the mediation.

R-10. Administrative Conference

At the request of any party or upon the AAA's own initiative, the AAA may conduct an administrative conference, in person or by telephone, with the parties and/or their representatives. The conference may address such issues as arbitrator selection, potential mediation of the dispute, potential exchange of information, a timetable for hearings and any other administrative matters. There is no administrative fee for this service.

R-11. Fixing of Locale

The parties may mutually agree on the locale where the arbitration is to be held. If any party requests that the hearing be held in a specific locale and the other party files no objection thereto within 15 days after notice of the request has been sent to it by the AAA, the locale shall be the one requested. If a party objects to the locale requested by the other party, the AAA shall have the power to determine the locale, and its decision shall be final and binding.

R-12. Qualifications of an Arbitrator

(a) Any neutral arbitrator appointed pursuant to Section R-13, R-14, R-15, or E-5, or selected by mutual choice of the parties or their appointees, shall be subject to disqualification for the reasons specified in Section R-19. If the parties specifically so agree in writing, the arbitrator shall not be subject to disqualification for those reasons.

(b) Unless the parties agree otherwise, an arbitrator selected unilaterally by one party is a party-appointed arbitrator and is not subject to disqualification pursuant to Section R-19.

R-13. Appointment from Panel

If the parties have not appointed an arbitrator and have not provided any other method of appointment, the arbitrator shall be appointed in the following manner:

(a) Immediately after the filing of the submission or the answering statement or the expiration of the time within which the answering statement is to be filed, the AAA shall send simultaneously to each party to the dispute an identical list of names of persons chosen from the panel. The parties are encouraged to agree to an arbitrator from the submitted list and to advise the AAA of their agreement.

(b) If the parties are unable to agree upon an arbitrator, each party to the dispute shall have 15 days from the transmittal date in which to strike names objected to, number the remaining names in order of preference, and return the list to the AAA. If a party does not return the list within the time specified, all persons named therein shall be deemed acceptable. From among the persons who have been approved on both lists, and in accordance with the designated order of mutual preference, the AAA shall invite the acceptance of an arbitrator to serve. If the parties fail to agree on any of the persons named, or if acceptable arbitrators are unable to act, or if for any other reason the appointment cannot be made from the submitted lists, the AAA shall have the power to make the appointment from among other members of the panel without the submission of additional lists.

(c) Unless the parties have agreed otherwise no later than 15 days after the commencement of an arbitration, if the notice of arbitration names two or more claimants or two or more respondents, the AAA shall appoint all the arbitrators.

R-14. Direct Appointment by a Party

(a) If the agreement of the parties names an arbitrator or specifies a method of appointing an arbitrator, that designation or method shall be followed. The notice of appointment, with the name and address of the arbitrator, shall be filed with the AAA by the appointing party. Upon the request of any appointing party, the AAA shall submit a list of members of the panel from which the party may, if it so desires, make the appointment.

(b) If the agreement specifies a period of time within which an arbitrator shall be appointed and any party fails to make the appointment within that period, the AAA shall make the appointment.

(c) If no period of time is specified in the agreement, the AAA shall notify the party to make the appointment. If within 15 days after such notice has been sent, an arbitrator has not been appointed by a party, the AAA shall make the appointment.

R-15. Appointment of Neutral Arbitrator by Party-Appointed Arbitrators or Parties

(a) If the parties have selected party-appointed arbitrators, or if such arbitrators have been appointed as provided in Section R-14, and the parties have authorized them to appoint a neutral arbitrator within a specified time and no appointment is made within that time or any agreed extension, the AAA may appoint a neutral arbitrator, who shall act as chairperson.

(b) If no period of time is specified for appointment of the neutral arbitrator and the party-appointed arbitrators or the parties do not make the appointment within 15 days from the date of the appointment of the last party-appointed arbitrator, the AAA may appoint the neutral arbitrator, who shall act as chairperson.

(c) If the parties have agreed that their party-appointed arbitrators shall appoint the neutral arbitrator from the panel, the AAA shall furnish to the party-appointed arbitrators, in the manner provided in Section R-13, a list selected from the panel, and the appointment of the neutral arbitrator shall be made as provided in that section.

R-16. Nationality of Arbitrator

Where the parties are nationals or residents of different countries, the AAA, at the request of any party or on its own initiative, may appoint as a neutral arbitrator a national of a country other than that of any of the parties. The request must be made prior to the time set for the appointment of the arbitrator as agreed by the parties or set by these rules.

R-17. Number of Arbitrators

If the arbitration agreement does not specify the number of arbitrators, the dispute shall be heard and determined by one arbitrator, unless the AAA, in its discretion, directs that three arbitrators be appointed. The parties may request three arbitrators in their demand or answer, which request the AAA will consider in exercising its discretion regarding the number of arbitrators appointed to the dispute.

R-18. Notice to Arbitrator of Appointment

Notice of the appointment of the neutral arbitrator, whether appointed mutually by the parties or by the AAA, shall be sent to the arbitrator by the AAA, together with a copy of these rules, and the signed acceptance of the arbitrator shall be filed with the AAA prior to the opening of the first hearing.

R-19. Disclosure and Challenge Procedure

(a) Any person appointed as a neutral arbitrator shall disclose to the AAA any circumstance likely to affect impartiality or independence, including any bias or any financial or personal interest in the result of the arbitration or any past or present relationship with the parties or their representatives. Upon receipt of such information from the arbitrator or another source, the AAA shall communicate the information to the parties and, if it deems it appropriate to do so, to the arbitrator and others.

(b) Upon objection of a party to the continued service of a neutral arbitrator, the AAA shall determine whether the arbitrator should be disqualified and shall inform the parties of its decision, which shall be conclusive.

R-20. Communication with Arbitrator

(a) No party and no one acting on behalf of any party shall communicate unilaterally concerning the arbitration with a neutral arbitrator or a candidate for neutral arbitrator. Unless the parties agree otherwise or the arbitrator so directs, any communication from the parties to a neutral arbitrator shall be sent to the AAA for transmittal to the arbitrator.

(b) The parties or the arbitrators may also agree that once the panel has been constituted, no party and no one acting on behalf of any party shall communicate unilaterally concerning the arbitration with any party-appointed arbitrator.

R-21. Vacancies

(a) If for any reason an arbitrator is unable to perform the duties of the office, the AAA may, on proof satisfactory to it, declare the office vacant. Vacancies shall be filled in accordance with the applicable provisions of these rules.

(b) In the event of a vacancy in a panel of neutral arbitrators after the hearings have commenced, the remaining arbitrator or arbitrators may continue with the hearing and determination of the controversy, unless the parties agree otherwise.

(c) In the event of the appointment of a substitute arbitrator, the panel of arbitrators shall determine in its sole discretion whether it is necessary to repeat all or part of any prior hearings.

R-22. Preliminary Hearing

(a) At the request of any party or at the discretion of the arbitrator or the AAA, the arbitrator may schedule as soon as practicable a preliminary hearing with the parties and/or their representatives. The preliminary hearing may be conducted by telephone at the arbitrator's discretion. There is no administrative fee for the first preliminary hearing.

(b) During the preliminary hearing, the parties and the arbitrator should discuss the future conduct of the case, including clarification of the issues and claims, a schedule for the hearings and any other preliminary matters.

R-23. Exchange of Information

(a) At the request of any party or at the discretion of the arbitrator, consistent with the expedited nature of arbitration, the arbitrator may direct (i) the production of documents and other information, and (ii) the identification of any witnesses to be called.

(b) At least five (5) business days prior to the hearing, the parties shall exchange copies of all exhibits they intend to submit at the hearing.

(c) The arbitrator is authorized to resolve any disputes concerning the exchange of information.

R-24. Date, Time, and Place of Hearing

The arbitrator shall set the date, time, and place for each hearing. The parties shall respond to requests for hearing dates in a timely manner, be cooperative in scheduling the earliest practicable date, and adhere to the established hearing schedule. The AAA shall send a notice of hearing to the parties at least 10 days in advance of the hearing date, unless otherwise agreed by the parties.

R-25. Attendance at Hearings

The arbitrator and the AAA shall maintain the privacy of the hearings unless the law provides to the contrary. Any person having a direct interest in the arbitration is entitled to attend hearings. The arbitrator shall otherwise have the power to require the exclusion of any witness, other than a party or other essential person, during the testimony of any other witness. It shall be discretionary with the arbitrator to determine the propriety of the attendance of any other person other than a party and its representatives.

R-26. Representation

Any party may be represented by counsel or other authorized representative. A party intending to be so represented shall notify the other party and the AAA of the name and address of the representative at least three days prior to the date set for the hearing at which that person is first to appear. When such a representative initiates an arbitration or responds for a party, notice is deemed to have been given.

R-27. Oaths

Before proceeding with the first hearing, each arbitrator may take an oath of office and, if required by law, shall do so. The arbitrator may require witnesses to testify under oath administered by any duly qualified person and, if it is required by law or requested by any party, shall do so.

R-28. Stenographic Record

Any party desiring a stenographic record shall make arrangements directly with a stenographer and shall notify the other parties of these arrangements at least three days in advance of the hearing. The requesting party or parties shall pay the cost of the record. If the transcript is agreed by the parties, or determined by the arbitrator to be the official record of the proceeding, it must be provided to the arbitrator and made available to the other parties for inspection, at a date, time, and place determined by the arbitrator.

R-29. Interpreters

Any party wishing an interpreter shall make all arrangements directly with the interpreter and shall assume the costs of the service.

R-30. Postponements

The arbitrator may postpone any hearing upon agreement of the parties, upon request of a party for good cause shown, or upon the arbitrator's own initiative. A party or parties causing a postponement of a hearing will be charged a postponement fee, as set forth in the administrative fee schedule.

R-31. Arbitration in the Absence of a Party or Representative

Unless the law provides to the contrary, the arbitration may proceed in the absence of any party or representative who, after due notice, fails to be present or fails to obtain a postponement. An award shall not be made solely on the default of a party. The arbitrator shall require the party who is present to submit such evidence as the arbitrator may require for the making of an award.

R-32. Conduct of Proceedings

(a) The claimant shall present evidence to support its claim. The respondent shall then present evidence to support its defense. Witnesses for each party shall also submit to questions from the arbitrator and the adverse party. The arbitrator has the discretion to vary this procedure, provided that the parties are treated with equality and that each party has the right to be heard and is given a fair opportunity to present its case.

(b) The arbitrator, exercising his or her discretion, shall conduct the proceedings with a view to expediting the resolution of the dispute and may direct the order of proof, bifurcate proceedings and direct the parties to focus their presentations on issues the decision of which could dispose of all or part of the case.

(c) The parties may agree to waive oral hearings in any case.

R-33. Evidence

(a) The parties may offer such evidence as is relevant and material to the dispute and shall produce such evidence as the arbitrator may deem necessary to an understanding and determination of the dispute. Conformity to legal rules of evidence shall not be necessary. All evidence shall be taken in the presence of all of the arbitrators and all of the parties, except where any of the parties is absent, in default or has waived the right to be present.

(b) The arbitrator shall determine the admissibility, relevance, and materiality of the evidence offered and may exclude evidence deemed by the arbitrator to be cumulative or irrelevant.

(c) The arbitrator shall take into account applicable principles of legal privilege, such as those involving the confidentiality of communications between a lawyer and client.

(d) An arbitrator or other person authorized by law to subpoena witnesses or documents may do so upon the request of any party or independently.

R-34. Evidence by Affidavit and Posthearing Filing of Documents or Other Evidence

(a) The arbitrator may receive and consider the evidence of witnesses by declaration or affidavit, but shall give it only such weight as the arbitrator deems it entitled to after consideration of any objection made to its admission.

(b) If the parties agree or the arbitrator directs that documents or other evidence be submitted to the arbitrator after the hearing, the documents or other evidence shall be filed with the AAA for transmission to the arbitrator. All parties shall be afforded an opportunity to examine and respond to such documents or other evidence.

R-35. Inspection or Investigation

An arbitrator finding it necessary to make an inspection or investigation in connection with the arbitration shall direct the AAA to so advise the parties. The arbitrator shall set the date and time and the AAA shall notify the parties. Any party who so desires may be present at such an inspection or investigation. In the event that one or all parties are not present at the inspection or investigation, the arbitrator shall make an oral or written report to the parties and afford them an opportunity to comment.

R-36. Interim Measures**

(a) The arbitrator may take whatever interim measures he or she deems necessary, including injunctive relief and measures for the protection or conservation of property and disposition of perishable goods.

(b) Such interim measures may take the form of an interim award, and the arbitrator may require security for the costs of such measures.

(c) A request for interim measures addressed by a party to a judicial authority shall not be deemed incompatible with the agreement to arbitrate or a waiver of the right to arbitrate.

R-37. Closing of Hearing

The arbitrator shall specifically inquire of all parties whether they have any further proofs to offer or witnesses to be heard. Upon receiving negative replies or if satisfied that the record is complete, the arbitrator shall declare the hearing closed.

** The Optional Rules may be found at the end of this document.

If briefs are to be filed, the hearing shall be declared closed as of the final date set by the arbitrator for the receipt of briefs. If documents are to be filed as provided in Section R-34 and the date set for their receipt is later than that set for the receipt of briefs, the later date shall be the closing date of the hearing. The time limit within which the arbitrator is required to make the award shall commence, in the absence of other agreements by the parties, upon the closing of the hearing.

R-38. Reopening of Hearing

The hearing may be reopened on the arbitrator's initiative, or upon application of a party, at any time before the award is made. If reopening the hearing would prevent the making of the award within the specific time agreed on by the parties in the contract(s) out of which the controversy has arisen, the matter may not be reopened unless the parties agree on an extension of time. When no specific date is fixed in the contract, the arbitrator may reopen the hearing and shall have 30 days from the closing of the reopened hearing within which to make an award.

R-39. Waiver of Rules

Any party who proceeds with the arbitration after knowledge that any provision or requirement of these rules has not been complied with and who fails to state an objection in writing shall be deemed to have waived the right to object.

R-40. Extensions of Time

The parties may modify any period of time by mutual agreement. The AAA or the arbitrator may for good cause extend any period of time established by these rules, except the time for making the award. The AAA shall notify the parties of any extension.

R-41. Serving of Notice

(a) Any papers, notices, or process necessary or proper for the initiation or continuation of an arbitration under these rules, for any court action in connection therewith, or for the entry of judgment on any award made under these rules may be served on a party by mail addressed to the party, or its representative at the last known address or by personal service, in or outside the state where the arbitration is to be held, provided that reasonable opportunity to be heard with regard to the dispute is or has been granted to the party.

(b) The AAA, the arbitrator and the parties may also use overnight delivery or electronic facsimile transmission (fax), to give the notices required by these rules. Where all parties and the arbitrator agree, notices may be transmitted by electronic mail (E-mail), or other methods of communication.

(c) Unless otherwise instructed by the AAA or by the arbitrator, any documents submitted by any party to the AAA or to the arbitrator shall simultaneously be provided to the other party or parties to the arbitration.

R-42. Majority Decision

When the panel consists of more than one arbitrator, unless required by law or by the arbitration agreement, a majority of the arbitrators must make all decisions.

R-43. Time of Award

The award shall be made promptly by the arbitrator and, unless otherwise agreed by the parties or specified by law, no later than 30 days from the date of closing the hearing, or, if oral hearings have been waived, from the date of the AAA's transmittal of the final statements and proofs to the arbitrator.

R-44. Form of Award

(a) Any award shall be in writing and signed by a majority of the arbitrators. It shall be executed in the manner required by law.

(b) The arbitrator need not render a reasoned award unless the parties request such an award in writing prior to appointment of the arbitrator or unless the arbitrator determines that a reasoned award is appropriate.

R-45. Scope of Award

(a) The arbitrator may grant any remedy or relief that the arbitrator deems just and equitable and within the scope of the agreement of the parties, including, but not limited to, specific performance of a contract.

(b) In addition to a final award, the arbitrator may make other decisions, including interim, interlocutory, or partial rulings, orders, and awards. In any interim, interlocutory, or partial award, the arbitrator may assess and apportion the fees, expenses, and compensation related to such award as the arbitrator determines is appropriate.

(c) In the final award, the arbitrator shall assess the fees, expenses, and compensation provided in Sections R-51, R-52, and R-53. The arbitrator may apportion such fees, expenses, and compensation among the parties in such amounts as the arbitrator determines is appropriate.

(d) The award of the arbitrator(s) may include: (a) interest at such rate and from such date as the arbitrator(s) may deem appropriate; and (b) an award of attorneys' fees if all parties have requested such an award or it is authorized by law or their arbitration agreement.

R-46. Award upon Settlement

If the parties settle their dispute during the course of the arbitration and if the parties so request, the arbitrator may set forth the terms of the settlement in a "consent award."

R-47. Delivery of Award to Parties

Parties shall accept as notice and delivery of the award the placing of the award or a true copy thereof in the mail addressed to the parties or their representatives at the last known addresses, personal or electronic service of the award, or the filing of the award in any other manner that is permitted by law.

R-48. Modification of Award

Within 20 days after the transmittal of an award, any party, upon notice to the other parties, may request the arbitrator, through the AAA, to correct any clerical, typographical, or computational errors in the award. The arbitrator is not empowered to redetermine the merits of any claim already decided. The other parties shall be given 10 days to respond to the request. The arbitrator shall dispose of the request within 20 days after transmittal by the AAA to the arbitrator of the request and any response thereto.

R-49. Release of Documents for Judicial Proceedings

The AAA shall, upon the written request of a party, furnish to the party, at the party's expense, certified copies of any papers in the AAA's possession that may be required in judicial proceedings relating to the arbitration.

R-50. Applications to Court and Exclusion of Liability

(a) No judicial proceeding by a party relating to the subject matter of the arbitration shall be deemed a waiver of the party's right to arbitrate.
(b) Neither the AAA nor any arbitrator in a proceeding under these rules is a necessary party in judicial proceedings relating to the arbitration.
(c) Parties to an arbitration under these rules shall be deemed to have consented that judgment upon the arbitration award may be entered in any federal or state court having jurisdiction thereof.
(d) Neither the AAA nor any arbitrator shall be liable to any party for any act or omission in connection with any arbitration conducted under these rules.

R-51. Administrative Fees

As a not-for-profit organization, the AAA shall prescribe filing and other administrative fees and service charges to compensate it for the cost of providing administrative services. The fees in effect when the fee or charge is incurred shall be applicable.

The filing fee shall be advanced by the party or parties making a claim or counterclaim, subject to final apportionment by the arbitrator in the award.

The AAA may, in the event of extreme hardship on the part of any party, defer or reduce the administrative fees.

R-52. Expenses

The expenses of witnesses for either side shall be paid by the party producing such witnesses. All other expenses of the arbitration, including required travel and other expenses of the arbitrator, AAA representatives, and any witness and the cost of any proof produced at the direct request of the arbitrator, shall be borne equally by the parties, unless they agree otherwise or unless the arbitrator in the award assesses such expenses or any part thereof against any specified party or parties.

R-53. Neutral Arbitrator's Compensation

(a) Unless the parties agree otherwise, members of the National Panel of Commercial Arbitrators appointed as neutrals on cases administered under the Expedited Procedures with claims not exceeding $10,000, will customarily serve without compensation for the first day of service. Thereafter, arbitrators shall receive compensation as set forth herein.

(b) Arbitrators shall be compensated at a rate consistent with the arbitrator's stated rate of compensation, beginning with the first day of hearing in all cases with claims exceeding $10,000.

(c) If there is disagreement concerning the terms of compensation, an appropriate rate shall be established with the arbitrator by the AAA and confirmed to the parties.

(d) Any arrangement for the compensation of a neutral arbitrator shall be made through the AAA and not directly between the parties and the arbitrator.

R-54. Deposits

The AAA may require the parties to deposit in advance of any hearings such sums of money as it deems necessary to cover the expense of the arbitration, including the arbitrator's fee, if any, and shall render an accounting to the parties and return any unexpended balance at the conclusion of the case.

R-55. Interpretation and Application of Rules

The arbitrator shall interpret and apply these rules insofar as they relate to the arbitrator's powers and duties. When there is more than one arbitrator and a difference arises among them concerning the meaning or application of these rules, it shall be decided by a majority vote. If that is not possible, either an arbitrator or a party may refer the question to the AAA for final decision. All other rules shall be interpreted and applied by the AAA.

R-56. Suspension for Nonpayment

If arbitrator compensation or administrative charges have not been paid in full, the AAA may so inform the parties in order that one of them may advance the required payment. If such payments are not made, the arbitrator may order the suspension or termination of the proceedings. If no arbitrator has yet been appointed, the AAA may suspend the proceedings.

Expedited Procedures

E-1. Applicability

Unless the parties or the AAA determines otherwise, these procedures shall apply in any case in which no disclosed claim or counterclaim exceeds $75,000, exclusive of interest and arbitration fees and costs. Parties may also agree to use these procedures in larger cases. Unless the parties agree otherwise, these procedures will not apply in cases in which there is no disclosed monetary claim or in cases involving more than two parties.

E-2. Limitation on Extensions

Except in extraordinary circumstances, the AAA or the arbitrator may grant a party no more than one seven-day extension of time to respond to the demand for arbitration or counterclaim as provided in Section R-4.

E-3. Changes of Claim or Counterclaim

A claim or counterclaim may be increased in amount, or a new or different claim or counterclaim added, upon the agreement of the other party, or the consent of the arbitrator. After the arbitrator is appointed, however, no new or different claim or counterclaim may be submitted except with the arbitrator's consent.

If an increased claim or counterclaim exceeds $75,000, the case will be administered under the regular procedures unless all parties and the arbitrator agree that the case may continue to be processed under the Expedited Procedures.

E-4. Serving of Notices

In addition to notice provided by Section R-41(b), the parties shall also accept notice by telephone. Telephonic notices by the AAA shall subsequently be confirmed in writing to the parties. Should there be a failure to confirm in writing any such oral notice, the proceeding shall nevertheless be valid if notice has, in fact, been given by telephone.

E-5. Appointment and Qualifications of Arbitrator

(a) The AAA shall simultaneously submit to each party an identical list of five proposed arbitrators drawn from its panel from which one arbitrator shall be appointed.

(b) The parties are encouraged to agree to an arbitrator from this list and to advise the AAA of their agreement. If the parties are unable to agree upon an arbitrator, each party may strike two names from the list and return it to the AAA within seven days from the date of the AAA's mailing to the parties. If for any reason the appointment of an arbitrator cannot be made from the list, the AAA may make the appoint-

ment from other members of the panel without the submission of
additional lists.

(c) The parties will be given notice by the AAA of the appointment of the
arbitrator, who shall be subject to disqualification for the reasons
specified in Section R-19. The parties shall notify the AAA within seven
days of any objection to the arbitrator appointed. Any such objection
shall be for cause and shall be confirmed in writing to the AAA with a
copy to the other party or parties.

E-6. Exchange of Exhibits

At least two business days prior to the hearing, the parties shall exchange copies
of all exhibits they intend to submit at the hearing. The arbitrator shall resolve
disputes concerning the exchange of exhibits.

E-7. Proceedings on Documents

Where no party's claim exceeds $10,000, exclusive of interest and arbitration
costs, and other cases in which the parties agree, the dispute shall be resolved by
submission of documents, unless any party requests an oral hearing, or the arbitrator determines that an oral hearing is necessary. The arbitrator shall establish
a fair and equitable procedure for the submission of documents.

E-8. Date, Time, and Place of Hearing

There shall not be an administrative conference. In cases in which a hearing is
to be held, the arbitrator shall set the date, time, and place of the hearing, to be
scheduled to take place within 30 days of confirmation of the arbitrator's
appointment. The AAA will notify the parties in advance of the hearing date.

E-9. The Hearing

(a) Generally, the hearing shall not exceed one day. Each party shall have
equal opportunity to submit its proofs and complete its case. The arbitrator shall determine the order of the hearing, and may require further
submission of documents within two days after the hearing. For good
cause shown, the arbitrator may schedule additional hearings within
seven business days after the initial day of hearings.

(b) Generally, there will be no stenographic record. Any party desiring a
stenographic record may arrange for one pursuant to the provisions of
Section R-28.

E-10. Time of Award

Unless otherwise agreed by the parties, the award shall be rendered not later
than fourteen days from the date of the closing of the hearing or, if oral hearings have been waived, from the date of the AAA's transmittal of the final statements and proofs to the arbitrator.

Optional Procedures for Large, Complex Commercial Disputes

L-1. Applicability

(a) Unless the parties agree otherwise, these Optional Procedures for Large, Complex Commercial Disputes (hereinafter "Procedures") shall apply to all cases administered by the AAA under the Commercial Arbitration Rules in which the disclosed claim or counterclaim of any party is at least $1,000,000 exclusive of claimed interest, arbitration fees and costs, and in which either (1) all parties have elected to have the Procedures apply to the resolution of their dispute; or (2) a court or governmental agency of competent jurisdiction has determined that a dispute should be resolved before the AAA pursuant to the procedures. Parties may also agree to using the Procedures in cases involving claims or counterclaims under $1,000,000, in non-monetary cases or in cases involving claims of undetermined amount. The Procedures are designed to complement the Regular Commercial Arbitration Rules. To the extent that there is any variance between such rules and these Procedures, the Procedures shall control. Any such cases are herein referred to as Large, Complex Cases.

(b) The parties to any arbitration proceeding that is to be subject to the Procedures may, prior to the appointment of the arbitrator(s) and by consent of all parties, agree to eliminate, modify or alter any of the Procedures, and, in such case, these Procedures as so modified or altered shall apply to that particular case. After appointment of the arbitrator(s), such modifications may be made only with the consent of the arbitrator(s).

L-2. Administrative Conference

Prior to the dissemination of a list of potential arbitrators, the AAA shall, unless it determines same to be unnecessary, conduct an administrative conference with the parties and/or their attorneys or other representatives, either in person or by conference call, at the discretion of the AAA. Such administrative conference shall be conducted for the following purposes and for such additional purposes as the parties or the AAA may deem appropriate:

(a) to obtain additional information about the nature and magnitude of the dispute and the anticipated length of hearing and scheduling;
(b) to discuss the views of the parties about the technical and other qualifications of the arbitrators;
(c) to obtain conflicts statements from the parties; and
(d) to consider, with the parties, whether mediation or other non-adjudicative methods of dispute resolution might be appropriate.

L-3. Arbitrators

(a) Large, Complex Commercial Cases shall be heard and determined by either one or three arbitrators, as may be agreed upon by the parties. If the parties are unable to agree upon the number of arbitrators, then three arbitrator(s) shall hear and determine the case.

(b) The AAA shall appoint arbitrator(s) as agreed by the parties. If they are unable to agree on a method of appointment, the AAA shall appoint arbitrators from the Large, Complex Commercial Case Panel, in the manner provided in the Regular Commercial Arbitration Rules. Absent agreement of the parties, the arbitrator(s) shall not have served as the mediator in the mediation phase of the instant proceeding.

L-4. Preliminary Hearing

As promptly as practicable after the selection of the arbitrator(s), a preliminary hearing shall be held among the parties and/or their attorneys or other representatives and the arbitrator(s). With the consent of the arbitrator(s) and the parties, the preliminary hearing may: (a) be conducted by the Chair of the panel rather than all the arbitrator(s); (b) be conducted by telephone conference call rather than in person; or (c) be omitted.

At the preliminary hearing the matters to be considered shall include, without limitation: (a) service of a detailed statement of claims, damages and defenses, a statement of the issues asserted by each party and positions with respect thereto, and any legal authorities the parties may wish to bring to the attention of the arbitrator(s); (b) stipulations to uncontested facts; (c) the extent to which discovery shall be conducted; (d) exchange and premarking of those documents which each party believes may be offered at the hearing; (e) the identification and availability of witnesses, including experts, and such matters with respect to witnesses including their biographies and expected testimony as may be appropriate; (f) whether, and the extent to which, any sworn statements and/or depositions may be introduced; (g) the extent to which hearings will proceed on consecutive days; (h) whether a stenographic or other official record of the proceedings shall be maintained; and (i) the possibility of utilizing mediation or other non-adjudicative methods of dispute resolution.

L-5. Management of Proceedings

(a) Arbitrators shall take such steps as they may deem necessary or desirable to avoid delay and to achieve a just, speedy and cost-effective resolution of Large, Complex Commercial Cases.

(b) Parties shall cooperate in the exchange of documents, exhibits and information within such party's control if the arbitrator(s) consider such production to be consistent with the goal of achieving a just, speedy and cost-effective resolution of a Large, Complex Commercial Case.

(c) The parties may conduct such document discovery as may be agreed to by all the parties provided, however, that the arbitrator(s) may place such limitations on the conduct of such discovery as the arbitrator(s) shall deem appropriate. If the parties cannot agree on document discovery, the arbitrator(s) for good cause shown and consistent with the expedited nature of arbitration, may establish the extent of same.

(d) The arbitrator(s) upon good cause shown may order the conduct of the deposition of, or the propounding of interrogatories to, such persons who may possess information determined by the arbitrator(s) to be necessary to a determination of a Large, Complex Commercial Case.

(e) Generally hearings will be scheduled on consecutive days or in blocks of consecutive days in order to maximize efficiency and minimize costs.

(f) The arbitrator(s) may direct the recording of the hearings, the cost of which shall be borne equally by the parties.

Optional Rules for Emergency Measures of Protection

O-1. Applicability

Where parties by special agreement or in their arbitration clause have adopted these rules for emergency measures of protection, a party in need of emergency relief prior to the constitution of the panel shall notify the AAA and all other parties in writing of the nature of the relief sought and the reasons why such relief is required on an emergency basis. The application shall also set forth the reasons why the party is entitled to such relief. Such notice may be given by facsimile transmission, or other reliable means, but must include a statement certifying that all other parties have been notified or an explanation of the steps taken in good faith to notify other parties.

O-2. Appointment of Emergency Arbitrator

Within one business day of receipt of notice as provided in Section O-1, the AAA shall appoint a single emergency arbitrator from a special AAA panel of emergency arbitrators designated to rule on emergency applications. The emergency arbitrator shall immediately disclose any circumstance likely, on the basis of the facts disclosed in the application, to affect such arbitrator's impartiality or independence. Any challenge to the appointment of the emergency arbitrator must be made within one business day of the communication by the AAA to the parties of the appointment of the emergency arbitrator and the circumstances disclosed.

O-3. Schedule

The emergency arbitrator shall as soon as possible, but in any event within two business days of appointment, establish a schedule for consideration of the application for emergency relief. Such schedule shall provide a reasonable opportunity to all parties to be heard, but may provide for proceeding by telephone conference or on written submissions as alternatives to a formal hearing.

O-4. Interim Award

If after consideration the emergency arbitrator is satisfied that the party seeking the emergency relief has shown that immediate and irreparable loss or damage will result in the absence of emergency relief, and that such party is entitled to such relief, the emergency arbitrator may enter an interim award granting the relief and stating the reasons therefor.

O-5. Constitution of the Panel

Any application to modify an interim award of emergency relief must be based on changed circumstances and may be made to the emergency arbitrator until the panel is constituted; thereafter such a request shall be addressed to the panel. The emergency arbitrator shall have no further power to act after the panel is constituted unless the parties agree that the emergency arbitrator is named as a member of the panel.

O-6. Security

Any interim award of emergency relief may be conditioned on provision by the party seeking such relief of appropriate security.

O-7. Special Master

A request for interim measures addressed by a party to a judicial authority shall not be deemed incompatible with the agreement to arbitrate or a waiver of the right to arbitrate. If the AAA is directed by a judicial authority to nominate a special master to consider and report on an application for emergency relief, the AAA shall proceed as provided in Section O-1 of this article and the references to the emergency arbitrator shall be read to mean the special master, except that the special master shall issue a report rather than an interim award.

O-8. Costs

The costs associated with applications for emergency relief shall initially be apportioned by the emergency arbitrator or special master, subject to the power of the panel to determine finally the apportionment of such costs.

Administrative Fees

The administrative fees of the AAA are based on the amount of the claim or counterclaim. Arbitrator compensation is not included in this schedule. Unless the parties agree otherwise, arbitrator compensation and administrative fees are subject to allocation by the arbitrator in the award.

Filing Fees

A nonrefundable filing fee is payable in full by a filing party when a claim, counterclaim or additional claim is filed, as provided below.

Amount of Claim	Filing Fee
Up to $10,000	$500
Above $10,000 to $50,000	$750
Above $50,000 to $100,000	$1,250
Above $100,000 to $250,000	$2,000
Above $250,000 to $500,000	$3,500
Above $500,000 to $l,000,000	$5,000
Above $1,000,000 to $5,000,000	$7,000
Above $5,000,000	Negotiated

When no amount can be stated at the time of filing, the minimum fee is $2,000, subject to increase when the claim or counterclaim is disclosed.

When a claim or counterclaim is not for a monetary amount, an appropriate filing fee will be determined by the AAA.

The minimum filing fee for any case having three or more arbitrators is $2,000.

Expedited Procedures are applied in any case where no disclosed claim or counterclaim exceeds $75,000, exclusive of interest and arbitration cost.

Hearing Fees

For each day of hearing held before a single arbitrator, an administrative fee of $150 is payable by each party.

For each day of hearing held before a multi-arbitrator panel, an administrative fee of $250 is payable by each party.

There is no AAA hearing fee for the initial Procedural Hearing.

There is no hearing fee for the initial hearing in cases in which no party's claim exceeds $10,000, administered under the Expedited Procedures.

Postponement/Cancellation Fees

A fee of $150 is payable by a party causing a postponement/cancellation of any hearing scheduled before a single arbitrator.

A fee of $250 is payable by a party causing a postponement/cancellation of any hearing scheduled before a multiarbitrator panel.

Hearing Room Rental

The Hearing Fees described above do not cover the rental of hearing rooms, which are available on a rental basis. Check with the AAA for availability and rates.

Appendix R.4
Comparison of Rules for Mediation Procedures

Kathleen M. Scanlon
CPR Institute for Dispute Resolution

(Private Procedures)	CPR Mediation Procedure*	AAA Rules for Commercial Mediation**	JAMS Agreement****	NASD Mediation Rules****
Selection of Mediator	Unless the parties agree otherwise, parties will select mediator from CPR Panel of Neutrals. The lists of the Panels of CPR Neutrals are on the Internet (CPR web site, www.cpradr.org) and otherwise readily available. Any party can directly retain a CPR Neutral without any involvement or payment to CPR. In the event the parties are unable to select a mediator promptly, CPR will assist in the selection process. (Rule 2).	Unless parties' agreement provides otherwise, upon receipt of request for mediation (Rule M3), AAA will appoint mediator. (Rule M4). AAA policy is to appoint a mediator only with the approval of all parties.	Parties select mediator with the assistance of a JAMS case administrator.	Mediator may be selected by parties from list supplied by NASD director or from list of parties' own choosing or by the NASD director if no mediator is selected after parties submit matter to mediation. (Rule 10404 (a)) "With respect to any mediator assigned or selected from a list provided by the Association, the parties will be provided with information relating to the mediator's employment, education, and professional background, as well as information on the mediator's experience, training, and credentials as a mediator." (Rule 10404(b))

421

(Private Procedures)	CPR Mediation Procedure*	AAA Rules for Commercial Mediation**	JAMS Agreement****	NASD Mediation Rules****
Impartiality and Conflicts of Interest Checks	Mediator "shall be neutral and impartial." (Rule 3(c)). If CPR assists in selection, a candidate with a clear conflict will not be proposed by CPR. Other circumstances a candidate discloses to CPR will be disclosed to parties. (Rule 2). Past and Concurrent Relationships: Mediator must disclose all business or professional relationships the mediator and/or the mediator's firm have had with the parties or their law firms within the past 5 years; any financial interest the mediator has in any party; any significant social, business or professional relationship the mediator has had with an officer or employee of a party or with an individual representing a party; and any other circumstances that may raise doubt regarding the mediator's impartiality in the proceeding. The disclosure obligations are continuing; the parties may waive any conflict and the mediator may serve if he/she agrees to do so. (CPR Model Mediation Agreement ¶ B) Concurrent and Future Relationships: The CPR Model Agreement further provides that neither the mediator nor the mediator's firm shall undertake any work for or against a party regarding the mediated dispute at any time; neither	No person shall serve as a mediator in any dispute in which that person has any financial or personal interest, except by written consent of parties. Mediator must disclose any circumstance likely to create a presumption of bias. (Rule M5).	Under JAMS Ethics Guidelines for Mediators, mediator must remain impartial throughout the process and disclose any actual or potential conflict of interest or other information which reasonably could question impartiality. Parties can waive any conflict of interest. However, if the conflict casts serious doubt on the integrity of the process, the mediator should withdraw notwithstanding receipt of a full waiver. Moreover, "[a]fter a mediation is completed, a mediator or should refrain from any conduct involving a party, insurer or counsel to the mediation that would cast reasonable doubt on the integrity of the mediation process, absent disclosure to and consent by all the parties to the mediation. This does not preclude the mediator from serving as a mediator or in another neutral capacity with a party, insurer or counsel involved in the prior mediation." (Section V).	"The mediator shall act as a neutral, impartial, facilitator of the mediation process . . . ." "Any mediator selected or assigned to mediate a matter shall comply with the provisions of Rule 10312(a), (b) and (c) [NASD Code of Arbitration Procedure disclosure requirements which includes any relationships that may affect impartiality or that might create an appearance of partiality or bias], unless, with respect to a mediator selected from a source other than the Association's lists, the parties elect to waive such disclosure." (Rule 10404(b)).

(Private Procedures)	CPR Mediation Procedure*	AAA Rules for Commercial Mediation**	JAMS Agreement****	NASD Mediation Rules****
Impartiality and Conflicts of Interest Checks *continued*	the mediator nor any person assisting the mediator with the mediated dispute shall personally work on any matter unrelated to the dispute for or against a party for 6 months following cessation of mediator's services; and the mediator's firms may work on matters for or against a party during the pendency of the mediation if such matters are unrelated and appropriate safeguards are in place. (CPR Model Mediation Agreement ¶ C)			
Mediator Availability	Before appointment, mediator will assure parties of availability to conduct proceeding expeditiously. (Rule 2).	Prior to selection, mediator must disclose any circumstance likely to prevent a prompt meeting with the parties. (Rule M5).	[Silent.]	"The parties and their representatives agree to cooperate with the mediator in ensuring that the mediation is conducted expeditiously, to make all reasonable efforts to be available for mediation sessions . . . ." (Rule 10406 (d)).
Vacancy Created by Mediator	Withdrawal of the mediator terminates the process. (See Rule 6).	If any mediator shall become unwilling or unable to serve, AAA will appoint another mediator, unless the parties agree otherwise. (Rule M6). AAA policy is to appoint a mediator only with the approval of all the parties.	[Silent.]	[Silent.]

(Private Procedures)	CPR Mediation Procedure*	AAA Rules for Commercial Mediation**	JAMS Agreement****	NASD Mediation Rules****
Mediator as Witness	Mediator disqualified as a witness, expert, consultant in any pending or future investigation relating to subject matter, unless parties and mediator agree otherwise. (Rule 3(j)).	Neither AAA nor mediator is a "necessary party" in judicial proceeding relating to the mediation. (Rule M15). Mediator "shall not be compelled to divulge such records or to testify in regard to the mediation in any adversary proceeding or judicial forum." (Rule M12).	Mediator disqualified as a witness or expert in any pending or future proceeding relating to subject matter. (¶ 4).	[Silent.]
Mediator Authority	"The mediator shall control the procedural aspects of the mediation" (Rule 3(d)). "The mediator may obtain assistance and independent expert advice" with the parties' prior consent. (Rule 3(l)). "The mediator may facilitate settlement in any manner the mediator believes is appropriate. . . . The mediator will decide when to hold joint meetings, and when to confer separately with each party." (Rule 6). If the parties are unable to develop their own settlement, "before terminating the procedure, and only with the consent of the parties, (a) the mediator may submit to the parties a final settlement proposal; and (b) if the mediator believes he/she is qualified to do so, the mediator may give the parties an evaluation (which if all the parties choose, and the mediator agrees,	"The mediator does not have the authority to impose a settlement on the parties but will attempt to help them reach a satisfactory resolution of their dispute. The mediator is authorized to conduct joint and separate meetings with the parties and to make oral and written recommendations for settlement." Mediator permitted to obtain expert advice concerning technical aspects of dispute with parties' agreement and to terminate mediation when in his/her judgment further efforts would not contribute to resolution. (Rule M10).	Mediator can recommend agenda; conduct joint and separate meetings. (¶ 2). At discretion of mediator or upon parties' request, mediator will provide an evaluation of the parties' case and of the likely resolution of the dispute if not settled. (Parties agree that mediator is not acting as an attorney or providing legal advice on behalf of any party.) (¶ 2).	"The mediator . . . shall not have any authority to determine issues, make decisions or otherwise resolve the matter." (Rule 10406(c). "Following the selection of a mediator, the mediator, all parties and their representatives will meet in person or by conference call for all mediation sessions, as determined by the mediator or by mutual agreement of the parties. The mediator shall facilitate, through joint sessions, caucuses and/or other means, discussions between the parties, with the goal of assisting the parties in reaching their own resolution of the matter. The mediator shall determine the procedure for the conduct

(Private Procedures)	CPR Mediation Procedure*	AAA Rules for Commercial Mediation**	JAMS Agreement****	NASD Mediation Rules****
Mediator Authority *continued*	may be in writing) of the likely outcome of the case if it were tried to final judgment" subject to any limitations under applicable statutes or rules. (Rule 6). Mediator has authority to end mediation if he/she concludes and informs parties that further efforts are not useful. (Rule 6).			of the mediation . . . . The mediator may meet with and communicate separately with each party or their representative. The mediator shall notify all other parties of any such separate meetings or other communications." (Rule 10406 (d),(e)).
Rule Interpretation	[Silent.]	Mediator interprets and applies mediation rules insofar as they relate to the mediator's duties and responsibilities. All other rules shall be interpreted and applied by AAA. (Rule M16).	[Silent.]	[Silent.]
Party Representation	By business executive or other person authorized to negotiate a resolution; by counsel to advise party in mediation, whether or not such counsel is present at mediation conferences. (Rule 3). Parties to exchange names and job titles of individuals who will attend. (Rule 4).	By "persons of the party's choice." Names and addresses of such persons shall be communicated in writing to all parties and AAA. (Rule M7).	By representatives of the parties with full settlement authority; sessions may be attended by counsel. (¶ 2).	The parties are to be represented at all scheduled mediation sessions either in person or through a person with authority to settle the matter. (Rule 10406 (d)).
Stay of Other Proceedings	Parties will refrain from pursuing litigation or any other administrative or judicial remedies on a without prejudice basis, unless agreed otherwise. (Rule 3(i)).	[Silent.]	[Silent.]	Unless parties agree otherwise, mediation shall not stay arbitration of matter under NASD code. (Rule 10403).

(Private Procedures)	CPR Mediation Procedure*	AAA Rules for Commercial Mediation**	JAMS Agreement****	NASD Mediation Rules****
Confidentiality	"Entire process is confidential." Unless agreed among parties or required to do so by law, parties and mediator shall not disclose any information, contents, settlement terms or outcome of proceeding. "Under this procedure, the entire process is a compromise negotiation subject to Federal Rule of Evidence 408 and all state counterparts, together with any applicable statute protecting the confidentiality of mediation. All offers, promises, conduct and statements, whether oral or written, made in the course of the proceeding . . . are confidential. Such offers . . . are privileged under any applicable mediation privilege and are inadmissible and not discoverable for any purpose, including impeachment, in litigation between the parties. However, evidence that is otherwise admissible or discoverable shall not be rendered inadmissible or non-discoverable solely as a result of its presentation or use during the mediation." (Rule 9). The mediator will not transmit information received in confidence from any party to any other party or any third party unless authorized to do so by the providing party or ordered to do so by court of competent jurisdiction. (Rule 3(h)).	Entire process is confidential. Confidential information disclosed to a mediator by the parties or witnesses in the course of the mediation shall not be divulged by the mediator. (Rule M12).	Entire process is a "compromise negotiation. All offers, promises, conduct and statements . . . made in the course of the mediation . . . are confidential . . . [and] will not be disclosed to third parties . . . and are privileged and inadmissible for any purposes. . . . However, evidence previously disclosed or known to a Party, or that is otherwise admissible or discoverable shall not be rendered confidential, inadmissible or not discoverable solely as a result of its use in the mediation." (¶ 3). If a party informs mediator that information conveyed in confidence, mediator will not disclose information. (¶ 2).	"(g)(1) Mediation is intended to be private and confidential. The parties and the mediator agree not to disclose, transmit, introduce, or otherwise use opinions, suggestions, proposals, offers, or admissions obtained or disclosed during the mediation by any party or the mediator as evidence in any action at law, or other proceeding, including a lawsuit or arbitration, unless authorized in writing by all other parties to the mediation or compelled by law, except that the fact that a mediation has occurred shall not be considered confidential. (2) Notwithstanding the foregoing, the parties agree and acknowledge that the provisions of this paragraph shall not operate to shield from disclosure to the Association or any other regulatory authority, documentary or other information that the Association of other regulatory authority would be entitled to obtain or examine in the exercise of its regulatory responsibilities.

(Private Procedures)	CPR Mediation Procedure*	AAA Rules for Commercial Mediation**	JAMS Agreement****	NASD Mediation Rules****
Confidentiality *continued*	The mediator will promptly advise the parties of any attempt to compel him/her to divulge information received in mediation. (Rule 9).			(3) The mediator will not transmit or otherwise disclose confidential information provided by one party to any other party unless authorized to do so by the party providing the confidential information." (Rule 10406 (g)).
Stenographic Record	"There will be no stenographic record of any meeting." (Rule 3(d)(ii)).	No stenographic record. (Rule M13).	[Silent.]	No stenographic record. (Rule 10326).
Mediation Statement and Exchange of Information	Procedure provides for the parties to prepare a short, written statement summarizing the background and present status for the mediator. The statement is to be submitted 10 days prior to first substantive meeting. Unless the parties otherwise agree, mediator shall keep confidential any written material or information that is submitted to him/her. A party is not entitled to receive any information submitted to mediator by another party without other party's consent. The parties are encouraged to discuss the exchange of all or certain materials that they submit to the mediator. (Rule 5).	At least 10 days prior to first session, each party shall provide mediator with a brief memorandum. At mediator's discretion, memoranda may be mutually exchanged. At first session, parties are expected to produce all information "reasonably required" for mediator to understand issues. (Rule M9).	Mediator may review written materials provided by parties. (¶ 2). If a party informs mediator that information conveyed in confidence, mediator will not disclose information. (¶ 2).	"The mediator will not transmit or otherwise disclose confidential information provided by one party to any other party unless authorized to do so by the party providing the confidential information." (Rule 10406 (g) (3)).

(Private Procedures)	CPR Mediation Procedure*	AAA Rules for Commercial Mediation**	JAMS Agreement****	NASD Mediation Rules****
Settlement Agreement	If settlement is reached, preliminary memorandum of understanding or term sheet normally prepared and signed before parties separate. Unless mediator undertakes to do so, representatives of parties will promptly draft a written settlement document. (Rule 7). Any written settlement agreement resulting from mediation may be disclosed for purposes of enforcement. (Rule 9).	Silent. AAA policy is to suggest that the relevant terms of the settlement be reduced to writing.	If the parties resolve the dispute in mediation, at the mediation session the parties will, with the assistance of the mediator, draft and execute a memorandum of agreement and, subject to the provisions of applicable law, be bound by that agreement. (Mediation/Arbitration Rules of Employment Disputes, Rule 9 (f)).	[Silent.]
Termination of Sessions	Session may be terminated in several ways: by execution of a settlement agreement; mediator concludes further efforts not useful; one of the parties or mediator withdraws from process. (Rule 6). Each party may withdraw at any time after attending first session by written notice. (Rule 3(b)). Mediator may withdraw at any time by written notice for serious personal reasons, if mediator doubts party's good faith or if mediator concludes further sessions are not useful. (Rule 3(n)).	By execution of a settlement agreement; written declaration by mediator that further efforts are futile; written declaration by parties or party that mediation proceedings are terminated. (Rule M14).	Any party may terminate its participation for any reason by written notification to JAMS and the other parties. (¶ 7). Under JAMS Ethics Guidelines for Mediators, a mediator should withdraw from process if mediation is being used to further illegal conduct, lack of informed consent by parties exists, a conflict of interest has not been waived, or an impairment exists of mediator's ability to maintain impartiality or his/her physical or mental ability. In addition, the mediator should be aware of potential need to withdraw if	"Mediation is voluntary and any party may withdraw from mediation at any time prior to the execution of a written settlement agreement by giving written notice of withdrawal to the mediator, the other parties, and the Director." (Rule 10406 (b)).

(Private Procedures)	CPR Mediation Procedure*	AAA Rules for Commercial Mediation**	JAMS Agreement****	NASD Mediation Rules****
Termination of Sessions *continued*			procedural or substantive unfairness "appears to have irrevocably impugned the integrity of the mediation process." (Section VII).	
Return of Materials Provided to Mediator	At end of process, upon request of party, mediator will return to that party all written materials and information provided by that party or certify destruction of same. (Rule 5).	[Silent.] AAA policy is to follow the agreement of the parties with respect to the return of materials.	Under JAMS Ethics Guidelines for Mediators, "the mediator's notes, briefs and other documents containing confidential or otherwise sensitive information should be stored in a reasonably secure location and may be destroyed 90 days after the mediation has been completed or sooner if all parties so request or consent." (Section IV).	[Silent.]
Mediator as Arbitrator	If resolution is not reached, mediator will discuss possibility of arbitration or another form of ADR. (Rule 8). If the parties proceed to arbitration, mediator shall not serve as arbitrator, unless parties and mediator agree otherwise. (Rule 3(k); Rule 8).	When parties have attempted mediation under AAA rules and have failed to reach a settlement, AAA will apply mediation administrative fee toward subsequent AAA arbitration, which is filed with AAA within 90 days of mediation termination. No explicit provision on appointment of mediator as arbitrator. However, once arbitration has commenced and parties	No explicit provision on appointment of mediator as arbitrator. Under J.A.M.S. Ethics Guidelines for Mediators, "[i]n the event that, prior to or during a mediation session, it becomes appropriate to discuss the possibility of combining mediation with binding arbitration, the mediator should explain how a mediator's role and relationship to the	"No mediator shall be permitted to serve as an arbitrator of any matter pending in NASD arbitration in which he served as a mediator, nor shall the mediator be permitted to represent any party or participant to the mediation in any subsequent NASD arbitration proceeding relating to the subject matter of the mediation." (Rule 10404 (c)).

(Private Procedures)	CPR Mediation Procedure*	AAA Rules for Commercial Mediation**	JAMS Agreement****	NASD Mediation Rules****
Mediator as Arbitrator *continued*		seek mediation, mediator shall not be arbitrator appointed to case (Rule R-9).	parties may be altered, as well as the impact such a shift may have on the disclosure of information to the mediator. The parties should be given the opportunity to select another neutral to conduct the arbitration procedure." (Section I)	
Immunity Issues	Neither CPR nor mediator "shall be liable for any act or omission in connection with the mediation, except for its/his/her own willful misconduct." (Rule 3(m)).	Neither AAA nor mediator shall be liable for "any act or omission in connection with any mediation conducted under these rules." (Rule M15).	Neither JAMS nor mediator shall be liable to any party "for any act or omission in connection with any mediation conducted under this Agreement." (¶ 4).	"The Association, its employees, and any mediator named to mediate a matter under this Rule 10400 Series, shall not be liable for any act or omission in connection with a mediation administered pursuant to these Procedures." (Rule 10405).

*The CPR Mediation Procedure. Revised and effective as of April 1, 1998. Reference also is made to the CPR Model Mediation Agreement.
**AAA Commercial Mediation Rules, reissued as of January 1, 1999.
***JAMS Rules, previously known as JAMS/Endispute, which contains a form Mediation Agreement. References also are made to JAMS Ethics Guidelines for Mediators and its Rules and Procedures for Mediation/Arbitration of Employment Disputes.
****NASD Regulation Inc., a subsidiary of the National Association of Securities Dealers Inc., has promulgated NASD Mediation Rules, which were adopted August 1, 1995. The rules, presented in the fourth column in the table above, are taken from its Code of Arbitration Procedure. While the NASD rules are more specialized than the other generally applicable rules here, they are presented because of their relevance to a specific category of business disputes. Furthermore, the percentage of NASD mediations as part of the regulatory body's ADR efforts has risen significantly in recent years, and can be expected to continue to grow.

Appendix R.5
Comparison of CPR and AAA Arbitration Procedures

Kathleen M. Scanlon, CPR Institute for Dispute Resolution

	CPR Arbitration Rules (Self-Administered)*	AAA Commercial Arbitration Rules (Administered)**
Administration	Self-managed by the arbitrator(s) and parties.	AAA manages—association manager is the administrator. Sets meeting and receives all filings.
Applicability of Rates	The CPR Arbitration Rules apply when parties to a contract or arbitration agreement provide for arbitration under the CPR Rules or have provided for CPR arbitration without further specification. The applicable CPR Rules are those in existence at the time the arbitration is commenced. The parties can agree in writing or on the record during the course of the proceedings to modify the CPR Rules. (Rule 1.1) The CPR Rules shall govern except when in conflict with a mandatory provision of applicable law. (Rule 1.2)	The AAA Arbitration Rules apply when parties to a contract or arbitration agreement provide for arbitration before AAA under its Commercial Arbitration Rules or for arbitration before AAA of a domestic dispute without specifying particular rules. The applicable AAA Rules are those in effect at the time the demand for arbitration is received by AAA; parties can modify rules by written agreement. (R-1) Unless parties determine otherwise, the arbitration provisions contained in the AAA Expedited Procedures "shall" apply in cases where no disclosed claim or counterclaim exceeds $75,000. (E-1) Unless parties agree otherwise, the arbitration provisions contained in the AAA Optional Procedures for Large, Complex Commercial Disputes "shall" apply to all cases where disclosed claim or counterclaim is at least $1 million and in which either (i) all parties have elected to have such procedures apply, or (ii) a court or government agency decides that the dispute should be resolved before AAA under such procedures. Parties can also agree to have such procedures apply to disputes under $1 million. (L-1)

431

	CPR Arbitration Rules (Self-Administered)*	**AAA Commercial Arbitration Rules (Administered)****
Initiating Arbitration	Party-to-party notice of arbitration. Notice shall include, *inter alia*, text of arbitration clause or separate arbitration agreement involved; statement of general nature of claimant's claim, relief or remedy sought; and name and address of the arbitrator appointed by the claimant, unless the parties have agreed that neither shall appoint an arbitrator or that the party-appointed arbitrators shall be appointed pursuant to a "screened" process as provided in Rule 5.4. (Rule 3)	Under a Contractual Arbitration Provision—claimant will provide party-to-party written notice of its intention to arbitrate. Notice shall include, *inter alia*, nature of dispute; names and addresses of other parties; amount involved; remedy sought; and hearing locale requested. Claimant shall file at any AAA office two copies of the demand, contract arbitration provisions and filing fee. (R-4 (a)). Parties are encouraged to provide descriptions of their claims in "sufficient detail to make the circumstances of the dispute clear." (R-4(d))

Initiation under a Submission—parties to "any existing dispute" may commence an arbitration by filing at any AAA office two copies of a written submission to arbitrate under AAA rules together with requisite filing fee. (R-5) |
| **Responses** | Respondent shall deliver a notice of defense within 20 days after receipt of notice of arbitration. The notice of defense shall include, *inter alia*, a statement of the general nature of the respondent's defense; the name and address of the arbitrator appointed by the respondent, unless the parties have agreed that neither shall appoint an arbitrator or that the party-appointed arbitrator shall be appointed pursuant to a "screened" process as provided in Rule 5.4.; and any counterclaim within scope of arbitration clause. However, failure to deliver a notice of defense shall not excuse respondent from notifying claimant of arbitrator selected if such party-appointment is required (Rule 3.4) nor delay the arbitration. In the event of such failure, all claims are deemed denied. (Rule 3.4; see also 3.7) If counterclaim is asserted, claimant shall deliver a reply within 20 days after receipt. (Rule 3.7) | A "respondent may file an answering statement in duplicate with AAA" within 15 days after confirmation of demand filing is sent by AAA. Respondent shall send a copy to claimant. If a counterclaim is asserted, party making counterclaim shall forward to AAA with the answering statement the appropriate fee. If no answering statement is filed, respondent will be deemed to deny the claim. Failure to file an answering statement will not delay arbitration. (R-4(b), (c)) |

	CPR Arbitration Rules (Self-Administered)*	AAA Commercial Arbitration Rules (Administered)**
Amendments	Claims or counterclaims within the scope of the arbitration clause may be freely added or amended prior to the establishment of the Tribunal and thereafter with the consent of the Tribunal. (Rule 3.8)	Claims or counterclaims may be made in writing and filed with the AAA, with a copy to the other party, prior to the appointment of an arbitrator. After the arbitrator is appointed, amendments are only permitted with arbitrator's consent. (R-6)
Representation	"Parties may be represented or assisted by persons of their choice." (Rule 4.1)	Any party "may be represented by counsel or other authorized representative." (R-26)
Administrative Conference	No provision, *see* Pre-Hearing Conference (Rule 9.3).	Before any arbitrator nominations or appointments, a meeting or conference call "may" be initiated by any party or on AAA's own initiative to discuss: • arbitrator selection/necessary qualifications • mediation or non-binding ADR applicability • potential exchange of information • timetable for hearings and other administrative matters. (R-10) No administrative conference under Expedited Procedures. (E-8) Under Large, Complex Procedures, AAA "shall" hold an administrative conference. (L-2)
Arbitrator Selection	*In absence of agreement; the Tribunal shall consist of 3 arbitrators (each party selects one and the chosen two select the third)—* Unless the parties have agreed in writing on a Tribunal consisting of a sole arbitrator or of 3 arbitrators not appointed by the parties or appointed pursuant to the "screened" process as provided in Rule 5.4, the Tribunal shall consist of two arbitrators appointed by the parties and a third arbitrator selected by the two party-appointed arbitrators. (Rule 5.1) Claimant provides notice of selection in its notice of arbitration (Rule 3.3(f)); respondent in its notice of defense. (Rule 3.5(c))	*One in the absence of agreement—* If the arbitration agreement does not specify the number of arbitrators, the dispute shall be heard and determined by one arbitrator, unless the AAA, in its discretion, directs that three arbitrators be appointed. The parties may request three arbitrators in their demand or answer, which request the AAA will consider in exercising its discretion. (R-17) Unless the parties have agreed otherwise, if arbitration notice names two or more claimants or two or more respondents, AAA "shall" appoint all arbitrators. (R-13(c)).

	CPR Arbitration Rules (Self-Administered)*	AAA Commercial Arbitration Rules (Administered)**
Arbitrator Selection *continued*	Arbitrators "shall be" deemed to agree that they have time available for expeditious processing of the case. (Rule 7.2)	Under Expedited Procedures, AAA "shall" submit a list of potential arbitrators from which one neutral arbitrator shall be selected; selection process involves party involvement. (E-5)
		Under Large, Complex Procedures, if parties cannot agree whether dispute will be heard by either one or three arbitrators, three arbitrators shall hear and determine case. (L-3)
	Within 30 days of appointment of second arbitrator, the two-party appointed arbitrator shall appoint a third arbitrator, who shall chair the Tribunal. (Rule 5.2)	If the party-appointed arbitrators are authorized to appoint the neutral arbitrator and have not done so within specified time period, AAA "may" appoint such neutral arbitrator to act as chairperson. (R-15(a)) If no time period is specified, 15 days after the date of appointment of last party-appointed arbitrator, AAA "may" appoint neutral arbitrator. (R-15(b))
	If parties have agreed on a Tribunal consisting of a sole arbitrator or of three arbitrators none of whom shall be appointed by either party, the parties shall attempt jointly to select such arbitrator(s) within 30 days after the notice of defense, but may extend such process until a deadlock occurs. (Rule 5.3)	
	If the parties have agreed on a Tribunal consisting of 3 arbitrators, two of whom are to be selected by the parties without knowing which party selected each of them, either party following the expiration of the time period for the notice of defense may request CPR in writing to conduct a "screened" selection of party-appointed arbitrators. The chair of the Tribunal is appointed by CPR in accordance with Rule 6.4. (Rule 5.4)	If the agreement of the parties names an arbitrator or specifies a method of appointing an arbitrator, that designation or method shall be followed. (R-14)
	Either party may request CPR in writing to appoint an arbitrator(s) under the circumstances enumerated in Rule 6.1, whereupon CPR shall convene the parties to attempt to select the arbitrator(s) by agreement and if that is not successful, CPR shall through a combination of a list ranking system and party involvement ensure an appointment. (Rule 6)	

	CPR Arbitration Rules (Self-Administered)*	**AAA Commercial Arbitration Rules (Administered)****
Arbitrator Selection *continued*	Where a party has failed to appoint the arbitrator to be appointed by it, CPR shall appoint a person whom it deems qualified to serve as such arbitrator. (Rule 6.5)	If the agreement specifies a relevant time period and any party fails to make the appointment within that period, AAA "shall" make the appointment. If no period is specified, AAA shall notify the party to make the appointment and if within 15 days after such notice, no appointment has been made, AAA "shall" make the appointment. (R-14)
Arbitrator Compensation	Each arbitrator is to be compensated on a reasonable basis determined at the time of the appointment. (Rule 16.1)	Compensation depends on case complexity and is set by agreement of AAA, parties and arbitrators before proceeding. (R-53)
	Tribunal fixes the costs of arbitration in its award, which includes fees and expenses of Tribunal members and other costs. (Rule 16.2) CPR does not charge filing fees or administrative hearing fees.	AAA charges filing fees that are relative to the amount of the claim or counterclaim. An administrative hearing fee is charged for each day of a hearing; hearing fees do not cover rental of hearing rooms. (R-51)
	Tribunal may request party deposits (Rule 16.4) and if such deposits are not made within 20 days after receipt of request, and after informing the parties of such failure, Tribunal may suspend or terminate the proceeding. (Rule 16.5)	The arbitrator (or AAA if none has been appointed) may suspend or terminate proceedings for non-payment of arbitrator compensation and/or administrative charges. (R-56)
	CPR charges an administrative fee only if the parties request assistance in selecting arbitrator(s) or a challenge is asserted. Arbitrator(s) are paid directly by the parties.	Payment to AAA which pays arbitrators.
Arbitrator Neutrality and Challenges	All arbitrators, including those appointed by either party, are required to be "independent and impartial." (Rule 7.1) (A departure from existing U.S. practice)	Unless the parties agree otherwise, an arbitrator selected unilaterally by one party is a party-appointed arbitrator and is not subject to disqualifications for bias, partiality or interest. (R-12(b)) Neutral arbitrators are required to reveal bias, partiality, or interest to the AAA. (R-19 (a)) Party-appointed arbitrators need not.

	CPR Arbitration Rules (Self-Administered)*	**AAA Commercial Arbitration Rules (Administered)****
Arbitrator Neutrality and Challenges *continued*	All arbitrators are subject to disqualification "if circumstances exist that give rise to justifiable doubt regarding that arbitrator's independence or impartiality. . . ." (Rule 7.5). Challenges are directed to CPR (Attention: CPR Challenge Officer). (Rule 7.6) The challenged arbitrator may agree to voluntarily withdraw or the other party may agree to the disqualification, both without accepting validity of challenge. (Rule 7.7) If neither agreed disqualification or voluntary withdrawal occurs, challenge shall be decided by CPR for an administrative fee (Rule 7.8).	Challenges are directed to and decided by AAA. (R-19 (b)).
Communications with Arbitrator(s)	Except as permitted by the Tribunal, no party shall have any *ex parte* communication concerning any matter of substance relating to the proceeding with any arbitrator or arbitrator candidate, except that a party may advise its party-appointed candidate of the general nature of the case and confer with its party-appointed arbitrator regarding the selection of the chair of the Tribunal. (Rule 7.4) As provided under the "screened" process set forth in Rule 5.4, no party shall have any *ex parte* communications relating to the case with any arbitrator or arbitrator candidates designated or appointed pursuant to Rule 5.4 (Rule 7.4)	No party or representative shall communicate unilaterally with a neutral arbitrator concerning the arbitration; any communications to a neutral arbitrator shall be sent to the AAA for transmittal unless the parties agree otherwise. (R-20 (a)) Unilaterally communications with party-appointed arbitrator permitted, unless otherwise agreed. The parties or the arbitrators may agree that once the panel has been constituted, no party or representative shall communicate unilaterally with the party-appointed arbitrator concerning the arbitration. (R-20(b))
Challenge to Jurisdiction of Arbitrator(s)	The Tribunal may decide challenges to its jurisdiction. (Rule 8.1) The Tribunal "shall have the power to determine the existence, validity or scope of the contract of which an arbitration clause forms a part, and/or of the arbitration clause itself." (Rule 8.2) Any jurisdictional challenges, except those based on an award itself, shall be made not later than the notice of defense or counterclaim reply, provided that if a claim or counterclaim is later added or amended such a challenge may be made not later than the response to such claim or counterclaim. (Rule 8.3)	The arbitrator has the power to rule on his/her own jurisdiction and "shall have the power to determine the existence or validity of a contract of which an arbitration clause forms a part." (R-8(a), (b)) Jurisdictional objections must be made no later than the filing of the answering statement to the claim or counterclaim. "The arbitrator may rule on such objections as a preliminary matter or as part of the final award." (R-8(c))

	CPR Arbitration Rules (Self-Administered)*	AAA Commercial Arbitration Rules (Administered)**
Vacancies	In event of death, resignation, or successful challenge of an arbitrator not appointed by a party, a substitute arbitrator shall be selected pursuant to the procedure by which the arbitrator being replaced was selected. (Rule 7.9) In the event of the death, resignation or successful challenge of an arbitrator appointed by a party, that party may appoint a substitute arbitrator. (Rule 7.9) If a sole arbitrator or chair of Tribunal is being replaced, successor shall decide the extent to which any hearings previously held shall be repeated. If any other arbitrator is replaced, the Tribunal in its discretion may require that some or all prior hearings be repeated. (Rule 7.11)	AAA may declare office vacant upon satisfactory proof that an arbitrator is unable to perform duties. (R-21(a)) If vacancy occurs in a panel of neutral arbitrators (not party-appointed), the remaining arbitrator or arbitrators may continue with the hearing and determination, unless parties agree otherwise. (R-21(b)) In the event of an appointment of a substitute arbitrator, the panel of arbitrators shall determine in its sole discretion whether it is necessary to repeat any portion of the hearing. (R-21(c)) (Presumably in the event if a party-appointed arbitrator, party appoints another candidate.)
Pre-Hearing Conference	*Mandatory*—After its constitution, the Tribunal "shall" "promptly" hold an initial pre-hearing conference to plan and schedule the proceeding, unless the Tribunal is of the view that further submissions from the parties are appropriate prior to such conference. (Rule 9.3) Among matters to consider: • Procedural matters—time limits for, and manner of, discovery; possible bifurcation/separation of issues; consolidation issues; scheduling; recording/transcript needs; time allotted for party presentations; mode, manner and order for presenting proof; need for experts; need for any on-site inspections. (Rule 9.3(a)) • Early identification and narrowing of issues. (Rule 9.3(b)) • Possibility of stipulations, admissions and simplification of document authentication. (Rule 9.3(c)) • Possibility of appointment of independent expert for Tribunal (Rule 9.3(d)) • Possibility of settlement negotiations, with or without assistance of a mediator. (Rule 9.3(e))	*Recommended*—At the request of any party or at an arbitrator's discretion, a preliminary hearing "may" be held in person or by telephone. (R-22) *Mandatory under Large, Complex Procedures*—a preliminary hearing "shall" be held as soon as practicable after selection of arbitrator(s). (L-4). Among items to consider: • Submission of a detailed statement of claims, positions, and legal authority • Stipulations to facts • Discovery issues • Exchange and premarking of documents • Identification and availability of witnesses • Use of sworn statements and/or depositions • Stenographic record • Utilizing mediation or other non-adjudicative process

	CPR Arbitration Rules (Self-Administered)*	**AAA Commercial Arbitration Rules (Administered)****
Location of Hearing; Scheduling	Unless the parties have agreed otherwise, the Tribunal "shall fix" the place of arbitration based upon the contentions of the parties and the circumstances of the arbitration. Tribunal holds and schedules hearings, including telephone meetings, wherever it deems appropriate. (Rule 9.5)	The parties may mutually agree on where the arbitration is to be held. If a party objects to the locale requested by the other party, the AAA "shall" have the power to determine the locale and "its decision shall be final and binding." (R-11) The arbitrator "shall" set the date, time and place for each hearing. (R-24) For hearings held under Expedited Procedures, arbitrator "shall set" the date, time and place; hearings also to be scheduled to occur within 30 days of confirmation of an arbitrator's appointment. (E-8)
Discovery or Exchange of Information	Tribunal "may require and facilitate such discovery as it shall determine is appropriate" taking into account parties' needs, expeditiousness and cost-effectiveness. (Rule 11) The Tribunal "may issue orders to protect the confidentiality of proprietary information, trade secrets and other sensitive information disclosed in discovery." (Rule 11)	Arbitrators are authorized to direct • production of documents and other information • production of the identity of any witnesses to be called. (R-23(a)) Parties shall exchange copies of all exhibits they intend to submit at the hearing at least five business days in advance. (R-23(b)) Two business days in advance under Expedited Procedures. (E-6) Under Large, Complex Procedures: • parties must exchange documents, exhibits and information if arbitrator(s) require such for a just and speedy resolution (L-5(b)) • arbitrator(s) may limit discovery agreed to by parties (L-5(c)) • for good cause shown, arbitrator(s) may order depositions or interrogatories for necessary information (L-5(d)) Arbitrator is authorized to resolve any disputes concerning the exchange of information. (R-23 (c))

	CPR Arbitration Rules (Self-Administered)*	**AAA Commercial Arbitration Rules (Administered)****
Applicable Laws and Remedies	Tribunal shall apply the substantive law(s) or rules of law designated by parties as applicable. Failing such designation, Tribunal shall apply law(s) it determines appropriate. (Rule 10.1) In arbitrations involving applications of contract, Tribunal "shall decide in accordance with the terms of the contract and shall take into account usage of the trade applicable to the contract." (Rule 10.2) The Tribunal "may grant any remedy or relief, including but not limited to specific performance of a contract, which is within the scope of the agreement of the parties and permissible under the law(s) or rules of law applicable to the dispute." (Rule 10.3) The Tribunal may award such pre-award or post-award interest, simple or compound, as it considers appropriate, taking into consideration contract and applicable law. (Rule 10.4) Costs of legal representation and assistance and experts incurred by a party to such extent as Tribunal may deem appropriate is part of arbitration costs to be fixed in the award. (Rule 16.2)	Arbitrator "may grant any remedy or relief that the arbitrator deems just and equitable and within the scope of the agreement of the parties, including, but not limited to, specific performance of a contract." (R-45 (a)) The award "may" include "interest at such rate and from such date as the arbitrator(s) may deem appropriate . . . [and] an award of attorneys' fees if all parties have requested such an award or it is authorized by law or their arbitration agreement." (R-45(d))
Interim Relief	*Permitted*—At the request of a party, the Tribunal may take such interim measures as its deems necessary, including measures for the preservation of assets, conservation of goods or the sale of perishable goods. Tribunal may require appropriate security as a condition of ordering such measures. (Rule 13.1) A request for interim measures by a party to a court shall not be deemed incompatible with an agreement to arbitrate or a waiver of such agreement. (Rule 13.2)	*Permitted*—The arbitrator "may take whatever interim measures he or she deems necessary, including injunctive relief and measures for the protection or conservation of property . . . " (R-36(a)) In addition to the final award, "the arbitrator may make other decisions, including interim, interlocutory, or partial rulings, orders and awards." (R-45(b)) A request for interim measures addressed by a party to a judicial authority shall not be deemed incompatible with an agreement to arbitrate or a waiver of such agreement. (R-36(c))

	CPR Arbitration Rules (Self-Administered)*	**AAA Commercial Arbitration Rules (Administered)***
Hearings and Evidence	The proceedings "shall" be conducted in an expeditious manner. Tribunal may set time limits for phases of the proceeding and for party presentation. (Rule 9.2)	The arbitrator shall conduct the proceedings "with a view to expediting the resolution of the dispute." (R-32(b)) (*See also* L-5)
	Tribunal shall determine the manner in which the parties shall present their cases. Unless determined otherwise by Tribunal or agreed by the parties, a pre-hearing memorandum is required. (Rule 12.1)	The claimant shall present evidence to support its claim; the respondent shall then present evidence to support its defense. (R-32(a)) Arbitrator has discretion to vary order. (R-32(b)) Arbitrator may exclude cumulative or irrelevant evidence at his/her discretion. (R-33)
	If either party so requests or Tribunal so directs, a hearing for presentation of evidence and oral argument shall be held. Testimony may be presented in written or oral form as the Tribunal deems appropriate. (Rule 12.2)	
	Tribunal in its discretion may require the parties to produce evidence in addition to that initially offered. It may also appoint experts. (Rule 12.3)	
	Tribunal shall determine the manner in which witnesses are to be examined; Tribunal has the right to exclude witnesses from hearing during testimony of other witnesses. (Rule 12.4).	
	Tribunal's powers with respect to subpoenas are determined by applicable law and are not dealt with specifically in the Rules. (Rule 12 Commentary)	An arbitrator or other person authorized by law to subpoena witnesses or documents may do so upon the request of any party or independently. (R-33(d))
	Tribunal is not required to apply rules of evidence, however, it "shall" apply the lawyer-client privilege and work product immunity. (Rule 12.2)	The arbitrator "shall" take into account applicable principles of legal privilege, such as the attorney-client privilege. (R-33(c))

	CPR Arbitration Rules (Self-Administered)*	AAA Commercial Arbitration Rules (Administered)**
Award and Costs	*Reasoned*—Reasoned award required unless parties otherwise agree. The award shall be deemed to be made at the seat of arbitration. (Rule 14.2)	*Bare*—Reasoned award need not be rendered unless parties request such an award in writing prior to appointment of the arbitrator or unless the arbitrator "determines that a reasoned award is appropriate." (R-44(b))
	When there are three arbitrators, award shall be made and signed by at least a majority. (Rule 14.2)	Majority decision required when panel comprised of more than one arbitrator, unless otherwise required by law or agreement. (R-42)
	Final award should in most circumstances be rendered within one month after close of hearing. (Rule 14.7)	Award should be made within 30 days from date of close of hearing, unless agreed otherwise or specified otherwise by law. (R-43) Under Expedited Procedures, within 14 days. (E-10)
	The Tribunal shall fix the costs of arbitration in its award. The costs include: • fees and expenses of Tribunal • costs of expert advice/other assistance engaged by Tribunal • witness travel expenses • reasonable legal costs and expert costs incurred by a party to extent Tribunal deems appropriate • charges and expenses of CPR, if any • transcript costs • meeting and hearing facility costs (Rule 16.2)	In final award, arbitrator shall assess administrative fees, expenses and arbitrator's compensation. (R-45(c)) Arbitrator's award may include an appropriate interest rate and/or award attorney's fees if authorized by parties. (R-45(d))
	Unless parties otherwise agree, Tribunal may apportion costs of arbitration between and among the parties in "such manner as its deems reasonable, taking into account the circumstances of the case, the conduct of the parties during the proceeding, and the result of the arbitration." (Rule 16.3)	Arbitrator may apportion fees, expenses and compensation among parties in manner deemed appropriate. (R-45(c)) Witness expenses shall be borne by the party bringing the witness. All other expenses, unless assigned to a party as part of the arbitrator's award, shall be divided equally among the parties. (R-52)
	Tribunal may request party deposits (Rule 16.4) and if such deposits are not made within 20 days after receipt of request, and after informing the parties of such failure, Tribunal may suspend or terminate the proceeding. (Rule 16.5)	The arbitrator (or AAA if none has been appointed) may suspend or terminate proceedings for non-payment of arbitrator compensation and/or administrative charges. (R-56)

	CPR Arbitration Rules (Self-Administered)*	AAA Commercial Arbitration Rules (Administered)**
Default Award	The Tribunal may issue an award on default pursuant to Rule 15 (failure to comply with Rules). Prior to entering a default award, the Tribunal "shall" require the non-defaulting party to produce evidence and legal argument in support of its positions as the Tribunal "may deem appropriate." (Rule 15)	An award shall not be made solely on the default of a party; the arbitrator shall require the party who is present to submit such evidence as the arbitrator may require for making such an award. (R-31)
Finality and Modification of Award	"The award shall be final and binding on the parties, and the parties will undertake to carry out the award without delay." (Rule 14.6) Within certain specified time frames, the Tribunal "shall make any interpretation, correction or additional award requested by either party that it deems justified. . . . " The Tribunal also "may make such corrections and additional awards on its own initiative as it deems appropriate." (Rule 14.5) "If an interpretation, correction or additional award is requested by a party, or a correction or additional award is made by the Tribunal on its own initiative . . . the award shall be final and binding on the parties" when such alteration is made or upon expiration of appropriate time periods set forth in Rule 14.5, whichever is earlier. (Rule 14.6)	Within 20 days after transmittal of an award, any party may request the arbitrator through the AAA and upon notice to other party to correct any clerical, typographical, or computational errors in the award. Arbitrator is not empowered to redetermine the merits of any claim already decided. Arbitrator shall dispose of request within 20 days after initial transmittal by the AAA to arbitrator. (R-48)
Confidentiality and Related Provisions	Unless parties otherwise agree, the parties, Tribunal and CPR "shall treat" the proceedings, any related discovery and Tribunal's decisions as confidential, except in connection with "judicial proceedings ancillary to the arbitration" and "unless otherwise required by law or to protect a legal right of a party." (Rule 17) "To the extent possible, any specific issues of confidentiality should be raised with and resolved by the Tribunal." (Rule 17) The Tribunal "may issue orders to protect the confidentiality of proprietary information, trade secrets and other sensitive information disclosed in discovery." (Rule 11)	Arbitrator and AAA "shall maintain the privacy of the hearings unless the law provides to the contrary. Any person having a direct interest in the arbitration is entitled to attend hearings." (R-25) "Neither AAA nor any arbitrator shall be considered a necessary party in a judicial proceedings related to the arbitration." (R-50(b))

	CPR Arbitration Rules (Self-Administered)*	**AAA Commercial Arbitration Rules (Administered)****
Confidentiality and Related Provisions *continued*	Tribunal is not required to apply rules of evidence, however, it "shall" apply the lawyer-client privilege and work product immunity. (Rule 11.2)	The arbitrator "shall" take into account applicable principles of legal privilege, such as the attorney-client privilege. (R-33(c))
Role of Negotiation/ Mediation	Either party at any time or Tribunal at such times that it deems appropriate can suggest conducting settlement negotiations. (Rule 18.1)	Potential mediation of the dispute may be addressed at administrative and preliminary hearings. (R-10; L-4)
	With parties' consent, Tribunal may arrange for mediation at any stage of proceeding; mediator shall be a person other than Tribunal member. (Rule 18.2)	At any stage of the proceedings, the parties may agree to conduct a mediation; mediator "shall not" be an arbitrator appointed to case. (R-9) However, under the Large, Complex Procedures, if the parties agree, the arbitrator can serve as mediator. (L-3(b))
	The Tribunal "will not be informed of any settlement offers or the statements made during settlement negotiations or a mediation between the parties, unless both parties consent." (Rule 18.3)	
		Arbitrators can enter "consent award" if parties settle case during arbitration. (R- 46)
Failure To Comply with Rules	If a party fails to comply with Rules or any order of the Tribunal in a manner deemed material by the Tribunal, the Tribunal shall fix a reasonable time for compliance, and if the party does not comply within that period, the Tribunal may impose a remedy it deems just, including a default judgment. However, prior to entering a default award, the Tribunal "shall" require the non-defaulting party to produce evidence and legal argument in support of its positions as the Tribunal "may deem appropriate." (Rule 15) Arbitrators may penalize dilatory tactics. (*See* Rule 16.3)	Unless the law provides to the contrary, the arbitration may proceed in the absence of any party who, after due notice, fails to be present or fails to obtain a postponement. An award shall not be made solely on the default of a party; the arbitrator shall require the party who is present to submit such evidence as the arbitrator may require for making such an award. (R-31)
Actions against Arbitrators	Neither CPR nor any arbitrator shall be liable to any party for any act or omission in connection with any arbitration conducted under the CPR Rules. (Rule 19)	Neither the AAA or any arbitrator shall be liable to any party for any act or omission in connection with any arbitration conducted under the AAA Rules. (R-50(d))

*CPR Rules for Non-Administered Arbitration (Rev. 2000). See also CPR Rules for Non-Administered Arbitration of International Disputes (Rev. 2000).
**Provisions reflect AAA Commercial Arbitration Rules (Effective January 1, 1999) (R-*); Expedited Procedures (E-*); Optional Procedures for Large, Complex Commercial Disputes (L-*)

Appendix R.6
CPR Institute for Dispute Resolution Rules for Non-Administered Arbitration of International Disputes

Revised and effective September 15, 2000

REVISION HISTORY

1992   CPR published Non-Administered International Arbitration Rules & Commentary.

1996   CPR published Mediation Procedure for Business Disputes in Europe, Minitrial Procedure for Disputes in Europe, and Dispute Resolution Clauses for Business Contracts in Europe.

1998   Bibliography updated.

2000   CPR Non-Administered International Arbitration Rules and Commentary revised.

STANDARD CONTRACTUAL PROVISIONS

The International Rules may be adopted by parties wishing to do so by using one of the following standard provisions:

A. Pre-Dispute Clause

"Any dispute arising out of or relating to, this contract, including the breach, termination or validity thereof, shall be finally resolved by arbitration in accordance with the CPR Institute for Dispute Resolution Rules for Non-Administered Arbitration of International Disputes, by (a sole arbitrator) (three arbitrators, of whom each party shall appoint one) (three arbitrators, none of whom shall be appointed by either party). Judgment upon the award rendered by the arbitrator(s) may be entered by any court having jurisdiction thereof. The seat of the arbitration shall be (city, country). The arbitration shall be conducted in (language). The Neutral Organization designated to perform the functions specified in Rules 5, 6 and 7 shall be (name of CPR or other organization)."

B. Existing Dispute Submission Agreement

"We, the undersigned parties, hereby agree to submit to arbitration in accordance with the CPR Institute for Dispute Resolution Rules for Non-

Administered Arbitration of International Disputes (the "International Rules") the following dispute: [Describe briefly]

We further agree that the above dispute shall be submitted to (a sole arbitrator) (three arbitrators, of whom each party shall appoint one) (three arbitrators, none of whom shall be appointed by either party). We further agree that we shall faithfully observe this agreement and the International Rules and that we shall abide by and perform any award rendered by the arbitrator(s). Judgment upon the award may be entered by any court having jurisdiction thereof. The seat of the arbitration shall be (city, country). The arbitration shall be conducted in (language). The Neutral Organization designated to perform the functions specified in Rules 5, 6 and 7 shall be (name of CPR or other organization)."

A. GENERAL AND INTRODUCTORY RULES

B. RULES WITH RESPECT TO THE TRIBUNAL

C. RULES WITH RESPECT TO THE CONDUCT OF THE ARBITRAL PROCEEDINGS

D. MISCELLANEOUS INTERNATIONAL RULES

A. GENERAL AND INTRODUCTORY RULES

Rule 1: Scope of Application

1.1   Where the parties to a contract have provided for arbitration under the CPR Institute for Dispute Resolution ("CPR") Rules for Non-Administered Arbitration of International Disputes (the "International Rules"), they shall be deemed to have made these International Rules a part of their arbitration agreement, except to the extent that they have agreed in writing, or on the record during the course of the arbitral proceeding, to modify these International Rules. Unless the parties otherwise agree, these International Rules, and any amendment thereof adopted by CPR, shall apply in the form in effect at the time the arbitration is commenced.

1.2   These International Rules shall govern the conduct of the arbitration except that where any of these International Rules is in conflict with a mandatory provision of applicable arbitration law of the seat of the arbitration, that provision of law shall prevail.

Rule 2:   Notices

2.1   Notices or other communications required under these International Rules shall be in writing and delivered to the address specified in writing by the recipient or, if no address has been specified, to the last known business or residence address of the recipient. Notices and communications may be given by registered mail, courier, telex, facsimile transmission, or any other means of telecommunication that provides a record thereof. Notices and communications shall be deemed to be effective as of the date of receipt. Proof of transmission shall be deemed *prima facie* proof of receipt of any notice or communication given under these International Rules.

2.2   Time periods specified by these International Rules or established by the Arbitral Tribunal (the "Tribunal") shall start to run on the day following the day when a notice or communication is received, unless the Tribunal shall specifically provide otherwise. If the last day of such period is an official holiday or a non-business day at the place where the notice or communication is received, the period is extended until the first business day which follows. Official holidays and non-business days occurring during the running of the period of time are included in calculating the period.

Rule 3:   Commencement of Arbitration

3.1   The party commencing arbitration (the "Claimant") shall address to the other party (the "Respondent") a notice of arbitration.

3.2   The arbitration shall be deemed commenced as to any Respondent on the date on which the notice of arbitration is received by the Respondent.

3.3   The notice of arbitration shall include in the text or in attachments thereto:

   a. The full names, descriptions and addresses of the parties;
   b. A demand that the dispute be referred to arbitration pursuant to the International Rules;
   c. The text of the arbitration clause or the separate arbitration agreement that is involved;
   d. A statement of the general nature of the Claimant's claim;
   e. The relief or remedy sought; and
   f. The name and address of the arbitrator appointed by the Claimant, unless the parties have agreed that neither shall appoint an arbitrator.

3.4   Within 30 days after receipt of the notice of arbitration, the Respondent shall deliver to the Claimant a notice of defense. Failure to deliver a notice of defense shall not delay the arbitration; in the event of such failure, all claims set forth in the demand shall be deemed denied. Failure to deliver a notice of defense shall not excuse the Respondent from notifying the Claimant in writing, within 30 days after receipt of the notice of arbitration, of the arbitrator appointed by the Respondent, unless the parties have agreed that neither party shall appoint an arbitrator.

3.5   The notice of defense shall include:

   a. Any comment on items (a), (b), and (c) of the notice of arbitration that the Respondent may deem appropriate;
   b. A statement of the general nature of the Respondent's defense; and
   c. The name and address of the arbitrator appointed by the Respondent, unless the parties have agreed that neither shall appoint an arbitrator.

3.6   The Respondent may include in its notice of defense any counterclaim within the scope of the arbitration clause. If it does so, the counterclaim in the notice of defense shall include items (a), (b), (c), (d) and (e) of Rule 3.3.

3.7   If a counterclaim is asserted, within 30 days after receipt of the notice of defense, the Claimant shall deliver to the Respondent a reply to counterclaim which shall have the same elements as provided in International Rule 3.5 for the notice of defense. Failure to deliver a reply to counterclaim shall not delay the arbitration; in the event of such failure, all counterclaims set forth in the notice of defense shall be deemed denied.

3.8   Claims or counterclaims within the scope of the arbitration clause may be freely added or amended prior to the establishment of the Tribunal and thereafter with the consent of the Tribunal. Notices of defense or replies to amended claims or counterclaims shall be delivered within 20 days after the addition or amendment.

3.9   If a dispute is submitted to arbitration pursuant to a submission agreement, this International Rule 3 shall apply to the extent that it is not inconsistent with the submission agreement.

Rule 4:   Representation

4.1   The parties may be represented or assisted by persons of their choice.

4.2   Each party shall communicate the name, address and function of such persons in writing to the other party and to the Tribunal.

B. RULES WITH RESPECT TO THE TRIBUNAL

Rule 5:   Selection of Arbitrators by the Parties

5.1   Unless the parties have agreed in writing on a Tribunal consisting of a sole arbitrator or of three arbitrators not appointed by parties, the Tribunal shall consist of two arbitrators, one appointed by each of the parties as provided in International Rules 3.3 and 3.5, and a third arbitrator who shall chair the Tribunal, selected as provided in International Rule 5.2.

5.2   Within 30 days of the appointment of the second arbitrator, the two party-appointed arbitrators shall appoint a third arbitrator, who shall chair the Tribunal. In the event the party-appointed arbitrators are unable to agree on the third arbitrator, the third arbitrator shall be selected as provided in International Rule 6.

5.3   If the parties have agreed on a Tribunal consisting of a sole arbitrator or of three arbitrators none of whom shall be appointed by either party, the parties shall attempt jointly to select such arbitrator(s) within 30 days after the notice of defense provided for in International Rule 3.4 is due. The parties may extend their selection process until one or both of them have concluded that a deadlock has been reached. In this event, the arbitrator(s) shall be selected as provided in International Rule 6.

5.4   Where the arbitration agreement entitles each party to appoint an arbitrator but there is more than one Claimant or Respondent to the dispute, and either the multiple Claimants or the multiple Respondents do not jointly appoint an arbitrator, the Neutral Organization shall appoint all of the arbitrators as provided in International Rule 6.4.

Rule 6:   Selection of Arbitrator(s) by Neutral Organization

6.1   Whenever (i) a party has failed to appoint the arbitrator to be appointed by it; (ii) the parties have failed to appoint the arbitrator(s) to be appointed by them acting jointly; (iii) the party-appointed arbitrators have failed to appoint the third arbitrator; (iv) the parties have provided that one or more arbitrators shall be appointed by a Neutral Organization agreed on by the parties; or (v) the multi-party nature of the dispute calls for the Neutral Organization to appoint all members of a three-member Tribunal pursuant to International Rule 5.4, the arbitrator(s) required to complete the Tribunal shall be selected as provided in this International Rule 6, and either party may request the Neutral Organization in writing, with copy to the other party, to proceed pursuant to this International Rule 6. In the event the parties have not agreed on a Neutral Organization, CPR shall serve as the Neutral Organization.

6.2   The written request may be made as follows:
    a.   If a party has failed to appoint the arbitrator to be appointed by it, or the parties have failed to appoint the arbitrator(s) to be appointed by them through agreement, at any time after such failure has occurred.
    b.   If the party-appointed arbitrators have failed to appoint the third arbitrator, as soon as the procedure contemplated by International Rule 5.2 has been completed.
    c.   If the arbitrator(s) are to be appointed by the Neutral Organization, as soon as the notice of defense is due.

6.3   The written request shall include complete copies of the notice of arbitration and the notice of defense or, if the dispute is submitted under a submission agreement, a copy of the agreement supplemented by the notice of arbitration and notice of defense if they are not part of the agreement.

6.4   Except where a party has failed to appoint the arbitrator to be appointed by it, the Neutral Organization shall submit to the parties a list of not less than five candidates if one arbitrator remains to be selected, and of not less than seven candidates if two or three arbitrators are to be selected. If either party shall so request, such candidates shall be of a nationality other than the nationality of the parties. Such list shall include a brief statement of each candidate's qualifications. Each party shall number the candidates in order of preference, shall note any objection it may have to any candidate, and shall deliver the list so marked to the Neutral Organization and to the other party. Any party failing without good cause to return the candidate list so marked within 10 days after receipt shall be deemed to have assented to all candidates listed thereon. The Neutral Organization shall designate as arbitrator(s) the nominee(s) willing to serve for whom the parties collectively have indicated the highest preference and who appear to meet the standards set forth in International Rule 7. If a tie should result between two candidates, the Neutral Organization may designate either candidate. If this procedure for any reason should fail to result in designation of the required number of arbitrators or if a party fails to participate in this procedure, the Neutral Organization shall appoint a person or persons whom it deems qualified to fill any remaining vacancy, and whom, if either party shall so request, shall be of a nationality other than the nationality of the parties.

6.5   Where a party has failed to appoint the arbitrator to be appointed by it, the Neutral Organization shall appoint a person whom it deems qualified to serve as such arbitrator, taking into account the nationalities of the parties and any other relevant circumstances.

Rule 7:   Qualifications, Challenges and Replacement of Arbitrator(s)

7.1   Each arbitrator shall be independent and impartial.

7.2   By accepting appointment, each arbitrator shall be deemed to be bound by these International Rules and any modification agreed to by the parties, and to have represented that he or she has the time available to devote to the expeditious process contemplated by these International Rules.

7.3   Each arbitrator shall disclose in writing to the Tribunal and the parties at the time of his or her appointment and promptly upon their arising during the course of the arbitration any circumstances that might give rise to justifiable doubt regarding the arbitrator's independence or impartiality. Such circumstances include bias, interest in the result of the arbitration, and past or present relations with a party or its counsel.

7.4   No party or anyone acting on its behalf shall have any ex parte communications concerning any matter of substance relating to the proceeding with any arbitrator or arbitrator candidate, except that a party may advise a candidate for appointment as its party-appointed arbitrator of the general nature of the case and discuss the candidate's qualifications, availability, and independence and impartiality with respect to the parties, and a party may confer with its party-appointed arbitrator regarding the selection of the chair of the Tribunal.

7.5   Any arbitrator may be challenged if circumstances exist or arise that give rise to justifiable doubt regarding that arbitrator's independence or impartiality, provided, that a party may challenge an arbitrator whom it has appointed only for reasons of which it becomes aware after the appointment has been made.

7.6   A party may challenge an arbitrator only by a notice in writing to the Neutral Organization, with copy to the Tribunal and the other party, given no later than 15 days after the challenging party (i) receives notification of the appointment of that arbitrator, or (ii) becomes aware of the circumstances specified in International Rule 7.5, whichever shall last occur. The notice shall state the reasons for the challenge with specificity.

7.7   When an arbitrator has been challenged by a party, the other party may agree to the challenge or the arbitrator may voluntarily withdraw. Neither of these actions implies acceptance of the validity of the challenge.

7.8   If neither agreed disqualification nor voluntary withdrawal occurs, the challenge shall be decided by the Neutral Organization, after providing the non-challenging party and each member of the Tribunal with an opportunity to comment on the challenge.

7.9   In the event of death, resignation or successful challenge of an arbitrator not appointed by a party, a substitute arbitrator shall be selected pursuant to the procedure by which the arbitrator being replaced was selected. In the event of the death, resignation or successful challenge of an arbitrator appointed by a party, that party may appoint a substitute arbitrator; provided, however, that should that party fail to notify the Tribunal and the other party of the substitute appointment within 20 days from the date on which it becomes aware that the opening arose, that party's right of appointment shall lapse and the Tribunal shall promptly request the Neutral Organization to appoint a substitute arbitrator forthwith.

7.10   In the event that an arbitrator fails to act or is de jure or de facto prevented from duly performing the functions of an arbitrator, the procedures provided in International Rule 7.9 shall apply to the selection of a replacement. If the parties do not agree on whether the arbitrator has failed to act or is prevented from performing the functions of an arbitrator, either party may request the Neutral Organization to make that determination forthwith.

7.11   If the sole arbitrator or the chair of the Tribunal is replaced, the successor shall decide the extent to which any hearings held previously shall be repeated. If any other arbitrator is replaced, the Tribunal in its discretion may require that some or all prior hearings be repeated.

Rule 8:   Challenges to the Jurisdiction of the Tribunal

8.1   The Tribunal shall have the power to hear and determine challenges to its jurisdiction, including any objections with respect to the existence, scope or validity of the arbitration agreement.

8.2   The Tribunal shall have the power to determine the existence, validity or scope of the contract of which an arbitration clause forms a part. For the purposes of challenges to the jurisdiction of the Tribunal, the arbitration clause shall be considered as separable from any contract of which it forms a part.

8.3   Any challenges to the jurisdiction of the Tribunal, except challenges based on the award itself, shall be made not later than the notice of defense or, with respect to a counterclaim, the reply to the counterclaim; provided, however, that if a claim or counterclaim is later added or amended such a challenge may be made not later than the response to such claim or counterclaim.

C. RULES WITH RESPECT TO THE CONDUCT OF THE ARBITRAL PROCEEDINGS

Rule 9:   General Provisions

9.1   Subject to these International Rules, the Tribunal may conduct the arbitration in such manner as it shall deem appropriate. The chair shall be responsible for the organization of arbitral conferences and hearings and arrangements with respect to the functioning of the Tribunal.

9.2   The proceedings shall be conducted in an expeditious manner. The Tribunal is empowered to impose time limits it considers reasonable on each phase of the proceeding, including without limitation the time allotted to each party for presentation of its case and for rebuttal. In setting time limits, the Tribunal should bear in mind its obligation to manage the proceeding firmly in order to complete proceedings as economically and expeditiously as possible.

9.3   The Tribunal shall hold an initial pre-hearing conference for the planning and scheduling of the proceeding. Such conference shall be held promptly after the constitution of the Tribunal, unless the Tribunal is of the view that further submissions from the parties are appropriate prior to such conference. The objective of this conference shall be to discuss all elements of the arbitration with a view to planning for its future conduct. Matters to be considered in the initial pre-hearing conference may include, *inter alia*, the following:

>   a.   Procedural matters (such as the timing and manner of any required disclosure; the desirability of bifurcation or other separation of the issues in the arbitration; the desirability and practicability of consolidating the arbitration with any other proceeding; the scheduling of conferences and hearings; the need for and costs of translations; the scheduling of pre-hearing memoranda; the need for and type of record of conferences and hearings, including the need for transcripts;

the amount of time allotted to each party for presentation of its case and for rebuttal; the mode, manner and order for presenting proof; the need for expert witnesses and how expert testimony should be presented; and the necessity for any on-site inspection by the Tribunal);
b. The early identification and narrowing of the issues in the arbitration;
c. The possibility of stipulations of fact and admissions by the parties solely for purposes of the arbitration, as well as simplification of document authentication;
d. The possibility of appointment of a neutral expert by the Tribunal; and
e. The possibility of the parties engaging in settlement negotiations, with or without the assistance of a mediator.

After the initial conference, further pre-hearing or other conferences may be held as the Tribunal deems appropriate.

9.4   In order to define the issues to be heard and determined, the Tribunal may, *inter alia*, make pre-hearing orders for the arbitration and instruct the parties to file more detailed statements of claim and of defense and pre-hearing memoranda.

9.5   Unless the parties have agreed upon the seat of arbitration, the Tribunal shall fix the seat of arbitration based upon the contentions of the parties and the circumstances of the arbitration. The award shall be deemed made at such place. The Tribunal may schedule meetings and hold hearings wherever it deems appropriate.

9.6   If the parties have not agreed otherwise, the language(s) of the arbitration shall be that of the documents containing the arbitration agreement, subject to the power of the Tribunal to determine otherwise based upon the contentions of the parties and the circumstances of the arbitration. The Tribunal may order that any documents submitted in other languages shall be accompanied by a translation into such language or languages.

Rule 10:   Applicable Law(s) and Remedies

10.1   The Tribunal shall apply the substantive law(s) or rules of law designated by the parties as applicable to the dispute. Failing such a designation by the parties, the Tribunal shall apply such law(s) or rules of law as it determines to be appropriate.

10.2   Subject to International Rule 10.1, in arbitrations involving the application of contracts, the Tribunal shall decide in accordance with the terms of the contract and shall take into account usages of the trade applicable to the contract.

10.3   The Tribunal shall not decide as *amiable compositeur* or *ex aequo et bono* unless the parties have expressly authorized it to do so.

10.4   The Tribunal may grant any remedy or relief, including but not limited to specific performance of a contract, which is within the scope of the agreement of the parties and permissible under the law(s) or rules of law applicable to the dispute pursuant to International Rule 10.1, or, if the parties have expressly so provided pursuant to International Rule 10.3, within the Tribunal's authority to decide as *amiable compositeur* or *ex aequo et bono*.

10.5   Unless the parties agree otherwise, the parties expressly waive and forego any right to punitive, exemplary or similar damages unless a statute requires that compensatory damages be increased in a specified manner. This provision shall not limit the Tribunal's authority under International Rule 16.3 to take into account a party's dilatory or bad faith conduct in the arbitration in apportioning arbitration costs between or among the parties.

10.6   A monetary award shall be in the currency or currencies of the contract unless the Tribunal considers another currency more appropriate, and the Tribunal may award such pre-award and post-award interest, simple or compound, as it considers appropriate, taking into consideration the contract and applicable law.

Rule 11:   Disclosure

The Tribunal may require and facilitate such disclosure as it shall determine is appropriate in the circumstances, taking into account the needs of the parties and the desirability of making disclosure expeditious and cost-effective. The Tribunal may issue orders to protect the confidentiality of proprietary information, trade secrets and other sensitive information disclosed.

Rule 12:   Evidence and Hearings

12.1   The Tribunal shall determine the manner in which the parties shall present their cases. Unless otherwise determined by the Tribunal or agreed by the parties, the presentation of a party's case shall include the submission of a pre-hearing memorandum including the following elements:

   a.   A statement of facts;
   b.   A statement of each claim being asserted;
   c.   A statement of the applicable law and authorities upon which the party relies;
   d.   A statement of the relief requested, including the basis for any damages claimed; and
   e.   The evidence to be presented, including documents relied upon and the name, capacity and subject of testimony of any witnesses to be called, the language in which each witness will testify, and an estimate of the amount of time required for the party's examination of the witness.

12.2   If either party so requests or the Tribunal so directs, a hearing shall be held for the presentation of evidence and oral argument. Testimony may be presented in written and/or oral form as the Tribunal may determine is appropriate. The Tribunal is not required to apply the rules of evidence used in judicial proceedings. The Tribunal shall determine the applicability of any privilege or immunity and the admissibility, relevance, materiality and weight of the evidence offered.

12.3   The Tribunal, in its discretion, may require the parties to produce evidence in addition to that initially offered. It may also appoint neutral experts whose testimony shall be subject to examination by the parties and the Tribunal and to rebuttal.

12.4   The Tribunal shall determine the manner in which witnesses are to be examined, including the need and arrangements for translation of any witness testimony in a language other than the language of the arbitration. The Tribunal shall have the right to exclude witnesses from hearings during the testimony of other witnesses.

Rule 13:   Interim Measures of Protection

13.1   At the request of a party, the Tribunal may take such interim measures as it deems necessary, including measures for the preservation of assets, the conservation of goods or the sale of perishable goods. The Tribunal may require appropriate security as a condition of ordering such measures.

13.2   A request for interim measures by a party to a court shall not be deemed incompatible with the agreement to arbitrate or as a waiver of that agreement.

Rule 14:   The Award

14.1   The Tribunal may make final, interim, interlocutory and partial orders or awards. With respect to any interim, interlocutory or partial award, the Tribunal may state in its award whether or not it views the award as final for purposes of any judicial proceedings in connection therewith.

14.2   All awards shall be in writing and shall state the reasoning on which the award rests unless the parties agree otherwise. The award shall be deemed to be made at the seat of arbitration and shall contain the date on which the award was made. When there are three arbitrators, the award shall be made and signed by at least a majority of the arbitrators. When one of three arbitrators does not sign, the award shall be accompanied by a statement of whether the third arbitrator was given the opportunity to sign.

14.3   A member of the Tribunal who does not join in an award may file a dissenting opinion. Such opinion shall not constitute part of the award.

14.4   Executed copies of awards and of any dissenting opinion shall be delivered by the Tribunal to the parties. If the arbitration law of the country where the award is made requires the award to be filed or registered, the Tribunal shall comply or arrange for compliance with such requirement.

14.5   Within 20 days after receipt of the award, either party, with notice to the other party, may request the Tribunal to interpret the award; to correct any clerical, typographical or computation errors, or any errors of a similar nature in the award; or to make an additional award as to claims or counterclaims presented in the arbitration but not determined in the award. The Tribunal shall make any interpretation, correction or additional award requested by either party that it deems justified within 30 days after receipt of such request. Within 20 days after delivery of the award to the parties or, if a party requests an interpretation, correction or additional award, within 30 days after receipt of such request, the Tribunal may make such corrections and additional awards on its own initiative as it deems appropriate. All interpretations, corrections and additional awards shall be in writing, and the provisions of this International Rule 14 shall apply to them.

14.6   The award shall be final and binding on the parties, and the parties will undertake to carry out the award without delay. If an interpretation, correction or additional award is requested by a party, or a correction or additional award is made by the Tribunal on its own initiative, as provided in International Rule 14.5, the award shall be final and binding on the parties when such interpretation, correction or additional award is made by the Tribunal or upon the expiration of the time periods provided in International Rule 14.5 for such interpretation, correction or additional award to be made, whichever is earlier.

14.7   The dispute should in most circumstances be heard and be submitted to the Tribunal for decision within nine months after the initial pre-hearing conference required by Rule 9.3. The final award should in most circumstances be rendered within three months thereafter. The parties and the Tribunal shall use their best efforts to comply with this schedule.

D. MISCELLANEOUS INTERNATIONAL RULES

Rule 15:   Failure to Comply with International Rules

Whenever a party fails to comply with these International Rules, or any order of the Tribunal pursuant to these International Rules, in a manner deemed material by the Tribunal, the Tribunal shall fix a reasonable period of time for compliance and, if the party does not comply within said period, the Tribunal may impose a remedy it deems just, including an award on default. Prior to entering an award on default, the Tribunal shall require the non-defaulting party to produce such evidence and legal argument in support of its contentions as the Tribunal may deem appropriate. The Tribunal may receive such evidence and argument without the defaulting party's presence or participation.

Rule 16:   Costs

16.1   Each arbitrator shall be compensated on a reasonable basis determined at the time of appointment for serving as an arbitrator and shall be reimbursed for any reasonable travel and other expenses.

16.2   The Tribunal shall fix the costs of arbitration in its award. The costs of arbitration include:

    a.   The fees and expenses of members of the Tribunal;
    b.   The costs of expert advice and other assistance engaged by the Tribunal;
    c.   The travel, translation, and other expenses of witnesses to such extent as the Tribunal may deem appropriate;
    d.   The costs for legal representation and assistance and experts incurred by a party to such extent as the Tribunal may deem appropriate;
    e.   The charges and expenses of the Neutral Organization with respect to the arbitration;
    f.   The costs of a transcript, if any; and
    g.   The costs of meeting and hearing facilities.

16.3   Subject to any agreement between the parties to the contrary, the Tribunal may apportion the costs of arbitration between or among the parties in such manner as it deems reasonable, taking into account the circumstances of the case, the conduct of the parties during the proceeding, and the result of the arbitration.

16.4   The Tribunal may request each party to deposit an appropriate amount as an advance for the costs referred to in International Rule 16.2 except those specified in subparagraph (d), and, during the course of the proceeding, it may request supplementary deposits from the parties. Any such funds shall be held and disbursed in such a manner as the Tribunal may deem appropriate.

16.5   If the requested deposits are not paid in full within 20 days after receipt of the request, the Tribunal shall so inform the parties in order that jointly or severally they may make the requested payment. If such payment is not made, the Tribunal may suspend or terminate the proceeding.

16.6   After the proceeding has been concluded, the Tribunal shall return any unexpended balance from deposits made to the parties as may be appropriate.

Rule 17:   Confidentiality

Unless the parties agree otherwise, the parties, the arbitrators and the Neutral Organization shall treat the proceedings, any related disclosure and the decisions of the Tribunal, as confidential, except in connection with judicial proceedings ancillary to the arbitration, such as a judicial challenge to, or enforcement of, an award, and unless otherwise required by law or to protect a legal right of a party. To the extent possible, any specific issues of confidentiality should be raised with and resolved by the Tribunal.

Rule 18:   Settlement and Mediation

18.1   Either party may propose settlement negotiations to the other party at any time. The Tribunal may suggest that the parties explore settlement at such times as the Tribunal may deem appropriate.

18.2   With the consent of the parties, the Tribunal at any stage of the proceeding may arrange for mediation of the claims asserted in the arbitration by a mediator acceptable to the parties. The mediator shall be a person other than a member of the Tribunal. Unless the parties agree otherwise, any such mediation shall be conducted under the CPR Mediation Procedure.

18.3   The Tribunal will not be informed of any settlement offers or other statements made during settlement negotiations or a mediation between the parties, unless both parties consent.

Rule 19:   Actions against the Neutral Organization or Arbitrator(s)

Neither the Neutral Organization nor any arbitrator shall be liable to any party for any act or omission in connection with any arbitration conducted under these International Rules, except that either may be liable to a party for the consequences of conscious and deliberate wrongdoing.

Rule 20:   Waiver

A party knowing of a failure to comply with any provision of these International Rules, or any requirement of the arbitration agreement or any direction of the Tribunal, and neglecting to state its objections promptly, waives any objection thereto.

For accompanying Commentary, see <www.cpradr.org> (Procedures and Clauses).

Appendix R.7
American Arbitration Association International Arbitration Rules

As amended and effective on September 1, 2000

INTRODUCTION

International Arbitration Rules: Article 1

I. COMMENCING THE ARBITRATION

Notice of Arbitration and Statement of Claim: Article 2
Statement of Defense and Counterclaim: Article 3
Amendments to Claims: Article 4

II. THE TRIBUNAL

Number of Arbitrators: Article 5
Appointment of Arbitrators: Article 6
Impartiality and Independence of Arbitrators: Article 7
Challenge of Arbitrators: Articles 8 and 9
Replacement of an Arbitrator: Articles 10 and 11

III. GENERAL CONDITIONS

Representation: Article 12
Place of Arbitration: Article 13
Language: Article 14
Pleas as to Jurisdiction: Article 15
Conduct of the Arbitration: Article 16
Further Written Statements: Article 17
Notices: Article 18
Evidence: Article 19
Hearings: Article 20
Interim Measures of Protection: Article 21
Experts: Article 22
Default: Article 23
Closure of Hearing: Article 24
Waiver of Rules: Article 25

ADMINISTRATIVE FEES

Introduction

The world business community uses arbitration to resolve commercial disputes arising in the global marketplace. Supportive laws are in place. The New York Convention of 1958 has been widely adopted, providing a favorable legislative climate. Arbitration clauses are enforced. International commercial arbitration awards are recognized by national courts in most parts of the world, even more than foreign court judgments.

Arbitration institutions have been established in many countries to administer international cases. Many have entered into cooperative arrangements with the American Arbitration Association.

These International Arbitration Rules have been developed to encourage greater use of such services. By providing for arbitration under these rules, parties can avoid the uncertainty of having to petition a local court to resolve procedural impasses.

These rules are intended to provide effective arbitration services to world business through the use of administered arbitration.

Parties can arbitrate future disputes under these rules by inserting the following clause into their contracts:

> "Any controversy or claim arising out of or relating to this contract shall be determined by arbitration in accordance with the International Arbitration Rules of the American Arbitration Association."

The parties may wish to consider adding:

(a) "The number of arbitrators shall be (one or three)";
(b) "The place of arbitration shall be (city and/or country)"; or
(c) "The language(s) of the arbitration shall be _____."

Parties are encouraged, when writing their contracts or when a dispute arises, to request a conference, in person or by telephone, with the AAA, to discuss an appropriate method for selection of arbitrators or any other matter that might facilitate efficient arbitration of the dispute.

Under these rules, the parties are free to adopt any mutually agreeable procedure for appointing arbitrators, or may designate arbitrators upon whom they agree. Parties can reach agreements concerning appointing arbitrators either when writing their contracts or after a dispute has arisen. This flexible procedure permits parties to utilize whatever method they consider best suits their needs. For example, parties may choose to have a sole arbitrator or a tribunal of three or more. They may agree that arbitrators shall be appointed by the AAA, or that each side shall designate one arbitrator and those two shall name a third, with the AAA making appointments if the tribunal is not promptly formed by that procedure. Parties may mutually request the AAA to submit to them a list of arbitrators from which each can delete names not acceptable to it, or the parties may instruct the AAA to appoint arbitrators without the submission of lists, or may leave that matter to the sole discretion of the AAA. Parties also may agree on a variety of other methods for establishing the tribunal. In any event, if parties are unable to agree on a procedure for appointing arbitrators or on the designation of arbitrators, the AAA, after inviting consultation by the parties, will appoint the arbitrators. The rules thus provide for the fullest exercise of party autonomy, while assuring that the AAA is available to act if the parties cannot reach mutual agreement.

Whenever a singular term is used in the rules, such as "party," "claimant" or "arbitrator," that term shall include the plural if there is more than one such entity.

Parties may wish to consider the possibility of mediation or conciliation. This too can be discussed with the AAA, either when the contract is being written or after a dispute arises, and the AAA is prepared to arrange for mediation or conciliation anywhere in the world.

Parties filing an international case with the American Arbitration Association may do so by contacting any one of the regional offices or by contacting the Association's International Center for Dispute Resolution located in New York, N.Y., which is staffed by multilingual attorneys who have the requisite expertise in international matters.

Further information about these rules can be secured by contacting the Association's Customer Service Department at 800-778-7879.

International Arbitration Rules
Article 1

1. Where parties have agreed in writing to arbitrate disputes under these International Arbitration Rules or have provided for arbitration of an international dispute by the American Arbitration Association without designating particular rules, the arbitration shall take place in accordance with these rules, as in effect at the date of commencement of the arbitration, subject to whatever modifications the parties may adopt in writing.

2. These rules govern the arbitration, except that, where any such rule is in conflict with any provision of the law applicable to the arbitration from which the parties cannot derogate, that provision shall prevail.

3. These rules specify the duties and responsibilities of the administrator, the American Arbitration Association. The administrator may provide services through its International Center, located in New York City, or through the facilities of arbitral institutions with which it has agreements of cooperation.

I. Commencing the Arbitration

Notice of Arbitration and Statement of Claim
Article 2

1. The party initiating arbitration ("claimant") shall give written notice of arbitration to the administrator and at the same time to the party against whom a claim is being made ("respondent").

2. Arbitral proceedings shall be deemed to commence on the date on which the administrator receives the notice of arbitration.

3. The notice of arbitration shall contain a statement of claim including the following:

    (a) a demand that the dispute be referred to arbitration;
    (b) the names and addresses of the parties;
    (c) a reference to the arbitration clause or agreement that is invoked;
    (d) a reference to any contract out of or in relation to which the dispute arises;
    (e) a description of the claim and an indication of the facts supporting it;
    (f) the relief or remedy sought and the amount claimed; and
    (g) may include proposals as to the means of designating and the number of arbitrators, the place of arbitration and the language(s) of the arbitration.

4. Upon receipt of the notice of arbitration, the administrator shall communicate with all parties with respect to the arbitration and shall acknowledge the commencement of the arbitration.

Statement of Defense and Counterclaim
Article 3

1. Within 30 days after the commencement of the arbitration, a respondent shall submit a written statement of defense, responding to the issues raised in the notice of arbitration, to the claimant and any other parties, and to the administrator.

2. At the time a respondent submits its statement of defense, a respondent may make counterclaims or assert setoffs as to any claim covered by the agreement to arbitrate, as to which the claimant shall within 30 days submit a written statement of defense to the respondent and any other parties and to the administrator.

3. A respondent shall respond to the administrator, the claimant and other parties within 30 days after the commencement of the arbitration as to any proposals the claimant may have made as to the number of arbitrators, the place of the arbitration or the language(s) of the arbitration, except to the extent that the parties have previously agreed as to these matters.

4. The arbitral tribunal, or the administrator if the arbitral tribunal has not yet been formed, may extend any of the time limits established in this article if it considers such an extension justified.

Amendments to Claims
Article 4

During the arbitral proceedings, any party may amend or supplement its claim, counterclaim or defense, unless the tribunal considers it inappropriate to allow such amendment or supplement because of the party's delay in making it, prejudice to the other parties or any other circumstances. A party may not amend or supplement a claim or counterclaim if the amendment or supplement would fall outside the scope of the agreement to arbitrate.

II. The Tribunal

Number of Arbitrators
Article 5

If the parties have not agreed on the number of arbitrators, one arbitrator shall be appointed unless the administrator determines in its discretion that three arbitrators are appropriate because of the large size, complexity or other circumstances of the case.

Appointment of Arbitrators
Article 6

1. The parties may mutually agree upon any procedure for appointing arbitrators and shall inform the administrator as to such procedure.

2. The parties may mutually designate arbitrators, with or without the assistance of the administrator. When such designations are made, the parties shall notify the administrator so that notice of the appointment can be communicated to the arbitrators, together with a copy of these rules.

3. If within 45 days after the commencement of the arbitration, all of the parties have not mutually agreed on a procedure for appointing the arbitrator(s) or have not mutually agreed on the designation of the arbitrator(s), the administrator shall, at the written request of any party, appoint the arbitrator(s) and designate the presiding arbitrator. If all of the parties have mutually agreed

upon a procedure for appointing the arbitrator(s), but all appointments have not been made within the time limits provided in that procedure, the administrator shall, at the written request of any party, perform all functions provided for in that procedure that remain to be performed.

4.   In making such appointments, the administrator, after inviting consultation with the parties, shall endeavor to select suitable arbitrators. At the request of any party or on its own initiative, the administrator may appoint nationals of a country other than that of any of the parties.

5.   Unless the parties have agreed otherwise no later than 45 days after the commencement of the arbitration, if the notice of arbitration names two or more claimants or two or more respondents, the administrator shall appoint all the arbitrators.

Impartiality and Independence of Arbitrators
Article 7

1.   Arbitrators acting under these rules shall be impartial and independent. Prior to accepting appointment, a prospective arbitrator shall disclose to the administrator any circumstance likely to give rise to justifiable doubts as to the arbitrator's impartiality or independence. If, at any stage during the arbitration, new circumstances arise that may give rise to such doubts, an arbitrator shall promptly disclose such circumstances to the parties and to the administrator. Upon receipt of such information from an arbitrator or a party, the administrator shall communicate it to the other parties and to the tribunal.

2.   No party or anyone acting on its behalf shall have any ex parte communication relating to the case with any arbitrator, or with any candidate for appointment as party-appointed arbitrator except to advise the candidate of the general nature of the controversy and of the anticipated proceedings and to discuss the candidate's qualifications, availability or independence in relation to the parties, or to discuss the suitability of candidates for selection as a third arbitrator where the parties or party-designated arbitrators are to participate in that selection. No party or anyone acting on its behalf shall have any ex parte communication relating to the case with any candidate for presiding arbitrator.

Challenge of Arbitrators
Article 8

1.   A party may challenge any arbitrator whenever circumstances exist that give rise to justifiable doubts as to the arbitrator's impartiality or independence. A party wishing to challenge an arbitrator shall send notice of the challenge to the administrator within 15 days after being notified of the appointment of the arbitrator or within 15 days after the circumstances giving rise to the challenge become known to that party.

2. The challenge shall state in writing the reasons for the challenge.

3. Upon receipt of such a challenge, the administrator shall notify the other parties of the challenge. When an arbitrator has been challenged by one party, the other party or parties may agree to the acceptance of the challenge and, if there is agreement, the arbitrator shall withdraw. The challenged arbitrator may also withdraw from office in the absence of such agreement. In neither case does withdrawal imply acceptance of the validity of the grounds for the challenge.

Article 9

If the other party or parties do not agree to the challenge or the challenged arbitrator does not withdraw, the administrator in its sole discretion shall make the decision on the challenge.

Replacement of an Arbitrator
Article 10

If an arbitrator withdraws after a challenge, or the administrator sustains the challenge, or the administrator determines that there are sufficient reasons to accept the resignation of an arbitrator, or an arbitrator dies, a substitute arbitrator shall be appointed pursuant to the provisions of Article 6, unless the parties otherwise agree.

Article 11

1. If an arbitrator on a three-person tribunal fails to participate in the arbitration for reasons other than those identified in Article 10, the two other arbitrators shall have the power in their sole discretion to continue the arbitration and to make any decision, ruling or award, notwithstanding the failure of the third arbitrator to participate. In determining whether to continue the arbitration or to render any decision, ruling or award without the participation of an arbitrator, the two other arbitrators shall take into account the stage of the arbitration, the reason, if any, expressed by the third arbitrator for such nonparticipation, and such other matters as they consider appropriate in the circumstances of the case. In the event that the two other arbitrators determine not to continue the arbitration without the participation of the third arbitrator, the administrator on proof satisfactory to it shall declare the office vacant, and a substitute arbitrator shall be appointed pursuant to the provisions of Article 6, unless the parties otherwise agree.

2. If a substitute arbitrator is appointed under either Article 10 or Article 11, the tribunal shall determine at its sole discretion whether all or part of any prior hearings shall be repeated.

III. General Conditions

Representation
Article 12

Any party may be represented in the arbitration. The names, addresses and telephone numbers of representatives shall be communicated in writing to the other parties and to the administrator. Once the tribunal has been established, the parties or their representatives may communicate in writing directly with the tribunal.

Place of Arbitration
Article 13

1. If the parties disagree as to the place of arbitration, the administrator may initially determine the place of arbitration, subject to the power of the tribunal to determine finally the place of arbitration within 60 days after its constitution. All such determinations shall be made having regard for the contentions of the parties and the circumstances of the arbitration.

2. The tribunal may hold conferences or hear witnesses or inspect property or documents at any place it deems appropriate. The parties shall be given sufficient written notice to enable them to be present at any such proceedings.

Language
Article 14

If the parties have not agreed otherwise, the language(s) of the arbitration shall be that of the documents containing the arbitration agreement, subject to the power of the tribunal to determine otherwise based upon the contentions of the parties and the circumstances of the arbitration. The tribunal may order that any documents delivered in another language shall be accompanied by a translation into the language(s) of the arbitration.

Pleas as to Jurisdiction
Article 15

1. The tribunal shall have the power to rule on its own jurisdiction, including any objections with respect to the existence, scope or validity of the arbitration agreement.

2. The tribunal shall have the power to determine the existence or validity of a contract of which an arbitration clause forms a part. Such an arbitration clause shall be treated as an agreement independent of the other terms of the contract. A decision by the tribunal that the contract is null and void shall not for that reason alone render invalid the arbitration clause.

3. A party must object to the jurisdiction of the tribunal or to the arbitrability of a claim or counterclaim no later than the filing of the statement of defense, as provided in Article 3, to the claim or counterclaim that gives rise to the objection. The tribunal may rule on such objections as a preliminary matter or as part of the final award.

Conduct of the Arbitration
Article 16

1. Subject to these rules, the tribunal may conduct the arbitration in whatever manner it considers appropriate, provided that the parties are treated with equality and that each party has the right to be heard and is given a fair opportunity to present its case.

2. The tribunal, exercising its discretion, shall conduct the proceedings with a view to expediting the resolution of the dispute. It may conduct a preparatory conference with the parties for the purpose of organizing, scheduling and agreeing to procedures to expedite the subsequent proceedings.

3. The tribunal may in its discretion direct the order of proof, bifurcate proceedings, exclude cumulative or irrelevant testimony or other evidence, and direct the parties to focus their presentations on issues the decision of which could dispose of all or part of the case.

4. Documents or information supplied to the tribunal by one party shall at the same time be communicated by that party to the other party or parties.

Further Written Statements
Article 17

1. The tribunal may decide whether the parties shall present any written statements in addition to statements of claims and counterclaims and statements of defense, and it shall fix the periods of time for submitting any such statements.

2. The periods of time fixed by the tribunal for the communication of such written statements should not exceed 45 days. However, the tribunal may extend such time limits if it considers such an extension justified.

Notices
Article 18

1. Unless otherwise agreed by the parties or ordered by the tribunal, all notices, statements and written communications may be served on a party by air mail, air courier, facsimile transmission, telex, telegram, or other written forms of electronic communication addressed to the party or its representative at its last known address or by personal service.

2. For the purpose of calculating a period of time under these rules, such period shall begin to run on the day following the day when a notice, statement or written communication is received. If the last day of such period is an official holiday at the place received, the period is extended until the first business day which follows. Official holidays occurring during the running of the period of time are included in calculating the period.

Evidence
Article 19

1. Each party shall have the burden of proving the facts relied on to support its claim or defense.

2. The tribunal may order a party to deliver to the tribunal and to the other parties a summary of the documents and other evidence which that party intends to present in support of its claim, counterclaim or defense.

3. At any time during the proceedings, the tribunal may order parties to produce other documents, exhibits or other evidence it deems necessary or appropriate.

Hearings
Article 20

1. The tribunal shall give the parties at least 30 days' advance notice of the date, time and place of the initial oral hearing. The tribunal shall give reasonable notice of subsequent hearings.

2. At least 15 days before the hearings, each party shall give the tribunal and the other parties the names and addresses of any witnesses it intends to present, the subject of their testimony and the languages in which such witnesses will give their testimony.

3. At the request of the tribunal or pursuant to mutual agreement of the parties, the administrator shall make arrangements for the interpretation of oral testimony or for a record of the hearing.

4. Hearings are private unless the parties agree otherwise or the law provides to the contrary. The tribunal may require any witness or witnesses to retire during the testimony of other witnesses. The tribunal may determine the manner in which witnesses are examined.

5. Evidence of witnesses may also be presented in the form of written statements signed by them.

6. The tribunal shall determine the admissibility, relevance, materiality and weight of the evidence offered by any party. The tribunal shall take into account applicable principles of legal privilege, such as those involving the confidentiality of communications between a lawyer and client.

Interim Measures of Protection
Article 21

1. At the request of any party, the tribunal may take whatever interim measures it deems necessary, including injunctive relief and measures for the protection or conservation of property.

2. Such interim measures may take the form of an interim award, and the tribunal may require security for the costs of such measures.

3. A request for interim measures addressed by a party to a judicial authority shall not be deemed incompatible with the agreement to arbitrate or a waiver of the right to arbitrate.

4. The tribunal may in its discretion apportion costs associated with applications for interim relief in any interim award or in the final award.

Experts
Article 22

1. The tribunal may appoint one or more independent experts to report to it, in writing, on specific issues designated by the tribunal and communicated to the parties.

2. The parties shall provide such an expert with any relevant information or produce for inspection any relevant documents or goods that the expert may require. Any dispute between a party and the expert as to the relevance of the requested information or goods shall be referred to the tribunal for decision.

3. Upon receipt of an expert's report, the tribunal shall send a copy of the report to all parties and shall give the parties an opportunity to express, in writing, their opinion on the report. A party may examine any document on which the expert has relied in such a report.

4. At the request of any party, the tribunal shall give the parties an opportunity to question the expert at a hearing. At this hearing, parties may present expert witnesses to testify on the points at issue.

Default
Article 23

1. If a party fails to file a statement of defense within the time established by the tribunal without showing sufficient cause for such failure, as determined by the tribunal, the tribunal may proceed with the arbitration.

2. If a party, duly notified under these rules, fails to appear at a hearing without showing sufficient cause for such failure, as determined by the tribunal, the tribunal may proceed with the arbitration.

3. If a party, duly invited to produce evidence or take any other steps in the proceedings, fails to do so within the time established by the tribunal without showing sufficient cause for such failure, as determined by the tribunal, the tribunal may make the award on the evidence before it.

Closure of Hearing
Article 24

1. After asking the parties if they have any further testimony or evidentiary submissions and upon receiving negative replies or if satisfied that the record is complete, the tribunal may declare the hearings closed.

2. The tribunal in its discretion, on its own motion or upon application of a party, may reopen the hearings at any time before the award is made.

Waiver of Rules
Article 25

A party who knows that any provision of the rules or requirement under the rules has not been complied with, but proceeds with the arbitration without promptly stating an objection in writing thereto, shall be deemed to have waived the right to object.

Awards, Decisions and Rulings
Article 26

1. When there is more than one arbitrator, any award, decision or ruling of the arbitral tribunal shall be made by a majority of the arbitrators. If any arbitrator fails to sign the award, it shall be accompanied by a statement of the reason for the absence of such signature.

2. When the parties or the tribunal so authorize, the presiding arbitrator may make decisions or rulings on questions of procedure, subject to revision by the tribunal.

Form and Effect of the Award
Article 27

1. Awards shall be made in writing, promptly by the tribunal, and shall be final and binding on the parties. The parties undertake to carry out any such award without delay.

2. The tribunal shall state the reasons upon which the award is based, unless the parties have agreed that no reasons need be given.

3. The award shall contain the date and the place where the award was made, which shall be the place designated pursuant to Article 13.

4. An award may be made public only with the consent of all parties or as required by law.

5. Copies of the award shall be communicated to the parties by the administrator.

6. If the arbitration law of the country where the award is made requires the award to be filed or registered, the tribunal shall comply with such requirement.

7. In addition to making a final award, the tribunal may make interim, interlocutory, or partial orders and awards.

Applicable Laws and Remedies
Article 28

1. The tribunal shall apply the substantive law(s) or rules of law designated by the parties as applicable to the dispute. Failing such a designation by the parties, the tribunal shall apply such law(s) or rules of law as it determines to be appropriate.

2. In arbitrations involving the application of contracts, the tribunal shall decide in accordance with the terms of the contract and shall take into account usages of the trade applicable to the contract.

3. The tribunal shall not decide as amiable compositeur or ex aequo et bono unless the parties have expressly authorized it to do so.

4. A monetary award shall be in the currency or currencies of the contract unless the tribunal considers another currency more appropriate, and the tribunal may award such pre-award and post-award interest, simple or compound, as it considers appropriate, taking into consideration the contract and applicable law.

5. Unless the parties agree otherwise, the parties expressly waive and forego any right to punitive, exemplary or similar damages unless a statute requires that compensatory damages be increased in a specified manner. This provision shall not apply to any award of arbitration costs to a party to compensate for dilatory or bad faith conduct in the arbitration.

Settlement or Other Reasons for Termination
Article 29

1. If the parties settle the dispute before an award is made, the tribunal shall terminate the arbitration and, if requested by all parties, may record the settlement in the form of an award on agreed terms. The tribunal is not obliged to give reasons for such an award.

2. If the continuation of the proceedings becomes unnecessary or impossible for any other reason, the tribunal shall inform the parties of its intention to terminate the proceedings. The tribunal shall thereafter issue an order terminating the arbitration, unless a party raises justifiable grounds for objection.

Interpretation or Correction of the Award
Article 30

1. Within 30 days after the receipt of an award, any party, with notice to the other parties, may request the tribunal to interpret the award or correct any clerical, typographical or computation errors or make an additional award as to claims presented but omitted from the award.

2. If the tribunal considers such a request justified, after considering the contentions of the parties, it shall comply with such a request within 30 days after the request.

Costs
Article 31

The tribunal shall fix the costs of arbitration in its award. The tribunal may apportion such costs among the parties if it determines that such apportionment is reasonable, taking into account the circumstances of the case.

Such costs may include:

(a) the fees and expenses of the arbitrators;
(b) the costs of assistance required by the tribunal, including its experts;
(c) the fees and expenses of the administrator;
(d) the reasonable costs for legal representation of a successful party; and
(e) any such costs incurred in connection with an application for interim or emergency relief pursuant to Article 21.

Compensation of Arbitrators
Article 32

Arbitrators shall be compensated based upon their amount of service, taking into account their stated rate of compensation and the size and complexity of the case. The administrator shall arrange an appropriate daily or hourly rate, based on such considerations, with the parties and with each of the arbitrators as soon as practicable after the commencement of the arbitration. If the parties fail to agree on the terms of compensation, the administrator shall establish an appropriate rate and communicate it in writing to the parties.

Deposit of Costs
Article 33

1. When a party files claims, the administrator may request the filing party to deposit appropriate amounts as an advance for the costs referred to in Article 31, paragraphs (a), (b) and (c).

2. During the course of the arbitral proceedings, the tribunal may request supplementary deposits from the parties.

3. If the deposits requested are not paid in full within 30 days after the receipt of the request, the administrator shall so inform the parties, in order that one or the other of them may make the required payment. If such payments are not made, the tribunal may order the suspension or termination of the proceedings.

4. After the award has been made, the administrator shall render an accounting to the parties of the deposits received and return any unexpended balance to the parties.

Confidentiality
Article 34

Confidential information disclosed during the proceedings by the parties or by witnesses shall not be divulged by an arbitrator or by the administrator. Unless otherwise agreed by the parties, or required by applicable law, the members of the tribunal and the administrator shall keep confidential all matters relating to the arbitration or the award.

Exclusion of Liability
Article 35

The members of the tribunal and the administrator shall not be liable to any party for any act or omission in connection with any arbitration conducted under these rules, except that they may be liable for the consequences of conscious and deliberate wrongdoing.

Interpretation of Rules
Article 36

The tribunal shall interpret and apply these rules insofar as they relate to its powers and duties. The administrator shall interpret and apply all other rules.

Administrative Fees

The administrative fees of the AAA are based on the amount of the claim or counterclaim. Arbitrator compensation is not included in this schedule. Unless the parties agree otherwise, arbitrator compensation and administrative fees are subject to allocation by the arbitrator in the award.

Fees

A nonrefundable initial filing fee is payable in full by a filing party when a claim, counterclaim or additional claim is filed.

A case service fee will be incurred for all cases that proceed to their first hearing. This fee will be payable in advance at the time that the first hearing is scheduled. This fee will be refunded at the conclusion of the case if no hearings have occurred.

However, if the Association is not notified at least 24 hours before the time of the scheduled hearing, the case service fee will remain due and will not be refunded.

These fees will be billed in accordance with the following schedule:

Amount of Claim	Initial Filing Fee	Case Service Fee
Above $0 to $10,000	$500	N/A
Above $10,000 to $75,000	$750	N/A
Above $75,000 to $150,000	$1,250	$750
Above $150,000 to $300,000	$2,750	$1,000
Above $300,000 to $500,000	$4,250	$1,250
Above $500,000 to $1,000,000	$6,000	$2,000
Above $1,000,000 to $7,000,000	$8,500	$2,500
Above $7,000,000 to $10,000,000	$13,000	$3,000
Above $10,000,000	*	*
No Amount Stated**	$3,250	$750

*Contact your local AAA office for fees for claims in excess of $10 million.

** This fee is applicable when no amount can be stated at the time of filing, or when a claim or counterclaim is not for a monetary amount. The fees are subject to increase or decrease when the claim or counterclaim is disclosed.

The minimum fees for any case having three or more arbitrators are $2,750 for the filing fee, plus a $1,000 case service fee.

Suspension for Nonpayment

If arbitrator compensation or administrative charges have not been paid in full, the administrator may so inform the parties in order that one of them may advance the required payment. If such payments are not made, the tribunal may order the suspension or termination of the proceedings. If no arbitrator has yet been appointed, the AAA may suspend the proceedings.

Hearing Room Rental

The fees described above do not cover the rental of hearing rooms, which are available on a rental basis. Check with the AAA for availability and rates.

Statutory Appendices

Appendix S.1
Federal Arbitration Act[1]

TITLE 9. ARBITRATION

CHAPTER 1. GENERAL PROVISIONS[2]

§ 1. "Maritime Transactions" and "Commerce" Defined; Exceptions to Operation of Title

"Maritime transactions", as herein defined, means charter parties, bills of lading of water carriers, agreements relating to wharfage, supplies furnished vessels or repairs to vessels, collisions, or any other matters in foreign commerce which, if the subject of controversy, would be embraced within admiralty jurisdiction; "commerce", as herein defined, means commerce among the several States or with foreign nations, or in any Territory of the United States or in the District of Columbia, or between any such Territory and another, or between any such Territory and any State or foreign nation, or between the District of Columbia and any State or Territory or foreign nation, but nothing herein contained shall apply to contracts of employment of seamen, railroad employees, or any other class of workers engaged in foreign or interstate commerce.

§ 2. Validity, Irrevocability, and Enforcement of Agreements to Arbitrate

A written provision in any maritime transaction or a contract evidencing a transaction involving commerce to settle by arbitration a controversy thereafter arising out of such contract or transaction, or the refusal to perform the whole or any part thereof, or an agreement in writing to submit to arbitration an existing controversy arising out of such a contract, transaction, or refusal, shall be valid, irrevocable, and enforceable, save upon such grounds as exist at law or in equity for the revocation of any contract.

---

1. 9 U.S.C. §§ 1 et scq.
2. F.A.A. §§ 1-14 were enacted into positive law by 61 Stat. 669, ch. 392, § 1 (July 30, 1947).

§ 3.   Stay of Proceedings Where Issue Therein Referable to Arbitration

If any suit or proceeding be brought in any of the courts of the United States upon any issue referable to arbitration under an agreement in writing for such arbitration, the court in which such suit is pending, upon being satisfied that the issue involved in such suit or proceeding is referable to arbitration under such an agreement, shall on application of one of the parties stay the trial of the action until such arbitration has been had in accordance with the terms of the agreement, providing the applicant for the stay is not in default in proceeding with such arbitration.

§ 4.   Failure to Arbitrate under Agreement; Petition to United States Court Having Jurisdiction for Order to Compel Arbitration; Notice and Service Thereof; Hearing and Determination

A party aggrieved by the alleged failure, neglect, or refusal of another to arbitrate under a written agreement for arbitration may petition any United States district court which, save for such agreement, would have jurisdiction under Title 28, in a civil action or in admiralty of the subject matter of a suit arising out of the controversy between the parties, for an order directing that such arbitration proceed in the manner provided for in such agreement. Five days' notice in writing of such application shall be served upon the party in default. Service thereof shall be made in the manner provided by the Federal Rules of Civil Procedure. The court shall hear the parties, and upon being satisfied that the making of the agreement for arbitration or the failure to comply therewith is not in issue, the court shall make an order directing the parties to proceed to arbitration in accordance with the terms of the agreement. The hearing and proceedings, under such agreement, shall be within the district in which the petition for an order directing such arbitration is filed. If the making of the arbitration agreement or the failure, neglect, or refusal to perform the same be in issue, the court shall proceed summarily to the trial thereof. If no jury trial be demanded by the party alleged to be in default, or if the matter in dispute is within admiralty jurisdiction, the court shall hear and determine such issue. Where such an issue is raised, the party alleged to be in default may, except in cases of admiralty, on or before the return day of the notice of application, demand a jury trial of such issue, and upon such demand the court shall make an order referring the issue or issues to a jury in the manner provided by the Federal Rules of Civil Procedure, or may specially call a jury for that purpose. If the jury find that no agreement in writing for arbitration was made or that there is no default in proceeding thereunder, the proceeding shall be dismissed. If the jury find that an agreement for arbitration was made in writing and that there is a default in proceeding thereunder, the court shall make an order summarily directing the parties to proceed with the arbitration in accordance with the terms thereof.

§ 5.   Appointment of Arbitrators or Umpire

If in the agreement provision be made for a method of naming or appointing an arbitrator or arbitrators or an umpire, such method shall be followed; but if no method be provided therein, or if a method be provided and any party thereto shall fail to avail himself of such method, or if for any other reason there shall be a lapse in the naming of an arbitrator or arbitrators or umpire, or in filling a vacancy, then upon the application of either party to the controversy the court shall designate and appoint an arbitrator or arbitrators or umpire, as the case may require, who shall act under the said agreement with the same force and effect as if he or they had been specifically named therein; and unless otherwise provided in the agreement the arbitration shall be by a single arbitrator.

§ 6.   Application Heard as Motion

Any application to the court hereunder shall be made and heard in the manner provided by law for the making and hearing of motions, except as otherwise herein expressly provided.

§ 7.   Witnesses before Arbitrators; Fees; Compelling Attendance

The arbitrators selected either as prescribed in this title or otherwise, or a majority of them, may summon in writing any person to attend before them or any of them as a witness and in a proper case to bring with him or them any book, record, document, or paper which may be deemed material as evidence in the case. The fees for such attendance shall be the same as the fees of witnesses before masters of the United States courts. Said summons shall issue in the name of the arbitrator or arbitrators, or a majority of them, and shall be signed by the arbitrators, or a majority of them, and shall be directed to the said person and shall be served in the same manner as subpoenas to appear and testify before the court; if any person or persons so summoned to testify shall refuse or neglect to obey said summons, upon petition the United States district court for the district in which such arbitrators, or a majority of them, are sitting may compel the attendance of such person or persons before said arbitrator or arbitrators, or punish said person or persons for contempt in the same manner provided by law for securing the attendance of witnesses or their punishment for neglect or refusal to attend in the courts of the United States.

§ 8.   Proceedings Begun by Libel in Admiralty and Seizure of Vessel or Property

If the basis of jurisdiction be a cause of action otherwise justiciable in admiralty, then, notwithstanding anything herein to the contrary, the party claiming to be aggrieved may begin his proceeding hereunder by libel and seizure of the vessel or other property of the other party according to the usual course of admiralty proceedings, and the court shall then have jurisdiction to direct the parties to proceed with the arbitration and shall retain jurisdiction to enter its decree upon the award.

§9.   Award of Arbitrators; Confirmation; Jurisdiction; Procedure

If the parties in their agreement have agreed that a judgment of the court shall be entered upon the award made pursuant to the arbitration, and shall specify the court, then at any time within one year after the award is made any party to the arbitration may apply to the court so specified for an order confirming the award, and thereupon the court must grant such an order unless the award is vacated, modified, or corrected as prescribed in sections 10 and 11 of this title. If no court is specified in the agreement of the parties, then such application may be made to the United States court in and for the district within which such award was made. Notice of the application shall be served upon the adverse party, and thereupon the court shall have jurisdiction of such party as though he had appeared generally in the proceeding. If the adverse party is a resident of the district within which the award was made, such service shall be made upon the adverse party or his attorney as prescribed by law for service of notice of motion in an action in the same court. If the adverse party shall be a nonresident, then the notice of the application shall be served by the marshal of any district within which the adverse party may be found in like manner as other process of the court.

§ 10.   Same; Vacation; Grounds; Rehearing

(a)   In any of the following cases the United States court in and for the district wherein the award was made may make an order vacating the award upon the application of any party to the arbitration—

(1)   Where the award was procured by corruption, fraud, or undue means.[3]

(2)   Where there was evident partiality or corruption in the arbitrators, or either of them.[4]

(3)   Where the arbitrators were guilty of misconduct in refusing to postpone the hearing, upon sufficient cause shown, or in refusing to hear evidence pertinent and material to the controversy; or of any other misbehavior by which the rights of any party have been prejudiced.[5]

(4)   Where the arbitrators exceeded their powers, or so imperfectly executed them that a mutual, final, and definite award upon the subject matter submitted was not made.[6]

(5)   Where an award is vacated and the time within which the agreement required the award to be made has not expired the court may, in its discretion, direct a rehearing by the arbitrators.[7]

---

3. Formerly FAA § 10(a)
4. Formerly FAA § 10(b).
5. Formerly FAA § 10(c).
6. Formerly FAA § 10(d).
7. Formerly FAA § 10(e).

(b)   The United States district court for the district wherein an award was made that was issued pursuant to section 580 of Title 5 may make an order vacating the award upon the application of a person, other than a party to the arbitration, who is adversely affected or aggrieved by the award, if the use of arbitration or the award is clearly inconsistent with the factors set forth in section 572 of Title 5.

§ 11.   Same; Modification or Correction; Grounds; Order

In either of the following cases the United States court in and for the district wherein the award was made may make an order modifying or correcting the award upon the application of any party to the arbitration

(a)   Where there was an evident material miscalculation of figures or an evident material mistake in the description of any person, thing, or property referred to in the award.

(b)   Where the arbitrators have awarded upon a matter not submitted to them, unless it is a matter not affecting the merits of the decision upon the matter submitted.

(c)   Where the award is imperfect in matter of form not affecting the merits of the controversy.

The order may modify and correct the award, so as to effect the intent thereof and promote justice between the parties.

§ 12.   Notice of Motions to Vacate or Modify; Service; Stay of Proceedings

Notice of a motion to vacate, modify, or correct an award must be served upon the adverse party or his attorney within three months after the award is filed or delivered. If the adverse party is a resident of the district within which the award was made, such service shall be made upon the adverse party or his attorney as prescribed by law for service of notice of motion in an action in the same court. If the adverse party shall be a nonresident then he notice of the application shall be served by the marshal of any district within which the adverse party may be found in like manner as other process of the court. For the purposes of the motion any judge who might make an order to stay the proceedings in an action brought in the same court may make an order, to be served with the notice of motion, staying the proceedings of the adverse party to enforce the award.

§ 13.   Papers Filed with Order on Motions; Judgment; Docketing; Force and Effect; Enforcement

The party moving for an order confirming, modifying, or correcting an award shall, at the time such order is filed with the clerk for the entry of judgment thereon, also file the following papers with the clerk:

(a)   The agreement; the selection or appointment, if any, of an additional arbitrator or umpire; and each written extension of the time, if any, within which to make the award.

> (b)   The award.
>
> (c)   Each notice, affidavit, or other paper used upon an application to confirm, modify, or correct the award, and a copy of each order of the court upon such an application.

The judgment shall be docketed as if it was rendered in an action. The judgment so entered shall have the same force and effect, in all respects, as, and be subject to all the provisions of law relating to, a judgment in an action; and it may be enforced as if it had been rendered in an action in the court in which it is entered.

§ 14.   Contracts Not Affected

This title shall not apply to contracts made prior to January 1, 1926.

§ 15.[8]   Inapplicability of the Act of State Doctrine

Enforcement of arbitral agreements, confirmation of arbitral awards, and execution upon judgments based on orders confirming such awards shall not be refused on the basis of the Act of State doctrine.

§ 16.[9]   Appeals

> (a)   An appeal may be taken from—
>
>> (1)   an order—
>>
>>> (A)   refusing a stay of any action under section 3 of this title,
>>>
>>> (B)   denying a petition under section 4 of this title to order arbitration to proceed,
>>>
>>> (C)   denying an application under section 206 of this title to compel arbitration,
>>>
>>> (D)   confirming or denying confirmation of an award or partial award, or
>>>
>>> (E)   modifying, correcting, or vacating an award;
>>
>> (2)   an interlocutory order granting, continuing, or modifying an injunction against an arbitration that is subject to this title; or
>>
>> (3)   a final decision with respect to an arbitration that is subject to this title.
>
> (b)   Except as otherwise provided in section 1292(b) of title 28, an appeal may not be taken from an interlocutory order—
>
>> (1)   granting a stay of any action under section 3 of this title;
>>
>> (2)   directing arbitration to proceed under section 4 of this title;

---

8.   There are two sections 15. This one was enacted on November 16, 1988, the second on November 19, 1988.
9.   This is the second of the two sections 15. It was enacted on November 19, 1988.

(3) compelling arbitration under section 206 of this title; or

(4) refusing to enjoin an arbitration that is subject to this title.

CHAPTER 2. CONVENTION ON THE RECOGNITION AND ENFORCEMENT OF FOREIGN ARBITRAL AWARDS[10]

§ 201. Enforcement of Convention

The Convention on the Recognition and Enforcement of Foreign Arbitral Awards of June 10, 1958, shall be enforced in United States courts in accordance with this chapter.

§ 202. Agreement or Award Falling under the Convention

An arbitration agreement or arbitral award arising out of a legal relationship, whether contractual or not, which is considered as commercial, including a transaction, contract, or agreement described in section 2 of this title, falls under the Convention. An agreement or award arising out of such a relationship which is entirely between citizens of the United States shall be deemed not to fall under the Convention unless that relationship involves property located abroad, envisages performance or enforcement abroad, or has some other reasonable relation with one or more foreign states. For the purpose of this section a corporation is a citizen of the United States if it is incorporated or has its principal place of business in the United States.

§ 203. Jurisdiction; Amount in Controversy

An action or proceeding falling under the Convention shall be deemed to arise under the laws and treaties of the United States. The district courts of the United States (including the courts enumerated in section 460 of title 28) shall have original jurisdiction over such an action or proceeding, regardless of the amount in controversy.

§ 204. Venue

An action or proceeding over which the district courts have jurisdiction pursuant to section 203 of this title may be brought in any such court in which save for the arbitration agreement an action or proceeding with respect to the controversy between the parties could be brought, or in such court for the district and division which embraces the place designated in the agreement as the place of arbitration if such place is within the United States.

---

10. Enacted July 31, 1970.

§ 205. Removal of Cases from State Courts

Where the subject matter of an action or proceeding pending in a State court relates to an arbitration agreement or award falling under the Convention, the defendant or the defendants may, at any time before the trial thereof, remove such action or proceeding to the district court of the United States for the district and division embracing the place where the action or proceeding is pending. The procedure for removal of causes otherwise provided by law shall apply, except that the ground for removal provided in this section need not appear on the face of the complaint but may be shown in the petition for removal. For the purposes of Chapter 1 of this title any action or proceeding removed under this section shall be deemed to have been brought in the district court to which it is removed.

§ 206. Order to Compel Arbitration; Appointment of Arbitrators

A court having jurisdiction under this chapter may direct that arbitration be held in accordance with the agreement at any place therein provided for, whether that place is within or without the United States. Such court may also appoint arbitrators in accordance with the provisions of the agreement.

§ 207. Award of Arbitrators; Confirmation; Jurisdiction; Proceeding

Within three years after an arbitral award falling under the Convention is made, any party to the arbitration may apply to any court having jurisdiction under this chapter for an order confirming the award as against any other party to the arbitration. The court shall confirm the award unless it finds one of the grounds for refusal or deferral of recognition or enforcement of the award specified in the said Convention.

§ 208. Chapter 1; Residual Application

Chapter 1 applies to actions and proceedings brought under this chapter to the extent that chapter is not in conflict with this chapter or the Convention as ratified by the United States.

CHAPTER 3.   INTER-AMERICAN CONVENTION ON INTERNATIONAL COMMERCIAL ARBITRATION[11]

§ 301. Enforcement of Convention

The Inter-American Convention on International Commercial Arbitration of January 30, 1975, shall be enforced in United States courts in accordance with this chapter.

---

11. Enacted August 15, 1990.

§ 302.   Incorporation by Reference

Sections 202, 203, 204, 205, and 207 of this title shall apply to this chapter as if specifically set forth herein, except that for the purposes of this chapter "the Convention" shall mean the Inter-American Convention.

§ 303.   Order to Compel Arbitration; Appointment of Arbitrators; Locale

(a)   A court having jurisdiction under this chapter may direct that arbitration be held in accordance with the agreement at any place therein provided for, whether that place is within or without the United States. The court may also appoint arbitrators in accordance with the provisions of the agreement.

(b)   In the event the agreement does not make provision for the place of arbitration or the appointment of arbitrators, the court shall direct that the arbitration shall be held and the arbitrators be appointed in accordance with Article 3 of the Inter-American Convention.

§ 304.   Recognition and Enforcement of Foreign Arbitral Decisions and Awards; Reciprocity

Arbitral decisions or awards made in the territory of a foreign State shall, on the basis of reciprocity, be recognized and enforced under this chapter only if that State has ratified or acceded to the Inter-American Convention.

§ 305.   Relationship between the Inter-American Convention and the Convention on the Recognition and Enforcement of Foreign Arbitral Awards of June 10, 1958

When the requirements for application of both the Inter-American Convention and the Convention on the Recognition and Enforcement of Foreign Arbitral Awards of June 10, 1958, are met, determination as to which Convention applies shall, unless otherwise expressly agreed, be made as follows:

(1)   If a majority of the parties to the arbitration agreement are citizens of a State or States that have ratified or acceded to the Inter-American Convention and are member States of the Organization of American States, the Inter-American Convention shall apply.

(2)   In all other cases the Convention on the Recognition and Enforcement of Foreign Arbitral Awards of June 10, 1958, shall apply.

§ 306.   Applicable Rules of Inter-American Commercial Arbitration Commission

(a)   For the purposes of this chapter the rules of procedure of the Inter-American Commercial Arbitration Commission referred to in Article 3 of the Inter-American Convention shall, subject to subsection (b) of this section, be those rules as promulgated by the Commission on July 1, 1988.

(b)   In the event the rules of procedure of the Inter-American Commercial Arbitration Commission are modified or amended in accordance with the procedures for amendment of the rules of that Commission, the Secretary of State, by regulation in accordance with section 553 of title 5, consistent with the aims and purposes of this Convention, may prescribe that such modifications or amendments shall be effective for purposes of this chapter.

§ 307. Chapter 1; Residual Application

Chapter 1 applies to actions and proceedings brought under this chapter to the extent chapter 1 is not in conflict with this chapter or the Inter-American Convention as ratified by the United States.

Appendix S.2
National Conference of Commissioners on Uniform State Laws
Uniform Arbitration Act[1]

§ 1.   Validity of Arbitration Agreement

A written agreement to submit any existing controversy to arbitration or a provision in a written contract to submit to arbitration any controversy thereafter arising between the parties is valid, enforceable and irrevocable, save upon such grounds as exist at law or in equity for the revocation of any contract. This act also applies to arbitration agreements between employers and employees or between their respective representatives (unless otherwise provided in the agreement).

§ 2.   Proceedings to Compel or Stay Arbitration

(a)   On application of a party showing an agreement described in Section 1, and the posing party's refusal to arbitrate, the Court shall order the parties to proceed with arbitration, but if the opposing party denies the existence of the agreement to arbitrate, the Court shall proceed summarily to the determination of the issue so raised and shall order arbitration if found for the moving party, otherwise, the application shall be denied.

(b)   On application, the court may stay an arbitration proceeding commenced or threatened on a showing that there is no agreement to arbitrate. Such an issue, when in substantial and bona fide dispute, shall be forthwith and summarily tried and the stay ordered if found for the moving party. If found for the opposing party, the court shall order the parties to proceed to arbitration.

(c)   If an issue referable to arbitration under the alleged agreement is involved in an action or proceeding pending in a court having jurisdiction to hear applications under subdivision (a) of this Section, the

---

1. As adopted by the National Conference of Commissioners on Uniform State Laws in 1955, and amended in 1956.

application shall be made therein. Otherwise and subject to Section 18, the application may be made in any court of competent jurisdiction.

(d) Any action or proceeding involving an issue subject to arbitration shall be stayed if an order for arbitration or an application therefor has been made under this section or, if the issue is severable, the stay may be with respect thereto only. When the application is made in such action or proceeding, the order for arbitration shall include such stay.

(e) An order for arbitration shall not be refused on the ground that the claim in issue lacks merit or bona fides or because any fault or grounds for the claim sought to be arbitrated have not been shown.

§ 3.   Appointment of Arbitrators by Court

If the arbitration agreement provides a method of appointment of arbitrators, this method shall be followed. In the absence thereof, or if the agreed method fails or for any reason cannot be followed, or when an arbitrator appointed fails or is unable to act and his successor has not been duly appointed, the court on application of a party shall appoint one or more arbitrators. An arbitrator so appointed has all the powers of one specifically named in the agreement.

§ 4.   Majority Action by Arbitrators

The powers of the arbitrators may be exercised by a majority unless otherwise provided by the agreement or by this act.

§ 5.   Hearing

Unless otherwise provided by the agreement:

(a) The arbitrators shall appoint a time and place for the hearing and cause notification to the parties to be served personally or by registered mail not less than five days before the hearing. Appearance at the hearing waives such notice. The arbitrators may adjourn the hearing from time to time as necessary and, on request of a party and for good cause, or upon their own motion may postpone the hearing to a time not later than the date fixed by the agreement for making the award unless the parties consent to a later date. The arbitrators may hear and determine the controversy upon the evidence produced notwithstanding the failure of a party duly notified to appear. The court on application may direct the arbitrators to proceed promptly with the hearing and determination of the controversy.

(b) The parties are entitled to be heard, to present evidence material to the controversy and to cross-examine witnesses appearing at the hearing.

(c) The hearing shall be conducted by all the arbitrators but a majority may determine any question and render a final award. If, during the course of the hearing, an arbitrator for any reason ceases to act, the remaining arbitrator or arbitrators appointed to act as neutrals may continue with the hearing and determination of the controversy.

§6. Representation by Attorney

A party has the right to be represented by an attorney at any proceeding or hearing under this act. A waiver thereof prior to the proceeding or hearing is ineffective.

§7. Witnesses, Subpoenas, Depositions

(a)   The arbitrators may issue (cause to be issued) subpoenas for the attendance of witnesses and for the production of books, records, documents and other evidence, and shall have the power to administer oaths. Subpoenas so issued shall be served, and upon application to the Court by a party or the arbitrators, enforced, in the manner provided by law for the service and enforcement of subpoenas in a civil action.

(b)   On application of a party and for use as evidence, the arbitrators may permit a deposition to be taken, in the manner and upon the terms designated by the arbitrators, of a witness who cannot be subpoenaed or is unable to attend the hearing.

(c)   All provisions of law compelling a person under subpoena to testify are applicable.

(d)   Fees for attendance as a witness shall be the same as for a witness in the _____Court.

§8. Award

(a)   The award shall be in writing and signed by the arbitrators joining in the award. The arbitrators shall deliver a copy to each party personally or by registered mail, or as provided in the agreement.

(b)   An award shall be made within the time fixed therefor by the agreement or, if not so fixed, within such time as the court orders on application of a party. The parties may extend the time in writing either before or after the expiration thereof. A party waives the objection that an award was not made within the time required unless he notifies the arbitrators of his objection prior to the delivery of the award to him.

§9. Change of Award by Arbitrators

On application of a party or, if an application to the court is pending under Sections 11, 12 or 13, on submission to the arbitrators by the court under such conditions as the court may order, the arbitrators may modify or correct the award upon the grounds stated in paragraphs (1) and (3) of subdivision (a) of Section 13, or for the purpose of clarifying the award. The application shall be made within twenty days after delivery of the award to the applicant. Written notice thereof shall be given forthwith to the opposing party, stating he must serve his objections thereto, if any, within ten days from the notice. The award so modified or corrected is subject to the provisions of Sections 11, 12 and 13.

§ 10.   Fees and Expenses of Arbitration

Unless otherwise provided in the agreement to arbitrate, the arbitrators' expenses and fees, together with other expenses, not including counsel fees, incurred in the conduct of the arbitration, shall be paid as provided in the award.

§ 11.   Confirmation of an Award

Upon application of a party, the Court shall confirm an award, unless within the time limits hereinafter imposed grounds are urged for vacating or modifying or correcting the award, in which case the court shall proceed as provided in Sections 12 and 13.

§ 12.   Vacating an Award

(a)   Upon application of a party, the court shall vacate an award where:

   (1)   The award was procured by corruption, fraud or other undue means;
   (2)   There was evident partiality by an arbitrator appointed as a neutral or corruption in any of the arbitrators or misconduct prejudicing the rights of any party;
   (3)   The arbitrators exceeded their powers;
   (4)   The arbitrators refused to postpone the hearing upon sufficient cause being therefor or refused to hear evidence material to the controversy or otherwise so conducted the earing, contrary to the provisions of Section 5, as to prejudice substantially the rights of a party; or
   (5)   There was no arbitration agreement and the issue was not adversely determined in proceedings under Section 2 and the party did not participate in the arbitration hearing without raising the objection; but the fact that the relief was such that it could not or would not be granted by a court of law or equity is not ground for vacating or refusing to confirm the award.

(b)   An application under this Section shall be made within ninety days after delivery of a copy of the award to the applicant, except that, if predicated upon corruption, fraud or other undue means, it shall be made within ninety days after such grounds are known or should have been known.

(c)   In vacating the award on grounds other than stated in clause (5) of Subsection (a) the court may order a rehearing before new arbitrators chosen as provided in the agreement, or in the absence thereof, by the court in accordance with Section 3, or if the award is vacated on grounds set forth in clauses (3) and (4) of Subsection (a) the court may order a rehearing before the arbitrators who made the award or their successors appointed in accordance with Section 3. The time within which the agreement requires the award to be made is applicable to the rehearing and commences from the date of the order.

(d)   If the application to vacate is denied and no motion to modify or correct the award is ending, the court shall confirm the award.

§ 13.   Modification or Correction of Award

(a)   Upon application made within ninety days after delivery of a copy of the award to the applicant, the court shall modify or correct the award where:

(1)   There was an evident miscalculation of figures or an evident mistake in the description of any person, thing or property referred to in the award;

(2)   The arbitrators have awarded upon a matter not submitted to them and the award may be corrected without affecting the merits of the decision upon the issues submitted; or

(3)   The award is imperfect in a matter of form, not affecting the merits of the controversy.

(b)   If the application is granted, the court shall modify and correct the award so as to effect its intent and shall confirm the award as so modified and corrected. Otherwise, the court shall confirm the award as made.

(c)   An application to modify or correct an award may be joined in the alternative with an application to vacate the award.

§ 14.   Judgment or Decree on Award

Upon the granting of an order confirming, modifying or correcting an award, judgment or decree shall be entered in conformity therewith and be enforced as any other judgment or decree. Costs of the application and of the proceedings subsequent thereto, and disbursements may be awarded by the court.

§ 15.   Judgment Roll, Docketing

(a)   On entry of judgment or decree, the clerk shall prepare the judgment roll consisting, to the extent filed, of the following:

(1)   The agreement and each written extension of the time within which to make the award;

(2)   The award;

(3)   A copy of the order confirming, modifying or correcting the award; and

(4)   A copy of the judgment or decree.

(b)   The judgment or decree may be docketed as if rendered in an action.

§ 16.   Applications to Court

Except as otherwise provided, an application to the court under this act shall be by motion and shall be heard in the manner and upon the notice provided by law or rule of court for the making and hearing of motions. Unless the parties have agreed otherwise, notice of an initial application for an order shall be served in the manner provided by law for the service of a summons in an action.

§ 17.   Court, Jurisdiction

The term "court" means any court of competent jurisdiction of this State. The making of an agreement described in Section 1 providing for arbitration in this State confers jurisdiction on the court to enforce the agreement under this Act and to enter judgment on an award thereunder.

§ 18.   Venue

An initial application shall be made to the court of the [county] in which the agreement provides the arbitration hearing shall be held or, if the hearing has been held, in the county in which it was held. Otherwise the application shall be made in the [county] where the adverse party resides or has a place of business or, if he has no residence or place of business in this State, to the court of any [county]. All subsequent applications shall be made to the court hearing the initial application unless the court otherwise directs.

§ 19.   Appeals

(a)   An appeal may be taken from:

(1)   An order denying an application to compel arbitration made under Section 2;
(2)   An order granting an application to stay arbitration made under Section 2(b);
(3)   An order confirming or denying confirmation of an award;
(4)   An order modifying or correcting an award;
(5)   An order vacating an award without directing a rehearing; or
(6)   A judgment or decree entered pursuant to the provisions of this act.

(b)   The appeal shall be taken in the manner and to the same extent as from orders or judgments in a civil action.

§ 20.   Act Not Retroactive

This act applies only to agreements made subsequent to the taking effect of this act.

§ 21.   Uniformity of Interpretation

This act shall be so construed as to effectuate its general purpose to make uniform the law of those states which enact it.

§ 22.   Constitutionality

If any provision of this act or the application thereof to any person or circumstance is held invalid, the invalidity shall not affect other provisions or applications of the act which can be given effect without the invalid provision or application, and to this end the provisions of this act are severable.

§ 23.   Short Title

This act may be cited as the Uniform Arbitration Act.

§ 24.   Repeal

All acts or parts of acts which are inconsistent with the provisions of this act are hereby repealed.

§ 25.   Time of Taking Effect

This act shall take effect _____

Appendix S.3
National Conference of Commissioners on Uniform State Laws
Uniform Arbitration Act (2000)

Revisions adopted by NCCUSL in August 2000

§ 1. Definitions

In this [Act]:

   (1) "Arbitration organization" means a neutral association, agency, board, commission, or other entity that initiates, sponsors, or administers arbitration proceedings or is involved in the appointment of arbitrators.
   (2) "Arbitrator" means an individual appointed to render an award in a controversy between persons who are parties to an agreement to arbitrate.
   (3) "Authenticate" means:

   (A) to sign; or
   (B) to execute or adopt a record by attaching to or logically associating with the record, an electronic sound, symbol or process with the intent to sign the record.

   (4) "Court" means [a court of competent jurisdiction in this State].
   (5) "Knowledge" means actual knowledge.
   (6) "Person" means an individual, corporation, business trust, estate, trust, partnership, limited liability company, association, joint venture, government; governmental subdivision, agency, or instrumentality; public corporation; or any other legal or commercial entity.
   (7) "Record" means information that is inscribed on a tangible medium or that is stored in an electronic or other medium and is retrievable in perceivable form.

§ 2. Notice

Unless the parties to an agreement to arbitrate otherwise agree or except as otherwise provided in this [Act], a person gives notice to another person by taking action that is reasonably necessary to inform the other person in ordinary course, whether or not the other person acquires knowledge of the notice. A person has notice if the person has knowledge of the notice or has received notice. A person receives notice when it comes to the person's attention or the notice is delivered at the person's place of residence or place of business, or at another location held out by the person as a place of delivery of such communications.

§ 3.   When [Act] Applies

(a)   Before [date], this [Act] governs agreements to arbitrate entered into:

    (1)   on or after [the effective date of this [Act]]; and

    (2)   before [the effective date of this [Act]], if all parties to the agreement to arbitrate or to arbitration proceedings agree in a record to be governed by this [Act].

(b)   On or after [date], this [Act] governs agreements to arbitrate even if the arbitration agreement was entered into prior to [the effective date of this [Act]].

§ 4.   Effect of Agreement to Arbitrate; Nonwaivable Provisions

(a)   Except as otherwise provided in subsection (b) and (c), the parties to an agreement to arbitrate or to an arbitration proceeding may waive or vary the requirements of this [Act] to the extent permitted by law.

(b)   Before a controversy arises that is subject to an agreement to arbitrate, the parties to the agreement may not:

    (1)   waive or vary the requirements of Section 5(a), 6(a), 8, 17(a), 17(b), 26, or 28;

    (2)   unreasonably restrict the right under Section 9 to notice of the initiation of an arbitration proceeding;

    (3)   unreasonably restrict the right under Section 12 to disclosure of any facts by a neutral arbitrator; or

    (4)   waive the right under Section 16 of a party to an agreement to arbitrate to be represented by a lawyer at any proceeding or hearing under this [Act], except that an employer and a labor organization may waive the right to representation by a lawyer in a labor arbitration.

(c)   The parties to an agreement to arbitrate may not waive or vary the requirements of this section or Section 3(a)(1), 3(b), 7, 14, 18, 20(c), 20(d), 22, 23, 24, 25(a), 25(b), 29, 30, 31, or 32.

§ 5.   [Application] to Court

(a)   Except as otherwise provided in Section 28, an [application] for judicial relief under this [Act] must be made by [motion] to the court and heard in the manner and upon the notice provided by law or rule of court for making and hearing [motions].

(b) Notice of an initial [motion] to the court under this [Act] must be served in the manner provided by law for the service of a summons in a civil action unless a civil action is already pending involving the agreement to arbitrate.

§ 6. Validity of Agreement to Arbitrate

(a) An agreement contained in a record to submit to arbitration any existing or subsequent controversy arising between the parties to the agreement is valid, enforceable, and irrevocable except upon a ground that exists at law or in equity for the revocation of contract.

(b) The court shall decide whether an agreement to arbitrate exists or a controversy is subject to an agreement to arbitrate.

(c) An arbitrator shall decide whether a condition precedent to arbitrability has been fulfilled and whether a contract containing a valid agreement to arbitrate is enforceable.

(d) If a party to a judicial proceeding challenges the existence of, or claims that a controversy is not subject to, an agreement to arbitrate, the arbitration proceeding may continue pending final resolution of the issue by the court, unless the court otherwise orders.

§ 7. [Motion] to Compel or Stay Arbitration

(a) On [motion] of a person showing an agreement to arbitrate and alleging another person's refusal to arbitrate pursuant to the agreement, the court shall order the parties to arbitrate if the refusing party does not appear or does not oppose the [motion]. If the refusing party opposes the [motion], the court shall proceed summarily to decide the issue. Unless the court finds that there is no enforceable agreement to arbitrate, it shall order the parties to arbitrate. If the court finds that there is no enforceable agreement, it may not order the parties to arbitrate.

(b) On [motion] of a person alleging that an arbitration proceeding has been initiated or threatened but that there is no agreement to arbitrate, the court shall proceed summarily to decide the issue. If the court finds that there is an enforceable agreement to arbitrate, it shall order the parties to arbitrate. If the court finds that there is no enforceable agreement, it may not order the parties to arbitrate.

(c) The court may not refuse to order arbitration because the claim subject to arbitration lacks merit or grounds for the claim have not been established.

(d) If a proceeding involving a claim referable to arbitration under an alleged agreement to arbitrate is pending in court, a [motion] under this section must be filed in that court. Otherwise a [motion] under this section may be filed in any court as required by Section 27.

(e) If a party files a [motion] with the court to order arbitration under this section, the court shall on just terms stay any judicial proceeding that involves a claim alleged to be subject to the arbitration until the court renders a final decision under this section.

(f) If the court orders arbitration, the court shall on just terms stay any judicial proceeding that involves a claim subject to the arbitration. If a claim subject to the arbitration is severable, the court may sever it and limit the stay to that claim.

§ 8.   Provisional Remedies

(a) Before an arbitrator is appointed and is authorized and able to act, the court, upon [motion] of a party to an arbitration proceeding and for good cause shown, may enter an order for provisional remedies to protect the effectiveness of the arbitration proceeding to the same extent and under the same conditions as if the controversy were the subject of a civil action.

(b) After an arbitrator is appointed and is authorized and able to act, the arbitrator may issue such orders for provisional remedies, including interim awards, as the arbitrator finds necessary to protect the effectiveness of the arbitration proceeding and to promote the fair and expeditious resolution of the controversy, to the same extent and under the same conditions as if the controversy were the subject of a civil action. After an arbitrator is appointed and is authorized and able to act, a party to an arbitration proceeding may move the court for a provisional remedy only if the matter is urgent and the arbitrator is not able to act timely or if the arbitrator cannot provide an adequate remedy.

(c) A [motion] to a court for a provisional remedy under subsection (a) or (b) does not waive any right of arbitration.

§ 9.   Initiation of Arbitration

(a) A person initiates an arbitration proceeding by giving notice in a record to the other parties to the agreement to arbitrate in the agreed manner between the parties or, in the absence of agreement, by mail certified or registered, return receipt requested and obtained, or by service as authorized for the initiation of a civil action. The notice must describe the nature of the controversy and the remedy sought.

(b) Unless a person interposes an objection as to lack or insufficiency of notice under Section 15(c) not later than the commencement of the arbitration hearing, the person's appearance at the hearing waives any objection to lack of or insufficiency of notice.

§ 10.   Consolidation of Separate Arbitration Proceedings

(a) Except as otherwise provided in subsection (c), upon [motion] of a party to an agreement to arbitrate or to an arbitration proceeding, the court may order consolidation of separate arbitration proceedings as to all or some of the claims if:

(1)   there are separate agreements to arbitrate or separate arbitration proceedings between the same persons or one of them is a party to a separate agreement to arbitrate or a separate arbitration proceeding with a third person;

(2)   the claims subject to the agreements to arbitrate arise in substantial part from the same transaction or series of related transactions;

(3)   the existence of a common issue of law or fact creates the possibility of conflicting decisions in the separate arbitration proceedings; and

(4)   prejudice resulting from a failure to consolidate is not outweighed by the risk of undue delay or prejudice to the rights of or hardship to parties opposing consolidation.

(b)   The court may order consolidation of separate arbitration proceedings as to certain claims and allow other claims to be resolved in separate arbitration proceedings.

(c)   The court may not order consolidation of the claims of a party to an agreement to arbitrate which prohibits consolidation.

§ 11.   Appointment of Arbitrator; Service As a Neutral Arbitrator

(a)   If the parties to an agreement to arbitrate agree on a method for appointing an arbitrator, that method must be followed, unless the method fails. If the parties have not agreed on a method, the agreed method fails, or an arbitrator appointed fails or is unable to act and a successor has not been appointed, the court, on [motion] of a party to the arbitration proceeding, shall appoint the arbitrator. The arbitrator so appointed has all the powers of an arbitrator designated in the agreement to arbitrate or appointed pursuant to the agreed method.

(b)   An arbitrator who has a known, direct, and material interest in the outcome of the arbitration proceeding or a known, existing, and substantial relationship with a party may not serve as a neutral arbitrator.

§ 12.   Disclosure by Arbitrator

(a)   Before accepting appointment, an individual who is requested to serve as an arbitrator, after making a reasonable inquiry, shall disclose to all parties to the agreement to arbitrate and arbitration proceeding and to any other arbitrators any known facts that a reasonable person would consider likely to affect the impartiality of the arbitrator in the arbitration proceeding, including:

(1)   a financial or personal interest in the outcome of the arbitration proceeding; and

(2)   an existing or past relationship with any of the parties to the agreement to arbitrate or the arbitration proceeding, their counsel or representatives, witnesses, or the other arbitrators.

(b)   An arbitrator has a continuing obligation to disclose to all parties to the agreement to arbitrate and arbitration proceedings and to any other arbitrators any facts that the arbitrator learns after accepting appointment which a reasonable person would consider likely to affect the impartiality of the arbitrator.

(c)   If an arbitrator discloses a fact required by subsection (a) or (b) to be disclosed and a party timely objects to the appointment or continued service of the arbitrator based upon the disclosure, the objection may be a ground to vacate the award under Section 23(a)(2).

(d)   If the arbitrator did not disclose a fact as required by subsection (a) or (b), upon timely objection of a party, an award may be vacated under Section 23(a)(2).

(e)   An arbitrator appointed as a neutral who does not disclose a known, direct, and material interest in the outcome of the arbitration proceeding or a known, existing, and substantial relationship with a party is presumed to act with evident partiality under Section 23(a)(2).

(f)   If the parties to an arbitration proceeding agree to the procedures of an arbitration organization or any other procedures for challenges to arbitrators before an award is made, substantial compliance with those procedures is a condition precedent to a [motion] to vacate an award on that ground under Section 23(a)(2).

§ 13.   Action by Majority

If there is more than one arbitrator, the powers of the arbitrators must be exercised by a majority of them.

§ 14.   Immunity of Arbitrator; Competency to Testify; Attorney's Fees and Costs

(a)   An arbitrator or an arbitration organization acting in such capacity is immune from civil liability to the same extent as a judge of a court of this State acting in a judicial capacity.

(b)   The immunity afforded by this section supplements any other immunity.

(c)   If an arbitrator does not make a disclosure required by Section 12, the nondisclosure does not cause a loss of immunity under this section.

(d)   In any judicial, administrative, or similar proceeding, an arbitrator or representative of an arbitration organization is not competent to testify or required to produce records as to any statement, conduct, decision, or ruling occurring during the arbitration proceeding to the same extent as a judge of a court of this State acting in a judicial capacity. This subsection does not apply:

(1)   to the extent necessary to determine the claim of an arbitrator or an arbitration organization or a representative of the arbitration organization against a party to the arbitration proceeding or

(2)   if a party to the arbitration proceeding files a [motion] to vacate an award under Section 23(a)(1) or (2) and establishes prima facie that a ground for vacating the award exists.

(e)   If a person commences a civil action against an arbitrator, an arbitration organization, or a representative of an arbitration organization arising from the services of the arbitrator, organization, or representative or if a person seeks to compel an arbitrator or a representative of an arbitration organization to testify in violation of subsection (d), and the court decides that the arbitrator, arbitration organization, or representative of an arbitration organization is immune from civil liability or that the arbitrator or representative of the organization is incompetent to testify, the court shall award to the arbitrator, organization, or representative reasonable attorney's fees and other reasonable expenses of litigation.

§ 15.   Arbitration Process

(a)   The arbitrator may conduct the arbitration in such manner as the arbitrator considers appropriate so as to aid in the fair and expeditious disposition of the proceeding. The authority conferred upon the arbitrator includes the power to hold conferences with the parties to the arbitration proceeding before the hearing and to determine the admissibility, relevance, materiality and weight of any evidence.

(b)   The arbitrator may decide a request for summary disposition of a claim or particular issue by agreement of all interested parties or upon request of one party to the arbitration proceeding if that party gives notice to all other parties to the arbitration proceeding and the other parties have a reasonable opportunity to respond.

(c)   The arbitrator shall set a time and place for a hearing and give notice of the hearing not less than five days before the hearing. Unless a party to the arbitration proceeding interposes an objection to lack of or insufficiency of notice not later than the commencement of the hearing, the party's appearance at the hearing waives the objection. Upon request of a party to the arbitration proceeding and for good cause shown, or upon the arbitrator's own initiative, the arbitrator may adjourn the hearing from time to time as necessary but may not postpone the hearing to a time later than that fixed by the agreement to arbitrate for making the award unless the parties to the arbitration proceeding consent to a later date. The arbitrator may hear and decide the controversy upon the evidence produced although a party who was duly notified of the arbitration proceeding did not appear. The court, on request, may direct the arbitrator to promptly conduct the hearing and render a timely decision.

(d)   If an arbitrator orders a hearing under subsection (c), the parties to the arbitration proceeding are entitled to be heard, to present evidence material to the controversy, and to cross-examine witnesses appearing at the hearing.

(e)   If there is more than one arbitrator, all of them shall conduct the hearing under subsection (c); however, a majority shall decide any issue and make a final award.

(f)   If an arbitrator ceases, or is unable, to act during the arbitration proceeding, a replacement arbitrator must be appointed in accordance with Section 11 to continue the hearing and to decide the controversy.

§ 16.   Representation by Lawyer

A party to an arbitration proceeding may be represented by a lawyer.

§ 17.   Witnesses; Subpoenas; Depositions; Discovery

(a)   An arbitrator may issue a subpoena for the attendance of a witness and for the production of records and other evidence at any hearing and may administer oaths. A subpoena must be served in the manner for service of subpoenas in a civil action and, upon [motion] to the court by a party to the arbitration proceeding or the arbitrator, enforced in the manner for enforcement of subpoenas in a civil action.

(b)   On request of a party to or a witness in an arbitration proceeding, an arbitrator may permit a deposition of any witness, including a witness who cannot be subpoenaed for or is unable to attend a hearing, to be taken under conditions determined by the arbitrator for use as evidence in order to make the proceeding fair, expeditious, and cost effective.

(c)   An arbitrator may permit such discovery as the arbitrator decides is appropriate in the circumstances, taking into account the needs of the parties to the arbitration proceeding and other affected persons and the desirability of making the proceeding fair, expeditious, and cost effective.

(d)   If an arbitrator permits discovery under subsection (c), the arbitrator may order a party to the arbitration proceeding to comply with the arbitrator's discovery-related orders, including the issuance of a subpoena for the attendance of a witness and for the production of records and other evidence at a discovery proceeding, and may take action against a party to the arbitration proceeding who does not comply to the extent permitted by law as if the controversy were the subject of a civil action in this State.

(e)   An arbitrator may issue a protective order to prevent the disclosure of privileged information, confidential information, trade secrets, and other information protected from disclosure as if the controversy were the subject of a civil action in this State.

(f)   All laws compelling a person under subpoena to testify and all fees for attending a judicial proceeding, a deposition, or a discovery proceeding as a witness apply to an arbitration proceeding as if the controversy were the subject of a civil action in this State.

(g)   The court may enforce a subpoena or discovery-related order for the attendance of a witness within this State and for the production of records and other evidence issued by an arbitrator in connection with an arbitration proceeding in another State upon conditions determined by the court in order to make the arbitration proceeding fair, expeditious, and cost effective. A subpoena or discovery-related order issued by an arbitrator must be served in the manner provided by law for service of subpoenas in a civil action in this State and, upon [motion] to the court by a party to the arbitration proceeding or the arbitrator, enforced in the manner provided by law for enforcement of subpoenas in a civil action in this State.

§ 18.   Court Enforcement of Pre-award Ruling by Arbitrator

If an arbitrator makes a pre-award ruling in favor of a party to the arbitration proceeding, the party may request the arbitrator to incorporate the ruling into an award under Section 19. The successful party may file a [motion] to the court for an expedited order to confirm the award under Section 22, in which case the court shall proceed summarily to decide the [motion]. The court shall issue an order to confirm the award unless the court vacates, modifies, or corrects the award of the arbitrator pursuant to Sections 23 and 24.

§ 19.   Award

(a)   An arbitrator shall make a record of an award. The record must be authenticated by any arbitrator who concurs with the award. The arbitrator or the arbitration organization shall give notice of the award, including a copy of the award, to each party to the arbitration proceeding.

(b)   An award must be made within the time specified by the agreement to arbitrate or, if not specified therein, within the time ordered by the court. The court may extend or the parties to the arbitration proceeding may agree in a record to extend the time. The court or the parties may do so within or after the time specified or ordered. A party waives any objection that an award was not timely made unless the party gives notice of the objection to the arbitrator before receiving notice of the award.

§ 20.   Change of Award by Arbitrator

(a)   On [motion] to an arbitrator by a party to the arbitration proceeding, the arbitrator may modify or correct an award:

   (1)   upon the grounds stated in Section 24(a)(1) or (3);
   (2)   because the arbitrator has not made a final and definite award upon a claim submitted by the parties to the arbitration proceeding; or
   (3)   to clarify the award.

(b)   A [motion] under subsection (a) must be made and served on all parties within 20 days after the movant receives notice of the award.

(c)   A party to the arbitration proceeding must serve any objections to the [motion] within 10 days after receipt of the notice.

(d)   If a [motion] to the court is pending under Section 22, 23, or 24, the court may submit the claim to the arbitrator to consider whether to modify or correct the award:

   (1)   upon the grounds stated in Section 24(a)(1) or (3);
   (2)   because the arbitrator has not made a final and definite award upon a claim submitted by the parties to the arbitration proceeding; or
   (3)   to clarify the award.

(e)   An award modified or corrected pursuant to this section is subject to Sections 22, 23, and 24.

§ 21.   Remedies; Fees and Expenses of Arbitration Proceeding

(a)   An arbitrator may award punitive damages or other exemplary relief if such an award is authorized by law in a civil action involving the same claim and the evidence produced at the hearing justifies the award under the legal standards otherwise applicable to the claim.

(b)   An arbitrator may award attorney's fees and other reasonable expenses of arbitration if such an award is authorized by law in a civil action involving the same claim or by the agreement of the parties to the arbitration proceeding.

(c)   As to all remedies other than those authorized by subsections (a) and (b), an arbitrator may order such remedies as the arbitrator considers just and appropriate under the circumstances of the arbitration proceeding. The fact that such a remedy could not or would not be granted by the court is not a ground for refusing to confirm an award under Section 22 or for vacating an award under Section 23.

(d)   An arbitrator's expenses and fees, together with other expenses, must be paid as provided in the award.

(e)   If an arbitrator awards punitive damages or other exemplary relief under subsection (a), the arbitrator shall specify in the award the basis in fact justifying and the basis in law authorizing the award and state separately the amount of the punitive damages or other exemplary relief.

§ 22. Confirmation of Award

After a party to the arbitration proceeding receives notice of an award, the party may file a [motion] with the court for an order confirming the award, at which time the court shall issue such an order unless the award is modified or corrected pursuant to Section 20 or 24 or is vacated pursuant to Section 23.

§ 23. Vacating Award

(a) Upon [motion] of a party to the arbitration proceeding, the court shall vacate an award if:

    (1) the award was procured by corruption, fraud, or other undue means;

    (2) there was:

        (A) evident partiality by an arbitrator appointed as a neutral;

        (B) corruption by an arbitrator; or

        (C) misconduct by an arbitrator prejudicing the rights of a party to the arbitration proceeding;

    (3) an arbitrator refused to postpone the hearing upon showing of sufficient cause for postponement, refused to consider evidence material to the controversy, or otherwise conducted the hearing contrary to Section 15, so as to prejudice substantially the rights of a party to the arbitration proceeding;

    (4) an arbitrator exceeded the arbitrator's powers;

    (5) (5) there was no agreement to arbitrate, unless the person participated in the arbitration proceeding without raising the objection under Section 15(c) not later than the commencement of the arbitration hearing; or

    (6) the arbitration was conducted without proper notice of the initiation of an arbitration as required in Section 9 so as to prejudice substantially the rights of a party to the arbitration proceeding.

(b) A [motion] under this section must be filed within 90 days after the movant receives notice of the award in a record pursuant to Section 19 or within 90 days after the movant receives notice of an arbitrator's award in a record on a [motion] to modify or correct an award pursuant to Section 20, unless the [motion] is predicated upon the ground that the award was procured by corruption, fraud, or other undue means, in which case it must be filed within 90 days after such a ground is known or by the exercise of reasonable care should have been known by the movant.

(c) In vacating an award on a ground other than that set forth in subsection (a)(5), the court may order a rehearing before a new arbitrator. If the award is vacated on a ground stated in subsection (a)(3), (4), or (6), the court may order a rehearing before the arbitrator who made the award or the arbitrator's successor. The arbitrator must render the decision in the rehearing within the same time as that provided in Section 19(b) for an award.

(d)   If a [motion] to vacate an award is denied and a [motion] to modify or correct the award is not pending, the court shall confirm the award.

§ 24.   Modification or Correction of Award

(a)   Upon [motion] filed within 90 days after the movant receives notice of the award in a record pursuant to Section 19 or within 90 days after the movant receives notice of an arbitrator's award in a record on a [motion] to modify or correct an award pursuant to Section 20, the court shall modify or correct the award if:

    (1)   there was an evident mathematical miscalculation or an evident mistake in the description of a person, thing, or property referred to in the award;

    (2)   the arbitrator has made an award on a claim not submitted to the arbitrator and the award may be corrected without affecting the merits of the decision upon the claims submitted; or

    (3)   the award is imperfect in a matter of form not affecting the merits of the decision on the claims submitted.

(b)   If a [motion] filed under subsection (a) is granted, the court shall modify or correct and confirm the award as modified or corrected. Otherwise, the court shall confirm the award.

(c)   A [motion] to modify or correct an award pursuant to this section may be joined with a [motion] to vacate the award.

§ 25.   Judgment on Award; Attorney's Fees and Litigation Expenses

(a)   Upon granting an order confirming, vacating without directing a rehearing, modifying, or correcting an award, the court shall enter a judgment in conformity therewith. The judgment may be recorded, docketed, and enforced as any other judgment in a civil action.

(b)   A court may allow reasonable costs of the [motion] and subsequent judicial proceedings.

(c)   On [application] of a prevailing party to a contested judicial proceeding under Section 22, 23, or 24, the court may add to a judgment confirming, vacating without directing a rehearing, modifying, or correcting an award, attorney's fees and other reasonable expenses of litigation incurred in a judicial proceeding after the award is made.

§ 26.   Jurisdiction

(a)   A court of this State having jurisdiction over the dispute and the parties may enforce an agreement to arbitrate.

(b)   An agreement to arbitrate providing for arbitration in this State confers exclusive jurisdiction on the court to enter judgment on an award under this [Act].

§ 27.   Venue

A [motion] pursuant to Section 5 must be filed in the court of the [county] in which the agreement to arbitrate specifies the arbitration hearing is to be held or, if the hearing has been held, in the court of the [county] in which it was held. Otherwise, the [motion] must be filed in any [county] in which an adverse party resides or has a place of business or, if no adverse party has a residence or place of business in this State, in the court of any [county] in this State. All subsequent [motions] must be filed in the court hearing the initial [motion] unless the court otherwise directs.

§ 28.   Appeals

(a)   An appeal may be taken from:

   (1)   an order denying a [motion] to compel arbitration;
   (2)   an order granting a [motion] to stay arbitration;
   (3)   an order confirming or denying confirmation of an award;
   (4)   an order modifying or correcting an award;
   (5)   an order vacating an award without directing a rehearing; or
   (6)   a final judgment entered pursuant to this [Act].

(b)   An appeal under this section must be taken as from an order or a judgment in a civil action.

§ 29.   Uniformity of Application and Construction

In applying and construing this Uniform Act, consideration must be given to the need to promote uniformity of the law with respect to its subject matter among States that enact it.

§ 30.   Effective Date

This [Act] takes effect on [effective date].

§ 31.   Repeal

Effective on [date], the [Uniform Arbitration Act] is repealed.

§ 32.   Savings Clause

This [Act] does not affect an action or proceeding commenced or right accrued before this [Act] takes effect.

§ 33.   Relationship to Electronic Signatures in Global and National Commerce Act

The provisions of this Act governing the legal effect, validity, and enforceability of electronic records or electronic signatures, and of contracts performed with the use of such records or signatures conform to the requirements of section 102 of the Electronic Signatures in Global and National Commerce Act.

Glossary of Relevant Terms and Arbitration Laws

RELEVANT BINDING AND NON-BINDING ADR PROCESSES

Alternative ("Appropriate") Dispute Resolution (ADR)

The acronym "ADR" refers collectively to the range of approaches, including binding arbitration and mediation, which provide alternatives to traditional court litigation—*alternative dispute resolution*. Some ADR proponents insist that because the label "alternative" conveys the mistaken impression suggests that court trial is the norm and not a last resort, ADR should be taken to stand for *"appropriate"* dispute resolution—that is, the approach best suited to resolving the problem at hand.

Appraisal

Parties sometimes agree to have experts *appraise*, or value, property (such as real estate or the assets of a business) for various purposes. Arrangements calling for binding appraisals may be functionally similar to binding arbitration, raising questions about the applicability of federal or state laws governing arbitration. Case law reflects varied approaches to this question; some states have addressed the issue by statute. See *Chapter 3*.

Conflict management programs

Conflict management programs involve a structured approach to the range of potential disputes that are likely to arise in a business relationship. Such programs evolve from deliberate planning at the start of the relationship, and typically result in a stepped conflict resolution scheme incorporating multiple forms of ADR. The potential advantages of a systematic approach to conflict management are discussed in *Chapter 1*.

Arbitration

Binding arbitration, the focus of this book, refers to any process in which parties have agreed to submit disputes to the judgment of a private tribunal, or panel, for binding resolution. Arbitrators often are chosen for pertinent commercial, technical or legal expertise. In addition to being more private and less formal than the courtroom, arbitration is often a faster and more efficient method of judging disputes. Under modern federal and state laws, courts liberally enforce agreements to arbitrate, as well as arbitrator decisions (awards). Parties have great flexibility in designing arbitration processes to suit their particular needs.

Non-binding abbreviated arbitration, used in many new court-sponsored programs in recent years, was also developed as a tool to spur settlement negotiations in court-bound cases. Like mini-trial, this model involves case presentations before a neutral or panel of neutrals. Although the resulting decision is not binding on the parties, applicable rules normally assess some amount (such as arbitrator costs and fees) against parties who thereafter seek trial and do not achieve a significantly better result. Again, the ultimate goal is to predict an adjudicated outcome based on objective criteria, thus providing a possible basis for settlement. The focus, however, is not on the negotiation process, but on exposing parties to the other side and to an outside view.

Early neutral evaluation; expert evaluation

An objective perspective on controversy sometimes promotes settlement. For this reason, some parties look to a neutral third party usually a business person, technical expert, or lawyer to evaluate the merits of their dispute. Used in the early stages of conflict resolution, *neutral evaluation* may prevent conflict from escalating, avoid or abbreviate discovery, and substantially reduce the cost and time necessary to resolve disputes. The process is sometimes used in conjunction with mediation. (See below.) In some cases, parties seek evaluations from mediators. See *Chapter 1*.

Mediation

In contrast to binding arbitration, *mediation* places primary emphasis on negotiation and mutual accommodation instead of adjudication. Using a variety of techniques, mediators facilitate informal discussions between disputing parties. In commercial contexts, the negotiated settlement of specific disputes is usually the primary goal of mediation. However, the process may also help to improve communications and/or promote understanding between parties. The use of mediation prior to or concurrent with arbitration is discussed in *Chapter 1*.

Med/arb and other hybrid approaches

The growing use of mediation before or during arbitration has caused some parties to experiment with *"med/arb"*—in which a third party neutral attempts to mediate disputes and, if unsuccessful in resolving all issues, serves as arbitrator. Mixing the roles of mediator and arbitrators raises a serious concerns, however. Med/arb and other approaches which combine elements of mediation and arbitration are discussed in *Chapter 1*.

Mini-trial

Mini-trial is not a trial in the ordinary sense, but an abbreviated proceeding that gives parties a foretaste of trial and, hopefully, some sense of the likely outcome. This predictive process, which exposes decision makers to a "best shot" presentation of each side of the case, is intended as a means of facilitating settlement negotiations by getting executives to the table and encouraging an objective assessment of the issues. Negotiations normally occur right after the "hearing." A neutral third party adviser supervises the process, and may render a nonbinding decision or even assist with negotiations if the parties so desire. Mini-trial has been successfully employed in the settlement of numerous commercial cases (including some very large ones). It is, however, a somewhat formal process that may require considerable preparation time.

Partnering

In *partnering*, parties entering into a contractual relationship take deliberate steps at the outset to identify and share individual and mutual goals, discuss performance expectations and potential problems, establish or improve channels of communication, and discuss methods of handling and avoiding controversies. Partnering processes usually include a pre-performance conference involving principals and a neutral facilitator, and facilitated follow-up sessions during the course of performance. Partnering has been successfully employed on many public as well as private contracts. Although it is usually used in the construction arena, partnering is adaptable to other commercial venues.

"Standing" neutrals

Where a premium is placed on getting contract disputes resolved quickly and efficiently, some parties designate one or more individuals as *"standing" neutrals* with ongoing responsibility to address conflicts as soon as possible. Standing neutrals may act as mediators or evaluators. One variant of the standing neutral approach is the "dispute review board" (DRB), in which a panel of neutrals meet periodically to evaluate disputes that have recently arisen. DRBs have proven very successful in resolving conflicts on a number of major construction projects.

Stepped conflict resolution processes

A growing number of commercial contracts now incorporate ADR processes in which disputes are "filtered" through several successive steps such as, for example, unassisted face-to-face negotiation, mediation and binding arbitration. The advantages of such approaches are discussed in *Chapter 1*.

Summary jury trial

Summary jury trial is similar in concept to mini-trial, but involves condensed adversary presentations before a jury which draws non-binding conclusions regarding issues in dispute. It is used by some courts as a means of facilitating pre-trial settlement of legal actions.

OTHER FREQUENTLY USED TERMS

Award

In arbitration, *award* refers to the decision rendered by the arbitrator(s). In the United States, arbitration awards are enforceable and subject to limited review under modern federal and state law. See *Chapter 7*.

Confirmation of award

Federal and state statutes provide a procedure by which courts may *confirm* arbitration awards that is, convert the arbitration awards into judgments of the court pursuant to the motion of a party. Among other things, confirmation is an important option where arbitration awards are not complied with voluntarily.

Functus officio

The principle of *functus officio* refers to the termination of the arbitrator's authority upon the rendition of a final award. The principle is subject to a number of exceptions.[1]

Vacatur (vacation) or modification of award

In addition to providing a procedure for confirmation of arbitration awards, federal and state statutes provide a mechanism for judicial *vacatur (vacation) or modification of awards* pursuant to a party's motion. Standards for judicial vacatur of award are very limited, as are standards for modification. See *Chapter 7*.

LAWS GOVERNING ARBITRATION

Federal Arbitration Act (FAA)

The Federal Arbitration Act (FAA), 9 U.S.C. §§ 1- 16, passed in 1925, is a federal statute governing arbitration agreements in federal courts, and in state courts under the Supremacy Clause. It provides for specific enforcement of (1) written arbitration agreements in, among other things, "any maritime transaction or contract evidencing a transaction involving [interstate] commerce," and (2) written agreements to submit to arbitration existing controversies under such agreements, subject to the normal contract defenses. Among other things, the FAA also provides for limited federal court intervention for the purpose of appointing arbitrators or enforcing arbitrator-issued summonses, and sets

---

1. *See* MACNEIL, ET AL, *supra* note 1, ch. 30.

out standards for review, vacatur, modification and/or confirmation of arbitration awards.[2]

Uniform Arbitration Act (UAA) and other state arbitration laws

The *Uniform Arbitration Act (UAA)*, a uniform statute published in 1955 by the National Conference of Commissioners on Uniform State Laws (NCCUSL), has been adopted by the great majority of U.S. states. Like the FAA, the UAA provides for the specific enforcement of written agreements to arbitrate future or existing controversies, subject to the usual contract defenses. Also like the FAA, the UAA provides for other forms of limited judicial intervention to facilitate arbitration, and for judicial vacatur, modification or confirmation of awards. In some cases, adopting states have made non-uniform amendments to the UAA. The UAA is currently being thoroughly revised by a committee of NCCUSL.

Some states, notably New York and California, have their own form of arbitration statute and have not adopted the UAA. Although similar in many respects to the FAA and UAA, these enactments are dissimilar in others. In addition, a number of states have developed legislation governing arbitration provisions in specific kinds of contracts, such as design and construction contracts.

United Nations (New York) Convention and other international conventions

The United Nations Convention on the Recognition and Enforcement of Foreign Arbitral Awards (New York Convention), adopted in 1958 by the United Nations Economic and Social Council, the primary international convention establishing a legal framework for the enforcement of arbitration agreements and awards, is in effect in the U.S. and more than 80 other countries. Under FAA §§ 201-208, the Convention is enforceable in United States courts.[3]

Another important international convention is the Inter-American Convention on International Commercial Arbitration, applicable in U.S. courts under FAA §§ 301-307.

UNCITRAL Model Law

The United Nations Council on International Trade Law (UNCITRAL) Model Law on International Commercial Arbitration, approved by UNCITRAL in 1985, was intended to serve as a model statute covering international arbitration. The Model Law, which has been adopted by a number of countries and, in whole or in part, by various U.S. states, "establishes a unified practice and procedure for international commercial transactions and strives to meet the essential requirements of party autonomy and basic fairness."[4]

---

2. *See generally* IAN R. MACNEIL, RICHARD E. SPEIDEL & THOMAS J. STIPANOWICH, FEDERAL ARBITRATION LAW: AGREEMENTS, AWARDS & REMEDIES UNDER THE FEDERAL ARBITRATION ACT (Aspen, 1994)(five-volume treatise addressing law and practice under the FAA).

3. *See id.*, § 44.8.

4. Washington Foreign L. Soc'y, Committee on the UNCITRAL Model Law on International Commercial Arbitration, Rep. Nov. 9, 1987 at 2.

Bibliography

GENERAL SOURCES ON COMMERCIAL ARBITRATION

Arbitration Rules

AMERICAN ARBITRATION ASSOCIATION, COMMERCIAL DISPUTE RESOLUTION PROCEDURES (1999).

CPR INSTITUTE FOR DISPUTE RESOLUTION, NON-ADMINISTERED ARBITRATION RULES & COMMENTARY (Rev. 2000).

CPR INSTITUTE FOR DISPUTE RESOLUTION, RULES FOR NON-ADMINISTERED ARBITRATION OF INTERNATIONAL DISPUTES & COMMENTARY (Rev. 2000).

CPR INSTITUTE FOR DISPUTE RESOLUTION, RULES FOR NON-ADMINISTERED ARBITRATION OF PATENT AND TRADE SECRET DISPUTES (1994).

CPR ARBITRATION APPEAL PROCEDURE (1999)

JAMS COMPREHENSIVE ARBITRATION RULES AND PROCEDURES FOR COMMERCIAL, REAL ESTATE AND CONSTRUCTION CASES (1999).

RULES FOR NON-ADMINISTERED ARBITRATION OF TRADEMARK AND UNFAIR COMPETITION DISPUTES (CPR/INTA, 1994).

Arbitration Forms and Clauses

CPR ONLINE FORM (2000), <www.cpradr.org>

Treatises

JAMES ACRET, CONSTRUCTION ARBITRATION HANDBOOK (1985).

IAN R. MACNEIL, AMERICAN ARBITRATION LAW: REFORMATION - NATIONALIZATION - INTERNATIONALIZATION (1992).

IAN R. MACNEIL, RICHARD E. SPEIDEL & THOMAS J. STIPANOWICH, FEDERAL ARBITRATION LAW: AGREEMENTS, AWARDS AND REMEDIES UNDER THE FEDERAL ARBITRATION ACT (ASPEN 1994). THOMAS H. OEHMKE, OEHMKE ON COMMERCIAL ARBITRATION (Rev. 1995).

Gabriel M. Wilner, Domke on Commercial Arbitration (Rev. 1999).

Empirical Studies

Lisa Brennan, *What Lawyers Like: Mediation*, Law News Network's Corporate Law Center, <http://www.lawnewsnetwork.com/stories/A917-1999Nov.8.html>.

S. Lazarus et al., Resolving Business Disputes: The Potential of Commercial Arbitration (1965).

David B. Lipsky & Ronald L. Seeber, The Appropriate Resolution of Corporate Disputes: A Report on the Growing Use of ADR by U.S. Corporations, Cornell/PERC Institute on Conflict Resolution (1998).

Soia Mentschikoff, *Commercial Arbitration*, 61 Colum. L. Rev. 846, 848-856 (1961)

Michael Segalla, Survey: *The Speed and Cost of Complex Commercial Arbitrations*, 46 Arb. J., Dec. 1991, at 12.

Thomas J. Stipanowich, *Beyond Arbitration: Innovation and Evolution in the United States Construction Industry*, 31 Wake Forest L. Rev. 65 (Spring 1996).

Thomas J. Stipanowich, *Rethinking American Arbitration*, 63 Ind. L. J. 425 (1998).

Dean B. Thomson, *Arbitration Theory and Practice: A Survey of AAA Construction Arbitrators*, 23 Hofstra L. Rev. 137 (1994).

User Perspectives

James H. Carter, *A User's Perspective on the Arbitral Process: What are the Current Needs?*, in Arbitration: Preparing for the 21st Century 822, Sept. 1998 A.B.A. Sec. Disp. Resol. and Ass'n. Bar City N.Y. (conference material).

CHAPTER 1   ARBITRATION IN THE ADR LANDSCAPE

Commercial Conflict Resolution; ADR Systems Design

Catherine Cronin-Harris, Building ADR into the Corporate Law Department: ADR Systems Design (CPR Institute, 1997).

CPR ADR Suitability Screen, CPR MAPP Series, Vol. I (2000).

Mediation

Mark D. Bennet and Michele S.G. Hermann, The Art of Mediation (1996).

CPR Institute For Dispute Resolution, Mediation Procedure (1998).

CPR Institute for Dispute Resolution, Confidentiality, CPR MAPP Series, Vol. I (2000).

CPR Institute for Dispute Resolution Mediation in Action: Resolving a Complex Business Dispute, Videotape and Videotape Study Guide (1994).

Richard M. Calkins, *Mediation: The Gentler Way*, 41 S.D. L. Rev. 277 (1996).

John W. Cooley, Mediation Advocacy (1996).

Eric Galton, Representing Clients in Mediation (1994).

Nancy H. Rogers and Craig A. McEwen, Mediation: Law, Policy, and Practice (2d ed. 1994).

Leonard L. Riskin, *Understanding Mediators' Orientations, Strategies and Techniques: A Grid for the Perplexed*, 1 Harv. Negotiation L. Rev. 7 (1996).

Kathleen M. Scanlon, CPR Institute for Dispute Resolution, MEDIATOR'S DESKBOOK (1999)

"Med-Arb"; Arbitrators as Mediators

Tom Arnold, *MEDALOA, The Dispute Resolution Process of Choice*, Dec. 27, 1996 (unpublished manuscript).

Barry C. Bartel, *Comment, Med-Arb as a Distinct Method of Dispute Resolution: History, Analysis, and Potential*, 27 Willamette L. Rev. 661 (1991).

David C. Elliott, Med/Arb: *Fraught with Danger or Ripe with Opportunity?*, 34 Alberta L. Rev. 163 (1995).

Richard P. Flake, *Nuances of Med/Arb: A Neutral's Perspective*, 3 ADR Currents, June 1998, at 8.

James T. Peter, *Note & Comment: Med-Arb in International Arbitration*, 8 Am. J. Int'l Arb. 83 (1997).

David W. Plant, *The Arbitrator as Settlement Facilitator*, 17 J. Int'l Arb. 143 (2000).

Irene C. Warshauer, *The Neutral in Multiple Roles: Practical and Ethical Issues*, in Arbitration Now: Opportunities for Fairness, Process Renewal and Invigoration 97 (Paul H. Haagen ed., 1999).

Partnering

Dispute Prevention Through Partnering, Construction, CPR Institute for Dispute Resolution MAPP Series (1998).

Thomas J. Stipanowich, *The Multi-Door Contract and Other Possibilities*, 13 Ohio St. J. on Disp. Resol. 303 (1998).

CHAPTER 2   DISPUTE RESOLUTION PROVISIONS

American Arbitration Association, Drafting Dispute Resolution Clauses—A Practical Guide (1998).

CPR Dispute Resolution Clauses, CPR MAPP Series, Vol. I (2000)

Tom Arnold, *Contracts to Arbitrate Patent and Other Commercial Disputes*, 10 Alternatives to High Cost Litig. (CPR Inst. for Disp. Resol., New York, N.Y.), Dec. 1992, at 191.

Stephen A. Hochman, *Model Dispute Resolution Provisions for Use in Commercial Agreements Between Parties with Equal Bargaining Power*, in Arbitration Now: Opportunities for Fairness, Process Renewal and Invigoration 129 (Paul H. Haagen ed., 1999).

Jarril F. Kaplan, *ADR Clauses Must Anticipate Contingencies*, 14 Alternatives to High Cost Litig. (CPR Inst. for Disp. Resol., New York, N.Y.), Feb. 1996, at 16.

Carl G. Love, *9th Circuit Gives Lesson about ADR Clauses: Very Narrow Wording Defeats the Purpose*, 13 Alternatives to High Cost Litig. (CPR Inst. for Disp. Resol., New York, N.Y.), July 1995, at 87.

Model Agreement Between Parties, Neutral, 12 Alternatives to High Cost Litig. (CPR Inst. for Disp. Resol., New York, N.Y.), June 1994, at 83.

Donald Lee Rome, *A New Approach to ADR for the Financial Services Industry*, Secured Lender, May-June 1998, at 23.

Donald Lee Rome, *Preserving Rights—and ADR—by Knowing When to Use a "Carve Out"* (Part III of III), 16 Alternatives to High Cost Litig. (CPR Inst. for Disp. Resol., New York, N.Y.), Jan. 1998, at 6 .

Donald Lee Rome, *Writing Rules: Eliminate the Boilerplate, and Draft According to the Terms of the Deal* (Part II of II), 15 Alternatives to High Cost Litig. (CPR Inst. for Disp. Resol., New York, N.Y.), Dec.1997, at 159.

John T. Sant, *How Contract Clauses Can Ensure ADR* (Part I of III), 15 Alternatives to High Cost Litig. (CPR Inst. for Disp. Resol., New York, N.Y.), Nov. 1997, at 146.

CHAPTER 3   FINDING THE RIGHT ARBITRATORS

Arbitrator Qualifications

American Arbitration Association Department of Neutrals' Education & Development, Role of the Panel Chair: Understanding Panel Dynamics (1999).

3 Ian R. Macneil, Richard E. Speidel & Thomas J. Stipanowich, Federal Arbitration Law: Agreements, Awards & Remedies Under the Federal Arbitration Act, ch. 26 (Aspen 1994).

Conflicts Of Interest; Disclosures

3 Ian R. Macneil, Richard E. Speidel & Thomas J. Stipanowich, Federal Arbitration Law: Agreements, Awards & Remedies Under the Federal Arbitration Act, ch. 28 (Aspen 1994).

Ethical Standards

American Arbitration Association/American Bar Association Code of Ethics for Arbitrators in Commercial Disputes (1977).

CPR - Georgetown Commission on Ethics and Standards in ADR, Proposed Model Rule of Professional Conduct for the Lawyer as Third Party Neutral (1999).

CHAPTER 4   PREPARING FOR THE HEARING

Managing Complex Arbitration

American Bar Association Litigation Section, Commercial Arbitration for the 1990's. (1991). Richard J. Medalie, Developing Innovative Procedures in a Complex Multiparty Arbitration, at 56.

Mark A. Buckstein, *Tailoring the Process: AAA's Large, Complex Case Dispute Resolution Program*, 48 Arb. J., Mar. 1993, at 17.

Robert H. Gorske, *An Arbitrator Looks at Expediting the Large, Complex Case*, 5 Ohio St. J. on Disp. Resol. 381 (1990).

James P. Groton, *The Arbitrator's Leadership Role in a Complex Arbitration Case*, Construction Superconference, San Francisco (Nov. 10, 1994).

James J. Myers, *Ten Techniques for Managing Arbitration Hearings*, 51 Disp. Resol. J., Jan.-Mar. 1996, at 28.

Allen Poppleton, *The Arbitrator's Role in Expediting the Large and Complex Commercial Case*, 36 Arb. J., Dec. 1981, at 6.

Pre-Hearing Conferences

Tom Arnold, Setting Up the Preliminary Administration Conference, The First Arbitrator-Party Communications (1999) (unpublished manuscript).

Robert H. Gorske, *An Arbitrator Looks at Expediting the Large, Complex Case*, 5 Ohio St. J. on Disp. Resol. 381, 383-84 (1990).

UNCITRAL NOTES ON ORGANIZING ARBITRAL PROCEEDINGS, U.N. Doc. V.96-84935 (1996). <http://www.transdata.ro/drept/uncitral/arbnotes.htm>.

Provisional Remedies

Committee on Arbitration and ADR, Association of the Bar, *The Advisability and Availability of Provisional Remedies in the Arbitration Process.* THE RECORD 625.

3 IAN R. MACNEIL, RICHARD E. SPEIDEL & THOMAS J. STIPANOWICH, FEDERAL ARBITRATION LAW: AGREEMENTS, AWARDS AND REMEDIES UNDER THE FEDERAL ARBITRATION ACT, ch. 25, § 36.6 (ASPEN 1994).

Discovery

Michael Hoellering and Peter Goetz, *Piercing the Veil: Document Discovery in Arbitration Hearings,* 47 Arb. J., Sept. 1992, at 58.

3 IAN R. MACNEIL, RICHARD E. SPEIDEL & THOMAS J. STIPANOWICH, FEDERAL ARBITRATION LAW: AGREEMENTS, AWARDS AND REMEDIES UNDER THE FEDERAL ARBITRATION ACT, ch. 34 (ASPEN 1994).

Consolidation

3 IAN R. MACNEIL, RICHARD E. SPEIDEL & THOMAS J. STIPANOWICH, FEDERAL ARBITRATION LAW: AGREEMENTS, AWARDS AND REMEDIES UNDER THE FEDERAL ARBITRATION ACT, ch. 33 (ASPEN 1994).

Jurisdictional Issues

CHAPTER 5   THE HEARING

Evidence

3 IAN R. MACNEIL, RICHARD E. SPEIDEL & THOMAS J. STIPANOWICH, FEDERAL ARBITRATION LAW: AGREEMENTS, AWARDS AND REMEDIES UNDER THE FEDERAL ARBITRATION ACT, ch. 35 (ASPEN 1994).

Technology In Arbitration

Deborah Enix-Ross & Thomas D. Halket, *ADR and On-Line Dispute Resolution,* in ARBITRATION NOW: OPPORTUNITIES FOR FAIRNESS, PROCESS RENEWAL AND INVIGORATION 69 (Paul H. Haagen ed., 1999).

Robert C. Field & Robert W. Robertson, *The Hearing,* in BETTE J. ROTH ET AL., THE ALTERNATIVE DISPUTE RESOLUTION PRACTICE GUIDE, § 12.15, at 21 (1993).

Arbitrator Sanctions

3 Ian R. Macneil, Richard E. Speidel & Thomas J. Stipanowich, Federal Arbitration Law: Agreements, Awards & Remedies Under the Federal Arbitration Act, ch. 36 (Aspen 1994).

CHAPTER 6   PRESERVING CONFIDENTIALITY

CPR Institute for Dispute Resolution, CPR Non-Administered Arbitration of Patent and Trade Secret Disputes Rules (1994).

James H. Carter, *The Attorney-Client Privilege in Arbitration*, ADR Currents, Winter 1996/1997, at 1.

IBM & Gartner Group Settle Trade Secret Suit by Creating Future Arbitration Panel, 2 Alternatives to High Cost Litig. (CPR Inst. for Disp. Resol., New York, N.Y.), Sept. 1984, at 8.

William L. Schaller, *Protecting Trade Secrets During Litigation: Policies and Procedures*, 88 Ill. Bar. J. 260 (May 2000).

CHAPTER 7   THE ARBITRATION AWARD: FINALITY VS. REVIEWABILITY

Arbitral Remedies

3 Ian R. Macneil, Richard E. Speidel & Thomas J. Stipanowich, Federal Arbitration Law: Agreements, Awards & Remedies Under the Federal Arbitration Act, ch. 36 (Aspen 1994).

Appeals; Judicial Review

Stephen L. Hayford, *Law in Disarray: Judicial Standards for Vacatur of Arbitration Awards*, 30 Ga. L. Rev. 731 (1996).

Stephen L. Hayford, *A New Paradigm for Commercial Arbitration: Rethinking the Relationship Between Reasoned Awards and the Judicial Standards for Vacatur*, 66 Geo. Wash. L. Rev. 443 (Mar. 1998).

4 Ian R. Macneil, Richard E. Speidel & Thomas J. Stipanowich, Federal Arbitration Law: Agreements, Awards & Remedies Under the Federal Arbitration Act, ch. 40 (Aspen 1994).

Bret F. Randall, The History, *Application and Policy of the Judicially Created Standards of Review for Arbitration Awards*, 1992 B.Y.U. L. Rev. 759.

Expanded Judicial Review

Hans Smit, *Contractual Modification of the Scope of Judicial Review of Arbitral Awards*, 8 AM. REV. INT'L ARB. 147 (1997).

Stephen P. Younger, *Agreements to Expand the Scope of Judicial Review of Arbitration Awards*, 63 ALB. L. REV. 241 (1999).

Appellate Arbitration

CPR INSTITUTE FOR DISPUTE RESOLUTION ARBITRATION APPEAL PROCEDURE (1999).

CHAPTER 8   INTERNATIONAL ARBITRATION

International Rules And Procedures

CPR INSTITUTE FOR DISPUTE RESOLUTION RULES FOR NON-ADMINISTERED ARBITRATION OF INTERNATIONAL DISPUTES (Rev. 2000).

SIMPSON THACHER & BARTLETT, A CHART COMPARING INTERNATIONAL COMMERCIAL ARBITRATION RULES (Juris Publishing, Inc., 1998)

General Sources, Treatises

ERIC BERGSTEN, INTERNATIONAL COMMERCIAL ARBITRATION (4 VOLS.)(1980 with updates)

GARY B. BORN, INTERNATIONAL COMMERCIAL ARBITRATION IN THE UNITED STATES (1994).

CHRISTIAN BUHRING-UHLE, ARBITRATION AND MEDIATION IN INTERNATIONAL BUSINESS (1996).

CENTRE OF CONSTRUCTION LAW AND MANAGEMENT, KING'S COLLEGE LONDON, INTERNATIONAL AND ICC ARBITRATION: CONFERENCE PAPERS AND SOURCE MATERIALS (John Uff & Elizabeth Jones eds., 1990).

YVES DEZALAY & BRYANT G. GARTH, DEALING IN VIRTUE: INTERNATIONAL COMMERCIAL ARBITRATION AND THE CONSTRUCTION OF A TRANSNATIONAL LEGAL ORDER (1996).

JAN PAULSSON, NIGEL RAWDING, LUCY REED, ERIC SCHWARTZ. THE FRESHFIELDS GUIDE TO ARBITRATION AND ADR: CLAUSES IN INTERNATIONAL CONTRACTS (2d, 1999).

IMPROVING THE EFFICIENCY OF ARBITRATION AGREEMENTS AND AWARDS: 40 YEARS OF APPLICATION OF THE NEW YORK CONVENTION, International Chamber of Commerce Arbitration Congress series no. 9 (Albert Jan van den Berg ed. 1999).

INTERNATIONAL COUNCIL FOR COMMERCIAL ARBITRATION, INTERNATIONAL HANDBOOK ON COMMERCIAL ARBITRATION (PIETER SANDERS ED. 1984).

PARKER SCHOOL OF FOREIGN AND COMPARATIVE LAW, COLUMBIA UNIVERSITY, COMMERCIAL ARBITRATION: AN INTERNATIONAL BIBLIOGRAPHY (1993).

ALAN REDFERN, MARTIN HUNTER & MURRAY SMITH, LAW AND PRACTICE OF INTERNATIONAL COMMERCIAL ARBITRATION (2d ed. 1991)

W. MICHAEL REISMAN, W. LAURENCE CRAIG, WILLIAM W. PARK & JAN PAULSSON, INTERNATIONAL COMMERCE ARBITRATION (1997).

Index

References are to sections.

A

Abuse of discretion standard, 7.7.3
Ad hoc arbitration. *See* Non-administered arbitration
Administered arbitration, 2.3
    decision for, 2.4.2
    fees for, 3.8.2, 8.2.3
    international, 8.2.3
    services available in, 2.4.1, 8.2.3
Administrative Procedure Act (APA), 7.7.3
Administrative services, 4.2, 4.11.4
    of international institutions, 8.2.3
    scope and nature of, 2.4.1
Admissions, 4.3.2
Advocacy, effective, 5.2
Affidavits, 4.5.2, 5.4.3
Agreement to arbitrate. *See* Dispute resolution provisions
Alternative dispute resolution (ADR), 1.1. *See also* specific types of ADR
    for international disputes, 8.1
    options for, 1.2
American Arbitration Association (AAA)
    Code of Ethics for Arbitrators in Commercial Disputes (AAA/ABA Code), 3.3.1, 3.9.4
    Commercial Arbitrator Development Program, 3.3.3

Commercial Dispute Resolution Procedures, 1.6, 2.4.1, 3.3.1
    expedited procedures, 2.8
    International Arbitration Rules, 8.3.1, 8.6.2
    International Center for Dispute Resolution, 8.2.2
    Large, Complex Case Procedures, 4.7.1
    Optional Rules for Emergency Measures of Protection, 2.5.8, 4.6.1
    resources by, 1.2.3, 2.3
American Bar Association (ABA)
    Code of Ethics for Arbitrators in Commercial Disputes (AAA/ABA Code), 3.3.1, 3.9.4
    Section of Dispute Resolution, 3.9.4
Ancillary services, 4.11.4
Appeal of decision, xx, 3.1.2. *See also* Judicial review; Private appeal
    international, 8.7.7
    separate systems for, 7.8.3
    standards for, 7.6, 7.7, 7.8.3
Appearance of bias, 3.3.1
Appraisal, 2.9
Arbitrability of issues, 2.5.2, 3.3.3
    court determination of, 4.4
    procedural, 2.5.5
    substantive, 2.5.5
Arbitrary and capricious standard, 7.6, 7.7.3, 7.7.5

About The Authors

Thomas J. Stipanowich, William L. Matthews Professor of Law at the University of Kentucky College of Law, and Counsel, Stites & Harbison, is a noted author and speaker on conflict resolution subjects. In January 2001, he will become the new president and CEO of the CPR Institute for Dispute Resolution, after having served as Director of the CPR Commission on the Future of Arbitration and the 1999-2000 Hewlett Scholar. He is chair of the Academic Advisory Committee for the American Arbitration Association's new International Global Research Center and, during the fall semester 2000, was the AAA's first Hoellering Scholar in Residence. He is also chair and public member of the Securities Industry Conference on Arbitration, the body charged with developing policies and procedures for securities arbitration and ADR. He is co-author, with Ian Macneil and Richard Speidel, of the award-winning 5-volume *Federal Arbitration Law: Agreements, Awards and Remedies under the Federal Arbitration Act* (Aspen Publishing (previously Little, Brown) 1994), which has been cited by the U.S. Supreme Court and a number of other federal and state courts. He is an honorary fellow of the American College of Civil Trial Mediators and was a co-founder of the Mediation Center of Kentucky, Inc.

Peter H. Kaskell is Senior Fellow of the CPR Institute for Dispute Resolution, which he has served since 1983. A graduate of Columbia College and Columbia Law School, he began his legal career at White & Case in New York. Mr. Kaskell held various legal positions at Olin Corporation in Stamford, Connecticut, and ultimately served as Olin's Vice President, Legal Affairs, for twelve years. He is also a past director of CARE and past member of the Advisory Committee of the U.S. District Court, Eastern District of New York, as well as a founder and President of the Westchester-Fairfield Corporate Counsel Association.